# Principles of Marketing

By
John F. Tanner Jr. and Mary Anne Raymond

S-45776-BW-2

# Principles of Marketing

John F. Tanner Jr. and Mary Anne Raymond

Published by:

Flat World Knowledge, Inc.
One Bridge Street
Irvington, NY 10533

# Brief Contents

# Contents

# About the Authors

## JEFF TANNER

John F. (Jeff) Tanner, Jr., is professor of marketing and associate dean of faculty development and research at the Hankamer School of Business, Baylor University. He is an internationally recognized expert in sales and sales management. He is the author or coauthor of twelve books, including two best-selling textbooks with McGraw-Hill—*Selling: Building Partnerships* and *Business Marketing: Connecting Strategy, Relationships and Learning*. His books have been translated into several languages and distributed in over thirty countries.

*Source: Photo by Lilly Tanner, used with permission.*

Dr. Tanner spent eight years in marketing and sales with Rockwell International and Xerox Corporation. In 1988, he earned his PhD from the University of Georgia and joined the faculty at Baylor University, where he currently serves as the research director of the Center for Professional Selling.

In addition to writing and research, Dr. Tanner maintains an active consulting and training practice. Recent clients include IBM, Hillcrest Medical System, and others. He is the managing partner of Team Fulcrum, which conducts sales training and marketing research, and he is a founder and research director of BPT Partners, the premier training and education company focused on advancing the skills and competency of professionals in the customer relationship management industry.

## MARY ANNE RAYMOND

Mary Anne Raymond is a professor of marketing at Clemson University. Prior to joining the faculty at Clemson, she served on the faculty at American University in Washington, DC, and helped coordinate the graduate marketing program at Johns Hopkins University. Previously, she was an invited Fulbright Professor of Marketing at Seoul National University in Seoul, Korea.

Dr. Raymond received her PhD from the University of Georgia. She has extensive industry experience doing strategic planning and acquisition analysis, marketing research, and investment analysis for Holiday Inns, Inc.; Freeport Sulphur; and Howard, Weil, Labouisse, Friedrichs. Dr. Raymond also does consulting, seminars, and marketing training for multinational companies, which have included organizations such as Merit Communications in Seoul, Korea; the Conference Center and Inn at Clemson University; and Sangyong Group.

Her research focuses on strategy in domestic and international markets, public policy issues, and social marketing. Dr. Raymond has published over one hundred papers appearing in journals such as *International Marketing Review*, the *Journal of Advertising Research*, the *Journal of Marketing Education*, the *Journal of Personal Selling and Sales Management*, and the *Journal of Public Policy and Marketing*, as well as numerous other journals and international conference proceedings. Dr. Raymond has also received numerous awards and recognition for her teaching and research. She received the Professor of the Year Award from Clemson University Panhellenic Association, the Undergraduate Teaching Excellence Award from the College of Business and Behavioral Science at Clemson three times, the Eli Lilly Faculty Excellence Awards for Outstanding Research and Outstanding Teaching, and the Eli Lilly Partnership Awards, and recognition for Leadership in Student Development from the Dow Chemical Company.

# Acknowledgments

The authors would like to thank Camille Schuster for her input, examples, and feedback on the chapters. The authors would also like to thank the following colleagues who have reviewed the text and provided comprehensive feedback and suggestions for improving the material:

- Christie Amaot, University of North Carolina, Charlotte
- Andrew Baker, Georgia State University
- Jennifer Barr, The Richard Stockton College of New Jersey
- George Bernard, Seminole Community College
- Patrick Bishop, Ferris State University
- Donna Crane, Northern Kentucky University
- Lawrence Duke, Drexel University
- Mary Ann Edwards, College of Mount St. Joseph
- Paulette Faggiano, Southern New Hampshire University
- Bob Farris, Mt. San Antonio College
- Leisa Flynn, Florida State University
- Renee Foster, Delta State University
- Alfredo Gomez, Broward College
- Jianwei Hou, Minnesota State University, Mankato
- Craig Kelley, California State University, Sacramento
- Marilyn Liebrenz-Himes, George Washington University
- Alicia Lupinacci, Tarrant County College
- John Miller, Pima Community College, Downtown
- Melissa Moore, Mississippi State University
- Kathy Rathbone, Tri-County Community College
- Michelle Reiss, Spalding University
- Tom Schmidt, Simpson College
- Richard Sharman, Lonestar College
- Karen Stewart, The Richard Stockton College of New Jersey
- Victoria Szerko, Dominican College
- Robert Winsor, Loyola Marymount University

# Preface

*Principles of Marketing* by Tanner and Raymond teaches the experience and process of actually doing marketing—not just the vocabulary. It carries five dominant themes throughout in order to expose students to marketing in today's environment:

1. **Service-dominant logic**—This textbook employs the term "offering" instead of the more traditional first *P*—product. That is because consumers don't sacrifice value when alternating between a product and a service. They are evaluating the entire experience, whether they interact with a product, a service, or a combination. So the fundamental focus is providing value throughout the value chain, whether that value chain encompasses a product, a service, or both.
2. **Sustainability**—Increasingly, companies are interested in their impact on their local community as well as on the overall environment. This is often referred to as the "triple bottom line" of financial, social, and environment performance.
3. **Ethics and social responsibility**—Following on the sustainability notion is the broader importance of ethics and social responsibility in creating successful organizations. The authors make consistent references to ethical situations throughout chapter coverage, and end-of-chapter material in most chapters will encompass ethical situations.
4. **Global coverage**—Whether it is today's price of gasoline, the current U.S. presidential race, or midwestern U.S. farming, almost every industry and company needs strong global awareness. And today's marketing professionals must understand the world in which they and their companies operate.
5. **Metrics**—Firms today have the potential to gather more information than ever before about their current and potential customers. That information gathering can be costly, but it can also be very revealing. With the potential to capture so much more detail about micro transactions, firms should now be more able to answer, "Was this marketing strategy really worth it?" and "What is the marketing ROI?" and finally, "What is this customer or set of customers worth to us over their lifetime?"

# CHAPTER 1
# What Is Marketing?

What makes a business idea work? Does it only take money? Why are some products a huge success and similar products a dismal failure? How was Apple, a computer company, able to create and launch the wildly successful iPod, yet Microsoft's first foray into MP3 players was a total disaster? If the size of the company and the money behind a product's launch were the difference, Microsoft would have won. But for Microsoft to have won, it would have needed something it's not had in a while—good marketing so it can produce and sell products that consumers want.

So how does marketing get done?

## 1. DEFINING MARKETING

### LEARNING OBJECTIVE

1. **Define marketing and outline its components.**

**Marketing** is defined by the American Marketing Association as "the activity, set of institutions, and processes for creating, communicating, delivering, and exchanging offerings that have value for customers, clients, partners, and society at large."[1] If you read the definition closely, you see that there are four activities, or components, of marketing:

1. **Creating**. The process of collaborating with suppliers and customers to create offerings that have value.
2. **Communicating**. Broadly, describing those offerings, as well as learning from customers.
3. **Delivering**. Getting those offerings to the consumer in a way that optimizes value.
4. **Exchanging**. Trading value for those offerings.

The traditional way of viewing the components of marketing is via the four Ps:

1. **Product.** Goods and services (creating offerings).
2. **Promotion**. Communication.
3. **Place.** Getting the product to a point at which the customer can purchase it (delivering).
4. **Price.** The monetary amount charged for the product (exchange).

Introduced in the early 1950s, the four Ps were called the marketing mix, meaning that a marketing plan is a mix of these four components.

If the four Ps are the same as creating, communicating, delivering, and exchanging, you might be wondering why there was a change. The answer is that they are *not* exactly the same. Product, price, place, and promotion are nouns. As such, these words fail to capture all the activities of marketing. For example, exchanging requires mechanisms for a transaction, which consist of more than simply a price or place. Exchanging requires, among other things, the transfer of ownership. For example, when you buy a car, you sign documents that transfer the car's title from the seller to you. That's part of the exchange process.

Even the term *product*, which seems pretty obvious, is limited. Does the product include services that come with your new car purchase (such as free maintenance for a certain period of time on some models)? Or does the product mean only the car itself?

Finally, none of the four Ps describes particularly well what marketing people do. However, one of the goals of this book is to focus on exactly what it is that marketing professionals do.

**marketing**

"The activity, set of institutions, and processes for creating, communicating, delivering, and exchanging offerings that have value for customers, clients, partners, and society at large."

**creating**

In marketing, a term that involves collaboration with suppliers and customers in order to generate offerings of value to customers.

**exchanging**

The act of transacting value between a buyer and a seller.

## 1.1 Value

Value is at the center of everything marketing does (Figure 1.1). What does value mean?

### FIGURE 1.1

Marketing is composed of four activities centered on customer value: creating, communicating, delivering, and exchanging value.

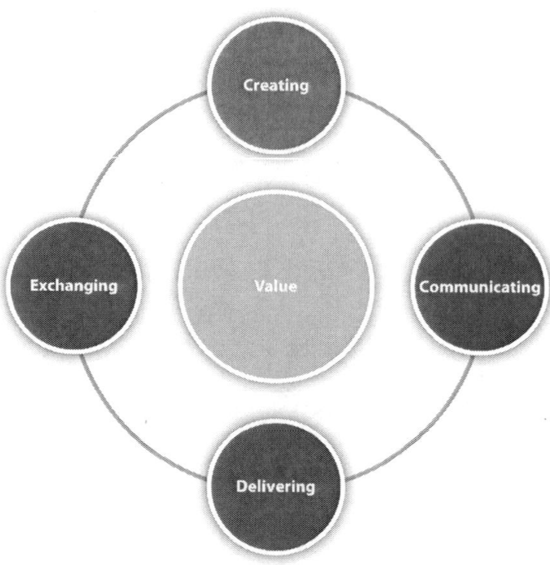


**value**

Total sum of benefits received that meet a buyer's needs. See personal value equation.

**personal value equation**

The net benefit a consumer receives from a product less the price paid for it and the hassle or effort expended to acquire it.

When we use the term **value**, we mean the benefits buyers receive that meet their needs. In other words, value is what the customer gets by purchasing and consuming a company's offering. So, although the offering is created by the company, the value is determined by the customer.

Furthermore, our goal as marketers is to create a profitable exchange for consumers. By profitable, we mean that the consumer's personal value equation is positive. The **personal value equation** is

$$\text{value} = \text{benefits received} - [\text{price} + \text{hassle}]$$

*Hassle* is the time and effort the consumer puts into the shopping process. The equation is a personal one because how each consumer judges the benefits of a product will vary, as will the time and effort he or she puts into shopping. Value, then, varies for each consumer.

One way to think of value is to think of a meal in a restaurant. If you and three friends go to a restaurant and order the same dish, each of you will like it more or less depending on your own personal tastes. Yet the dish was exactly the same, priced the same, and served exactly the same way. Because your tastes varied, the benefits you received varied. Therefore the value varied for each of you. That's why we call it a *personal* value equation.

**marketing concept**

A philosophy underlying all that marketers do, driven by satisfying customer wants and needs.

**market oriented**

The degree to which a company follows the marketing concept.

Value varies from customer to customer based on each customer's needs. The **marketing concept**, a philosophy underlying all that marketers do, requires that marketers seek to satisfy customer wants and needs. Firms operating with that philosophy are said to be **market oriented**. At the same time, market-oriented firms recognize that exchange must be profitable for the company to be successful. A marketing orientation is not an excuse to fail to make profit.

Firms don't always embrace the marketing concept and a market orientation. Beginning with the Industrial Revolution in the late 1800s, companies were **production oriented**. They believed that the best way to compete was through product innovation and by reducing production costs. In other words, companies thought that good products would sell themselves. Perhaps the best example of such a product was Henry Ford's Model A automobile, the first product of his production line innovation. Ford's production line made the automobile cheap and affordable for just about everyone. The **production era** lasted until the 1920s, when production-capacity growth began to outpace demand growth and new strategies were called for.

From the 1920s until after World War II, companies tended to be **selling oriented**, meaning they believed it was necessary to push their products by heavily emphasizing advertising and selling. Consumers during the Great Depression and World War II did not have as much money, so the competition for their available dollars was stiff. The result was this push approach during the **selling era**.

In the post–World War II environment, demand for goods increased as the economy soared. Some products, limited in supply during World War II, were now plentiful to the point of surplus. Consumers had many choices available to them, so companies had to find new ways to compete. During this time, the marketing concept was developed, and from about 1950 to 1990, businesses operated in the **marketing era**.

So what era would you say we're in now? Some call it the **value era**: a time when companies emphasize creating value for customers. Is that really different from the marketing era, in which the emphasis was on fulfilling the marketing concept? Maybe not. Others call today's business environment the **one-to-one era**, meaning that the way to compete is to build relationships with customers one at a time and seek to serve each customer's needs individually. Yet is that substantially different from the marketing concept?

**production orientation**

A belief that the way to compete is a function of product innovation and reducing production costs, as good products appropriately priced sell themselves.

**production era**

A period beginning with the Industrial Revolution and concluding in the 1920s in which production-orientation thinking dominated the way in which firms competed.

**selling orientation**

A philosophy that products must be pushed through selling and advertising in order for a firm to compete successfully.

**selling era**

A period running from the 1920s to until after World War II in which the selling orientation dominated the way firms competed.

**marketing era**

From 1950 to at least 1990 (see service-dominant logic era, value era, and one-to-one era), the dominant philosophy among businesses is the marketing concept.

**value era**

From the 1990s to the present, some argue that firms moved into the value era, competing on the basis of value; others contend that the value era is simply an extension of the marketing era and is not a separate era.

**one-to-one era**

From the 1990s to the present, the idea of competing by building relationships with customers one at a time and seeking to serve each customer's needs individually.

Still others argue that this is the time of **service-dominant logic** and that we are in the **service-dominant logic era**. Service-dominant logic is an approach to business that recognizes that consumers want value no matter how it is delivered, whether it's via a product, a service, or a combination of the two. Although there is merit in this belief, there is also merit to the value approach and the one-to-one approach. As you will see throughout this book, all three are intertwined. Perhaps, then, the name for this era has yet to be devised.

**service-dominant logic**

An approach to business that recognizes that customers do not distinguish between the tangible and the intangible aspects of a good or service, but rather see a product in terms of its total value.

**service-dominant logic era**

The period from 1990 to the present in which some believe that the philosophy of service-dominant logic dominates the way firms compete.

Whatever era we're in now, most historians would agree that defining and labeling it is difficult. Value and one-to-one are both natural extensions of the marketing concept, so we may still be in the marketing era. To make matters more confusing, not all companies adopt the philosophy of the era. For example, in the 1800s Singer and National Cash Register adopted strategies rooted in sales, so they operated in the selling era forty years before it existed. Some companies are still in the selling era. Many consider automobile manufacturers to be in the trouble they are in because they work too hard to sell or push product and not hard enough on delivering value.

## Creating Offerings That Have Value

Marketing creates those goods and services that the company offers at a price to its customers or clients. That entire bundle consisting of the tangible good, the intangible service, and the price is the company's **offering**. When you compare one car to another, for example, you can evaluate each of these dimensions—the tangible, the intangible, and the price—separately. However, you can't buy one manufacturer's car, another manufacturer's service, and a third manufacturer's price when you actually make a choice. Together, the three make up a single firm's offer.

**offering**

The entire bundle of a tangible good, intangible service, and price that composes what a company offers to customers.

Marketing people do not create the offering alone. For example, when the iPhone was created, Apple's engineers were also involved in its design. Apple's financial personnel had to review the costs of producing the offering and provide input on how it should be priced. Apple's operations group needed to evaluate the manufacturing requirements the iPhone would need. The company's logistics managers had to evaluate the cost and timing of getting the offering to retailers and consumers. Apple's dealers also likely provided input regarding the iPhone's service policies and warranty structure. Marketing, however, has the biggest responsibility because it is marketing's responsibility to ensure that the new phone delivers value. Creating and managing offerings will be the focus of Chapter 5 and Chapter 6 in this book.

## Communicating Offerings

**Communicating** is a broad term in marketing that means describing the offering and its value to your potential and current customers, as well as learning from customers what it is they want and like. Sometimes communicating means educating potential customers about the value of an offering, and sometimes it means simply making customers aware of where they can find a product. Communicating also means that customers get a chance to tell the company what they think. Today companies are finding that to be successful, they need a more interactive dialog with their customers. For example, Comcast customer service representatives will watch consumer Web sites like Twitter. When they observe consumers "tweeting" (posting) problems with Comcast, the customer service reps will post resolutions to their problems. Similarly, JCPenney has created consumer groups that talk among themselves on JCPenney-monitored Web sites. The company might post questions, send samples, or engage in other activities designed to solicit feedback from customers.

**communicating**

In marketing, a broad term meaning describing the offering and its value to potential customers, as well as learning from customers.

**FIGURE 1.2**

A Porsche Boxster can cost three times as much as a Pontiac Solstice, but why is it worth more? What makes up the complete offering?

*Source: Wikimedia Commons.*

Companies use many forms of communication, including advertising on the Web or television, on billboards or in magazines, through product placements in movies, and through salespeople. Other forms of communication include attempting to have news media cover the company's actions (part of public relations [PR]), participating in special events such as the annual International Consumer Electronics Show in which Apple and other companies introduce their newest gadgets, and sponsoring special events like the Susan G. Komen Race for the Cure.

**FIGURE 1.3**

Apple's Web site featured the iPhone 3G when it was first launched. Web site communication included details regarding the phone's features, speed, and price.

### Delivering Offerings

Marketing can't just promise value, it also has to deliver value. **Delivering** an offering that has value is much more than simply getting the product into the hands of the user; it is also making sure that the user understands how to get the most out of the product and is taken care of if he or she requires service later. Value is delivered in part through a company's supply chain. The **supply chain** includes a number of organizations and functions that mine, make, assemble, or deliver materials and products from a manufacturer to consumers. The actual group of organizations can vary greatly from industry to industry, and include wholesalers, transportation companies, and retailers. **Logistics**, or the actual transportation and storage of materials and products, is the primary component of supply chain management, but there are other aspects of supply chain management that we will discuss later.

### Exchanging Offerings

In addition to creating an offering, communicating its benefits to consumers, and delivering the offering, there is the actual transaction, or **exchange**, that has to occur. In most instances, we consider the exchange to be cash for products and services. However, if you were to fly to Louisville, Kentucky, for the Kentucky Derby, you could "pay" for your airline tickets using frequent-flier miles. You could also use Hilton Honors points to "pay" for your hotel, and cash back points on your Discover card to pay for meals. None of these transactions would actually require cash. Other exchanges, such as information about your preferences gathered through surveys, might not involve cash.

When consumers acquire, consume (use), and dispose of products and services, exchange occurs, including during the consumption phase. For example, via Apple's "One-to-One" program, you can pay a yearly fee in exchange for additional periodic product training sessions with an Apple professional. So, each time a training session occurs, another transaction takes place. A transaction also occurs when you are finished with a product. For example, you might sell your old iPhone to a friend, trade in a car, or ask the Salvation Army to pick up your old refrigerator.

Disposing of products has become an important ecological issue. Batteries and other components of cell phones, computers, and high-tech appliances can be very harmful to the environment, and many consumers don't know how to dispose of these products properly. Some companies, such as Office Depot, have created recycling centers to which customers can take their old electronics.

Apple has a Web page where consumers can fill out a form, print it, and ship it along with their old cell phones and MP3 players to Apple. Apple then pulls out the materials that are recyclable and properly disposes of those that aren't. By lessening the hassle associated with disposing of products, Office Depot and Apple add value to their product offerings.

**delivering**

In marketing, as in delivering value, a broad term that means getting the product to the consumer and making sure that the user gets the most out of the product and service.

**supply chain**

All of the organizations that participate in the production, promotion, and delivery of a product or service from the producer to the end consumer.

**logistics**

The physical flow of materials in the supply chain.

**exchange**

The transaction of value, usually economic, between a buyer and seller.

### KEY TAKEAWAY

The focus of marketing has changed from emphasizing the product, price, place, and promotion mix to one that emphasizes creating, communicating, delivering, and exchanging value. Value is a function of the benefits an individual receives and consists of the price the consumer paid and the time and effort the person expended making the purchase.

### REVIEW QUESTIONS

1. What is the marketing mix?
2. How has marketing changed from the four Ps approach to the more current value-based perspective?
3. What is the personal value equation?

# 2. WHO DOES MARKETING?

LEARNING OBJECTIVE

1. Describe how the various institutions and entities that engage in marketing use marketing to deliver value.

The short answer to the question of who does marketing is "everybody!" But that answer is a bit glib and not too useful. Let's take a moment and consider how different types of organizations engage in marketing.

## 2.1 For-Profit Companies

The obvious answer to the question, "Who does marketing?" is for-profit companies like McDonald's, Procter & Gamble (the makers of Tide detergent and Crest toothpaste), and Walmart. For example, McDonald's creates a new breakfast chicken sandwich for $1.99 (the offering), launches a television campaign (communicating), makes the sandwiches available on certain dates (delivering), and then sells them in its stores (exchanging). When Procter & Gamble (or P&G for short) creates a new Crest tartar control toothpaste, it launches a direct mail campaign in which it sends information and samples to dentists to offer to their patients. P&G then sells the toothpaste through retailers like Walmart, which has a panel of consumers sample the product and provide feedback through an online community. These are all examples of marketing activities.

For-profit companies can be defined by the nature of their customers. A B2C (business-to-consumer) company like P&G sells products to be used by consumers like you, while a B2B (business-to-business) company sells products to be used within another company's operations, as well as by government agencies and entities. To be sure, P&G sells toothpaste to other companies like Walmart (and probably to the Army and prisons and other government agencies), but the end user is an individual person.

Other ways to categorize companies that engage in marketing is by the functions they fulfill. P&G is a manufacturer, Walmart is a retailer, and Grocery Supply Company (http://www.grocerysupply.com) is a wholesaler of grocery items and buys from companies like P&G in order to sell to small convenience store chains. Though they have different functions, all these types of for-profit companies engage in marketing activities. Walmart, for example, advertises to consumers. Grocery Supply Company salespeople will call on convenience store owners and take orders, as well as build in-store displays. P&G might help Walmart or Grocery Supply Company with templates for advertising or special cartons to use in an in-store display, but all the companies are using marketing to help sell P&G's toothpaste.

Similarly, all the companies engage in dialogs with their customers in order to understand what to sell. For Walmart and Grocery Supply, the dialog may result in changing what they buy and sell; for P&G, such customer feedback may yield a new product or a change in pricing strategy.

## 2.2 Nonprofit Organizations

Nonprofit organizations also engage in marketing. When the American Heart Association (AHA) created a heart-healthy diet for people with high blood pressure, it bound the diet into a small book, along with access to a special Web site that people can use to plan their meals and record their health-related activities. The AHA then sent copies of the diet to doctors to give to patients. When does an exchange take place, you might be wondering? And what does the AHA get out of the transaction?

From a monetary standpoint, the AHA does not directly benefit. Nonetheless, the organization is meeting its mission, or purpose, of getting people to live heart-healthy lives and considers the campaign a success when doctors give the books to their patients. The point is that the AHA is engaged in the marketing activities of creating, communicating, delivering, and exchanging. This won't involve the same kind of exchange as a for-profit company, but it is marketing. When a nonprofit organization engages in marketing activities, this is called **nonprofit marketing**. Some schools offer specific courses in nonprofit marketing, and many marketing majors begin their careers with nonprofit organizations.

**nonprofit marketing**

Marketing activities conducted to meet the goals of nonprofit organizations.

Government entities also engage in marketing activities. For example, when the U.S. Army advertises to parents of prospective recruits, sends brochures to high schools, or brings a Bradley Fighting Vehicle to a state fair, the Army is engaging in marketing. The U.S. Army also listens to its constituencies, as evidenced by recent research aimed at understanding how to serve military families more effectively. One result was advertising aimed at parents and improving their response to their children's interest in joining the Army; another was a program aimed at encouraging spouses of military personnel to access counseling services when their spouse is serving overseas.

Similarly, the Environmental Protection Agency (EPA) runs a number of advertising campaigns designed to promote environmentally friendly activities. One such campaign promoted the responsible disposal of motor oil instead of simply pouring it on the ground or into a storm sewer.

There is a difference between these two types of activities. When the Army is promoting the benefits of enlisting, it hopes young men and women will join the Army. By contrast, when the EPA runs commercials about how to properly dispose of motor oil, it hopes to change people's attitudes and behaviors so that social change occurs. Marketing conducted in an effort to achieve certain social objectives can be done by government agencies, nonprofit institutions, religious organizations, and others and is called **social marketing**. Convincing people that global warming is a real threat via advertisements and commercials is social marketing, as is the example regarding the EPA's campaign to promote responsible disposal of motor oil.

**social marketing**

Marketing conducted in an effort to achieve social change.

## 2.3 Individuals

If you create a résumé, are you using marketing to communicate the value you have to offer prospective employers? If you sell yourself in an interview, is that marketing? When you work for a wage, you are delivering value in exchange for pay. Is this marketing, too?

Some people argue that these are not marketing activities and that individuals do not necessarily engage in marketing. (Some people also argue that social marketing really isn't marketing either.) Can individuals market themselves and their ideas?

In some respects, the question is a rhetorical one, designed for academics to argue about in class. Our point is that in the end, it may not matter. If, as a result of completing this book, you can learn how to more effectively create value, communicate and deliver that value to the receiver, and receive something in exchange, then we've achieved our purpose.

### KEY TAKEAWAY

Marketing can be thought of as a set of business practices that for-profit organizations, nonprofit organizations, government entities, and individuals can utilize. When a nonprofit organization engages in marketing activities, this is called *nonprofit marketing*. Marketing conducted in an effort to achieve certain social objectives is called *social marketing*.

### REVIEW QUESTIONS

1. What types of companies engage in marketing?
2. What is the difference between nonprofit marketing and social marketing?
3. What can individuals do for themselves that would be considered marketing?

# 3. WHY STUDY MARKETING?

### LEARNING OBJECTIVE

1. **Explain the role marketing plays in individual firms and society as a whole.**

## 3.1 Marketing Enables Profitable Transactions to Occur

Products don't, contrary to popular belief, sell themselves. Generally, the "build it and they will come" philosophy doesn't work. Good marketing educates customers so that they can find the products they want, make better choices about those products, and extract the most value from them. In this way, marketing helps facilitate exchanges between buyers and sellers for the mutual benefit of both parties.

Likewise, good social marketing provides people with information and helps them make healthier decisions for themselves and for others.

Of course, all business students should understand all functional areas of the firm, including marketing. There is more to marketing, however, than simply understanding its role in the business. Marketing has tremendous impact on society.

## 3.2 Marketing Delivers Value

Not only does marketing deliver value to customers, but also that value translates into the value of the firm as it develops a reliable customer base and increases its sales and profitability. So when we say that marketing delivers value, marketing delivers value to both the customer and the company. Franklin D. Roosevelt, the U.S. president with perhaps the greatest influence on our economic system, once said, "If I were starting life over again, I am inclined to think that I would go into the advertising business in preference to almost any other. The general raising of the standards of modern civilization among all groups of people during the past half century would have been impossible without the spreading of the knowledge of higher standards by means of advertising."[2] Roosevelt referred to advertising, but advertising alone is insufficient for delivering value. Marketing finishes the job by ensuring that what is delivered is valuable.

## 3.3 Marketing Benefits Society

Marketing benefits society in general by improving people's lives in two ways. First, as we mentioned, it facilitates trade. As you have learned, or will learn, in economics, being able to trade makes people's lives better. Otherwise people wouldn't do it. (Imagine what an awful life you would lead if you had to live a Robinson Crusoe–like existence as did Tom Hanks's character in the movie *Castaway.*) In addition, because better marketing means more successful companies, jobs are created. This generates wealth for people, who are then able to make purchases, which, in turn, creates more jobs.

The second way in which marketing improves the quality of life is based on the value delivery function of marketing, but in a broader sense. When you add all the marketers together who are trying to deliver offerings of greater value to consumers and are effectively communicating that value, consumers are able to make more informed decisions about a wider array of choices. From an economic perspective, more choices and smarter consumers are indicative of a higher quality of life.

## 3.4 Marketing Costs Money

Marketing can sometimes be the largest expense associated with producing a product. In the soft drink business, marketing expenses account for about one-third of a product's price—about the same as the ingredients used to make the soft drink itself. At the bottling and retailing level, the expenses involved in marketing a drink to consumers like you and me make up the largest cost of the product.

Some people argue that society does not benefit from marketing when it represents such a huge chunk of a product's final price. In some cases, that argument is justified. Yet, when marketing results in more informed consumers receiving a greater amount of value, then the cost is justified.

## 3.5 Marketing Offers People Career Opportunities

Marketing is the interface between producers and consumers. In other words, it is the one function in the organization in which the entire business comes together. Being responsible for both making money for your company and delivering satisfaction to your customers makes marketing a great career. In addition, because marketing can be such an expensive part of a business and is so critical to its success, companies actively seek good marketing people. At the beginning of each chapter in this book, we profile a person in the marketing profession and let that person describe for you what he or she does. As you will learn, there's a great variety of jobs available in the marketing profession. These positions represent only a few of the opportunities available in marketing.

- **Marketing research.** Personnel in marketing research are responsible for studying markets and customers in order to understand what strategies or tactics might work best for firms.
- **Merchandising.** In retailing, merchandisers are responsible for developing strategies regarding what products wholesalers should carry to sell to retailers such as Target and Walmart.
- **Sales.** Salespeople meet with customers, determine their needs, propose offerings, and make sure that the customer is satisfied. Sales departments can also include sales support teams who work on creating the offering.

- **Advertising.** Whether it's for an advertising agency or inside a company, some marketing personnel work on advertising. Television commercials and print ads are only part of the advertising mix. Many people who work in advertising spend all their time creating advertising for electronic media, such as Web sites and their pop-up ads, podcasts, and the like.
- **Product development.** People in product development are responsible for identifying and creating features that meet the needs of a firm's customers. They often work with engineers or other technical personnel to ensure that value is created.
- **Direct marketing.** Professionals in direct marketing communicate directly with customers about a company's product offerings via channels such as e-mail, chat lines, telephone, or direct mail.
- **Event marketing.** Some marketing personnel plan special events, orchestrating face-to-face conversations with potential and current customers in a special setting.

A career in marketing can begin in a number of different ways. Entry-level positions for new college graduates are available in many of the positions mentioned above. A growing number of CEOs are people with marketing backgrounds. Some legendary CEOs like Ross Perot and Mary Kay Ash got their start in marketing. More recently, CEOs like Mark Hurd, who runs Hewlett-Packard, and Jeffrey Immelt at GE are showing how marketing careers can lead to the highest pinnacles of the organization.

**KEY TAKEAWAY**

By facilitating transactions, marketing delivers value to both consumers and firms. At the broader level, this process creates jobs and improves the quality of life in a society. Marketing can be costly, so firms need to hire good people to manage their marketing activities. Being responsible for both making money for your company and delivering satisfaction to your customers makes marketing a great career.

**REVIEW QUESTIONS**

1. Why study marketing?
2. How does marketing provide value?
3. Why does marketing cost so much? Is marketing worth it?

# 4. THEMES AND ORGANIZATION OF THIS BOOK

**LEARNING OBJECTIVE**

1. **Understand and outline the elements of a marketing plan as a planning process.**

## 4.1 Marketing's Role in the Organization

We previously discussed marketing as a set of activities that anyone can do. Marketing is also a functional area in companies, just like operations and accounting are. Within a company, marketing might be the title of a department, but some marketing functions, such as sales, might be handled by another department. Marketing activities do not occur separately from the rest of the company, however.

As we have explained, pricing an offering, for example, will involve a company's finance and accounting departments in addition to the marketing department. Similarly, a marketing strategy is not created solely by a firm's marketing personnel. Instead, it flows from the company's overall strategy. We'll discuss strategy much more completely in Chapter 2.

## 4.2 Everything Starts with Customers

Most organizations start with an idea of how to serve customers better. Apple's engineers began working on the iPod by looking at the available technology and thinking about how customers would like to have their music more available, as well as more affordable, through downloading.

Many companies think about potential markets and customers when they start. John Deere, for example, founded his company on the principle of serving customers. When admonished for making constant improvements to his products even though farmers would take whatever they could get, Deere reportedly replied, "They haven't got to take what we make and somebody else will beat us, and we will lose our trade."[3] He recognized that if his company failed to meet customers' needs, someone else would. The mission of the company then became the one shown in Figure 1.4.

**FIGURE 1.4** Mission Statement of Deere and Company

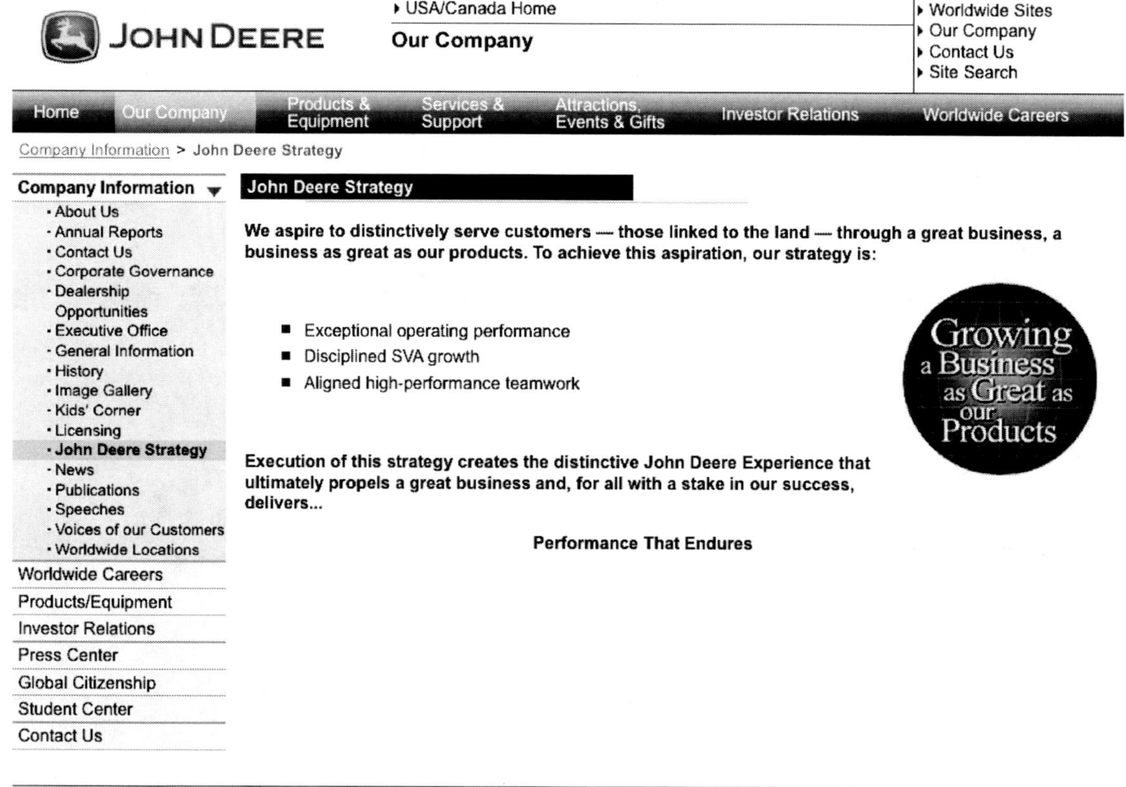


*Source: Deere and Company, used with permission.*

Here are a few mission statements from other companies. Note that they all refer to their customers, either directly or by making references to relationships with them. Note also how these are written to inspire employees and others who interact with the company and may read the mission statement.

*IBM*

*IBM will be driven by these values:*

- *Dedication to every client's success.*
- *Innovation that matters, for our company and for the world.*
- *Trust and personal responsibility in all relationships.*[4]

*Coca-Cola*

*Everything we do is inspired by our enduring mission:*

- *To refresh the world...in body, mind, and spirit.*
- *To inspire moments of optimism...through our brands and our actions.*
- *To create value and make a difference...everywhere we engage.*[5]

*McDonald's*

> *To be our customers' favorite place and way to eat.*[6]

*Merck*

> *To provide innovative and distinctive products and services that save and improve lives and satisfy customer needs, to be recognized as a great place to work, and to provide investors with a superior rate of return.*[7]

Not all companies create mission statements that reflect a marketing orientation. Note Apple's mission statement: "Apple ignited the personal computer revolution in the 1970s with the Apple II and reinvented the personal computer in the 1980s with the Macintosh. Today, Apple continues to lead the industry in innovation with its award-winning computers, OS X operating system and iLife and professional applications. Apple is also spearheading the digital media revolution with its iPod portable music and video players and iTunes online store, and has entered the mobile phone market with its revolutionary iPhone."[8] This mission statement reflects a production orientation, or an operating philosophy based on the premise that Apple's success is due to great products and that simply supplying them will lead to demand for them. The challenge, of course, is how to create a "great" product without thinking too much about the customer's wants and needs. Apple, and for that matter, many other companies, have fallen prey to thinking that they knew what a great product was without asking their customers. In fact, Apple's first attempt at a graphic user interface (GUI) was the LISA, a dismal failure.

## 4.3 The Marketing Plan

The **marketing plan** is the strategy for implementing the components of marketing: creating, communicating, delivering, and exchanging value. Once a company has decided what business it is in and expressed that in a mission statement, the firm then develops a corporate strategy. Marketing strategists subsequently use the corporate strategy and mission and combine that with an understanding of the market to develop the company's marketing plan. This is the focus of Chapter 2. Figure 1.5 shows the steps involved in creating a marketing plan.

**marketing plan**

A document that is designed to communicate the marketing strategy for an offering. The purpose of the plan is to influence executives, suppliers, distributors, and other important stakeholders of the firm so they will invest money, time, and effort to ensure the plan is a success.

The book then moves into understanding customers. Understanding the customer's wants and needs; how the customer wants to acquire, consume, and dispose of the offering; and what makes up their personal value equation are three important goals. Marketers want to know their customers—who they are and what they like to do—so as to uncover this information. Generally, this requires marketing researchers to collect sales and other related customer data and analyze it.

**FIGURE 1.5** Steps in Creating a Marketing Plan

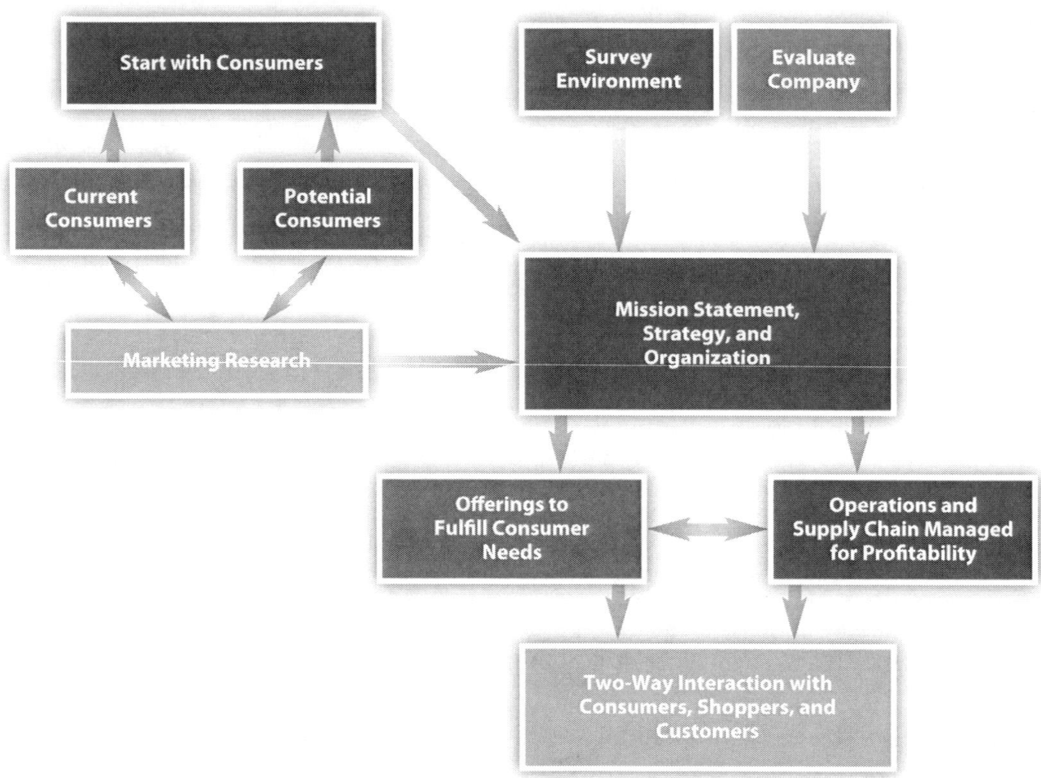


Once this information is gathered and digested, the planners can then work to create the right offering. Products and services are developed, bundled together at a price, and then tested in the market. Decisions have to be made as to when to alter the offerings, add new ones, or drop old ones. These decisions are the focus of the next set of chapters and are the second step in marketing planning.

Following the material on offerings, we explore the decisions associated with building the value chain. Once an offering is designed, the company has to be able to make it and then be able to get it to the market. This step, planning for the delivery of value, is the third step in the marketing plan.

The fourth step is creating the plan for communicating value. How does the firm make consumers aware of the value it has to offer? How can it help them recognize that value and decide that they should purchase products? These are important questions for marketing planners.

Once a customer has decided that her personal value equation is likely to be positive, then she will decide to purchase the product. That decision still has to be acted on, however, which is the exchange. The details of the exchange are the focus of the last few chapters of the book. As exchanges occur, marketing planners then refine their plans based on the feedback they receive from their customers, what their competitors are doing, and how market conditions are changing.

## 4.4 The Changing Marketing Environment

At the beginning of this chapter, we mentioned that the view of marketing has changed from a static set of four Ps to a dynamic set of processes that involve marketing professionals as well as many other employees in an organization. The way business is being conducted today is changing, too, and marketing is changing along with it. There are several themes, or important trends, that you will notice throughout this book.

- **Ethics and social responsibility.** Businesses exist only because society allows them to. When businesses begin to fail society, society will punish them or revoke their license. The crackdown on companies in the subprime mortgage-lending industry is one example. The collapse of Enron and the jailing of its executives is another. Scandals such as these illustrate how society responds to unethical business practices. However, whereas ethics require that you only do no harm, the concept of **social responsibility** requires that you must actively seek to improve the lot of others. Today, people are demanding businesses take a proactive stance in terms of social responsibility, and they are being held to ever-higher standards of conduct.
- **Sustainability. Sustainability** is an example of social responsibility and involves engaging in practices that do not diminish the earth's resources. SC Johnson, the company that makes Pledge and Windex, was among the first companies to engage in manufacturing practices that reduced or eliminated pollution. Right now, companies do not *have* to engage in these practices, but because firms really represent the people behind them (their owners and employees), forward-thinking executives are seeking ways to reduce the impact their companies are having on the planet.
- **Service-dominant logic.** You might have noticed that we use the word *offering* a lot instead of the term *product*. That's because of service-dominant logic, the approach to business that recognizes that consumers want value no matter how it is delivered. That emphasis on value is what drives the functional approach to value that we've taken—that is, creating, communicating, delivering, and exchanging value.
- **Metrics.** Technology has increased the amount of information available to decision makers. As such, the amount and quality of data for evaluating a firm's performance is increasing. Earlier in our discussion of the marketing plan, we explained that customers communicate via transactions. Although this sounds both simple and obvious, better information technology has given us a much more complete picture of each exchange. Using this data, we can build more effective metrics that can then be used to create better offerings, better communication plans, and so forth.
- **A global environment.** Every business is influenced by global issues. The price of oil, for example, is a global concern that affects everyone's prices and even the availability of some offerings. Many companies, though, source some or all their offerings from companies in other countries or else face some sort of direct competition from companies based in other countries. Every business professional, whether marketing or otherwise, has to have some understanding of the global environment in which companies operate.

**social responsibility**

The idea that companies should manage their businesses not just to earn profits but to advance the well-being of society.

**sustainability**

An example of social responsibility that involves engaging in practices that do not diminish the earth's resources.

## KEY TAKEAWAY

A company's marketing plan flows from its strategic plan. Both begin with a focus on customers. The essential components of the plan are understanding customers, creating an offering that delivers value, communicating the value to the customer, exchanging with the customer, and evaluating the firm's performance. A marketing plan is influenced by environmental trends such as social responsibility, sustainability, service-dominant logic, the increased availability of data and effective metrics, and the global nature of the business environment.

## REVIEW QUESTIONS

1. Why does everything start with customers? Or is it only marketing that starts with customers?
2. What are the key parts of a marketing plan?
3. What is the relationship between social responsibility, sustainability, service-dominant logic, and the global business environment? How does the concept of metrics fit?

# 5. DISCUSSION QUESTIONS AND ACTIVITIES

## DISCUSSION QUESTIONS

1. Compare and contrast a four Ps approach to marketing versus the value approach (creating, communicating, and delivering value). What would you expect to be the same and what would you expect to be different between two companies that apply one or the other approach?
2. Assume you are about to graduate. How would you apply marketing principles to your job search? In what ways would you be able to create, communicate, and deliver value as a potential employee, and what would that value be, exactly? How would you prove that you can deliver that value?
3. Is marketing always appropriate for political candidates? Why or why not?
4. How do the activities of marketing for value fulfill the marketing concept for the market-oriented organization?
5. This chapter introduces the personal value equation. How does that concept apply to people who buy for the government or for a business or for your university? How does that concept apply when organizations are engaged in social marketing?
6. This chapter addresses several reasons why marketing is an important area of study. Should marketing be required for all college students, no matter their major? Why or why not?
7. Of the four marketing functions, where does it look like most of the jobs are? What are the specific positions? How are the other marketing functions conducted through those job positions, even though in a smaller way?
8. Why is service-dominant logic important?
9. What is the difference between a need and a want? How do marketers create wants? Provide several examples.
10. The marketing concept emphasizes satisfying customer needs and wants. How does marketing satisfy your needs as a college student? Are certain aspects of your life influenced more heavily by marketing than others? Provide examples.
11. A company's offering represents the bundling of the tangible good, the intangible service, and the price. Describe the specific elements of the offering for an airline carrier, a realtor, a restaurant, and an online auction site.
12. The value of a product offering is determined by the customer and varies accordingly. How does a retailer like Walmart deliver value differently than Banana Republic?
13. Explain how Apple employed the marketing concept in designing, promoting, and supplying the iPhone. Identify the key benefit(s) for consumers relative to comparable competitive offerings.

## ACTIVITIES

1. One of your friends is contemplating opening a coffee shop near your college campus. She seeks your advice about size of the prospective customer base and how to market the business according to the four Ps. What strategies can you share with your friend to assist in launching the business?
2. You are considering working for United Way upon graduation. Explain how the marketing goals, strategies, and markets for the nonprofit differ from a for-profit organization.
3. Think about the last time you ate at McDonald's. Evaluate your experience using the personal value equation.
4. Marketing benefits organizations, customers, and society. Explain how an organization like DuPont benefits the community in which it operates as well as society at large.

# ENDNOTES

1. American Marketing Association, "Definition of Marketing," http://www.marketingpower.com/AboutAMA/Pages/DefinitionofMarketing.aspx?sq=definition+of+marketing (accessed December 3, 2009).

2. Famous Quotes and Authors, "Franklin D. Roosevelt Quotes and Quotations," http://www.famousquotesandauthors.com/authors/franklin_d__roosevelt_quotes.html (accessed December 7, 2009).

3. John Deere, "John Deere: A Biography," http://www.deere.com/en_US/compinfo/history/johndeere2.html (accessed December 3, 2009).

4. IBM, "About IBM," http://www.ibm.com/ibm/us/en (accessed December 3, 2009).

5. The Coca-Cola Company, "Mission, Vision & Values," http://www.thecoca-colacompany.com/ourcompany/mission_vision_values.html (accessed December 3, 2009).

6. McDonald's, "Our Company," http://aboutmcdonalds.com/mcd/our_company/mcd_faq/student_research.html#1 (accessed December 3, 2009).

7. Merck & Co., Inc., "The New Merck," http://www.merck.com/about/Merck%20Vision%20Mission.pdf (accessed December 7, 2009).

8. Apple, Inc., "Apple's App Store Downloads Top 1.5 Billion in First Year," http://www.apple.com/hk/en/pr/library/2009/07/14apps.html (accessed December 3, 2009).

# CHAPTER 2
# Strategic Planning

Have you ever wondered how an organization decides which products and services to develop, price, promote, and sell? Organizations typically develop plans and strategies that outline how they want to go about this process. Such a plan must take into account a company's current internal conditions, such as its resources, capabilities, technology, and so forth. The plan must also take into account conditions in the external environment, such as the economy, competitors, and government regulations that could affect what the firm wants to do.

Just as your personal plans—such as what you plan to major in or where you want to find a job—are likely to change, organizations also have contingency plans. Individuals and organizations both must develop long-term (longer than a year) strategic plans, match their strengths and resources to available opportunities, and adjust their plans to changing circumstances as necessary.

## 1. THE VALUE PROPOSITION

**LEARNING OBJECTIVES**

1. **Explain what a value proposition is.**
2. **Understand why a company may develop different value propositions for different target markets.**

### 1.1 What Is a Value Proposition?

Individual buyers and organizational buyers both evaluate products and services to see if they provide desired benefits. For example, when you're exploring your vacation options, you want to know the benefits of each destination and the value you will get by going to each place. Before you (or a firm) can develop a strategy or create a strategic plan, you first have to develop a value proposition. A **value proposition** is a thirty-second "elevator speech" stating the specific benefits a product or service offering provides a buyer. It shows why the product or service is superior to competing offers.

The following is an example of a value proposition developed by a sales consulting firm: "Our clients grow their business, large or small, typically by a minimum of 30–50% over the previous year. They accomplish this without working 80 hour weeks and sacrificing their personal lives."[1]

Note that although a value proposition will hopefully lead to profits for a firm, when the firm presents its value proposition to its customers, it doesn't mention its own profits. That's because the goal is to focus on the external market, or what customers want.

**value proposition**

A statement that summarizes the key benefits or value for target customers. It explains why customers should buy a product, why stakeholders should donate, or why prospective employees may want to work for an organization.

Firms typically identify different **target markets**, or groups of customers, they want to reach when they are developing their value propositions. Target markets will be discussed in more detail in Chapter 5. For now, be aware that companies sometimes develop different value propositions for different target markets. The value proposition tells each group of customers why they should buy a product or service, vacation to a particular destination, donate to an organization, and so forth.

Once the benefits of a product or service are clear, the firm must develop strategies that support the value proposition. The value proposition serves as a guide for this process. In the case of our sales consulting firm, the strategies it develops must help clients improve their sales by 30–50 percent. Likewise, if a company's value proposition states that the firm is the largest retailer in the region with the most stores and best product selection, opening stores or increasing the firm's inventory might be a key part of the company's strategy.

Individuals and students should also develop their own personal value propositions. Tell companies why they should hire you or why a graduate school should accept you. Show the value you bring to the situation. A value proposition will help you in different situations. Think about if you were to ask your parents for money to go on an overseas trip or study abroad program. You would need to explain to them the benefits and value of going abroad. Perhaps studying abroad will make you better prepared to find a good job. This, in turn, could help you more quickly repay any college money you might owe your parents—something that they might very much value.

**FIGURE 2.1**

Like any other company, Beaches, an all-inclusive chain of resorts for families, must explain what its value proposition is to customers. In other words, why does a Beaches resort provide more value to vacationing families than do other resorts?

*Source: Wikimedia Commons.*

**target market**

The group of customers toward which an organization directs its marketing efforts.

## KEY TAKEAWAY

A value proposition is a thirty-second "elevator speech" stating the specific value a product or service provides to a target market. Firms may develop different value propositions for different groups of customers. The value proposition shows why the product or service is superior to competing offers and why the customer should buy it or why a firm should hire you.

## REVIEW QUESTIONS

1. What is a value proposition?
2. You are interviewing for an internship. Create a value proposition for yourself that you may use as your thirty-second "elevator speech" to get the company interested in hiring you or talking to you more.

# 2. WHERE STRATEGIC PLANNING OCCURS WITHIN FIRMS

**LEARNING OBJECTIVES**

1. Identify the different levels at which strategic planning may occur within firms.
2. Understand how strategic planning that occurs at multiple levels in an organization helps a company achieve its overall corporate objectives.

Strategic planning is a process that helps an organization allocate its resources to capitalize on opportunities in the marketplace. Typically, it is a long-term process. So how and where does strategic planning occur within organizations? In large organizations, strategic planning is likely to occur at a number of different levels. For example, top executives will develop strategic plans for the corporation as a whole. These are **corporate level plans**. In addition, many large firms have different divisions, or businesses, called strategic business units. A **strategic business unit (SBU)** is a business or product line within an organization that has its own competitors, customers, and profit center for accounting purposes. A firm's SBUs may also have their own mission statement (purpose) and will generally develop strategic plans for themselves. These are called **business level plans**. The different departments, or functions (accounting, finance, marketing, and so forth) within a company or SBU, might also develop strategic plans. For example, a company may develop a marketing plan or a financial plan, which are functional level plans.

**corporate level plans**

Plans developed for the corporation as a whole take place at the corporate level.

**strategic business unit (SBU)**

Businesses or product lines within an organization that have their own competitors, customers, and profit centers.

**business level plans**

Plans developed for each strategic business unit typically have their own mission statement.

Figure 2.3 shows an example of different strategic planning levels that can exist within an organization's structure. The number of levels can vary, depending on the size and structure of an organization. Not every organization will have every level or have every type of plan. An overview of the marketing (or functional) plan is presented briefly at the end of this chapter but will be discussed in detail in Chapter 16 so you can see how the information discussed throughout the text may be used in developing a marketing plan.

**FIGURE 2.2**

Many consumers recognize the Goodyear blimp. Goodyear's strategic business units are North American Tire; Latin American Tire; Asia Pacific Tire; and Europe, Middle East, and Africa Tire. Goodyear's SBUs are set up to satisfy customers' needs in different worldwide markets.[2]

*Source: Wikimedia Commons.*

**FIGURE 2.3** Strategic Planning Levels in an Organization

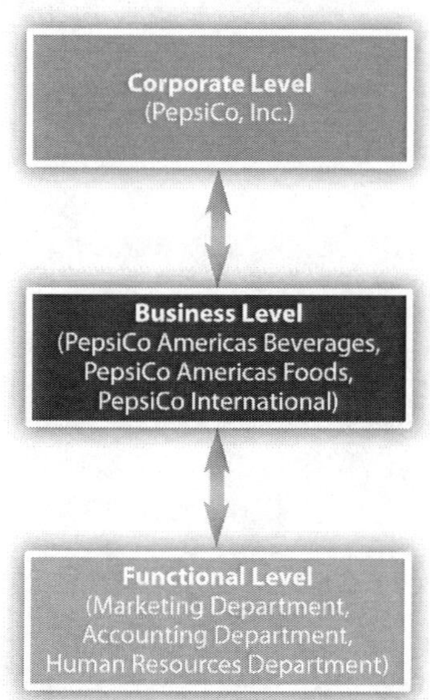


The strategies and actions implemented at the functional (department) level must be consistent with and help an organization achieve its objectives at both the business and corporate levels and vice versa. The SBUs at the business level must also be consistent with and help an organization achieve its corporate level objectives. For example, if a company wants to increase its profits at the corporate level and owns multiple business units, each unit might develop strategic plans to increase its own profits and thereby the firm's profits as a whole. At the functional level, a firm's marketing department might develop strategic plans to increase sales and the market share of the firm's most profitable products, which will increase profits at the business level and help the corporation's profitability. Both business level and functional plans should help the firm increase its profits, so that the company's corporate level strategic objectives can be met.

For example, take PepsiCo, which has committed itself to achieving business and financial success while leaving a positive imprint on society. PepsiCo identifies its three divisions (business units) as (1) PepsiCo Americas Beverages, which is responsible for products such as Pepsi soft drinks, Aquafina waters, Tropicana juices, and Gatorade products; (2) PepsiCo Americas Foods, which is responsible for Frito-Lay and Quaker Oats products; and (3) PepsiCo International, which consists of PepsiCo's businesses in Asia, Africa, Europe, and Australia.[3] To support PepsiCo's overall corporate strategy, all three business units must develop strategic plans to profitably produce offerings while demonstrating that they are committed to society and the environment.

At the functional (marketing) level, to increase PepsiCo's profits, employees responsible for different products or product categories such as beverages or foods might focus on developing healthier products and making their packaging more environmentally friendly so the company captures more market share. For example, the new Aquafina bottle uses less plastic and has a smaller label, which helps the environment by reducing the amount of waste.

**FIGURE 2.4**

The new Aquafina bottle uses less plastic and has a smaller label, reducing waste and helping the environment.

*Source: Wikipedia.*

Organizations can utilize multiple methods and strategies at different levels in the corporation to accomplish their various goals just as you may use different strategies to accomplish your goals. However, the basic components of the strategic planning process are the same at each of the different levels. Next, we'll take a closer look at the components of the strategic planning process.

## KEY TAKEAWAY

Strategic planning can occur at different levels (corporate, business, and functional) in an organization. The number of levels may vary. However, if a company has multiple planning levels, the plans must be consistent, and all must help achieve the overall goals of the corporation.

## REVIEW QUESTIONS

1. What different levels of planning can organizations utilize?
2. Give an example and explain how a corporation that wants to help protect the environment can do so at its corporate, business, and functional levels.

# 3. COMPONENTS OF THE STRATEGIC PLANNING PROCESS

**LEARNING OBJECTIVES**

1. Explain how a mission statement helps a company with its strategic planning.
2. Describe how a firm analyzes its internal environment.
3. Describe the external environment a firm may face and how it is analyzed.

The **strategic planning process** includes conducting a situation analysis and developing the organization's mission statement, objectives, value proposition, and strategies. Figure 2.5 shows the components of strategic planning. Let's now look at each of these components.

**strategic planning process**

A process that helps an organization allocate its resources under different conditions to accomplish its objectives, deliver value, and be competitive in a market-driven economy.

**FIGURE 2.5** The Strategic Planning Process

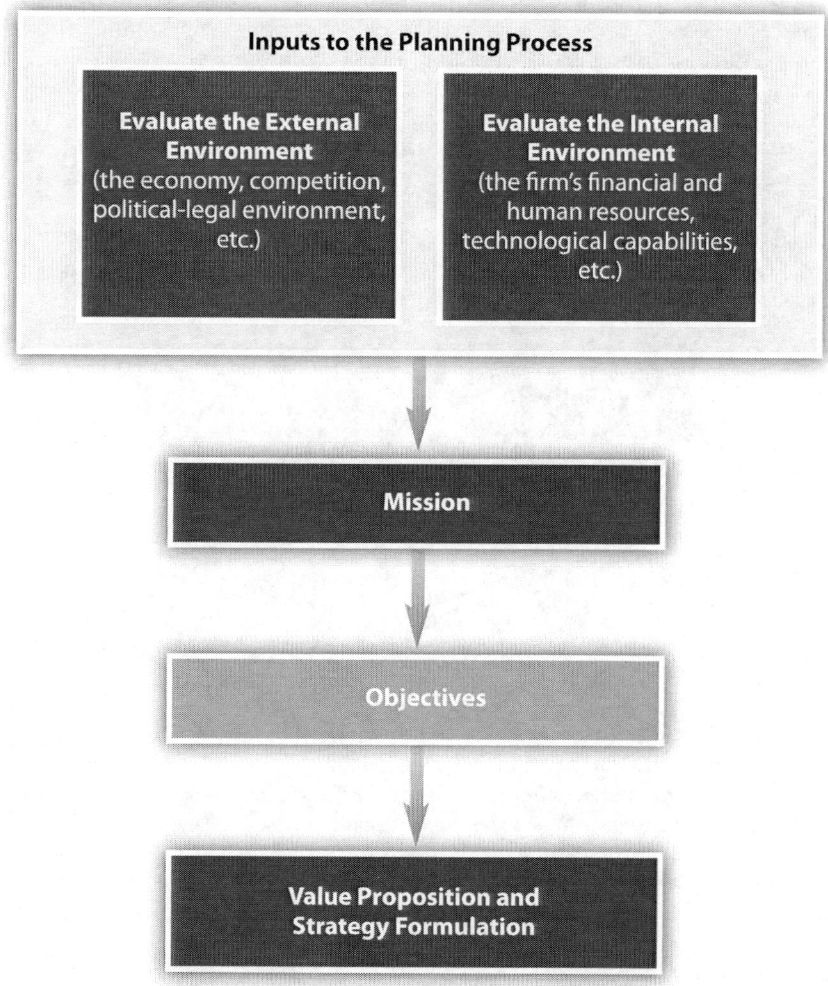


## 3.1 Conducting a Situation Analysis

As part of the strategic planning process, a **situation analysis** must be conducted before a company can decide on specific actions. A situation analysis involves analyzing both the external (outside the organization) and the internal (company) environments, as Figure 2.5 shows. The firm's internal environment—such as its financial resources, technological resources, and the capabilities of its personnel and their performance—has to be examined. It is also critical to examine the external environment the firm faces, such as the economy and its competitors. The external environment significantly affects the decisions a firm makes, and thus must be continuously evaluated. For example, during the economic

**situation analysis**

An assessment of an organization's internal and external environments.

downturn in 2008–2009, businesses found that many competitors cut the prices of their products drastically. Other companies reduced package sizes or the amount of product in packages. Firms also offered customers incentives (free shipping, free gift cards with purchase, rebates, etc.) to purchase their goods and services online, which allowed businesses to cut back on the personnel needed to staff their brick-and-mortar stores. While a business cannot control what competitors do, they must decide what actions to take to remain competitive—actions that depend in part on their internal environment.

## 3.2 Conducting a SWOT Analysis

**SWOT analysis**

An acronym for strengths, weaknesses, opportunities, and threats, the SWOT analysis is a tool that frames the situational analysis.

Based on the situation analysis, organizations analyze their strengths, weaknesses, opportunities, and threats, or conduct what's called a **SWOT analysis**. Strengths and weaknesses are internal factors and are somewhat controllable. For example, an organization's strengths might include its brand name, efficient distribution network, reputation for great service, and strong financial position. A firm's weaknesses might include lack of awareness of its products in the marketplace, a lack of human resources talent, and a poor location. Opportunities and threats are factors that are external to the firm and largely uncontrollable. Opportunities might entail the international demand for the type of products the firm makes, few competitors, and favorable social trends such as people living longer. Threats might include a bad economy, high interest rates that increase a firm's borrowing costs, and an aging population that makes it hard for the business to find workers.

You can conduct a SWOT analysis of yourself to help determine your competitive advantage. Perhaps your strengths include strong leadership abilities and communication skills, whereas your weaknesses include a lack of organization. Opportunities for you might exist in specific careers and industries; however, the economy and other people competing for the same position might be threats. Moreover, what is a strength for one person (say, strong accounting skills) might be a weakness for another person (poor accounting skills). The same is true for businesses. See Figure 2.6 for an illustration of some of the factors examined in a SWOT analysis.

**FIGURE 2.6** Elements of a SWOT Analysis

The easiest way to determine if a factor is external or internal is to take away the company, organization, or individual and see if the factor still exists. Internal factors such as strengths and weaknesses are specific to a company or individual, whereas external factors such as opportunities and threats affect multiple individuals and organizations in the marketplace. For example, if you are doing a situation analysis on PepsiCo and are looking at the weak economy, take PepsiCo out of the picture and see what factors remain. If the factor—the weak economy—is still there, it is an external factor. Even if PepsiCo hadn't been around in 2008–2009, the weak economy reduced consumer spending and affected a lot of companies.

## 3.3 Assessing the Internal Environment

As we have indicated, when an organization evaluates which factors are its strengths and weaknesses, it is assessing its internal environment. Once companies determine their strengths, they can use those strengths to capitalize on opportunities and develop their competitive advantage. For example, strengths for PepsiCo are what are called "mega" brands, or brands that individually generate over $1 billion in sales.[4] These brands are also designed to contribute to PepsiCo's environmental and social responsibilities.

PepsiCo's brand awareness, profitability, and strong presence in global markets are also strengths. Especially in foreign markets, the loyalty of a firm's employees can be a major strength, which can provide it with a competitive advantage. Loyal and knowledgeable employees are easier to train and tend to develop better relationships with customers. This helps organizations pursue more opportunities.

Although the brand awareness for PepsiCo's products is strong, smaller companies often struggle with weaknesses such as low brand awareness, low financial reserves, and poor locations. When organizations assess their internal environments, they must look at factors such as performance and costs as well as brand awareness and location. Managers need to examine both the past and current strategies of their firms and determine what strategies succeeded and which ones failed. This helps a company plan its future actions and improves the odds they will be successful. For example, a company might look at packaging that worked very well for a product and use the same type of packaging for new products. Firms may also look at customers' reactions to changes in products, including packaging, to see what works and doesn't work. When PepsiCo changed the packaging of major brands in 2008, customers had mixed responses. Tropicana switched from the familiar orange with the straw in it to a new package and customers did not like it. As a result, Tropicana changed back to their familiar orange with a straw after spending $35 million for the new package design.

**Video Clip**

**Tropicana's New Ad**

Tropicana's new ad left out the familiar orange with a straw.

View the video online at: http://www.youtube.com/embed/LDnkqlnhGGI

Individuals are also wise to look at the strategies they have tried in the past to see which ones failed and which ones succeeded. Have you ever done poorly on an exam? Was it the instructor's fault, the strategy you used to study, or did you decide not to study? See which strategies work best for you and perhaps try the same type of strategies for future exams. If a strategy did not work, see what went wrong and change it. Doing so is similar to what organizations do when they analyze their internal environments.

## 3.4 Assessing the External Environment

Analyzing the external environment involves tracking conditions in the marketplace that, although largely uncontrollable, affect the way an organization does business. As we have mentioned, these factors include competition and the economy. Other external factors include cultural and social trends, political and legal regulations, technological changes, and the price and availability of natural resources. Each of these factors is discussed separately in the next section. When firms globalize, analyzing the environment becomes more complex because they must examine the external environment in each country in which they do business. Regulations, competitors, technological development, and the economy may be different in each country and will affect how firms do business. To see how factors in the external environment such as technology may change education and lives of people around the world, watch the videos "Did You Know 2.0?" and "Did You Know 3.0?" which provide information on things such as the number of people on MySpace compared to populations in the world. Originally created in 2006, the video has been updated and translated into other languages. The latest edition of "Did You Know?" was created in Rome in 2008 and shows how information may change the world.

**Video Clip**

**Did You Know 2.0?**

To see how the external environment and world are changing and in turn affecting marketing strategies, check out "Did You Know 2.0?"

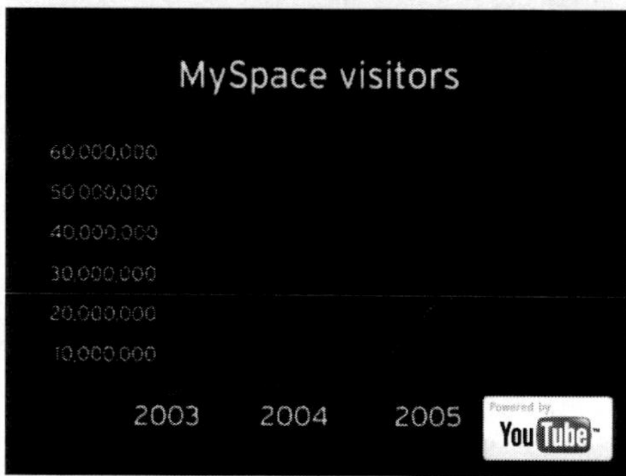


View the video online at: http://www.youtube.com/embed/pMcfrLYDm2U

**Video Clip**

**Did You Know 3.0?**

To see how fast things changed in two years, visit "Did You Know 3.0?"

View the video online at: http://www.youtube.com/embed/PHmwZ96_Gos

Although the external environment affects all organizations, companies must focus on factors that are relevant for their operations. For example, government regulations on food packaging will affect PepsiCo but not Goodyear. Similarly, students getting a business degree don't need to focus on job opportunities for registered nurses.

### The Competitive Environment

All organizations must consider their competition, whether it is direct or indirect competition vying for the consumer's dollar. Both nonprofit and for-profit organizations compete for customers' resources. Coke and Pepsi are direct competitors in the soft drink industry, Hilton and Sheraton are competitors in the hospitality industry, and organizations such as United Way and the American Cancer Society compete for resources in the nonprofit sector. However, hotels must also consider other options that people have when selecting a place to stay, such as hostels, dorms, bed and breakfasts, or rental homes.

A group of competitors that provide similar products or services form an industry. Michael Porter, a professor at Harvard University and a leading authority on competitive strategy, developed an approach for analyzing industries. Called the five forces model[5] and shown in Figure 2.7, the framework helps organizations understand their current competitors as well as organizations that could become competitors in the future. As such, firms can find the best way to defend their position in the industry.

**FIGURE 2.7** Five Forces Model[6]

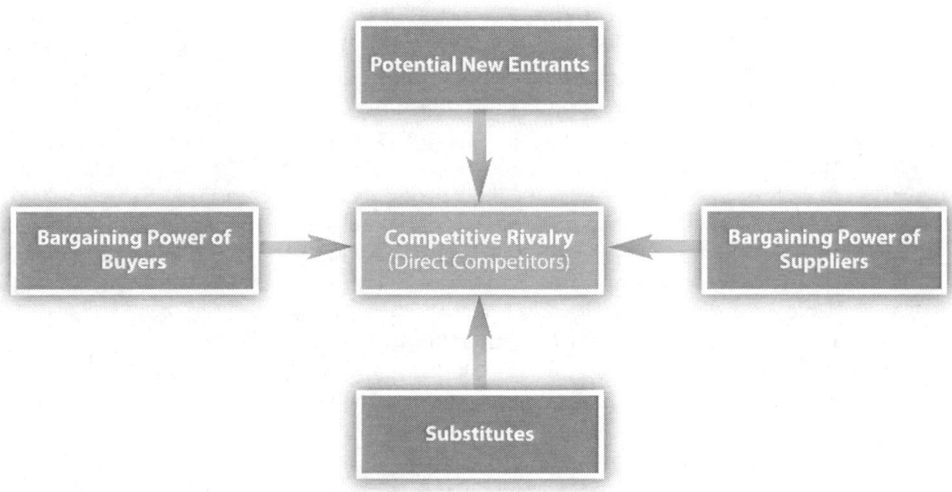


## Competitive Analysis

When a firm conducts a competitive analysis, they tend to focus on direct competitors and try to determine a firm's strengths and weaknesses, its image, and its resources. Doing so helps the firm figure out how much money a competitor may be able to spend on things such as research, new product development, promotion, and new locations. Competitive analysis involves looking at any information (annual reports, financial statements, news stories, observation details obtained on visits, etc.) available on competitors. **Mystery shoppers**, or people who act like customers, might visit competitors to learn about their customer service and their products. Imagine going to a competitor's restaurant and studying the menu and the prices and watching customers to see what items are popular and then changing your menu to better compete. Competitors battle for the customer's dollar and they must know what other firms are doing. Individuals and teams also compete for jobs, titles, and prizes and must figure out the competitors' weaknesses and plans in order to take advantage of their strengths and have a better chance of winning.

**mystery shopper**

A person who is paid to shop at a firm's establishment or one of its competitors' to observe the level of service, cleanliness of the facility, and so forth, and report his or her findings to the firm.

According to Porter, in addition to their direct competitors (competitive rivals), organizations must consider the strength and impact the following could have:[7]

- Substitute products
- Potential entrants (new competitors) in the marketplace
- The bargaining power of suppliers
- The bargaining power of buyers

When any of these factors change, companies may have to respond by changing their strategies. For example, because buyers are consuming fewer soft drinks these days, companies such as Coke and Pepsi have had to develop new, substitute offerings such as vitamin water and sports drinks. However, other companies such as Dannon or Nestlé may also be potential entrants in the flavored water market. When you select a hamburger fast-food chain, you also had the option of substitutes such as getting food at the grocery or going to a pizza place. When computers entered the market, they were a substitute for typewriters. Most students may not have ever used a typewriter, but some consumers still use typewriters for forms and letters.

Suppliers, the companies that supply ingredients as well as packaging materials to other companies, must also be considered. If a company cannot get the supplies it needs, it's in trouble. Also, sometimes suppliers see how lucrative their customers' markets are and decide to enter them. Buyers, who are the focus of marketing and strategic plans, must also be considered because they have bargaining power and must be satisfied. If a buyer is large enough, and doesn't purchase a product or service, it can affect a selling company's performance. Walmart, for instance, is a buyer with a great deal of bargaining power. Firms that do business with Walmart must be prepared to make concessions to them if they want their products on the company's store shelves.

**FIGURE 2.8**

When personal computers were first invented, they were a serious threat to typewriter makers such as Smith Corona.

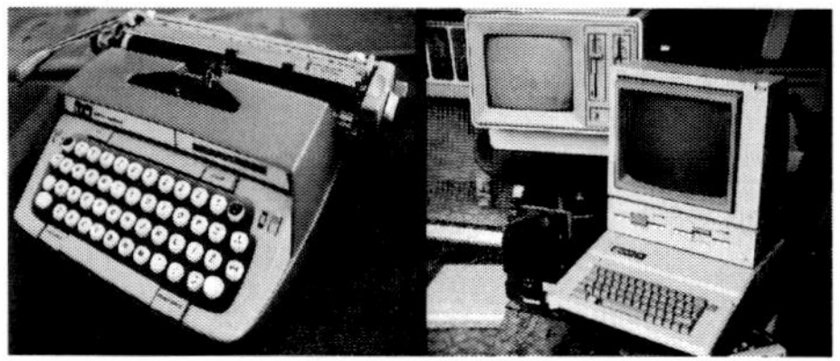

*Source: Flickr.*

Lastly, the world is becoming "smaller" and a more of a global marketplace. Companies everywhere are finding that no matter what they make, numerous firms around the world are producing the same "widget" or a similar offering (substitute) and are eager to compete with them. Employees are in the same position. The Internet has made it easier than ever for customers to find products and services and for workers to find the best jobs available, even if they are abroad. Companies are also acquiring foreign firms. These factors all have an effect on the strategic decisions companies make.

### The Political and Legal Environment

All organizations must comply with government regulations and understand the political and legal environments in which they do business. Different government agencies enforce the numerous regulations that have been established to protect both consumers and businesses. For example, the Sherman Act (1890) prohibits U.S. firms from restraining trade by creating monopolies and cartels. The regulations related to the act are enforced by the Federal Trade Commission (FTC), which also regulates deceptive advertising. The U.S. Food and Drug Administration (FDA) regulates the labeling of consumable products, such as food and medicine. One organization that has been extremely busy is the Consumer Product Safety Commission, the group that sets safety standards for consumer products. Unsafe baby formula and toys with lead paint caused a big scare among consumers in 2008 and 2009.

As we have explained, when organizations conduct business in multiple markets, they must understand that regulations vary across countries and across states. Many states and countries have different laws that affect strategy. For example, suppose you are opening up a new factory because you cannot keep up with the demand for your products. If you are considering opening the factory in France (perhaps because the demand in Europe for your product is strong), you need to know that it is illegal for employees in that country to work more than thirty-five hours per week.

**FIGURE 2.9**

The U.S. Food and Drug Administration prohibits companies from using unacceptable levels of lead in toys and other household objects, such as utensils and furniture. Mattel voluntarily recalled Sarge cars made in mid-2000.

*Source: U.S. Consumer Product Safety Commission.*

### The Economic Environment

The economy has a major impact on spending by both consumers and businesses, which, in turn, affects the goals and strategies of organizations. Economic factors include variables such as inflation, unemployment, interest rates, and whether the economy is in a growth period or a recession. Inflation occurs when the cost of living continues to rise, eroding the purchasing power of money. When this happens, you and other consumers and businesses need more money to purchase goods and services. Interest rates often rise when inflation rises. Recessions can also occur when inflation rises because higher prices sometimes cause low or negative growth in the economy.

During a recessionary period, it is possible for both high-end and low-end products to sell well. Consumers who can afford luxury goods may continue to buy them, while consumers with lower incomes tend to become more value conscious. Other goods and services, such as products sold in traditional department stores, may suffer. In the face of a severe economic downturn, even the sales of luxury goods can suffer. The economic downturn that began in 2008 affected consumers and businesses at all levels worldwide. Consumers reduced their spending, holiday sales dropped, financial institutions went bankrupt, the mortgage industry collapsed, and the "Big Three" U.S. auto manufacturers (Ford, Chrysler, and General Motors) asked for emergency loans.

### The Social and Cultural Environment

The social and cultural environment—including social trends, such as people's attitudes toward fitness and nutrition; demographic characteristics, such as people's age, income, marital status, education, and occupation; and culture, which relates to people's beliefs and values—is changing in the global marketplace. Fitness, nutrition, and health trends are affecting the product offerings of many firms. For example, PepsiCo produces vitamin water and sports drinks. More women are working, which has led to a rise in the demand for services such as house cleaning and daycare. U.S. baby boomers are reaching retirement age, sending their children to college, and trying to care of their elderly parents all at the same time. Firms are responding to the time constraints their buyers face by creating products that are more convenient, such as frozen meals and nutritious snacks.

The composition of the population is also constantly changing. Hispanics are the fastest-growing minority in the United States. Consumers in this group and other diverse groups prefer different types of products and brands. In many cities, stores cater specifically to Hispanic customers.

**FIGURE 2.10**

A small condiment business in California caters to Hispanic customers.

© 2010 Jupiterimages Corporation

### Technology

The technology available in the world is changing the way people communicate and the way firms do business. Everyone is affected by technological changes. Self-scanners and video displays at stores, ATMs, the Internet, and mobile phones are a few examples of how technology is affecting businesses and consumers. Many consumers get information, read the news, use text messaging, and shop online. As a result, marketers have begun allocating more of their promotion budgets to online ads and mobile marketing and not just to traditional print media such as newspapers and magazines.

**FIGURE 2.11**

Technology changes the way we do business. Banking on a cell phone adds convenience for customers. Bar codes on merchandise speed the checkout process.

© 2010 Jupiterimages Corporation

### Natural Resources

Natural resources are scarce commodities, and consumers are becoming increasingly aware of this fact. Today, many firms are doing more to engage in "sustainable" practices that help protect the environment and conserve natural resources. **Green marketing** involves marketing environmentally safe products and services in a way that is good for the environment. Water shortages often occur in the summer months, so many restaurants now only serve patrons water upon request. Hotels voluntarily conserve water by not washing guests' sheets and towels every day unless they request it. Reusing packages (refillable containers) and reducing the amount of packaging, paper, energy, and water in the production of goods and services are becoming key considerations for many organizations, whether they sell their products to other businesses or to final users (consumers). Green marketing not only helps the environment but also saves the company, and ultimately the consumer, money. Sustainability, ethics (doing the right things), and social responsibility (helping society, communities, and other people) influence an organization's planning process and the strategies they implement.

Once the situation analysis is complete, it becomes a critical input to an organization's or an individual's strategic plan. Let's look at the other components of the strategic planning process.

**green marketing**

Marketing environmentally safe products and services in a way that is good for the environment.

## 3.5 The Mission Statement

The firm's **mission statement** states the purpose of the organization and why it exists. Both profit and nonprofit organizations have mission statements, which they often publicize. The following are examples of mission statements:

**mission statement**

Defines the purpose of the organization and answers the question of how a company defines its business.

*PepsiCo's Mission Statement*

*"Our mission is to be the world's premier consumer products company focused on convenient foods and beverages. We seek to produce financial rewards to investors as we provide opportunities for growth and enrichment to our employees, our business partners and the communities in which we operate. And in everything we do, we strive for honesty, fairness and integrity."[8] "*

*The United Way's Mission Statement*

*"To improve lives by mobilizing the caring power of communities."[9] "*

Sometimes SBUs develop separate mission statements. For example, PepsiCo Americas Beverages, PepsiCo Americas Foods, and PepsiCo International might each develop a different mission statement.

**KEY TAKEAWAY**

A firm must analyze factors in the external and internal environments it faces throughout the strategic planning process. These factors are inputs to the planning process. As they change, the company must be prepared to adjust its plans. Different factors are relevant for different companies. Once a company has analyzed its internal and external environments, managers can begin to decide which strategies are best, given the firm's mission statement.

**REVIEW QUESTIONS**

1. What factors in the external environment are affecting the "Big Three" U.S. automobile manufacturers?
2. What are some examples of Walmart's strengths?
3. Suppose you work for a major hotel chain. Using Porter's five forces model, explain what you need to consider with regard to each force.

# 4. DEVELOPING ORGANIZATIONAL OBJECTIVES AND FORMULATING STRATEGIES

**LEARNING OBJECTIVES**

1. **Explain how companies develop the objectives driving their strategies.**
2. **Describe the different types of product strategies and market entry strategies that companies pursue.**

## 4.1 Developing Objectives

**objectives**

What organizations want to accomplish (the end results) in a given time frame.

**Objectives** are what organizations want to accomplish—the end results they want to achieve—in a given time frame. In addition to being accomplished within a certain time frame, objectives should be realistic (achievable) and be measurable, if possible. "To increase sales by 2 percent by the end of the year" is an example of an objective an organization might develop. You have probably set objectives for yourself that you want to achieve in a given time frame. For example, your objectives might be to maintain a certain grade point average and get work experience or an internship before you graduate.

Objectives help guide and motivate a company's employees and give its managers reference points for evaluating the firm's marketing actions. Although many organizations publish their mission statements, most for-profit companies do not publish their objectives. Accomplishments at each level of the organization have helped PepsiCo meet its corporate objectives over the course of the past few years. PepsiCo's business units (divisions) have increased the number of their facilities to grow their brands and enter new markets. PepsiCo's beverage and snack units have gained market share by developing healthier products and products that are more convenient to use.

A firm's marketing objectives should be consistent with the company's objectives at other levels, such as the corporate level and business level. An example of a marketing objective for PepsiCo might be "to increase by 4 percent the market share of Gatorade by the end of the year." The way firms analyze their different divisions or businesses will be discussed later in the chapter.

## 4.2 Formulating Strategies

**Strategies** are the means to the ends, or what a firm's going to do to meet its objectives. Successful strategies help organizations establish and maintain a competitive advantage that competitors cannot imitate easily. PepsiCo attempts to sustain its competitive advantage by constantly developing new products and innovations, including "mega brands," which are eighteen individual brands that generate over $1 billion in sales each.

**strategies**

Actions (means) taken to accomplish objectives.

Firms often use multiple strategies to accomplish their objectives and capitalize on marketing opportunities. For example, in addition to pursuing a low cost strategy (selling products inexpensively), Walmart has simultaneously pursued a strategy of opening new stores rapidly around the world. Many companies develop marketing strategies as part of their general, overall business plans. Other companies prepare separate marketing plans. We'll look at marketing plans here and discuss them more completely in Chapter 16.

A **marketing plan** is a strategic plan at the functional level that provides a firm's marketing group with direction. It is a road map that improves the firm's understanding of its competitive situation. The marketing plan also helps the firm allocate resources and divvy up the tasks that employees need to do for the company to meet its objectives. The different components of marketing plans will be discussed throughout the book and then discussed together at the end of the book. Next, let's take a look at the different types of basic market strategies firms pursue before they develop their marketing plans.

**marketing plan**

A document that is designed to communicate the marketing strategy for an offering. The purpose of the plan is to influence executives, suppliers, distributors, and other important stakeholders of the firm so they will invest money, time, and effort to ensure the plan is a success.

**FIGURE 2.12** Product and Market Entry Strategies

The different types of product and market entry strategies a firm can pursue in order to meet their objectives.

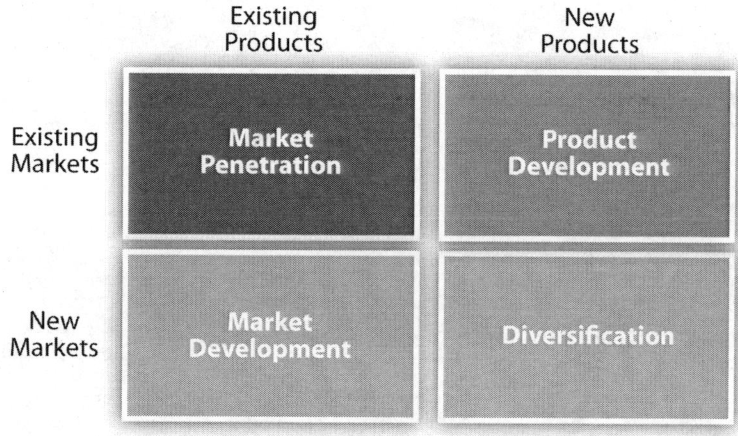


**Market penetration strategies** focus on increasing a firm's sales of its existing products to its existing customers. Companies often offer consumers special promotions or low prices to increase their usage and encourage them to buy products. When Frito-Lay distributes money-saving coupons to customers or offers them discounts to buy multiple packages of snacks, the company is utilizing a penetration strategy. The Campbell Soup Company gets consumers to buy more soup by providing easy recipes using their soup as an ingredient for cooking quick meals.

**market penetration strategy**

Selling more of existing products and services to existing customers.

**Product development strategies** involve creating new products for existing customers. A new product can be a totally new innovation, an improved product, or a product with enhanced value, such as one with a new feature. Cell phones that allow consumers to charge purchases with the phone or take pictures are examples of a product with enhanced value. A new product can also be one that comes in different variations, such as new flavors, colors, and sizes. Mountain Dew Voltage, introduced by PepsiCo Americas Beverages in 2009, is an example. Keep in mind, however, that what works for one company might not work for another. For example, just after Starbucks announced it was cutting back on the number of its lunch offerings, Dunkin' Donuts announced it was adding items to its lunch menu.

**product development strategy**

Creating new products or services for existing markets.

**market development strategy**

Selling existing products or services to new customers. Foreign markets often present opportunities for organizations to expand. Exporting, licensing, franchising, joint ventures, and direct investment are methods that companies use to enter international markets.

**export**

Sell products to buyers in foreign markets.

**license**

Sell the right to use some aspect of the production process, trademark, or patent to individuals in foreign markets.

**Market development strategies** focus on entering new markets with existing products. For example, during the recent economic downturn, manufacturers of high-end coffee makers began targeting customers who go to coffee shops. The manufacturers are hoping to develop the market for their products by making sure consumers know they can brew a great cup of coffee at home for a fraction of what they spend at Starbucks.

New markets can include any new groups of customers such as different age groups, new geographic areas, or international markets. Many companies, including PepsiCo and Hyundai, have entered—and been successful in—rapidly emerging markets such as Russia, China, and India. As Figure 2.12 shows, there are different ways, or strategies, by which firms can enter international markets. The strategies vary in the amount of risk, control, and investment that firms face. Firms can simply **export**, or sell their products to buyers abroad, which is the least risky and least expensive method but also offers the least amount of control. Many small firms export their products to foreign markets.

Firms can also **license**, or sell the right to use some aspect of their production processes, trademarks, or patents to individuals or firms in foreign markets. Licensing is a popular strategy, but firms must figure out how to protect their interests if the licensee decides to open its own business and void the license agreement. The French luggage and handbag maker Louis Vuitton faced this problem when it entered China. Competitors started illegally putting the Louis Vuitton logo on different products, which cut into Louis Vuitton's profits.

## FIGURE 2.13

The front of a KFC franchise in Asia may be much larger than KFC stores in the United States. Selling franchises is a popular way for firms to enter foreign markets.

*Source: Wikimedia Commons.*

**franchising**

Granting an independent operator the right to use your company's business model, techniques, and trademarks for a fee.

**contract manufacturing**

When companies hire manufacturers to produce their products in another country.

**Franchising** is a longer-term form of licensing that is extremely popular with service firms, such as restaurants like McDonald's and Subway, hotels like Holiday Inn Express, and cleaning companies like Stanley Steamer. Franchisees pay a fee for the franchise and must adhere to certain standards; however, they benefit from the advertising and brand recognition the franchising company provides.

**Contract manufacturing** allows companies to hire manufacturers to produce their products in another country. The manufacturers are provided specifications for the products, which are then manufactured and sold on behalf of the company that contracted the manufacturing. Contract manufacturing may provide tax incentives and may be more profitable than manufacturing the products in the home country. Examples of products in which contract manufacturing is often used include cell phones, computers, and printers.

**Joint ventures** combine the expertise and investments of two companies and help companies enter foreign markets. The firms in each country share the risks as well as the investments. Some countries such as China often require companies to form a joint venture with a domestic firm in order to enter the market. After entering the market in a partnership with a domestic firm and becoming established in the market, some firms may decide to separate from their partner and become their own business. Fuji Xerox Co., Ltd., is an example of a joint venture between the Japanese Fuji Photo Film Co. and the American document management company Xerox. Another example of a joint venture is Sony Ericsson. The venture combined the Japanese company Sony's electronic expertise with the Swedish company Ericsson's telecommunication expertise.

**joint venture**

An entity that is created when two parties agree to share their profits, losses, and control with one another in an economic activity they jointly undertake.

**Direct investment** (owning a company or facility overseas) is another way to enter a foreign market. For example, In Bev, the Dutch maker of Beck's beer, was able to capture market share in the United States by purchasing St. Louis-based Anheuser-Busch. A direct investment strategy involves the most risk and investment but offers the most control. Other companies such as advertising agencies may want to invest and develop their own businesses directly in international markets rather than trying to do so via other companies.

**direct investment**

Owning a company or facility overseas.

**FIGURE 2.14** Market Entry Methods

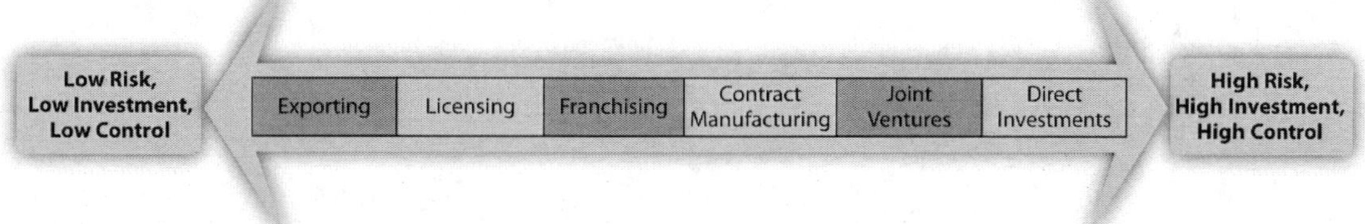


**Diversification strategies** involve entering new markets with new products or doing something outside a firm's current businesses. Firms that have little experience with different markets or different products often diversify their product lines by acquiring other companies. Diversification can be profitable, but it can also be risky if a company does not have the expertise or resources it needs to successfully implement the strategy. Warner Music Group's purchase of the concert promoter Bulldog Entertainment is an example of a diversification attempt that failed.

**diversification strategy**

Offering products that are unrelated to other existing products produced by the organization.

## KEY TAKEAWAY

The strategic planning process includes a company's mission (purpose), objectives (end results desired), and strategies (means). Sometimes the different SBUs of a firm have different mission statements. A firm's objectives should be realistic (achievable) and measurable. The different product market strategies firms pursue include market penetration, product development, market development, and diversification.

## REVIEW QUESTIONS

1. How do product development strategies differ from market development strategies?
2. Explain why some strategies work for some companies but not others.
3. What factors do firms entering foreign markets need to consider?
4. How do franchising and licensing strategies differ?

# 5. STRATEGIC PORTFOLIO PLANNING APPROACHES

**LEARNING OBJECTIVES**

1. **Explain how SBUs are evaluated using the Boston Consulting Group matrix.**
2. **Explain how businesses and the attractiveness of industries are evaluated using the General Electric approach.**

**portfolio**

A group of business units owned by a single firm.

**portfolio planning approach**

An approach to analyzing various businesses relative to one another.

When a firm has multiple strategic business units like PepsiCo does, it must decide what the objectives and strategies for each business are and how to allocate resources among them. A group of businesses can be considered a **portfolio**, just as a collection of artwork or investments compose a portfolio. In order to evaluate each business, companies sometimes utilize what's called a portfolio planning approach. A **portfolio planning approach** involves analyzing a firm's entire collection of businesses relative to one another. Two of the most widely used portfolio planning approaches include the Boston Consulting Group (BCG) matrix and the General Electric (GE) approach.

## 5.1 The Boston Consulting Group Matrix

**FIGURE 2.15** The Boston Consulting Group (BCG) Matrix

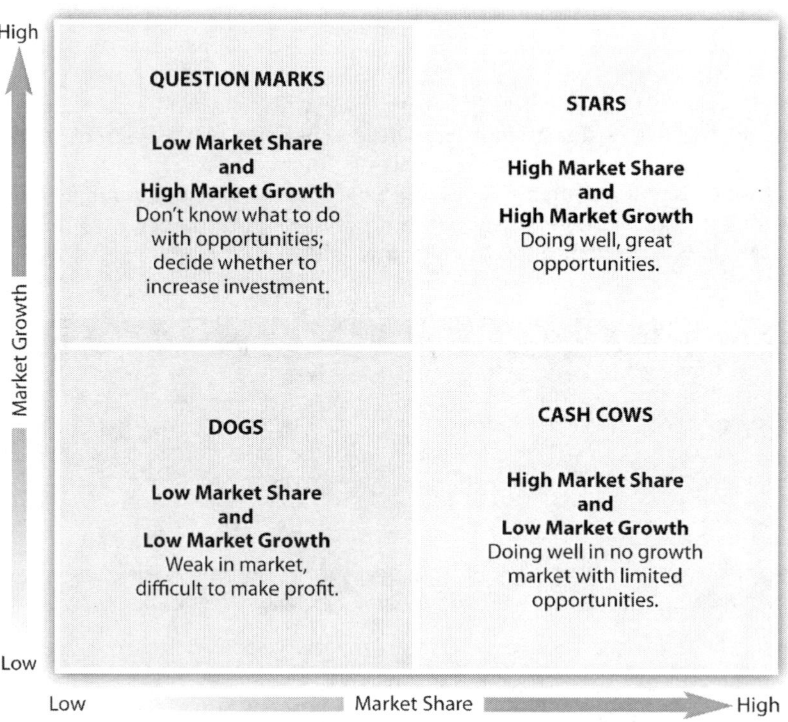


**Boston Consulting Group (BCG) matrix**

A portfolio planning approach that examines strategic business units based on their relative market shares and growth rates. Businesses are classified as stars, cash cows, question marks (problem children), or dogs.

The **Boston Consulting Group (BCG) matrix** helps companies evaluate each of its strategic business units based on two factors: (1) the SBU's market growth rate (i.e., how fast the unit is growing compared to the industry in which it competes) and (2) the SBU's relative market share (i.e., how the unit's share of the market compares to the market share of its competitors). Because the BCG matrix assumes that profitability and market share are highly related, it is a useful approach for making business and investment decisions. However, the BCG matrix is subjective and managers should also use their judgment and other planning approaches before making decisions. Using the BCG matrix, managers can categorize their SBUs (products) into one of four categories, as shown in Figure 2.15.

### Stars

Everyone wants to be a star. A **star** is a product with high growth and a high market share. To maintain the growth of their star products, a company may have to invest money to improve them and how they are distributed as well as promote them. The iPod, when it was first released, was an example of a star product.

**star**

Business or offering with high growth and a high market share.

### Cash Cows

A **cash cow** is a product with low growth and a high market share. Cash cows have a large share of a shrinking market. Although they generate a lot of cash, they do not have a long-term future. For example, DVD players are a cash cow for Sony. Eventually, DVDs are likely to be replaced by digital downloads, just like MP3s replaced CDs. Companies with cash cows need to manage them so that they continue to generate revenue to fund star products.

**cash cow**

Business or offering with a large share of a shrinking market.

### Questions Marks or Problem Children

Did you ever hear an adult say they didn't know what to do with a child? The same question or problem arises when a product has a low share of a high-growth market. Managers classify these products as **question marks or problem children**. They must decide whether to invest in them and hope they become stars or gradually eliminate or sell them. For example, as the price of gasoline soared in 2008, many consumers purchased motorcycles and mopeds, which get better gas mileage. However, some manufacturers have a very low share of this market. These manufacturers now have to decide what they should do with these products.

**question marks or problem children**

Businesses or offerings with a low share of a high-growth market.

### Dogs

In business, it is not good to be considered a dog. A **dog** is a product with low growth and low market share. Dogs do not make much money and do not have a promising future. Companies often get rid of dogs. However, some companies are hesitant to classify any of their products as dogs. As a result, they keep producing products and services they shouldn't or invest in dogs in hopes they'll succeed.

**dog**

Business or offering with low growth and a low market share.

The BCG matrix helps managers make resource allocation decisions once different products are classified. Depending on the product, a firm might decide on a number of different strategies for it. One strategy is to build market share for a business or product, especially a product that might become a star. Many companies invest in question marks because market share is available for them to capture. The success sequence is often used as a means to help question marks become stars. With the success sequence, money is taken from cash cows (if available) and invested into question marks in hopes of them becoming stars.

Holding market share means the company wants to keep the product's share at the same level. When a firm pursues this strategy, it only invests what it has to in order to maintain the product's market share. When a company decides to **harvest** a product, the firm lowers its investment in it. The goal is to try to generate short-term profits from the product regardless of the long-term impact on its survival. If a company decides to **divest** a product, the firm drops or sells it. That's what Procter & Gamble did in 2008 when it sold its Folgers coffee brand to Smuckers. Proctor & Gamble also sold Jif peanut butter brand to Smuckers. Many dogs are divested, but companies may also divest products because they want to focus on other brands they have in their portfolio.

**harvest**

When a firm lowers investment in a product or business.

**divest**

When a firm drops or sells a product or business.

As competitors enter the market, technology advances, and consumer preferences change, the position of a company's products in the BCG matrix is also likely to change. The company has to continually evaluate the situation and adjust its investments and product promotion strategies accordingly. The firm must also keep in mind that the BCG matrix is just one planning approach and that other variables can affect the success of products.

## 5.2 The General Electric Approach

Another portfolio planning approach that helps a business determine whether to invest in opportunities is the **General Electric (GE) approach**. The GE approach examines a business's strengths and the attractiveness of the industry in which it competes. As we have indicated, a business' strengths are factors internal to the company, including strong human resources capabilities (talented personnel), strong technical capabilities, and the fact that the firm holds a large share of the market. The attractiveness of an industry can include aspects such as whether or not there is a great deal of growth in the industry, whether the profits earned by the firms competing within it are high or low, and whether or not it is difficult to enter the market. For example, the automobile industry is not attractive in times of economic downturn such as the recession in 2009, so many automobile manufacturers don't want to

**General Electric (GE) approach**

A portfolio planning approach that examines a business' strengths and the attractiveness of industries.

invest more in production. They want to cut or stop spending as much as possible to improve their profitability. Hotels and airlines face similar situations.

Companies evaluate their strengths and the attractiveness of industries as high, medium, and low. The firms then determine their investment strategies based on how well the two correlate with one another. As Figure 2.16 shows, the investment options outlined in the GE approach can be compared to a traffic light. For example, if a company feels that it does not have the business strengths to compete in an industry and that the industry is not attractive, this will result in a low rating, which is comparable to a red light. In that case, the company should harvest the business (slowly reduce the investments made in it), divest the business (drop or sell it), or stop investing in it, which is what happened with many automotive manufacturers.

**FIGURE 2.16** The General Electric (GE) Approach

- ✓ Red: Harvest or divest products; stop investing in new products, markets, or technology
- ✓ Yellow: Hold market share
- ✓ Green: Build market share; invest in new products, market, or technology

Although many people may think a yellow light means "speed up," it actually means caution. Companies with a medium rating on industry attractiveness and business strengths should be cautious when investing and attempt to hold the market share they have. If a company rates itself high on business strengths and the industry is very attractive (also rated high), this is comparable to a green light. In this case, the firm should invest in the business and build market share. During bad economic times, many industries are not attractive. However, when the economy improves businesses must reevaluate opportunities.

**KEY TAKEAWAY**

A group of businesses is called a portfolio. Organizations that have multiple business units must decide how to allocate resources to them and decide what objectives and strategies are feasible for them. Portfolio planning approaches help firms analyze the businesses relative to each other. The BCG and GE approaches are two or the most common portfolio planning methods.

**REVIEW QUESTIONS**

1. How would you classify a product that has a low market share in a growing market?
2. What does it mean to hold market share?
3. What factors are used as the basis for analyzing businesses and brands using the BCG and the GE approaches?

# 6. DISCUSSION QUESTIONS AND ACTIVITIES

**DISCUSSION QUESTIONS**

1. Explain how a marketing objective differs from a marketing strategy. How are they related?
2. Explain how an organization like McDonald's can use licensing to create value for the brand.
3. How has PepsiCo employed a product development strategy?
4. Discuss how conducting a SWOT (strengths, weaknesses, opportunities, threats) analysis helps a firm develop its strategic plan.
5. Describe the value propositions the social networking sites YouTube and MySpace offer Web users.

## ACTIVITIES

1. Outline a strategic plan for yourself to begin planning for a job after graduation. Include your value proposition, targeted organizations, objectives, strategies, and the internal and external factors that may affect your plans.
2. Assume you have an interview for an entry-level sales position. Write a value proposition emphasizing why you are the best candidate for the position relative to other recent college graduates.
3. A mission statement outlines an organization's purpose and answers the question of how a company defines its business. Write a mission statement for a campus organization.
4. The Web site "My M&Ms" (http://www.mymms.com) allows customers to personalize M&M candies with words, faces, and colors and select from multiple packaging choices. Identify and explain the product market or market development strategies Mars pursued when it introduced personalized M&Ms.
5. Explain how the social and cultural environment has impacted the health care industry. Identify new venues for health care that didn't exist a decade ago. (Hint: emergency care services are available outside a hospital's emergency room today.)
6. Select an organization for which you would like to work. Look up its mission statement. What do you think the organization's objectives and strategies are? What environmental and internal factors might affect its success?
7. Break up into teams. Come up with as many real-world examples as you can of companies that pursued market penetration, market development, product development, or diversification strategies.

# ENDNOTES


1. Laura Lake, "Develop Your Value Proposition," http://marketing.about.com/od/marketingplanandstrategy/a/valueprop.htm (accessed December 7, 2009).
2. Goodyear Tire & Rubber Company, http://goodyear.com.
3. PepsiCo, Inc., "The PepsiCo Family," http://www.pepsico.com/Company/The-Pepsico-Family.html (accessed December 7, 2009).
4. PepsiCo, Inc., "PepsiCo Brands," http://www.pepsico.com/Company/Our-Brands.html (accessed December 7, 2009).
5. Michael E. Porter, *Competitive Strategy* (New York: The Free Press, 1980), 3–33.
6. Michael E. Porter, *Competitive Strategy* (New York: The Free Press, 1980), 4.
7. Michael E. Porter, *Competitive Strategy* (New York: The Free Press, 1980), 3–33.
8. PepsiCo, Inc., "Our Mission and Vision," http://www.pepsico.com/Company/Our-Mission-and-Vision.html (accessed December 7, 2009).
9. United Way Worldwide, "Mission and Vision," http://www.liveunited.org/about/missvis.cfm (accessed December 7, 2009).

# CHAPTER 3
# Consumer Behavior: How People Make Buying Decisions

Why do you buy the things you do? How did you decide to go to the college you're attending? Where do like to shop and when? Do your friends shop at the same places or different places?

Marketing professionals want to know the answers to these questions. They know that once they do have those answers, they will have a much better chance of creating and communicating about products that you and people like you will want to buy. That's what the study of consumer behavior is all about. **Consumer behavior** considers the many reasons why—personal, situational, psychological, and social—people shop for products, buy and use them, and then dispose of them.

**consumer behavior**

The study of when, where, and how people buy things and then dispose of them.

Companies spend billions of dollars annually studying what makes consumers "tick." Although you might not like it, Google, AOL, and Yahoo! monitor your Web patterns—the sites you search, that is. The companies that pay for **search advertising**, or ads that appear on the Web pages you pull up after doing an online search, want to find out what kind of things you're interested in. Doing so allows these companies to send you popup ads and coupons you might actually be interested in instead of ads and coupons for products such as Depends or Viagra.

**search advertising**

Advertising that appears on the Web pages pulled up when online searches are conducted.

Massachusetts Institute of Technology (MIT), in conjunction with a large retail center, has tracked consumers in retail establishments to see when and where they tended to dwell, or stop to look at merchandise. How was it done? By tracking the position of the consumers' mobile phones as the phones automatically transmitted signals to cellular towers. MIT found that when people's "dwell times" increased, sales increased, too.[1]

Researchers have even looked at people's brains by having them lie in scanners and asking them questions about different products. What people *say* about the products is then compared to what their brains scans show—that is, what they are really thinking. Scanning people's brains for marketing purposes might sound nutty. But maybe not when you consider the fact is that eight out of ten new consumer products fail, even when they are test marketed. Could it be that what people say about potentially new products and what they think about them are different? Marketing professionals want to find out.[2]

Studying people's buying habits isn't just for big companies, though. Even small businesses and entrepreneurs can study the behavior of their customers with great success. For example, by figuring out what zip codes their customers are in, a business might determine where to locate an additional store. Customer surveys and other studies can also help explain why buyers purchased what they did and what their experiences were with a business. Even small businesses such as restaurants use coupon codes. For example, coupons sent out in newspapers are given one code. Those sent out via the Internet are given another. Then when the coupons are redeemed, the restaurants can tell which marketing avenues are having the biggest effect on their sales.

**FIGURE 3.1**

Tony Hsieh, the chief executive of the shoe company Zappos.com, reportedly has thirty thousand followers on Twitter and his Zappos blog. Dell has begun making millions on Twitter by providing followers with exclusive deals, outlet offers, and product updates. To see the top users of Twitter, go to http://www.twitterholic.com.

© *Zappos.com, Inc.*

Some businesses, including a growing number of startups, are using blogs and social networking Web sites to gather information about their customers at a low cost. For example, Proper Cloth, a company based in New York, has a site on the social networking site Facebook. Whenever the company posts a new bulletin or photos of its clothes, all its Facebook "fans" automatically receive the information on their own Facebook pages. "We want to hear what our customers have to say," says Joseph Skerritt, the young MBA graduate who founded Proper Cloth. "It's useful to us and lets our customers feel connected to Proper Cloth."[3] Skerritt also writes a blog for the company. Twitter and podcasts that can be downloaded from iTunes are two other ways companies are amplifying the "word of mouth" about their products.[4]

# 1. THE CONSUMER'S DECISION-MAKING PROCESS

**LEARNING OBJECTIVES**

1. **Understand what the stages of the buying process are.**
2. **Distinguish between low-involvement buying decisions and high-involvement buying decisions.**

You've been a consumer with purchasing power for much longer than you probably realize—since the first time you were asked which cereal or toy you wanted. Over the years, you've developed a systematic way you choose among alternatives, even if you aren't aware of it. Other consumers follow a similar process. The first part of this chapter looks at this process. The second part looks at the situational, psychological, and other factors that affect what, when, and how people buy what they do.

Keep in mind, however, that different people, no matter how similar they are, make different purchasing decisions. You might be very interested in purchasing a Smart Car. But your best friend might want to buy a Ford 150 truck. Marketing professionals understand this. They don't have unlimited budgets that allow them to advertise in all types of media to all types of people, so what they try to do is figure out *trends* among consumers. Doing so helps them reach the people most likely to buy their products in the most cost effective way possible.

## 1.1 Stages in the Buying Process

Figure 3.2 outlines the buying stages consumers go through. At any given time, you're probably in some sort of buying stage. You're thinking about the different types of things you want or need to eventually buy, how you are going to find the best ones at the best price, and where and how will you buy them. Meanwhile, there are other products you have already purchased that you're evaluating. Some might be better than others. Will you discard them, and if so, how? Then what will you buy? Where does that process start?

**FIGURE 3.2** Stages in the Consumer's Purchasing Process

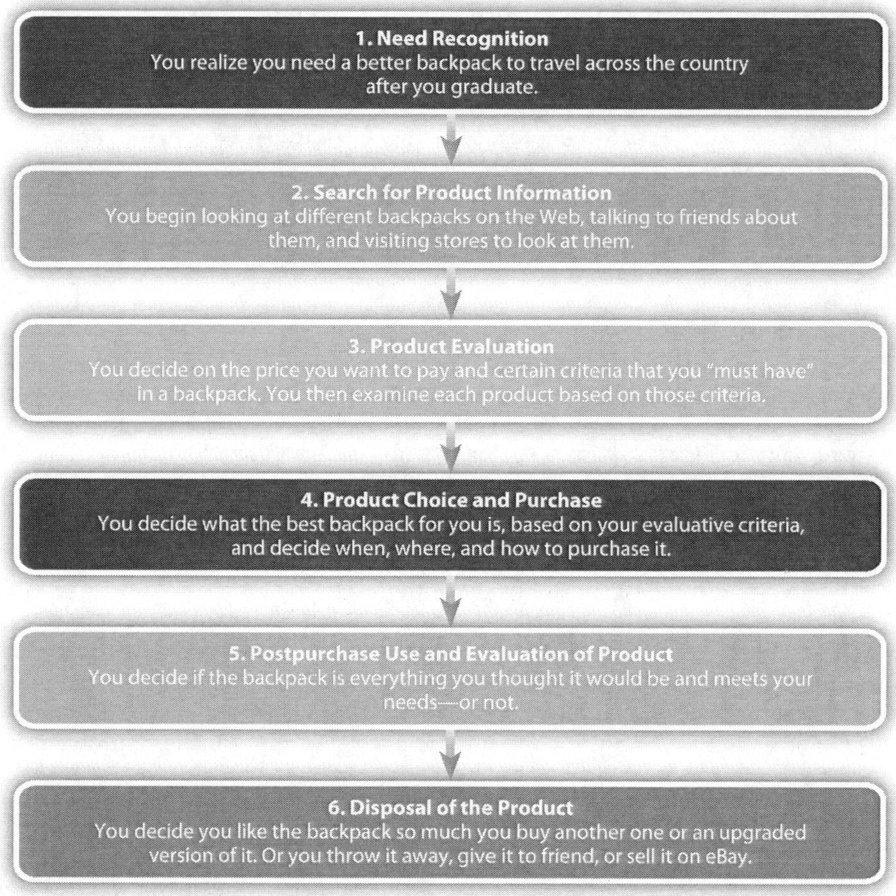


## Stage 1. Need Recognition

Perhaps you're planning to backpack around the country after you graduate, but you don't have a particularly good backpack. Marketers often try to stimulate consumers into realizing they have a need for a product. Do you think it's a coincidence that Gatorade, Powerade, and other beverage makers locate their machines in gymnasiums so you see them after a long, tiring workout? Previews at movie theaters are another example. How many times have you have heard about a movie and had no interest in it—until you saw the preview? Afterward, you felt like *had* to see it.

## Stage 2. Search for Information

Maybe you have owned several backpacks and know what you like and don't like about them. Or, there might be a particular brand that you've purchased in the past that you liked and want to purchase in the future. This is a great position for the company that owns the brand to be in—something firms strive for. Why? Because it often means you will limit your search and simply buy their brand again.

If what you already know about backpacks doesn't provide you with enough information, you'll probably continue to gather information from various sources. Frequently people ask friends, family, and neighbors about their experiences with products. Magazines such as *Consumer Reports* or *Backpacker Magazine* might also help you.

Internet shopping sites such as Amazon.com have become a common source of information about products. Epinions.com is an example of consumer-generated review site. The site offers product ratings, buying tips, and price information. Amazon.com also offers product reviews written by consumers. People prefer "independent" sources such as this when they are looking for product information. However, they also often consult nonneutral sources of information, such advertisements, brochures, company Web sites, and salespeople.

## Stage 3. Product Evaluation

Obviously, there are hundreds of different backpacks available to choose from. It's not possible for you to examine all of them. (In fact, good salespeople and marketing professionals know that providing you with too many choices can be so overwhelming, you might not buy anything at all.) Consequently, you develop what's called evaluative criteria to help you narrow down your choices.

**evaluative criteria**

Certain characteristics of products consumers consider when they are making buying decisions.

**Evaluative criteria** are certain characteristics that are important to you such as the price of the backpack, the size, the number of compartments, and color. Some of these characteristics are more important than others. For example, the size of the backpack and the price might be more important to you than the color—unless, say, the color is hot pink and you hate pink.

Marketing professionals want to convince you that the evaluative criteria you are considering reflect the strengths of their products. For example, you might not have thought about the weight or durability of the backpack you want to buy. However, a backpack manufacturer such as Osprey might remind you through magazine ads, packaging information, and its Web site that you should pay attention to these features—features that happen to be key selling points of its backpacks.

**FIGURE 3.3**

Osprey backpacks are known for their durability. The company has a special design and quality control center, and Osprey's salespeople annually take a "canyon testing" trip to see how well the company's products perform.

*© 2010 Jupiterimages Corporation*

### Stage 4. Product Choice and Purchase

Stage 4 is the point at which you decide what backpack to purchase. However, in addition to the backpack, you are probably also making other decisions at this stage, including where and how to purchase the backpack and on what terms. Maybe the backpack was cheaper at one store than another, but the salesperson there was rude. Or maybe you decide to order online because you're too busy to go to the mall. Other decisions, particularly those related to big ticket items, are made at this point. If you're buying a high-definition television, you might look for a store that will offer you credit or a warranty.

### Stage 5. Postpurchase Use and Evaluation

At this point in the process you decide whether the backpack you purchased is everything it was cracked up to be. Hopefully it is. If it's not, you're likely to suffer what's called **postpurchase dissonance**. You might call it *buyer's remorse*. You want to feel good about your purchase, but you don't. You begin to wonder whether you should have waited to get a better price, purchased something else, or gathered more information first. Consumers commonly feel this way, which is a problem for sellers. If you don't feel good about what you've purchased from them, you might return the item and never purchase anything from them again. Or, worse yet, you might tell everyone you know how bad the product was.

**postpurchase dissonance**

A situation in which consumers rethink their decisions after purchasing products and wonder if they made the best decision.

Companies do various things to try to prevent buyer's remorse. For smaller items, they might offer a money back guarantee. Or, they might encourage their salespeople to tell you what a great purchase you made. How many times have you heard a salesperson say, "That outfit looks so great on you!"? For larger items, companies might offer a warranty, along with instruction booklets, and a toll-free troubleshooting line to call. Or they might have a salesperson call you to see if you need help with product.

### Stage 6. Disposal of the Product

There was a time when neither manufacturers nor consumers thought much about how products got disposed of, so long as people bought them. But that's changed. How products are being disposed is becoming extremely important to consumers and society in general. Computers and batteries, which leech chemicals into landfills, are a huge problem. Consumers don't want to degrade the environment if they don't have to, and companies are becoming more aware of the fact.

Take for example, Crystal Light, a water-based beverage that's sold in grocery stores. You can buy it in a bottle. However, many people buy a concentrated form of it, put it in reusable pitchers or bottles, and add water. That way, they don't have to buy and dispose of plastic bottle after plastic bottle, damaging the environment in the process. Windex has done something similar with its window cleaner. Instead of buying new bottles of it all the time, you can purchase a concentrate and add water. You have probably noticed that most grocery stores now sell cloth bags consumers can reuse instead of continually using and discarding of new plastic or paper bags.

**planned obsolescence**

A deliberate effort by companies to make their products obsolete, or unusable, after a period of time.

Other companies are less concerned about conservation than they are about **planned obsolescence**. Planned obsolescence is a deliberate effort by companies to make their products obsolete, or unusable, after a period of time. The goal is to improve a company's sales by reducing the amount of time between the repeat purchases consumers make of products. When a software developer introduces a new version of product, older versions of it are usually designed to be incompatible with it. For example, not all the formatting features are the same in Microsoft Word 2003 and 2007. Sometimes documents do not translate properly when opened in the newer version. Consequently, you will be more inclined to upgrade to the new version so you can open all Word documents you receive.

Products that are disposable are another way in which firms have managed to reduce the amount of time between purchases. Disposable lighters are an example. Do you know anyone today that owns a nondisposable lighter? Believe it or not, prior to the 1960s, scarcely anyone could have imagined using a cheap disposable lighter. There are many more disposable products today than there were in years past—including everything from bottled water and individually wrapped snacks to single-use eye drops and cell phones.

**FIGURE 3.4**

Disposable lighters came into vogue in the United States in the 1960s. You probably don't own a cool, nondisposable lighter like one of these, but you don't have to bother refilling it with lighter fluid either.

## 1.2 Low-Involvement versus High-Involvement Buying Decisions

Consumers don't necessarily go through all the buying stages when they're considering purchasing product. You have probably thought about many products you want or need but never did much more than that. At other times, you've probably looked at dozens of products, compared them, and then decided not to purchase any one of them. At yet other times, you skip stages 1 through 3 and buy products on impulse. As Nike would put, you "just do it." Perhaps you see a magazine with Angelina Jolie and Brad Pitt on the cover and buy it on the spot simply because you want it. Purchasing a product with no planning or forethought is called **impulse buying**.

**impulse buying**

Purchases that occurs with no planning or forethought.

Impulse buying brings up a concept called *level of involvement*—that is, how personally important or interested you are in consuming a product. For example, you might see a roll of tape at a check-out stand and remember you need one. Or you might see a bag of chips and realize you're hungry. These are items you need, but they are low-involvement products. **Low-involvement products** aren't necessarily purchased on impulse, although they can be. Low-involvement products are, however, inexpensive and pose a low risk to the buyer if she makes a mistake by purchasing them.

**low-involvement products**

Products that carry a low risk of failure and/or have a low price tag for a specific individual or group making the decision.

Consumers often engage in **routine response behavior** when they buy low-involvement products—that is, they make automatic purchase decisions based on limited information or information they have gathered in the past. For example, if you always order a Diet Coke at lunch, you're engaging in routine response behavior. You may not even think about other drink options at lunch because your routine is to order a Diet Coke, and you simply do it. If you're served a Diet Coke at lunchtime, and it's flat, oh well. It's not the end of the world.

**routine response behavior**

When consumers make automatic purchase decisions based on limited information or information they have gathered in the past.

**high-involvement products**

Products that carry a high price tag or high level of risk to the individual or group making the decision.

**extended problem solving**

Purchasing decisions in which a consumer gathers a significant amount of information before making a decision.

By contrast, **high-involvement products** carry a high risk to buyers if they fail, are complex, or have high price tags. A car, a house, and an insurance policy are examples. These items are not purchased often. Buyers don't engage in routine response behavior when purchasing high-involvement products. Instead, consumers engage in what's called **extended problem solving**, where they spend a lot of time comparing the features of the products, prices, warrantees, and so forth.

High-involvement products can cause buyers a great deal of postpurchase dissonance if they are unsure about their purchases. Companies that sell high-involvement products are aware of that postpurchase dissonance can be a problem. Frequently, they try to offer consumers a lot of information about their products, including why they are superior to competing brands and how they won't let the consumer down. Salespeople are typically utilized to do a lot of customer "hand-holding."

**FIGURE 3.5**

Allstate's "You're in Good Hands" advertisements are designed to convince consumers that the insurance company won't let them down.

© 2010 Jupiterimages Corporation

**limited problem solving**

Purchasing decisions made based on consideration of some outside information.

Limited problem solving falls somewhere in the middle. Consumers engage in **limited problem solving** when they already have some information about a good or service but continue to search for a bit more information. The backpack you're looking to buy is an example. You're going to spend at least some time looking for one that's decent because you don't want it to fall apart while you're traveling and dump everything you've packed on a hiking trail. You might do a little research online and come to a decision relatively quickly. You might consider the choices available at your favorite retail outlet but not look at every backpack at every outlet before making a decision. Or, you might rely on the advice of a person you know who's knowledgeable about backpacks. In some way you shorten the decision-making process.

Brand names can be very important regardless of the consumer's level of purchasing involvement. Consider a low- versus high-involvement product—say, purchasing a tube of toothpaste versus a new car. You might routinely buy your favorite brand of toothpaste, not thinking much about the purchase (engage in routine response behavior), but not be willing to switch to another brand either. Having a brand you like saves you "search time" and eliminates the evaluation period because you know what you're getting.

When it comes to the car, you might engage in extensive problem solving but, again, only be willing to consider a certain brands or brands. For example, in the 1970s, American-made cars had such a poor reputation for quality, buyers joked that a car that's "not Jap [Japanese made] is crap." The quality of American cars is very good today, but you get the picture. If it's a high-involvement product you're purchasing, a good brand name is probably going to be very important to you. That's why the makers of high-involvement products can't become complacent about the value of their brands.

## Video Clip

**1970s American Cars**

Today, Lexus is the automotive brand that experiences the most customer loyalty. For a humorous, tongue-in-cheek look at why the brand reputation of American carmakers suffered in the 1970s, check out this clip.

View the video online at: http://www.youtube.com/embed/pjzpx_jUUA0

**KEY TAKEAWAY**

Consumer behavior looks at the many reasons why people buy things and later dispose of them. Consumers go through distinct buying phases when they purchases products: (1) realizing the need or want something, (2) searching for information about the item, (3) evaluating different products, (4) choosing a product and purchasing it, (5) using and evaluating the product after the purchase, and (6) disposing of the product. A consumer's level of involvement is how interested he or she is in buying and consuming a product. Low-involvement products are usually inexpensive and pose a low risk to the buyer if she makes a mistake by purchasing them. High-involvement products carry a high risk to the buyer if they fail, are complex, or have high price tags. Limited-involvement products fall somewhere in between.

**REVIEW QUESTIONS**

1. What is consumer behavior? Why do companies study it?
2. What stages do people go through in the buying process?
3. How do low-involvement products differ from high-involvement products in terms of the risks their buyers face? Name some products in each category that you've recently purchased.

# 2. SITUATIONAL FACTORS THAT AFFECT PEOPLE'S BUYING BEHAVIOR

**LEARNING OBJECTIVES**

1. **Describe the situational factors that affect what consumers buy and when.**
2. **Explain what marketing professionals can do to make situational factors work to their advantage.**

Situational influences are temporary conditions that affect how buyers behave—whether they actually buy your product, buy additional products, or buy nothing at all from you. They include things like physical factors, social factors, time factors, the reason for the buyer's purchase, and the buyer's mood. You have undoubtedly been affected by all these factors at one time or another. Because businesses very much want to try to control these factors, let's now look at them in more detail.

## 2.1 The Consumer's Physical Situation

Have you ever been in a department store and couldn't find your way out? No, you aren't necessarily directionally challenged. Marketing professionals take physical factors such as a store's design and layout into account when they are designing their facilities. Presumably, the longer you wander around a facility, the more you will spend. Grocery stores frequently place bread and milk products on the opposite ends of the stores because people often need both types of products. To buy both, they have to walk around an entire store, which of course, is loaded with other items they might see and purchase.

Store locations are another example of a physical factor. Starbucks has done a good job in terms of locating its stores. It has the process down to a science; you can scarcely drive a few miles down the road without passing a Starbucks. You can also buy cups of Starbucks coffee at many grocery stores and in airports—virtually any place where there is foot traffic.

Physical factors like these—the ones over which firms have control—are called **atmospherics**. In addition to store locations, they include the music played at stores, the lighting, temperature, and even the smells you experience. Perhaps you've visited the office of an apartment complex and noticed how great it looked and even smelled. It's no coincidence. The managers of the complex were trying to get you to stay for a while and have a look at their facilities. Research shows that "strategic fragrancing" results in customers staying in stores longer, buying more, and leaving with better impression of the quality of stores' services and products. Mirrors near hotel elevators are another example. Hotel operators have found that when people are busy looking at themselves in the mirrors, they don't feel like they are waiting as long for their elevators.[5]

**atmospherics**

The physical aspects of the selling environment retailers try to control.

Not all physical factors are under a company's control, however. Take weather, for example. Rain and other types of weather can be a boon to some companies, like umbrella makers such as London Fog, but a problem for others. Beach resorts, outdoor concert venues, and golf courses suffer when the weather is rainy. So do a lot of retail organizations—restaurants, clothing stores, and automobile dealers. Who wants to shop for a car in the rain or snow?

Firms often attempt to deal with adverse physical factors such as bad weather by making their products more attractive during unattractive times. For example, many resorts offer consumers discounts to travel to beach locations during hurricane season. Having an online presence is another way to cope with weather-related problems. What could be more comfortable than shopping at home? If it's too cold and windy to drive to the GAP, REI, or Abercrombie & Fitch, you can buy these companies' products online. You can shop online for cars, too, and many restaurants take orders online and deliver.

Crowding is another situational factor. Have you ever left a store and not purchased anything because it was just too crowded? Some studies have shown that consumers feel better about retailers who attempt to prevent overcrowding in their stores. However, other studies have shown that to a certain extent, crowding can have a positive impact on a person's buying experience. The phenomenon is often referred to as "herd behavior."

If people are lined up to buy something, you want to know why. Should you get in line to buy it too? Herd behavior helped drive up the price of houses in the mid-2000s before the prices for them rapidly fell. Unfortunately, herd behavior has also led to the deaths of people. In 2008, a store employee was trampled to death by an early morning crowd rushing into a Walmart to snap up holiday bargains.

To some extent, how people react to crowding depends on their personal tolerance levels. Which rock concert would you rather attend: A sold-out concert in which the crowd is having a rocking good time? Or a half-sold-out concert where you can perhaps move to a seat closer to the stage and not have to stand in line at the restrooms?[6]

## 2.2 The Consumer's Social Situation

The social situation you're in can significantly affect what you will buy, how much of it, and when. Perhaps you have seen Girl Scouts selling cookies outside grocery stores and other retail establishments and purchased nothing from them. But what if your neighbor's daughter is selling the cookies? Are you going to turn her down, or be a friendly neighbor and buy a box (or two)?

**Video Clip**

**Thin Mints, Anyone?**

Are you going to turn down this cute Girl Scout's cookies? What if she's your neighbor's daughter? Pass the milk, please!

View the video online at: http://www.youtube.com/embed/GJHN4eutKjY

Companies like Avon and Tupperware that sell their products at parties understand that the social situation you're in makes a difference. When you're at a Tupperware party a friend is having, you don't want to disappoint her by not buying anything. Plus, everyone at the party will think you're cheap.

Certain social situations can also make you less willing to buy products. You might spend quite a bit of money each month eating at fast-food restaurants like McDonald's and Subway. But suppose you've got a hot first date? Where do you take your date? Some people might take a first date to Subway, but that first date might also be the last. Other people would perhaps choose a restaurant that's more upscale. Likewise, if you have turned down a drink or dessert on a date because you were worried about what the person you were with might have thought, your consumption was affected by your social situation.[7]

## 2.3 The Consumer's Time Situation

The time of day, the time of year, and how much time consumers feel like they have to shop also affects what they buy. Researchers have even discovered whether someone is a "morning person" or "evening person" affects shopping patterns. Seven-Eleven Japan is a company that's extremely in tune to physical factors such as time and how it affects buyers. The company's point-of-sale systems at its checkout counters monitor what is selling well and when, and stores are restocked with those items immediately—sometimes via motorcycle deliveries that zip in and out of traffic along Japan's crowded streets. The goal is to get the products on the shelves when and where consumers want them. Seven-Eleven Japan also knows that, like Americans, its customers are "time starved." Shoppers can pay their utility bills, local taxes, and insurance or pension premiums at Seven-Eleven Japan stores, and even make photocopies.[8]

Companies worldwide are aware of people's lack of time and are finding ways to accommodate them. Some doctors' offices offer drive-through shots for patients who are in a hurry and for elderly patients who find it difficult to get out of their cars. Tickets.com allows companies to sell tickets by sending them to customers' mobile phones when they call in. The phones' displays are then read by barcode scanners when the ticket purchasers arrive at the events they're attending. Likewise, if you need customer service from Amazon.com, there's no need to wait on hold on the telephone. If you have an account with Amazon, you just click a button on the company's Web site and an Amazon representative calls you immediately.

## 2.4 The Reason for the Consumer's Purchase

The reason you are shopping also affects the amount of time you will spend shopping. Are you making an emergency purchase? Are you shopping for a gift? In recent years, emergency clinics have sprung up in strip malls all over the country. Convenience is one reason. The other is sheer necessity. If you cut yourself and you are bleeding badly, you're probably not going to shop around much to find the best clinic to go to. You will go to the one that's closest to you.

What about shopping for a gift? Purchasing a gift might not be an emergency situation, but you might not want to spend much time shopping for it either. Gift certificates have been a popular way to purchase for years. But now you can purchase them as cards at your corner grocery store. By contrast, suppose you need to buy an engagement ring. Sure, you could buy one online in a jiffy, but you probably wouldn't, because it's a high-involvement product. What if it were a fake? How would you know until after you purchased it? What if your significant other turned you down and you had to return the ring? How hard would it be to get back online and return the ring?[9]

## 2.5 The Consumer's Mood

Have you ever felt like going on a shopping spree? At other times wild horses couldn't drag you to a mall. People's moods temporarily affect their spending patterns. Some people enjoy shopping. It's entertaining for them. At the extreme are compulsive spenders who get a temporary "high" from spending.

A sour mood can spoil a consumer's desire to shop. The crash of the U.S. stock market in 2008 left many people feeling poorer, leading to a dramatic downturn in consumer spending. Penny pinching came into vogue, and conspicuous spending was out. Costco and Walmart experienced heightened sales of their low-cost Kirkland Signature and Great Value brands as consumers scrimped.[10]

Saks Fifth Avenue wasn't so lucky. Its annual release of spring fashions usually leads to a feeding frenzy among shoppers, but spring 2009 was different. "We've definitely seen a drop-off of this idea of shopping for entertainment," says Kimberly Grabel, Saks Fifth Avenue's senior vice president of marketing.[11]

To get buyers in the shopping mood, companies resorted to different measures. The upscale retailer Neiman Marcus began introducing more midpriced brands. By studying customer's loyalty cards, the French hypermarket Carrefour hoped to find ways to get its customers to purchase nonfood items that have higher profit margins.

The glum mood wasn't bad for all businesses though. Discounters like Half-Priced books saw their sales surge. So did seed sellers as people began planting their own gardens. Finally, those products you see being hawked on television? Aqua Globes, Snuggies, and Ped Eggs? Their sales were the best ever.

Apparently, consumers too broke to go to on vacation or shop at Saks were instead watching television and treating themselves to the products.[12]

**KEY TAKEAWAY**

Situational influences are temporary conditions that affect how buyers behave. They include physical factors such as a store's buying locations, layout, music, lighting, and even smells. Companies try to make the physical factors in which consumers shop as favorable as possible. If they can't, they utilize other tactics such as discounts. The consumer's social situation, time situation, the reason for their purchases, and their moods also affect their buying behavior.

**REVIEW QUESTIONS**

1. Why and how does the social situation the consumer is in play a role in behavior?
2. Outline the types of physical factors companies try to affect and how they go about it.
3. What social situations have you been in that affected what you purchased?
4. What types of moods and time situations are likely to affect people's buying behavior?

# 3. PERSONAL FACTORS THAT AFFECT PEOPLE'S BUYING BEHAVIOR

**LEARNING OBJECTIVES**

1. **Explain how a person's self-concept and ideal self affects what he or she buys.**
2. **Describe how companies market products to people based on their genders, life stages, and ages.**
3. **Explain how looking at the lifestyles of consumers helps firms understand what they want to purchase.**

## 3.1 The Consumer's Personality

**personality**

An individual's disposition as other people see it.

**Personality** describes a person's disposition as other people see it. The following are the "Big Five" personality traits that psychologists discuss frequently:

1. **Openness.** How open you are to new experiences.
2. **Conscientiousness.** How diligent you are.
3. **Extraversion.** How outgoing or shy you are.
4. **Agreeableness.** How easy you are to get along with.
5. **Neuroticism.** How prone you are to negative mental states.

The question marketing professionals want answered is do the traits predict people's purchasing behavior? Can companies successfully target certain products at people based on their personalities? And how do you find out what personalities they have? Are the extraverts you know wild spenders and the introverts you know penny pinchers? Maybe not.

The link between people's personalities and their buying behavior is somewhat unclear, but market researchers continue to study it. For example, some studies have shown that "sensation seekers," or people who exhibit extremely high levels of openness, are more likely to respond well to advertising that's violent and graphic. The practical problem for firms is figuring out "who's who" in terms of their personalities.

## 3.2 The Consumer's Self-Concept

Marketers have had better luck linking people's self-concept to their buying behavior. Your **self-concept** is how you see yourself—be it positive or negative. Your **ideal self** is how you would *like* to see yourself—whether it's prettier, more popular, more eco-conscious, or more "goth."

Marketing researchers believe people buy products to enhance how they feel about themselves—to get themselves closer to their ideal selves, in other words. The slogan "Be All That You Can Be," which for years was used by the U.S. Army to recruit soldiers, is an attempt to appeal to the self-concept. Presumably, by joining the U.S. Army, you will become a better version of yourself, which will, in turn, improve your life. Many beauty products and cosmetic procedures are advertised in a way that's supposed to appeal to the ideal selves people are searching for. All of us want products that improve our lives.

**self-concept**

How a person sees himself or herself.

**ideal self**

How a person would like to view himself or herself.

## 3.3 The Consumer's Gender

Everyone knows that men and women buy different products. Physiologically speaking, they simply need different product—different underwear, shoes, toiletries, and a host of other products.[13] Men and women also shop differently. One study by Resource Interactive, a technology research firm, found that when shopping online, men prefer sites with lots of pictures of products; women prefer to see products online in lifestyle context—say, a lamp in a living room. Women are also twice as likely as men to use viewing tools such as the zoom and rotate buttons and links that allow them to change the color of products.

In general, men have a different attitude about shopping than women do. You know the old stereotypes: Men see what they a want and buy it, but women "shop 'til they drop." There's some truth to the stereotypes. Otherwise, you wouldn't see so many advertisements directed at one sex or the other—beer commercials that air on ESPN and commercials for household products that air on Lifetime. In fact, women influence fully two-thirds of all household product purchases, whereas men buy about three-quarters of all alcoholic beverages.[14]

### Video Clip

**What Women Want versus What Men Want**

Check out this Heineken commercial which highlights the differences between "what women want" and "what men want" when it comes to products.

View the video online at: http://www.youtube.com/embed/ylutgtzwhAc

The shopping differences between men and women seem to be changing, though. For example, younger, well-educated men are less likely to believe grocery shopping is a woman's job. They would also be more inclined to bargain shop and use coupons if the coupons were properly targeted at them.[15] One survey found that approximately 45 percent of married men actually *like* shopping and consider it relaxing.

FIGURE 3.6

Marketing to men is big business. Some advertising agencies specialize in advertisements designed specifically to appeal to male consumers.

© 2010 Jupiterimages Corporation

Many businesses today are taking greater pains to figure out "what men want." Products such as face toners and body washes for men, such as the Axe brand, are a relatively new phenomenon. So are hair salons such as the Men's Zone and Weldon Barber. Some advertising agencies specialize in advertising directed at men. Keep in mind that there are also many items targeted toward women that weren't in the past, including products such as kayaks and mountain bikes.

## 3.4 The Consumer's Age and Stage of Life

You have probably noticed that the things you buy have changed as you age. When you were a child, the last thing you probably wanted as a gift was clothing. As you became a teen, however, cool clothes probably became a bigger priority. Don't look now, but depending on the stage of life you're currently in, diapers and wrinkle cream might be just around the corner.

Companies understand that people buy different things based on their ages and life stages. Aging baby boomers are a huge market that companies are trying to tap. Ford and other car companies have created "aging suits" for young employees to wear when they're designing automobiles.[16] The suit simulates the restricted mobility and vision people experience as they get older. Car designers can then figure out how to configure the automobiles to better meet the needs of these consumers.

Lisa Rudes Sandel, the founder of Not Your Daughter's Jeans (NYDJ), created a multimillion-dollar business by designing jeans for baby boomers with womanly bodies. Since its launch seven years ago, NYDJ has become the largest domestic manufacturer of women's jeans under $100. "The truth is," Rudes Sandel says, "I've never forgotten that woman I've been aiming for since day one." Sandel "speaks to" every one of her customers via a note tucked into each pair of jean that reads, "NYDJ (Not Your Daughter's Jeans) cannot be held responsible for any positive consequence that may arise due to your fabulous appearance when wearing the Tummy Tuck jeans. You can thank me later."[17]

FIGURE 3.7

You're only as old as you feel—and the things you buy.

© 2010 Jupiterimages Corporation

Your **chronological age**, or actual age in years, is one thing. Your **cognitive age**, or how old you perceive yourself to be, is another. In other words, how old do you *really* feel? A person's cognitive age affects the activities one engages in and sparks interests consistent with the person's perceived age.[18] Cognitive age is a significant predictor of consumer behaviors, including people's dining out, watching television, going to bars and dance clubs, playing computer games, and shopping.[19] How old people "feel" they are has important implications for marketing professionals. For example, companies have found that many "aged" consumers don't take kindly to products that feature "old folks." The consumers can't identify with them because they see themselves as being younger. We will discuss more about the various age groups and how marketing professionals try to target them in Chapter 5.

**chronological age**

A person's age in years.

**cognitive age**

The age a buyer perceives himself or herself to be.

## 3.5 The Consumer's Lifestyle

At the beginning of the chapter, we explained that two consumers (say, you and your best friend) can be similar in age, personality, gender, and so on but still purchase very different products. If you have ever watched the television show *Wife Swap*, you can see that despite people's similarities (e.g., being middle-class Americans who are married with children), their lifestyles can differ radically.

To better understand consumers and connect with them, companies have begun looking more closely at consumers' lifestyles. This often includes asking consumers to fill out extensive questionnaires or conducting in-depth interviews with them. The questionnaires go beyond asking people about the products they like, where they live, and what sex they are. Instead, researchers ask people what they *do*—that is, how they spend their time and what their priorities, values, and general outlooks on the world are. Where do they go other than work? Who do they like to talk to? What do they talk about? Researchers hired by Procter & Gamble have gone so far as to follow women around for weeks as they shop, run errands, and socialize with one another.[20] Other companies have paid people to keep a daily journal of their activities and routines.

**Audio Clip**

**Interview with Joy Mead**

Joy Mead is an associate director of marketing for Procter & Gamble. Listen to this audio clip to learn about the approach Procter & Gamble takes to understand customers.

A number of research organizations examine lifestyle and psychographic characteristics of consumers. **Psychographics** combines the lifestyle traits of consumers (for example, whether they are single or married, wealthy or poor, well-educated or high school dropouts) and their personality styles with an analysis of their attitudes, activities, and values to determine groups of consumers with similar characteristics. We will talk more about psychographics and what companies do to develop further insight into what consumers want in Chapter 5.

**psychographics**

Measuring the attitudes, values, lifestyles, and opinions of consumers using demographics.

### KEY TAKEAWAY

Your personality describes your disposition as other people see it. Market researchers believe people buy products to enhance how they feel about themselves. Your gender also affects what you buy and how you shop. Women shop differently than men. However, there's some evidence that this is changing. Younger men and women are beginning to shop more alike. People buy different things based on their ages and life stages. A person's cognitive age is how old he "feels" himself to be. To further understand consumers and connect with them, companies have begun looking more closely at their lifestyles (what they do, how they spend their time, what their priorities and values are, and how they see the world).

### REVIEW QUESTIONS

1. Explain how someone's personality differs from his or her self-concept. How does the person's ideal self come into play in a consumer-behavior context?
2. Describe the buying patterns women exhibit versus men.
3. Why are companies interested in consumers' cognitive ages?
4. What are some of the consumer lifestyle factors firms examine?

# 4. PSYCHOLOGICAL FACTORS THAT AFFECT PEOPLE'S BUYING BEHAVIOR

### LEARNING OBJECTIVES

1. **Explain how Maslow's hierarchy of needs works.**
2. **Outline the additional psychological factors that affect people's buying behavior.**

## 4.1 Motivation

**Motivation** is the inward drive we have to get what we need. In the mid-1900s, Abraham Maslow, an American psychologist, developed the hierarchy of needs shown in Figure 3.8.

**motivation**

The inward drive people have to get what they need.

**FIGURE 3.8** Maslow's Hierarchy of Needs

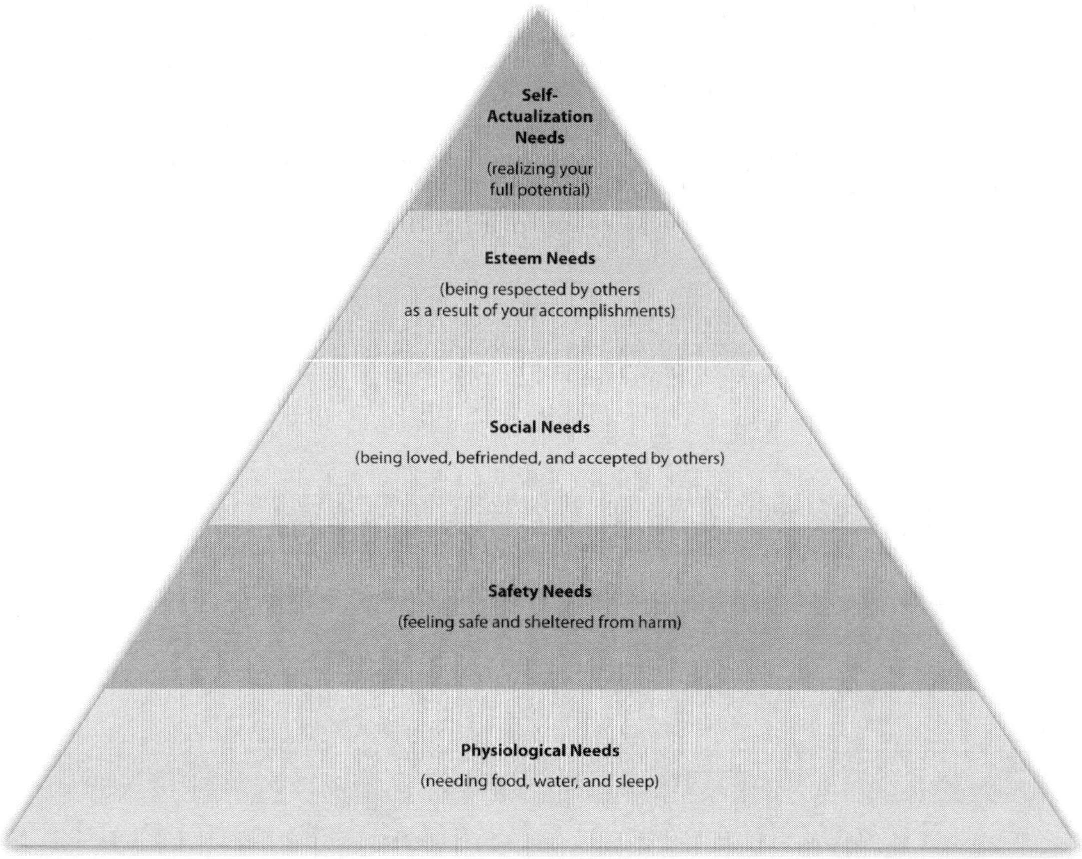


Maslow theorized that people have to fulfill their basic needs—like the need for food, water, and sleep—before they can begin fulfilling higher-level needs. Have you ever gone shopping when you were tired or hungry? Even if you were shopping for something that would make you envy of your friends (maybe a new car) you probably wanted to sleep or eat even worse. (Forget the car. Just give me a nap and a candy bar.)

People's needs can be recurring, such as the physiological need for hunger. You eat breakfast and are hungry at lunchtime and then again in the evening. Other needs tend to be enduring, such as the need for shelter, clothing, and safety. Still other needs arise at different points in time in a person's life. For example, during grade school and high school, your *social* needs probably rose to the forefront. You wanted to have friends and get a date. Perhaps this prompted you to buy certain types of clothing or electronic devices. After high school, you began thinking about how people would view you in your "station" in life, so you decided to pay for college and get a professional degree, thereby fulfilling your need for *esteem*. If you're lucky, at some point you will realize Maslow's state of *self-actualization*: You will believe you have become the person in life that you feel you were meant to be.

Marketing professionals understand Maslow's hierarchy. Take the need for people to feel secure and safe. Following the economic crisis that began in 2008, the sales of new automobiles dropped sharply virtually everywhere around the world—except the sales of Hyundai vehicles. Hyundai ran an ad campaign that assured car buyers they could return their vehicles if they couldn't make the payments on them without damaging their credit. Other carmakers began offering similar programs after they saw how successful Hyundai had been.

Likewise, banks began offering "worry-free" mortgages to ease the minds of would-be homebuyers. For a fee of about $500, First Mortgage Corp., a Texas-based bank, offered to make a homeowner's mortgage payment for six months if he or she got laid off.[21]

## 4.2 The Consumer's Perception

**perception**

How people interpret the world around them.

**Perception** is how you interpret the world around you and make sense of it in your brain. You do so via stimuli that affect your different senses—sight, hearing, touch, smell, and taste. How you combine these senses also makes a difference. For example, in one study, consumers were blindfolded and asked to drink a new brand of clear beer. Most of them said the product tasted like regular beer. However, when the blindfolds came off and they drank the beer, many of them described it as "watery" tasting.[22]

Using different types of stimuli, marketing professionals try to make you more perceptive to their products whether you need them or not. It's not an easy job. Consumers today are bombarded with all types of marketing from every angle—television, radio, magazines, the Internet, and even bathroom walls. It's been estimated that the average consumer is exposed to about three thousand advertisements per day.[23] Consumers are also multitasking more today than in the past. They are surfing the Internet, watching television, and checking their cell phones for text messages simultaneously. All day, every day, we are receiving information. Some, but not all, of it makes it into our brains.

Have you ever read or thought about something and then started noticing ads and information about it popping up everywhere? That's because your perception of it had become heightened. Many people are more perceptive to advertisements for products they need. **Selective perception** is the process of filtering out information based on how relevant it is to you. It's been described as a "suit of armor" that helps you filter out information you *don't* need. At other times, people forget information, even if it's quite relevant to them, which is called **selective retention**. Usually the information contradicts the person's belief. A longtime chain smoker who forgets much of the information communicated during an antismoking commercial is an example.

**selective perception**

The process whereby a person filters information based on how relevant it is to them.

**selective retention**

The process whereby a person retains information based on how well it matches their values and beliefs.

To be sure their advertising messages get through to you, companies use repetition. How tired of iPhone commercials were you before they tapered off the tube? How often do you see the same commercial aired during a single television show?

**Video Clip**

**A Parody of an iPhone Commercial**

Check out this parody on Apple's iPhone commercial.

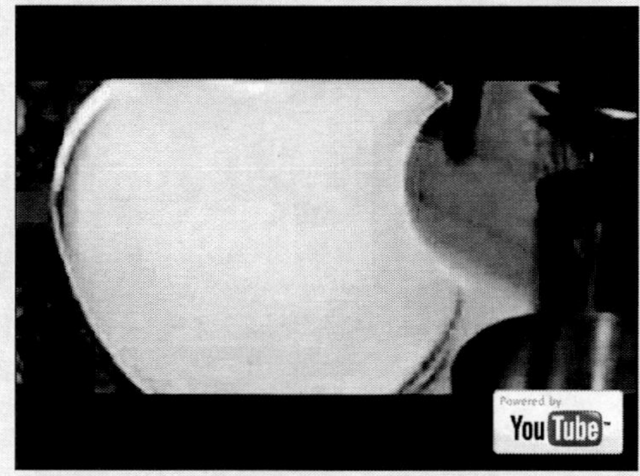


View the video online at: http://www.youtube.com/embed/4vle73VqtHw

Using surprising stimuli is also a technique. Sometimes this is called **shock advertising**. The clothing makers Benetton and Calvin Klein are probably best known for their shocking advertising. Calvin Klein sparked an uproar when it featured scantily clad prepubescent teens in its ads. There's evidence that shock advertising actually works, though. One study found that shocking content increased attention, benefited memory, and positively influenced behavior among a group of university students.[24]

**shock advertising**

Advertising designed to startle people so as to get their attention.

**Subliminal advertising** is the opposite of shock advertising. It involves exposing consumers to marketing stimuli—photos, ads, message, and so forth—by stealthily embedding them in movies, ads, and other media. For example, the words *Drink Coca-Cola* might be flashed for a millisecond on a movie screen. Consumers were thought to perceive the information subconsciously, and it would make them buy products. Keep in mind that today it's common to see brands such as Coke being consumed in movies and television programs, but there's nothing subliminal about it. Coke and other companies often pay to have their products in the shows.

**subliminal advertising**

Advertising that is not apparent to consumers but is thought to be perceived subconsciously by them.

The general public became aware of subliminal advertising in the 1960s. Many people considered the practice to be subversive, and in 1974, the Federal Communications Commission condemned it. Its effectiveness is somewhat sketchy, in any case. It didn't help that much of the original research on it, conducted in the 1950s by a market researcher who was trying to drum up business for his market research firm, was fabricated.[25]

People are still fascinated by subliminal advertising, however. To create "buzz" about the television show *The Mole* in 2008, ABC began hyping it by airing short commercials composed of just a few frames. If you blinked, you missed it. Some television stations actually called ABC to figure out what was going on. One-second ads were later rolled out to movie theaters.[26]

Even if your marketing effort reaches consumers and they retain it, different consumers can perceive it differently. Show two people the same product and you'll get two different perceptions of it. One man sees Pledge, an outstanding furniture polish, while another sees a can of spray no different from any other furniture polish. One woman sees a luxurious Gucci purse, and the other sees an overpriced bag to hold keys and makeup.[27] A couple of frames about *The Mole* might make you want to see the television show. However, your friend might see the ad, find it stupid, and never tune in to watch the show.

## 4.3 Learning

**learning**

The process by which consumers change their behavior after they gain information or experience with a product.

**Learning** refers to the process by which consumers change their behavior after they gain information or experience a product. It's the reason you don't buy a crummy product twice. Learning doesn't just affect what you buy, however. It affects how you shop. People with limited experience about a product or brand generally seek out more information about it than people who have used it before.

Companies try to get consumers to learn about their products in different ways. Car dealerships offer test drives. Pharmaceutical reps leave behind lots of free items at doctor's offices with medication names and logos written all over them—pens, coffee cups, magnets, and so on. Free samples of products that come in the mail or are delivered with newspapers are another example. To promote its new line of coffees, McDonald's offered customers free samples to try.

**operant conditioning**

A type of behavior that's repeated when it's rewarded.

Another kind of learning is **operant conditioning**, which is what occurs when researchers are able to get a mouse to run through a maze for a piece cheese or a dog to salivate just by ringing a bell. Companies engage in operant conditioning by rewarding consumers, too. The prizes that come in Cracker Jacks and with McDonald's Happy Meals are examples. The rewards cause consumers to want to repeat their purchasing behaviors. Other rewards include free tans offered with gym memberships, punch cards that give you a free Subway sandwich after a certain number of purchases, and free car washes when you fill up your car with a tank of gas.

## 4.4 Consumer's Attitude

**attitudes**

"Mental positions" or emotional feelings people have about products, services, companies, ideas, issues, or institutions.

**Attitudes** are "mental positions" or emotional feelings people have about products, services, companies, ideas, issues, or institutions.[28] Attitudes tend to be enduring, and because they are based on people's values and beliefs, they are hard to change. That doesn't stop sellers from trying, though. They want people to have positive rather than negative feelings about their offerings. A few years ago, KFC began running ads to the effect that fried chicken was healthy—until the U.S. Federal Trade Commission told the company to stop. Wendy's slogan to the effect that its products are "way better than fast food" is another example. Fast food has a negative connotation, so Wendy's is trying to get consumers to think about its offerings as being better.

A good example of a shift in the attitudes of consumers relates to banks. The taxpayer-paid government bailouts of big banks that began in 2008 provoked the wrath of Americans, creating an opportunity for small banks not involved in the credit derivates and subprime mortgage mess. The Worthington National Bank, a small bank in Fort Worth, Texas, ran billboards reading: "Did Your Bank Take a Bailout? We didn't." Another read: "Just Say NO to Bailout Banks. Bank Responsibly!" The Worthington Bank received tens of millions in new deposits soon after running these campaigns.[29]

**FIGURE 3.9**

Worthington National, a small Texas bank, capitalized on people's bad attitudes toward big banks that accepted bailouts from the government in 2008–2009. After running billboards with this message, the bank received millions of dollars in new deposits.

Did Your Bank Take a Bailout?
We didn't.
Discover the Worthington National Bank difference.

Just say NO to Bailout Banks.
Bank Responsibly!
Discover the Worthington National Bank difference.

*© WorthingtonBank.com*

**KEY TAKEAWAY**

Psychologist Abraham Maslow theorized that people have to fulfill their basic needs—like the need for food, water, and sleep—before they can begin fulfilling higher-level needs. Perception is how you interpret the world around you and make sense of it in your brain. To be sure their advertising messages get through to you, companies often resort to repetition. Shocking advertising and subliminal advertising are two other methods. Learning is the process by which consumers change their behavior after they gain information about or experience with a product. Consumers' attitudes are the "mental positions" people take based on their values and beliefs. Attitudes tend to be enduring and are often difficult for companies to change.

**REVIEW QUESTIONS**

1. How does Maslow's Hierarchy of Needs help marketing professionals?
2. How does the process of perception work and how can companies use it to their advantage in their marketing?
3. What types of learning do companies try to get consumers to engage in?

# 5. SOCIETAL FACTORS THAT AFFECT PEOPLE'S BUYING BEHAVIOR

**LEARNING OBJECTIVES**

1. **Explain why the culture, subcultures, social classes, and families consumers belong to affect their buying behavior.**
2. **Describe what reference groups and opinion leaders are.**

Situational factors—the weather, time of day, where you are, who you are with, and your mood—influence what you buy, but only on a temporary basis. So do personal factors, such as your gender, as well as psychological factors, such as your self-concept. Societal factors are a bit different. They are more outward. They depend on the world around you and how it works.

## 5.1 The Consumer's Culture

**culture**

The shared beliefs, customs, behaviors, and attitudes that characterize a society used to cope with their world and with one another.

**Culture** refers to the shared beliefs, customs, behaviors, and attitudes that characterize a society. Your culture prescribes the way in which you should live. As a result, it has a huge effect on the things you purchase. For example, in Beirut, Lebanon, women can often be seen wearing miniskirts. If you're a woman in Afghanistan wearing a miniskirt, however, you could face bodily harm or death. In Afghanistan women generally wear *burqas*, which cover them completely from head to toe. Similarly, in Saudi Arabia, women must wear what's called an *abaya*, or long black garment. Interestingly, abayas have become big business in recent years. They come in many styles, cuts, and fabrics. Some are encrusted with jewels and cost thousands of dollars.

To read about the fashions women in Muslim countries wear, check out the following article: http://www.time.com/time/world/article/0,8599,1210781,00.html.

Even cultures that share many of the same values as the United States can be quite different from the United States in many ways. Following the meltdown of the financial markets in 2008, countries around the world were pressed by the United States to engage in deficit spending so as to stimulate the worldwide economy. But the plan was a hard sell both to German politicians and the German people in general. Most Germans don't own credit cards, and running up a lot of debt is something people in that culture generally don't do. Companies such as Visa and MasterCard and businesses that offer consumers credit to purchase items with high ticket prices have to deal with factors such as these.

## 5.2 The Consumer's Subculture(s)

**subculture**

A group of people within a culture who are different from the dominant culture but have something in common with one another, such as common interests, vocations or jobs, religions, ethnic backgrounds, or sexual orientations.

A **subculture** is a group of people within a culture who are different from the dominant culture but have something in common with one another—common interests, vocations or jobs, religions, ethnic backgrounds, sexual orientations, and so forth. The fastest-growing subculture in the United States consists of people of Hispanic origin, followed by Asian Americans, and blacks. The purchasing power of U.S. Hispanics is growing by leaps and bounds. By 2010 it is expected to reach more than $1 trillion.[30] This is a lucrative market that companies are working to attract. Home Depot has launched a Spanish version of its Web site. Walmart is in the process of converting some of its Neighborhood Markets into stores designed to appeal to Hispanics. The Supermarcado de Walmart stores are located in Hispanic neighborhoods and feature elements such as cafés serving Latino pastries and coffee and full meat and fish counters.[31]

**FIGURE 3.10**

Care to join the subculture of the "Otherkin"? Otherkins are primarily Internet users who believe they are reincarnations of mythological or legendary creatures—angels, demons, vampires—you name it. To read more about the Otherkins and seven other bizarre subcultures, visit http://www.oddee.com/item_96676.aspx.

Marketing products based the ethnicity of consumers is useful. However, it could become harder to do in the future because the boundaries between ethnic groups are blurring. For example, many people today view themselves as multiracial. (Golfer Tiger Woods is a notable example.) Also, keep in mind that ethnic and racial subcultures are not the only subcultures marketing professionals look at. As we have indicated, subcultures can develop in response to people's interest. You have probably heard of the hip-hop subculture, people who in engage in extreme types of sports such as helicopter skiing, or people who play the fantasy game Dungeons and Dragons. The people in these groups have certain interests and exhibit certain behaviors that allow marketing professionals design specific products for them.

## 5.3 The Consumer's Social Class

A **social class** is a group of people who have the same social, economic, or educational status in society.[32] To *some* degree, consumers in the same social class exhibit similar purchasing behavior. Have you ever been surprised to find out that someone you knew who was wealthy drove a beat-up old car or wore old clothes and shoes? If so, it was because the person, given his or her social class, was behaving "out of the norm" in terms of what you thought his or her purchasing behavior should be.

**social class**

A group of people who have the same social, economic, or educational status in society.

Table 3.1 shows seven classes of American consumers along with the types of car brands they might buy. Keep in mind that the U.S. market is just a fraction of the world market. As we explained in Chapter 2, to sustain their products, companies often launch their products in other parts of the world. The rise of the middle class in India and China is creating opportunities for many companies to successfully do this. For example, China has begun to overtake the United States as the world's largest auto market.[33]

**TABLE 3.1** Social Classes and Buying Patterns: An Example

| Class | Type of Car | Definition of Class |
|---|---|---|
| Upper-Upper Class | Rolls-Royce | People with inherited wealth and aristocratic names (the Kennedys, Rothschilds, Windsors, etc.) |
| Lower-Upper Class | Mercedes | Professionals such as CEOs, doctors, and lawyers |
| Upper-Middle Class | Lexus | College graduates and managers |
| Middle Class | Toyota | Both white-collar and blue-collar workers |
| Working Class | Pontiac | Blue-collar workers |
| Lower but Not the Lowest | Used Vehicle | People who are working but not on welfare |
| Lowest Class | No vehicle | People on welfare |

The makers of upscale brands in particular walk a fine line in terms of marketing to customers. On the one hand, they want their customer bases to be as large as possible. This is especially tempting in a recession when luxury buyers are harder to come by. On the other hand, if the companies create products the middle class can better afford, they risk "cheapening" their brands. That's why, for example, Smart Cars, which are made by BMW, don't have the BMW label on them. For a time, Tiffany's sold a cheaper line of silver jewelry to a lot of customers. However, the company later worried that its reputation was being tarnished by the line. Keep in mind that a product's price is to some extent determined by supply and demand. Luxury brands therefore try to keep the supply of their products in check so their prices remain high.

Some companies have managed to capture market share by introducing "lower echelon" brands without damaging their luxury brands. Johnnie Walker is an example. The company's whiskeys come in bottles with red, green, blue, black, and gold labels. The blue label is the company's best product. Every blue-label bottle has a serial number and is sold in a silk-lined box, accompanied by a certificate of authenticity.[34]

**FIGURE 3.11**

The whiskey brand Johnnie Walker has managed to expand its market share without cheapening the brand by producing a few lower-priced versions of the whiskey and putting them in bottles with different labels.

*© 2010 Jupiterimages Corporation*

## 5.4 Reference Groups and Opinion Leaders

Of course, you probably know people who aren't wealthy but who still drive a Mercedes or other upscale vehicle. That's because consumers have reference groups. **Reference groups** are groups a consumer identifies with and wants to join. If you have ever dreamed of being a professional player of basketball or another sport, you have a reference group. Marketing professionals are aware of this. That's why, for example, Nike hires celebrities such as Michael Jordan to pitch the company's products.

**Opinion leaders** are people with expertise in certain areas. Consumers respect these people and often ask their opinions before they buy goods and services. An information technology specialist with a great deal of knowledge about computer brands is an example. These people's purchases often lie at the forefront of leading trends. For example, the IT specialist we mentioned is probably a person who has the latest and greatest tech products, and his opinion of them is likely to carry more weight with you than any sort of advertisement.

Today's companies are using different techniques to reach opinion leaders. Network analysis using special software is one way of doing so. Orgnet.com has developed software for this purpose. Orgnet's software doesn't mine sites like Facebook and LinkedIn, though. Instead, it's based on sophisticated techniques that unearthed the links between Al Qaeda terrorists. Explains Valdis Krebs, the company's founder: "Pharmaceutical firms want to identify who the key opinion leaders are. They don't want to sell a new drug to everyone. They want to sell to the 60 key oncologists."[35] As you can probably tell from this chapter, exploring the frontiers of people's buying patterns is a fascinating and constantly evolving field.

**reference groups**

Groups a consumer identifies with and wants to join.

**opinion leaders**

People with expertise certain areas. Consumers respect these people and often ask their opinions before they buy goods and services.

## 5.5 The Consumer's Family

Most market researchers consider a person's family to be one of the biggest determiners of buying behavior. Like it or not, you are more like your parents than you think, at least in terms of your consumption patterns. The fact is that many of the things you buy and don't buy are a result of what your parents do and do not buy. The soap you grew up using, toothpaste your parents bought and used, and even the "brand" of politics you lean toward (Democratic or Republican) are examples of the products you are likely to favor as an adult.

Family buying behavior has been researched extensively. Companies are also interested in which family members have the most influence over certain purchases. Children have a great deal of influence over many household purchases. For example, in 2003 nearly half (47 percent) of nine- to seventeen-year-olds were asked by parents to go online to find out about products or services, compared to 37 percent in 2001. IKEA used this knowledge to design their showrooms. The children's bedrooms feature fun beds with appealing comforters so children will be prompted to identify and ask for what they want.[36]

Marketing to children has come under increasing scrutiny. Some critics accuse companies of deliberating manipulating children to nag their parents for certain products. For example, even though tickets for Hannah Montana concerts ranged from hundreds to thousands of dollars, the concerts often still sold out. However, as one writer put it, exploiting "pester power" is not always ultimately in the long-term interests of advertisers if it alienates kids' parents.[37]

### KEY TAKEAWAY

Culture prescribes the way in which you should live and affects the things you purchase. A subculture is a group of people within a culture who are different from the dominant culture but have something in common with one another—common interests, vocations or jobs, religions, ethnic backgrounds, sexual orientations, and so forth. To some degree, consumers in the same social class exhibit similar purchasing behavior. Most market researchers consider a person's family to be one of the biggest determiners of buying behavior. Reference groups are groups that a consumer identifies with and wants to join. Companies often hire celebrities to endorse their products to appeal to people's reference groups. Opinion leaders are people with expertise in certain areas. Consumers respect these people and often ask their opinions before they buy goods and services.

### REVIEW QUESTIONS

1. Why do people's cultures affect what they buy?
2. How do subcultures differ from cultures? Can you belong to more than one culture or subculture?
3. How are companies trying to reach opinion leaders today?

# 6. DISCUSSION QUESTIONS AND ACTIVITIES

### DISCUSSION QUESTIONS

1. Why do people in different cultures buy different products? Discuss with your class the types of vehicles you have seen other countries. Why are they different, and how do they better meet buyers' needs in those countries? What types of cars do you think should be sold in the United States today?
2. What is your opinion of companies like Google that gather information about your browsing patterns? What advantages and drawbacks does this pose for consumers? If you were a business owner, what kinds of information would you gather on your customers and how would you use it?
3. Are there any areas in which you consider yourself an opinion leader? What are they?
4. What purchasing decisions have you been able to influence in your family and why? Is marketing to children a good idea? If not, what if one of your competitors were successfully do so? Would it change your opinion?
5. How do you determine what is distinctive about different groups? What distinguishes one group from other groups?
6. Name some products that have led to postpurchase dissonance on your part. Then categorize them as high- or low-involvement products.
7. Describe the decision process for impulse purchases at the retail level. Would they be classified as high- or low-involvement purchases?
8. How do you think the manufacturers of products sold through infomercials reduce postpurchase dissonance?
9. Explain the relationship between extensive, limited, and routine decision making relative to high and low involvement. Identify examples of extensive, limited, and routine decision making based on your personal consumption behavior.

### ACTIVITIES

1. Go to http://www.ospreypacks.com and enter the blog site. Does the blog make you more or less inclined to purchase an Osprey backpack?
2. Select three advertisements and describe the needs identified by Maslow that each ad addresses.
3. Break up into groups and visit an ethnic part of your town that differs from your own ethnicity(ies). Walk around the neighborhood and its stores. What types of marketing and buying differences do you see? Write a report of your findings.
4. Using Maslow's Hierarchy of Needs, identify a list of popular advertising slogans that appeal to each of the five levels.
5. Identify how McDonald's targets both users (primarily children) and buyers (parents, grandparents, etc.). Provide specific examples of strategies used by the fast-food marketer to target both groups. Make it a point to incorporate Happy Meals and Mighty Kids Meals into your discussion.

# ENDNOTES


1. "The Way the Brain Buys," *Economist*, December 20, 2009, 105–7.
2. "The Way the Brain Buys," *Economist*, December 20, 2009, 105–7.
3. Rebecca Knight, "Custom-made for E-tail Success," *Financial Times*, March 18, 2009, 10.
4. Rebecca Knight, "Custom-made for E-tail Success," *Financial Times*, March 18, 2009, 10.
5. Patricia Moore, "Smells Sell," *NZ Business*, February 2008, 26–27.
6. Carol J. Gaumer and William C. Leif, "Social Facilitation: Affect and Application in Consumer Buying Situations," *Journal of Food Products Marketing* 11, no. 1 (2005): 75–82.
7. Anna S. Matilla and Jochen Wirtz, "The Role of Store Environmental Stimulation and Social Factors on Impulse Purchasing," *Journal of Services Marketing* 22, no. 7 (2008): 562–67.
8. Allan Bird, "Retail Industry," *Encyclopedia of Japanese Business and Management* (London: Routledge, 2002), 399–400.
9. Jacob Hornik and Giulia Miniero, "Synchrony Effects on Customers' Responses and Behaviors," *International Journal of Research in Marketing* 26, no. 1 (2009): 34–40.
10. "Wal-Mart Unveils Plans for Own-Label Revamp," *Financial Times*, March 17, 2009, 15.
11. Stephanie Rosenbloom (New York Times News Service), "Where Have All the Shoppers Gone?" *Fort Worth Star-Telegram*, March 18, 2009, 5E.
12. Alyson Ward, "Products of Our Time," *Fort Worth Star-Telegram*, March 7, 2009, 1E.
13. Cheryl B. Ward and Tran Thuhang, "Consumer Gifting Behaviors: One for You, One for Me?" *Services Marketing Quarterly* 29, no. 2 (2007): 1–17.
14. Genevieve Schmitt, "Hunters and Gatherers," *Dealernews* 44, no. 8 (2008): 72. The article references the 2006 Behavioral Tracking Study by Miller Brewing Company.
15. Jeanne Hill and Susan K. Harmon, "Male Gender Role Beliefs, Coupon Use and Bargain Hunting," *Academy of Marketing Studies Journal* 11, no. 2 (2007): 107–21.
16. "Designing Cars for the Elderly: A Design Story," http://www.businessweek.com/globalbiz/content/may2008/gb2008056_154197.htm (accessed April 13, 2012).
17. Sarah Saffian, "Dreamers: The Making of Not Your Daughter's Jeans," *Reader's Digest*, March 2009, 53–55.
18. Benny Barak and Steven Gould, "Alternative Age Measures: A Research Agenda," in *Advances in Consumer Research*, vol. 12, ed. Elizabeth C. Hirschman and Morris B. Holbrook (Provo, UT: Association for Consumer Research, 1985), 53–58.
19. Benny Barak and Steven Gould, "Alternative Age Measures: A Research Agenda," in *Advances in Consumer Research*, vol. 12, ed. Elizabeth C. Hirschman and Morris B. Holbrook (Provo, UT: Association for Consumer Research, 1985), 53–58.
20. Robert Berner, "Detergent Can Be So Much More," *BusinessWeek*, May 1, 2006, 66–68.
21. Andrea Jares, "New Programs Are Taking Worries from Home Buying," *Fort Worth Star-Telegram*, March 7, 2010, 1C–2C.
22. Laura Ries, *In the Boardroom: Why Left-Brained Management and Right-Brain Marketing Don't See Eye-to-Eye* (New York: HarperCollins, 2009).
23. Kalle Lasn, *Culture Jam: The Uncooling of America* (New York: William Morrow & Company, 1999).
24. Darren W. Dahl, Kristina D. Frankenberger, and Rajesh V. Manchanda, "Does It Pay to Shock? Reactions to Shocking and Nonshocking Advertising Content among University Students," *Journal of Advertising Research* 43, no. 3 (2003): 268–80.
25. Cynthia Crossen, "For a Time in the '50s, A Huckster Fanned Fears of Ad 'Hypnosis,'" *Wall Street Journal*, November 5, 2007, eastern edition, B1.
26. Josef Adalian, "ABC Hopes 'Mole' Isn't Just a Blip," *Television Week*, June 2, 2008, 3.
27. James Chartrand, "Why Targeting Selective Perception Captures Immediate Attention," http://www.copyblogger.com/selective-perception (accessed October 14, 2009).
28. "Dictionary of Marketing Terms," http://www.allbusiness.com/glossaries/marketing/4941810-1.html (accessed October 14, 2009).
29. Joe Mantone, "Banking on TARP Stigma," *SNLi*, March 16, 2009, http://www.snl.com/Interactivex/article.aspx?CdId=A-9218440-12642 (accessed October 14, 2009).
30. Larry Watrous, "Illegals: The New N-Word in America," *Fort Worth Star-Telegram*, March 16, 2009, 9B.
31. Jonathan Birchall, "Wal-Mart Looks to Hispanic Market in Expansion Drive," *Financial Times*, March 13, 2009, 18.
32. Princeton University, "WordNet," http://wordnetweb.princeton.edu/perl/webwn?s=social+class&sub=Search+WordNet&o2=&o0=1&o7=&o5=&o1=1&o6=&o4=&o3=&h= (accessed October 14, 2009).
33. "More Cars Sold in China than in January," *France 24*, February 10, 2009, http://www.france24.com/en/20090210-more-cars-sold-china-us-january-auto-market (accessed October 14, 2009).
34. "Johnnie Walker," http://en.wikipedia.org/wiki/Johnnie_Walker (accessed October 14, 2009).
35. Anita Campbell, "Marketing to Opinion Leaders," *Small Business Trends*, June 28, 2004, http://smallbiztrends.com/2004/06/marketing-to-opinion-leaders.html (accessed October 13, 2009).
36. "Teen Market Profile," Mediamark Research, 2003, http://www.magazine.org/content/files/teenprofile04.pdf (accessed December 4, 2009).
37. Ray Waddell, "Miley Strikes Back," *Billboard*, June 27, 2009, 7–8.

# CHAPTER 4
# Business Buying Behavior

In the last chapter, we talked about the buying behavior of consumers—people like you and me who buy products for our own personal use. However, many businesses don't offer their goods and services to individual consumers at all. Instead, their customers are other businesses, institutions, or government organizations. These are the business-to-business (B2B) markets we talked about in Chapter 1.

## 1. THE CHARACTERISTICS OF BUSINESS-TO-BUSINESS (B2B) MARKETS

### LEARNING OBJECTIVES

1. **Identify the ways in which business-to-business (B2B) markets differ from business-to-consumer (B2C) markets.**
2. **Explain why business buying is acutely affected by the behavior of consumers.**

Business-to-business (B2B) markets differ from business-to-consumer (B2C) markets in many ways. For one, the number of products sold in business markets dwarfs the number sold in consumer markets. Suppose you buy a five-hundred-dollar computer from Dell. The sale amounts to a single transaction for you. But think of all the transactions Dell had to go through to sell you that one computer. Dell had to purchase many parts from many computer component makers. It also had to purchase equipment and facilities to assemble the computers, hire and pay employees, pay money to create and maintain its Web site and advertise, and buy insurance and accounting and financial services to keep its operations running smoothly. Many transactions had to happen before yours could.

Business products can also be very complex. Some need to be custom built or retrofitted for buyers. The products include everything from high-dollar construction equipment to commercial real estate and buildings, military equipment, and billion-dollar cruise liners used in the tourism industry. There are few or no individual consumers in the market for many of these products. Moreover, a single customer can account for a huge amount of business. Some businesses, like those that supply the U.S. auto industry around Detroit, have just a handful of customers—General Motors, Chrysler, and/or Ford. Consequently, you can imagine why these suppliers become very worried when the automakers fall on hard times.

Not only can business products be complex, but so can figuring out the buying dynamics of organizations. Many people within an organization can be part of the buying process and have a say in ultimately what gets purchased, how much of it, and from whom. This is perhaps the most complicated part of the business. In fact, it's a bit like a chess match. And because of the quantities each business customer is capable of buying, the stakes are high. For some organizations, losing a big account can be financially devastating and winning one can be a financial bonanza.

How high are the stakes? Table 4.1 shows a recent ranking of the top five corporations in the world in terms of the sales they generate annually. Believe it or not, these companies earn more in a year than all the businesses of some countries do. Imagine the windfall you could gain as a seller by landing an exclusive account with any one of them.

**TABLE 4.1** Top Five Corporations Worldwide in Terms of Their Revenues

| Company | Sales (Billions of Dollars) |
|---|---|
| Royal Dutch Shell | 458 |
| ExxonMobil | 426 |
| Walmart Stores | 405 |
| British Petroleum (BP) | 361 |
| Toyota Motor Company | 263 |
| **Note: Numbers have been rounded to the nearest billion.** | |

Generally, the more high-dollar and complex the item being sold is, the longer it takes for the sale to be made. The sale of a new commercial jet to an airline company such as U.S. Airways, Delta, or American Airlines can take literally years to be completed. Sales such as these are risky for companies. The buyers are concerned about many factors, such as the safety, reliability, and efficiency of the planes. They also generally want the jets customized in some way. Consequently, a lot of time and effort is needed to close these deals.

Unlike many consumers, most business buyers demand that the products they buy meet strict standards. Take, for example, the Five Guys burger chain, based in Virginia. The company taste-tested eighteen different types of mayonnaise before settling on the one it uses. Would you be willing to taste eighteen different brands of mayonnaise before buying one? Probably not.[1]

Another characteristic of B2B markets is the level of personal selling that goes on. Salespeople personally call on business customers to a far greater extent than they do consumers. Most of us have had door-to-door salespeople call on us occasionally. However, businesses often have multiple salespeople call on them in person daily, and some customers even provide office space for key vendors' salespeople. Table 4.2 outlines the main differences between B2C and B2B markets.

**TABLE 4.2** Business-to-Consumer Markets versus Business-to-Business Markets: How They Compare

| Consumer Market | Business Market |
|---|---|
| Many customers, geographically dispersed | Fewer customers, often geographically concentrated, with a small number accounting for most of the company's sales |
| Smaller total dollar amounts due to fewer transactions | Larger dollar amounts due to more transactions |
| Shorter decision cycles | Longer decision cycles |
| More reliance on mass marketing via advertising, Web sites, and retailing | More reliance on personal selling |
| Less-rigid product standards | More-rigid product standards |

## 1.1 The Demand for B2B Products

**derived demand**

Demand that springs from, or is derived from, a secondary source other than the primary buyer of the product.

**fluctuating demand**

Demand that fluctuates sharply in response to a change in consumer demand.

Even though they don't sell their products to consumers like you and me, B2B sellers carefully watch general economic conditions to anticipate consumer buying patterns. The firms do so because the demand for business products is based on derived demand. **Derived demand** is demand that springs from, or is derived from, a source other than the primary buyer of a product. When it comes to B2B sales, that source is consumers. If consumers aren't demanding the products produced by businesses, the firms that supply products to these businesses are in big trouble.

**Fluctuating demand** is another characteristic of B2B markets: a small change in demand by consumers can have a big effect throughout the chain of businesses that supply all the goods and services that produce it. Often, a bullwhip type of effect occurs. If you have ever held a whip, you know that a slight shake of the handle will result in a big snap of the whip at its tip. Essentially, consumers are the handle and businesses along the chain compose the whip—hence the need to keep tabs on end consumers. They are a powerful purchasing force.

For example, Cisco makes routers, which are specialized computers that enable computer networks to work. If Google uses five hundred routers and replaces 10 percent of them each year, that means Google usually buys fifty routers in a given year. What happens if consumer demand for the Internet falls by 10 percent? Then Google needs only 450 routers. Google's demand for Cisco's routers therefore becomes zero. Suppose the following year the demand for the Internet returns to normal. Google now needs to replace the fifty routers it didn't buy in the first year plus the fifty it needs to replace in the second year. So in year two, Cisco's sales go from zero to a hundred, or twice normal. Thus, Cisco experiences a bullwhip effect, whereas Google's sales vary only by 10 percent.

Because consumers are such a powerful force, some companies go so far as to try to influence their B2B sales by directly influencing consumers even though they don't sell their products to them. Intel is a classic case. Do you really care what sort of microprocessing chip gets built into your computer? Intel would like you to, which is why it runs TV commercials like the Homer Simpson commercial shown in the video clip below. The commercial isn't likely to persuade a computer manufacturer to buy Intel's chips. But the manufacturer might be persuaded to buy them if it's important to you. Derived demand is also the reason Intel demands that the buyers of its chips put a little "Intel Inside" sticker on each computer they make—so you get to know Intel and demand its products.

### Video Clip

**Intel Animations Over the Years**

Does this commercial make you want to buy a computer with "Intel Inside"? Intel hopes so.

View the video online at: http://www.youtube.com/embed/VRcAdXd-TRU

B2B buyers also keep tabs on consumers to look for patterns that could create joint demand. **Joint demand** occurs when the demand for one product increases the demand for another. For example, when a new video console like the Xbox comes out, it creates demand for a whole new crop of video games.

**joint demand**

When the demand for one product increases the demand for another.

### Video Clip

**The History of Pong**

Watch this video to see the first video game ever invented, Pong, and learn about its maker. Of course, Pong got old pretty fast, so more games were quickly developed and continue to be, especially when new gaming systems hit the market.

View the video online at: http://www.youtube.com/embed/ShyRGWRcagY

**KEY TAKEAWAY**

B2B markets differ from B2C markets in many ways. There are more transactions in B2B markets and more high-dollar transactions because business products are often costly and complex. There are also fewer buyers in B2B markets, but they spend much more than the typical consumer does and have more-rigid product standards. The demand for business products is based on derived demand. Derived demand is demand that springs from, or is derived from, a secondary source other than the primary buyer of a product. For businesses, this source is consumers. Fluctuating demand is another characteristic of B2B markets: a small change in demand by consumers can have a big effect throughout the chain of businesses that supply all the goods and services that produce it.

**REVIEW QUESTIONS**

1. Why are there more transactions in B2B markets than B2C markets? Why are there fewer buyers?
2. Explain what derived demand is.
3. Why do firms experience a bullwhip effect in the demand for their products when consumers demand changes?

# 2. TYPES OF B2B BUYERS

**LEARNING OBJECTIVES**

1. **Describe the major categories of business buyers.**
2. **Explain why finding decision makers in business markets is challenging for sellers.**

Business buyers can be either nonprofit or for-profit businesses. To help you get a better idea of the different types of business customers in B2B markets, we've put them into four basic categories: producers, resellers, governments, and institutions.

## 2.1 Producers

**FIGURE 4.1**

Your local tattoo parlor is a producer.

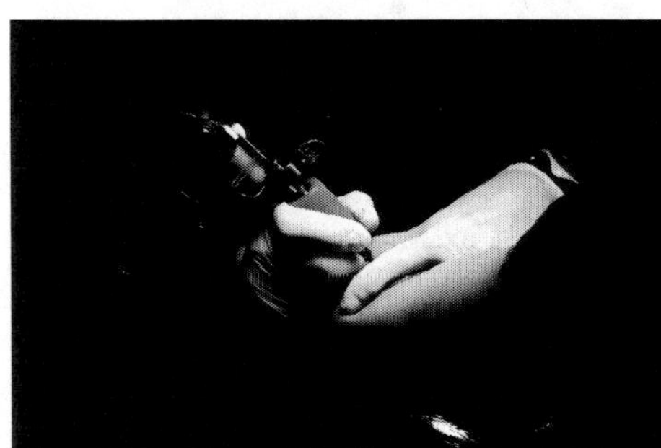

*© 2010 Jupiterimages Corporation*

**Producers** are companies that purchase goods and services that they transform into other products. They include both manufacturers and service providers. Procter & Gamble, General Motors, McDonald's, Dell, and Delta Airlines are examples. So are the restaurants around your campus, your dentist, your doctor, and the local tattoo parlor. All these businesses have to buy certain products to produce the goods and services they create. General Motors needs steel and hundreds of thousands of other products to produce cars. McDonald's needs beef and potatoes. Delta Airlines needs fuel and planes. Your dentist needs drugs such as Novocain, oral tools, and X-ray machinery. Your local tattoo parlor needs special inks and needles and a bright neon sign that flashes "open" in the middle of the night.

**producers**

Companies that purchase goods and services that they transform into other products.

## 2.2 Resellers

**resellers**

Companies that sell goods and services produced by other firms without materially changing them.

**Resellers** are companies that sell goods and services produced by other firms without materially changing them. They include wholesalers, brokers, and retailers. Walmart and Target are two big retailers you are familiar with. Large wholesalers, brokers, and retailers have a great deal of market power. If you can get them to buy your products, your sales can exponentially increase.

Every day, retailers flock to Walmart's corporate headquarters in Bentonville, Arkansas, to try to hawk their products. But would it surprise you that not everybody wants to do business with a powerhouse like Walmart? Jim Wier, one-time CEO of the company that produces Snapper-brand mowers and snow blowers, actually took a trip to Walmart's headquarters to *stop* doing business with the company. Why? Snapper products are high-end, heavy-duty products. Wier knew that Walmart had been selling his company's products for lower and lower prices and wanted deeper and deeper discounts from Snapper. He believed Snapper products were too expensive for Walmart's customers and always would be, unless the company started making cheaper-quality products or outsourced their manufacturing overseas, which is something he didn't want to do.

"The whole visit to Wal-Mart's headquarters is a great experience," said Wier about his trip. "It's so crowded, you have to drive around, waiting for a parking space. You have to follow someone who is leaving, walking back to their car, and get their spot. Then you go inside this building, you register for your appointment, they give you a badge, and then you wait in the pews with the rest of the peddlers, the guy with the bras draped over his shoulder." Eventually, would-be suppliers were taken into small cubicles where they had thirty minutes to make their case. "It's a little like going to see the principal, really," he said.[2]

## 2.3 Governments

**business-to-government (B2G) markets**

Markets in which local, state, and federal governments buy products.

Can you guess the biggest purchaser of goods and services in the world? It is the U.S. government. It purchases everything you can imagine, from paper and fax machines to tanks and weapons, buildings, toilets for NASA (the National Aeronautics and Space Administration), highway construction services, and medical and security services. State and local governments buy enormous amounts of products, too. They contract with companies that provide citizens with all kinds of services from transportation to garbage collection. (So do foreign governments, provinces, and localities, of course.) **Business-to-government (B2G) markets**, or when companies sell to local, state, and federal governments, represent a major selling opportunity, even for smaller sellers. In fact, many government entities specify that their agencies must award a certain amount of business to small businesses, minority- and women-owned businesses, and businesses owned by disabled veterans.

There is no one central department or place in which all these products are bought and sold. Companies that want to sell to the U.S. government should first register with the Central Contractor Registry at http://www.CCR.gov. They should then consult the General Services Administration (GSA) Web site (http://www.gsa.gov). The GSA helps more than two hundred federal agencies buy a wide variety of products purchased routinely. The products can include office supplies, information technology services, repair services, vehicles, and many other products purchased by agencies on a regular basis. Consequently, it is a good starting point. However, the GSA won't negotiate a contract for the NASA toilet or a fighter jet. It sticks to routine types of purchases.

## FIGURE 4.2

The General Services Administration (GSA) is a good starting point for companies that want to do business with the federal government. The U.S. Small Business Administration (SBA) also offers sellers a great deal of information on marketing to the government, including online courses that explain how to do it.

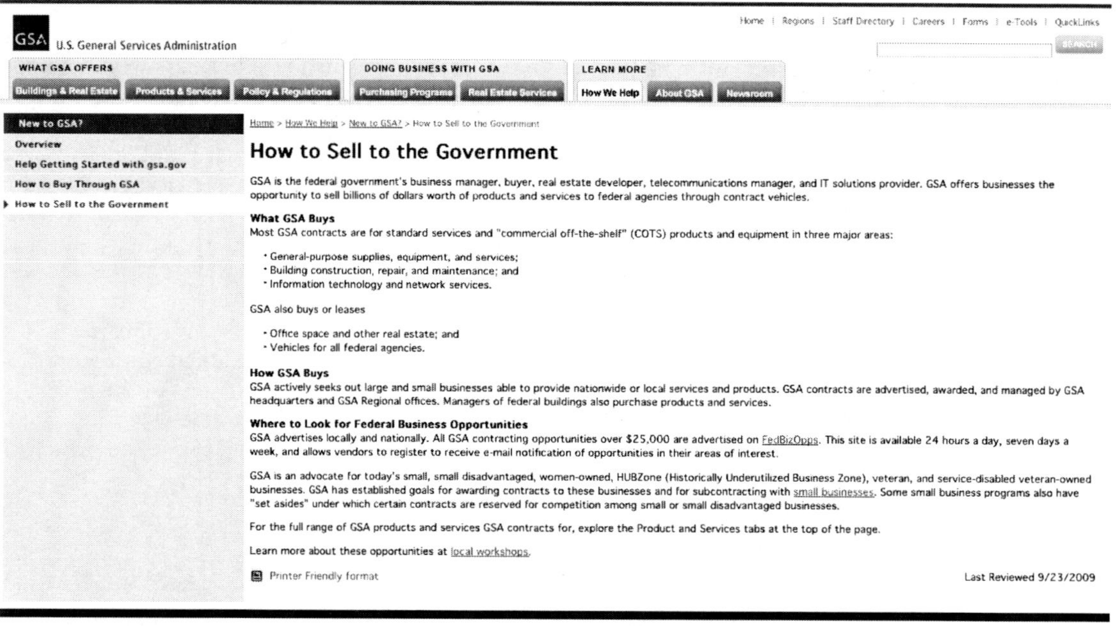


*Source: http://www.gsa.gov/Portal/gsa/ep/contentView.do?contentType=GSA_BASIC&contentId=13439&noc=T.*

The existence of the GSA doesn't mean the agencies it works with don't have any say over what is purchased for them. The agencies themselves have a big say, so B2B sellers need to contact them and aggressively market their products to them. After all, agencies don't buy products, people do. Fortunately, every agency posts on the Internet a forecast of its budget, that is, what it is planning on spending money on in the coming months. The agencies even list the names, addresses, and e-mails of contact persons responsible for purchasing decisions. Many federal agencies are able to purchase as much as $25,000 of products at a time by simply using a government credit card. This fact makes them a good target for small businesses.

It's not unusual for each agency or department to have its own procurement policies that must be followed. Would-be sellers are often asked to submit sealed bids that contain the details of what they are willing to provide the government and at what price. But contrary to popular belief, it's not always the lowest bid that's accepted. Would the United States want to send its soldiers to war in the cheapest planes and tanks, bearing the lowest-cost armor? Probably not. Like other buyers, government buyers look for the best value.

**FIGURE 4.3**

Politics can come into play when it comes to large government purchases: Although the F-22 is the most sophisticated fighter jet in the world, it has never been used in battle. But when the Pentagon wanted to stop production on seven of the jets so it could spend the money on other conventional weapons being used in the wars the United States is currently fighting, it had a fight on its hands from the members of Congress. They didn't want the companies in their states that helped produce the plane to lose business.

## 2.4 Institutions

**Institutional markets** include nonprofit organizations such as the American Red Cross, churches, hospitals, charitable organizations, private colleges, civic clubs, and so on. Like government and for-profit organizations, they buy a huge quantity of products and services. Holding costs down is especially important to them. The lower their costs are, the more people they can provide their services to.

**institutional markets**

Nonprofit organizations such as the American Red Cross, churches, hospitals, charitable organizations, private colleges, and civic clubs.

The businesses and products we have mentioned so far are broad generalizations to help you think about the various markets in which products can be sold. In addition, not all products a company buys are high dollar or complex. Businesses buy huge quantities of inexpensive products, too. McDonald's, for example, buys a lot of toilet paper, napkins, bags, employee uniforms, and so forth. Pretty much any product you and I use is probably used for one or more business purposes (cell phones and cell-phone services, various types of food products, office supplies, and so on). Some of us own real estate, and so do many businesses. But very few of us own many of the other products businesses sell to one another: cranes, raw materials such as steel, fiber-optic cables, and so forth.

That said, a smart B2B marketer will look at all the markets we have mentioned, to see if they represent potential opportunities. The Red Cross will have no use for a fighter jet, of course. However, a company that manufactures toilet paper might be able to market it to both the Red Cross and the U.S. government. B2B opportunities abroad and online B2B markets can also be successfully pursued. We will discuss these topics later in the chapter.

## 2.5 Who Makes the Purchasing Decisions in Business Markets?

Figuring out who exactly in B2B markets is responsible for what gets purchased and when often requires some detective work for marketing professionals and the salespeople they work with. Think about the college textbooks you buy. Who decides which ones ultimately are purchased by the students at your school? Do publishers send you e-mails about certain books they want you to buy? Do you see ads for different types of chemistry or marketing books in your school newspaper or on TV? Generally, you do not. The reason is that even though you buy the books, the publishers know that professors ultimately decide which textbooks are going to be used in the classroom. Consequently, B2B sellers largely concentrate their efforts on those people.

That's not to say that to some extent the publishers don't target you. They may offer you a good deal by packaging a study guide with your textbook or some sort of learning supplement online you can purchase. They might also offer your bookstore manager a discount for buying a certain number of textbooks. However, a publishing company that focused on selling its textbooks directly to you or to a bookstore manager would go out of business. They know the true revenue generators are professors.

The question is, which professors? Some professors choose their own books. Adjunct professors often don't have a choice—their books are chosen by a course coordinator or the dean or chair of the department. Still other decisions are made by groups of professors, some of whom have more say over the final decision than others. Are you getting the picture? Figuring out where to start in B2B sales can be a little bit like a scavenger hunt.

**FIGURE 4.4**

Who ya gonna call? Click on http://blogs.bnet.com/salesmachine/?p=2308&page=1&tag=col1;post-2308 to play an online game that will help you understand why finding the right decision makers in a company is so tricky. Are you up to the challenge?

## KEY TAKEAWAY

Business buyers can be either nonprofit or for-profit businesses. There are four basic categories of business buyers: producers, resellers, governments, and institutions. Producers are companies that purchase goods and services that they transform into other products. They include both manufacturers and service providers. Resellers are companies that sell goods and services produced by other firms without materially changing them. They include wholesalers, brokers, and retailers. Local, state, and national governments purchase large quantities of goods and services. Institutional markets include nonprofit organizations such as the American Red Cross, churches, hospitals, charitable organizations, private colleges, civic clubs, and so on. Holding costs down is especially important to them because it enables them to provide their services to more people. Figuring out who exactly in B2B markets is responsible for what gets purchased and when often requires some detective work by marketing professionals and the salespeople they work with.

## REVIEW QUESTIONS

1. What sorts of products do producers buy?
2. What role do resellers play in B2B markets, and why are they important to sellers?
3. How do sellers find government buyers? Institutional buyers?
4. Why is it difficult to figure out whom to call on in business markets?

# 3. BUYING CENTERS

## LEARNING OBJECTIVES

1. Explain what a buying center is.
2. Explain who the members of buying centers are and describe their roles.
3. Describe the duties of professional buyers.
4. Describe the personal and interpersonal dynamics that affect the decisions buying centers make.

The professors who form a committee at your school to choose textbooks are acting like a buying center. **Buying centers** are groups of people within organizations who make purchasing decisions. Large organizations often have permanent departments that consist of the people who, in a sense, shop for a living. They are professional buyers, in other words. Their titles vary. In some companies, they are simply referred to as *buyers*. In other companies, they are referred to as *purchasing agents*, *purchasing managers*, or *procurement officers*. Retailers often refer to their buyers as *merchandisers*. Most of the people who do these jobs have bachelor's of science degrees. Some undergo additional industry training to obtain an advanced purchasing certification designation.[3]

**buying centers**

Groups of people within organizations who make purchasing decisions.

Buyers can have a large impact on the expenses, sales, and profits of a company. Pier 1's purchasing agents literally comb the entire world looking for products the company's customers want most. What happens if the products the purchasing agents pick don't sell? Pier 1's sales fall, and people get fired. This doesn't happen in B2C markets. If you pick out the wrong comforter for your bed, you don't get fired. Your bedroom just looks crummy.

Consequently, professional buyers are shrewd. They have to be because their jobs depend on it. Their jobs depend on their choosing the best products at the best prices from the best vendors. Professional buyers are also well informed and less likely to buy a product on a whim than consumers. The sidebar below outlines the tasks professional buyers generally perform.

### The Duties of Professional Buyers

- Considering the availability of products, the reliability of the products' vendors, and the technical support they can provide
- Studying a company's sales records and inventory levels
- Identifying suppliers and obtaining bids from them
- Negotiating prices, delivery dates, and payment terms for goods and services
- Keeping abreast of changes in the supply and demand for goods and services their firms need
- Staying informed of the latest trends so as to anticipate consumer buying patterns
- Determining the media (TV, the Internet, newspapers, and so forth) in which advertisements will be placed
- Tracking advertisements in newspapers and other media to check competitors' sales activities

Increasingly, purchasing managers have become responsible for buying not only products but also functions their firms want to outsource. The functions aren't limited to manufacturing. They also include product innovation and design services, customer service and order fulfillment services, and information technology and networking services to name a few. Purchasing agents responsible for finding offshore providers of goods and services often take trips abroad to inspect the facilities of the providers and get a better sense of their capabilities.

## 3.1 Other Players

Purchasing agents don't make all the buying decisions in their companies, though. As we explained, other people in the organization often have a say, as well they should. Purchasing agents frequently need their feedback and help to buy the best products and choose the best vendors. The people who provide their firms' buyers with input generally fall into one or more of the following groups:

### Users

**users**

The people and groups within the organization that actually use the product.

**Users** are the people and groups within the organization that actually use the product. Frequently, they initiated the purchase in the first place in an effort to improve what they produce or how they produce it. Users often have certain specifications in mind for products and how they want them to perform. An example of a user might be a professor at your school who wants to adopt an electronic book and integrate it into his or her online course.

### Influencers

**influencers**

People who may or may not use the product but actively participate in the purchasing process in order to secure a decision they consider favorable.

**Influencers** are people who may or may not use the product but have experience or expertise that can help improve the buying decision. For example, an engineer may prefer a certain vendor's product platform and try to persuade others that it is the best choice.

### Gatekeepers

**gatekeepers**

People who decide if and when a salesperson gets access to members of the buying center.

If you want to sell a product to a large company like Walmart, you can't just walk in the door of its corporate headquarters and demand to see a purchasing agent. You will first have to get past of a number of **gatekeepers**, or people who will decide if and when you get access to members of the buying center. These are people such as buying assistants, personal assistants, and other individuals who have some say about which sellers are able to get a foot in the door.

Gatekeepers often need to be courted as hard as prospective buyers do. They generally have a lot of information about what's going on behind the scenes and a certain amount of informal power. If they like you, you're in a good position as a seller. If they don't, your job is going to be *much* harder. In the case of textbook sales, the gatekeepers are often faculty secretaries. They know in advance which instructors will be teaching which courses and the types of books they will need. It is not uncommon for faculty secretaries to screen the calls of textbook sales representatives.

**FIGURE 4.5**

Warning: Do not be rude to or otherwise anger the faculty secretary. This is good advice for salespeople and students as well as faculty members.

*© 2010 Jupiterimages Corporation*

### Deciders

**decider**

The person who makes the final purchasing decision.

The **decider** is the person who makes the final purchasing decision. The decider might or might not be the purchasing manager. Purchasing managers are generally solely responsible for deciding upon routine purchases and small purchases. However, the decision to purchase a large, expensive product that will have a major impact on a company is likely to be made by or with the help of other people in the organization, perhaps even the CEO. Sellers, of course, pay special attention to what deciders want. "Who makes the buying decision?" is a key question B2B sales and marketing personnel are trained to quickly ask potential customers.

## 3.2 The Interpersonal and Personal Dynamics of B2B Marketing

We made it a point earlier in our discussion to explain how rational and calculating business buyers are. So would it surprise you to learn that sometimes the dynamics that surround B2B marketing don't lead to the best purchasing decisions? Interpersonal factors among the people making the buying decision often have an impact on the products chosen, good or bad. (You can think of this phenomenon as "office politics.") For example, one person in a buying unit might wield a lot of power and greatly influence the purchasing decision. However, other people in the unit might resent the power he or she wields and insist on a different offering, even if doesn't best meet the organization's needs. Savvy B2B marketers are aware of these dynamics and try their best to influence the outcome.

Personal factors play a part. B2B buyers are overwhelmed with choices, features, benefits, information, data, and metrics. They often have to interview dozens of potential vendors and ask them hundreds of questions. No matter how disciplined they are in their buying procedures, they will often find a way to simplify their decision making either consciously or subconsciously.[4] For example, a buyer deciding upon multiple vendors running neck and neck might decide to simply choose the vendor whose sales representative he likes the most.

Factors such as these can be difficult for a company to control. However, branding—how successful a company is at marketing its brands—*is* a factor under a company's control, says Kevin Randall of Movéo Integrated Branding, an Illinois-based marketing-consulting firm. Sellers can use their brands to their advantage to help business buyers come to the conclusion that their products are the best choice. IBM, for example, has long had a strong brand name when it comes to business products. The company's reputation was so solid that for years the catchphrase "Nobody ever got fired for buying IBM" was often repeated among purchasing agents—and by IBM salespeople of course![5]

In short, B2B marketing is very strategic. Selling firms try to gather as much information about their customers as they can and use that information to their advantage. As an analogy, imagine if you were interested in asking out someone you had seen on campus. Sure, you could simply try to show up at a party or somewhere on campus in the hopes of meeting the person. But if you were thinking strategically, you might try to find out everything you could about the person, what he or she likes to do and so forth, and then try to arrange a meeting. That way when you did meet the person, you would be better able to strike up a conversation and develop a relationship with him or her. B2B selling is similarly strategic. Little is left to chance.

**KEY TAKEAWAY**

Buying centers are groups of people within organizations who make purchasing decisions. The buying centers of large organizations employ professional buyers who, in a sense, shop for a living. They don't make all the buying decisions in their companies, though. The other people who provide input are users, or the people and groups within the organization that actually use the product; influencers, or people who may or may not use the product but have experience or expertise that can help improve the buying decision; gatekeepers, or people who will decide if and when a seller gets access to members of the buying center; and deciders, or the people who make the final purchasing decision. Interpersonal dynamics between the people in a buying center will affect the choices the center makes. Personal factors, such as how likeable a seller is, play a part because buyers are often overwhelmed with information and will find ways to simplify their decision making.

**REVIEW QUESTIONS**

1. Which people do you think have the most influence on the decisions a buying center makes? Why?
2. Describe the duties of professional buyers. What aspects of their jobs seem attractive? Which aspects seem unattractive to you?
3. How do personal and interpersonal dynamics affect the decisions buying centers make?

# 4. STAGES IN THE B2B BUYING PROCESS AND B2B BUYING SITUATIONS

**LEARNING OBJECTIVES**

1. **Outline the stages in the B2B buying process.**
2. **Explain the scorecard process of evaluating proposals.**
3. **Describe the different types of B2B buying situations and how they affect sellers.**

## 4.1 Stages in the B2B Buying Process

Next, let's look at the stages in the B2B buying process. They are similar to the stages in the consumer's buying process.

**1. A need is recognized.** Someone recognizes that the organization has a need that can be solved by purchasing a good or service. Users often drive this stage. In the case of the electronic textbook, it could be, for example, the professor assigned to teach the online course. However, it could be the dean or chairman of the department in which the course is taught.

**2. The need is described and quantified.** Next, the buying center, or group of people brought together to help make the buying decision, work to put some parameters around what needs to be purchased. In other words, they describe what they believe is needed, the features it should have, how much of it is needed, where, and so on. For more technical or complex products the buyer will define the product's technical specifications. Will an off-the-shelf product do, or must it be customized?

Users and influencers come into play here. In the case of our electronic book, the professor who teaches the online course, his teaching assistants, and the college's information technology staff would try to describe the type of book best suited for the course. Should the book be posted on the Web as this book is? Should it be downloadable? Maybe it should be compatible with Amazon's Kindle. Figure 4.6 shows the specifications developed for a janitorial-services purchase by the state of Kentucky.

**FIGURE 4.6** Product Specifications Developed for a B2B Purchase: An Example

**Who:** Division of Building Services

**What:** Janitorial Services for State Office Building at High and Mero Streets, Frankfort, Kentucky

**Background:**

Past experience with various contractors indicates that not all vendors are prepared to handle buildings the size of the State Office Building. Building Services indicated that staff and materials supported by a quality review program have been the common elements of the more successful vendors.

- Gross area: 384,586 sq. ft
- Total area to be cleaned: 322,585 sq. ft
- Rest room areas: 7,801 sq. ft
- Carpeted areas: 126,304 sq. ft
- Basement areas: 22,734 sq. ft
- Computer areas: 1,104 sq. ft
- Stairways: 4 sets
- Passenger elevators: 6
- Freight elevators: 1

**Specifications:**

- Daily cleaning for waste baskets, ashtrays, trash can liners, glass partitions, floors (sweep, mop, and buff), carpets (vacuum), and restrooms
- All cleaning conducted after hours
- Sign–in sheets and identification on badges for contractor's employees
- Current insurance

DIVISION OF PURCHASES

*Source: http://www.state.ky.us/agencies/adm/leadership/best/sld047.htm.*

**3. Potential suppliers are searched for**. At this stage, the people involved in the buying process seek out information about the products they are looking for and the vendors that can supply them. Most buyers look online first to find vendors and products, then attend industry trade shows and conventions and telephone or e-mail the suppliers with whom they have relationships. The buyers might also consult trade magazines, the blogs of industry experts, and perhaps attend Webinars conducted by vendors or visit their facilities. Purchasing agents often play a key role when it comes to deciding which vendors are the most qualified. Are they reliable and financially stable? Will they be around in the future? Do they need to be located near the organization or can they be in another region of the country or in a foreign country? The vendors that don't make the cut are quickly eliminated from the running.

**request for proposal (RFP)**

An invitation to submit a bid to supply the good or service.

**4. Qualified suppliers are asked to complete responses to requests for proposal (RFPs)**. Each vendor that makes the cut is sent a **request for proposal (RFP)**, which is an invitation to submit a bid to supply the good or service. An RFP outlines what the vendor is able to offer in terms of its product—its quality, price, financing, delivery, after-sales service, whether it can be customized or returned, and even the product's disposal, in some cases. Good sales and marketing professionals do more than just provide basic information to potential buyers in RFPs. They focus on the buyer's problems and how to adapt their offers to solve those problems.

Oftentimes the vendors formally present their products to the people involved in the buying decision. If the good is a physical product, the vendors generally provide the purchaser with samples, which are then inspected and sometimes tested. They might also ask satisfied customers to make testimonials or initiate a discussion with the buyer to help the buyer get comfortable with the product and offer advice on how best to go about using it.

**5. The proposals are evaluated and supplier(s) selected**. During this stage, the RFPs are reviewed and the vendor or vendors selected. RFPs are best evaluated if the members agree on the criteria being evaluated and the importance of each. Different organizations will weight different parts of a proposal differently, depending on their goals and the products they purchase. The price might be very important to some sellers, such as discount and dollar stores. Other organizations might be more focused on top-of-the-line goods and the service a seller provides. Recall that the maker of Snapper mowers and snow blowers was more focused on purchasing quality materials to produce top-of-the-line equipment that could be sold at a premium. Still other factors include the availability of products and the reliability with which vendors can supply them. Reliability of supply is extremely important because delays in the supply chain can shut down a company's production of goods and services and cost the firm its customers and reputation.

For high-priced, complex products, after-sales service is likely to be important. A fast-food restaurant might not care too much about the after-sales service for the paper napkins it buys—just that they are inexpensive and readily available. However, if the restaurant purchases a new drive-thru system, it wants to be assured that the seller will be on hand to repair the system if it breaks down and perhaps train its personnel to use the system.

A scorecard approach can help a company rate the RFPs. Figure 4.7 is a simple example of a scorecard completed by one member of a buying team. The scorecards completed by all the members of the buying team can then be tabulated to help determine the vendor with the highest rating.

**FIGURE 4.7** A Scorecard Used to Evaluate RFPs

| Reviewer: Jose Martinez | | Vendor A | | Vendor B | | Vendor C | |
|---|---|---|---|---|---|---|---|
| Criteria | Weight | Score (scale of 1–3) | Points (score x weight) | Score (scale of 1–3) | Points (score x weight) | Score (scale of 1–3) | Points (score x weight) |
| Product Performance | 3 | 1 | 3 | 3 | 9 | 2 | 6 |
| Product Durability | 3 | 3 | 9 | 2 | 6 | 3 | 9 |
| Price | 3 | 3 | 9 | 2 | 6 | 2 | 6 |
| On-Time Delivery | 3 | 3 | 9 | 2 | 6 | 2 | 6 |
| Customer Service | 3 | 2 | 6 | 2 | 6 | 2 | 6 |
| Returns Policy | 2 | 2 | 6 | 2 | 6 | 2 | 6 |
| TOTAL SCORE | | | 42 | | 39 | | 39 |

*Selecting Single versus Multiple Suppliers.* Sometimes organizations select a single supplier to provide the good or service. This can help streamline a company's paperwork and other buying processes. With a single supplier, instead of negotiating two contracts and submitting two purchase orders to buy a particular offering, the company only has to do one of each. Plus, the more the company buys from one vendor, the bigger the volume discount it gets. Single sourcing can be risky, though, because it leaves a firm at the mercy of a sole supplier. What if the supplier doesn't deliver the goods, goes out of business, or jacks up its prices? Many firms prefer to do business with more than one supplier to avoid problems such as these. Doing business with multiple suppliers keeps them on their toes. If they know their customers can easily switch their business over to another supplier, they are likely to compete harder to keep the business.

**6. An order routine is established.** This is the stage in which the actual order is put together. The order includes the agreed-upon price, quantities, expected time of delivery, return policies, warranties, and any other terms of negotiation.[6] The order can be made on paper, online, or sent electronically from the buyer's computer system to the seller's. It can also be a one-time order or consist of multiple orders that are made periodically as a company needs a good or service. Some buyers order products continuously by having their vendors electronically monitor their inventory for them and ship replacement items as the buyer needs them. (We'll talk more about inventory management in Chapter 9.)

**7. A postpurchase evaluation is conducted and the feedback provided to the vendor.** Just as consumers go through an evaluation period after they purchase goods and services, so do businesses. The buying unit might survey users of the product to see how satisfied they were with it. Cessna Aircraft Company, a small U.S. airplane maker, routinely surveys the users of the products it buys so they can voice their opinions on a supplier's performance.[7]

Some buyers establish on-time performance, quality, customer satisfaction, and other measures for their vendors to meet, and provide those vendors with the information regularly, such as trend reports that show if their performance is improving, remaining the same, or worsening. (The process is similar to a performance evaluation you might receive as an employee.) For example, Food Lion shares a wide variety of daily retail data and performance calculations with its suppliers in exchange for their commitment to closely collaborate with the grocery-store chain.

Keep in mind that a supplier with a poor performance record might not be entirely to blame. The purchasing company might play a role, too. For example, if the U.S. Postal Service contracts with FedEx to help deliver its holiday packages on time, but a large number of the packages are delivered late, FedEx may or may not be to blame. Perhaps a large number of loads the U.S. Postal Service delivered to FedEx were late, weather played a role, or shipping volumes were unusually high. Companies need to collaborate with their suppliers to look for ways to improve their joint performance. Some companies hold annual symposiums with their suppliers to facilitate cooperation among them and to honor their best suppliers.[8]

## 4.2 Types of B2B Buying Situations

**straight rebuy**

When a purchaser buys the same product in the same quantities from the same vendor.

To some extent the stages an organization goes through and the number of people involved depend on the buying situation. Is this the first time the firm has purchased the product or the fiftieth? If it's the fiftieth time, the buyer is likely to skip the search and other phases and simply make a purchase. A **straight rebuy** is a situation in which a purchaser buys the same product in the same quantities from the same vendor. Nothing changes, in other words. Postpurchase evaluations are often skipped, unless the buyer notices an unexpected change in the offering such as a deterioration of its quality or delivery time.

Sellers like straight rebuys because the buyer doesn't consider any alternative products or search for new suppliers. The result is a steady, reliable stream of revenue for the seller. Consequently, the seller doesn't have to spend a lot of time on the account and can concentrate on capturing other business opportunities. Nonetheless, the seller cannot ignore the account. The seller still has to provide the buyer with top-notch, reliable service or the straight-rebuy situation could be jeopardized.

If an account is especially large and important, the seller might go so far as to station personnel at the customer's place of business to be sure the customer is happy and the straight-rebuy situation continues. IBM and the management consulting firm Accenture station employees all around the world at their customers' offices and facilities.

**new buy**

When a firm purchases a product for the first time.

By contrast, a **new-buy** selling situation occurs when a firm purchases a product for the first time. Generally speaking, all the buying stages we described in the last section occur. New buys are the most time consuming for both the purchasing firm and the firms selling to them. If the product is complex, many vendors and products will be considered, and many RFPs will be solicited.

New-to-an-organization buying situations rarely occur. What is more likely is that a purchase is new to the people involved. For example, a school district owns buildings. But when a new high school needs to be built, there may not be anyone in management who has experience building a new school. That purchase situation is a new buy for those involved.

**modified rebuy**

When a company wants to buy the same type of product it has in the past but make some modifications to it.

A **modified rebuy** occurs when a company wants to buy the same type of product it has in the past but make some modifications to it. Maybe the buyer wants different quantities, packaging, or delivery, or the product customized slightly differently. For example, your instructor might have initially adopted this textbook "as is" from its publisher, Flat World Knowledge, but then decided to customize it later with additional questions, problems, or content that he or she created or that was available from Flat World Knowledge.

A modified rebuy doesn't necessarily have to be made with the same seller, however. Your instructor may have taught this course before, using a different publisher's book. High textbook costs, lack of customization, and other factors may have led to dissatisfaction. In this case, she might visit with some other textbook suppliers and see what they have to offer. Some buyers routinely solicit bids from other sellers when they want to modify their purchases in order to get sellers to compete for their business. Likewise, savvy sellers look for ways to turn straight rebuys into modified buys so they can get a shot at the business. They do so by regularly visiting with customers and seeing if they have unmet needs or problems a modified product might solve.

### KEY TAKEAWAY

The stages in the B2B buying process are as follows: Someone recognizes that the organization has a need that can be solved by purchasing a good or service. The need is described and quantified. Qualified suppliers are searched for, and each qualified supplier is sent a request for proposal (RFP), which is an invitation to submit a bid to supply the good or service. The proposals suppliers submit are evaluated, one or more supplier(s) selected, and an order routine with each is established. A postpurchase evaluation is later conducted and the feedback provided to the suppliers. The buying stages an organization goes through often depend on the buying situation—whether it's a straight rebuy, new buy, or modified rebuy.

### REVIEW QUESTIONS

1. What buying stages do buying centers typically go through?
2. Why should business buyers collaborate with the companies they buy products from?
3. Explain how a straight rebuy, new buy, and modified rebuy differ from one another.

# 5. INTERNATIONAL B2B MARKETS AND E-COMMERCE

**LEARNING OBJECTIVES**

1. Describe the reasons why firms in the same industries are often located in the same geographic areas.
2. Explain the effect e-commerce is having on the firms, the companies they do business with, where they are located, and the prices they charge.
3. Outline the different types of e-commerce sites and what each type of site is used for.

## 5.1 International B2B Markets

Another characteristic of B2B markets that you may or may not have noticed or thought about is that firms in the same industry tend to cluster in the same geographic areas. In the United States, many banks and financial companies are located on or near Wall Street in New York City. Many film and television companies operate out of Hollywood. Is it just by chance that this has occurred? No.

The clustering occurs because the resources these firms need—both human and natural—are located in some areas and not others. For example, the Gulf of Mexico is rich with oil deposits. As a result, many oil companies and facilities are located along or near the Gulf in cities such as Houston. Likewise, many high-tech companies are located in Silicon Valley (California). One reason is that nearby Stanford University is one of the top computer-science schools in the country, and the firms want to hire graduates from the school.

But that's not the only reason businesses in the same industry cluster together. Another reason is the sellers want to be close to their buyers. Bentonville, Arkansas, the world headquarters of Walmart, used to be a sleepy little rural town. As Walmart grew, so have the number of companies moving into the area to do business with Walmart. In the last twenty years, the size of the town has nearly tripled.

Why do companies want to be near their buyers? Let's go back to our date analogy. Suppose you hit it off with the person you're interested in and you become "an item." You probably wouldn't want to be half the world away from the person for a long period of time because you would miss the person and because you wouldn't want a rival moving in on your turf! Companies also want to be close to their suppliers because it can help them get inventory more quickly. Dell's suppliers are located right next to the company's assembly plants. And, as you have learned, some companies actually locate their personnel on their customers' sites.

**FIGURE 4.8**

Bollywood, which refers to the film industry in India, has become one of the largest film centers in the world. It's growing faster than Hollywood and is beginning to rival its size.

## 5.2 B2B E-Commerce

Not all B2B buyers and sellers are cozying up to one another location-wise today, though: **e-commerce**, or commerce conducted electronically, such as over the Internet, has made locating near buyers less important. Consider the Hubert Company, a Cincinnati-based firm that sells supplies to the food industry. "Just ten years ago the Internet didn't exist for the Hubert Company, and today almost 30 percent of our business comes through the Internet as an ordering mechanism," says Bart Kohler, president of the company.[9] However, the Hubert Company can no longer protect the market in and around Cincinnati just because it's headquartered there. "Whereas in the past, I was somewhat insulated to just people in my area, now there really are no geographic boundaries anymore, and anyone can compete with me anywhere," Kohler explains. The advantage is that whereas the United States is a mature market in which growth is limited, other countries, like Brazil, India, and China, are growing like crazy and represent huge opportunities for the Hubert Company, he says.

**e-commerce**

Commerce conducted electronically, such as over the Internet.

## FIGURE 4.9

The Hubert Company sells to companies all over the globe, including the U.S. government. Notice the GSA link in the upper right-hand corner of its Web page.

*Source: http://www.hubert.com.*

B2B e-commerce was actually a little slower to take hold than B2C e-commerce, though. Initially, the Web sites of many B2B firms were static. There was no interactivity. "We put our first Web site up in 1998, and it really didn't do anything," Kohler explains. "All it did was it had the picture of the company. I think it had a picture of me holding a catalog with a toll-free number at the bottom, and said, 'Hey, call this number and we'll send you a catalog.'"

Things have changed. Companies have since developed sophisticated e-commerce systems that allow their customers to do many things for themselves. As a result, they have been able to cut down on the amount of customer service they need to provide. Does your business want to ship your products cheaply across the country via rail? You can sign up online for an account with a railroad like Union Pacific (UP), reserve some rail cars on UP's site, and choose the route you want them to travel. Later, after you ship the goods, you can check your account balance on the Web site and track the rail cars online like you can packages shipped with FedEx and UPS. The office supply chain Staples has special Web sites set up for each of its business customers, which are customized with online catalogs containing the types of products they buy at the prices they seem to be willing to pay, based on their past purchases on StaplesLink.com.[10] Today's B2B sites are far from static.

## Types of B2B Web Sites

**FIGURE 4.10** An Example of a Sell-Side B2B Web site

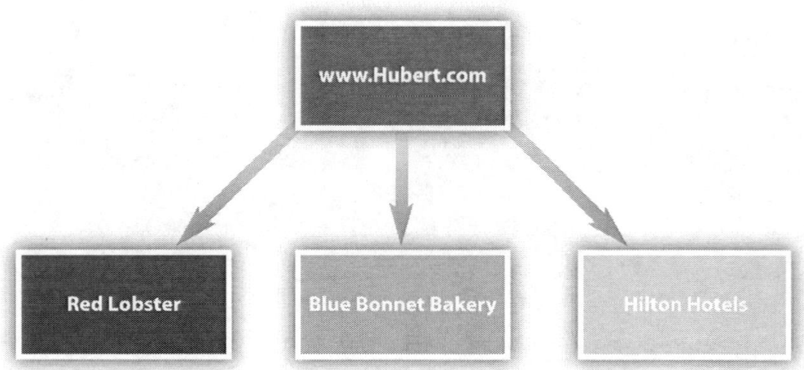


Most of the examples we've described so far are examples of *sell-side* e-commerce sites. A **sell-side site** is a site in which a single seller sells products to many different buyers. Figure 4.10 shows the direction of the sale of goods and services sold on a sell-side site, such as the Hubert Company has.

But there are buy-side e-commerce sites as well. A **buy-side site** is one in which a business *buys* products from multiple sellers that go there to do business with the firm. Some government agencies have buy-side sites. **B2B exchanges** are e-commerce sites where multiple buyers and sellers go to find and do business with one another. (You can think of the exchanges as being somewhat like Craigslist but composed solely of business buyers and sellers.) Sites such as these make their money by charging buyers and sellers a fee when they conduct transactions with one another. In the late 1990s and early 2000s, B2B exchanges sprouted up on the Internet like weeds. Cyber entrepreneurs took a "build it and they will come" attitude, hoping to earn a fee off the transactions conducted on site. Many of these sites have failed, but not all of them. One of the most successful and largest exchanges is Alibaba.com, founded in 1999 as a trading platform for small and medium manufacturers to sell their wares.[11] ChemNet.com is a global exchange where companies go to buy and sell chemicals of all kinds. The homepage for ChemNet is shown in Figure 4.11. (Ammonium, sodium, or potassium, anyone?)

**sell-side site**

A Web site in which a single seller sells products to many different buyers.

**buy-side site**

A Web site in which a business buys products from multiple sellers that go there to do business with the firm.

**B2B exchanges**

E-commerce Web sites where multiple buyers and sellers go to find and do business with one another.

**FIGURE 4.11**

Need chemicals? You can find them on the B2B exchange Web site ChemNet.

*Source: http://www.chemnet.com.*

**B2B auctions**

Web-based auctions that occur between businesses.

**B2B auctions** are Web-based auctions that occur between businesses. The auctions can be either sell side or buy side. An example of a sell-side auction is a B2B auction that occurs on eBay or a site like AssetAuctions.com where surplus industrial equipment is sold. Motorola regularly sells small quantities of products at the end of their life cycles on eBay. Motorola has found that eBay is a good way to make some money from products that businesses are reluctant to buy otherwise because they are being discontinued.[12] Sell-side auctions are sometimes referred to as forward auctions.

**reverse auction**

When the buyer lists what he or she wants to buy and also states how much he or she is willing to pay. The reverse auction is finished when at least one firm is willing to accept the buyer's price.

Buy-side auctions, by contrast, reverse the traditional auction formula, which is to help the seller get the highest price for the product. Instead, the buyer initiates the auction in order to find the cheapest supplier of a product. Sellers then bid against one another, offering the lowest prices they can for their products, in order to get the buyer's business. Because the roles of the buyers and sellers are reversed in buy-side auctions, they are often referred to as **reverse auctions**.

Not all companies use an intermediary like eBay or AssetAuctions to conduct their auctions, though. Some companies conduct their own auctions on their Web sites so they don't have to pay a fee to an intermediary. For example, General Motors auctions off reconditioned vehicles to auto dealers on its own Web site, http://www.gmonlineauctions.com.

## Pricing in E-commerce Markets

One of the consequences of e-commerce is that B2B customers can easily shop around from the convenience of their cubicles or offices, bid on products, and read blogs about products from industry experts. That's what buyers generally do before they get on the phone or personally meet with sellers. E-commerce has made it especially easy for buyers to compare prices. And the cheapest price often attracts the most attention.

The result is that B2B sellers (and B2C sellers) have found their ability to raise prices limited. The problem is more acute when products are very similar to one another (commodities) and B2B auctions and exchanges are utilized. If you are a buyer of chemicals looking for a supplier on ChemNet, do you want to pay more for one brand of a chemical that has the same molecular formula as every other brand? Maybe not. However, if you believe you can get better service from one company than from another, you might pay more. "Everything has become much more of a commodity, commodity meaning that it's basically more and more about price," says Kohler about e-commerce competition. "So my challenge as a distributor is that I have got to constantly find new ways to try to create value for Hubert's customers."

To avoid e-commerce price wars, some companies refuse to sell their products directly online or put prices on them. Snapper products are an example. Go to Snapper.com, and you will find a lot of information about Snapper mowers and snow blowers online and dealers where you can buy them. But you won't see any prices listed. Nor can you buy a product directly from the Web site.

**KEY TAKEAWAY**

Firms in the same industry tend to cluster in the same geographic areas because the resources these firms need—both human and natural—are located in some areas and not others. Sellers also want to be close to their buyers. E-commerce, or commerce conducted electronically such as over the Internet, has made locating near buyers less important for business-to-business sellers and opened up opportunities for them to sell their products around the world. However, e-commerce has also led to more competition and made it difficult for sellers to raise their prices. B2B e-commerce was slower to take hold than B2C e-commerce. Companies have since developed sophisticated e-commerce systems, including sell-side and buy-side Web sites, exchanges, and B2B auctions.

**REVIEW QUESTIONS**

1. Name some other industries you're aware of in which companies tend to cluster geographically. Why are the companies in these industries located near one another?
2. How do B2B exchange sites differ from B2B auction sites?
3. How can firms that sell their products on the Internet prevent their prices from being driven down by competitors?

# 6. ETHICS IN B2B MARKETS

**LEARNING OBJECTIVES**

1. **Explain how the ethical dilemmas B2B marketers face differ from the ethical dilemmas B2C marketers face.**
2. **Outline the measures companies take to encourage their employees and executives to act in ethical ways.**

It's likely that every topic we have talked about so far in this chapter has an ethical dimension to it. Take procurement, for example: unlike B2C markets, offering customers free dinners, golf games, and so forth is very common in B2B settings. In many foreign countries, business and government buyers not only expect perks such as these but also actually demand bribes be paid if you want to do business with them. And firms pay them, even though some countries prohibit them. (The United States is one such country.) Which countries have a penchant for bribery? In a report called the "Bribe Payers Index," Transparency International, a watchdog organization, annually ranks the likelihood of firms from the world's industrialized countries to bribe abroad. The top five countries are shown in Table 4.3.

**TABLE 4.3** Transparency International's Bribe Payers Index, 2008

| 1. Russia |
|---|
| 2. China |
| 3. Mexico |
| 4. India |
| 5. Italy |

Or take, for example, the straight-rebuy situation we discussed earlier. Recall that in a straight rebuy, buyers repurchase products automatically. Recently, Dean Foods, which manufactures the Silk brand of soy milk, experienced a lot of negative press after the company changed the word "organic" to "natural" on the labels of its milk, and quietly switched to conventional soybeans, which are often grown with pesticides. But Dean didn't change the barcode for the product, the packaging of the product, or the price much. So stores kept ordering what they thought was the same product—making a straight rebuy—but it wasn't. Many stores and consumers felt as though they had been duped. Some grocers dropped the entire Silk lineup of products.[13]

And remember Intel's strategy to increase the demand for its chips by insisting that PC makers use "Intel Inside" stickers? Recently Intel paid a competitor more than a billion dollars to settle a court case contending that it strong-armed PC makers into doing business exclusively with Intel. (Does that make you feel less warm and fuzzy about the "Intel Inside" campaign?)

What Dean Foods and Intel did might strike you as being wrong. However, what is ethical and what is not is often not clear-cut. Walmart has a reputation for using its market power to squeeze its suppliers for the best deals possible, in some cases putting them out of business. Is that ethical? What about companies that hire suppliers abroad, putting U.S. companies and workers out of business? Is that wrong? It depends on whom you ask. Some economists believe Walmart's ability to keep costs low has benefited consumers far more than it has hurt the suppliers of products. Is it fair to prohibit U.S. companies from offering bribes when their foreign competitors can?

Clearly, people have very different ideas about what's ethical and what's not. So how does a business get all of its employees on the same page in terms of how they behave? Laws and regulations—state, federal, and international—are an obvious starting point for companies, their executives, and employees wanting to do the right thing. The U.S. Federal Trade Commission (FTC) often plays a role when it comes to B2B laws and regulations. The FTC regulates companies in an effort to prevent them from engaging in unfair trade practices that can harm consumers and hamper competition.

Companies are also adopting ethics codes that provide general guidelines about how their employees should behave. Many firms require employees to go through ethics training so they know what to do when they face tricky ethical dilemmas. Large corporations have begun hiring "chief ethics officers" to ensure ethics are properly implemented within their organizations. The Business Marketing Association has also developed a code of ethics that discourages bribery and other practices, such as disparaging a competitor's products unfairly, and encourages treating one's suppliers equitably.

## FIGURE 4.12

Click on the following link to read the Business Marketing Association's entire code of ethics: http://www.marketing.org/i4a/pages/Index.cfm?pageID=3286.

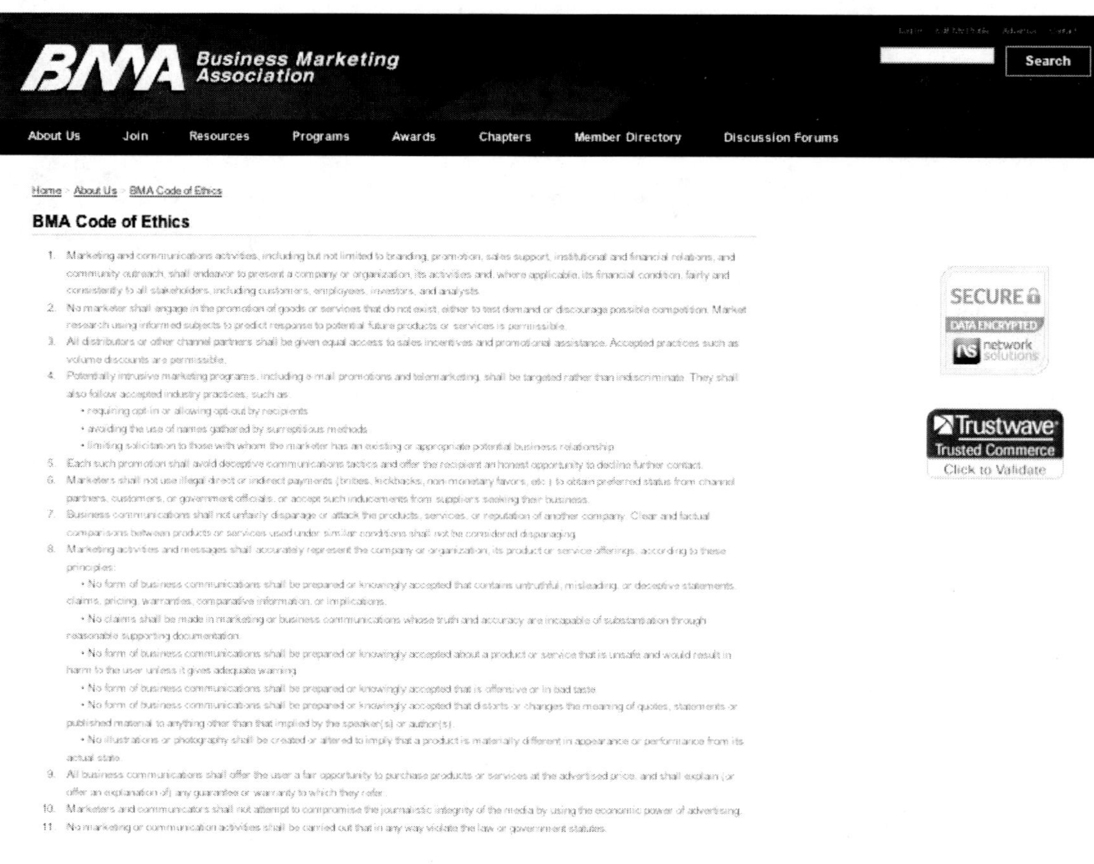

BMA Business Marketing Association

Search

About Us | Join | Resources | Programs | Awards | Chapters | Member Directory | Discussion Forums

Home > About Us > BMA Code of Ethics

### BMA Code of Ethics

1. Marketing and communications activities, including but not limited to branding, promotion, sales support, institutional and financial relations, and community outreach, shall endeavor to present a company or organization, its activities and, where applicable, its financial condition, fairly and consistently to all stakeholders, including customers, employees, investors, and analysts.
2. No marketer shall engage in the promotion of goods or services that do not exist, either to test demand or discourage possible competition. Market research using informed subjects to predict response to potential future products or services is permissible.
3. All distributors or other channel partners shall be given equal access to sales incentives and promotional assistance. Accepted practices such as volume discounts are permissible.
4. Potentially intrusive marketing programs, including e-mail promotions and telemarketing, shall be targeted rather than indiscriminate. They shall also follow accepted industry practices, such as:
   - requiring opt-in or allowing opt-out by recipients
   - avoiding the use of names gathered by surreptitious methods
   - limiting solicitation to those with whom the marketer has an existing or appropriate potential business relationship
5. Each such promotion shall avoid deceptive communications tactics and offer the recipient an honest opportunity to decline further contact.
6. Marketers shall not use illegal direct or indirect payments (bribes, kickbacks, non-monetary favors, etc.) to obtain preferred status from channel partners, customers, or government officials, or accept such inducements from suppliers seeking their business.
7. Business communications shall not unfairly disparage or attack the products, services, or reputation of another company. Clear and factual comparisons between products or services used under similar conditions shall not be considered disparaging.
8. Marketing activities and messages shall accurately represent the company or organization, its product or service offerings, according to these principles:
   - No form of business communications shall be prepared or knowingly accepted that contains untruthful, misleading, or deceptive statements, claims, pricing, warranties, comparative information, or implications.
   - No claims shall be made in marketing or business communications whose truth and accuracy are incapable of substantiation through reasonable supporting documentation.
   - No form of business communications shall be prepared or knowingly accepted about a product or service that is unsafe and would result in harm to the user unless it gives adequate warning.
   - No form of business communications shall be prepared or knowingly accepted that is offensive or in bad taste.
   - No form of business communications shall be prepared or knowingly accepted that distorts or changes the meaning of quotes, statements or published material to anything other than that implied by the speaker(s) or author(s).
   - No illustrations or photography shall be created or altered to imply that a product is materially different in appearance or performance from its actual state.
9. All business communications shall offer the user a fair opportunity to purchase products or services at the advertised price, and shall explain (or offer an explanation of) any guarantee or warranty to which they refer.
10. Marketers and communicators shall not attempt to compromise the journalistic integrity of the media by using the economic power of advertising.
11. No marketing or communication activities shall be carried out that in any way violate the law or government statutes.

As for Walmart, you can't fault the company's procurement practices. Walmart's purchasing agents aren't allowed to accept a lunch, dinner, golf game, or so much as a cup of coffee from potential vendors. Walmart is not the only company to have implemented such a policy. More and more firms have followed suit because (1) they realize that perks such as these drive up product costs and (2) they don't want their buyers making decisions based on what they personally can get out of them rather than what's best for the company.

All things equal, companies want to do business with firms that are responsible. They don't want to be associated with firms that are not. Why is this important? Because that's what consumers are increasingly demanding. A few years ago, Nike and a number of other apparel makers were lambasted when it came to light that the factories they contracted with were using child labor and keeping workers toiling for long hours under terrible conditions. Nike didn't own the factories, but it still got a bad rap. Today, Nike, Inc., uses a "balanced scorecard." When evaluating suppliers, it looks at their labor-code compliance along with measures such as price, quality, and delivery time. During crunch times, it allows some Chinese factories latitude by, for example, permitting them to adjust when employees can take days off.[14]

Similarly, Walmart has developed a scorecard to rate its suppliers on how their packaging of products affects the environment.[15] Walmart does so because its customers are becoming more conscious of environmental damage and see value in products that are produced in as environmentally friendly a way as possible.

### KEY TAKEAWAY

Ethics come into play in almost all business settings. Business-to-business markets are no different. For example, unlike B2C markets, offering customers perks is very common in B2B settings. In many foreign countries, government buyers demand bribes be paid if a company wants to do business with them. Understanding the laws and regulations that apply to their firms is an obvious starting point for companies, their executives, and employees in terms of knowing how to act ethically. Companies are also adopting ethics codes that provide general guidelines about how their employees should behave, requiring their employees to go through ethics training, and hiring chief ethics officers. Companies want to do business with firms that are responsible. They don't want to be associated with firms that are not. Why? Because they know ethics are important to consumers and that they are increasingly demanding firms behave responsibly.

### REVIEW QUESTIONS

1. Name some of the types of ethical dilemmas facing firms in B2B markets.
2. Why is it difficult for employees and firms to know what's considered to be ethical behavior and what is not?

# 7. DISCUSSION QUESTIONS AND ACTIVITIES

## DISCUSSION QUESTIONS

1. Assume your company makes shop towels, hand-washing stations, and similar products. Make a list of all the companies that could be potential customers of your firm. Then identify all the markets from which their demand is derived. (Who are their customers and their customers' customers?) What factors might influence the success or failure of your business in these markets?
2. How might a buying center be different for a company that is considering building a new plant versus choosing a new copier?
3. Imagine you are a salesperson for a company that sells maintenance items used in keeping a manufacturing plant running. There is a large plant in your territory that buys 60 percent of its products from one competitor and the other 40 percent from another competitor. What could you do to try to make a sale in that plant? How would your answer change if you were the 40 percent vendor and wanted to increase your share of the buyer's business?
4. When your family makes a major purchase, such as choosing a vacation destination or buying furniture, does it resemble a buying center? If so, who plays what roles?
5. Katie is a forklift operator who is tired of her forklift breaking down. She points out to her boss, the plant supervisor, that her forklift is broken down at least 20 percent of the time, and it is beginning to impact production. The plant supervisor tells the purchasing agent that a new forklift is needed and asks the purchasing agent to get three bids on new ones with similar features. The purchasing agent calls three companies and gets bids, which the plant supervisor uses to narrow it down to two. He then has Katie test drive the two and since she liked the Yamamatsu best, he decides to purchase that one. What roles do the supervisor and Katie play in this firm's buying center? Does the process followed resemble the process outlined in the chapter? If not, why not?
6. Someone who works in a company is also a consumer at home. You have already learned about how consumers buy. How does what you already know about how consumers buy relate to what you would expect those same people to do at work when making a purchase?

## ACTIVITIES

1. Interview someone you know who makes purchasing decisions as part of the job. The person may or may not be a professional purchasing agent, as long as business purchasing decisions are a fairly regular part of his or her position. What are the key principles to making good purchasing decisions at work? How do those principles influence people's purchases for their own personal consumption?
2. Locate three different types of Web sites that cater to markets discussed in this chapter. How do these differ from sites like eBay or Overstock.com? How are they similar?

# ENDNOTES


1. Michael Steinberg, "A Fine Diner," *Financial Times*, November 21–22, 2009, 5.
2. Charles Fishman, "The Man Who Said No to Wal-Mart," *Fast Company*, December 19, 2007, http://www.fastcompany.com/magazine/102/open_snapper.html?page=0%2C2 (accessed December 13, 2009).
3. U.S. Bureau of Labor Statistics, "Purchasing Managers, Buyers, and Purchasing Agents," *Occupational Outlook Handbook*, 2010–11 ed., December 17, 2009, http://www.bls.gov/oco/ocos023.htm (accessed January 8, 2010).
4. Jon Miller, "Why B2B Branding Matters in B2B Marketing," *Marketo.com*, March 18, 2007, http://blog.marketo.com/blog/2007/03/b2b_branding_wh.html (accessed December 13, 2009).
5. Jon Miller, "Why B2B Branding Matters in B2B Marketing," *Marketo.com*, March 18, 2007, http://blog.marketo.com/blog/2007/03/b2b_branding_wh.html (accessed December 13, 2009).
6. Ron Brauner, "The B2B Process: Eight Stages of the Business Sales Funnel," Ron Brauner Integrated Marketing (Web site), July 31, 2008, http://www.ronbrauner.com/?p=68 (accessed December 13, 2009).
7. "Cessna Expands Scorecard to Indirect Suppliers," *Purchasing* 138, no. 6 (June 2009): 58.
8. William Copacino, "Unlocking Value through the Supplier Scorecard," *Supply Chain Management Review*, July 8, 2009, http://www.scmr.com/article/329960-Unlocking_Value_through_the_Supplier_Scorecard.php (accessed December 13, 2009).
9. Information from Bart Kohler based on a telephone interview conducted by Dr. Camille Schuster.
10. Efraim Turban, Jae K. Lee, David King, Ting Peng Liang, and Deborrah Turban, *Electronic Commerce 2010*, 6th ed. (Upper Saddle River, NJ: Prentice Hall, 2009), 203.
11. "Company Overview," *Alibaba.com*, http://news.alibaba.com/specials/aboutalibaba/index.html (accessed December 13, 2009).
12. "Motorola Finds Higher Return in B2B Auctions on eBay," *internetretailer.com*, March 23, 2002, http://www.internetretailer.com/dailyNews.asp?id=8291 (accessed December 13, 2009).
13. Richard Waters and Nikki Tait, "Intel Settles Antitrust AMD Case for $1.2 Billion," *Financial Times*, November 13, 2009, http://www.ft.com/cms/s/0/789729c2-cff4-11de-a36d-00144feabdc0.html (accessed December 13, 2009).
14. Dexter Roberts, Pete Engardio, Aaron Bernstein, Stanley Holmes, and Xiang Ji, "How to Make Factories Play Fair," *BusinessWeek*, November 27, 2006, http://www.businessweek.com/magazine/content/06_48/b4011006.htm (accessed December 13, 2009).
15. Mark Arzoumanian, "Wal-Mart Updates *Scorecard* Status," *Official Board Markets* 84, no. 46 (November 15, 2008): 1, 4.

# CHAPTER 5
# Market Segmenting, Targeting, and Positioning

Suppose you've created a great new offering you hope will become a hot seller. Before you quit your day job to market it, you'll need to ask yourself, "Who's going to buy my product?" and "Will there be enough of these people to make it worth my while?"

Certain people will be more interested in what you have to offer than others. Not everyone needs homeowners' insurance, not everyone needs physical therapy services, and not every organization needs to purchase vertical lathes or CT scanners. Among those that do, some will buy a few, and a few will buy many. In other words, in terms of your potential buyers, not all of them are "created equal." Some customers are more equal than others, however. A number of people might be interested in your product if it's priced right. Other people might be interested if they simply are aware of the fact that your product exists.

Your goal is to figure out who these people and organizations are. To do this you will need to divide them up into different categories. The process of breaking down all consumers into groups of potential buyers with similar characteristics is called **market segmentation**. The key question you have to ask yourself when segmenting markets is, *What groups of buyers are similar enough that the same product or service will appeal to all of them?*[1] After all, your marketing budget is likely to be limited. You need to get the biggest bang for your buck by focusing on those people you truly have a shot at selling to and tailoring your offering toward them.

**market segmentation**

The process of breaking down all consumers into groups of potential buyers with similar characteristics.

## 1. TARGETED MARKETING VERSUS MASS MARKETING

### LEARNING OBJECTIVES

1. Distinguish between targeted marketing and mass marketing and explain what led to the rise of each.
2. Describe how targeted marketing can benefit firms.
3. Explain why companies differentiate among their customers.

Choosing select groups of people and organizations to sell to is called **targeted marketing**, or *differentiated marketing*. It is a relatively new phenomenon. **Mass marketing**, or *undifferentiated marketing*, came first. It evolved along with mass production and involves selling the same product to everybody. You can think of mass marketing as a shotgun approach: you blast out as many marketing messages as possible on every medium available as often as you can afford.[2] (By contrast, targeted marketing is more like shooting a rifle; you take careful aim at one type of customer with your message.)

**targeted marketing**

Choosing select groups of people to sell to.

**mass marketing**

Selling the same product to all consumers.

Automaker Henry Ford was very successful at both mass production and mass marketing. Ford pioneered the modern-day assembly line early in the twentieth century, which helped him cost-effectively pump out huge numbers of identical Model T automobiles. They came in only one color: black. "Any customer can have a car painted any color he wants, so long as it is black," Ford used to joke. He also advertised in every major newspaper and persuaded all kinds of publications to carry stories about the new, inexpensive cars. By 1918, half of all cars on America's roads were Model Ts.[3]

Then Alfred P. Sloan, the head of General Motors (GM), appeared on the scene. Sloan began to segment consumers in the automobile market—to divide them up by the prices they wanted to pay and the different cars they wanted to buy. His efforts were successful, and in the 1950s, GM overtook Ford in the as the nation's top automaker.[4] (You might be interested to know that before GM declared bankruptcy in 2009, it was widely believed the automaker actually had too many car models. Apparently, "old habits die hard," as the saying goes.)

**FIGURE 5.1**

You could forget about buying a custom Model T from Ford in the early 1900s. The good news? The price was right.

## 1.1 Benefits of Segmenting and Targeting Markets

The story of General Motors raises an important point, which is that segmenting and targeting markets doesn't necessarily mean "skinnying down" the number of your customers. In fact, it can help you enlarge your customer base by giving you information with which to successfully adjust some component of your offering—the offering itself, its price, the way you service and market it, and so on. More specifically, the process can help you do the following:

- Avoid head-on competition with other firms trying to capture the same customers
- Develop new offerings and expand profitable brands and products lines
- Remarket older, less-profitable products and brands
- Identify early adopters
- Redistribute money and sales efforts to focus on your most profitable customers
- Retain "at-risk" customers in danger of defecting to your competitors

The trend today is toward more precise, targeted marketing. Figuring out "who's who" in terms of your customers involves some detective work, though—often market research. A variety of tools and research techniques can be used to segment markets. Government agencies, such as the U.S. Census Bureau, collect and report vast amounts of population information and economic data that can reveal changing consumption trends. We will talk more about market research in Chapter 10.

Technology is also making it easier for even small companies and entrepreneurs to gather information about potential customers. For example, the online game company GamePUMA.com originally believed its target market consisted of U.S. customers. But when the firm looked more closely at who was downloading games from its Web site, they were people from all over the globe.

The great product idea you had? As we explained in Chapter 3, companies are now using the Internet to track people's Web browsing patterns and segment them into groups that can be marketed to. Even small businesses are able to do this cost effectively now because they don't need their own software and programs. They can simply sign up online for products like Google's AdSense and AdWords programs. You can locate potential customers by looking at blog sites and discussion forums on the Web. Big-boards.com has thousands of discussion forums you can mine to find potential customers interested in your product. Do you have a blog? Go to BlogPoll.com, and you can embed a survey in your blog to see what people think of your idea. If you have a Web site, you can download an application onto your iPhone that will give you up-to-the-minute information and statistics on your site's visitors.

Getting a read on potential target markets doesn't necessarily have to involve technology, though. Your own personal experience and talking to would-be buyers is an important part of the puzzle. Go where you think would-be buyers go—restaurants, malls, gyms, subways, grocery stores, daycare centers, and offices. Ask questions: What do they do during the day? What do they talk about? What products or services do you see them using? Are they having an enjoyable experience when using those products or are they frustrated?

Healthy Choice frozen dinners were conceived as a result of questioning potential customers. The food-maker ConAgra launched the dinners in the late 1980s after its CEO, Charlie Harper, suffered a heart attack. One day a colleague complimented Harper on his wife's tasty low-fat turkey stew. That's when Harper realized there were people like him who wanted healthy convenience foods, so he began talking to them about what they wanted. Two years after the Healthy Choice line was launched, it controlled 10 percent of the frozen-dinner market.[5]

**FIGURE 5.2**

The Healthy Choice line of frozen dinners was launched by a heart attack victim.

## 1.2 Segmenting and Targeting a Firm's Current Customers

Finding and attracting new customers is generally far more difficult than retaining your current customers. People are creatures of habit. Think about how much time and energy you spend when you switch your business from one firm to another—even when you're buying something as simple as a haircut. If you aren't happy with your hair and want to find a new hairdresser, you first have to talk to people with haircuts you like or read reviews of salons. Once you decide to go to a particular salon, you have to look it up on the Internet or your GPS device and hope you don't get lost on the way. When you get to the salon, you must try to explain to the new hairdresser how you want your hair cut and hope he or she gets it right. You might also have to jump through some different hoops when you pay the bill. Perhaps the new salon won't accept your American Express card or won't let you put the tip on your card. However, once you have learned the ropes at the new salon, doing business with it gets much easier.

The same is true for firms when it comes to finding new customers. Finding customers, getting to know them, and figuring out what they really want is a difficult process—one that's fraught with trial and error. That's why it's so important to get to know and form close relationships with your current customers. Broadly speaking, your goal is to do as much business with each one of them as possible.

The most recent economic downturn drove home the point of making the most of one's current customers. During the downturn, new customers were hard to find, and firms' advertising and marketing budgets were cut. Expensive, untargeted, shotgunlike marketing campaigns that would probably produce spotty results were out of the question. Consequently, many organizations chose to focus their selling efforts on their current customers.[6]

This is the situation in which the adventure-based travel firm Backroads found itself in 2009. The California-based company increased its revenues by creating a personalized marketing campaign for people who had done business with Backroads in the past. The firm looked at information such as customers' past purchases, the seasons in which they took their trips, the levels of activity associated with them, and whether or not the customers tended to vacation with children. The company then created three relevant trip suggestions for each customer based on the information. The information was sent to customers via postcards and e-mails with links to customized Web pages reminding them of the trips they had previously booked with Backroads and suggesting new ones. "In terms of past customers, it was like off-the-charts better [than past campaigns]," says Massimo Prioreschi, the vice president of Backroads' sales and marketing group.[7]

In addition to studying their buying patterns, firms also try to get a better read on their customers by surveying them or hiring marketing research firms to do so. (A good source for finding marketing research companies is http://www.greenbook.org.) Firms also utilize loyalty programs to find out about their customers. For example, if you sign up to become a frequent flier with a certain airline, the airline will likely ask to you a number of questions about your likes and dislikes. This information will then be entered into a customer relationship management (CRM) system, and you might be e-mailed special deals based on the routes you tend to fly. British Airways goes so far as to track the magazines its most elite fliers like to read so the publications are available to them on its planes.

Many firms—even small ones—are using Facebook to develop closer relationships with their customers. Hansen Cakes, a Beverly Hills (California) bakery, has about two thousand customers who visit its Facebook page. During her downtime at the bakery, employee Suzi Finer posts "cakes updates" and photos of the goodies she's working on to the site. Along with information about the cakes, Finer extends special offers to customers and mixes in any gossip about Hollywood celebrities she's spotted in the area. After Hansen Cakes launched its Facebook page, the bakery's sales shot up 15–20 percent. "And that's during the recession," notes Finer, who is obviously proud of the results she's gotten.[8] Twitter is another way companies are keeping in touch with their customers and boosting their revenues. For example, when the homemaking maven Martha Stewart schedules a book signing, she tweets her followers, and voilà—many of them show up at the bookstore she's appearing at to buy copies. Finding ways to interact with customers that they enjoy—whether it's meeting or "tweeting" them, or putting on events and tradeshows they want to attend—is the key to forming relationships with them.

Remember what you learned in Chapter 3, however: not all customers are created equal, including your *current* customers. Some customers are highly profitable, and others aren't. Still others will actually end up costing your firm money to serve. Consequently, you will want to interact with some of them more than others.

Believe it or not, some firms deliberately "untarget" unprofitable customers. That's what Best Buy did. In 2004, Best Buy got a lot of attention (not all of it good) when it was discovered the company had categorized its buyers into "personas," or types of buyers, and created customized sales approaches for each. For example, an upper-middle-class woman was referred to as a "Jill." A young urban man was referred to as a "Buzz." And pesky, bargain-hunting customers that Best Buy couldn't make much of a profit from? They were referred to as "devils" and taken off the company's mailing lists.[9]

The knife cuts both ways, though. Not all firms are equal in the minds of consumers, who will choose to do business with some companies rather than others. To consumers, market segmentation means: meet *my* needs—give me what *I* want.[10]

**FIGURE 5.3**

Are you a "high maintenance" customer? Always trying to "work a deal"? Then don't call Best Buy. They'll call you.

*© 2010 Jupiterimages Corporation*

"Steps in One-to-One Marketing" outlines the steps companies can take to target their best customers, form close, personal relationships with them, and give them what they want—a process called **one-to-one marketing**. In terms of our shotgun versus rifle approach, you can think of one-to-one marketing as a rifle approach, but with an added advantage: now you have a scope on your rifle.

**one-to-one marketing**

Forming close, personal relationships with customers and giving them exactly what they want.

One-to-one marketing is an idea proposed by Don Peppers and Martha Rogers in their 1994 book *The One to One Future*. The book described what life would be like after mass marketing. We would all be able to get exactly what we want from sellers, and our relationships with them would be collaborative, rather than adversarial. Are we there yet? Not quite. But it does seem to be the direction the trend toward highly targeted marketing is leading.

## Steps in One-to-One Marketing

1. ***Establish short-term measures to evaluate your efforts***. Determine how you will measure your effort. For example, will you use higher customer satisfaction ratings, increased revenues earned per customer, number of products sold to customers, transaction costs, or another measure?
2. ***Identify your customers***. Gather all the information you can about your current customers, including their buying patterns, likes, and dislikes. When conducting business with them, include an "opt in" question that allows you to legally gather and use their phone numbers and e-mail addresses so as to can remain in contact with them.
3. ***Differentiate among your customers***. Determine who your best customers are in terms of what they spend and will spend in the future (their customer lifetime value), and how easy or difficult they are to serve. Identify and target customers that spend only small amounts with you but large amounts with your competitors.
4. ***Interact with your customers, targeting your best ones***. Find ways and mediums in which to talk to customers about topics they're interested in and enjoy. Spend the bulk of your resources interacting with your best (high-value) customers. Minimize the time and money you spend on low-value customers with low growth potential.
5. ***Customize your products and marketing messages to meet their needs***. Try to customize your marketing messages and products in order to give your customers exactly what they want—whether it's the product itself, its packaging, delivery, or the services associated with it.[11]

### Audio Clip

**Interview with Apurva Ghelani**

Listen to Apurva Ghelani, a senior sales engineer, from the marketing company Air2Web, discuss how companies like NASCAR get permission from consumers to them send advertisements via their wireless devices.

### KEY TAKEAWAY

Choosing select groups of people to sell to is called targeted marketing, or *differentiated marketing*. Mass marketing, or *undifferentiated marketing*, involves selling the same product to everyone. The trend today is toward more precise, targeted marketing. Finding and attracting new customers is generally far more difficult than retaining one's current customers, which is why organizations try to interact with and form relationships with their current customers. The goal of firms is to do as much business with their best customers as possible. Forming close, personal relationships with customers and giving them exactly what they want is a process called one-to-one marketing. It is the opposite of mass marketing.

REVIEW QUESTIONS

1. Using the shotgun and rifle analogy, how do mass marketing, targeted marketing, and one-to-one marketing compare with one another?
2. How is technology making it easier for firms to target potential customers?
3. Outline the steps companies need to take to engage in one-to-one marketing with their customers.

# 2. HOW MARKETS ARE SEGMENTED

LEARNING OBJECTIVES

1. **Understand and outline the ways in which markets are segmented.**
2. **Explain why marketers use some segmentation bases versus others.**

As you learned in Chapter 4, sellers can choose to pursue consumer markets, business-to-business (B2B) markets, or both. Consequently, one obvious way to begin the segmentation process is to segment markets into these two types of groups. Next, we look primarily at the ways in which consumer markets can be segmented. Later in the chapter, we look at the ways in which B2B markets can be segmented.

In Chapter 3, we mentioned that certain factors drive consumers to buy certain things. Many of the same factors can also be used to segment customers. A firm will often use multiple **segmentation bases**, or criteria to classify buyers, to get a fuller picture of its customers and create real value for them. Each variable adds a layer of information. Think of it as being similar to the way in which your professor builds up information on a PowerPoint slide to the point at which you are able to understand the material being presented.

**segmentation bases**

Criteria used to classify buyers.

There are all kinds of characteristics you can use to slice and dice a market. You might not immediately think of some of them. What about the physical sizes of people? "Big-and-tall" stores cater to the segment of population that's larger sized. What about people with wide or narrow feet, or people with medical conditions, certain hobbies, or different sexual orientations? Next, we'll look at some of the more common characteristics market researchers look at when segmenting buyers—rather than, say, the width of their feet, although this could certainly be something you might look at, depending on your offering.

## 2.1 Types of Segmentation Bases

Table 5.1 shows some of the different types of buyer characteristics used to segment markets. Notice that the characteristics fall into one of four segmentation categories: *behavioral*, *demographic*, *geographic*, or *psychographic*. We'll discuss each of these categories in a moment. For now, you can get a rough idea of what the categories consist of by looking at them in terms of how marketing professionals might answer the following questions:

- **Behavioral segmentation.** What benefits do customers want, and how do they use our product?
- **Demographic segmentation.** How do the ages, races, and ethnic backgrounds of our customers affect what they buy?
- **Geographic segmentation.** Where are our customers located, and how can we reach them? What products do they buy based on their locations?
- **Psychographic segmentation.** What do our customers think about and value? How do they live their lives?

**TABLE 5.1** Common Ways of Segmenting Buyers

| By Behavior | By Demographics | By Geography | By Psychographics |
|---|---|---|---|
| ■ Benefits sought from the product<br>■ How often the product is used (usage rate)<br>■ Usage situation (daily use, holiday use, etc.)<br>■ Buyer's status and loyalty to product (nonuser, potential user, first-time users, regular user) | ■ Age/ generation<br>■ Income<br>■ Gender<br>■ Family life cycle<br>■ Ethnicity<br>■ Family size<br>■ Occupation<br>■ Education<br>■ Nationality<br>■ Religion<br>■ Social class | ■ Region (continent, country, state, neighborhood)<br>■ Size of city or town<br>■ Population density<br>■ Climate | ■ Activities<br>■ Interests<br>■ Opinions<br>■ Values<br>■ Attitudes<br>■ Lifestyles |

## 2.2 Segmenting by Behavior

**behavioral segmentation**

Dividing people and organization into groups according to how they behave with or act toward products.

**Behavioral segmentation** divides people and organization into groups according to how they behave with or act toward products. *Benefits segmentation*—segmenting buyers by the benefits they want from products—is very common. Take toothpaste, for example. Which benefit is most important to you when you buy a toothpaste: The toothpaste's price, ability to whiten your teeth, fight tooth decay, freshen your breath, or something else? Perhaps it's combination of two or more benefits. If marketing professionals know what those benefits are, they can then tailor different toothpaste offerings to you (and other people like you). For example, Colgate 2-in-1 Toothpaste & Mouthwash, Whitening Icy Blast is aimed at people who want the benefits of both fresher breath and whiter teeth.

**Video Clip**

**A Vintage Colgate Commercial from the 1950s**

Watch the YouTube video to see a vintage Colgate toothpaste ad that describes the product's various benefits to consumers. (Onscreen kissing was evidently too racy for the times.)

View the video online at: http://www.youtube.com/embed/9QrFa3tDwvY

Another way in which businesses segment buyers is by their usage rates—that is, how often, if ever, they use certain products. For example, the entertainment and gaming company Harrah's gathers information about the people who gamble at its casinos. High rollers, or people who spend a lot of money, are considered "VIPs." VIPs people get special treatment, including a personal "host" who looks after their needs during their casino visits. Companies are interested in frequent users because they want to reach other people like them. They are also keenly interested in nonusers and how they can be persuaded to use products.

The way in which people use products is also be a basis for segmentation. Avon Skin So Soft was originally a beauty product. But after Avon discovered that some people were using it as a mosquito repellant, the company began marketing it for that purpose. Eventually, Avon created a separate product called Skin So Soft Bug Guard, which competes with repellents like Off! Similarly, Glad, the company that makes plastic wrap and bags, found out customers were using its Press 'n Seal wrap in ways the company could never have imagined. The personnel in Glad's marketing department subsequently launched a Web site called 1000uses.com that contains both the company and consumer's use tips. Some of the ways in which people use the product are pretty unusual, as evidenced by the following comment posted on the site: "I have a hedgehog who likes to run on his wheel a lot. After quite a while of cleaning a gross wheel every morning, I got the tip to use 'Press 'n Seal wrap' on his wheel, making clean up much easier! My hedgie can run all he wants, and I don't have to think about the cleanup. Now we're both GLAD!"

Although we doubt Glad will ever go to great lengths to segment the Press 'n Seal market by hedgehog owners, the firm has certainly gathered a lot of good consumer insight about the product and publicity from its 1000uses.com Web site. (Incidentally, one rainy day, the author of this chapter made "rain boots" out of Press 'n Seal for her dog. But when she later tried to tear them off of the dog's paws, he bit her. She is now thinking of trading him in for a hedgehog.)

**FIGURE 5.4**

Encouraging consumers to use your products for multiple purposes is a smart marketing strategy.

© 2010 *Jupiterimages Corporation*

## 2.3 Segmenting by Demographics

Segmenting buyers by tangible, personal characteristics such as their ages, incomes, ethnicity, family sizes, and so forth is called **demographic segmentation**. This section will discuss some prominent demographic characteristics used to segment buyers, including age, income, gender, and family life cycles. Other demographic characteristics include occupation, education, nationality, religion, and social class.

Demographics are commonly utilized to segment markets because a mountain of demographic information is publicly available in databases around the world. You can obtain a great deal of demographic information on the U.S. Census Bureau's Web site (http://www.census.gov). Other government Web sites you can tap include FedStats (http://www.fedstats.gov) and *The World Factbook* (http://www.cia.gov/cia/publications/factbook), which contains statistics about countries around the world. In addition to current statistics, the sites contain forecasts of demographic trends, such as whether some segments of the population are expected to grow or decline.

**demographic segmentation**

Segmenting buyers by tangible, personal characteristics such as their ages, incomes, ethnicity, family sizes, and so forth.

### Age

At this point in your life, you are probably more likely to buy a car than a funeral plot. Marketing professionals know this. That's why they try to segment consumers by their ages. You're probably familiar with some of the age groups most commonly segmented in the United States. They are shown in Table 5.2. Into which category do you fall?

**TABLE 5.2** U.S. Generations and Characteristics

| Generation | Also Known As | Birth Years | Characteristics |
|---|---|---|---|
| Seniors | "The Silent Generation," "Matures," "Veterans," and "Traditionalists" | 1945 and prior | ▪ Experienced very limited credit growing up<br>▪ Tend to live within their means<br>▪ Spend more on health care than any other age group<br>▪ Internet usage rates increasing faster than any other group |
| Baby Boomers | | 1946–1964 | ▪ Second-largest generation in the United States<br>▪ Grew up in prosperous times before the widespread use of credit<br>▪ Account for 50 percent of U.S. consumer spending<br>▪ Willing to use new technologies as they see fit |
| Generation X | | 1965–1979 | ▪ Comfortable but cautious about borrowing<br>▪ Buying habits characterized by their life stages<br>▪ Embrace technology and multitasking |
| Generation Y | "Millennials," "Echo Boomers," includes "Tweens" (preteens) | 1980–2000 | ▪ Largest U.S. generation<br>▪ Grew up with credit cards<br>▪ Adept at multitasking; technology use is innate<br>▪ Ignore irrelevant media |
| **Note: Not all demographers agree on the cutoff dates between the generations.** | | | |

*Sources: U.S. Census Bureau, http://www.census.gov/population/www/popdata.html; Richard K. Miller and Kelli Washington, The 2009 Entertainment, Media & Advertising Market Research Handbook, 10th ed. (Loganville, GA: Richard K. Miller & Associates, 2009), 157–66; Sydney Jones and Susannah Fox, "Generations Online in 2009," Pew Research Center, http://www.pewinternet.org/Reports/2009/Generations-Online-in-2009.aspx; Maria Panaritas, "Generation Gap: Boomers, Xers Are Reining in Spending," Philadelphia Inquirer, August 2, 2009, http://articles.philly.com/2009-08-02/business/25275378_1_spending-habits-boomers-consumer-economy.*

**retro brands**

Old brands or products companies "bring back" for a period of time.

Today's college-age students (Generation Y) compose the largest generation. The baby boomer generation is the second largest, and over the course of the last thirty years or so, has been a very attractive market for sellers. **Retro brands**—old brands or products that companies "bring back" for a period of time—were aimed at baby boomers during the recent economic downturn. Pepsi Throwback and Mountain Dew Throwback, which are made with cane sugar—like they were "back in the good old days"—instead of corn syrup, are examples.[12] Marketing professionals believe they appealed to baby boomers because they reminded them of better times—times when they didn't have to worry about being laid off, about losing their homes, or about their retirement funds and pensions drying up.

But baby boomers are aging, and the size of the group will eventually decline. By contrast, the members of Generation Y have a lifetime of buying still ahead of them, which translates to a lot of potential customer lifetime value (CLV) for marketers if they can capture this group of buyers. However, a recent survey found that the latest recession had forced teens to change their spending habits and college plans and that roughly half of older Generation Yers reported they had no savings.[13]

So which group or groups should your firm target? Although it's hard to be all things to all people, many companies try to broaden their customer bases by appealing to multiple generations so they don't lose market share when demographics change. Several companies have introduced lower-cost brands targeting Generation Xers, who have less spending power than boomers. For example, kitchenware and home-furnishings company Williams-Sonoma opened the Elm Street chain, a less-pricey version of the Pottery Barn franchise. The Starwood hotel chain's W hotels, which feature contemporary designs and hip bars, are aimed at Generation Xers.[14]

The video game market is very proud of the fact that along with Generation X and Generation Y, so many older Americans still play video games. (You probably know some baby boomers who own a Nintendo Wii.) The spa market is another example. Products and services in this market used to be aimed squarely at adults. Not anymore. Parents are now paying for their tweens to get facials, pedicures, and other pampering in numbers no one in years past could have imagined.

**Video Clip**

**Evian Water: Roll, Baby, Roll!**

Watch the YouTube video to see a fun generational type of advertisement. No, the ad isn't designed to appeal to babies. It's aimed at adults!!

View the video online at: http://www.youtube.com/embed/_PHnRln74Ag

Staying abreast of changing demographics can be a matter of life or death for many companies. As early as the 1970s, U.S. automakers found themselves in trouble because of demographic reasons. Many of the companies' buyers were older Americans inclined to "buy American." These people hadn't forgotten that Japan bombed Pearl Harbor during World War II and weren't about buy Japanese vehicles. But younger Americans were. Plus, Japanese cars had developed a better reputation. Despite the challenges U.S. automakers face today, they have taken great pains to cater to the "younger" generation—today's baby boomers who don't think of themselves as being old. If you are a car buff, you perhaps have noticed that the once-stodgy Cadillac now has a sportier look and stiffer suspension. Likewise, the Chrysler 300 looks more like a muscle car than the old Chrysler Fifth Avenue your great-grandpa might have driven.

And what about Generations X and Y? Automakers have begun reaching out to them, too. General Motors (GM) has sought to revamp the century-old company by hiring a new younger group of managers—managers who understand how Generation X and Y consumers are wired and what they want. "If you're going to appeal to my daughter, you're going to have to be in the digital world," explained one GM vice president.[15]

Companies have to not only develop new products designed to appeal to Generations X and Y but also find new ways to reach them. People in these generations not only tend ignore traditional advertising but also are downright annoyed by it. To market to Scion drivers, who are generally younger, Toyota created Scion Speak, a social networking site where they can communicate, socialize, and view cool new models of the car. Online events such as the fashion shows broadcast over the Web are also getting the attention of younger consumers, as are text, e-mail, and Twitter messages they can sign up to receive so as to get coupons, cash, and free merchandise. Advergames are likewise being used to appeal to the two demographic groups. **Advergames** are electronic games sellers create to promote a product or service. Would you like to play one now? Click on the following link to see a fun one created by Burger King to advertise its Tender Crisp Chicken.

**advergames**

Electronic games sellers create to promote a product or service.

**Burger King Advergame**

http://web.archive.org/web/20110426194400/http://www.bk.com/en/us/campaigns/subservient-chicken.html

You can boss the "subservient chicken" around in this advergame. He will do anything you want—well, *almost* anything.

### Income

Tweens might appear to be a very attractive market when you consider they will be buying products for years to come. But would you change your mind if you knew that baby boomers account for 50 percent of all consumer spending in the United States? Americans *over* sixty-five now control nearly three-quarters of the net worth of U.S. households; this group spends $200 billion a year on major "discretionary" (optional) purchases such as luxury cars, alcohol, vacations, and financial products.[16]

Income is used a segmentation variable because it indicates a group's buying power. People's incomes also tend to reflect their education levels, occupation, and social classes. Higher education levels usually result in higher paying jobs and greater social status.

The makers of upscale products such as Rolexes and Lamborghinis aim their products at high-income groups. However, a growing number of firms today are aiming their products at lower-income consumers. The fastest-growing product in the financial services sector is prepaid debit cards, most of which are being bought and used by people who don't have bank accounts. Firms are finding that this group is a large, untapped pool of customers who tend to be more brand loyal than most. If you capture enough of them, you can earn a profit.[17]

Sometimes income isn't always indicative of who will buy your product, however. Companies are aware that many consumers want to be in higher income groups and behave like they are already part of them (recall the reference groups discussed in Chapter 3). Mercedes Benz's cheaper line of "C" class vehicles is designed to appeal to these consumers.

**FIGURE 5.5**

Do you ever wonder if your neighbors can really afford to drive the cars they do?

### Gender

Gender is another way to segment consumers. As we explained in Chapter 3, men and women have different physiological and other needs. They also shop differently. Consequently, the two groups are often, but not always, segmented and targeted differently. Marketing professionals don't stop there, though. For example, because women make many of the purchases for their households, market researchers sometimes try to further divide them into subsegments. (Men are also often subsegmented.) For women, those segments might include *stay-at-home* housewives, *plan-to-work* housewives, *just-a-job* working women, and *career-oriented* working women. Women who are solely homemakers tend to spend more money research has found—perhaps because they have more time.

In addition to segmenting by gender, market researchers might couple people's genders along with their marital statuses and other demographic characteristics. For, example, did you know that more women in America than ever before (51 percent) now live without spouses? Can you think of any marketing opportunities this might present?[18]

**FIGURE 5.6**

Considering the rising number of U.S. women who live without spouses, should some smart entrepreneur consider launching a "hunky handyman" service?

### Family Life Cycle

**Family life cycle** refers to the stages families go through over time and how it affects people's buying behavior. For example, if you have no children, your demand for pediatric services (medical care for children) is likely to be slim to none. But if you have children or adopt them, your demand might be very high because children frequently get sick. You will be part of the target market not only for pediatric services but also for a host of other products, such as children's clothing, entertainment services, and educational products. A secondary segment of interested consumers might be grandparents who are likely to spend less on day-to-day childcare items but more on special-occasion gifts for children. In fact, many markets are segmented based on the special events in people's lives. Think about brides (and wannabe brides) and all the products targeted at them, including Web sites and television shows such as *Platinum Weddings*, *Married Away*, *Whose Wedding Is It Anyway*, and *Bridezilla*.

**family life cycle**

The stages families go through over time and how it affects people's buying behavior.

Resorts also segment vacationers depending on where they are in their family life cycles. When you think of family vacations, you probably think of Disney resorts. Some vacation properties, such as Sandals, exclude children from some of their resorts. Perhaps they do so because some studies show that the market segment with greatest financial potential is married couples without children.[19]

**FIGURE 5.7**

Many markets are segmented based on people's family life cycle needs.

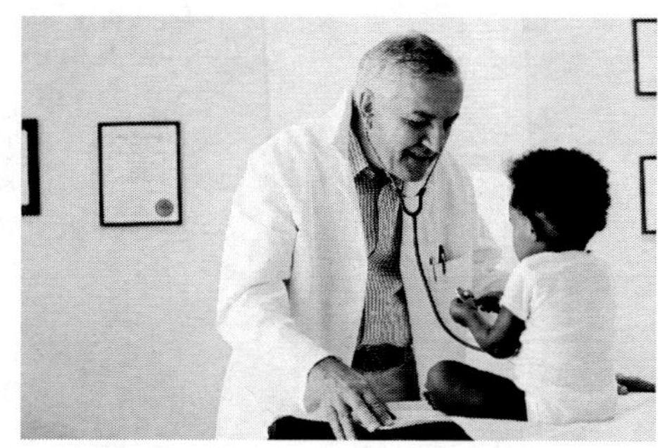

© 2010 Jupiterimages Corporation

Keep in mind that although you might be able to isolate a segment in the marketplace, including one based on family life cycle, you can't make necessarily make assumptions about what the people in it will want. Just like people's demographics change, so do their tastes. For example, over the past few decades U.S. families have been getting smaller. Households with a single occupant are more commonplace than ever. But until recently, that hasn't stopped people from demanding bigger cars (and more of them) as well as larger houses, or what some people jokingly refer to as "McMansions."

But like the trend toward larger cars, the trend toward larger houses appears to be reversing. High energy costs, the credit crunch, and concern for the environment are leading people to demand smaller houses. To attract people such as these, D. R. Horton, the nation's leading homebuilder, and other construction firms are now building smaller homes.

### Ethnicity

People's ethnic backgrounds have a big impact on what they buy. If you've visited a grocery store that caters to a different ethnic group than your own, you were probably surprised to see the types of products sold there.

It's no secret that the United States is becoming—and will continue to become—more diverse. Hispanic Americans are the largest and the fastest-growing minority in the United States. Companies are going to great lengths to court this once overlooked group. In California, the health care provider Kaiser Permanente runs television ads letting members of this segment know that they can request Spanish-speaking physicians and that Spanish-speaking nurses, telephone operators, and translators are available at all of its clinics.[20]

African Americans are the second-largest ethnic group in America. Collectively, they have the most buying power of any ethnic group in America. Many people of Asian descent are known to be early adapters of new technology and have above-average incomes. As a result, companies that sell electronic products, such as AT&T, spend more money segmenting and targeting the Asian community.[21] Table 5.3 contains information about the number of people in these groups and their buying power.

**TABLE 5.3** Major U.S. Ethnic Segments and Their Spending

| Group | Percentage of U.S. Population | Annual Spending Power (Billions of Dollars) |
|---|---|---|
| Hispanic | 13.7 | 736 |
| African American | 13.0 | 761 |
| Asian | 5.0 | 397 |

*Source: New American Dimensions, LLC.*

As you can guess, even within various ethnic groups there are many differences in terms of the goods and services buyers choose. Consequently, painting each group with a broad brush would leave you with an incomplete picture of your buyers. For example, although the common ancestral language among the Hispanic segment is Spanish, Hispanics trace their lineages to different countries. Nearly 70 percent of Hispanics in the United States trace their lineage to Mexico; others trace theirs to Central America, South America, and the Caribbean.

All Asians share is race. Chinese, Japanese, and Korean immigrants do not share the same language.[22] Moreover, both the Asian and Hispanic market segments include new immigrants, people who immigrated to the United States years ago, and native-born Americans. So what language will you use to communicate your offerings to these people, and where?

Subsegmenting the markets could potentially help you. New American Dimension, a multicultural research firm, has further divided the Hispanic market into the following subsegments:

- **Just moved in'rs.** Recent arrivals, Spanish dependent, struggling but optimistic.
- **FOBrs (fashionistas on a budget).** Spanish dominant, traditional, but striving for trendy.
- **Accidental explorers.** Spanish preferred, not in a rush to embrace U.S. culture.
- **The englightened.** Bilingual, technology savvy, driven, educated, modern.
- **Doubting Tomáses.** Bilingual, independent, skeptical, inactive, shopping uninvolved.
- **Latin flavored.** English preferred, reconnecting with Hispanic traditions.
- **SYLrs (single, young latinos).** English dominant, free thinkers, multicultural.

You could go so far as to break down segments to the individual level (which is the goal behind one-to-one marketing). However, doing so would be dreadfully expensive, notes Juan Guillermo Tornoe, a marketing expert who specializes in Hispanic marketing issues. After all, are you really going to develop different products for each of the groups? Different marketing campaigns and communications? Perhaps not. However, "you need to perform your due diligence and understand where the majority of the people you are trying to reach land on this matrix, modifying your message according to this insight," Tornoe explains.[23]

## 2.4 Segmenting by Geography

Where will your customers come from? Suppose your great new product or service idea involves opening a local store. Before you open the store, you will probably want to do some research to determine which geographical areas have the best potential. For instance, if your business is a high-end restaurant, should it be located near the local college or country club? If you sell ski equipment, you probably will want to locate your shop somewhere in the vicinity of a mountain range where there is skiing. You might see a snowboard shop in the same area but probably not a surfboard shop. By contrast, a surfboard shop is likely to be located along the coast, but you probably would not find a snowboard shop on the beach.

**geographic segmentation**

Segmenting buyers by where they are located.

**geocoding**

The process of plotting geographic marketing information takes on a map.

**geodemographics**

Combining both demographic and geographic information for marketing purposes.

**customer profile**

The description of a type of customer based on market segmentation criteria.

**Geographic segmentation** explains why the checkout clerks at stores sometimes ask you what your zip code is. It's also why businesses print codes on coupons that correspond to zip codes. When the coupons are redeemed, the store can then find out where its customers are located—or not located. **Geocoding** is a process that takes data such as this and plots it on a map. Geocoding can help businesses see where prospective customers might be clustered and target them with various ad campaigns, including direct mail, for example. One of the most popular geocoding software programs is PRIZM NE, which is produced by a company called Claritas. PRIZM NE uses zip codes and demographic information to classify the American population into segments. The idea behind PRIZM is that "you are where you live." Combining both demographic and geographic information is referred to as **geodemographics**. To see how geodemographics works, visit the following page on Claritas' Web site: http://www.claritas.com/MyBestSegments/Default.jsp?ID=20.

Type in your zip code, and you will see **customer profiles** of the types of buyers who live in your area. Table 5.4 shows the profiles of buyers who can be found the zip code 76137—the "Brite Lites, Li'l City" bunch, Home Sweet Home" set, and so on. Click on the profiles on the Claritas site to see which one most resembles you.

**TABLE 5.4** An Example of Geodemographic Segmentation for 76137 (Fort Worth, TX)

| Number | Profile Name |
|---|---|
| 12 | *Brite Lites, Li'l City* |
| 19 | *Home Sweet Home* |
| 24 | *Up-and-Comers* |
| 13 | *Upward Bound* |
| 34 | *White Picket Fences* |

The tourism bureau for the state of Michigan was able to identify different customer profiles and target them using PRIZM. Michigan's biggest travel segment are Chicagoans in certain zip codes consisting of upper-middle-class households with children—or the "kids in cul-de-sacs" group, as Claritas puts it. The bureau was also able to identify segments significantly different from the Chicago segment, including blue-collar adults in the Cleveland area who vacation without their children. The organization then created significantly different marketing campaigns to appeal to each group.

City size and **population density** (the number of people per square mile) are also used for segmentation purposes. Have you ever noticed that in rural towns, McDonald's restaurants are hard to find? But Dairy Queens are usually easy to locate. McDonald's generally won't put a store in a town of fewer than five thousand people. However, this is prime turf for the "DQ"—for one, because it doesn't have to compete with bigger franchises like McDonald's.

**population density**

The number of people per square mile.

**Proximity marketing** is an interesting new technology firms are using to segment buyers geographically and target them within a few hundred feet of their businesses using wireless technology. In some areas, you can switch your mobile phone to a "discoverable mode," while you're shopping and, if you want, get ads and deals from stores as you pass by them. And it's often less expensive than hiring people to hand you a flier as you walk by.[24]

### Audio Clip

**Interview with Apurva Ghelani**

To learn about how proximity marketing works at a real company, listen to Apurva Ghelani in this audio clip. Ghelani is a senior sales engineer for Air2Web, a company that helps businesses promote their brands and conduct transactions with people via their mobile phones.

**FIGURE 5.8**

Virgin Mobile is helping stores capitalize on proximity marketing by sending text messages to Virgin Mobile users when they opt to receive them. Billboards outside stores tell Virgin Mobile users to "switch your Bluetooth on to get free stuff here!" (Who wouldn't want free stuff?)

*© 2010 Jupiterimages Corporation*

In addition to figuring out where to locate stores and advertise to customers in that area, geographic segmentation helps firms tailor their products. Chances are you won't be able to find the same heavy winter coat you see at a Walmart in Montana at a Walmart in Florida because of the climate differences between the two places. Market researchers also look at migration patterns to evaluate opportunities. TexMex restaurants are more commonly found in the southwestern United States. However, northern states are now seeing more of them as more people of Hispanic descent move northward.

## 2.5 Segmenting by Psychographics

If your offering fulfills the needs of a specific demographic group, then the demographic can be an important basis for identifying groups of consumers interested in your product. But what if your product crosses several market segments? Take cereal, for example. The group of potential consumers could be "almost" everyone. However, there are groups of people who have different needs with regard to their cereal. Some consumers might be interested in the fiber, some consumers (especially children) may be interested in the prize that comes in the box, other consumers may be interested in the added vitamins, and still other consumers may be interested in the type of grains. Associating these specific needs with consumers in a particular demographic group could be difficult. Marketing professionals often desire more information about consumers than just demographic data. You want to know *why* consumers behave the way they do, what is of high priority to them, or how they rank the importance of specific buying criteria. Think about some of your friends who seem a lot like you. Have you ever gone their homes and been shocked by their lifestyles and how vastly different they are from yours? Why are their families so much different from yours?

**proximity marketing**

The process of segmenting buyers geographically and target them within a few hundred feet of a business businesses using wireless technology.

**Psychographic segmentation** can help fill in some of the blanks. Recall that we first mentioned psychographics in Chapter 3. Psychographic information is frequently gathered via extensive surveys that ask people about their activities, interests, opinion, attitudes, values, and lifestyles. One of the most well-known psychographic surveys is VALS (which originally stood for "Values, Attitudes, and Lifestyles"), developed by a company called SRI International in the late 1980s. Thousands of Americans were asked by the California company the extent to which they agreed or disagreed with questions similar to the following ones: "My idea of fun at a national park would be to stay at an expensive lodge and dress up for dinner" and "I could stand to skin a dead animal."[25] (Which category do you fall into?) Consumers were then divided up into the following categories, each characterized by certain buying behaviors.

**psychographic segmentation**

Segmenting people by their activities, interests, opinion, attitudes, values, and lifestyles.

- **Innovators.** Innovators are successful, sophisticated, take-charge people with high self-esteem. Because they have such abundant resources, they exhibit all three primary motivations in varying degrees. They are change leaders and are the most receptive to new ideas and technologies. Innovators are very active consumers, and their purchases reflect cultivated tastes for upscale, niche products and services. Image is important to Innovators, not as evidence of status or power but as an expression of their taste, independence, and personality. Innovators are among the established and emerging leaders in business and government, yet they continue to seek challenges. Their lives are characterized by variety. Their possessions and recreation reflect a cultivated taste for the finer things in life.

- **Thinkers.** Thinkers are motivated by ideals. They are mature, satisfied, comfortable, and reflective people who value order, knowledge, and responsibility. They tend to be well educated and actively seek out information in the decision-making process. They are well informed about world and national events and are alert to opportunities to broaden their knowledge. Thinkers have a moderate respect for the status quo institutions of authority and social decorum but are open to consider new ideas. Although their incomes allow them many choices, Thinkers are conservative, practical consumers; they look for durability, functionality, and value in the products they buy.
- **Achievers.** Motivated by the desire for achievement, Achievers have goal-oriented lifestyles and a deep commitment to career and family. Their social lives reflect this focus and are structured around family, their place of worship, and work. Achievers live conventional lives, are politically conservative, and respect authority and the status quo. They value consensus, predictability, and stability over risk, intimacy, and self-discovery. With many wants and needs, Achievers are active in the consumer marketplace. Image is important to Achievers; they favor established, prestige products and services that demonstrate success to their peers. Because of their busy lives, they are often interested in a variety of timesaving devices.
- **Experiencers.** Experiencers are motivated by self-expression. As young, enthusiastic, and impulsive consumers, Experiencers quickly become enthusiastic about new possibilities but are equally quick to cool. They seek variety and excitement, savoring the new, the offbeat, and the risky. Their energy finds an outlet in exercise, sports, outdoor recreation, and social activities. Experiencers are avid consumers and spend a comparatively high proportion of their income on fashion, entertainment, and socializing. Their purchases reflect the emphasis they place on looking good and having "cool" stuff.
- **Believers.** Like Thinkers, Believers are motivated by ideals. They are conservative, conventional people with concrete beliefs based on traditional, established codes: family, religion, community, and the nation. Many Believers express moral codes that are deeply rooted and literally interpreted. They follow established routines, organized in large part around home, family, community, and social or religious organizations to which they belong. As consumers, Believers are predictable; they choose familiar products and established brands. They favor American products and are generally loyal customers.
- **Strivers.** Strivers are trendy and fun loving. Because they are motivated by achievement, Strivers are concerned about the opinions and approval of others. Money defines success for Strivers, who don't have enough of it to meet their desires. They favor stylish products that emulate the purchases of people with greater material wealth. Many see themselves as having a job rather than a career, and a lack of skills and focus often prevents them from moving ahead. Strivers are active consumers because shopping is both a social activity and an opportunity to demonstrate to peers their ability to buy. As consumers, they are as impulsive as their financial circumstance will allow.
- **Makers.** Like Experiencers, Makers are motivated by self-expression. They express themselves and experience the world by working on it—building a house, raising children, fixing a car, or canning vegetables—and have enough skill and energy to carry out their projects successfully. Makers are practical people who have constructive skills and value self-sufficiency. They live within a traditional context of family, practical work, and physical recreation and have little interest in what lies outside that context. Makers are suspicious of new ideas and large institutions such as big business. They are respectful of government authority and organized labor but resentful of government intrusion on individual rights. They are unimpressed by material possessions other than those with a practical or functional purpose. Because they prefer value to luxury, they buy basic products.
- **Survivors.** Survivors live narrowly focused lives. With few resources with which to cope, they often believe that the world is changing too quickly. They are comfortable with the familiar and are primarily concerned with safety and security. Because they must focus on meeting needs rather than fulfilling desires, Survivors do not show a strong primary motivation. Survivors are cautious consumers. They represent a very modest market for most products and services. They are loyal to favorite brands, especially if they can purchase them at a discount.[26]

You can take a VALS survey at http://www.sric-bi.com/vals/surveynew.shtml to find out which category you're in. VALS surveys have been adapted and used to study buying behavior in other countries, too. Note that both VALS and PRIZM group buyers based on their values and lifestyles. But PRIZM also overlays the information with geographic data. As a result, you can gauge what the buying habits of people in certain zip codes are, which can be helpful if you are trying to figure out where to locate stores and retail outlets.

The segmenting techniques we've discussed so far in this section require gathering quantitative information—data, in other words. Quantitative information can be improved with and *qualitative* information you gather by talking to your customers and getting to know them. (Recall that this is how Healthy Choice frozen dinners were created.) **Consumer insight** is what results when you use both types of information. You want to be able to answer the following questions:

**consumer insight**

An understanding of consumers that results when both quantitative and qualitative information are gathered about them.

- Am I looking at the consumers they way they see themselves?
- Am I looking at life from their point of view?

Best Buy asked store employees to develop insight about local consumer groups in order to create special programs and processes for them. Employees in one locale invited a group of retirees to their store to explain how to make the switch to digital television. The store sold $350,000 worth of equipment and televisions in just two hours' time. How much did it cost? Ninety-nine dollars in labor costs plus coffee and donuts.

Intuit, the company that makes the tax software Quicken, has a "follow me home" program. Teams of engineers from Intuit visit people's homes and spend a couple of hours watching consumers use Quicken. Then they use the insights they gain to improve the next version of Quicken. Contrast this story with that of a competing firm: When a representative of the firm was asked if he had ever observed consumers installing or using his company's product, he responded, "I'm not sure I'd want to be around when they were trying to use it."[27] This company is now struggling to stay in business.

To read about some of the extreme techniques Nokia uses to understand cell phone consumers around the world, click on the following link: http://www.nytimes.com/2008/04/13/magazine/13anthropology-t.html?pagewanted=all.

## 2.6 Segmentation in B2B Markets

Many of the same bases used to segment consumer markets are also used to segment B2B markets. Demographic criteria are used. For example, Goya Foods is a U.S. food company that sells different ethnic products to grocery stores, depending on the demographic groups the stores serve—Hispanic, Mexican, or Spanish. Likewise, B2B sellers often divide their customers by geographic areas and tailor their products to them accordingly. Segmenting by behavior is common as well. B2B sellers frequently divide their customers based on their product usage rates. Customers that order many goods and services from a seller often receive special deals and are served by salespeople who call on them in person. By contrast, smaller customers are more likely to have to rely on a firm's Web site, customer service people, and salespeople who call on them by telephone.

However, researchers Matthew Harrison, Paul Hague, and Nick Hague have theorized that there are fewer behavioral and needs-based segments in B2B markets than in business-to-consumer (B2C) markets for two reasons: (1) business markets are made up of a few hundred customers whereas consumer markets can be made up of hundreds of thousands of customers, and (2) businesses aren't as fickle as consumers. Unlike consumers, they aren't concerned about their social standing, influenced by their families and peers, and so on. Instead, businesses are concerned solely with buying products that will ultimately increase their profits.

According to Harrison, Hague, and Hague, the behavioral, or needs-based, segments in B2B markets include the following:

- **A price-focused segment** composed of small companies that have low profit margins and regard the good or service being sold as not being strategically important to their operations
- **A quality and brand-focused segment** composed of firms that want the best possible products and are prepared to pay for them
- **A service-focused segment** composed of firms that demand high-quality products and have top-notch delivery and service requirements
- **A partnership-focused segment** composed of firms that seek trust and reliability on the part of their suppliers and see them as strategic partners[28]

B2B sellers, like B2C sellers, are exploring new ways to reach their target markets. Trade shows, which we discuss in more detail later in the book, and direct mail campaigns are two traditional ways of reaching B2B markets. Now, however, firms are finding they can target their B2B customers more cost effectively via e-mail campaigns, search-engine marketing, and "fan pages" on social networking sites like Facebook. Companies are also creating blogs with cutting-edge content about new products and business trends their customers are interested in. And for the fraction of the cost of attending a trade show to exhibit their products, B2B sellers are holding Webcasts and conducting online product demonstrations for potential customers.

**KEY TAKEAWAY**

Segmentation bases are criteria used to classify buyers. The main types of buyer characteristics used to segment consumer markets are behavioral, demographic, geographic, and psychographic. Behavioral segmentation divides people and organization into groups according to how they behave with or toward products. Segmenting buyers by tangible, personal characteristics such as their age, income, ethnicity, family size, and so forth is called demographic segmentation. Geographic segmentation involves segmenting buyers based on where they live. Psychographic segmentation seeks to differentiate buyers based on their activities, interests, opinions, attitudes, values, and lifestyles. Oftentimes a firm uses multiple bases to get a fuller picture of its customers and create value for them. Marketing professionals develop consumer insight when they gather both quantitative and qualitative information about their customers. Many of the same bases used to segment consumer markets are used to segment business-to-business (B2B) markets. However, there are generally fewer behavioral-based segments in B2B markets.

**REVIEW QUESTIONS**

1. What buyer characteristics do companies look at when they segment markets?
2. Why do firms often use more than one segmentation base?
3. What two types of information do market researchers gather to develop consumer insight?

# 3. SELECTING TARGET MARKETS AND TARGET-MARKET STRATEGIES

**LEARNING OBJECTIVES**

1. **Describe the factors that make some markets more attractive targets than others.**
2. **Describe the different market-segmenting strategies companies pursue and why.**
3. **Outline the market-segmentation strategies used in global markets.**

## 3.1 Selecting Target Markets

After you segment buyers and develop a measure of consumer insight about them, you can begin to see those that have more potential. Now you are hunting with a rifle instead of a shotgun. The question is, do you want to spend all day hunting squirrels or ten-point bucks? An attractive market has the following characteristics:

- **It's sizeable enough to be profitable given your operating cost.** Only a tiny fraction of the consumers in China can afford to buy cars. However, because the country's population is so large (nearly 1.5 billion people), more cars are sold in China than in Europe (and in the United States, depending on the month). Three billion people in the world own cell phones. But that still leaves three billion who don't.[29]
- **It's growing.** For example, the middle class of India is growing rapidly, making it a very attractive market for consumer products companies. People under thirty make up the majority of the Indian population, fueling the demand for "Bollywood" (Indian-made) films.
- **It's not already swamped by competitors, or you have found a way to stand out in a crowd.** IBM used to make PCs. However, after the marketplace became crowded with competitors, IBM sold the product line to a Chinese company called Lenovo. (Recall from Chapter 2 that this is part of assessing the competitive environment.)
- **Either it's accessible or you can find a find a way to reach it.** Accessibility, or the lack of it, could include geographic accessibility, political and legal barriers, technological barriers, or social barriers. For example, to overcome geographic barriers, the consumer products company Unilever hires women in third-world countries to distribute the company's products to rural consumers who lack access to stores. (See the discussion in Chapter 2 about assessing the external environment.)

- **You have the resources to compete in it.** You might have a great idea to compete in the wind-power market. However, it is a business that is capital intensive. What this means is that you will either need a lot of money or must be able to raise it. You might also have to compete with the likes of T. Boone Pickens, an oil tycoon who is attempting to develop and profit from the wind-power market. Does your organization have the resources to do this? (See the discussion in Chapter 2 about assessing the internal environment.)
- **It "fits in" with your firm's objectives and mission.** Consider TerraCycle, which has made its mark by selling organic products in recycled packages. Fertilizer made from worm excrement and sold in discarded plastic beverage bottles is just one of its products. It wouldn't be a good idea for TerraCycle to open up a polluting, coal-fired power plant, no matter how profitable the market for the service might be.

**Video Clip**

**Yogurt, Anyone? I Mean, Any Woman?**

Are women an attractive target market for yogurt sellers? The maker of this humorous YouTube video thinks so. (She seems to imply they are the only market.)

View the video online at: http://www.youtube.com/embed/qMRDLCR8vAE

## 3.2 Target-Market Strategies: Choosing the Number of Markets to Target

Henry Ford proved that mass marketing can work—at least for a while. Mass marketing is also efficient because you don't have to tailor any part of the offering for different groups of consumers, which is more work and costs more money. The problem is that buyers are not all alike. If a competitor comes along and offers these groups a product (or products) that better meet their needs, you will lose business.

## 3.3 Multisegment Marketing

Most firms tailor their offerings in one way or another to meet the needs of different segments of customers. Because these organizations don't have all their eggs in one basket, they are less vulnerable to competition. Marriott International is an example of a company that operates in a multisegment market. The company has fifteen different types of facilities designed to meet the needs of different types of market segments, including the following:

- **Marriott Courtyard.** Targeted at over-the-road travelers.
- **Ritz-Carlton Hotels.** Targeted at luxury travelers.
- **Marriott Conference Centers.** Targeted at businesses hosting small- and midsized meetings.
- **Marriott ExecuStay.** Targeted at executives needing month-long accommodations.
- **Marriott Vacation Clubs.** Targeted at travelers seeking to buy timeshares.

A **multisegment marketing** strategy can allow you to respond to demographic and other changes in markets. For example, the growing number of people too old to travel have the option of moving into one of Marriott's "Senior Living Services" facilities, which cater to retirees who need certain types of care. A multisegment strategy can also help you weather an economic downturn by allowing customers

**multisegment marketing**

Targeting multiple groups of consumers.

to trade up or down among your brands and products. Suppose you take a pay cut and can't afford to stay at Marriott's Ritz-Carlton hotels anymore. A room at a JW Marriott—the most luxurious of the Marriott-brand hotels but cheaper than the Ritz—is available to you. A multisegment strategy can also help you deal with the product life cycle issues discussed in Chapter 2. If one of your products is "dying out," you have others to fall back on.

## 3.4 Concentrated Marketing

**concentrated marketing**

Targeting a very select group of customers.

Some firms—especially smaller ones with limited resources—engage in concentrated marketing. **Concentrated marketing** involves targeting a very select group of customers. Concentrated marketing can be a risky strategy because you really *do* have all of your eggs in one basket. The auto parts industry is an example. Traditionally, many North American auto parts makers have supplied parts exclusively to auto manufacturers. But when General Motors, Ford, Chrysler, and other auto companies experienced a slump in sales following the recession that began in 2008, the auto parts makers found themselves in trouble. Many of them began trying to make and sell parts for wind turbines, aerospace tools, solar panels, and construction equipment.[30]

**niche marketing**

Targeting an extremely select group of consumers.

**Niche marketing** involves targeting an even more select group of consumers. When you're engaging in niche marketing, your goal is to be a big fish in a small pond instead of a small fish in a big pond.[31] Some examples of companies operating in niche markets include those shown in Table 5.5.

**TABLE 5.5** Companies That Operate in Niche Markets

| Company | Niche | Market Share (%) |
|---|---|---|
| Hohner | Harmonicas | 85 |
| Tetra | Tropical fish food | 80 |
| Swarovski | Crystal jewels | 65 |
| Uwatec | Snorkeling equipment | 60 |
| St. Jude Medical Center | Artificial heart valves | 60 |

*Source: José María Manzanedo, "Market Segmentation Strategies. How to Maximize Opportunities on the Potential Market," February 20, 2005, http://www.daemonquest.com/en/research_and_insight/2006/10/11/market_segmentation_strategies_how_to_maximize_opportunities_on_the_potential_market (accessed April 13, 2012).*

**microtargeting**

The process of gathering multiple sources of data available on people, everything from their tax and phone records to the catalogs they receive, so as to market to them.

**Microtargeting**, or narrowcasting, is a new effort to isolate markets and target them. It was originally used to segment voters during elections, including the 2004 U.S. presidential election. Microtargeting involves gathering all kinds of data available on people—everything from their tax and phone records to the catalogs they receive. One company that compiles information such as this is Acxiom. For a fee, Acxiom can provide you with a list of Hispanic consumers who own two pets, have caller ID, drive a sedan, buy certain personal care products, subscribe to certain television cable channels, read specified magazines, and have income and education levels within a given range.[32] Clearly, microtargeting has ethical implications. Data privacy issues will be discussed more in Chapter 14.

## 3.5 Targeting Global Markets

Firms that compete in the global marketplace can use any combination of the segmenting strategies we discussed or none at all. A microcosm of the targeting strategies used in global markets is shown in Figure 5.9. If you're a seller of a metal like iron ore, you might sell the same product across the entire world via a metals broker. The broker would worry about communicating with customers around the world and devising different marketing campaigns for each of them.

**FIGURE 5.9** Targeting Strategies Used in Global Markets

Most companies, however, tailor their offerings to some extent to meet the needs of different buyers around the world. For example, Mattel sells Barbie dolls all around the world—but not the same Barbie. Mattel has created thousands of different Barbie offerings designed to appeal to all kinds of people in different countries.

Pizza Hut has franchises around the world, but its products, packaging, and advertising are tailored to different markets. Squid is a popular topping in Asia, for instance. Companies tailor products not only for different countries but also for different customers in different countries. For example, Procter & Gamble's China division now offers products designed for different local market segments in that country. P&G has an advanced formulation of laundry detergent for the premium segment, a modified product for the second (economy) segment, and a very basic, inexpensive product created for the third (rural) segment.[33]

Sellers are increasingly targeting consumers in China, Russia, India, and Brazil because of their fast-growing middle classes. Take the cosmetics maker Avon. Avon's largest market is no longer the United States. It is Brazil. Brazilians are extremely looks-conscious and increasingly able to afford cosmetic products as well as plastic surgery.[34] So attractive are these countries that firms are changing how they develop goods and services, too. "Historically, American companies innovated in the U.S. and took those products abroad," says Vjay Govindarahan, a professor at Dartmouth's Tuck School of Business. Now, says Govindarahan, companies are creating low-cost products to capture large markets in developing countries and then selling them in developed countries. Acer's $250 laptop and General Electric's ultrainexpensive $1,000 electrocardiogram device are examples. The world's cheapest car, the $2,500 Tato Nano, was developed for India but is slated to be sold in the United States.[35]

Other strategies for targeting markets abroad include acquiring (buying) foreign companies or companies with large market shares there. To tap the Indian market, Kraft made a bid to buy the candymaker Cadbury, which controls about one-third of India's chocolate market. Likewise, to compete against Corona beer, the Dutch brewer Heineken recently purchased Mexico's Femsa, which makes the beer brands Dos Equis, Tecate, and Sol.[36] However, some countries don't allow foreign firms to buy domestic firms. They can only form partnerships with them. Other regulatory and cultural barriers sometimes prevent foreign firms from "invading" a country. IKEA, the Swedish home-furnishings maker, eventually left Russia because it found it too hard to do business there. By contrast, McDonald's efforts to expand into Russia have been quite successful. Having saturated other markets, the hamburger chain is hoping to continue to grow by opening hundreds of new stores in the country.

**KEY TAKEAWAY**

A market worth targeting has the following characteristics: (1) It's sizeable enough to be profitable, given your operating costs; (2) it's growing; (3) it's not already swamped by competitors, or you have found a way to stand out in the crowd; (4) it's accessible, or you can find a way to reach it; (5) you have the resources to compete in it; and (6) it "fits in" with your firm's mission and objectives. Most firms tailor their offerings in one way or another to meet the needs of different segments of customers. A multisegment marketing strategy can allow a company to respond to demographic and other changes in markets, including economic downturns. Concentrated marketing involves targeting a very select group of customers. Niche marketing involves targeting an even more select group of consumers. Microtargeting, or *narrowcasting*, is a new, effort to "super target" consumers by gathering all kinds of data available on people—everything from their tax and phone records to the catalogs they receive. Firms that compete in the global marketplace can use any combination of these segmenting strategies or none at all. Sellers are increasingly targeting consumers in China, Russia, India, and Brazil because of their fast-growing middle classes. Firms are creating low-cost products to capture large markets in developing countries such as these and then selling the products in developed countries. Other strategies for targeting markets abroad include acquiring foreign companies or forming partnerships with them.

**REVIEW QUESTIONS**

1. What factors does a firm need to examine before deciding to target a market?
2. Which of the segmenting strategies discussed in this section is the broadest? Which is the narrowest?
3. Why might it be advantageous to create low-cost products for developing countries and then sell them in nations such as the United States? Do you see any disadvantages of doing so?

# 4. POSITIONING AND REPOSITIONING OFFERINGS

**LEARNING OBJECTIVES**

1. **Explain why positioning is an important element when it comes to targeting consumers.**
2. **Describe how a product can be positioned and mapped.**
3. **Explain what repositioning is designed is to do.**

**positioning**

Tailoring a product or its marketing so that it stands out from the competition and people want to buy it.

**perceptual map**

A two-dimensional graph that visually shows where a product stands, or should stand, relative to its competitors.

Why should buyers purchase your offering versus another? If your product faces competition, you will need to think about how to "position" it in the marketplace relative to competing products. After all you don't want the product to be just another "face in the crowd" in the minds of consumers. **Positioning** involves tailoring your product so that it stands out from the competition and people want to buy it.

One way to position your product is to plot customer survey data on a perceptual map. A **perceptual map** is a two-dimensional graph that visually shows where your product stands, or should stand, relative to your competitors, based on criteria important to buyers. The criteria can involve any number of characteristics—price, quality, level of customer service associated with the product, and so on. An example of a perceptual map is shown in Figure 5.10. To avoid head-to-head competition with your competitors, you want to position your product somewhere on the map where your competitors aren't clustered.

**FIGURE 5.10** An Example of a Perceptual Map

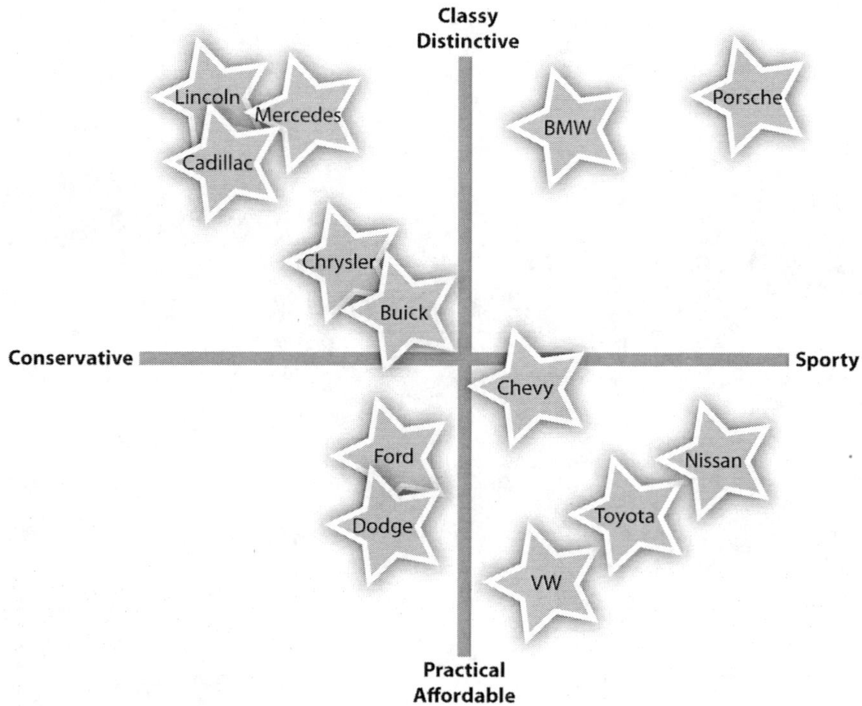


*Source: Adapted from http://en.wikipedia.org/wiki/Perceptual_mapping.*

Many companies use taglines in their advertising to try to position their products in the minds of the buyer—where they want them, of course. A **tagline** is a catchphrase designed to sum up the essence of a product. You perhaps have heard Wendy's tagline "It's better than fast food." The tagline is designed to set Wendy's apart from restaurants like McDonald's and Burger King—to plant the idea in consumers' heads that Wendy's offerings are less "fast foodish," given the bad rap fast food gets these days.

**tagline**

A catchphrase designed to sum up the essence of a product.

Sometimes firms find it advantageous to reposition their products—especially if they want the product to begin appealing to different market segments. **Repositioning** is an effort to "move" a product to a different place in the minds of consumers. The i-house, a prefab house built by Clayton Homes, a mobile home manufacturer, is an example. According to the magazine *Popular Mechanics*, the i-house "looks like a house you'd order from IKEA, sounds like something designed by Apple, and consists of amenities—solar panels, tankless water heaters and rainwater collectors—that one would expect to come from an offbeat green company out of California selling to a high-end market."[37] A Clayton Homes spokesperson says, "Are we repositioning to go after a new market? I would think we are maintaining our value to our existing market and expanding the market to include other buyers that previously wouldn't have considered our housing product."[38]

**repositioning**

The process of "moving" a product to a different place in the minds of consumers.

**FIGURE 5.11** The Clayton i-house: "A Giant Leap from the Trailer Park"

*Source: http://www.claytonihouse.com.*

Recently, Porsche unveiled its new line of Panamera vehicles at a Shanghai car show. The car is a global model, but unlike Porsche's other cars, it's longer. Why? Because rich car buyers in China prefer to be driven by chauffeurs.[39] How do you think Porsche is trying to reposition itself for the future?

### Audio Clip

**Interview with Apurva Ghelani**

Listen to Ghelani's advice to students interested in working in his area of marketing.

## KEY TAKEAWAY

If a product faces competition, its producer will need to think about how to "position" it in the marketplace relative to competing products. Positioning involves tailoring a product or its marketing so that it stands out from the competition and people want to buy it. A perceptual map is a two-dimensional graph that visually shows where a product stands, or should stand, relative to its competitors, based on criteria important to buyers. Sometimes firms find it advantageous to reposition their products. Repositioning is an effort to "move" a product to a different place in the minds of consumers.

## REVIEW QUESTIONS

1. Why do companies position products?
2. Explain what a tagline is designed to do.
3. Why might an organization reposition a product?

# 5. DISCUSSION QUESTIONS AND ACTIVITIES

## DISCUSSION QUESTIONS

1. Think about some of your friends and what you have discovered by visiting their homes. Do they buy different things than you do? If so, why? How might a company distinguish you from them in terms of its targeting?
2. Staples and The Limited have attempted to thwart shoppers who abuse store return policies. When a customer returns items, store clerks swipe the customer's driver's license through electronic card readers that track buying and return patterns for any suspicious activity.[40] What drawbacks do you think such a strategy could have?
3. Is it always harder to find new customers than it is to retain old ones? Or does it depend on the business you're in?
4. Does one-to-one marketing have to be expensive? How can small organizations interact with their customers in a cost-effective way?
5. Are large companies better off using multisegment strategies and small companies better off using niche strategies? Why or why not?

## ACTIVITIES

1. Visit http://aclu.org/pizza/images/screen.swf to see a video created by the American Civil Liberties Union in an effort to warn consumers about the information being collected about them. Do you think the video is far-fetched? Or do you think consumers should be alarmed? In your opinion, do the potential benefits of CRM databases exceed the potential downsides—or not?
2. Form groups of three students. Think of a product or service that one of you purchased recently on campus. How might you go about developing a customer profile for the product? List the sources you would use.
3. Describe a product you like that you believe more people should use. As a marketer, how would you reposition the product to increase its use? Outline your strategy.

# ENDNOTES


1. Bruce R. Barringer and Duane Ireland, *Entrepreneurship: Successfully Launching New Ventures*, 3rd ed. (Upper Saddle River, NJ: Prentice Hall, 2010).
2. Robert Spellings, Jr., "Mass Marketing Is Dead. Make Way for Personal Marketing," *The Direct Marketing Voice*, March 20, 2009, http://thedirectmarketingvoice.com/2009/03/20/mass-marketing-is-dead-make-way-for-personal-marketing (accessed December 2, 2009).
3. Henry Ford, *My Life and Work* (Garden City, NY: Garden City Publishing Co., 1922), 72.
4. José María Manzanedo, "Market Segmentation Strategies. How to Maximize Opportunities on the Potential Market," February 20, 2005, http://www.daemonquest.com/en/research_and_insight/2006/10/11/market_segmentation_strategies_how_to_maximize_opportunities_on_the_potential_market (accessed April 13, 2012).
5. John Birchall, "Out to Launch in a Downturn," *Financial Times*, June 4, 2009, 10.
6. John Birchall, "Value Trend Tests Brand Loyalty," *Financial Times*, March 31, 2009, 12.
7. "Lift Sales with Personalized, Multi-channel Messages: 6 Steps," July 9, 2009, http://www.marketingsherpa.com/article.php?ident=31299 (accessed December 2, 2009).
8. Jefferson Graham, "Cade Decoratero Finds Twitter a Sweet Recipe for Success," *USA Today*, April 1, 2009, 5B.
9. Meg Marco, "LEAKS: Best Buy's Internal Customer Profiling Document," *The Consumerist*, March 18, 2008, http://consumerist.com/368894/leaks-best-buys-internal-customer-profiling-document (accessed December 2, 2009).
10. "Market Segmentation," *The Market Segmentation Company*, http://www.marketsegmentation.co.uk/segmentation_tmsc.htm (accessed December 2, 2009).
11. Curt Harler, "Reaching the Unreachable," *Smart Business Cleveland*, December 2008, 92; Don Peppers and Martha Rogers, "The Short Way to Long-Term Relationships," *Sales and Marketing Management*, May 1, 1999, 24; Don Peppers, Martha Rogers, and Bob Dorf, "Is Your Company Ready for One-to-One Marketing?" *Harvard Business Review*, January–February 1999, 151–60.
12. Barry Schlacter, "Sugar-Sweetened Soda Is Back in the Mainstream," *Fort Worth Star-Telegram*, April 22, 2009, 1C, 5C.
13. "Generation Y Lacking Savings," *Fort Worth Star-Telegram*, September 13, 2009, 2D.
14. Richard K. Miller and Kelli Washington, *The 2009 Entertainment, Media & Advertising Market Research Handbook*, 10th ed. (Loganville, GA: Richard K. Miller & Associates, 2009), 157–66.
15. Bob Cox, "GM Hopes Its New Managers Will Energize It," *Fort Worth Star-Telegram*, August 29, 2009, 1C–4C.
16. Tim Reisenwitz, Rajesh Iyer, David B. Kuhlmeier, and Jacqueline K. Eastman, "The Elderly's Internet Usage: An Updated Look," *Journal of Consumer Marketing*, 24, no. 7 (2007): 406–18.
17. Constantine von Hoffman, "For Some Marketers, Low Income Is Hot," *Brandweek*, September 11, 2006, http://www.allbusiness.com/marketing-advertising/branding-brand-development/4670054-1.html (accessed December 2, 2009).
18. Thomas Barry, Mary Gilly, and Lindley Doran, "Advertising to Women with Different Career Orientations," *Journal of Advertising Research* 25 (April–May 1985): 26–35.
19. Brian J. Hill, Carey McDonald, and Muzzafer Uysal, "Resort Motivations for Different Family Life Cycle Stages," *Visions in Leisure and Business Number* 8, no. 4 (1990): 18–27.
20. Eric N. Berkowitz, *The Essentials of Health Care Marketing*, 2nd ed. (Sudbury, MA: Jones & Bartlett Publishers, 2006), 13.
21. "Telecommunications Marketing Opportunities to Ethnic Groups: Segmenting Consumer Markets by Ethnicity, Age, Income and Household Buying Patterns, 1998–2003," The Insight Research Corporation, 2003, http://www.insight-corp.com/reports/ethnic.asp (accessed December 2, 2009).
22. "Telecommunications Marketing Opportunities to Ethnic Groups: Segmenting Consumer Markets by Ethnicity, Age, Income and Household Buying Patterns, 1998–2003," The Insight Research Corporation, 2003, http://www.insight-corp.com/reports/ethnic.asp (accessed December 2, 2009).
23. Juan Guillermo Tornoe, "Hispanic Marketing Basics: Segmentation of the Hispanic Market," January 18, 2008, http://network.latpro.com/profiles/blogs/hispanic-marketing-basics (accessed December 2, 2009).
24. "Bluetooth Proximity Marketing," April 24, 2007, http://bluetomorrow.com/bluetooth-articles/marketing-technologies/bluetooth-proximity-marketing.html (accessed December 2, 2009).
25. James H. Donnelly, preface to *Marketing Management*, 9th ed., by J. Paul Peter (New York: McGraw-Hill Professional, 2002), 79.
26. "U.S. Framework and VALS™ Type," *Strategic Business Insights*, http://www.strategicbusinessinsights.com/vals/ustypes.shtml (accessed December 2, 2009).
27. Eric Nee, "Due Diligence: The Customer Is Always Right," *CIO Insight*, May 23, 2003.
28. Matthew Harrison, Paul Hague, and Nick Hague, "Why Is Business-to-Business Marketing Special?"(whitepaper), *B2B International*, http://www.b2binternational.com/library/whitepapers/whitepapers04.php (accessed January 27, 2010).
29. Sara Corbett, "Can the Cellphone Help End Global Poverty?" *New York Times Magazine*, April 13, 2008, http://www.nytimes.com/2008/04/13/magazine/13anthropology-t.html?pagewanted=all (accessed December 2, 2009).
30. Bernad Simon, "Alternative Routes For Survival," *Financial Times*, April 23, 2009, 8.
31. "Niche Marketing," BusinessDictionary.com, http://www.businessdictionary.com/definition/niche-marketing.html (accessed December 2, 2009).
32. Leon Schiffman and Leslie Kanuk, *Consumer Behavior*, 10th ed. (Upper Saddle River, NJ: Prentice Hall, 2010), 80.
33. Dan Sewell, "P&G May Make Changes as it Faces Challenges," *The Associated Press*, June 9, 2009.
34. Jonathan Wheatley, "Business of Beauty Is Turning Heads in Brazil," *Financial Times*, January 20, 2010, 5.
35. Daniel, McGinn, "Cheap, Cheap, Cheap," *Newsweek*, February 2010, 10.
36. Michael J. de la Merced and Chris V. Nicholson, "Heineken in Deal to Buy Big Mexican Brewer," *New York Times*, January 11, 2010, http://www.nytimes.com/2010/01/12/business/global/12beer.html (accessed January 26, 2010).
37. Ariel Schwartz, "Clayton Homes' i-house Combines Energy Efficiency and Modular Affordability," *Fast Company*, May 4, 2009, http://www.fastcompany.com/blog/ariel-schwartz/sustainability/clayton-homes-75k-energy-efficient-i-house (accessed December 9, 2009).
38. "Clayton 'i-house' is giant leap from trailer park," *Knoxvillebiz.com*, May 6, 2009, http://www.knoxnews.com/news/2009/may/06/clayton-i-house-giant-leap-trailer-park/ (accessed April 13, 2012).
39. John Gapper, "Why Brands Now Rise in the East," *Financial Times*, April 23, 2009, 9.
40. Liz Pulliam Weston, "The Basics: Are You a Bad Customer?" *MSN Money*, http://moneycentral.msn.com/content/Savinganddebt/consumeractionguide/P103694.asp (accessed December 2, 2009).

# CHAPTER 6
# Creating Offerings

Why do buyers purchase something? Why do you own anything? Many of us own iPods, but few of us do for the sake of owning an iPod. We own one because it delivers music, and we want the music. Or we own one because we have been influenced to buy one. Shortly after the iPod's introduction, some people undoubtedly purchased the devices because other people thought they were "cool," and they wanted to be cool by owning one. Now iPods are so ubiquitous that no one gives them a second glance. Yet the impact that iPods have had on the music and entertainment industry has been huge because the product revolutionized how we purchase entertainment.

## 1. WHAT COMPOSES AN OFFERING?

**LEARNING OBJECTIVES**

1. **Distinguish between the three major components of an offering—product, price, and service.**
2. **Explain, from both a product-dominant and a service-dominant approach, the mix of components that compose different types of offerings.**
3. **Distinguish between technology platforms and product lines.**

People buy things to solve needs. In the case of the iPod, the need is to have better access to music, to look cool, or both. **Offerings** are products and services designed to deliver value to customers—either to fulfill their needs, satisfy their "wants," or both. Recall that you learned about people's needs in earlier chapters. In this chapter, we discuss how marketing fills those needs through the creation and delivery of offerings.

**offering**

The entire bundle of a tangible good, intangible service, and price that composes what a company offers to customers.

### 1.1 Product, Price, and Service

Most offerings consist of a **product**, or a tangible good people can buy, sell, and own. Purchasing a classic iPod, for example, will allow you store up to forty thousand songs or two hundred hours of video. The amount of storage is an example of a **feature**, or characteristic of the offering. If your playlist consists of twenty thousand songs, then this feature delivers a benefit to you—the benefit of plenty of storage. However, the feature will only benefit you up to a point. For example, you won't be willing to pay more for the extra storage if you only need half that much. When a feature satisfies a need or want, then there is a **benefit**. Features, then, matter differently to different consumers based on each individual's needs. Remember the value equation, which is different for every customer!

An offering also consists of a **price**, or the amount people pay to receive the offering's benefits. The price paid can consist of a one-time payment, or it can consist of something more than that. Many consumers think of a product's price as only the amount they paid; however, the true cost of owning an iPod, for example, is the cost of the device itself plus the cost of the music or videos downloaded onto it. The **total cost of ownership (TCO)**, then, is the total amount someone pays to own, use, and eventually dispose of a product.

TCO is usually thought of as a concept businesses use to compare offerings. However, consumers also use the concept. For example, suppose you are comparing two sweaters, one that can be hand-washed and one that must be dry-cleaned. The hand-washable sweater will cost you less to own in dollars but may cost more to own in terms of your time and hassle. A smart consumer would take that into consideration. When we first introduced the personal value equation in Chapter 1, we discussed hassle as the time and effort spent making a purchase. A TCO approach, though, would also include the time and effort related to owning the product—in this case, the time and effort to hand wash the sweater.

**product**

A tangible good that can be bought, sold, and owned.

**feature**

A characteristic of an offering.

**benefit**

The degree to which a feature satisfies a buyer's need or desire.

**price**

The amount exchanged by the buyer to receive the value offered by the product or service.

**total cost of ownership (TCO)**

The total amount of time and money spent to acquire, use, and dispose of an offering.

A **service** is an action that provides a buyer with an intangible benefit. A haircut is a service. When you purchase a haircut, it's not something you can hold, give to another person, or resell. "Pure" services are offerings that don't have any tangible characteristics associated with them. Skydiving is an example of a pure service. You are left with nothing after the jump but the memory of it (unless you buy a DVD of the event). Yes, a plane is required, and it is certainly tangible. But it isn't the product—the jump is. At times people use the term "product" to mean an offering that's either tangible or intangible. Banks, for example, often advertise specific types of loans, or financial "products," they offer consumers. Yet truly these products are financial services. The term "product" is frequently used to describe an offering of either type.

**FIGURE 6.1**

Neiman-Marcus sells sweaters for over $1,000! But that's just the purchase price. The total cost of ownership would also include the cost of having the sweater professionally cleaned or the value of the time and effort needed to hand wash it.

*© 2010 Jupiterimages Corporation*

**service**

An intangible component of an offering.

**FIGURE 6.2**

Skydiving is an example of a pure service. You are left with nothing after the jump but the memory of it (unless you buy a DVD of the event).

*© 2010 Jupiterimages Corporation*

Many tangible products have an intangible service components attached to them, however. When Hewlett-Packard (HP) introduced its first piece of audio testing equipment, a key concern for buyers was the service HP could offer with it. Could a new company such as HP back up the product, should something go wrong with it? As you can probably tell, a service does not have to be consumed to be an important aspect of an offering. HP's ability to provide good after-sales service in a timely fashion was an important selling characteristic of the audio oscillator, even if buyers never had to use the service.

**Audio Clip**

**René Guess**

Listen to René Guess of Curves International describe her job. What does Curves International sell? What are the benefits that they provide? Do they provide a product or a service?

### FIGURE 6.3

Sport Clips is a barbershop with a sports-bar atmosphere. The company's slogan is "At Sport Clips, guys win." So, although you may walk out of Sport Clips with the same haircut you could get from Pro Cuts, the experience you had getting it was very different, which adds value for some buyers.

*Source: Sport Clips, used with permission.*

What services do you get when you purchase a can of soup? You might think that a can of soup is as close to a "pure" product devoid of services that you can get. But think for a moment about your choices in terms of how to purchase the can of soup. You can buy it at a convenience store, a grocery store like Publix, or online. Your choice of how to get it is a function of the product's intangible service benefits, such as the way you are able to shop for it.

### FIGURE 6.4

Even what seems like a "pure" product like a can of soup can have an intangible service component associated with it, such as the way you are able to shop for it—say, at a convenience store, a grocery store like Publix, or perhaps online.

*Source: Wikimedia Commons.*

## 1.2 The Product-Dominant Approach to Marketing

**product-oriented**

An approach to business that centers on capturing business by focusing on creating and manufacturing better products at lower prices.

From the traditional product-dominant perspective of business, marketers consider products, services, and prices as three separate and distinguishable characteristics. To some extent, they are. HP could, for example, add or strip out features from a piece of testing equipment and not change its service policies or the equipment's price. The product-dominant marketing perspective has its roots in the Industrial Revolution. During this era, businesspeople focused on the development of products that could be mass produced cheaply. In other words, firms became **product-oriented**, meaning that they believed the best way to capture market share was to create and manufacture better products at lower prices. Marketing remained oriented that way until after World War II.

## 1.3 The Service-Dominant Approach to Marketing

Who determines which products are better? Customers do, of course. Thus, taking a product-oriented approach can result in marketing professionals focusing too much on the product itself and not enough on the customer or service-related factors that customers want. Most customers will compare tangible products and the prices charged for them in conjunction with the services that come with them. In other words, the *complete* offering is the basis of comparison. So, although a buyer will compare the price of product A to the price of product B, in the end, the prices are compared in conjunction with the other features and services of the products. The dominance of any one of these dimensions is a function of the buyer's needs.

**FIGURE 6.5**

King Ranch Chicken is a casserole made with chicken, RO*TEL tomatoes, cream of mushroom soup, and cream of chicken soup. If you eat the casserole at your school's cafeteria, you are consuming both a product and a service. Consequently, separating the product from the service is often an artificial exercise.

*© 2010 Jupiterimages Corporation*

The advantage of the service-dominant approach is that it integrates the product, price, and service dimensions of an offering. This helps marketers think more like their customers, which can help them add value to their firm's products. In addition to the offering itself, marketers should consider what services it takes for the customer to acquire their offerings (e.g., the need to learn about the product from a sales clerk), to enjoy them, and to dispose of them (e.g., someone to move the product out of the house and haul it away), because each of these activities create costs for their customers—either monetary costs or time and hassle costs.

Customers are now becoming more involved in the creation of benefits. Let's go back to that "pure" product, Campbell's Cream of Chicken Soup. The consumer may prepare that can as a bowl of soup, but it could also be used as an ingredient in making King Ranch Chicken. As far as the consumer goes, no benefit is experienced until the soup is eaten; thus, the consumer played a part in the creation of the final "product" when the soup was an ingredient in the King Ranch Chicken. Or suppose your school's cafeteria made King Ranch Chicken for you to consume; in that case you both ate a product and consumed a service.

Some people argue that focusing too much on the customer can lead to too little product development or poor product development. These people believe that customers often have difficulty seeing how an innovative new technology can create benefits for them. Researchers and entrepreneurs frequently make many discoveries and then products are created as a result of those discoveries. 3M's Post-it Notes are an example. The adhesive that made it possible for Post-it Notes to stick and restick was created by a 3M scientist who was actually in the process of trying to make something else. Post-it Notes came later.

**FIGURE 6.6**

Few consumers could have envisioned that a new type of adhesive would lead to the development of a product as successful as Post-it Notes.

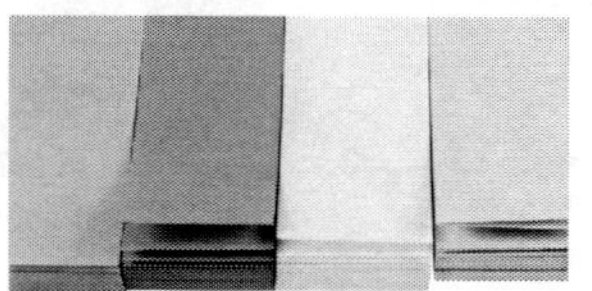

*© 2010 Jupiterimages Corporation*

## 1.4 Product Levels and Product Lines

A product's **technology platform** is the core technology on which it is built. Take for example, the iPod, which is based on MP3 technology. In many cases, the development of a new offering is to take a technology platform and rebundle its benefits in order to create a different version of an already-existing offering. For example, in addition to the iPod Classic, Apple offers the Shuffle and the Nano. Both are based on the same core technology.

**technology platform**

The core technology that is the basis for an offering or product.

In some instances, a new offering is based on a technology platform originally designed to solve different problems. For example, a number of products originally were designed to solve the problems facing NASA's space-traveling astronauts. Later, that technology was used to develop new types of offerings. EQyss's Micro Tek pet spray, which stops pets from scratching and biting themselves, is an example. The spray contains a trademarked formula developed by NASA to decontaminate astronauts after they return from space.

**FIGURE 6.7**

The formula in EQyss's Micro Tek pet grooming spray was originally developed by NASA to decontaminate astronauts after they return from space.

*Source: Photo by Amy Ray, used with permission.*

A technology platform isn't limited to tangible products. Knowledge can be a type of technology platform in a pure services environment. For example, the "bioesthetic" treatment model was developed to help people who suffer from TMJ, a jaw disorder that makes chewing painful. A dentist can be trained on the bioesthetic technology platform and then provide services based on it. There are, however, other ways to treat TMJ that involve other platforms, or bases of knowledge and procedures, such as surgery.

Few firms survive by selling only one product. Most firms sell several offerings designed to work together to satisfy a broad range of customers' needs and desires. A **product line** is group of related offerings. Product lines are created to make marketing strategies more efficient. Campbell's condensed soups, for example, are basic soups sold in cans with red labels. But Campbell's Chunky is a ready-to-eat soup sold in cans that are labeled differently. Most consumers expect there to be differences between Campbell's red-label chicken soup and Chunky chicken soup, even though they are both made by the same company.

**product line**

A group of offerings that serve similar needs and are sold under the same name.

**line depth**

The number of variations in a single product line.

**line extension**

A new idea or offering that occurs when a company comes out with another model (related product or service) based on the same platform and brand as one of its other products.

**line breadth**

The number of different, or distinct, product lines offered by a company.

**product mix**

The entire assortment of products that a firm offers.

A product line can be broad, as in the case of Campbell's condensed soup line, which consists of several dozen different flavors. Or, a product line can be narrow, as in the case of Apple's iPod line, which consists of only a few different MP3 devices. How many offerings there are in a single product line—that is, whether the product line is broad or narrow—is called **line depth**. When new but similar products are added to the product line, it is called a **line extension**. If Apple introduces a new MP3 player to the iPod family, that would be a line extension. Companies can also offer many different product lines. **Line breadth** (or width) is a function of how many different, or distinct, product lines a company has. For example, Campbell's has a Chunky soup line, condensed soup line, Kids' soup line, Lower Sodium soup line, and a number of nonsoup lines like Pace Picante sauces, Prego Italian sauces, and crackers. The entire assortment of products that a firm offers is called the **product mix**.

As Figure 6.8 shows, there are four offering levels. Consider the iPod Shuffle. There is (1) the basic offering (the device itself), (2) the offering's technology platform (the MP3 format or storage system used by the Shuffle), (3) the product line to which the Shuffle belongs (Apple's iPod line of MP3 music players), and (4) the product category to which the offering belongs (MP3 players as opposed to iPhones, for example).

**FIGURE 6.8** Product Levels

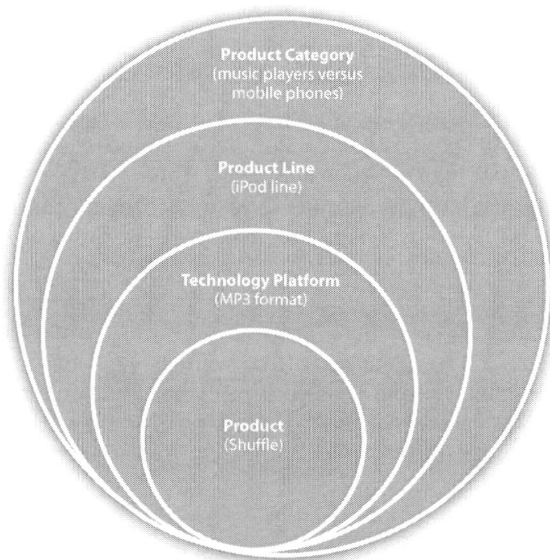


So how does a technology platform become a new product or service or line of new products and services? In Chapter 7, we will take a closer look at how companies design and develop new offerings.

**KEY TAKEAWAY**

Companies market offerings composed of a combination of tangible and intangible characteristics for certain prices. During the Industrial Revolution, firms focused primarily on products and not so much on customers. The service-dominant perspective to marketing integrates three different dimensions of an offering—not only the product but also its price and the services associated with it. This perspective helps marketers think more like their customers, which helps firms add value to their offerings. An offering is based on a technology platform, which can be used to create a product line. A product line is a group of similar offerings. A product line can be deep (many offerings of a similar type) and/or broad (offerings that are very different from one another and cover a wide range of customers' needs). The entire assortment of products that a company offers is called the product mix.

**REVIEW QUESTIONS**

1. How do the product-dominant and service-dominant approaches to marketing differ?
2. Do "product-dominant" and "product-oriented" mean the same thing?
3. What is the difference between a technology platform and a product line?
4. Does a product line have to be built on one technology platform?
5. What is the difference between product depth and product breadth?

# 2. TYPES OF CONSUMER OFFERINGS

**LEARNING OBJECTIVES**

1. **Define the various types of offerings marketed to individual consumers.**
2. **Explain why a single offering might be marketed differently to different types of consumers.**

Products and services can be categorized in a number of ways. We will use these categories throughout the book because they are the most commonly referred to categories by marketers and because there are marketing implications for each. Consumer offerings fall into four general categories:

1. Convenience offerings
2. Shopping offerings
3. Specialty offerings
4. Unsought offerings

In this section, we will discuss each of these categories. Keep in mind that the categories are not a function of the characteristic of the offerings themselves. Rather, they are a function of how consumers want to purchase them, which can vary from consumer to consumer. What one consumer considers a shopping good might be a convenience good to another consumer.

## 2.1 Convenience Offerings

**Convenience offerings** are products and services consumers generally don't want to put much effort into shopping for because they see little difference between competing brands. For many consumers, bread is a convenience offering. A consumer might choose the store in which to buy the bread but be willing to buy whatever brand of bread the store has available. Marketing convenience items is often limited to simply trying to get the product in as many places as possible where a purchase could occur.

**convenience offering**

Low-priced, frequently purchased products and services that require little shopping effort.

Closely related to convenience offerings are **impulse offerings**, or items purchased without any planning. The classic example is Life Savers, originally manufactured by the Life Savers Candy Company, beginning in 1913. The company encouraged retailers and restaurants to display the candy next to their cash registers and to always give customers a nickel back as part of their change so as to encourage them to buy one additional item—a roll of Life Savers, of course!

**FIGURE 6.9**

The Life Savers Candy Company was formed in 1913. Its primary sales strategy was to create an impulse to buy Life Savers by encouraging retailers and restaurants to place them next to their cash registers and include a nickel—the purchase price of a roll of Life Savers—in the customer's change.

*Source: Wikimedia Commons.*

**impulse offering**

An offering that is purchased on impulse, without prior planning.

## 2.2 Shopping Offerings

A **shopping offering** is one for which the consumer will make an effort to compare and select a brand. Consumers believe there are differences between shopping offerings and want to find the right one or the best price. Buyers might visit multiple retail locations or spend a considerable amount of time visiting Web sites and reading reviews about the product, such as the reviews found in *Consumer Reports*.

Consumers often care about brand names when they're deciding on shopping goods. If a store is out of a particular brand, then another brand might not do. For example, if you prefer Crest Whitening Expressions toothpaste and the store you're shopping at is out if it, you might put off buying the toothpaste until your next trip to the store. Or, you might go to a different store or buy a small tube of some other toothpaste until you can get what you want. Note that even something as simple as toothpaste can become a shopping good for someone very interested in her dental health—perhaps after she's read online product reviews or consulted with her dentist. That's why companies like Procter & Gamble, the maker of Crest, work hard to influence not only consumers but also people like dentists who influence the sale of their products.

**shopping offering**

An offering for which the consumer will make an effort to compare various firms' offerings and select a brand.

**FIGURE 6.10**

If your favorite toothpaste is Crest's Whitening Fresh Mint, you might change stores if you don't find it on the shelves of your regular store.

*Source: Wikimedia Commons.*

## 2.3 Specialty Offerings

**Specialty offerings** are highly differentiated offerings, and the brands under which they are marketed are very different across companies, too. For example, an Orange County Chopper or Iron Horse motorcycle is likely to be far different feature-wise than a Kawasaki or Suzuki motorcycle. Typically, specialty items are available only through limited channels. For example, exotic perfumes available only in exclusive outlets are considered specialty offerings. Specialty offerings are purchased less frequently than convenience offerings. Therefore, the profit margin on them tends to be greater.

**specialty offering**

An offering that is highly differentiated from other offerings and is designed to satisfy a similar need or want.

**FIGURE 6.11**

Specialty offerings, such as this custom-made motorcycle, are highly differentiated. People will go to greater lengths to shop for these items and are willing to pay more for them.

*Source: Wikimedia Commons.*

Marketing specialty goods requires building brand name recognition in the minds of consumers and educating them about your product's key differences. This is critical. For fashion goods, the only point of difference may be the logo on the product (for example, an Izod versus a Polo label). Even so, marketers spend a great deal of money and effort to try to get consumers to perceive these products differently than their competitors'.

### 2.4 Unsought Offerings

**Unsought offerings** are those that buyers do not generally want to have to shop for until they need them. Towing services and funeral services are generally considered unsought offerings. Marketing unsought items is difficult. Some organizations try to presell the offering, such as preneed sales in the funeral industry or towing insurance in the auto industry. Other companies, such as insurance companies, try to create a strong awareness among consumers so that when the need arises for these products, consumers think of their organizations first.

**unsought offering**

An offering consumers don't typically shop for until it is needed. Examples include funeral and towing services.

#### KEY TAKEAWAY

Convenience offerings, shopping offerings, specialty offerings, and unsought offerings are the major types of consumer offerings. Convenience offerings often include life's necessities (bread, milk, fuel, and so forth), for which there is little difference across brands. Shopping goods do vary, and many consumers develop strong preferences for some brands versus others. Specialty goods are even more exclusive. Unsought goods are a challenge for marketers because customers do not want to have to shop for them until they need them.

#### REVIEW QUESTIONS

1. What are the four types of consumer offerings? How do they differ from one another?
2. Is it possible for cemetery plots or caskets to be a shopping good or a specialty good? Or are they always unsought goods?

## 3. TYPES OF BUSINESS-TO-BUSINESS (B2B) OFFERINGS

#### LEARNING OBJECTIVES

1. **Define the various types of offerings marketed to businesses.**
2. **Identify some of the differences with regard to how the various types of business offerings are marketed.**

Just like there are different types of consumer offerings, there are different types of business-to-business (B2B) offerings as well. But unlike consumer offerings, which are categorized by how consumers shop, B2B offerings are categorized by how they are used. The primary categories of B2B offerings are

- capital equipment offerings,
- raw materials offerings,
- original equipment manufacturer (OEM) offerings,
- maintenance, repair, and operations (MRO) offerings,
- facilitating offerings.

### 3.1 Capital Equipment Offerings

A **capital equipment offering** is any equipment purchased and used for more than one year and depreciated over its useful life. Machinery used in a manufacturing facility, for example, would be considered capital equipment. Professionals who market capital equipment often have to direct their communications to many people within the firms to which they are selling because the buying decisions related to the products can be rather complex and involve many departments. From a marketing standpoint, deciding who should get what messages and how to influence the sale can be very challenging.

**capital equipment offering**

Tangible equipment business purchases that are depreciated.

## 3.2 Raw Materials Offerings

**FIGURE 6.12**

The grade of raw leather used to cover the sofa is purchased from suppliers as a commodity—that is, a certain grade is the same across vendors, which compete on the basis of price and the availability of the product.

**raw materials offering**

Raw material products firms offer other firms so they can make a product or provide a service. These offerings are processed only to the point required for economic handling and distribution.

**manufactured material**

A material that has been processed into a finished good but is not a stand-alone product; it still has to be incorporated into something else to be usable.

**Raw materials offerings** are materials firms offer other firms so they can make a product or provide a service. Raw materials offerings are processed only to the point required to economically distribute them. Lumber is generally considered a raw material, as is iron, nickel, copper, and other ores. If iron is turned into sheets of steel, it is called a **manufactured material** because it has been processed into a finished good but is not a stand-alone product; it still has to be incorporated into something else to be usable. Both raw and manufactured materials are then used in the manufacture of other offerings.

Raw materials are often thought of as commodities, meaning that there is little difference among them. Consequently, the competition to sell them is based on price and availability. Natuzzi is an Italian company that makes leather furniture. The wood Natuzzi buys to make its sofas is a commodity. By contrast, the leather the company uses is graded, meaning each piece of leather is rated based on quality. To some extent, the leather is still a commodity, because once a firm decides to buy a certain grade of leather, every company's leather within that grade is virtually the same.

## 3.3 OEM Offerings or Components

**original equipment manufacturer (OEM)**

A company that assembles and manufactures a product into its final form.

**OEM offerings or components**

Products, or parts, sold by one manufacturer to another that get built into a final product without further modification.

An **original equipment manufacturer (OEM)** is a manufacturer or assembler of a final product. An OEM purchases raw materials, manufactured materials, and component parts and puts them together to make a final product. **OEM offerings or components**, like an on/off switch, are components, or parts, sold by one manufacturer to another that get built into a final product without further modification. If you look at that picture of the Natuzzi couch, you may notice that it sits on metal feet. The metal feet are probably made by a manufacturer other than Natuzzi, making the feet an OEM component. Dell's hard drives installed in computer kiosks like the self-service kiosks in airports that print your boarding passes are another example of OEM components.

## 3.4 MRO Offerings

**Maintenance, repair, and operations (MRO)** offerings refer to products and services used to keep a company functioning. Janitorial supplies are MRO offerings as is hardware used to repair any part of a building or equipment. MRO items are often sold by distributors. However, you can buy many of the same products at a retail store. For example, you can buy nuts and bolts at a hardware store. A business buyer of nuts and bolts, however, will also need repair items that you don't, such as very strong solder used to weld metal. For convenience sake, the buyer would prefer to purchase multiple products from one vendor rather than driving all over town to buy them. So the distributor sends a salesperson to see the buyer. Most distributors of MRO items sell thousands of products, set up online purchasing Web sites for their customers, and provide a number of other services to make life easier for them.

**FIGURE 6.13**

These janitorial products are examples of MRO items. Because most businesses buy MRO items in large quantities and because these firms also need products not available to the general public, they will generally buy these products from a distributor such as T&G Chemical rather than from a retailer.

*© 2010 Jupiterimages Corporation*

## 3.5 Facilitating Offerings

**Facilitating offerings** include products and services that support a company's operations but are not part of the final product it sells. Marketing research services, banking and transportation services, copiers and computers, and other similar products and services fall into this category. Facilitating offerings might not be central to the buyer's business, at least not the way component parts and raw materials are. Yet to the person who is making the buying decision, these offerings can be very important. If you are a marketing manager who is selecting a vendor for marketing research or choosing an advertising agency, your choice could be critical to your own personal success. For this reason, many companies that supply facilitating offerings try to build strong relationships with their clients.

**maintenance, repair, and operations (MRO)**

Offerings used to maintain, repair, and operate the physical assets of an organization.

**facilitating offerings**

Offerings that support an organization's ability to do business but do not go into the final product.

### KEY TAKEAWAY

Business buyers purchase various types of offerings to make their own offerings. Some of the types of products they use are raw materials, manufactured materials, and component parts and assemblies, all of which can become part of an offering. MRO (maintenance, repair, and operations) offerings are those that keep a company's depreciable assets in working order. Facilitating offerings are products and services a company purchases to support its operations but are not part of the firm's final product.

### REVIEW QUESTIONS

1. What types of offerings do businesses buy? How do the offerings differ in terms of how they are marketed?
2. As you learned early in the chapter, consumer offering can belong to different categories depending on how the buyer wants to purchase them. Is the same true for business offerings?

# 4. BRANDING, LABELING, AND PACKAGING

**LEARNING OBJECTIVES**

1. **Understand the branding decisions firms make when they're developing new products.**
2. **Identify the various levels of packaging for new products.**

What comes to mind when someone says Coke or Nike or Microsoft? According to *BusinessWeek* magazine, the Coca-Cola brand is the *strongest* brand in the world. However, a global study of consumers sponsored by Reuters found that Apple has the *best* brand. What is a "brand" and what do these studies mean when they report that one brand is the strongest or the best?

## 4.1 Branding

**brand**

A name, picture, design, or symbol, or combination of those elements, used by a seller to differentiate its offerings from competitors'.

**branding**

A set of activities designed to create a brand and position it in the minds of consumers.

We have mentioned brands periodically throughout this chapter. But what is a brand? A **brand** is a name, picture, design, or symbol, or combination of those items, used by a seller to identify its offerings and to differentiate them from competitors' offerings. **Branding** is the set of activities designed to create a brand and position it in the minds of consumers. Did you know that The Beatles started a recording studio called Apple? When Apple Computer (the iPod company) was formed, Apple Corp., Ltd. (the Beatles' recording studio), sued Apple Computer because two companies with the same name can create confusion among consumers. This wasn't much of a problem when Apple was only selling computers, but following the release of the iPod and launch of Apple's iTunes program, a case could be made that the companies' offerings are similar enough for consumers to confuse the two companies and their products. In fact, it wasn't until very recently that the lawsuit over the name was settled, some thirty years after the initial lawsuit was filed. Nonetheless, the situation signifies how important brand names are to the companies that own them.

A successful branding strategy is one that accomplishes what Coke and Apple have done—it creates consumer recognition of what the brand (signified by its name, picture, design, symbol, and so forth) means. Consequently, when marketing professionals are considering whether a potential new offering fits a company's image, they are very concerned about whether the offering supports the organization's brand and position in the mind of the consumer.

**brand name**

The spoken part of an identity used to describe of a brand.

**brand mark**

A symbol or logo used to identify a brand.

A **brand name**, like Apple, is the spoken part of a brand's identity. A **brand mark** is the symbol, such as Coke's wave or Apple Computer's multicolor apple (not to be confused with Apple Records' green apple), associated with a brand. Brand names and brand marks are important to companies because consumers use them to make choices. That's why it was important to sort out the Apple brand. Each company wanted to make sure that consumers were getting what they wanted and would know what each brand meant.

**brand extension**

The process of utilizing an existing brand name or brand mark for a new product category.

An important decision companies must make is under which brand a new offering will be marketed. For example, Black & Decker makes power tools for consumers under its Black & Decker brand, while tools for more serious do-it-yourselfers and professionals are under its Dewalt brand. If Black & Decker decided to add to its Dewalt line new products such as coolers, portable radios, CD players, and other accessories construction professionals might find useful at a job site, the company would be creating a brand extension. A **brand extension** involves utilizing an existing brand name or brand mark for a new product category.

Why would Black & Decker add these accessories to the Dewalt line? If the company did, it would be because Dewalt already has a good reputation for high quality, long-lasting durability, and performance among construction professionals. These same professionals would trust the Dewalt brand to deliver. How a company like Black & Decker goes about building this trust is the subject of later chapters. For now, let's consider whether it is better for a company to market a new product via a brand extension or create an entirely new brand for the product.

**cannibalization**

When a new product takes sales away from the same company's existing products.

One thing firms have to consider when they're branding a new offering is the degree of cannibalization that can occur across products. **Cannibalization** occurs when a firm's new offering eats into the sales of one of its older offerings. (Ideally, when you sell a new product, you hope that all of its sales come from your competitors' buyers or buyers that are new to the market.) A completely new offering will not result in cannibalization, whereas a line extension likely will. A brand extension will also result in some cannibalization if you sell similar products under another brand. For example, if Black & Decker already had an existing line of coolers, portable radios, and CD players when the Dewalt line of them was launched, the new Dewalt offerings might cannibalize some of the Black & Decker offerings.

Some marketers argue that cannibalization can be a good thing because it is a sign that a company is developing new and better offerings. These people believe that if you don't cannibalize your own line, then your competitors will.

## 4.2 Packaging Decisions

Another set of questions to consider involves the packaging on which a brand's marks and name will be prominently displayed. Sometimes the package itself is part of the brand. For example, the curvaceous shape of Coca-Cola's Coke bottle is a registered trademark. If you decide to market your beverage in a similar-shaped bottle, Coca-Cola's attorneys will have grounds to sue you.

### FIGURE 6.14

Sometimes the package itself is part of a licensed brand. Coke's curvaceous bottle is an example.

*Source: Wikimedia Commons.*

Packaging has to fulfill a number of important functions, including

- communicating the brand and its benefits;
- protecting the product from damage and contamination during shipment, as well as damage and tampering once it's in retail outlets;
- preventing leakage of the contents;
- presenting government-required warning and information labels.

Sometimes packaging can fulfill other functions, such as serving as part of an in-store display designed to promote the offering.

**Primary packaging** holds a single retail unit of a product. For example, a bottle of Coke, a bag of M&Ms, or a ream of printer paper (five hundred sheets) are all examples of primary packages. Primary packaging can be used to protect and promote products and get the attention of consumers. Primary packaging can also be used to demonstrate the proper use of an offering, provide instructions on how to assemble the product, or any other needed information. If warning or nutrition labels are required, they must be on the primary packaging. Primary packaging can be bundled together as well. Consumers can buy bottles of Coke sold in six-packs or cans of Coke in twelve-packs, for example.

**primary packaging**

Packaging designed to hold a single retail unit of a product.

## FIGURE 6.15

A single wholesale unit of a product, such as these empty cartons shown here, is an example of secondary packaging. Each of these boxes might hold, for example, twenty-four cans of car polish or thirty-six cans of bug spray.

**secondary packaging**

Packaging designed to hold a single wholesale unit of a product.

**tertiary packaging**

Packaging designed for the shipping and efficiently handling of large quantities of a product.

**Secondary packaging** holds a single wholesale unit of a product. A case of M&M bags is an example, as are cartons of reams of paper. Secondary packaging is designed more for retailers than consumers. It does not have to carry warning or nutrition labels but is still likely to have brand marks and labels. Secondary packaging further protects the individual products during shipping.

**Tertiary packaging** is packaging designed specifically for shipping and efficiently handling large quantities. When a Coca-Cola bottler ships cases of Cokes to a grocery store, they are stacked on pallets (wooden platforms) and then wrapped in plastic. Pallets can be easily moved by a forklift truck and can even be moved within the grocery store by a small forklift.

## FIGURE 6.16

This product is bound in tertiary packaging so that mass quantities of it can be stacked on pallets and moved with a forklift.

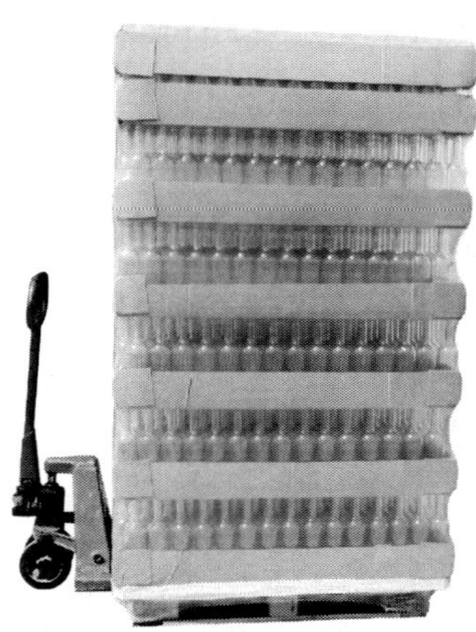

A product's packaging can benefit the customer beyond just protecting the offering while it's being shipped. No-spill caps, for example, can make it easier for you to use your laundry detergent or prevent spills when you're adding oil to your car's engine. And, as we have noted, secondary packaging (and also tertiary packaging) can serve as part of an in-store display, thereby adding value for your retailers.

### KEY TAKEAWAY

A brand is a name, picture, design, or symbol, or combination of those items, used by a seller to identify its offerings and differentiate them from competitors' offerings. Branding is the set of activities designed to create a brand and position it relative to competing brands in the minds of consumers. An important decision companies must make is under which brand a new offering will be marketed. A brand extension involves utilizing an existing brand name or brand mark for a new product or category (line) of products. Cannibalization occurs when a company's new offering eats into the sales of one of its older offerings. It is something to be avoided in most cases, but it can also be a sign of progress because it means a company is developing new and better products. Packaging protects products from damage, contamination, leakage, and tampering, but it is also used to communicate the brand and its benefits, product warnings, and proper use.

### REVIEW QUESTIONS

1. How do brands help companies market their products?
2. What is the purpose of a brand extension?
3. Name the basic types of packaging used in marketing.

# 5. MANAGING THE OFFERING

### LEARNING OBJECTIVES

1. **Understand the people involved in creating and managing offerings.**
2. **Recognize the differences in organizing product marketing for consumer versus B2B companies.**

Managing all of a company's offerings presents a number of challenges. Depending on the size of the company and the breadth of the company's offerings, several positions may be needed.

A brand manager is one such position. A **brand manager** is the person responsible for all business decisions regarding offerings within one brand. By business decisions, we mean making decisions that affect profit and loss, which include such decisions as which offerings to include in the brand, how to position the brand in the market, pricing options, and so forth. Indeed, a brand manager is often charged with running the brand as if it were its own separate business.

**brand manager**

A person responsible for all business decisions regarding offerings within one brand. A brand manager is often charged with running his or her brand as if it is its own separate business.

A brand manager is much more likely to be found in consumer marketing companies. Typically, B2B companies do not have multiple brands so the position is not common in the B2B environment. What you often find in a B2B company is a **product manager**, someone with business responsibility for a particular product or product line. Like the brand manager, the product manager must make many business decisions, such as which offerings to include, advertising selection, and so on. Companies with brand managers include Microsoft, Procter & Gamble, SC Johnson, Kraft, Target, General Mills, and ConAgra Foods. Product managers are found at Xerox, IBM, Konica-Minolta Business Solutions, Rockwell International, and many others.

**product manager**

Someone with business responsibility for a particular product or product line. Like brand managers, product managers must make decisions, such as which offerings to include, advertising selection, and others.

The University of Georgia was the first to launch a graduate program in brand management, but the only major program now being taught in the United States is at the University of Wisconsin. The program is managed through the university's Center for Brand and Product Management. Most brand managers simply have an undergraduate degree in marketing, but it helps to have a strong background in either finance or accounting because of the profitability and volume decisions brand managers have to make. In the United Kingdom, a number of school have undergraduate degree programs specializing in brand management, as does Seneca College in Toronto, Canada.

**category manager**

Someone responsible for managing a broad group of products that may belong to multiple manufacturers.

**market manager**

Someone responsible for managing efforts within a particular market, such as a geographic market or another grouping of customers into a market (e.g., a single industry or size).

**vertical market**

B2B customers that compose a particular industry, such as the health care industry.

**vertical market managers**

Marketing managers who oversee B2B products sold to a particular industry.

In some companies, a **category manager** has responsibility for business decisions within a broad grouping of offerings. For example, a category manager at SC Johnson may have all home cleaning products, which would mean that brands such as Pledge, Vanish, Drano, Fantastik, Windex, Scrubbing Bubbles, and Shout would be that person's responsibility. Each of those brands may be managed by brand manager who then reports directly to the category manager.

At the retail level, a category manager at each store is responsible for more than just one manufacturer's products. The home cleaning category manager would have responsibility for offerings from SC Johnson, as well as Procter & Gamble, Colgate-Palmolive, and many other producers.

Another option is to create a **market manager**, who is responsible for business decisions within a market. In this case, a market can be defined as a geographic market or region; a market segment, such as a type of business; or a channel of distribution. For example, SC Johnson could have regional insect control managers. Regional market managers would make sense for insect control because weather has an influence on which bugs are pests at any given time. For example, a southern regional manager would want more inventory of the repellent Off! in March because it is already warm and the mosquitoes are already breeding and biting in the southern United States.

In B2B markets, a market manager is more likely to be given responsibility for a particular market segment, such as all hospital health care professionals or doctor's offices. All customers such as these (retail, wholesale, and so forth) in a particular industry compose what's called a **vertical market**, and the managers of these markets are called **vertical market managers**. B2B companies organize in this way because

- buying needs and processes are likely to be similar within an industry,
- channels of communication are likely to be the same within an industry but different across industries.

Because magazines, Web sites, and trade shows are organized to serve specific industries or even specific positions within industries, B2B marketers find vertical market structures for marketing departments to be more efficient than organizing by geography.

Market managers sometimes report to brand managers or are a part of their firms' sales organizations and report to sales executives. Market managers are less likely to have as much flexibility in terms of pricing and product decisions and have no control over the communication content of marketing campaigns or marketing strategies. These managers are more likely to be tasked with implementing a product or brand manager's strategy and be responsible for their markets. Some companies have market managers but no brand managers. Instead, marketing vice presidents or other executives are responsible for the brands.

### KEY TAKEAWAY

Brand managers decide what products are to be marketed and how. Other important positions include category managers, market managers, and vertical market managers. Category managers are found in consumer markets, usually in retail. Market managers can be found in both consumer markets and B2B markets. However, vertical market managers are found only in B2B markets. Some companies have market managers but no brand managers. Instead, a vice president of marketing or other executive is responsible for the brands.

### REVIEW QUESTIONS

1. What is a brand manager?
2. How do brand managers differ from category managers?
3. What is a market manager?
4. Which type of manager has the most marketing responsibility?

# 6. DISCUSSION QUESTIONS AND ACTIVITIES

## DISCUSSION QUESTIONS

1. How is marketing capital equipment different from marketing MRO offerings?
2. What are the marketing implications for your company if buyers stop viewing your primary offering as a shopping good and begin considering it a convenience good? How would you respond to the change?
3. Can you market unsought goods? If so, how?
4. How does packaging add value for consumers and retailers?

## ACTIVITIES

1. Identify three television commercials designed to persuade buyers to view the products being advertised as shopping items rather than convenience items. What is similar about the strategies employed in the commercials? Do you think the commercials are successful? Why or why not?
2. Identify a product for which packaging adds value and describe how that value is added for the consumer. Identify a second brand for which the organization uses primary packaging to distinguish the brand at the point of purchase, and describe how the package contributes to the branding. Do not use brands used as examples in the chapter. Finally, identify a pure service brand and describe how that service is "packaged."
3. Coach has successfully reinvented and expanded its brand to appeal to new markets in previously untapped categories. Explain how the company has used a brand extension strategy and provide specific examples. (Hint: Coach partnered with Lexus.)

# CHAPTER 7
# Developing and Managing Offerings

Having something that customers want to buy is important to any company. Most companies are started by people who get an idea about how to make something better. Hewlett-Packard, for example, began in 1939 in a garage (now a California Historic Landmark) when two young engineers, Bill Hewlett and Dave Packard, thought they had a better idea for designing and making a precision audio oscillator, which is an electronic device that tests sound. Their product was so much more precise than competitors' products that it was manufactured and sold around the world for over thirty years. In fact, it is probably one of the longest-selling electronic devices ever. It also sold for just $54, whereas competing products sold for over $200. Hewlett-Packard, now more commonly known as HP, has not been located in a little garage for many years. Yet the company's ability to grow by successfully designing and marketing new offerings continues.

Developing new offerings is a constant process in most companies. In some instances, a company starts with a price and then develops products and services to fit that price. IKEA is an example of a company that does this. IKEA looks at the various prices consumers want to pay for home furnishings and then works backward to design products that match those prices (using a demand backward pricing strategy is discussed in Chapter 15). In other situations, the goal is simply to develop a better product that adds value to existing products, and the price comes later. Hewlett-Packard's audio oscillator is an example of this type of product.

**FIGURE 7.1**

Hewlett-Packard was founded in this California garage, which is now a national landmark.

*Source: Wikimedia Commons.*

Keep in mind that a "new" product can be a "new and improved" product, such as laundry detergent; an addition to a product or service line, such as Marriott adding the Courtyard by Marriott and the Fairfield Inn (see Chapter 6) or Capri Sun adding new flavors; a repositioned product or company, such as Hyundai Motor Company trying to change the perceptions of Hyundai automobiles from being inexpensive to being "an overachieving, underappreciated brand that smart people are discovering";[1] or a totally new innovation, such as the mobile phone. What is new for one company may not be new to another. For example, one hotel may already have budget properties, but when a luxury hotel adds a budget property, that property is considered a new offering for them.

# 1. THE NEW OFFERING DEVELOPMENT PROCESS

**LEARNING OBJECTIVES**

1. Identify an effective process for creating offerings and bringing them to market.
2. Understand the relative importance of each step in the new offering development process and the functions within each step.
3. Distinguish between the various forms of testing and analysis that take place before a new offering is brought to the market.

Most new offerings go through similar stages in their development process. Although the size of a company will affect how the different stages of their new product development process are conducted and whether products are test marketed before being introduced, the steps are generally the same. Figure 7.2 summarizes these steps.

**FIGURE 7.2** The New Offering Development Process

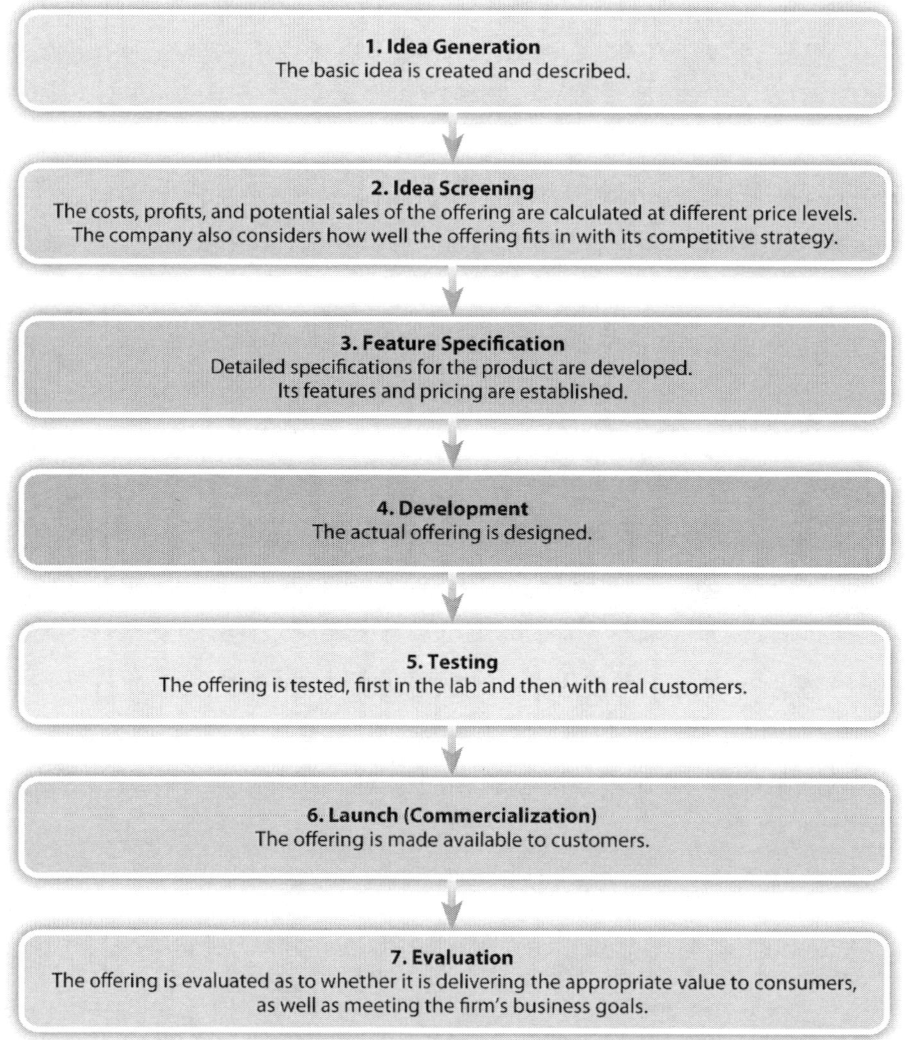


## 1.1 Idea Generation

Many companies, HP and Apple included, were launched in someone's garage after the founders got an idea for a product and then tried to make and sell it. HP's first product was an audio oscillator that two Stanford University students developed. While there was some debate, Apple's Macintosh microcomputer appeared to be a low-cost knockoff of the Xerox Star, a software-equipped workstation. Apple's cofounder, Steve Jobs, saw the product demonstrated at a Xerox research center.[2]

## FIGURE 7.3

Ideas can come from anywhere. A Motorola employee came up with an idea for a new cell phone while rollerblading. His idea was to use the wheels of the roller blades to generate electricity to charge a cell phone or MP3 player.

Employees often come up with new product ideas, too. At Motorola, engineers are working on a mobile phone that can be recharged by rubbing it on smooth surface. A Motorola engineer came up with the idea while rollerblading. He wondered if a small generator could be created to capture and store the energy generated by rollerblade wheels. This idea, in turn, led to the development of a small roller ball (like you would find on an old-style computer mouse) built into the mobile phone. To power up the phone, you just give it a roll.

Ideas can come from anywhere, including your customers. In fact, in business-to-business (B2B) markets, customers are probably the biggest source of new product ideas. Customers know what customers need and want, which provides organizations an indication of market needs. Customers who are good at generating new product ideas or applications of products are called **lead users**. These people are often courted by manufacturers for this purpose. Lead users exist in consumer markets, too. JCPenney, for example, utilizes a panel of women who help develop the company's Ambrielle line of lingerie products.

**lead users**

Potential customers who are innovative and develop new applications or new products for their own use without the aid of a supplier.

Customers are particularly important cocreators of offerings when they are consuming products with service components. For example, if you provide your hairdresser with feedback while your hair is being cut, your input will alter the final style you receive. Similarly, a businessperson who provides her certified public accountant (CPA) with information and feedback about her firm will help the CPA develop better financial and tax plans for her business.

Suppliers provide another source of ideas for new products. A supplier might develop a new product or technology that can be used to make yet another product, and then go to the makers of those products and suggest new versions of them. For example, McClancy Seasoning Co. makes spices that restaurants and food processing companies use in their food products. McClancy's research and development department works with companies such as Campbell's to help them develop new and better offerings (for more information, visit http://www.mcclancy.com/research_and_development.asp).

**FIGURE 7.4**

Campbell's creates many new products, including varieties of their Pace products, that may result from working with their suppliers.

*Source: Wikimedia Commons.*

**line extension**

A new idea or offering that occurs when a company comes out with another model (related product or service) based on the same platform and brand as one of its other products.

Of course, companies also watch their competitors to see what they're doing. Some offerings are protected by patents or copyrights and can't be legally duplicated. The software that runs Apple's iPhone is an example. There are, however, different ways to achieve the same results as Apple has with its iPhone. The Omnia, manufactured by Samsung, and the G1, a T-Mobile product, are devices similar to the iPhone that operate with software serving the same purpose.

Figure 7.5 shows some product ideas that came from each of the sources we have discussed—employees, customers, suppliers, and one's competitors. Innovations like the iPhone are rare. However, many new ideas (and consequently new products) aren't actually new but rather are versions of products and services already available. A **line extension** occurs when a company comes out with another model (related product) based on the same platform and brand as one of its other products. When Apple added the Nano and the Shuffle to its iPod line, these were line extensions.

**FIGURE 7.5** New Offering Ideas

**And Then There Was ... Sources of New Offering Ideas**

Customers: Kraft maintains a discussion board at its Web site (http://www.kraft.com), from which new product ideas are gathered from customers.

Employees: A FedEx manager wonders if customers would like to track their shipments themselves after realizing that the company's customer service department is having difficulty handling the number of tracking-request calls it's receiving, most of which are routine. FedEx's online tracking system is the result (although they started with sending the information on a disk).

Suppliers: DuPont creates a new livelier rubber, a product it then sells to Titleist, which makes the rubber into the center for a new golf ball brand.

Competitors: Microsoft sees the success of the iPod and develops the Zune.

Keep in mind that idea generation is typically the least expensive step in the process of developing a new offering, whether you involve customers or not. As you move through the product development process, each step is usually more expensive than the last. Ideas for new products are relatively cheap and easy to generate; what is difficult and expensive is making them a reality.

## 1.2 Idea Screening

Not all new product ideas are good ones. Famous product blunders include Ford Motor Company's Edsel, Clear Pepsi, and Coca-Cola's New Coke. Less famous is Dell's cell phone for aging baby boomers. The phone's large size, large buttons, and large screen screamed "I'm old and blind!" leading potential users to shun it in droves. Yes, even the big companies make mistakes.

The purpose of idea screening is to try to avoid mistakes early in the development process. The sooner bad ideas are discarded, the less the investment made and lost. In the idea screening stage, the company tries to evaluate the new offering by answering these questions:

- Does the proposed product add value for the customer? Does it satisfy a market need?
- Can the product be made within a stated time period to get it to market when needed?
- How many units of it will sell and at what price?
- Can we manufacture and sell the product within budget and still make money?
- Do we need to provide the customer with after-sales service? If so, do we have the resources to do that?
- Does the product fit our image and corporate strategy?

Some organizations conduct concept testing at this stage. **Concept testing** involves running the idea of the offering by potential consumers. The purpose is to get early consumer feedback before investing too much money in an offering that won't work. Some of the methods used to test concepts include **focus groups**, in which groups of eight to twelve consumers gather and react to the concept, and **depth interviews**, in which individuals are presented with the concept and can react to it individually. Focus groups and depth interviews are research techniques that can also be used later in the offering development process to test ideas, or for other purposes. Focus groups working virtually on the Web and by phone actually helped to develop this textbook. Concepts may also be tested online by creating an image and having people representative of the target market provide feedback. Whether using focus groups, depth interviewing, or online methods, concepts must be evaluated by people representative of the target market or the feedback is not relevant.

Because screening considers the feasibility of actually making and servicing an offering, price and cost are important components. If the company cannot sell the product in sufficient quantities to generate a profit, the idea must be scrapped. Understanding the customer's personal value equation (defined in Chapter 1) is an important consideration, too. If the value consumers receive from the product is less than the price the company charges for it, they will not buy it. In other words, the offering must be financially feasible to justify investing in it.

The offering must also have process feasibility. **Process feasibility** is the degree to which the company can actually make and service the product. Process feasibility affects **financial feasibility**. If the product's costs cannot be controlled when it's being made or serviced, the firm's financial goals won't be met. Process feasibility also affects customer satisfaction. For example, many manufacturers make great-looking faucets, yet one of your authors had to have the "guts" of one faucet replaced three times before it would work, only to find two other friends had the same experience with the same model. A great-looking design is really only great if it works right.

**FIGURE 7.6**

Better idea screening might have helped Coca-Cola avoid the problems it encountered marketing its "New Coke" formula.

*Source: Wikimedia Commons.*

**concept testing**

Presenting an idea for an offering (including possible marketing communication ideas) to consumers for their reaction early in the offering development process.

**focus group**

A group of potential buyers brought together to discuss a marketing research topic with one another.

**depth interview**

An exploratory research technique of engaging in detailed, one-on-one, question-and-answer sessions with potential buyers.

**process feasibility**

The degree to which the manufacturing of a product or the delivery of a service can be done within the proper quality specifications on a repeatable basis; the degree to which an organization can actually make and service an offering.

**financial feasibility**

A new offering's ability to make money.

FIGURE 7.7

A good product doesn't just look right. It also works right, which is the idea behind process feasibility.

*Source: Wikimedia Commons.*

The question of strategic fit is a difficult one. The history of business is rife with examples of companies failing to develop winning new products only to see their competitors do so. For example, when the inventor Chester Carlson approached IBM executives with the idea of photocopying—the technology platform that later became the heart of Xerox Corporation—they turned Carlson down. IBM did not see the product fitting with its strategy and stopped before they fully considered the potential. Nor did IBM see the moneymaking opportunity the product presented.

At this point in the process, the company begins to assess two types of risk. The first is **investment risk**, or the possibility that the company will fail to earn the appropriate return on the money and effort (the investment) it puts into the new product. The second is **opportunity risk**, or the risk that there is a better idea that gets ignored because the firm has invested in the idea at hand. When a company is assessing fit, it is assessing its opportunity risk. When it is assessing feasibility (both financial and process), it is assessing its investment risk. Other risk-related questions include whether or not the offering can be developed on time and within budget. Assessing a product's feasibility continues throughout the entire new product development process.

**investment risk**

The potential of losing one's money and time should a new offering fail.

**opportunity risk**

The potential loss of revenue a company risks when it chooses an alternative course of action such as launching a different offering.

## 1.3 Feature Specification

The next step involves narrowing down the product's features. Again, price enters the picture as the company considers which features are important to consumers at different price points. A premium (high-priced) offering is likely to be loaded with extra features. By contrast, a low-priced offering is likely to be a "bare-bones" product with few features.

**Quality function deployment (QFD)** is a process whereby a company begins with the customer's desired benefits and then designs an offering that delivers those benefits. The benefits are linked to certain characteristics of the offering, which are then broken down into component-part characteristics. From this list of component parts, the product is designed. Thus, the feature specifications process begins with a strong understanding of what consumers want and need.

**quality function deployment (QFD)**

A specific process for designing new offerings that begins by specifying a customer's requirements and then designing a product to meet those needs.

HP has developed a number of computer printers using the QFD process. The QFD process has been particularly helpful when it comes to bundling the right features within the HP's printer line because each printer model can be targeted to specific customer needs. Customers can then purchase the model that best suits their needs and doesn't have a bunch of features that don't add value for them.

## 1.4 Development

In the development stage, the actual offering is designed, specifications for it are written, and prototypes of it are developed. It is also during this stage that the firm considers the product's manufacturing process. For example, when a restaurant is developing a new dish, it must not only taste good; it must also be a dish that can be made in a reasonable amount of time once it's ordered and prepared at a cost that earns the restaurant a profit. In terms of a manufacturer's offerings, using the same technology platform as another product (like Apple has done with iPods) can be very effective and cheaper. Using the same platform also generally makes it easier for a company to train its technicians to service a new product.

## 1.5 Testing

During the testing stage, the offering is tested, first in the lab and then with real customers. Lab testing is also called **alpha testing**. Alpha testing ensures that the offering works like it's supposed to in a variety of different environments—that it meets its specifications, that is. For example, Kraft might launch a new food product that has to work in hot climates, cold climates, high humidity, dry climates, and high altitudes—all conditions that can change how well the product works.

**alpha testing**

The testing of a product in a laboratory setting.

The next step is beta testing. During **beta testing**, actual customers make sure the offering works under real-world conditions. Beta testing not only tests whether the offering works as advertised but also tests the offering's delivery mechanisms, service processes, and other aspects of marketing the product. This step can be an expensive. Depending on the product, some companies might find it better to simply launch the product and let the market respond to, or test, it once it is available for purchase.

**beta testing**

The testing of a product by real customer in the customer's location.

In B2B settings, beta tests are usually conducted with lead users and preferred customers. The developer of the product needs a strong relationship with these customers because the product might still have bugs that need to be ironed out. If the relationship between the parties is "iffy," and the product or service needs a significant amount of changes, beta testing could damage the relationship between the two parties and hurt the developer of the product's sales.

Simultaneous to testing the offering's ability to meet its specs, the company is also developing and testing the marketing communication plan that will be used to launch the product. Many companies involve consumer panels or user communities, both for testing the offering and the communication plan. As we mentioned, JCPenney solicits the advice of a user community for its Ambrielle line of lingerie (you can listen to Laura Carros, who developed the community, in Chapter 14). The company frequently runs concepts by the group as well as sends actual prototypes to users to try on and report back to the company. Similarly, the data warehousing company Teradata has a "partners" organization that consists of a community of users who participate in the firm's product design and testing.

## 1.6 Launch or Commercialization

Once an offering has been designed and tested, it is made available to customers. Sometimes a company launches the offering to all of its markets at once. Other companies may use a **rolling launch** in which the offering is made available to certain markets first and then other markets later. A rolling launch might make sense if the company's service technicians need training. The company makes the offering available to one market after the first batch of its employees are prepared to service the product; then as new batches of employees are prepared to service the product, the company enters more markets. See the following video clip for an example of a new product launch.

**rolling launch**

Introducing a new offering across markets one by one in order to work out any challenges or problems related to marketing and supporting the offering.

**Video Clip**

**Example of a Successful New Product Launch**

This YouTube video documents the launch of Apple's iPhone 3G.

View the video online at: http://www.youtube.com/embed/4yVQJ6jJPak

Some companies test the complete launch of a product's marketing plan to ensure that it reaches buyers, gets positive feedback, and generates sales of the product or service. This is called a **market test**. Companies may conduct market tests in limited markets or nationwide. For example, when one beverage maker tested the marketing plan for a new wine cooler, the firm first launched the product on the east coast, where the beverage was promoted as a "Polynesian" drink; on the west coast, the beverage was promoted as an "Australian" drink. The Polynesian version proved more popular, so in other new markets, that's how the beverage was advertised and packaged.

**market test**

The test launch of a product's complete marketing plan to ensure that it reaches buyers, gets positive reactions, and generates sales of the product.

## 1.7 Evaluation

Once an offering is launched, a firm's executives carefully monitor its progress. You have probably heard about the "box office" sales for new movies the first weekend following their release. The first weekend is a good predictor of how much money a movie will make overall. If the ticket sales for it are high during the first weekend, a studio's executives might decide to beef up the promotions for it. If the ticket sales for the movie are low, the studio might stop screening the movie in theaters altogether and release it on DVD instead. For other types of offerings, important milestones might be the first ninety days after the product is launched, followed by a second period of ninety days, and so forth. However, be aware that firms are constantly in the process of evaluating their offerings and modifying them by either adding or subtracting the features and services associated with them, changing their prices, or how they are marketed. The length of time for milestones used to evaluate products may vary depending on the organization and other products or services being developed.

**KEY TAKEAWAY**

Most companies put new offering ideas through a seven-step process, beginning with the idea generation stage. Ideas for new offerings can come from anywhere including one's customers, employees, customers, suppliers, and competitors. The next step in the process is the idea screening stage, followed by the feature specifications, development, testing, and launching stages. After an offering is launched, it is evaluated. A company must balance an offering's investment risk (the risk associated with losing the time and money put into developing the offering) against the offering's opportunity risk (the risk associated with missing the opportunity to market the product and profit from it).

**REVIEW QUESTIONS**

1. What are the seven steps in the offering development process? What are the key activities in each step?
2. Who are lead users?
3. How should a company evaluate new ideas? What are the criteria?
4. How does quality function deployment work?

# 2. MANAGING NEW PRODUCTS: THE PRODUCT LIFE CYCLE

**LEARNING OBJECTIVES**

1. **Explain how organizations manage offerings after being introduced to the marketplace.**
2. **Explain how managing an offering may be different in international markets.**
3. **Explain the product life cycle and the objectives and strategies for each stage.**

Over 20,000 new offerings, including convenience foods, health and beauty aids, electronics, automobiles, pharmaceutical products, hotels, restaurants, and so on, enter the marketplace each year. For example, in 2006 almost 1,400 food products making a "whole grain claim" were introduced.[3] Other recent new product introductions include many technological products such as Nintendo's Wii, iPods, and digital video recorders (DVRs); many new personal care products such as new fragrances of shampoo and conditioner and new flavors of toothpaste; and new convenience foods such as frozen meals, "100 calorie pack" snacks, and cereal bars.[4]

**Video Clip**

**Oreo 100 Calorie Pack**

The 100 Calorie Packs offered by Nabisco proved to be extremely popular.

View the video online at: http://www.youtube.com/embed/ZNfqKHSkL7o

Once a product is created and introduced in the marketplace, the offering must be managed effectively for the customer to receive value from it. Only if this is done will the product's producer achieve its profit objectives and be able to sustain the offering in the marketplace. The process involves making many complex decisions, especially if the product is being introduced in global markets. Before introducing products in global markets, an organization must evaluate and understand factors in the external environment, including laws and regulations, the economy and stage of economic development, the competitors and substitutes, cultural values, and market needs. Companies also need expertise to successfully launch products in foreign markets. Given many possible constraints in international markets, companies might initially introduce a product in limited areas abroad. Other organizations, such as Coca-Cola, decide to compete in markets worldwide.[5]

**product life cycle (PLC)**

The stages (introduction, growth, maturity, decline) that a product may go through over time.

The **product life cycle (PLC)** includes the stages the product goes through after development, from introduction to the end of the product. Just as children go through different phases in life (toddler, elementary school, adolescent, young adult, and so on), products and services also age and go through different stages. The PLC is a beneficial tool that helps marketers manage the stages of a product's acceptance and success in the marketplace, beginning with the product's introduction, its growth in market share, maturity, and possible decline in market share. Other tools such as the Boston Consulting Group matrix and the General Electric approach (see Chapter 2 for discussion) may also be used to manage and make decisions about what to do with products. For example, when a market is no longer growing but the product is doing well (cash cow in the BCG approach), the company may decide to use the money from the cash cow to invest in other products they have rather than continuing to invest in the product in a no-growth market (see Chapter 2).

The product life cycle can vary for different products and different product categories. Figure 7.8 illustrates an example of the product life cycle, showing how a product can move through four stages. However, not all products go through all stages and the length of a stage varies. For example, some products never experience market share growth and are withdrawn from the market.

**FIGURE 7.8** Life Cycle

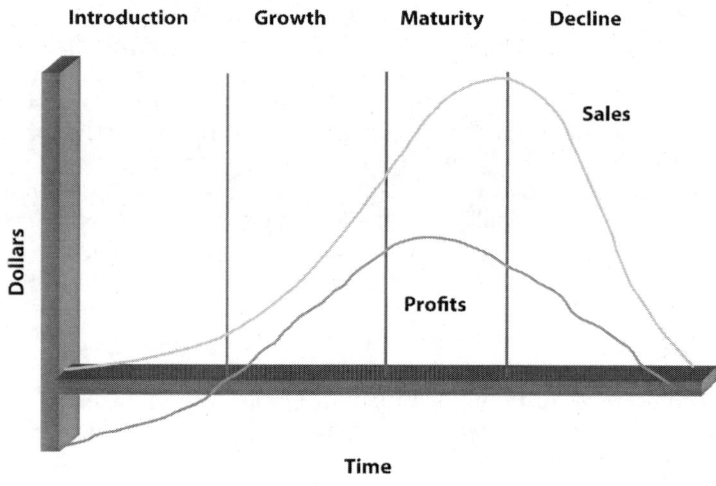

FIGURE 7.9

Diet Coke changed its can to keep from getting outdated.

*Source: Wikimedia Commons.*

Other products stay in one stage longer than others. For example, in 1992, PepsiCo introduced a product called Clear Pepsi, which went from introduction to decline very rapidly. By contrast, Diet Coke entered the growth market soon after its introduction in the early 1980s and then entered (and remains in) the mature stage of the product life cycle. New computer products and software and video games often have limited life cycles, whereas product categories such as diamonds and durable goods (kitchen appliances) generally have longer life cycles. How a product is promoted, priced, distributed, or modified can also vary throughout its life cycle. Let's now look at the various product life cycle stages and what characterizes each.

## 2.1 The Introduction Stage

**introduction stage**

The first stage of the product life cycle after a product is launched.

The first stage in a product's life cycle is the **introduction stage**. The introduction stage is the same as commercialization, or the last stage of the new product development process. Marketing costs are typically higher in this stage than in other stages. As an analogy, think about the amount of fuel a plane needs for takeoff relative to the amount it needs while in the air. Just as an airplane needs more fuel for takeoff, a new product or service needs more funds for introduction into the marketplace. Communication (promotion) is needed to generate awareness of the product and persuade consumers to try it, and placement alternatives and supply chains are needed to deliver the product to the customers. Profits are often low in the introductory stage due to the research and development costs and the marketing costs necessary to launch the product.

The length of the introductory stage varies for different products. However, by law in the United States, a company is only allowed to use the label "new" on a product's package for six months. An organization's objectives during the introductory stage often involve educating potential customers about its value and benefits, creating awareness, and getting potential customers to try the product or service. Getting products and services, particularly multinational brands, accepted in foreign markets can take even longer. Consequently, companies introducing products and services abroad generally must have the financial resources to make a long-term (longer than one year) commitment to their success.

The specific promotional strategies a company uses to launch a product vary depending on the type of product and the number of competitors it faces in the market. Firms that manufacture products such as cereals, snacks, toothpastes, soap, and shampoos often use mass marketing techniques such as television commercials and Internet campaigns and promotional programs such as coupons and sampling to reach consumers (pull strategy; see Chapter 11). To reach wholesalers and retailers such as Walmart, Target, and grocery stores, firms utilize personal selling (push strategy; see Chapter 11). Many firms promote to customers, retailers, and wholesalers. Sometimes other, more targeted advertising strategies are employed, such as billboards and transit signs (signs on buses, taxis, subways, and so on). For more technical or expensive products such as computers or plasma televisions, many firms utilize personal selling, informational promotions, and in-store demonstrations so consumers can see how the products work.

FIGURE 7.10

Many new convenient snack packages, such as jelly snacks and packages of different sizes, are available in China and the United States.

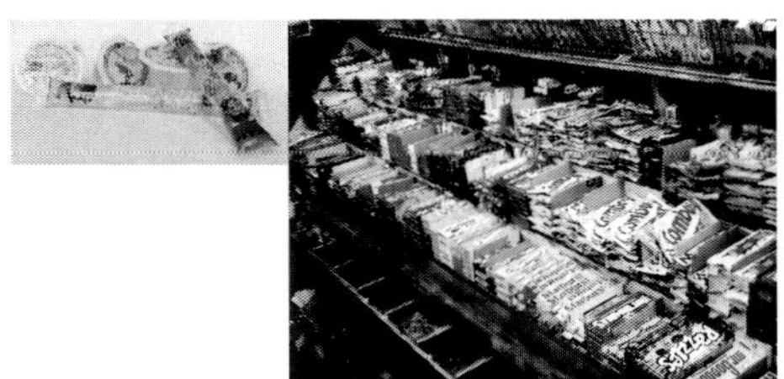

*Source: Wikimedia Commons.*

During introduction, an organization must have enough distribution outlets (places where the product is sold or the service is available) to get the product or service to the customers. The product quantities must also be available to meet demand. For example, IBM's ThinkPad was a big hit when it was first introduced, but the demand for it was so great that IBM wasn't able to produce enough of the product. Cooperation from a company's supply chain members—its manufacturers, wholesalers, and so forth—helps ensure that supply meets demand and that value is added throughout the process.

When you were growing up, you may remember eating Rice Krispies Treats cereal, a very popular product. The product was so popular that Kellogg's could not keep up with initial demand and placed ads to consumers apologizing for the problem. When demand is higher than supply, the door opens for competitors to enter the market, which is what happened when the microwave was introduced. Most people own a microwave, and prices have dropped significantly since Amana introduced the first microwave at a price of almost $500. As consumers in the United States initially saw and heard about the product, sales increased from forty thousand units to over a million units in only a few years. Sales in Japan increased even more rapidly due to a lower price. As a result of the high demand in both countries, many competitors entered the market and prices dropped.[6]

Product pricing strategies in the introductory stage can vary depending on the type of product, competing products, the extra value the product provides consumers versus existing offerings, and the costs of developing and producing the product. Organizations want consumers to perceive that a new offering is better or more desirable than existing products. Two strategies that are widely used in the introductory stage are penetration pricing and skimming. A **penetration pricing strategy** involves using a low initial price to encourage many customers to try a product. The organization hopes to sell a high volume in order to generate substantial revenues. New varieties of cereals, fragrances of shampoo, scents of detergents, and snack foods are often introduced at low initial prices. Seldom does a company utilize a high price strategy with a product such as this. The low initial price of the product is often combined with advertising, coupons, samples, or other special incentives to increase awareness of the product and get consumers to try it.

**penetration pricing strategy**

A strategy in which an organization offers a low initial price on a product so that it captures as much market share as possible.

A company uses a **skimming pricing strategy**, which involves setting a high initial price for a product, to more quickly recoup the investment related to its development and marketing. The skimming strategy attracts the top, or high end, of the market. Generally this market consists of customers who are not as price sensitive or who are early adopters of products. Firms that produce electronic products such as DVRs, plasma televisions, and digital cameras set their prices high in the introductory stage. However, the high price must be consistent with the nature of the product as well as the other marketing strategies being used to promote it. For example, engaging in more personal selling to customers, running ads targeting specific groups of customers, and placing the product in a limited number of distribution outlets are likely to be strategies firms use in conjunction with a skimming approach.

**skimming pricing strategy**

A high initial price that companies set when introducing new products in order to get back money invested.

## 2.2 The Growth Stage

If a product is accepted by the marketplace, it enters the growth stage of the product life cycle. The **growth stage** is characterized by increasing sales, more competitors, and higher profits. Unfortunately for the firm, the growth stage attracts competitors who enter the market very quickly. For example, when Diet Coke experienced great success, Pepsi soon entered with Diet Pepsi. You'll notice that both Coca-Cola and Pepsi have similar competitive offerings in the beverage industry, including their own brands of bottled water, juice, and sports drinks. As additional customers begin to buy the product, manufacturers must ensure that the product remains available to customers or run the risk of them buying competitors' offerings. For example, the producers of video game systems such as Nintendo's Wii could not keep up with consumer demand when the product was first launched. Consequently, some consumers purchased competing game systems such as Microsoft's Xbox.

**growth stage**

The stage of the life cycle in which sales increase and more competitors enter the market.

A company sometimes increases its promotional spending on a product during its growth stage. However, instead of encouraging consumers to try the product, the promotions often focus on the specific benefits the product offers and its value relative to competitive offerings. In other words, although the company must still inform and educate customers, it must counter the competition. Emphasizing the advantages of the product's brand name can help a company maintain its sales in the face of competition. Although different organizations produce personal computers, a highly recognized brand such as IBM strengthens a firm's advantage when competitors enter the market. New offerings that utilize the same successful brand name as a company's already existing offerings, which is what Black & Decker does with some of its products, can give a company a competitive advantage. Companies typically begin to make a profit during the growth stage because more units are being sold and more revenue is generated.

The number of distribution outlets (stores and dealers) utilized to sell the product can also increase during the growth stage as a company tries to reach as much of the marketplace as possible. Expanding a product's distribution and increasing its production to ensure its availability at different outlets usually results in a product's costs remaining high during the growth stage. The price of the product itself typically remains at about the same level during the growth stage, although some companies reduce their prices slightly to attract additional buyers and meet the competitors' prices. Companies hope by increasing their sales, they also improve their profits.

**FIGURE 7.11**

Demand for the Nintendo Wii increased sharply after the product's introduction.

*Source: Wikimedia Commons.*

## 2.3 The Maturity Stage

**maturity stage**

The stage of the product life cycle at which sales begin to level off and competitors have saturated the market.

After many competitors enter the market and the number of potential new customers declines, the sales of a product typically begin to level off. This indicates that a product has entered the **maturity stage** of its life cycle. Most consumer products are in the mature stage of their life cycle; their buyers are repeat purchasers versus new customers. Intense competition causes profits to fall until only the strongest players remain. The maturity stage lasts longer than other stages. Quaker Oats and Ivory Soap are products in the maturity stage—they have been on the market for over one hundred years.

### Video Clip

**Quaker Oats Packaging**

Quaker Oats was introduced over one hundred years ago and is still in the maturity stage although the package has been changed.

View the video online at: http://www.youtube.com/embed/a0Q8jp1-ehE

Given the competitive environment in the maturity stage, many products are promoted heavily to consumers by stronger competitors. The strategies used to promote the products often focus on value and benefits that give the offering a competitive advantage. The promotions aimed at a company's distributors may also increase during the mature stage. Companies may decrease the price of mature products to counter the competition. However, they must be careful not to get into "price wars" with their competitors and destroy all the profit potential of their markets, threatening a firm's survival. Intel and Advanced Micro Devices (AMD) have engaged in several price wars with regard to their microprocessors. Likewise, Samsung added features and lowered the price on its Instinct mobile phone, engaging in a price war with Apple's iPhone. With the weakened economy, many online retailers engaged in price wars during the 2008 holiday season by cutting prices on their products and shipping costs. Although large organizations such as Amazon.com can absorb shipping costs, price wars often hurt smaller retailers. Many retailers learned from their mistakes and ordered less inventory for the 2009 holiday season.

Companies are challenged to develop strategies to extend the maturity stage of their products so they remain competitive. Many firms do so by modifying their target markets, their offerings, or their marketing strategies. Next, we look at each of these strategies.

Modifying the target market helps a company attract different customers by seeking new users, going after different market segments, or finding new uses for a product in order to attract additional customers. Financial institutions and automobile dealers realized that women have increased buying power and now market to them. With the growth in the number of online shoppers, more organizations sell their products and services through the Internet. Entering new markets provides companies an opportunity to extend the product life cycles of their different offerings.

Many companies enter different geographic markets or international markets as a strategy to get new users. A product that might be in the mature stage in one country might be in the introductory stage in another market. For example, when the U.S. market became saturated, McDonald's began opening restaurants in foreign markets. Cell phones were very popular in Asia before they were introduced in the United States. Many cell phones in Asia are being used to scan coupons and to charge purchases. However, the market in the United States might not be ready for that type of technology.

FIGURE 7.12 McDonald's in China

*Source: Wikimedia Commons.*

Modifying the product, such as changing its packaging, size, flavors, colors, or quality can also extend the product's maturity stage. The 100 Calorie Packs created by Nabisco provide an example of how a company changed the packaging and size to provide convenience and one-hundred-calorie portions for consumers. While the sales of many packaged foods fell, the sales of the 100 Calorie Packs increased to over $200 million, prompting Nabisco to repackage more products.[7] Kraft Foods extended the mature stage of different crackers such as Wheat Thins and Triscuits by creating different flavors. Although not popular with consumers, many companies **downsize** (or decrease) the package sizes of their products or the amount of the product in the packages to save money and keep prices from rising too much.

Car manufacturers modify their vehicles slightly each year to offer new styles and new safety features. Every three to five years, automobile manufacturers do more extensive modifications. Changing the package or adding variations or features are common ways to extend the mature stage of the life cycle. Pepsi recently changed the design and packaging of its soft drinks and Tropicana juice products. However, consumers thought the new juice package looked like a less expensive brand, which made the quality of the product look poorer. As a result, Pepsi resumed the use of the original Tropicana carton. Pepsi's redesigned soda cans also received negative consumer reviews.

FIGURE 7.13

Older consumers in international markets are being targeted with different products.

© 2010 Jupiterimages Corporation

## Video Clip

**Pepsi Rebranding**

Changing packing designs does not always help the brand.

View the video online at: http://www.youtube.com/embed/tZJRJy0UK4g

**downsize**

To decrease the size of the package or the amount of product in the package.

FIGURE 7.14 Pepsi's New Can

*Source: Wikimedia Commons.*

## Video Clip

**Tropicana's New Packaging**

Tropicana's new (and now abandoned) packaging look didn't compare well with the "orange and the straw" but is still used on the lower-calorie Tropicana.

View the video online at: http://www.youtube.com/embed/_GzVpG3jfR4

**standardized**

Keeping a product or service the same in all markets.

**adaptation**

The changes that an organization must make for a product or service to fit the local culture.

When introducing products to international markets, firms must decide if the product can be **standardized** (kept the same) or how much, if any, **adaptation**, or changing, of the product to meet the needs of the local culture is necessary. Although it is much less expensive to standardize products and promotional strategies, cultural and environmental differences usually require some adaptation. Product colors and packages as well as product names must often be changed because of cultural differences. For example, in many Asian and European countries, Coca-Cola's diet drinks are called "light," not diet. GE makes smaller appliances such as washers and dryers for the Japanese market. Hyundai Motor Company had to improve the quality of its automobiles in order to compete in the U.S. market. Companies must also examine the external environment in foreign markets since the regulations, competition, and economic conditions vary as well as the cultures.

**FIGURE 7.15**

In Europe, diet drinks are called "light," not diet. This Coca-Cola product is available in Germany.

*Source: Wikimedia Commons.*

Some companies modify the marketing strategy for one or more marketing variables of their products. For example, many coffee shops and fast-food restaurants such as McDonald's now offer specialty coffee that competes with Starbucks. As a result, Starbucks' managers a decided it was time to change the company's strategy. Over the years, Starbucks had added lunch offerings and moved away from grinding coffee in the stores to provide faster service for its customers. However, customers missed the coffee shop atmosphere and the aroma of freshly brewed coffee and didn't like the smell of all the lunch items.

As a result of falling market share, Starbucks' former CEO and founder Howard Schultz returned to the company. Schultz hired consultants to determine how to modify the firm's offering and extend the maturity stage of their life cycle. Subsequently, Starbucks changed the atmosphere of many of its stores back to that of traditional coffee shops, modified its lunch offerings in many stores, and resumed grinding coffee in stores to provide the aroma customers missed. The company also modified some of its offerings to provide health-conscious consumers lower-calorie alternatives.[8] After the U.S. economy weakened in 2009, Starbucks announced it would begin selling instant coffee for about a dollar a cup to appeal to customers who were struggling financially but still wanted a special cup of coffee. The firm also changed its communication with customers by utilizing more interactive media such as blogs.

Whereas Starbucks might have overexpanded, McDonald's plans to add fourteen thousand coffee bars to selected stores.[9] In addition to the coffee bars, many McDonald's stores are remodeling their interiors to feature flat screen televisions, recessed lighting, and wireless Internet access. Other McDonald's restaurants kept their original design, which customers still like.

FIGURE 7.16

The oldest operating McDonald's is in California.

*Source: Wikimedia Commons.*

## 2.4 The Decline Stage

When sales decrease and continue to drop to lower levels, the product has entered the **decline stage** of the product life cycle. In the decline stage, changes in consumer preferences, technological advances, and alternatives that satisfy the same need can lead to a decrease in demand for a product. How many of your fellow students do you think have used a typewriter, adding machine, or slide rule? Computers replaced the typewriter and calculators replaced adding machines and the slide rule. Ask your parents about eight-track tapes, which were popular before cassette tapes, which were popular before CDs. Some products decline slowly. Others go through a rapid level of decline. Many fads and fashions for young people tend to have very short life cycles and go "out of style" very quickly. (If you've ever asked your parents to borrow clothes from the 1990s, you may be amused at how much the styles have changed.) Similarly, many students don't have landline phones or VCR players and cannot believe that people still use the "outdated" devices. Similarly, payphones are rapidly becoming obsolete.

**decline stage**

The stage of the life cycle at which sales drop and companies must decide whether to keep, modify, or drop a product.

Technical products such as digital cameras, cell phones, and video games that appeal to young people often have limited life cycles. Companies must decide what strategies to take when their products enter the decline stage. To save money, some companies try to reduce their promotional expenditures on these products and the number of distribution outlets in which they are sold. They might implement price cuts to get customers to buy the product. **Harvesting** the product entails gradually reducing all costs spent on it, including investments made in the product and marketing costs. By reducing these costs, the company hopes that the profits from the product will increase until their inventory runs out. Another option for the company is **divesting** (dropping or deleting) the product from its offerings. The company might choose to sell the brand to another firm or simply reduce the price drastically in order to get rid of all remaining inventory. If a company decides to keep the product, it may lose money or make money if competitors drop out. Many companies decide the best strategy is to modify the product in the maturity stage to avoid entering the decline stage.

FIGURE 7.17

Your parents or grandparents might still use a videocassette recorder (VCR) like this.

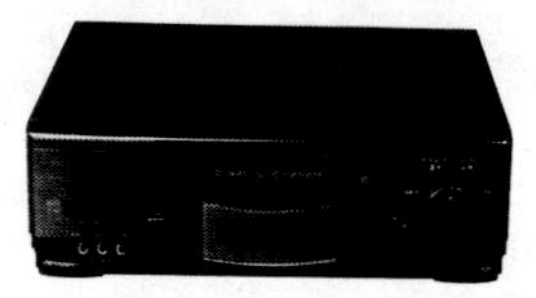

© 2010 Jupiterimages Corporation

**harvesting**

Companies reduce investment in a product, service, or business.

**divesting**

Companies get rid of a product, service, or business.

### KEY TAKEAWAY

The product life cycle helps a company understand the stages (introduction, growth, maturity, and decline) a product or service may go through once it is launched in the marketplace. The number and length of stages can vary. When a product is launched or commercialized, it enters the introduction stage. Companies must try to generate awareness of the product and encourage consumers to try it. During the growth stage, companies must demonstrate the product's benefits and value to persuade customers to buy it versus competing products. Some products never experience growth. The majority of products are in the mature stage. In the mature stage, sales level off and the market typically has many competitors. Companies modify the target market, the offering, or the marketing mix in order to extend the mature stage and keep from going into decline. If a product goes into decline, a company must decide whether to keep the product, harvest and reduce the spending on it until all the inventory is sold, or divest and get rid of the product.

**REVIEW QUESTIONS**

1. Explain what a firm that sells a product with a limited life cycle (such as software) should do in each stage so there is not a lot of inventory left over when a newer version is introduced?
2. Explain why the marketing costs related to a product are typically higher during the introduction stage and why companies must generate awareness of the new product or service and encourage consumers to try it.
3. Explain why and when penetration and skimming pricing are used in the introduction stage.
4. What stage of the life cycle is a product in when the company cannot meet the demand for it and competitors begin to enter the market?
5. What different strategies do firms use to extend the life cycles of their products throughout the maturity stage?
6. How did Kraft extend the mature stage of the product life cycle of Wheat Thins crackers?
7. Explain the difference between harvesting and a divesting when a firm enters the decline stage.

# 3. DISCUSSION QUESTIONS AND ACTIVITIES

**DISCUSSION QUESTIONS**

1. Who owns an idea? If a customer comes up with an innovation involving your product, and your company thinks that innovation can be commercialized, who owns the new product?
2. Assume you come up with an idea for a new electronic product you think your fellow students would really like. How would you go through the product development process? How would you accomplish each step within that process?
3. Select a product you are familiar with and explain the stages of the product's life cycle and different ways in which a company can extend its mature stage.

**ACTIVITIES**

1. Take two existing offerings and combine them to create a new one. What type of offering is it? To whom would you sell it? What new benefits does the product offer, and how would you communicate them to potential buyers? What evidence could you generate to predict the likelihood of the new offering being successful?
2. Identify two new consumer products sold in a grocery store or by a mass merchandiser such as Walmart. Explain the strategies used to introduce each of the products and which strategy you feel will be most successful.
3. Identify three products that are sold in international markets and explain any differences in how the products have been changed to meet the needs of consumers in the international markets.

# ENDNOTES

1. "At Hyundai, Branding Is Job 2," *BusinessWeek*, May 21, 2007, http://www.businessweek.com/magazine/content/07_21/b4035069.htm (accessed January 20, 2010).

2. Lawrence M. Fisher, "Xerox Sues Apple Computer Over Macintosh Copyright," *New York Times*, December 15, 1989, http://www.nytimes.com/1989/12/15/business/company-news-xerox-sues-apple-computer-over-macintosh-copyright.html?pagewanted=1 (accessed January 20, 2010).

3. Nick Roskelly, "Partial to Whole Grains," *New Products Online*, http://www.newproductsonline.com/Archives_Davinci?article=1979 (accessed January 20, 2010).

4. Molly Hunter, "The True Cost of the 100-Calorie Snack Pack," *ABC News*, July 15, 2008, http://abcnews.go.com/Health/story?id=5373173&page=1&mediakit=adgallery10 (accessed January 20, 2010).

5. "Best Global Brands," *Interbrand*, 2009, http://www.interbrand.com/best_global_brands.aspx?langid=1000 (accessed January 20, 2010).

6. "Microwave oven," *Wikipedia*, http://en.wikipedia.org/wiki/Microwave_oven (accessed January 20, 2010).

7. Molly Hunter, "The True Cost of the 100-Calorie Snack Pack," *ABC News*, July 15, 2008, http://abcnews.go.com/Health/story?id=5373173&page=1&mediakit=adgallery10 (accessed January 20, 2010).

8. Bruce Horovitz, "Starbucks Orders an Extra Shot; Founder Takes Over as CEO to Perk Up Coffee Chain," *USA Today*, January 8, 2008, 1B.

9. "Starbucks v McDonald's," *Economist*, January 10, 2008, http://www.economist.com/business/displaystory.cfm?story_id=10498747 (accessed January 20, 2010).

# CHAPTER 8
# Using Marketing Channels to Create Value for Customers

Sometimes when you buy a good or service, it passes straight from the producer to you. But suppose every time you purchased something, you had to contact its maker? For some products, such as a haircut, this would work. But what about the products you purchase at the grocery store? You couldn't begin to contact and buy from all the makers of those products. It would be an incredibly inefficient way to do business.

Fortunately, companies partner with one another, alleviating you of this burden. So, for example, instead of Procter & Gamble selling individual toothbrushes to consumers, it sells many of them to a drugstore close to you, which then sells them to you and other people.

The specific avenue a seller uses to make a finished good or service available to you for purchase—for example, whether you are able to buy it directly from the seller, at a store, online, from a salesperson, and so on—is referred to as the product's **marketing channel** (or *distribution channel*). All of the people and organizations that buy, resell, and promote the product "downstream" as it makes its way to you are part of the marketing channel. This chapter focuses on downstream channels. In the next chapter, we look not only "downstream" but also "upstream" at the people and organizations that supply the materials and services and that allow products to be made in the first place.

**marketing channel**

The group of organizations involved in selling and promoting goods from the time they are produced until they reach end users.

## 1. MARKETING CHANNELS AND CHANNEL PARTNERS

**LEARNING OBJECTIVES**

1. **Explain why marketing channel decisions can result in the success or failure of products.**
2. **Describe the different types of organizations that work together as channel partners and what each does.**

Today, marketing channel decisions are as important as the decisions companies make about the features and prices of products.[1] Consumers have become more demanding. They are used to getting what they want. If you can't get your product to them when, where, and how they want it, they will simply buy a competing product. In other words, *how* companies sell has become as important as *what* they sell.[2]

The firms a company partners with to actively promote and sell a product as it travels through its marketing channel to users are referred to by the firm as its **channel members** (or partners). Companies strive to choose not only the best marketing channels but also the best channel partners. A strong channel partner like Walmart can promote and sell the heck out of a product that might not otherwise turn a profit for its producer. In turn, Walmart wants to work with strong channel partners it can depend on to continuously provide it with great products that fly off the shelves. By contrast, a weak channel partner, like a bad spouse, can be a liability.

**channel members**

The firms a company partners with to actively promote and sell a product as it travels through its marketing channel to users.

**intermediaries**

Third parties that facilitate the supply and sale of products from manufacturers to users.

The simplest marketing channel consists of just two parties—a producer and a consumer. Your haircut is a good example. When you get a haircut, it travels straight from your hairdresser to you. No one else owns, handles, or remarkets the haircut to you before you get it. However, many other products and services pass through multiple organizations before they get to you. These organizations are called **intermediaries** (or *middlemen* or *resellers*).

Companies partner with intermediaries not because they necessarily want to (ideally they could sell their products straight to users) but because the intermediaries can help them sell the products better than they could working alone. In other words, they have some sort of capabilities the producer needs; contact with many customers or the right customers, marketing expertise, shipping and handling capabilities, and the ability to lend the producer credit are among the types of help a firm can get by utilizing a channel partner.

Intermediaries also create efficiencies by streamlining the number of transactions an organization must make, each of which takes time and costs money to conduct. As Figure 8.1 shows, by selling the tractors it makes through local farm machinery dealers, the farm machinery manufacturer John Deere can streamline the number of transactions it makes from eight to just two.

**FIGURE 8.1** Using Intermediaries to Streamline the Number of Transactions

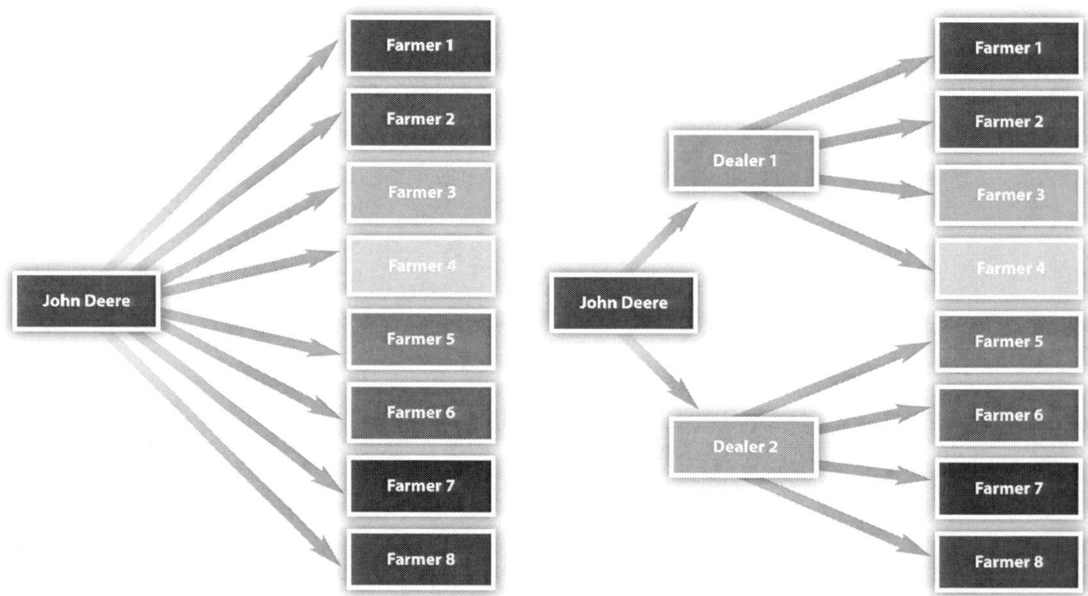


The marketing environment is always changing, so what was a great channel or channel partner yesterday might not be a great channel partner today. Changes in technology, production techniques, and your customer's needs mean you have to continually reevaluate your marketing channels and the channel partners you ally yourself with. Moreover, when you create a new product, you can't assume the channels that were used in the past are the best ones.[3] A different channel or channel partner might be better.

Consider Microsoft's digital encyclopedia, Encarta, which was first sold on CD and via online subscription in the early 1990s. Encarta nearly destroyed Encyclopedia Britannica, a firm that had dominated the print encyclopedia business for literally centuries. Ironically, Microsoft had actually tried to partner with Encyclopedia Britannica to use its encyclopedia information to make Encarta but was turned down.

But today, Encarta no longer exists. It's been put out of business by the free online encyclopedia Wikipedia. The point is that products and their marketing channels are constantly evolving. Consequently, you and your company have to be ready to evolve, too.

FIGURE 8.2

Neither Encyclopedia Britannica nor Microsoft saw Wikipedia on the horizon.

© 2010 Jupiterimages Corporation

## 1.1 Types of Channel Partners

Let's now look at the basic types of channel partners. To help you understand the various types of channel partners, we will go over the most common types of intermediaries. The two types you hear about most frequently are wholesalers and retailers. Keep in mind, however, that the categories we discuss in this section are just that—categories. In recent years, the lines between wholesalers, retailers, and producers have begun to blur considerably. Microsoft is a producer of goods, but recently it began opening up its own retail stores to sell products to consumers, much as Apple has done.[4] As you will learn later in the chapter, Walmart and other large retailers now produce their own store brands and sell them to other retailers. Similarly, many producers have outsourced their manufacturing, and although they still call themselves manufacturers, they act more like wholesalers. Wherever organizations see an opportunity, they are beginning to take it, regardless of their positions in marketing channels.

### Wholesalers

**Wholesalers** obtain large quantities of products from producers, store them, and break them down into cases and other smaller units more convenient for retailers to buy, a process called "breaking bulk." Wholesalers get their name from the fact that they resell goods "whole" to other companies without transforming the goods. If you are trying to stock a small electronics store, you probably don't want to purchase a truckload of iPods. Instead, you probably want to buy a smaller assortment of iPods as well as other merchandise. Via wholesalers, you can get the assortment of products you want in the quantities you want. Some wholesalers carry a wide range of different products. Other carry narrow ranges of products.

**wholesalers**

Businesses that purchase products in large quantities, can store the products, can break the pallets down into cases or units, and can deliver the desired quantity of a product to distributors, retailers, and/or consumers.

Most wholesalers "take title" to goods—or own them until purchased by other sellers. Wholesalers such as these assume a great deal of risk on the part of companies further down the marketing channel as a result. For example, if the iPods you plan to purchase are stolen during shipment, damaged, or become outdated because a new model has been released, the wholesaler suffers the loss—not you. Electronic products, in particular, become obsolete very quickly. Think about the cell phone you owned just a couple of years ago. Would you want to have to use it today?

**Video Clip**

**Marketing Channels and Products That Become Obsolete**

Good thing you don't have to use the cell phone shown in this YouTube video. You could forget about putting it in your purse or pocket. But in 1973, the phone was the latest and greatest of gadgets. Martin Cooper, who championed the development of the device, was a lead engineer at Motorola. To whom do you think Cooper made his first phone call on the device? To his rivals at AT&T, which at the time manufactured only "land-line" phones. He wanted to let them know he and Motorola had changed the telephone game.

View the video online at: http://www.youtube.com/embed/8iE0OH5FmiU

There are many types of wholesalers. The three basic types of wholesalers are merchant wholesalers, brokers, and manufacturers' agents, each of which we discuss next.

## Merchant Wholesalers

**merchant wholesalers**

Wholesalers that take title to the goods.

**distributors**

Businesses that purchase large quantities of products, can store products, can sell products, can deliver desired quantities of products, and can offer services. Distributors generally take title to products and employ a sales force to actively market their products.

**Merchant wholesalers** are wholesalers that take title to the goods. They are also sometimes referred to as **distributors**, *dealers*, and *jobbers*. The category includes both full-service wholesalers and limited-service wholesalers. Full-service wholesalers perform a broad range of services for their customers, such as stocking inventories, operating warehouses, supplying credit to buyers, employing salespeople to assist customers, and delivering goods to customers. Maurice Sporting Goods is a large North American full-service wholesaler of hunting and fishing equipment. The firm's services include helping customers figure out which products to stock, how to price them, and how to display them.[5]

*Limited-service wholesalers* offer fewer services to their customers but lower prices. They might not offer delivery services, extend their customers' credit, or have sales forces that actively call sellers. *Cash-and-carry wholesalers* are an example. Small retailers often buy from cash-and-carry wholesalers to keep their prices as low as big retailers that get large discounts because of the huge volumes of goods they buy.

*Drop shippers* are another type of limited-service wholesaler. Although drop shippers take title to the goods, they don't actually take possession of them or handle them, oftentimes because they deal with goods that are large or bulky. Instead, they earn a commission by finding sellers and passing their orders along to producers, who then ship them directly to the sellers. *Mail-order wholesalers* sell their products using catalogs instead of sales forces and then ship the products to buyers. *Truck jobbers* (or *truck wholesalers*) actually store products, which are often highly perishable (e.g., fresh fish), on their trucks. The trucks make the rounds to customers, who inspect and select the products they want straight off the trucks.

*Rack jobbers* sell specialty products, such as books, hosiery, and magazines that they display on their own racks in stores. Rack jobbers retain the title to the goods while the merchandise is in the stores for sale. Periodically, they take count of what's been sold off their racks and then bill the stores for those items.

## Brokers

**FIGURE 8.3**

Good brokers with excellent contacts are able to quickly match up buyers and sellers.

*© 2010 Jupiterimages Corporation*

**brokers (agents)**

Representatives of one or more manufacturers who sell products on their behalf to consumers, wholesalers, and distributors but do not take title to them.

**Brokers**, or *agents*, don't purchase the products they sell (take title to them). Their role is limited to negotiating sales contracts for producers. Clothing, furniture, food, and commodities such as lumber and steel are often sold by brokers. They are generally paid a commission for what they sell and are assigned to different geographical territories by the producers with whom they work. Because they have excellent industry contacts, brokers and agents are a "go-to" resource for both consumers and companies trying to buy and sell products.

### Manufacturers' Sales Offices or Branches

**Manufacturers' sales offices or branches** are selling units that work directly for manufacturers. They are a type of factory outlet store. They sell products to stores and sometimes to consumers, often at a discount.

### Retailers

**Retailers** buy products from wholesalers, agents, or distributors and then sell them to consumers. Retailers vary by the types of products they sell, their sizes, the prices they charge, the level of service they provide consumers, and the convenience or speed they offer. You are familiar with many of these types of retailers because you have purchased products from them.

**Supermarkets**, or grocery stores, are self-service retailers that provide a full range of food products to consumers, as well as some household products. Supermarkets can be high, medium, or low range in terms of the prices they charge and the service and variety of products they offer. Whole Foods and Central Market are grocers that offer a wide variety of products, generally at higher prices. Midrange supermarkets include stores like Albertsons and Kroger. Aldi and Sack 'n Save are examples of supermarkets with a limited selection of products and service but low prices. **Drugstores** specialize in selling over-the-counter medications, prescriptions, and health and beauty products and offer services such as photo developing.

**Convenience stores** are miniature supermarkets. Many of them sell gasoline and are open twenty-four hours a day. Often they are located on corners, making it easy and fast for consumers to get in and out. Some of these stores contain fast-food franchises like Church's Chicken and Jack in the Box. Consumers pay for the convenience in the form of higher markups on products.

**Specialty stores** sell a certain type of product, but they usually carry a deep line of it. Zales, which sells jewelry, and Williams-Sonoma, which sells an array of kitchen and cooking-related products, are examples of specialty stores. The personnel who work in specialty stores are usually knowledgeable and often provide customers with a high level of service. Specialty stores vary by size. Many are small. However, in recent years, giant specialty stores called category killers have emerged. A **category killer** sells a high volume of a particular type of product and, in doing so, dominates the competition, or "category." PETCO and PetSmart are category killers in the retail pet-products market. Best Buy is a category killer in the electronics-product market.

**Department stores**, by contrast, carry a wide variety of household and personal types of merchandise such as clothing and jewelry. Many are chain stores. The prices department stores charge range widely, as does the level of service shoppers receive. Neiman Marcus, Saks Fifth Avenue, and Nordstrom sell expensive products and offer extensive personal service to customers. The prices department stores such as JCPenney, Sears, and Macy's charge are midranged, as is the level of service shoppers receive. Walmart, Kmart, and Target are discount department stores with cheaper goods and a limited amount of service.

**Superstores** are oversized department stores that carry a broad array of general merchandise as well as groceries. Banks, hair and nail salons, and restaurants such as Starbucks are often located within these stores for the convenience of shoppers. You have probably shopped at a SuperTarget or a huge Walmart with offerings such as these. Superstores are also referred to as *hypermarkets* and *supercenters*.

**manufacturers' sales offices or branches**

Selling units that work directly for manufacturers. A type of factory outlet store.

**retailers**

Businesses that purchase products from manufacturers, wholesalers, agents, or distributors and then sell them to consumers.

**supermarkets**

Self-service retailers that provide a full range of food products to consumers as well as some household products.

**drugstores**

Stores that specialize in selling over-the-counter medication, prescriptions, and health and beauty products and offer services such as photo developing.

**convenience stores**

Miniature supermarkets that stock a limited assortment of products. Many of them sell gasoline and are open twenty-four hours a day.

**specialty stores**

Stores that sell a certain type of product.

**category killer**

A firm that sells a high volume of a product in a particular category.

**department stores**

Stores that carry a wide variety of household and personal types of merchandise such as clothing and jewelry.

**superstores**

Large department stores that carry a broad array of general merchandise as well as groceries. Superstores are also referred to as *hypermarkets* and *supercenters*.

**warehouse clubs**

Supercenters that sell products at a discount to people who pay an annual membership fee to join them.

**off-price retailers**

Stores that sell a variety of discount merchandise that consists of seconds, overruns, and the previous season's stock other stores have liquidated.

**pop-up store**

Small temporary stores designed to generate "buzz" for a retailer and drive customers to its regular stores.

**nonstore retailing**

Retailing not conducted in stores.

**direct marketing**

Delivering personalized promotional materials directly to individual consumers. Materials may be delivered via mail, catalogs, Internet, e-mail, or telephone, or in person.

**Warehouse clubs** are supercenters that sell products at a discount. They require people who shop with them to become members by paying an annual fee. Costco and Sam's Club are examples. **Off-price retailers** are stores that sell a variety of discount merchandise that consists of seconds, overruns, and the previous season's stock other stores have liquidated. Big Lots, Ross Dress for Less, and dollar stores are off-price retailers.

A new type of retail store that turned up in the last few years is the **pop-up store**. Pop-up stores are small temporary stores. They can be kiosks or temporarily occupy unused retail space. The goal is to create excitement and "buzz" for a retailer that then drives customers to their regular stores. In 2006, JCPenney created a pop-up store in Times Square for a month. Kate Coultas, a spokesperson for JCPenney, said the store got the attention of Manhattan's residents. Many hadn't been to a JCPenney store in a long time. "It was a real dramatic statement," Coultas says. "It kind of had a halo effect" on the company's stores in the surrounding boroughs of New York City.[6]

Not all retailing goes on in stores, however. **Nonstore retailing**—retailing not conducted in stores—is a growing trend. Door-to-door sales; party selling; selling to consumers via television, catalogs, the Internet, and vending machines; and telemarketing are examples of nonstore retailing. So is direct marketing. Companies that engage in **direct marketing** develop and send promotional materials such as catalogs, letters, leaflets, e-mails, and online ads straight to consumers urging them to contact their firms directly to buy products.

## KEY TAKEAWAY

The specific way in which you are able to buy a product is referred to as its marketing channel. Marketing channel decisions are as important as the decisions companies make about the features and prices of products. Channel partners are firms that actively promote and sell a product as it travels through its channel to its user. Companies try to choose the best channels and channel partners to help them sell products because doing so can give them a competitive advantage.

## REVIEW QUESTIONS

1. Why are marketing channel decisions as important as pricing and product feature decisions?
2. Why do channel partners rely on each other to sell their products and services?
3. How do companies add value to products via their marketing channels?

# 2. TYPICAL MARKETING CHANNELS

## LEARNING OBJECTIVES

1. **Describe the basic types of channels in business-to-consumer (B2C) and business-to-business (B2B) markets.**
2. **Explain the advantages and challenges companies face when using multiple channels and alternate channels.**
3. **Explain the pros and cons of disintermediation.**
4. **List the channels firms can use to enter foreign markets.**

Figure 8.4 shows the typical channels in business-to-consumer (B2C) markets. As we explained, the shortest marketing channel consists of just two parties—a producer and a consumer. A channel such as this is a **direct channel**. By contrast, a channel that includes one or more intermediaries—say, a wholesaler, distributor, or broker or agent—is an **indirect channel**. In an indirect channel, the product passes through one or more intermediaries. That doesn't mean the producer will do no marketing directly to consumers. Levi's runs ads on TV designed to appeal directly to consumers. The makers of food products run coupon ads. However, the seller also has to focus its selling efforts on these intermediaries because the intermediary can help with the selling effort. Not everyone wants to buy Levi's online.

**direct channel**

A marketing channel that consists of a producer and a consumer.

**indirect channel**

A marketing channel that consists of a producer, a consumer, and one or more intermediaries.

**FIGURE 8.4** Typical Channels in Business-to-Consumer (B2C) Markets

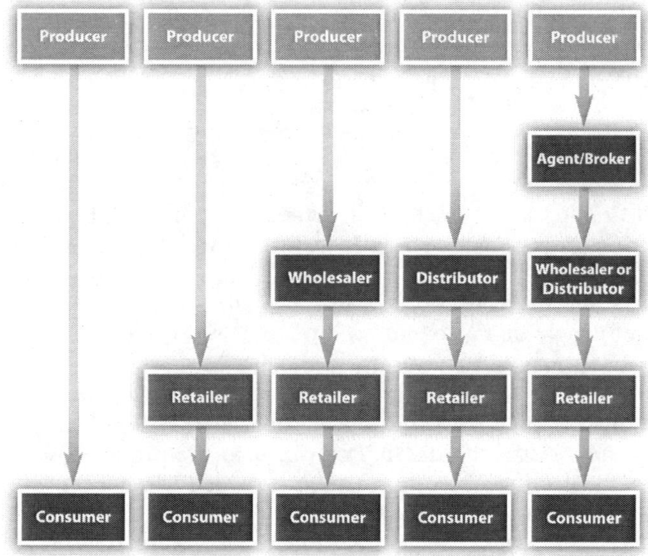

**FIGURE 8.5** Typical Channels in Business-to-Business (B2B) Markets

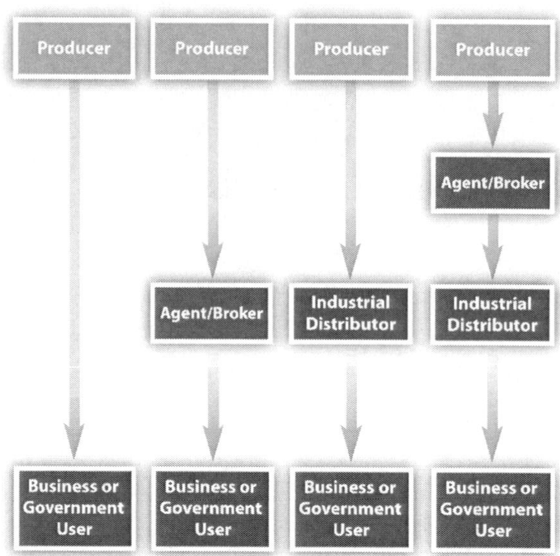


**FIGURE 8.6**

Name it, and your company can probably buy it from Grainger Industrial Supply.

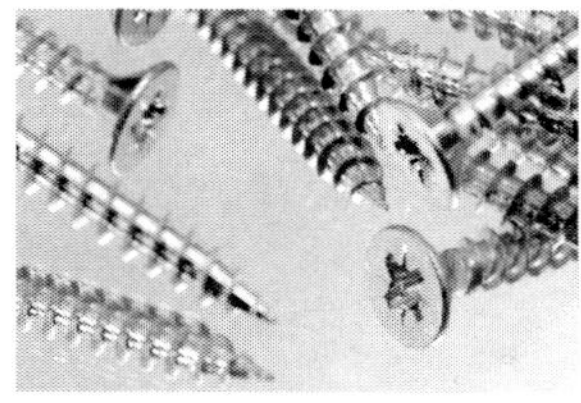

*© 2010 Jupiterimages Corporation*

Figure 8.5 shows the marketing channels common in business-to-business (B2B) markets. Notice how the channels resemble those in B2C markets, except that the products are sold to businesses and governments instead of consumers like you. The **industrial distributors** shown in Figure 8.5 are firms that supply products that businesses or government departments and agencies use but don't resell. Grainger Industrial Supply, which sells tens of thousands of products, is one of the world's largest industrial distributors. Nearly two million businesses and institutions in 150 countries buy products from the company, ranging from padlocks to painkillers.

**industrial distributors**

Intermediary firms that sell products that businesses or government departments and agencies use but don't resell.

**disintermediation**

A situation that occurs when intermediaries are cut out of marketing channels.

## 2.1 Disintermediation

You might be tempted to think middlemen, or intermediaries, are bad. If you can cut them out of the deal—a process marketing professionals call **disintermediation**—products can be sold more cheaply, can't they? Large retailers, including Target and Walmart, sometimes bypass middlemen. Instead, they buy their products directly from manufacturers and then store and distribute them to their own retail outlets. Walmart is increasingly doing so and even purchasing produce directly from farmers around the word.[7] However, sometimes cutting out the middleman is desirable but not always. A wholesaler with buying power and excellent warehousing capabilities might be able to purchase, store, and deliver a product to a seller more cheaply than its producer could acting alone. Likewise, hiring a distributor will cost a producer money. But if the distributor can help the producer sell greater quantities of a product, it can increase the producer's profits. Moreover, when you cut out the middlemen you work with, you have to perform the functions they once did. Maybe it's storing the product or dealing with hundreds of retailers. More than one producer has ditched its intermediaries only to rehire them later because of the hassles involved.

The trend today is toward disintermediation. The Internet has facilitated a certain amount of disintermediation by making it easier for consumers and businesses to contact one another without going through any middlemen. The Internet has also made it easier for buyers to shop for the lowest prices on products. Today, most people book trips online without going through travel agents. People also shop for homes online rather than using real estate agents. To remain in business, resellers need to find new ways to add value to products.

**FIGURE 8.7**

Be glad you're not the owner of this parking lot because it's going to need a lot of cleanup. This Nationwide Insurance ad drives home the point that close personal contact with your insurance agent might be a good idea.

*Source: Courtesy of Nationwide, used with permission.*

However, for some products, disintermediation via the Internet doesn't work so well. Insurance is an example. You can buy it online directly from companies, but many people want to buy through an agent they can talk to for advice.

Sometimes it's simply impossible to cut out middlemen. Would the Coca-Cola Company want to take the time and trouble to personally sell you an individual can of Coke? No. Coke is no more capable of selling individual Cokes to people than Santa is capable of delivering toys to children around the globe. Even Dell, which initially made its mark by selling computers straight to users, now sells its products through retailers such as Best Buy as well. Dell found that to compete effectively, its products needed to be placed in stores alongside Hewlett-Packard, Acer, and other computer brands.[8]

**FIGURE 8.8**

Michael Dell, founder of the worldwide corporation Dell, Inc., initially made and sold computers to buyers by telephone out of his college dorm room.

*Source: Courtesy of Dell, Inc., used with permission.*

## 2.2 Multiple Channels and Alternate Channels

Marketing channels can get a lot more complex than the channels shown in Figure 8.4 and Figure 8.5, though. Look at the channels in Figure 8.9. Notice how in some situations, a wholesaler will sell to brokers, who then sell to retailers and consumers. In other situations, a wholesaler will sell straight to retailers or straight to consumers. Manufacturers also sell straight to consumers, and, as we explained, sell straight to large retailers like Target.

**FIGURE 8.9** Alternate Channel Arrangements

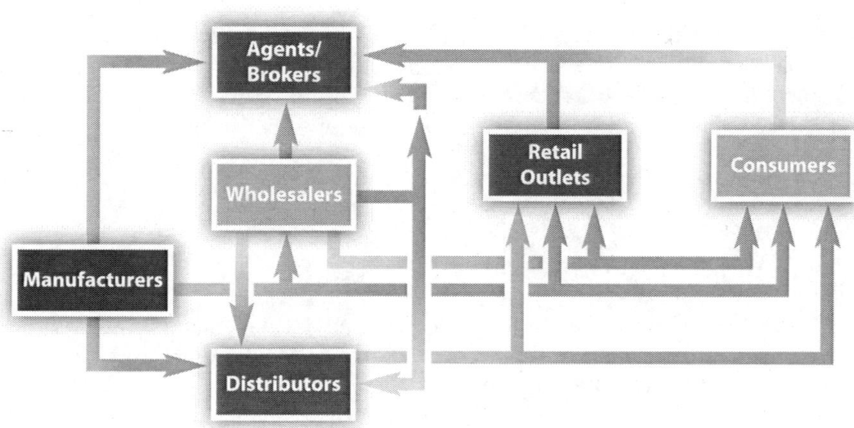

The point is that firms can and do utilize multiple channels. Take Levi's, for example. You can buy a pair of Levi's from a retailer such as Kohl's, or you can buy a pair directly from Levi's at one of the outlet stores it owns around the country. You can also buy a pair from the Levi's Web site.

The key is understanding the different target markets for your product and designing the best channel to meet the needs of customers in each. Is there a group of buyers who would purchase your product if they could shop online from the convenience of their homes? Perhaps there is a group of customers interested in your product but they do not want to pay full price. The ideal way to reach these people might be with an outlet store and low prices. Each group then needs to be marketed to accordingly. Many people regularly interact with companies via numerous channels before making buying decisions.

**FIGURE 8.10**

In addition to selling products on TV and on the Web, QVC also sells them via its mobile message service. Customers can sign up to get alerts about products for sale and buy them on their cell phones.

*© 2010 Jupiterimages Corporation*

Using multiple channels can be effective. At least one study has shown that the more marketing channels your customers utilize, the more loyal they are likely to be to your products.[9] Companies work hard to try to integrate their selling channels so users get a consistent experience. For example, QVC's TV channel, Web site, and mobile service—which sends alerts to customers and allows them to buy products via their cell phones—all have the same look and feel.

A company can also use a marketing channel to set itself apart from the crowd. Jones Soda Co. initially placed its own funky-looking soda coolers in skate and surf shops, tattoo and piercing parlors, individual fashion stores, and national retail clothing and music stores. The company then began an up-and-down-the-street "attack," placing product in convenience and food stores. Finally, the company was able to sell its drinks to bigger companies like Starbucks, Barnes & Noble, Safeway, Target, and 7-Eleven stores.[10]

Would you like to purchase gold from a vending machine? Soon you will be able to—in Germany. Germans like to purchase gold because it's considered a safe alternative to paper money, which can become devalued during a period of hyperinflation. So, in addition to selling gold the usual way, TG-Gold-Super-Markt company is planning to install "gold to go" machines in five hundred locations in German-speaking countries. The gold is dispensed in metal boxes, and cameras on the machine monitor the transactions to prevent money laundering.[11]

**Video Clip**

**Gold to Go: Germany's Version of an ATM Machine?**

Check out this YouTube clip to get a look at how a gold vending machine works.

View the video online at: http://www.youtube.com/embed/WIZ6N49mFX0

**strategic channel alliance**

An agreement formed by two or more firms to deliver their products via a channel. The products and organizations can be similar or different.

Some companies find ways to increase their sales by forming **strategic channel alliances** with one another. Harley-Davidson has a strategic channel alliance with Best Western. Click on Harley-Davidson's "Ride Planner" tab on its Web site, and you can sign up to receive points and other discounts by staying at Best Western hotels and motels.[12] Starbucks now dispenses its beverages in some of Safeway's grocery stores. Starbucks wants grocery shoppers at Safeway craving a cup of coffee to grab one; Safeway hopes customers dropping in for a Starbucks cup of coffee will buy some grocery products.

## 2.3 International Marketing Channels

Consumer and business markets in the United States are well developed and growing slowly. However, the opportunities for growth abound in other countries. Coca-Cola, in fact, earns most of its income abroad—not in the United States. The company's latest push is into China, where the per-person consumption of ready-to-drink beverages is only about a third of the global average.[13]

The question is how to enter these markets? Via what marketing channels? Some third-world countries lack good intermediary systems. In these countries, firms are on their own in terms of selling and distributing products downstream to users. Other countries have elaborate marketing channels that must be navigated. Consider Japan, for example. Japan has an extensive, complicated system of intermediaries, each of which demands a cut of a company's profits. Carrefour, a global chain of hypermarkets, tried to expand there but eventually left the country because its marketing channel system was so complicated.

Walmart managed to develop a presence in Japan, but only after acquiring the Japanese supermarket operator Seiyu.[14] As you learned in Chapter 2 and Chapter 5, acquiring part or all of a foreign company is a common strategy for companies. It is referred to as making a direct foreign investment. However, as you learned some nations don't allow foreign companies to do business within their borders or buy local companies. The Chinese government blocked Coca-Cola from buying Huiyuan Juice, that country's largest beverage maker.

Corruption and unstable governments also make it difficult to do business in some countries. The banana company Chiquita found itself in the bad position of having to pay off rebels in Colombia to prevent them from seizing the banana plantations of one of its subsidiaries.

One of the easier ways of utilizing intermediaries to expand abroad is a joint venture. You first learned about joint ventures in Chapter 2. A joint venture is an entity created when two parties agree to share their profits, losses, and control with one another in an economic activity they jointly undertake. The German automaker Volkswagen has struggled to penetrate Asian markets. It recently signed an agreement with Suzuki, the Japanese company, in an effort to challenge Toyota's dominance in Asia. Will it work? Time will tell. Many joint ventures fail, particularly when they involve companies from different countries. Daimler-Chrysler, the union between the German car company and U.S. automaker Chrysler, is one of many joint ventures that fell by the wayside.[15] However, in some countries, such as India, it is the only way companies are allowed to do business within their borders.

An even easier way to enter markets is to simply export your products. Microsoft hasn't done well with its Zune MP3 player in the United States. It subsequently redesigned the product and launched it in other countries.[16] Companies can sell their products directly to other firms abroad, or they can hire intermediaries such as brokers and agents that specialize in international exporting to help them find potential buyers for their products.

Recall that many companies, particularly those in the United States, have expanded their operations via franchising. Franchising grants an independent operator the right to use a company's business model, name, techniques, and trademarks for a fee. McDonald's is the classic example of a franchise. Unlike Walmart, McDonald's has had no trouble making headway in Japan. It has done so by selling thousands of franchises there. In fact, Japan is McDonald's second-largest market next to the United States. The company also has thousands of franchises in Europe and other countries. There is even a McDonald's franchise in the Louvre, the prestigious museum in Paris that houses the *Mona Lisa*. Licensing is similar to franchising. For a fee, a firm can buy the right to use another firm's manufacturing processes, trade secrets, patents, and trademarks for a certain period of time.

**FIGURE 8.11**

McDonald's opened a franchise in the Louvre. How about a little art with your Big Mac?

## KEY TAKEAWAY

A direct marketing channel consists of just two parties—a producer and a consumer. By contrast, a channel that includes one or more intermediaries (wholesaler, distributor, or broker or agent) is an indirect channel. Firms often utilize multiple channels to reach more customers and increase their effectiveness. Some companies find ways to increase their sales by forming strategic channel alliances with one another. Other companies look for ways to cut out the middlemen from the channel, a process known as disintermediation. Direct foreign investment, joint ventures, exporting, franchising, and licensing are some of the channels by which firms attempt to enter foreign markets.

**REVIEW QUESTIONS**

1. Why are direct marketing channels possible for some products and not others?
2. Explain the value middlemen can add to products.
3. Name some companies that have multiple marketing channels for their products. What are those channels?
4. How do marketing channels differ around the world? Why is it sometimes hard for firms to penetrate foreign markets?

# 3. FUNCTIONS PERFORMED BY CHANNEL PARTNERS

**LEARNING OBJECTIVES**

1. **Describe the activities performed in channels.**
2. **Explain which organizations perform which functions.**

Different organizations in a marketing channel are responsible for different value-adding activities. The following are some of the most common functions channel members perform. However, keep in mind that "who does what" can vary, depending on what the channel members actually agree to in their contracts with one another.

## 3.1 Disseminate Marketing Communications and Promote Brands

**push strategy**

A strategy in which businesses are the target of promotions so products get "pushed" through their marketing channels and sold to consumers.

Somehow wholesalers, distributors, retailers, and consumers need to be informed—via marketing communications—that an offering exists and that there's a good reason to buy it. Sometimes, a push strategy is used to help marketing channels accomplish this. A **push strategy** (which is discussed in greater detail in Chapter 12) is one in which a manufacturer convinces wholesalers, distributors, or retailers to sell its products. Consumers are informed via advertising and other promotions that the product is available for sale, but the main focus is to sell to intermediaries.

The problem with a push strategy is that it doesn't focus on the needs of the actual users of the products. Coca-Cola used a push strategy for years before realizing that instead of focusing on moving beverages through a retailer's back door, it needed to help them sell to shoppers through the retailer's front door.[17] College textbook publishers are in a similar position today. Traditionally, they have concentrated their selling efforts on professors and bookstore managers. (Has a textbook company ever asked you what you want out of a textbook?) It's no secret that the price of textbooks is climbing and students are purchasing fewer of them. Like Coca-Cola, textbook publishers are probably going to have to rethink their sales and marketing channel strategies.[18]

By contrast, a **pull strategy** focuses on creating demand for a product among consumers so that businesses agree to sell the product. A good example of an industry that utilizes both pull and push strategies is the pharmaceutical industry. Pharmaceutical companies promote their drugs to pharmacies and doctors, but they now also run ads designed to persuade individual consumers to ask their physicians about drugs that might benefit them.

In many cases, two or more organizations in a channel jointly promote a product to retailers, purchasing agents, and consumers and work out which organization is responsible for what type of communication to whom. The actual forms and styles of communication will be discussed more in the promotions and sales section of the book.

**FIGURE 8.12**

Entrepreneurs Jeff Shelstad and Eric Frank launched Flat World Knowledge, the publisher of this textbook. Shelstad and Frank believe they have found a way to add more value to the textbooks you buy. One of their strategies is to deliver their products via a marketing channel that's different from those used to sell traditional textbooks.

## 3.2 Sorting and Regrouping Products

As we explained, many businesses don't want to receive huge quantities of a product. One of the functions of wholesalers and distributors is to break down large quantities of products into smaller units and provide an assortment of different products to businesses.

## 3.3 Storing and Managing Inventory

If a channel member has run out of a product when a customer wants to buy it, the result is often a lost sale. That's why most channel members stock, or "carry," reserve inventory. However, storing products is not free. Warehouses cost money to build or rent and heat and cool; employees have to be paid to stock shelves, pick products, ship them, and so forth. Some companies, including Walmart, put their suppliers in charge of their inventory. The suppliers have access to Walmart's inventory levels and ship products when and where the retailer's stores need them.

**pull strategy**

A strategy in which consumers are targeted with sales promotions such as coupons, contests, games, rebates, mail-in offers.

### Video Clip

**Warehouse Robots at Work**

Not all warehouses utilize humans to pluck products from shelves. Some of them use robots, as this video shows. Robots cost money, too, though.

View the video online at: http://www.youtube.com/embed/IWsMdN7HMuA

## 3.4 Distributing Products

Physical goods that travel within a channel need to be moved from one member to another and sometimes back again. Some large wholesalers, distributors, and retailers own their own fleets of trucks for this purpose. In other cases, they hire third-party transportation providers—trucking companies, railroads, and so forth—to move their products.

**FIGURE 8.13**

Walmart doesn't just own its own warehouses. It also owns its own fleet of semi-trucks.

Being able to track merchandise like you can track a FedEx package is extremely important to channel partners. They want to know where their products are at all times and what shape they are in. Losing inventory or having it damaged or spoiled can wreak havoc on a company's profits. So can not getting products on time or being able to get them at all when your competitors can.

## 3.5 Assume Ownership Risk and Extend Credit

If products *are* damaged during transit, one of the first questions asked is who owned the product at the time. In other words, who suffers the loss? Generally, no one channel member assumes all of the ownership risk in a channel. Instead, it is distributed among channel members depending on the contracts they have with one another and their free on board provisions. A **free on board (FOB)** provision designates who is responsible for what shipping costs and who owns the title to the goods and when. However, the type of product, the demand for it, marketing conditions, and the clout of the various organizations in its marketing channel can affect the contract terms channel members are willing to agree to. Some companies try to wait as long as possible to take ownership of products so they don't have to store them. During the economic downturn, many channel members tried to hold as little inventory as possible for fear it would go unsold or become obsolete.[19]

**free on board (FOB)**

A contract term that designates which party is responsible for a product's shipping costs and owns the title to the goods and when.

## 3.6 Share Marketing and Other Information

Each of the channel members has information about the demand for products, trends, inventory levels, and what the competition is doing. The information is valuable and can be doubly valuable if channel partners trust one another and share it. More information can help each firm in the marketing channel perform its functions better and overcome competitive obstacles.[20]

That said, confidentiality is a huge issue among supply chain partners because they share so much information with one another, such as sales and inventory data. For example, a salesperson who sells Tide laundry detergent for Procter & Gamble will have a good idea of how many units of Tide Walmart and Target are selling. However, it would be unethical for the salesperson to share Walmart's numbers with Target or Target's numbers with Walmart. Many business buyers require their channel partners to sign nondisclosure agreements or make the agreements part of purchasing contracts. A **nondisclosure agreement (NDA)** is a contract that specifies what information is proprietary, or owned by the partner, and how, if at all, the partner can use that information.

**nondisclosure agreement**

A contract that specifies information that is proprietary, or owned by a channel partner, and how, if at all, the other partners can use that information.

### KEY TAKEAWAY

Different organizations in a marketing channel are responsible for different value-adding activities. These activities include disseminating marketing communications and promoting brands, sorting and regrouping products, storing and managing inventory, distributing products, assuming the risk of products, and sharing information.

### REVIEW QUESTIONS

1. Explain the difference between a pull and a push strategy when it comes to marketing communications.
2. Why is taking ownership of products an important marketing channel function?
3. Which firms manage inventory in marketing channels?

# 4. MARKETING CHANNEL STRATEGIES

**LEARNING OBJECTIVES**

1. **Describe the factors that affect a firm's channel decisions.**
2. **Explain how intensive, exclusive, and selective distribution differ from one another.**
3. **Explain why some products are better suited to some distribution strategies than others.**

## 4.1 Channel Selection Factors

Selecting the best marketing channel is critical because it can mean the success or failure of your product. One of the reasons the Internet has been so successful as a marketing channel is because customers get to make some of the channel decisions themselves. They can shop virtually for any product in the world when and where they want to, as long as they can connect to the Web. They can also choose how the product is shipped.

### Type of Customer

The Internet isn't necessarily the best channel for every product, though. For example, do you want to closely examine the fruits and vegetables you buy to make sure they are ripe enough or not overripe? Then online grocery shopping might not be for you. Clearly, how your customers want to buy products will have an impact on the channel you select. In fact, it should be your prime consideration.

First of all, are you selling to a consumer or a business customer? Generally, these two groups want to be sold to differently. Most consumers are willing to go to a grocery or convenience store to purchase toilet paper. The manager of a hospital trying to replenish its supplies would not. The hospital manager would also be buying a lot more toilet paper than an individual consumer and would expect to be called upon by a distributor, but perhaps only semiregularly. Thereafter, the manager might want the toilet paper delivered on a regular basis and billed to the hospital via automatic systems. Likewise, when businesses buy expensive products such as machinery and computers or products that have to be customized, they generally expect to be sold to personally via salespeople. And often they expect special payment terms.

### Type of Product

The type of product you're selling will also affect your marketing channel choices. Perishable products often have to be sold through shorter marketing channels than products with longer shelf lives. For example, a yellowfin tuna bound for the sushi market will likely be flown overnight to its destination and handled by few intermediaries. By contrast, canned tuna can be shipped by "slow boat" and handled by more intermediaries. Valuable and fragile products also tend to have shorter marketing channels. Automakers generally sell their cars straight to car dealers (retailers) rather than through wholesalers. The makers of corporate jets often sell them straight to corporations, which demand they be customized to certain specifications.

### Channel Partner Capabilities

Your ability versus the ability of other types of organizations that operate in marketing channels can affect your channel choices. If you are a massage therapist, you are quite capable of delivering your product straight to your client. If you produce downloadable products like digital books or recordings, you can sell your products straight to customers on the Internet. Hypnotic World, a UK producer of self-hypnosis recordings, is a company such as this. If you want to stop smoking or lose weight, you can pay for and download a recording to help you do this at http://www.hypnoticworld.com.

But suppose you've created a great new personal gadget—something that's tangible, or physical. You've managed to sell it via two channels—say, on TV (via the Home Shopping Network, perhaps) and on the Web. Now you want to get the product into retail stores like Target, Walgreens, and Bed Bath & Beyond. If you can get the product into these stores, you can increase your sales exponentially. In this case, you might want to contract with an intermediary—perhaps an agent or a distributor who will convince the corporate buyers of those stores to carry your product.

## Video Clip

**Ped Egg Commercial**

View the video online at: http://www.youtube.com/embed/FB3LzVQGsDk

Where would the world be today without "As Seen on TV" products such as the Ped Egg, designed to remove calluses on feet? Lucky for us, products such as these are now sold both on the Web and in stores. (There have been a few jokes to the effect that a cheese grater might work as well as the Ped Egg, but . . .)

### The Business Environment and Technology

The general business environment, such as the economy, can also affect the marketing channels chosen for products. For example, think about what happens when the value of the dollar declines relative to the currencies of other countries. When the dollar falls, products imported from other countries cost more to buy relative to products produced and sold in the United States. Products "made in China" become less attractive because they have gotten more expensive. As a result, some companies then look closer to home for their products and channel partners.

Technological changes affect marketing channels, too, of course. We explained how the Internet has changed how products are bought and sold. Many companies like selling products on the Internet as much as consumers like buying them. For one, an Internet sales channel gives companies more control over how their products are sold and at what prices than if they leave the job to another channel partner such as a retailer. Plus, a company selling on the Internet has a digital footprint, or record, of what shoppers look at, or click on, at its site. As a result, it can recommend products they appear to be interested in and target them with special offers and even prices.[21]

Some sites let customers tailor products to their liking. On the Domino's Web site, you can pick your pizza ingredients and then watch them as they fall onto your virtual pizza. The site then lets you know who is baking your pizza, how long it's taking to cook, and who's delivering it. Even though interaction is digital, it somehow feels a lot more personal than a basic phone order. Developing customer relationships is what today's marketing is about. The Internet is helping companies do this.

### Competing Products' Marketing Channels

How your competitors sell their products can also affect your marketing channels. As we explained, Dell now sells computers to firms like Best Buy so the computers can compete with other brands on store shelves.

You don't always have to choose the channels your competitors rely on, though. Netflix is an example. Netflix turned the video rental business on its head by coming up with a new marketing channel that better meets the needs of many consumers. Maybelline and L'Oréal products are sold primarily in retail stores. However, Mary Kay and Avon use salespeople to personally sell their products to consumers.

## 4.2 Factors That Affect a Product's Intensity of Distribution

**intensive distribution**

A strategy of selling a product in as many outlets as possible.

Firms that choose an **intensive distribution** strategy try to sell their products in as many outlets as possible. Intensive distribution strategies are often used for convenience offerings—products customers purchase on the spot without much shopping around. Soft drinks and newspapers are an example. You see them sold in all kinds of different places. Redbox, which rents DVDs out of vending machines, has made headway using a distribution strategy that's more intensive than Blockbuster's: the machines are located in fast-food restaurants, grocery stores, and other places people go frequently.

By contrast, **selective distribution** involves selling products at select outlets in specific locations. For instance, Sony TVs can be purchased at a number of outlets such as Circuit City, Best Buy, or Walmart, but the same models are generally not sold at all the outlets. By selling different models with different features and price points at different outlets, a manufacturer can appeal to different target markets.

**Exclusive distribution** involves selling products through one or very few outlets. For instance, supermodel Cindy Crawford's line of furniture is sold exclusively at the furniture company Rooms To Go. Designer Michael Graves has a line of products sold exclusively at Target. To purchase those items you need to go to one of those retailers. TV series are distributed exclusively. A company that produces a TV series will sign an exclusive deal with a network like ABC, CBS, or Showtime, and the series will initially appear only on that network. Later, reruns of the shows are often distributed selectively to other networks.

To control the image of their products and the prices at which they are sold, the makers of upscale products often prefer to distribute their products more exclusively. Expensive perfumes and designer purses are an example. During the economic downturn, the makers of some of these products were disappointed to see retailers had slashed the products' prices, "cheapening" their prestigious brands.

**FIGURE 8.14**

Because installing a vending machine is less expensive than opening a retail outlet, redbox has been able to locate its DVD vending machines in more places than Blockbuster can its stores.

**FIGURE 8.15**

What's for sale at Rooms To Go, Cindy?

*© 2010 Jupiterimages Corporation*

**selective distribution**

A strategy of selling products at specific outlets and/or locations.

**exclusive distribution**

A strategy of selling products through one or a few retailers in a specific location.

Distributing a product exclusively to a limited number of organizations under strict terms can help prevent a company's brand from deteriorating, or losing value. It can also prevent products from being sold cheaply in gray markets. A **gray market** is a market in which a producer hasn't authorized its products to be sold.[22]

**gray market**

A market in which a producer hasn't authorized its products to be sold.

## KEY TAKEAWAY

Selecting the best marketing channel is critical because it can mean the success or failure of your product. The type of customer you're selling to will have an impact on the channel you select. In fact, this should be your prime consideration. The type of product, your organization's capabilities versus those of other channel members, the way competing products are marketed, and changes in the business environment and technology can also affect your marketing channel decisions. Various factors affect a company's decisions about the intensity of a product's distribution. An intensive distribution strategy involves selling a product in as many outlets as possible. Selective distribution involves selling a product at select outlets in specific locations. Exclusive distribution involves selling a product through one or very few outlets.

**REVIEW QUESTIONS**

1. Why are good channel decisions critical to a product's success?
2. Name the factors that affect channel-selection decisions.
3. Which kinds of products are more likely to be distributed using exclusive marketing strategies?

# 5. CHANNEL DYNAMICS

**LEARNING OBJECTIVES**

1. **Explain what channel power is and the types of firms that wield it.**
2. **Describe the types of conflicts that can occur in marketing channels.**
3. **Describe the ways in which channel members achieve cooperation with one another.**

## 5.1 Channel Power

**channel power**

The ability to influence a channel partner's goals and efforts.

**channel leader**

A strong channel member that wields channel power.

Strong channel partners often wield what's called **channel power** and are referred to as **channel leaders**, or *channel captains*. In the past, big manufacturers like Procter & Gamble and Dell were often channel captains. But that is changing. More often today, big retailers like Walmart and Target are commanding more channel power. They have millions of customers and are bombarded with products wholesalers and manufacturers want them to sell. As a result, these retailers increasingly are able to call the shots. In other words, they get what they want.

Category killers are in a similar position. Consumers like you are gaining marketing channel power, too. Regardless of what one manufacturer produces or what a local retailer has available, you can use the Internet to find whatever product you want at the best price available and have it delivered when, where, and how you want.

## 5.2 Channel Conflict

**channel conflict**

A dispute among channel members.

A dispute among channel members is called a **channel conflict**. Channel conflicts are common. Part of the reason for this is that each channel member has its own goals, which are unlike those of any other channel member. The relationship among them is not unlike the relationship between you and your boss (assuming you have a job). Both of you want to serve your organization's customers well. However, your goals are different. Your boss might want you to work on the weekend, but you might not want to because you need to study for a Monday test.

All channel members want to have low inventory levels but immediate access to more products. Who should bear the cost of holding the inventory? What if consumers don't purchase the products? Can they be returned to other channel members, or is the organization in possession of the products responsible for disposing of them? Channel members try to spell out details such as these in their contracts.

No matter how "airtight" their contracts are, there will still be points of contention among channel members. Channel members are constantly asking their partners, "What have you done (or not done) for me lately?" Wholesalers and retailers frequently lament that the manufacturers they work with aren't doing more to promote their products—for example, distributing coupons for them, running TV ads, and so forth—so they will move off store shelves more quickly. Meanwhile, manufacturers want to know why wholesalers aren't selling their products faster and why retailers are placing them at the bottom of shelves where they are hard to see. Apple opened its own retail stores around the country, in part because it didn't like how its products were being displayed and sold in other companies' stores.

Channel conflicts can also occur when manufacturers sell their products online. When they do, wholesalers and retailers often feel like they are competing for the same customers when they shouldn't have to. Likewise, manufacturers often feel slighted when retailers dedicate more shelf space to their own store brands. **Store brands** are products retailers produce themselves or pay manufacturers to produce for them. Dr. Thunder is Walmart's store-brand equivalent of Dr. Pepper, for example. Because a retailer doesn't have to promote its store brands to get them on its own shelves like a "regular" manufacturer would, store brands are often priced more cheaply. And some retailers sell their store brands to other retailers, creating competition for manufacturers.

**FIGURE 8.16**

Dr. Thunder is Walmart's store-brand equivalent of Dr. Pepper. Store brands create competition for "regular" manufacturers.

### Vertical versus Horizontal Conflict

The conflicts we've described so far are examples of vertical conflict. A **vertical conflict** is conflict that occurs between two different types of members in a channel—say, a manufacturer, an agent, a wholesaler, or a retailer. By contrast, a **horizontal conflict** is conflict that occurs between organizations of the same type—say, two manufacturers that each want a powerful wholesaler to carry only its products.

Horizontal conflict can be healthy because it's competition driven. But it can create problems, too. In 2005, Walmart experienced a horizontal conflict among its landline telephone suppliers. The suppliers were in the middle of a price war and cutting the prices to all the retail stores they sold to. Walmart wasn't selling any additional phones due to the price cuts. It was just selling them for less and making less of a profit on them.[23]

Channel leaders like Walmart usually have a great deal of say when it comes to how channel conflicts are handled, which is to say that they usually get what they want. But even the most powerful channel leaders strive for cooperation. A manufacturer with channel power still needs good retailers to sell its products; a retailer with channel power still needs good suppliers from which to buy products. One member of a channel can't squeeze all the profits out of the other channel members and still hope to function well. Moreover, because each of the channel partners is responsible for promoting a product through its channel, to some extent they are all in the same boat. Each one of them has a vested interest in promoting the product, and the success or failure of any one of them can affect that of the others.

Flash back to Walmart and how it managed to solve the conflict among its telephone suppliers: Because the different brands of landline telephones were so similar, Walmart decided it could consolidate and use fewer suppliers. It then divided its phone products into market segments—inexpensive phones with basic functions, midpriced phones with more features, and high-priced phones with many features. The suppliers chosen were asked to provide products for one of the three segments. This gave Walmart's customers the variety they sought. And because the suppliers selected were able to sell more phones and compete for different types of customers, they stopped undercutting each other's prices.[24]

**store brands**

Products retailers produce themselves or pay manufacturers to produce for them.

**vertical conflict**

Conflict that occurs between two different types of members of the channel.

**horizontal conflict**

Conflict that occurs between organizations of the same type.

## 5.3 Achieving Channel Cooperation Ethically

What if you're not Walmart or a channel member with a great deal of power? How do you build relationships with channel partners and get them to cooperate with you? One way is by emphasizing the benefits of working with your firm. For example, if you are a seller whose product and brand name are in demand, you want to point out how being one of its "authorized sellers" can boost a retailer's store traffic and revenues.

Oftentimes companies produce informational materials and case studies showing their partners how they can help boost their sales volumes and profits. Channel partners also want to feel assured that the products coming through the pipeline are genuine and not knockoffs and that there will be a steady supply of them. Your goal is to show your channel partners that you understand issues such as these and help them generate business.

Sometimes the shoe is on the other foot—retailers have to convince the makers of products to do business with them instead of the other way around. Beauty.com, an online retailer, is an example. Selling perfumes and cosmetics online can be difficult because people want to be able to smell and feel the products like they can at a department store. But Beauty.com has been able to convince the makers of more than two hundred upscale cosmetic brands that selling their products on its Web site is a great deal and can increase their revenues. To reassure sellers that shoppers can get personalized service, Beauty.com offers the site's visitors free samples of products and the ability to chat live online with skin and hair care consultants.[25]

**FIGURE 8.17**

Boar's Head creates in-store displays like the banner shown here to help its channel partners sell its products.

Producing marketing and promotional materials their channel partners can use for sales purposes can also facilitate cooperation among companies. In-store displays, brochures, banners, photos for Web sites, and advertisements the partners can customize with their own logos and company information are examples. Look at the banner in Figure 8.17. Although it looks like it was made by the grocery store displaying it, it wasn't. It was produced by Boar's Head, a meat supplier, for the grocer and others like it.

Educating your channel members' sales representatives is an extremely important part of facilitating cooperation, especially when you're launching a new product. The reps need to be provided with training and marketing materials in advance of the launch so their activities are coordinated with yours. Microsoft is a company that does a good job of training its partners. Before launching operating systems such as Windows XP and Vista, Microsoft provides thousands of its partners with sales and technical training.[26]

In addition, companies run sales contests to encourage their channel partners' sales forces to sell what they have to offer. Offering your channel partners certain monetary incentives, such as discounts for selling your product, can help, too. We'll talk more about incentive programs such as these in Chapter 12.

**Audio Clip**

**Interview with Joy Mead**

Recall from Chapter 3 that Joy Mead is an associate marketing director with Procter & Gamble. Listen to this audio clip to hear Mead discuss how Procter & Gamble has developed insight about consumers and shared that insight with its retailers to help both them and the manufacturer succeed.

What shouldn't you do when it comes to your channel partners? Take them for granted, says John Addison, the author of the book *Revenue Rocket: New Strategies for Selling with Partners*. Addison suggests creating a dialogue with them via one-on-one discussions and surveys and developing "partner advisory councils" to better understand their needs.

You also don't want to "stuff the channel," says Addison. Stuffing the channel occurs when, in order to meet its sales numbers, a company offers its channel partners deep discounts and unlimited returns to buy a lot of a product. The problem is that such a strategy can lead to a buildup of inventory that gets steeply discounted and dumped on the market and sometimes on gray markets. This can affect people's perceptions of the product and its brand name. And what happens to any unsold inventory? It gets returned back up in the channel in the next accounting period, taking a toll on the "stuffers'" sales numbers.

**resale price maintenance agreement**

An agreement whereby a producer of a product restricts the price a retailer can charge for it.

Lastly, you don't want to risk breaking the law or engage in unfair business practices when dealing with your channel partners.[27] We have already discussed confidentiality issues. Another issue channel partners sometimes encounter relates to resale price maintenance agreements. A **resale price maintenance agreement** is an agreement whereby a producer of a product restricts the price a retailer can charge for it.

The producers of upscale products often want retailers to sign resale price maintenance agreements because they don't want the retailers to deeply discount their products. Doing so would "cheapen" their brands, producers believe. Producers also contend that resale price maintenance agreements prevent price wars from breaking out among their retailers, which can lead to the deterioration of prices for all of a channel's members.

Both large companies and small retail outlets have found themselves in court as a result of price maintenance agreements. Although the U.S. Supreme Court hasn't ruled that all price maintenance agreements are illegal, some states have outlawed them on the grounds that they stifle competition. In some countries, such as the United Kingdom, they are banned altogether. The safest bet for a manufacturer is to provide a "suggested retail price" to its channel partners.

## 5.4 Channel Integration: Vertical and Horizontal Marketing Systems

**vertical marketing system**

A system in which channel members formally agree to cooperate with one another.

Another way to foster cooperation in a channel is to establish a vertical marketing system. In a **vertical marketing system**, channel members formally agree to closely cooperate with one another. (You have probably heard the saying, "If you can't beat 'em, join 'em.") A vertical marketing system can also be created by one channel member taking over the functions of another member.

Procter & Gamble (P&G) has traditionally been a manufacturer of household products, not a retailer of them. But the company's long-term strategy is to compete in every personal-care channel, including salons, where the men's business is underdeveloped. In 2009, P&G purchased The Art of Shaving, a seller of pricey men's shaving products located in upscale shopping malls. P&G also runs retail boutiques around the globe that sell its prestigious SK-II skin-care line.[28]

Franchises are another type of vertical marketing system. They are used not only to lessen channel conflicts but also to penetrate markets. Recall that a franchise gives a person or group the right to market a company's goods or services within a certain territory or location.[29] McDonald's sells meat, bread, ice cream, and other products to its franchises, along with the right to own and operate the stores. And each of the owners of the stores signs a contract with McDonald's agreeing to do business in a certain way.

By contrast, in a **conventional marketing system** the channel members have no affiliation with one another. All the members operate independently. If the sale or the purchase of a product seems like a good deal at the time, an organization pursues it. But there is no expectation among the channel members that they have to work with one another in the future.

**conventional marketing system**

A marketing system in which the channel members have no affiliation with one another.

A **horizontal marketing system** is one in which two companies at the same channel level—say, two manufacturers, two wholesalers, or two retailers—agree to cooperate with another to sell their products or to make the most of their marketing opportunities. The Internet phone service Skype and the mobile-phone maker Nokia created a horizontal marketing system by teaming up to put Skype's service on Nokia's phones. Skype hopes it will reach a new market (mobile phone users) this way. And Nokia hopes to sell its phones to people who like to use Skype on their personal computers (PCs).[30]

**horizontal marketing system**

A system in which two companies at the same channel level agree to cooperate with one another to sell their products.

Similarly, Via Technologies, a computer-chip maker that competes with Intel, has teamed up with a number of Chinese companies with no PC-manufacturing experience to produce $200 netbooks. Via Technologies predicts that the new, cheaper netbooks the Chinese companies sell will quickly capture 20 percent of the market.[31] Of course, the more of them that are sold, the more computer chips Via Technologies sells.

## KEY TAKEAWAY

Channel partners that wield channel power are referred to as channel leaders. A dispute among channel members is called a channel conflict. A vertical conflict is one that occurs between two different types of members in a channel. By contrast, a horizontal conflict is one that occurs between organizations of the same type. Channel leaders are often in the best position to resolve channel conflicts. Vertical and horizontal marketing systems can help foster channel cooperation, as can creating marketing programs to help a channel's members all generate greater revenues and profits.

## REVIEW QUESTIONS

1. What gives some organizations more channel power than others?
2. Why do channel conflicts occur?
3. Which organization(s) has the most power to resolve channel conflicts?
4. How can setting up vertical and horizontal marketing systems prevent channel conflicts?

# 6. MARKETING CHANNELS VERSUS SUPPLY CHAINS

## LEARNING OBJECTIVES

1. **Understand how supply chains differ from marketing channels.**
2. **Describe the types of organizations that are part of supply chains.**

**supply chain**

All the organizations that participate in the production, promotion, and delivery of a product or service from the producer to the end consumer.

In the past few decades, organizations have begun taking a more holistic look at their marketing channels. Instead of looking at only the firms that sell and promote their products, they have begun looking at *all* the organizations that figure into any part of the process of producing, promoting, and delivering an offering to its user. All these organizations are considered part of the offering's **supply chain**.

For instance, the supply chain includes producers of the raw materials that go into a product. If it's a food product, the supply chain extends back through the distributors all the way to the farmers who grew the ingredients and the companies from which the farmers purchased the seeds, fertilizer, or animals. A product's supply chain also includes transportation companies such as railroads that help physically move the product and companies that build Web sites for other companies. If a software maker hires a company in India to help it write a computer program, the Indian company is part of the partner's supply chain. These types of firms aren't considered channel partners because it's not their job to actively sell the products being produced. Nonetheless, they all contribute to a product's success or failure.

**supply chain management**

The process of managing and refining supply chains so as to make them as efficient as possible.

Firms are constantly monitoring their supply chains and tinkering with them so they're as efficient as possible. This process is called **supply chain management**. Supply chain management is challenging. Done well, it's practically an art. We'll talk more about supply chains in the next chapter and what companies can do to improve them to better satisfy customers and gain a competitive edge.

## KEY TAKEAWAY

All of the organizations that figure into any part of the process of producing, promoting, and delivering an offering to its user are part of the offering's supply chain. In recent decades, firms have begun looking at these organizations in addition to the organizations that sell and promote their products. The process of managing and improving supply chains is called supply chain management.

## REVIEW QUESTION

1. What are the benefits of looking at all of the organizations that contribute to the production of a product versus just the organizations that sell them?

# 7. DISCUSSION QUESTIONS AND ACTIVITIES

## DISCUSSION QUESTIONS

1. What's the ideal number of marketing channels a firm should have?
2. Is a pull strategy superior in all markets?
3. Is selling power the only source of channel power? From what other sources could an organization derive channel power?
4. The chapter listed a number of scenarios that can cause channel conflicts. What other factors can you think of that might cause channel conflicts?
5. Amazon.com has carved out a unique niche for itself as an intermediary. Amazon sells products on behalf of manufacturers such as Dell, Sony, and Calvin Klein, as well as retailers such as Macy's and Toys"R"Us. How should Amazon be categorized? As a retailer, wholesaler, or broker?

## ACTIVITIES

1. Think of some products you currently use. Are there any you would like to buy via different marketing channels? Do you think the products could be successfully marketed this way?
2. Describe a time in which you did business with a company and received conflicting information from its different channels (for example, a store's Web site versus a visit to the store). How did it affect your buying experience? Have you done business with the company since?
3. Break into groups and make a list of four to five different types of products. Decide which channels should be used to distribute each product. Present your findings to your class and see if they agree with you.
4. Make a list of products you believe failed because of poor marketing channel choices.

# ENDNOTES


1. Randy Littleson, "Supply Chain Trends: What's In, What's Out," *Manufacturing.net*, February 6, 2007, http://www.manufacturing.net/articles/2007/02/supply-chain-trends-whats-in-whats-out (accessed April 13, 2012).
2. "Developing a Channel Strategy," *CBSNews.com*, http://www.cbsnews.com/8301-505125_162-51168339/developing-a-channel-strategy/?tag=mncol;lst;1 (accessed April 13, 2012).
3. Geoff Lancaster and Frank Withey, *Marketing Fundamentals* (Burlington, MA: Butterworth-Heinemann, 2007), 173.
4. Daniel Lyons, "The Lost Decade," *Newsweek*, November 9, 2009, 27.
5. "Developing a Channel Strategy," *CBSNews.com*, http://www.cbsnews.com/8301-505125_162-51168339/developing-a-channel-strategy/?tag=mncol;lst;1 (accessed April 13, 2012).
6. John Austin, "Pop-Up Stores Offer Long-Term Strategy," *Fort Worth Star-Telegram*, November 27, 2009, 1C–2C.
7. Jonathan Birchall, "Walmart Aims to Cut Supply Chain Cost," *Financial Times*, January 4, 2010, 4.
8. Kenneth L. Kraemeer and Jason Dedrick, "Dell Computer: Organization of a Global Production Network," Center for Research on Information Technology and Organizations, University of California, Irvine, 2008, http://escholarship.org/uc/item/89x7p4ws#page-2 (accessed April 13, 2012).
9. Michele Fitzpatrick, "The Seven Myths of Channel Integration," *Chief Marketer*, October 1, 2005, http://chiefmarketer.com/multi_channel/myths_integration_1001 (accessed December 12, 2009).
10. "About Jones Soda Co.," *JonesSoda.com*, http://www.jonessoda.com/company/about-us (accessed April 13, 2012).
11. James Wilson and Javier Blas, "Machines with Midas Touch Swap Chocolate for Gold Bars," *Financial Times*, June 17, 2009, http://www.ft.com/cms/s/0/5232dc6c-5ad4-11de-8c14-00144feabdc0.html?nclick_check=1 (accessed December 12, 2009).
12. Cristene Gonzalez-Wertz, "Ten Examples of Smarter Customer Focus" (blog), *WordPress.com*, February 11, 2009, http://museandmaven.wordpress.com/2009/02/11/10-examples-of-smarter-customer-focus (accessed December 12, 2009).
13. Patt Waldmeir, "Coca-Cola in New China Push," *Financial Times*, March 7, 2009, 10.
14. Matthew Boyle, "Walmart's Painful Lessons," *BusinessWeek*, October 13, 2009, http://www.businessweek.com/managing/content/oct2009/ca20091013_227022.htm (accessed December 12, 2009).
15. Daniel Shafer, "Asia Is Final Frontier for VW Empire," *Financial Times*, December 10, 2009, 17.
16. Tim Bradshaw, "Zune to Launch Outside U.S.," *Financial Times*, November 16, 2009, http://www.ft.com/cms/s/0/76f98ae8-d205-11de-a0f0-00144feabdc0.html (accessed December 11, 2009).
17. "Bottling Success," *Packaging-Gateway.com*, September 1, 2006, http://www.packaging-gateway.com/features/feature738 (accessed December 12, 2009).
18. Goldie Blumenstyk, "Kaplan U.'s Catchy Ad Provokes a Question: Do Colleges Serve Today's Students?" *Chronicle of Higher Education*, June 29, 2009, http://chronicle.com/article/Kaplan-Us-Question-Do/46956 (accessed December 12, 2009).
19. Barbara Jorgensen, "Distributors' Services Help Keep Customers Afloat," *EDN* 54, no. 8 (April 23, 2009): 60.
20. Gary L. Frazier, Elliot Maltz, Kersi D. Antia, and Aric Rindfleisch, "Distributor Sharing of Strategic Information with Suppliers," *Journal of Marketing*, July 1, 2009, http://www.atypon-link.com/AMA/doi/abs/10.1509/jmkg.73.4.31?cookieSet=1&journalCode=jmkg (accessed December 12, 2009).
21. "Pizza Hut's Online Ordering Called 'Virtual Waiter,'" *The Food Channel*, http://www.foodchannel.com/stories/421-pizza-hut-s-online-ordering-called-virtual-waiter (accessed December 12, 2009).
22. Peter Burrows, "Inside the iPhone Gray Market," *BusinessWeek*, February 12, 2008, http://www.businessweek.com/technology/content/feb2008/tc20080211_152894.htm (accessed December 12, 2009).
23. Michael Hitt, Stewart Black, and Lyman Porter, *Management*, 2nd ed. (Upper Saddle River, NJ: Prentice Hall, 2009), chap. 5.
24. Michael Hitt, Stewart Black, and Lyman Porter, *Management*, 2nd ed. (Upper Saddle River, NJ: Prentice Hall, 2009), chap. 5.
25. Matthew W. Evans, "Beauty.com Undergoes a Revamp," *Women's Wear Daily* 194, no. 66 (September 26, 2007): 17.
26. "Ten Mistakes to Avoid with Channel Partners," *irieAuctions.com*, http://www.irieauctions.com/Alternate_Distribution_Channel.htm (accessed December 12, 2009).
27. "Ten Mistakes to Avoid with Channel Partners," *irieAuctions.com*, http://www.irieauctions.com/Alternate_Distribution_Channel.htm (accessed December 12, 2009).
28. Jack Neff, "P&G Acquires the Upscale *Art of Shaving* Retail Chain," *Advertising Age* 80, no. 2118 (June 8, 2009): 2.
29. Don Daszkowski, "What Is a Franchise," *About.com*, http://franchises.about.com/od/franchisebasics/a/what-franchises.htm (accessed December 12, 2009).
30. "Skype Expands Mobile Push," *Financial Times*, March 31, 2009, 20.
31. Kathrin Hill, "Via to Help New PC Makers Enter the Netbook Market," *Financial Times*, May 18, 2009, 16.

# CHAPTER 9
# Using Supply Chains to Create Value for Customers

Suppose you have developed a great new product like *Ghostbusters: The Video Game*. Not only is the game terrific, but you've managed to maximize to get it sold in every marketing channel you can. The product is selling at GameStop, Walmart, Best Buy, and Amazon, and it's slated to come out on Sony's PlayStation Portable console. That's the end of the story, right? Not quite. Sooner rather than later, in addition to focusing on the firms "downstream" that sell *your product*, you will also look "upstream" at your suppliers and "sideways" at potential firms to partner with. It's only natural. (Or in the case of *Ghostbusters: The Video Game*, should we say *supernatural*?)

**Video Clip**

**Who Ya Gonna Call?**

Mark Randel, John O'Keefe, and Brendan Goss, the founders of the company that produced the new Ghostbusters video game, say they had to satisfy two types of customers with the product—gamers and fans of the original *Ghostbusters* movie. Check out the demo.

View the video online at: http://www.youtube.com/embed/xGgHJdz8WT8

As we explained in Chapter 8, your product's supply chain includes not only the downstream companies that actively sell the product but also all the other organizations that have an impact on it before, during, and after it's produced. Those companies include the providers of the raw materials your firm uses to produce it, the transportation company that physically moves it, and the firm that helped build the Web pages to promote it. If you hired a programmer in India to help write computer code for the game, the Indian programmer is also part of the product's supply chain. If you hired a company to process copies of the game returned by customers, that company is part of the supply chain as well. Large organizations with many products can have literally thousands of supply chain partners. Service organizations also need supplies to operate, so they have supply chains, too.

As you learned at the end of the last chapter, the process of designing, monitoring, and altering supply chains to make them as efficient as possible is called **supply chain management**. The term supply chain management was first coined by an American industry consultant in the early 1980s, but it's an old idea. Part of Henry Ford's strategy in the early 1900s was to extract as much efficiency (and money) as he could by taking ownership of the supply chains for his automobiles. Ford owned the foundries that converted raw iron ore to steel for his cars. He also owned the plantations from which rubber was extracted to produce his automobiles' tires, and the ships on which the materials and finished products were transported.[1]

Today, many companies still take a narrow view of their supply chains; they look at supply chains mainly in terms of the costs they can save. Cost reduction is definitely an important part of supply chain management. After all, if your competitors can produce their products at a lower cost, they could put you out of business.

Keep in mind, however, that a firm can produce a product so cheaply that no one will buy it because it's shoddy. That's why smart companies view their supply chains as an integral part of their marketing plans. In other words, these companies also look at the ways their supply chains can create value for customers so as to give their firms a competitive edge.

**value chain**

A term that is sometimes used interchangeably with the term supply chain. The idea behind the value chain is that your supply chain partners should do more for you than perform just basic functions.

Today, the term **value chain** is sometimes used interchangeably with the term *supply chain*. The idea behind the value chain is that your supply chain partners should do more for you than perform just basic functions; each one should help you create more value for customers as the product travels along the chain—preferably more value than your competitors' supply chain partners can add to their products.

**FIGURE 9.1**

There are no fuddy-duddy fashions at Zara stores. Out with the old, in with the new—or whatever is selling well.

Zara, a trendy but inexpensive clothing chain in Europe, is a good example of a company that has managed to create value for its customers with smart supply chain design and execution. Originally, it took six months for Zara to design a garment and get it delivered to stores. To get the hottest fashions in the hands of customers as sooner, Zara began working more closely with its supply chain partners and internal design teams. It also automated its inventory systems so it could quickly figure out what was selling and what was not. As a result, it's now able to deliver its customers the most cutting-edge fashion in just two weeks. Not only that, but the company set a new standard for the clothing industry in the process.[2]

# 1. SOURCING AND PROCUREMENT

## LEARNING OBJECTIVES

1. **Explain why sourcing and procurement activities are an important part of supply chain management.**
2. **Describe the reasons why the use of outsourcing and offshoring has grown.**
3. **Explain some of the drawbacks companies face when they outsource their activities.**

**Sourcing** is the process of evaluating and hiring individual businesses to supply goods and services to your business. **Procurement** is the process of actually purchasing those goods and services. Sourcing and procurement have become a bigger part of a supply manager's job in recent years, in part because businesses keep becoming more specialized. Just like Ford's workers became more efficient by performing specialized tasks, so, too have companies.

Ford Motor Company no longer produces its own tires for its cars. It buys them from tire producers like Michelin and Goodyear. It's still possible to "own" your supply chain, though. The diamond company DeBeers owns its own mines, distributorships, and retail diamond stores. The problem is that it's very costly to own multiple types of companies and difficult to run them all well, too.

Firms look up and down their supply chains and outside them to see which companies can add the most value to their products at the least cost. If a firm can find a company that can add more value than it can to a function, it will often **outsource** the task to that company. After all, why do something yourself if someone else can do it better or more cost effectively?

Rather than their own fleets of trucks, ships, and airplanes, most companies outsource at least some of their transportation tasks to shippers such as Roadway and FedEx. Other companies hire freight forwarders to help them. You can think of **freight forwarders** as travel agents for freight.[3] Their duties include negotiating rates for shipments and booking space for them on transportation vehicles and in warehouses. A freight forwarder also combines small loads from various shippers into larger loads that can be shipped by more economically. However, it doesn't own its own transportation equipment or warehouses.

Other companies go a step further and outsource their entire order processing and shipping departments to **third-party logistics (3PLs) firms**. FedEx Supply Chain Services and UPS Supply Chain Solutions (which are divisions of FedEx and UPS, respectively) are examples of 3PLs. A 3PL is one-stop shipping solution for a company that wants to focus on other aspects of its business. Firms that receive and ship products internationally often hire 3PLs so they don't have to deal with the headaches of transporting products abroad and completing import and export paperwork for them.

**sourcing**

The process of evaluating and hiring individual businesses to supply goods and services to your organization.

**procurement**

The process of purchasing goods and services for your organization.

**outsource**

Hiring an organization to do a task your firm previously performed.

**freight forwarder**

An organization whose duties include consolidating small loads of freight, negotiating rates for their shipment, and booking space for them on transportation vehicles and in warehouses.

**third-party logistics (3PLs) firms**

Firms to which other companies outsource their entire order processing and shipping departments.

## 1.1 The Growth of Outsourcing and Offshoring

Beginning in the 1990s, companies began to outsource a lot of other activities besides transportation.[4] Their goal was twofold: (1) to lower their costs and (2) to focus on the activities they do best. You might be surprised by the functions firms outsource. In fact, many "producers" of products no longer produce them at all but outsource their production instead.

Most clothing companies, including Nike, design products, but they don't make them. Instead, they send their designs to companies in nations with low labor costs. Likewise, many drug companies no longer develop their own drugs. They outsource the task to smaller drug developers, which in recent years have had a better track record of developing best-selling pharmaceuticals. The Crest SpinBrush (toothbrush) wasn't developed by Procter & Gamble, the maker of Crest. A small company called Church & Dwight Co. developed the technology for the SpinBrush, and P&G purchased the right to market and sell the product.

Outsourcing work to companies abroad is called **offshoring**. Figure 9.2 shows the percentage of supply chain functions three hundred global manufacturers and service organizations say they now offshore and the percentages these organizations expect to offshore by 2010.

**offshoring**

Outsourcing work to a company abroad.

**FIGURE 9.2** Percentage of Supply Chain Functions Offshored in 2008[5]

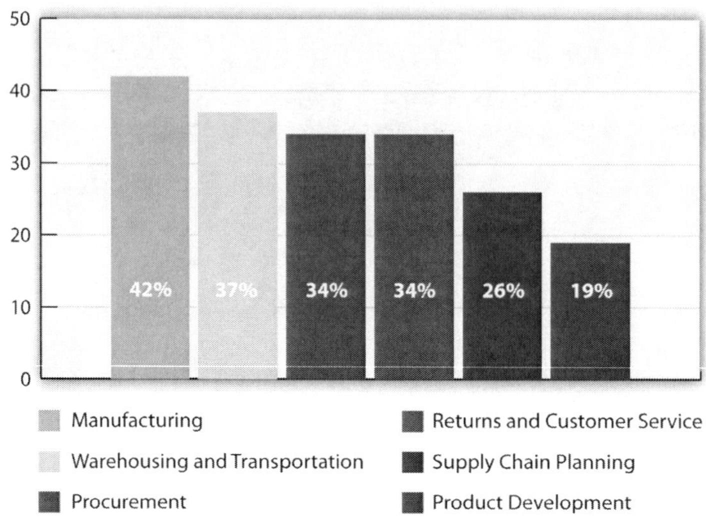


## Some of the Ins and Outs of Outsourcing

A company faces a number of tradeoffs when it outsources an activity. The loss of control—particularly when it comes to product quality and safety—is one of them. Just ask Mattel. Beginning in 2007, Mattel was forced to recall tens of millions of toys it had outsourced for production because they were tainted with lead. But Mattel isn't the only company to experience problems. In a recent global survey, more than one-fifth of the companies that outsource their production said they have experienced "frequent" and "serious" quality problems.[6]

The U.S. Consumer Products Safety Commission randomly inspects products, but there is no way the commission's personnel can begin to test them all. To protect their customers, many companies either test their suppliers' products themselves or contract with independent labs to do so. For example, if you sell a product to Walmart, you need to be prepared to send it to such a lab, should Walmart ask you to.[7] Companies also do on-site audits, or checks, of their suppliers. Other companies station employees with their suppliers on a permanent basis to be sure that the quality of the products they're producing is acceptable.

The loss of control of their technology is another outsourcing risk that companies face. Some countries are better about protecting patented technologies and designs than others, and some supply chain partners are more trustworthy than others. How can you be sure your supply chain partner won't steal your technology? A few years ago, General Motors began working with a Chinese firm to produce a car called the Spark for the Chinese market. But before GM could even get the automobile plant up and running, the U.S. automaker alleged that the design of the car had been stolen, sold to another company, and knockoffs of it were being driven around China's streets.[8]

**social responsibility**

The idea that companies should manage their businesses not just to earn profits but to advance the well-being of society.

**environmental sustainability**

The idea that firms should engage in business practices that have the least impact on the environment so that it is sustained for future generations.

Another aspect of outsourcing relates to the social responsibility and environmental sustainability companies exhibit in terms of how they manage their supply chains. **Social responsibility** is the idea that companies should manage their businesses not just to earn profits but to advance the well-being of society. Both issues are becoming increasingly important to consumers. **Environmental sustainability** is the idea that firms should engage in business practices that have the least impact on the environment so that it's sustained for future generations.

To demonstrate to consumers they are socially responsible, Starbucks and other companies have joined the Fair Trade movement. Members of the Fair Trade movement pay farmers and other third-world producers higher prices for their products so they don't have to live in poverty. The prices consumers pay for products with fair-trade labels are often higher, but one Harvard study has showed that consumers expect them to be and that sales actually increased when the prices of them went up.[9]

The push for environmental sustainability is also having an impact on supply chains, partly because the stricter environmental laws in many counties are demanding it. But companies are seeing the upside of producing "greener" products and disposing of them in ethical ways. First, it improves a company's image and makes it stand out among its competitors. Second, many consumers are willing to pay more for green products, even during a recession.[10] Walmart recently announced that it's planning to require its suppliers to measure the environmental costs of producing their products. The "green" ratings will then be put on the products labels.[11] Figure 9.3 shows the reasons why firms "go green" with their supply chains.

**FIGURE 9.3** Why Firms Say They Are "Going Green" with Their Supply Chains[12]

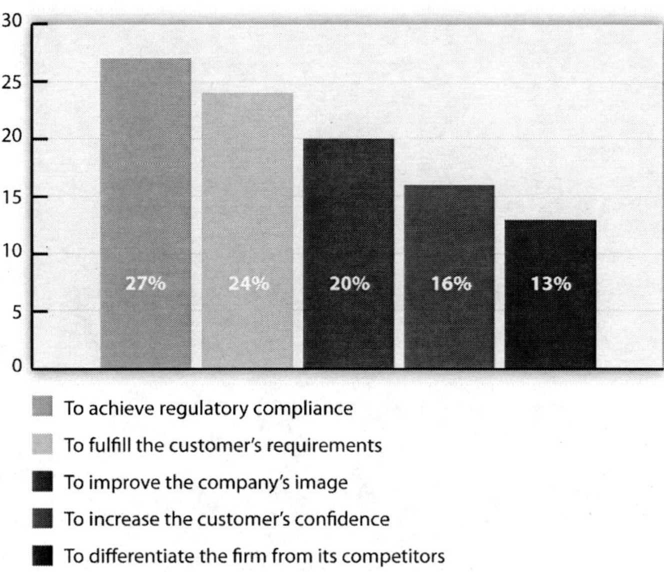


To achieve regulatory compliance
To fulfill the customer's requirements
To improve the company's image
To increase the customer's confidence
To differentiate the firm from its competitors

The outdoor clothing company Patagonia takes both social responsibility and environmental sustainability seriously. Patagonia tries to design, source, produce, and recycle its products so they cause the least environmental damage possible. The company also audits it supply chain partners to ensure they treat workers fairly.

## Video Clip

**Hewlett-Packard = Hazardous Products**

Not going green can be hazardous to a company's reputation. After Hewlett-Packard (HP) broke a promise to eliminate toxic materials in its computers by 2009, Greenpeace activists painted the words "Hazardous Products" on the roof of the company's headquarters in Palo Alto, California. Meanwhile, a voicemail message from *Star Trek* actor William Shatner was delivered to all the phones in the building. "Please ask your leader [HP CEO Mark Hurd]" to make computers that are toxin free like Apple has done, Shatner said in the message. You can hear the message by going to the following link: http://www.greenpeace.org/international/news/hp-reminder-28-07-09. An HP spokesman said that eliminating the toxic materials would have disrupted the company's supply chain.

View the video online at: http://www.youtube.com/embed/D5qlemzD0iY

One of the drawbacks of outsourcing is the time it takes for products to make their way to the United States and into the hands of consumers. The time it takes is a big issue because it affects how responsive a company is to its customers. Retailers don't like to wait for products. Waiting might mean their customers will shop elsewhere if they can't find what they want. As we explained in Chapter 8, for this reason and others, some companies are outsourcing their activities closer to home.

**FIGURE 9.4**

Click on the link below to track the environmental and social impact of Patagonia's various products throughout the supply chain—from their design to their delivery: http://www.patagonia.com/web/us/footprint/index.jsp.

**insourcing**

When firms move activities, such as logistics, in-house.

When firms that can't resolve their supplier problems, they find other suppliers to work with or they move the activities back in-house, which is a process called **insourcing**. Insourcing can actually help set your company apart these days. The credit card company Discover doesn't outsource its customer service to companies abroad. Perhaps that helps explain why one survey ranked Discover number one in customer loyalty.

## 1.2 Matching a Company's Sourcing Strategies with the Needs of Its Customers

Your customer should ultimately be the focus of any insourcing and outsourcing decision you make. After all, unless the product gets recycled, the customer is the last link in the supply chain. Not all customers have the same product and service requirements, though. It might be acceptable for a company that sells PCs to individual consumers to outsource its tech support, perhaps to a firm in India that can perform the function at lower cost. However, a company that buys an expensive, customized computer network is probably going to want to deal directly with the maker of the product if the network goes down—not another company in another country.

Similarly, if you're producing an expensive car for Ferrari-type buyers, purchasing bargain-basement-priced parts could leave your customers dissatisfied—especially if the parts fail and their cars break down. Conversely, if you're designing a low-end automobile, top-of-the-line parts could make it too expensive for low-end buyers. High-end car buyers are likely to demand better after-sales service than low-end car buyers, too.

**FIGURE 9.5**

Many of Patagonia's customers are outdoor enthusiasts willing to pay $100 or more for a fleece jacket made from recycled plastic bottles. A customer at Walmart might not be. The trick for Walmart and its green index will be to satisfy customers who want low prices as well as to save the planet.

*© 2010 Jupiterimages Corporation*

## KEY TAKEAWAY

Sourcing is the process of evaluating and hiring individual businesses to supply goods and services to your business. Procurement is the process of actually purchasing those goods and services. Sourcing and procurement have become a bigger part of a supply manager's job in recent years, in part because businesses keep becoming more specialized. Companies outsource activities to lower their costs to focus on the activities they do best. Companies face numerous tradeoffs when they outsource activities, which can include a loss of control and product-quality and safety problems. When firms that can't resolve their supplier problems, they find other suppliers to work with or they move the activities back in-house, which is a process called insourcing. Customer should be the focus of any insourcing and outsourcing decisions companies make.

## REVIEW QUESTIONS

1. What are some of the supply chain functions firms outsource and offshore?
2. How does outsourcing differ from offshoring?
3. Why might a company be better off insourcing an activity?

# 2. DEMAND PLANNING AND INVENTORY CONTROL

**LEARNING OBJECTIVES**

1. Explain why demand planning adds value to products.
2. Describe the role inventory control plays when it comes marketing products.
3. List the reasons why firms collaborate with another for the purposes of inventory control and demand planning.

## 2.1 Demand Planning

Imagine you are a marketing manager who has done everything in your power to help develop and promote a product—and it's selling well. But now your company is running short of the product because the demand forecasts for it were too low. Recall that this is the scenario Nintendo faced when the Wii first came out. The same thing happened to IBM when it launched the popular ThinkPad laptop in 1992.

Not only is the product shortage going to adversely affect the profitably of your company, but it's going to adversely affect you, too. Why? Because you, as a marketing manager, probably earn either a bonus or commission from the products you work to promote, depending on how well they sell. And, of course, you can't sell what you don't have.

As you can probably tell, the best marketing decisions and supplier selections aren't enough if your company's demand forecasts are wrong. **Demand planning** is the process of estimating how much of a good or service customers will buy from you. If you're a producer of a product, this will affect not only the amount of goods and services you have to produce but also the materials you must purchase to make them. It will also affect your **production scheduling**, or the management of the resources, events, and processes need to create an offering. For example, if demand is heavy, you might need your staff members to work overtime. Closely related to demand forecasting are lead times. A product's **lead time** is the amount of time it takes for a customer to receive a good or service once it's been ordered. Lead times also have to be taken into account when a company is forecasting demand.

**FIGURE 9.6**

IBM ThinkPads were hard to find in 1992. But NASA didn't have any trouble getting one. In 1993, astronauts used it to repair the Hubble Space Telescope, which orbits Earth.

*© 2010 Jupiterimages Corporation*

**demand planning**

The process of estimating how much of a good or service customers will buy from you.

**production scheduling**

The management of the resources, events, and processes need to create an offering.

**lead time**

The amount of time it takes for a customer to receive a good or service once it's been ordered.

*Sourcing decisions*—deciding which suppliers to use—are generally made periodically. *Forecasting decisions* must be made more frequently—sometimes daily. One way for you to predict the demand for your product is to look at your company's past sales. This is what most companies do. But they don't stop there. Why? Because changes in many factors—the availability of materials to produce a product and their prices, global competition, oil prices (which affect shipping costs), the economy, and even the weather—can change the picture.

For example, when the economy hit the skids in 2008, the demand for many products fell. So if you had based your production, sales, and marketing forecasts on 2007 data alone, chances are your forecasts would have been wildly wrong. Do you remember when peanut butter was recalled in 2009 because of contamination? If your firm were part of the supply chain for peanut butter products, you would have needed to quickly change your forecasts.

The promotions you run will also affect demand for your products. Consider what happened to KFC when it first came out with its new grilled chicken product. As part of the promotion, KFC gave away coupons for free grilled chicken via Oprah.com. Just twenty-four hours after the coupons were uploaded to the Web site, KFC risked running out of chicken. Many customers were turned away. Others were given "rain checks" (certificates) they could use to get free grilled chicken later.[13]

In addition to looking at the sales histories of their firms, supply chain managers also consult with marketing managers and sales executives when they are generating demand forecasts. Sales and marketing personnel know what promotions are being planned because they work more closely with customers and know what customers' needs are and if those needs are changing.

Firms also look to their supply chain partners to help with their demand planning. **Collaborative planning, forecasting, and replenishment (CPFR)** is a practice whereby supply chain partners share information and coordinate their operations. Walmart has developed a Web-based CPFR system called Retail Link. Retailers can log into Retail Link to see how well their products are selling at various Walmart stores, how soon more products need to be shipped to the company and where, how any promotions being run are affecting the profitability of their products, and so forth. Because different companies often use different information technology systems and software, Web-based tools like Retail Link are becoming a popular way for supply chain partners to interface with one another.

Not all firms are wild about sharing every piece of information they can with their supply chains partners. Some retailers view their sales information as an asset—something they can sell to information companies like Information Resources, Inc., which provides competitive data to firms that willing to pay for it.[14] By contrast, other firms go so far as to involve their suppliers before even producing a product so they can suggest design changes, material choices, and production recommendations.

**FIGURE 9.7**

KFC's new Kentucky Grilled Chicken was finger-lickin' good—if you could get it. Reportedly, the chain nearly ran out of the birds following a promotion on Oprah.com.

© 2010 *Jupiterimages Corporation*

## Video Clip

**Take a Test Drive of the Tato Nano**

Priced at about $2,500 the Tata Nano is the least expensive car ever produced in the world. To make a safe, reliable car at such a low cost, Tata Motors, an Indian company, sought new, innovative design approaches from its suppliers. The elimination of one of the car's two windshield wipers was one result of the collaboration that occurred between Tata and its supply chain partners.[15]

View the video online at: http://www.youtube.com/embed/3sZitve3SUw

**collaborative planning, forecasting, and replenishment (CPFR)**

A practice whereby supply chain partners share information and coordinate their operations.

The trend is clearly toward more shared information, or what businesspeople refer to as **supply chain visibility**. After all, it makes sense that a supplier will be not only more reliable but also in a better position to add value to your products if it knows what your sales, operations, and marketing plans are—and what your customers want. By sharing more than just basic transaction information, companies can see how well operations are proceeding, how products are flowing through the chain, how well the partners are performing and cooperating with one another, and the extent to which value is being built in to the product.

**supply chain visibility**

A situation in which supply chain partners share information with one another so they can see how well the chain is working.

Demand-planning software can also be used to create more accurate demand forecasts. **Demand-planning software** can synthesize a variety of factors to better predict a firm's demand—for example, the firm's sales history, point-of-sale data, warehouse, suppliers, and promotion information, and economic and competitive trends. So a company's demand forecasts are as up-to-date as possible, some of the systems allow sales and marketing personnel to input purchasing information into their mobile devices after consulting with customers.

**demand-planning software**

Software that can synthesize a variety of factors to better predict a firm's demand.

Litehouse Foods, a salad dressing manufacturer, was able to improve its forecasts dramatically by using demand-planning software. Originally the company was using a traditional sales database and spreadsheets to do the work. "It was all pretty much manual calculations. We had no engine to do the heavy lifting for us," says John Shaw, the company's Information Technology director. In a short time, the company was able to reduce its inventory by about one-third while still meeting its customers' needs.[16]

## 2.2 Inventory Control

**inventory control**

The process of ensuring your firm has an adequate amount of products and a wide enough assortment of them meet your customers' needs.

**stockout**

A situation that occurs when a firm runs out of a product a customer wants to buy.

Demand forecasting is part of a company's overall inventory control activities. **Inventory control** is the process of ensuring your firm has an adequate supply of products and a wide enough assortment of them meet your customers' needs. One of the goals of inventory management is to avoid stockouts. A **stockout** occurs when you run out of a product a customer wants to buy. Customers will simply look elsewhere to buy the product—a process the Internet has made easier than ever

When the attack on the World Trade Center occurred, many Americans rushed to the store to buy batteries, flashlights, American flags, canned goods, and other products in the event that the emergency signaled a much bigger attack. Target sold out of many items and could not replenish them for several days, partly because its inventory tracking system only counted up what was needed at the end of the day. Walmart, on the other hand, took count of what was needed every five minutes. Before the end of the day, Walmart had purchased enough American flags, for example, to meet demand and in so doing, completely locked up all their vendors' flags. Meanwhile, Target was out of flags and out of luck—there were no more to be had.

**safety stock**

Backup inventory that serves as a buffer in case the demand for a product surges or the supply of it drops off for some reason.

**shrinkage**

A term used to describe a reduction or loss in inventory due to shoplifting, employee theft, paperwork errors, and supplier fraud.

To help avoid stockouts, most companies keep a certain amount of safety stock on hand. **Safety stock** is backup inventory that serves as a buffer in case the demand for a product surges or the supply of it drops off for some reason. Maintaining too much inventory, though, ties up money that could be spent other ways—perhaps on marketing promotions. Inventory also has to be insured, and in some cases, taxes must be paid on it. Products in inventory can also become obsolete, deteriorate, spoil, or "shrink." **Shrinkage** is a term used to describe a reduction or loss in inventory due to shoplifting, employee theft, paperwork errors, or supplier fraud.[17]

When the economy went into its most recent slide, many firms found themselves between a rock and a hard place in terms of their inventory levels. On the one hand, because sales were low, firms were reluctant to hold much safety stock. Many companies, including Walmart, cut the number of brands they sold in addition to holding a smaller amount of inventory. On the other hand, because they didn't know when business would pick up, they ran the risk of running out of products. Many firms dealt with the problem by maintaining larger amounts of key products. Companies also watched their supply chain partners struggle to survive. Forty-five percent of firms responding to one survey about the downturn reported providing financial help to their critical supply chain partners—often in the form of credit and revised payment schedules.[18]

## 2.3 Just-in-Time Inventory Systems

**just-in-time inventory systems**

A system in which a firm keeps very little inventory on hand. Instead, its suppliers ship it inventory as needed.

**vendor-managed inventory (VMI)**

The practice of having your suppliers monitor your inventory levels.

To lower the amount of inventory and still maintain they stock they need to satisfy their customers, some organizations use **just-in-time inventory systems** in both good times and bad. Firms with just-in-time inventory systems keep very little inventory on hand. Instead, they contract with their suppliers to ship them inventory as they need it—and even sometimes manage their inventory for them—a practice called **vendor-managed inventory (VMI)**. Dell is an example of a company that utilizes a just-in-time inventory system that's vendor managed. Dell carries very few component parts. Instead, its suppliers carry them. They are located in small warehouses near Dell's assembly plants worldwide and provide Dell with parts "just-in-time" for them to be assembled.[19]

**mass customization**

Mass producing goods customized to the specifications of individual consumers.

Dell's inventory and production system allows customers to get their computers built exactly to their specifications, a production process that's called **mass customization**. This helps keep Dell's inventory levels low. Instead of a huge inventory of expensive, already-assembled computers consumers may or may not buy, Dell simply has the parts on hand, which can be configured or reconfigured should consumers' preferences change. Dell can more easily return the parts to its suppliers if at some point it redesigns its computers to better match what its customers want. And by keeping track of its customers and what they are ordering, Dell has a better idea of what they might order in the future and the types of inventory it should hold. Because mass customization lets buyers "have it their way," it also adds value to products, for which many customers are willing to pay.

## 2.4 Product Tracking

Some companies, including Walmart, are beginning to experiment with new technologies such as electronic product codes in an effort to better manage their inventories. An **electronic product code (EPC)** is similar to a barcode, only better, because the number on it is truly unique. You have probably watched a checkout person scan a barcode off of a product identical to the one you wanted to buy—perhaps a pack of gum—because the barcode on your product was missing or wouldn't scan. Electronic product codes make it possible to distinguish between two identical packs of gum. The codes contain information about when the packs of gum were manufactured, where they were shipped from, and where they were going to. Being able to tell the difference between "seemingly" identical products can help companies monitor their expiration dates if they are recalled for quality of safety reasons. EPC technology can also be used to combat "fake" products, or knockoffs, in the marketplace.

**electronic product code (EPC)**

A barcode that can distinguish between two seemingly identical products. It contains information about where the product was manufactured and where it was shipped from and bound to.

### Video Clip

**The Basics of RFID and EPC Technology**

To understand how EPC and RFID technology can help marketers, watch this YouTube video.

View the video online at: http://www.youtube.com/embed/k-w6ZYlo37E

Electronic product codes are stored on radio-frequency identification (RFID) tags. A **radio-frequency identification (RFID) tag** emits radio signals that can record and track a shipment as it comes in and out of a facility. If you have unlocked your car door remotely, microchipped your dog, or waved a toll-way tag at a checkpoint, you have used RFID technology.[20] Because each RFID tag can cost anywhere from $0.50 to $50 each, they are generally used to track larger shipments, such cases and pallets of goods rather than individual items. See Figure 9.8 to get an idea of how RFID tags work.

**radio-frequency identification (RFID) tag**

A tag that emits radio signals that can record and track a shipment as it comes in and out of a facility.

**FIGURE 9.8** How RFID Tagging Works

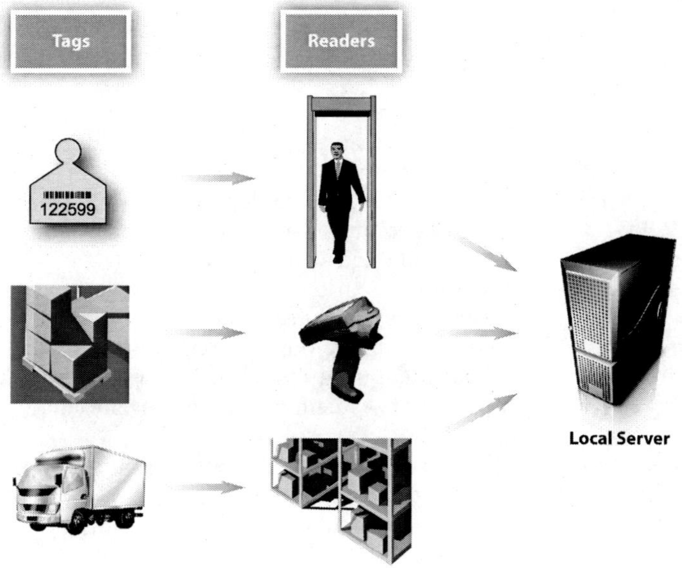

Some consumer groups worry that RFID tags and electronic product codes could be used to track their consumption patterns or for the wrong purposes. But keep in mind that like your car-door remote, the codes and tags are designed to work only within short ranges. (You know that if you try to unlock your car from a mile away using such a device, it won't work.)

Proponents of electronic product codes and RFID tags believe they can save both consumers and companies time and money. These people believe consumers benefit because the information embedded in the codes and tags help prevent stockouts and out-of-date products from remaining on store shelves. In addition, the technology doesn't require cashiers to scan barcodes item by item. Instead an electronic product reader can automatically tally up the entire contents of a shopping cart—much like a wireless network can detect your computer within seconds. As a customer, wouldn't that add value to your shopping experience?

### KEY TAKEAWAY

The best marketing decisions and supplier selections aren't enough if your company's demand forecasts are wrong. Demand forecasting is the process of estimating how much of a good or service a customer will buy from you. If you're a producer of a product, this will affect not only the amount of goods and services you have to produce but also the materials you must purchase to make them. Demand forecasting is part of a company's overall inventory control activities. Inventory control is the process of ensuring your firm has an adequate amount of products and a wide enough assortment of them meet your customers' needs. One of the goals of inventory control is to avoid stockouts without keeping too much of a product on hand. Some companies are beginning to experiment with new technologies such as electronic product codes and RFID tags in an effort to better manage their inventories and meet their customers' needs.

### REVIEW QUESTIONS

1. Why are demand forecasts made more frequently than sourcing decisions?
2. How can just-in-time and vendor-managed inventories add value to products for customers?
3. Why and how do companies track products?

# 3. WAREHOUSING AND TRANSPORTATION

### LEARNING OBJECTIVES

1. **Understand the role warehouses and distribution centers play in the supply chain.**
2. **Outline the transportation modes firms have to choose from and the advantages and disadvantages of each.**

## 3.1 Warehousing

At times, the demand and supply for products can be unusually high. At other times, it can be unusually low. That's why companies generally maintain a certain amount of safety stock, oftentimes in warehouses. As a business owner, it would be great if you didn't have excess inventory you had to store in a warehouse. In an ideal world, materials or products would arrive at your facility just in time for you to assemble or sell them. Unfortunately, we don't live in an ideal world.

Toys are a good example. Most toymakers work year round to be sure they have enough toys available for sale during the holidays. However, retailers don't want to buy a huge number of toys in July. They want to wait until November and December to buy large amounts of them.

Consequently, toymakers warehouse them until that time. Likewise, during the holiday season, retailers don't want to run out of toys, so they maintain a certain amount of safety stock in their warehouses.

Some firms store products until their prices increase. Oil is an example. Speculators, including investment banks and hedge funds, have been known to buy, and hold, oil if they think its price is going to rapidly rise. Sometimes they go so far as to buy oil tankers and even entire oil fields.[21]

A **distribution center** is a warehouse or storage facility where the emphasis is on processing and moving goods on to wholesalers, retailers, or consumers.[23] A few years ago, companies were moving toward large, centralized warehouses to keep costs down. In 2005, Walmart opened a four-million-square-foot distribution center in Texas. (Four million square feet is about the size of eighteen football fields.)

Today, however, the trend has shifted back to smaller warehouses. Using smaller warehouses is a change that's being driven by customer considerations rather than costs. The long lead times that result when companies transport products from Asia, the Middle East, and South America are forcing international manufacturers and retailers to shorten delivery times to consumers.[24] Warehousing products regionally, closer to consumers, can also help a company tailor its product selection to better match the needs of customers in different regions.

**FIGURE 9.9**

You might not know where the tiny town of Cushing, Oklahoma, is. But oil producers and traders around the world do. Cushing is one of the largest oil storage areas in the United States. Storage tanks like these cover more than nine square miles on the outskirts of the town.[22]

*© 2010 Jupiterimages Corporation*

## How Warehouses and Distribution Centers Function

So how do you begin to find a product or pallet of products in a warehouse or distribution center the size of eighteen football fields? To begin with, each type of product that is unique because of some characteristic—say, because of its manufacturer, size, color, or model—must be stored and accounted for separate from other items. To help distinguish it, its manufacturer gives it its own identification number, called a **SKU (stock-keeping unit)**.[25] Figure 9.10 shows an example of a SKU that appears on a box of products. When the product enters the warehouse, it is scanned and given an "address," or location, in the warehouse where it is stored until it is plucked from its shelf and shipped.

Warehouses and distribution centers are also becoming increasingly automated and wired. As you learned in Chapter 8, some warehouses use robots to picks products from shelves. At other warehouses, employees use voice-enabled headsets to pick products. Via the headsets, the workers communicate with a computer that tells them where to go and what to grab off of shelves. As a result, the employees are able to pick products more accurately than they could by looking at a sheet of paper or computer screen.

The process we just described is an extremely simple explanation of a *very* complicated operation. The video below shows how one of Amazon.com's distribution centers works.

**distribution center**

A warehouse or storage facility where the emphasis is on processing and moving goods on to wholesalers, retailers, or consumers rather than on storage.

**SKU (stock-keeping unit)**

A label used to distinguish a product that is unique because of some characteristic, such as manufacturer, size, color, or model.

**Video Clip**

**Order Fulfillment at Amazon**

Amazon.com's mission is "to be Earth's most customer-centric company where people can find and discover anything they want to buy online." Watch the following video to see one of Amazon's order-fulfillment centers in action.

View the video online at: http://www.youtube.com/embed/Qt9hkZmbNfU&NR

**FIGURE 9.10**

**An Example of an SKU**

*© 2010 Jupiterimages Corporation*

It's pretty amazing when you think about how the thousands of products that come in and out of Amazon's distribution centers every day ultimately end up in the right customer's hands. After all, how many times have you had to look really hard to find something you put in your own closet or garage? Processing orders—order fulfillment—is a key part of the job in supply chains. Why? Because delivering what was promised, when it was promised, and the way it was promised are key drivers of customer satisfaction.[26]

**electronic data interchange (EDI)**

A special electronic format companies use to exchange business documents from computer to computer.

One of the ways companies are improving their order fulfillment and other supply chain processes is by getting rid of paper systems and snail mail. So, for instance, instead of companies receiving paper orders and sending paper invoices to one another, they send and receive the documents via electronic data interchange (EDI). **Electronic data interchange (EDI)** is a special electronic format that companies use to exchange business documents from computer to computer. It also makes for greater visibility among supply chain partners because they can all check the status of orders electronically rather than having to fax or e-mail documents back and forth.

**FIGURE 9.11** How Cross-Docking Works

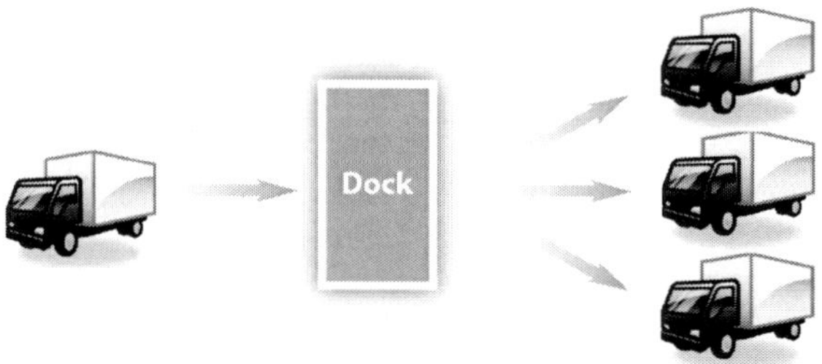


**cross-docking**

The practice of moving products between supply chain intermediaries so that they spend little or no time in warehouses as they are transported.

Another new trend is **cross-docking**. Products that are cross-docked spend little or no time in warehouses. As Figure 9.11 shows, a product being cross-docked will be delivered via truck to a dock at a warehouse where it is unloaded and put on other trucks bound for retail outlets.

## 3.2 Transportation

Not all goods and services need to be physically transported. When you get a massage, oil change, or a manicure, the services pass straight from the provider to you. Other products can be transported electronically via electronic networks, computers, phones, or fax machines. Downloads of songs, software, and books are an example. So are cable and satellite television and psychic hotline readings delivered over the phone.

### Video Clip

**Motorbike Delivery**

The types of delivery vehicles used around the world might surprise you.

View the video online at: http://www.youtube.com/embed/Lry6c4RudbM

**logistics**

The physical flow of materials in the supply chain.

Other products, of course, have to be physically shipped. **Logistics** refers to the physical flow of materials in the supply chain. You might be surprised by some of physical distribution methods that companies use. To get through crowded, narrow streets in Tokyo, Seven-Eleven Japan delivers products to its retail stores via motorcycles. In some countries, Coca-Cola delivers syrup to its bottlers via camelback. More commonly, though, products that need to be transported physically to get to customers are moved via air, rail, truck, water, or pipeline.

### Trucks

More products are shipped by truck than by another means. Trucks can go anywhere there are roads, including straight to customer's homes. By contrast, planes, trains, and ships are limited as to where they can go. Shipping by truck is also fast relative to other modes (except for air transportation). However, it's also fairly expensive. Some goods—especially those that are heavy or bulky—would require so many trucks and drivers it would be economically unfeasible to use them over long distances. Coal is a good example of such a product. It would take four to five hundred trucks and drivers to haul the amount of freight that one coal train can. The amount of $CO_2$ emitted by trucks is also high relative to some of the other transportation modes, so it's not the greenest solution.

### Water

International trade could scarcely be conducted without cargo shipping. Cargo ships transport "loose" cargo such as grain, coal, ore, petroleum, and other mined products. But they also transport consumer products—everything from televisions to toys. Consumer goods are often shipped in intermodal containers. **Intermodal containers** are metal boxes. The largest containers are fifty-three feet long and one hundred inches tall. The biggest cargo ships are huge and carry as many 15,000 containers. By contrast, the maximum a train can carry is around 250 containers stacked on top of each other. Figure 9.12 shows a picture of a cargo ship carrying intermodal containers. The good news about shipping via waterway is that inexpensive. The bad news is that it's very slow. In addition, many markets aren't accessible by water, so another method of transportation has to be utilized

**FIGURE 9.12**

Cargo ships like this one can transport thousands of intermodal containers.

*© 2010 Jupiterimages Corporation*

### Air

Air freight is the fastest way to ship goods. However, it can easily cost ten times as much to ship a product by air as by sea.[27] High-dollar goods and a small fraction of perishable goods are shipped via air. Freshly cut flowers and fresh seafood bound for sushi markets are examples of the latter. Keeping perishable products at the right temperature and humidity levels as they sit on runways and planes can be a challenge. They often have to be shipped in special types of containers with coolants. Freight forwarders are often hired to arrange the packing for perishables traveling by air and to ensure they don't deteriorate while they are in transit. Despite the fact that it is expensive, air transportation is growing faster than any other transportation mode, thanks to companies like FedEx.

**intermodal containers**

Metal boxes used to ship consumer goods.

### Railroads

Railroads carry many of the same products as cargo ships—only over land. A significant percentage of intermodal containers offloaded from ships end up on railcars bound for inland destinations. The containers are then are trucked shorter distances to distribution centers, warehouses, and stores. Businesses that need to ship heavy, bulky goods often try to locate their facilities next to railroads. Lumber mills are an example.

In terms of speed and cost, shipping by rail falls somewhere between truck and water transportation. It's not as slow and inexpensive as moving goods by water. However, it's not as fast as shipping them by truck. Nor is it as expensive. So, when the price of gasoline rose in to record highs in 2008, shippers that traditionally used trucks began to look at other transportation alternatives such as rail.

### Pipelines

Pipelines are generally used to transport oil, natural gas, and chemicals. Two-thirds of petroleum products are transported by pipeline, including heating oil, diesel, jet fuel, and kerosene. Pipelines are costly to build, but once they are constructed, they can transport products cheaply. For example, for about one dollar you can transport a barrel of petroleum products via pipeline from Houston to New York. The oil will move three to eight miles per hour and arrive in two to three weeks depending on the size of the pipe, its pressure, and the density of the liquid.[28] Like other products, products shipped via pipelines often have to be moved using two different transportation modes. Once your barrel of oil has made it to New York, to get it to service stations, you will need to move it by rail or truck. The material in pipelines can also be stolen like other products can. In Mexico, for example, drug gangs have tapped into pipelines in remote areas and stolen millions of dollars in oil.[29]

Companies face different tradeoffs when choosing transportation methods. Which is most important? Speed? Cost? Frequency of delivery? The flexibility to respond to different market conditions? Again, it depends on your customers.

Goya Foods has many challenges due to the variety of customers it serves. The company sells more than 1,600 canned food products. Because the types of beans people prefer often depends on their cultures—whether they are of Cuban, Mexican, or Puerto Rican descent, and so forth—Goya sells thirty-eight varieties of beans alone. Almost daily, Goya's truck drivers deliver products to tens of thousands of U.S. food stores, from supermarket chains in Texas to independent mom-and-pop bodegas in New York City. Delivering daily is more costly than dropping off jumbo shipments once a week and letting stores warehouse goods, says the company's CEO Peter Unanue. However, it's more of a just-in-time method that lets Goya offer stores a greater variety and ensure that products match each store's demographics. "Pink beans might sell in New York City but not sell as well in Texas or California," says Unanue.[30]

**KEY TAKEAWAY**

Some firms store products until their prices increase. A distribution center is a warehouse or storage facility where the emphasis is on processing and moving goods on to other parts of the supply chain. Warehousing products regionally can help a company tailor its product selection to better match the needs of customers in different regions. Logistics refers to the physical flow of materials in the supply chain. Not all goods and services need to be physically transported. Some are directly given to customers or sent to them electronically. Products that need to be transported physically to get to customers are moved via, air, rail, truck, water, and pipelines. The transportation modes a firm uses should be based on what its customers want and are willing to pay for.

**REVIEW QUESTIONS**

1. How do warehouses and distribution centers differ?
2. What is cross-docking and why might a company choose to cross-dock a product?
3. What kinds of products can be delivered electronically? What kinds need to be physically transported?

# 4. TRACK AND TRACE SYSTEMS AND REVERSE LOGISTICS

**LEARNING OBJECTIVES**

1. **Understand why being able to trace products is important to organizations and their customers.**
2. **Explain what reverse logistics is and why firms utilize it.**

As we have explained, shippers are highly anxious when their products are in transit because the merchandise is valuable and because it is exposed to more risks when it's traveling across the country than when it's sitting in a warehouse or store. Shippers want to know where the goods are, when they will arrive, and what kind of shape they are in. After all, they can end up in the wrong place, be damaged, or stolen. (Do you remember the 2008 incident in which when Somali pirates captured the *Maersk Alabama* and held its captain hostage? The cargo ship was carrying seventeen thousand metric tons of freight at the time.) The result can be unhappy customers and lost sales and profits.

## 4.1 Track and Trace Systems

**track and trace systems**

Systems that electronically record the paths shipments take.

In recent years, **track and trace systems** that electronically record the paths shipments take has become almost as important to businesses as shipping costs themselves. Being able to help trace products helps a company anticipate events that could disrupt the supply chain, including order shipping mistakes, bad weather, and accidents so they can be averted.

Today most product shipments can be traced. GPS devices are sometimes placed on containers, railcars, and trucks to track the movement of expensive shipments. Tracing individual products is harder, though. Systems that utilize electronic product codes and RFID tags are not yet in widespread use. Produce is a product that's hard to trace. You have probably noticed that the bananas, peaches, and other types of produce don't have barcodes slapped on them. Products that are combined to make other products are also hard to trace

Being able to trace products is important not only to businesses but also to consumers. Consumers are more interested than ever in knowing where their products come from—particularly when there is a contamination problem with an offering. Products containing salmonella infested peanuts, tomatoes, and contaminated milk have sickened and caused the deaths of consumers and their pets across the globe. Even if the source of the contaminated product is known, consumers can't tell exactly where the products originated from, so they stop buying them altogether. This can devastate the livelihood of producers whose products aren't to blame.

Companies are working to develop systems that may one day make it possible to trace all products. The Chinese government is working toward that goal in conjunction with a Norwegian company called TraceTracker. TraceTracker is testing an online service that can identify and track each batch of every product that is merged together in the global food chain, from raw ingredients to products on supermarket shelves.[31]

## 4.2 Reverse Logistics

So what happens if products end up broken or unusable as they travel through their supply chains? And what do companies do with scrap materials and other "junk" produced, such as packaging? Increasingly, firms now run products and materials such as these backward through the supply chain to extract value from them. The process is known as **reverse logistics**.

**reverse logistics**

Running broken, defective, and scrap products backward through the supply chain so as to extract value from them.

Patagonia developed a reverse logistics systems for environmental reasons. After garments made by Patagonia are worn out, consumers can mail them to the company or return them to a Patagonia store. Patagonia then sends them to Japan to be recycled into usable fibers that are later made into new garments. The company has also convinced other clothing makers to do the same, even though it can add to the cost of products.

Most companies set up reverse logistics systems to "turn trash into cash." Pittsburgh-based Genco is firm that specializes in reverse logistics. Companies like Best Buy, Sears, and Target hire Genco to find buyers for defective or broken products. A recent study suggests companies can recover up to 0.3 percent of their annual sales this way, which for Best Buy would amount to $100 million a year.[33]

TerraCycle, which we mentioned in Chapter 5, is a company dedicated to extracting value from waste and using it to create new products—a process that's being called "upcycling." In addition to selling fertilizer in used (but relabeled) plastic bottles, TerraCycle makes backpacks and pencil cases out of the metallic juice pouches used in drink boxes. The company also creates tote bags out of plastic bags, and contracted with Target to make clocks out of old vinyl records.

**FIGURE 9.13**

The first product collected and recycled by Patagonia was its polyester-spandex underwear. The underwear was chosen because it has no buttons or zippers that have to be removed.[32]

*© 2010 Jupiterimages Corporation*

### Video Clip

**TerraCycle Turns Garbage into Gold**

TerraCycle founder Tom Szaky explains how his company makes money while saving the planet, too.

View the video online at: http://www.youtube.com/embed/zEND9KG67PM

**KEY TAKEAWAY**

Being able to trace products helps a company anticipate events that could disrupt the supply chain, including shipping mistakes, bad weather, and accidents so they can be averted. Most shippers have track and trace systems that can track product loads. Tracking individual products, especially after they are combined to make other products, is more difficult.

Consumers are more interested than ever in knowing where their products come from—particularly when there is a contamination problem with an offering. Reverse logistics is the process of running damaged and defective products and scrap materials backward through the supply chain to extract value from them. Companies are increasingly employing reverse logistics not only to save money but for environmental reasons.

**REVIEW QUESTIONS**

1. Why is being able to track products important to companies? Why is it important to consumers? How can it add value to products?
2. What place does reverse logistics have in a company's supply chain?

# 5. DISCUSSION QUESTIONS AND ACTIVITIES

**DISCUSSION QUESTIONS**

1. Why do marketing professionals care about and participate in supply chain decisions?
2. What criteria do you think companies look at when evaluating the performance of their supply chain partners? Make a list of them.
3. Is the electronic delivery of products always better? To what extent does it depend on the customer?
4. Discuss the supply chain for education at your college. What elements does it consist of? What aspects of its delivery could be improved opinion? What sort of alternate sourcing and delivery methods might be used? Can education be warehoused? How?

**ACTIVITIES**

1. Research the distribution system for Coca-Cola at http://www.thecoca-colacompany.com/ourcompany/the_cocacola_system.html. What elements of Coca-Cola's supply chain were you unaware of?
2. Get into groups of four. Then choose a product and outline the supply chain for it. If you need to, use the Web to research the product. Then discuss with your group how you believe the supply chain could be used to create additional value for customers. Present your findings to your class.

# ENDNOTES


1. Donald J. Bowersox and David J. Closs, "Ten Mega-Trends That Will Revolutionize Supply Chain Logistics," *Journal of Business Logistics* 21, no. 2 (2000): 1.
2. Jeremy N. Smith, "Fast Fashion," *World Trade* 21, no. 12 (2008): 54.
3. Skip McGrath, "China Shipping Advice," *Smart China Sourcing*, December 14, 2007, http://www.smartchinasourcing.com/shipping/china-shipping-advice-cif-shipping-terms-explained.html (accessed April 13, 2012).
4. Skip McGrath, "China Shipping Advice," *Smart China Sourcing*, December 14, 2007, http://www.smartchinasourcing.com/shipping/china-shipping-advice-cif-shipping-terms-explained.html (accessed April 13, 2012).
5. Adapted from PRTM Management Consultants, "Global Supply Chain Trends 2008–2010," http://www.prtm.com/uploadedFiles/Strategic_Viewpoint/Articles/Article_Content/Global_Supply_Chain_Trends_Report_%202008.pdf (accessed December 2, 2009).
6. PRTM Management Consultants, "Global Supply Chain Trends 2008–2010," http://www.prtm.com/uploadedFiles/Strategic_Viewpoint/Articles/Article_Content/Global_Supply_Chain_Trends_Report_%202008.pdf (accessed December 2, 2009).
7. "Quality Assurance through Testing," *Walmartstores.com*, http://walmartstores.com/Suppliers/248.aspx (accessed December 2, 2009).
8. Bureau of International Information Programs, U.S. Department of State, "China Pressed to Forcefully Attack Intellectual Property Theft," America.gov, January 13, 2005, http://www.america.gov/st/washfile-english/2005/January/20050113180002asesuark0.9782831.html#ixzz0Mada2mLk (accessed December 2, 2009).
9. Jeff Chu, "Are Fair-Trade Goods Recession Proof?" *Fast Company*, March 27, 2009, http://www.organicconsumers.org/articles/article_17395.cfm (accessed December 2, 2009).
10. John Birchall, "Greener Apple Helps Clean Up," *Financial Times*, March 24, 2009, 11.
11. Steve Rosen, "Wal-Mart to Create Green Index to Rate Products," *Kansas City Star*, July 15, 2009, http://economy.kansascity.com/?q=node/2844 (accessed December 2, 2009).
12. Adapted from PRTM Management Consultants, "Global Supply Chain Trends 2008–2010," http://www.prtm.com/uploadedFiles/Strategic_Viewpoint/Articles/Article_Content/Global_Supply_Chain_Trends_Report_%202008.pdf (accessed December 2, 2009).
13. Joe Weisenthal, "Slammed KFC 'Scrambling to Source More Chicken,'" *The Business Insider*, May 6, 2009, http://www.businessinsider.com/kfc-2009-5 (accessed December 2, 2009).
14. Donald J. Bowersox and David J. Closs, "Ten Mega-Trends That Will Revolutionize Supply Chain Logistics," *Journal of Business Logistics* 21, no. 2 (2000): 11.
15. Steven Wingett, "Capro, Saint-Gobain, Denso Win Big with Tata Nano," *Automotive News Europe*, March 3, 2008, 16.
16. Carol Casper, "Demand Planning Comes of Age," *Food Logistics* 101 (January/February 2008): 19–24.
17. Shari Waters, "Shrinkage," About.com, http://retail.about.com/od/glossary/g/shrinkage.htm (accessed December 2, 2009).
18. PRTM Management Consultants, "Global Supply Chain Trends 2008–2010," http://www.prtm.com/uploadedFiles/Strategic_Viewpoint/Articles/Article_Content/Global_Supply_Chain_Trends_Report_%202008.pdf (accessed December 2, 2009).
19. Sameer Kumar and Sarah Craig, "Dell, Inc.'s Closed Loop Supply Chain for Computer Assembly Plants," *Information Knowledge Systems Management* 6, no. 3 (2007): 197–214.
20. "FAQs," *EPCglobal*, http://www.epcglobalinc.org/consumer_info/faq (accessed December 2, 2009).
21. Robert Winnett, "Soaring Prices: Speculators Hijack the Oil Market," *TimesOnline*, September 12, 2004, http://business.timesonline.co.uk/tol/business/article481363.ece (accessed December 2, 2009).
22. Ann Davis, "Where Has All the Oil Gone?" *Wall Street Journal*, October 6, 2007, http://online.wsj.com/article/SB119162309507450611.html (accessed December 2, 2009).
23. "Distribution Center," Wikipedia, http://en.wikipedia.org/wiki/Distribution_center (accessed April 13, 2012).
24. Sara Pearson Specter, "Industry Outlook: Mostly Cloudy, with a Few Bright Spots," *Modern Materials Handling* 64, no. 3 (2009): 22–26.
25. "Stock-Keeping Unit (SKU)," BusinessDictionary.com, http://www.businessdictionary.com/definition/stock-keeping-unit-SKU.html (accessed December 2, 2009).
26. Sriram Thirumalai and Kingshuk K. Sinha, "Customer Satisfaction with Order Fulfillment in Retail Supply Chains: Implications of Product Type in Electronic B2C Transactions," *Journal of Operations Management* 23, no. 3–4 (2005): 291–303.
27. James F. Thompson, C. F. H. Bishop, and Patrick E. Brecht, "Air Transport of Perishable Products," Division of Agriculture and Natural Resources, University of California, Publication 2168 (Oakland: ANR Communication Services): 1.
28. "Oil Pipelines: Small Price, Big Value," *In the Pipe*, April 15, 2005, http://www.enewsbuilder.net/aopl/e_article000391720.cfm (accessed December 2, 2009).
29. Martha Mendoza, "Millions of Dollars in Stolen Mexican Oil Sold to U.S. Refineries," *Fort Worth Star-Telegram*, April 11, 2009, 6A.
30. Barbara De Lollis, "CEO Profile: At Goya, It's All in La Familia," *USA Today*, http://abcnews.go.com/Business/Story?id=4507435&page=1 (accessed December 2, 2009).
31. Jennifer L. Schenker, "TraceTracker Tracks Food Safety on the Net," December 4, 2008, http://www.businessweek.com/globalbiz/content/dec2008/gb2008124_501139.htm (accessed December 2, 2009).
32. "Patagonia's Clothing Recycling Program: Lessons Learned, Challenges Ahead," *GreenerDesign*, March 9, 2009, http://www.greenbiz.com/news/2009/03/09/patagonias-clothing-recycling-program-lessons-learned-challenges-ahead (accessed December 2, 2009).
33. "Reverse Logistics: From Trash to Cash," *BusinessWeek*, July 24, 2008, http://www.businessweek.com/magazine/content/08_31/b4094046657076.htm (accessed December 2, 2009).

CHAPTER 10

# Gathering and Using Information: Marketing Research and Market Intelligence

Once you have come up with a great idea for an offering, how will you know if people will want to buy it? If they *are* willing to buy it, what will they want to pay? Will they be willing to pay enough so that you can earn a profit from the product? Wouldn't it be great if you had some sort of crystal ball that would give you the answers to these questions? After all, you don't want to quit your day job to develop a product that's going to be a flop.

In a sense, you do have such a crystal ball. It's called marketing research. **Marketing research** is the process of collecting, analyzing, and reporting marketing information that can be used to answer questions or solve problems so as to improve a company's bottom line. Marketing research includes a wide range of activities. (By contrast, **market research** is a narrower activity. It is the process of researching a specific market to determine its size and trends.)

**marketing research**

The process of collecting, analyzing, and reporting marketing information that can be used to improve a company's bottom line.

**market research**

The process of researching a specific market to determine its size and trends.

Although marketing research isn't foolproof, it can take some of the guesswork out of decision making. Back to your great product idea: what, for example, should you name your product? Naming a product might sound like a minor decision, but it's not. In some cases it can be a deal breaker. Just ask the bug-spray maker Out! International, Inc. In the 1990s, Out! International came up with what it thought was a really cute name for bug spray that would appeal to children. The product was called "Hey! There's a Monster in My Room!" The problem was that the name itself scared kids. They wanted nothing to do with it.[1]

**FIGURE 10.1**

A little marketing research might have helped: In 1966, Capitol Records released hundreds of thousands of the Beatles' album *Yesterday and Today* with the cover shown here. Do you think it was well received? No. The public was appalled. Capitol Records quickly realized it had made a mistake, recalled the albums, and pasted a different cover over what became known as the "butcher cover." (Note: Some of the albums slipped through the cracks and didn't get the paste-over. If you can find one, it could be worth thousands of dollars.)

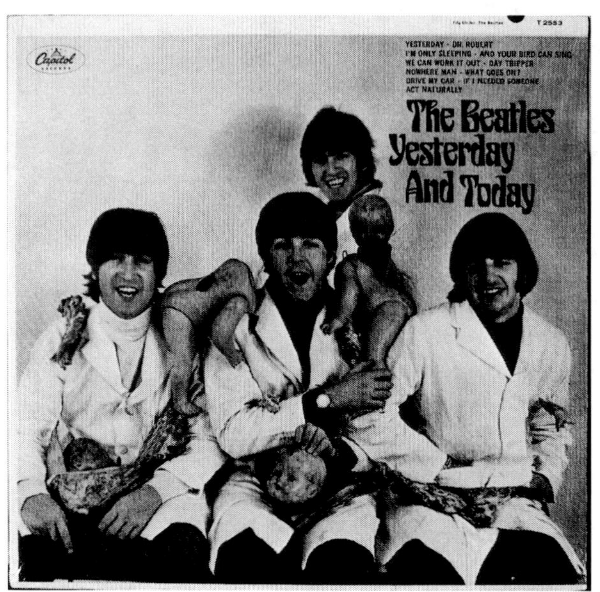


*Source: Wikipedia.*

Marketing research can help you with many tasks:

- Developing product ideas and designs
- Determining if there is demand for your product so you know whether or not to produce it
- Identifying market segments for your product
- Making pricing decisions
- Evaluating packaging types
- Evaluating in-store promotions
- Measuring the satisfaction of your customers
- Measuring the satisfaction of your channel partners
- Evaluating the effectiveness of your Web site
- Testing the effectiveness of ads and their placement
- Making marketing channel decisions

**market intelligence**

Information gathered on a regular, ongoing basis to enable a firm's decision makers to stay in touch with what's happening in the marketplace.

Closely related to marketing research is market intelligence, which is often referred to as *competitive intelligence*. Whereas marketing research involves solving a specific marketing problem at a specific point in time, **market intelligence** involves gathering information on a regular, ongoing basis to stay in touch with what's happening in the marketplace. For example, if you own a convenience store, part of your daily market intelligence gathering would include driving around to see what competing stores are charging for gasoline or checking to see what types of products are being sold and advertised by them.

If you're a small business owner, and you're talking to your customers and suppliers about new product ideas, you're engaging in market intelligence. If you go so far as to survey your customers with a questionnaire about a new type of service you're considering offering, you are engaging in marketing research. In big companies, marketing departments are often responsible for gathering market intelligence. But they are by no means the only group to do so. (We'll discuss more about who in the organization does which activities in a moment.) Students also gather market intelligence when they question other students about the best professors to take classes from.

# 1. MARKETING INFORMATION SYSTEMS

## LEARNING OBJECTIVES

1. **Describe the components of a marketing information system and each component's purpose.**
2. **Explain the situations in which marketing research should be used versus market intelligence.**
3. **Describe the limitations of market intelligence and its ethical boundaries.**
4. **Explain when marketing research should and should not be used.**

A certain amount of marketing information is being gathered all the time by companies as they engage in their daily operations. When a sale is made and recorded, this is marketing information that's being gathered. When a sales representative records the shipping preferences of a customer in a firm's customer relationship management (CRM) system, this is also marketing information that's being collected. When a firm gets a customer complaint and records it, this too is information that should be put to use. All this data can be used to generate consumer insight. However, truly understanding customers involves not just collecting quantitative data (numbers) related to them but qualitative data, such as comments about what they think.

### Audio Clip

**Interview with Joy Mead**

Recall from Chapter 3 that Joy Mead is an associate director of marketing with Procter & Gamble. Listen to this clip to hear Mead talk about the research techniques and methods Procter & Gamble uses to develop consumer insight. You will learn that the company isn't just interested in what consumers want now but also years in the future.

The trick is integrating all the information you collect so it can be used by as many people as possible in your organization to make good decisions. Unfortunately, in many organizations, information isn't shared very well among departments. Even within departments, it can be a problem. For example, one group in a marketing department might research a problem related to a brand, uncover certain findings that would be useful to other brand managers, but never communicate them.

A **marketing information system (MIS)** is a way to manage the vast amount of information firms have on hand—information marketing professionals and managers need to make good decisions. Marketing information systems range from paper-based systems to very sophisticated computer systems. Ideally, however, a marketing information system should include the following components:

- A system for recording internally generated data and reports
- A system for collecting market intelligence on an ongoing basis
- Marketing analytics software to help managers with their decision making
- A system for recording marketing research information

**marketing information system (MIS)**

A system, either paper or electronic, used to manage information a firm's marketing professionals and managers need to make good decisions.

## 1.1 Internally Generated Data and Reports

**clickstream data**

Data collected from Web sites showing the Web pages visitors clicked on and the order of their clicks.

As we explained, an organization generates and records a lot of information as part of its daily business operations, including sales and accounting data, and data on inventory levels, back orders, customer returns, and complaints. Firms are also constantly gathering information related to their Web sites, such as clickstream data. **Clickstream data** is data generated about the number of people who visit a Web site and its various pages, how long they dwell there, and what they buy or don't buy. Companies use clickstream data in all kinds of ways. They use it to monitor the overall traffic of visitors that a site gets, to see which areas of the site people aren't visiting and explore why, and to automatically offer visitors products and promotions by virtue of their browsing patterns. Software can be used to automatically tally the vast amounts of clickstream data gathered from Web sites and generate reports for managers based on that information. Netflix recently awarded a $1 million prize to a group of scientists to plow through Web data generated by millions of Netflix users so as to improve Netflix's predictions of what users would like to rent.[2] (That's an interesting way to conduct marketing research, don't you think?)

Being able to access clickstream data and other internally generated information quickly can give a company's decision makers a competitive edge. Remember our discussion in Chapter 9 about how Walmart got a leg up on Target after 9/11? Walmart's inventory information was updated by the minute (the retailer's huge computing center rivals the Pentagon's, incidentally); Target's was only updated daily. When Walmart's managers noticed American flags began selling rapidly immediately following the terrorist attacks on 9/11, the company quickly ordered as many flags as possible from various vendors—leaving none for Target.

Click on the following link to watch a fascinating documentary about how Walmart, the world's most powerful retailer, operates: http://www.hulu.com/watch/103756/cnbc-originals-the-new-age-of-walmart.

**intranet**

A private, internal Web site accessible only to a firm's employees.

Many companies make a certain amount of internal data available to their employees and managers via intranets. An **intranet** looks like the Web and operates like it, but only an organization's employees have access to the information. So, for example, instead of a brand manager asking someone in accounting to run a report on the sales of a particular product, the brand manager could look on her firm's intranet for the information.

However, big companies with multiple products, business units, and databases purchased and installed in different places and at different times often have such vast amounts of information that they can't post it all on an intranet. Consequently, getting hold of the right information can be hard. The information could be right under your nose and you might not know it. Meet people like Gary Pool: Pool works for BNSF Railway and is one of BNSF's "go-to" employees when it comes to gathering marketing data. Pool knows how to access different databases and write computer programs to extract the right information from the right places at BNSF, a process known as **data mining**. Pool captures the information in spreadsheets such as Excel, which managers can use to detect marketing trends.

**FIGURE 10.2**

Gary Pool is an expert at data mining—hunting up information for decision makers at BNSF Railway. And no, he doesn't wear a headlamp. Nor does he wear a pocket protector! Pool's title: Manager, Marketing Systems Support & Marketing Decision Support & Planning.

**data mining**

The process of extracting information from large databases so as to uncover patterns and trends.

## 1.2 Analytics Software

Increasingly, companies are purchasing analytics software to help them pull and make sense of internally generated information. **Analytics software** allows managers who are not computer experts to gather all kinds of different information from a company's databases—information not produced in reports regularly generated by the company. The software incorporates regression models, linear programming, and other statistical methods to help managers answer "what if" types of questions. For example, "If we spend 10 percent more of our advertising on TV ads instead of magazine ads, what effect will it have on sales?" Oracle Corporation's Crystal Ball is one brand of analytical software.

**analytics software**

Software that utilizes a firm's data, regression models, linear programming, and other statistical methods to help managers who are not computer experts make decisions.

The sporting goods retailer Cabela's has managed to refine its marketing efforts considerably using analytics software developed by the software maker SAS. "Our statisticians in the past spent 75 percent of their time just trying to manage data. Now they have more time for analyzing the data with SAS, and we have become more flexible in the marketplace," says Corey Bergstrom, director of marketing research and analysis for Cabela's. "That is just priceless."[3]

The software analyzes the company's sales transactions, market research, and demographic data associated with its large database of customers. It uses the information to gain a better understanding of the marketing channels Cabela's prefers and to make other marketing decisions. For example, does the customer prefer Cabela's' one-hundred-page catalogs or the seventeen-hundred-page catalogs? The software has helped Cabela's employees figure this out.[4]

**FIGURE 10.3**

Cabela's' analytics software has helped the outdoor sporting retailer reach the right customers with the right catalogs.

*© 2010 Jupiterimages Corporation*

## 1.3 Market Intelligence

A good internal reporting system can tell a manager what happened inside his firm. But what about what's going on *outside* the firm? What is the business environment like? Are credit-lending terms loose or tight, and how will they affect what you and your customers are able to buy or not buy? How will rising fuel prices and alternate energy sources affect your firm and your products? Do changes such as these present business obstacles or opportunities? Moreover, what are your competitors up to?

Not gathering market intelligence leaves a company vulnerable. Remember in Chapter 8 when we discussed Encyclopedia Britannica, the market leader in print encyclopedia business for literally centuries? Encyclopedia Britannica didn't see the digital age coming and nearly went out of business as a result. (Suffice it to say, you can now access Encyclopedia Britannica online.) By contrast, when fuel prices hit an all-time high in 2008, unlike other passenger airline companies, Southwest Airlines was prepared. Southwest had anticipated the problem, and early on locked in contracts to buy fuel for its planes at much lower prices. Other airlines weren't as prepared and lost money because their fuel expenses skyrocketed. Meanwhile, Southwest Airlines managed to eke out a profit. Collecting market intelligence can also help a company generate ideas or product concepts that can then be tested by conducting market research.

Gathering market intelligence involves a number of activities, including scanning newspapers, trade magazines, and economic data produced by the government to find out about trends and what the competition is doing. In big companies, personnel in a firm's marketing department are primarily responsible for their firm's market intelligence and making sure it gets conveyed to decision makers. Some companies subscribe to news service companies that regularly provide them with this information. LexisNexis is one such company. It provides companies with news about business and legal developments that could affect their operations. Let's now examine some of the sources of information you can look at to gather market intelligence.

### Search Engines and Corporate Web Sites

An obvious way to gain market intelligence is by examining your competitors' Web sites as well as doing basic searches with search engines like Google. If you want to find out what the press is writing about your company, your competitors, or any other topic you're interested in, you can sign up to receive free alerts via e-mail by going to Google Alerts at http://www.google.com/alerts. Suppose you want to monitor what people are saying about you or your company on blogs, the comment areas of Web sites, and social networks such as Facebook and Twitter. You can do so by going to a site like WhosTalkin.com, typing a topic or company name into the search bar, and voilà! All the good (and bad) things people have remarked about the company or topic turn up. What a great way to seek out the shortcomings of your competitors. It's also a good way to spot talent. For example, designers are using search engines like WhosTalkin.com to search the blogs of children and teens who are "fashion forward" and then involve them in designing new products.

**FIGURE 10.4**

Type a company's name (or anything else you want) into the search bar and see what comes up. (Note: It takes a little while for all of the results to show up.)

*Source: http://www.whostalkin.com.*

### Publications

The *Economist*, the *Wall Street Journal*, *Forbes*, *Fortune*, *BusinessWeek*, the *McKinsey Report*, *Sales and Marketing Management*, and the *Financial Times* are good publications to read to learn about general business trends. All of them discuss current trends, regulations, and consumer issues that are relevant for organizations doing business in the domestic and global marketplace. All of the publications are online as well, although you might have to pay a subscription fee to look at some of the content. If your firm is operating in a global market, you might be interested to know that some of these publications have Asian, European, and Middle Eastern editions.

Other publications provide information about marketplace trends and activities in specific industries. *Consumer Goods and Technology* provides information consumer packaged-goods firms want to know. Likewise, *Progressive Grocer* provides information on issues important to grocery stores. *Information Week* provides information relevant to people and businesses working in the area of technology. *World Trade* provides information about issues relevant to organizations shipping and receiving goods from other countries. *Innovation: America's Journal of Technology Commercialization* provides information about innovative products that are about to hit the marketplace.

### Trade Shows and Associations

Trade shows are another way companies learn about what their competitors are doing. (If you are a marketing professional working a trade show for your company, you will want to visit all of your competitors' booths and see what they have to offer relative to what you have to offer.) And, of course, every field has a trade association that collects and disseminates information about trends, breakthroughs, new technology, new processes, and challenges in that particular industry. The American Marketing Association, Food Marketing Institute, Outdoor Industry Association, Semiconductor Industry Association, Trade Promotion Management Association, and Travel Industry Association provide their member companies with a wealth of information and often deliver them daily updates on industry happenings via e-mail.

### Salespeople

A company's salespeople provide a vital source of market intelligence. Suppose one of your products is selling poorly. Will you initially look to newspapers and magazines to figure out why? Will you consult a trade association? Probably not. You will first want to talk to your firm's salespeople to get their "take" on the problem.

Salespeople are the eyes and ears of their organizations. Perhaps more than anyone else, they know how products are faring in the marketplace, what the competition is doing, and what customers are looking for.

A system for recording this information is crucial, which explains why so many companies have invested in customer relationship management (CRM) systems. Some companies circulate lists so their employees have a better idea of the market intelligence they might be looking for. Textbook publishers are an example. They let their sales representatives know the types of books they want to publish and encourage their representatives to look for good potential textbook authors among the professors they sell to.

### Suppliers and Industry Experts

Your suppliers can provide you with a wealth of information. Good suppliers know which companies are moving a lot of inventory. And oftentimes they have an idea why. In many instances, they will tell you, if the information you're looking for is general enough so they don't have to divulge any information that's confidential or that would be unethical to reveal—an issue we'll talk more about later in the book. Befriending an expert in your industry, along with business journalists and writers, can be helpful, too. Often these people are "in the know" because they get invited to review products.[5]

### Customers

Lastly, when it comes to market intelligence don't neglect observing how customers are behaving. They can provide many clues, some of which you will be challenged to respond to. For example, during the latest economic downturn, many wholesalers and retailers noticed consumers began buying smaller amounts of goods—just what they needed to get by during the week. Seeing this trend, and realizing that they couldn't pass along higher costs to customers (because of, say, higher fuel prices), a number of consumer-goods manufacturers "shrank" their products slightly rather than raise prices. You have perhaps noticed that some of the products you buy got smaller—but not cheaper.

## 1.4 Can Market Intelligence Be Taken Too Far?

Can market intelligence be taken too far? The answer is yes. In 2001, Procter & Gamble admitted it had engaged in "dumpster diving" by sifting through a competitors' garbage to find out about its hair care products. Although the practice isn't necessarily illegal, it cast P&G in a negative light. Likewise, British Airways received a lot of negative press in the 1990s after it came to light that the company had hacked into Virgin Atlantic Airways' computer system.[7]

Gathering corporate information illegally or unethically is referred to as **industrial espionage**. Industrial espionage is not uncommon. Sometimes companies hire professional spies to gather information about their competitors and their trade secrets or even bug their phones. Former and current employees can also reveal a company's trade secret either deliberately or unwittingly. Microsoft recently sued a former employee it believed had divulged trade secrets to its competitors.[8] It's been reported that for years professional spies bugged Air France's first-class seats to listen in on executives' conversations.[9]

**FIGURE 10.5**

Don't get caught doing this—unless you work for the natural-cosmetics maker Burt's Bees. To get across to employees the amount of material being wasted, Burt's Bees had its employees put on hazmat suits and sort through garbage for a couple of weeks. (No, employees weren't engaging in industrial espionage, which is discussed below.) The recycling opportunities they spotted as part of the exercise ended up saving the natural-cosmetics maker $25,000 annually.[6]

### Video Clip

**Spying at Work—Espionage: Who, How, Why, and How to Stop It**

To learn more about the hazards of industrial espionage and how it's done, check out this YouTube video.

View the video online at: http://www.youtube.com/embed/kooznkqQ1GQ

**industrial espionage**

The process of gathering corporate information illegally or unethically.

To develop standards of conduct and create respect for marketing professionals who gather market intelligence, the Society of Competitive Intelligence Professionals has developed a code of ethics. It is as follows:

- To continually strive to increase the recognition and respect of the profession.
- To comply with all applicable laws, domestic and international.
- To accurately disclose all relevant information, including one's identity and organization, prior to all interviews.

- To avoid conflicts of interest in fulfilling one's duties.
- To provide honest and realistic recommendations and conclusions in the execution of one's duties.
- To promote this code of ethics within one's company, with third-party contractors and within the entire profession.
- To faithfully adhere to and abide by one's company policies, objectives and guidelines.[10]

## 1.5 Marketing Research

Marketing research is what a company has to resort to if it can't answer a question by using any of the types of information we have discussed so far—market intelligence, internal company data, or analytics software. As we have explained, marketing research is generally used to answer specific questions. The name you should give your new product is an example. Unless your company has previously done some specific research on product names—what consumers think of them, good or bad—you're probably not going to find the answer to that question in your internal company data. Also, unlike internal data, which is generated on a regular basis, marketing research is not ongoing. Marketing research is done on an as-needed or project basis. If an organization decides that it needs to conduct marketing research, it can either conduct marketing research itself or hire a marketing research firm to do it.

So when exactly is marketing research needed? Keep in mind marketing research can be expensive. You therefore have to weigh the costs of the research against the benefits. What questions will the research answer, and will knowing the answer result in the firm earning or saving more money than the research costs?

Marketing research can also take time. If a quick decision is needed for a pressing problem, it might not be possible to do the research. Lastly, sometimes the answer is obvious, so there is no point in conducting the research. If one of your competitors comes up with a new offering and consumers are clamoring to get it, you certainly don't need to undertake a research study to see if such a product would survive in the marketplace.

Alex J. Caffarini, the president and founder of the marketing research firm Analysights, believes there are a number of other reasons companies mistakenly do marketing research. Caffarini's explanations (shown in parentheses) about why a company's executives sometimes make bad decisions are somewhat humorous. Read through them:

- "*We've always done this research.*" (The research has taken on a life of its own; this particular project has continued for years and nobody questioned whether it was still relevant.)
- "*Everyone's doing this research.*" (Their competitors are doing it, and they're afraid they'll lose competitive advantage if they don't; yet no one asks what value the research is creating.)
- "*The findings are nice to know.*" (Great—spend a lot of money to create a wealth of useless information. If the information is nice to know, but you can't do anything with it, you're wasting money.)
- "*If our strategy fails, having done the research will show that we made our best educated guess.*" (They're covering their butts. If things go wrong, they can blame the findings, or the researcher.)
- "*We need to study the problem thoroughly before we decide on a course of action.*" (They're afraid of making a tough decision. Conducting marketing research is a good way to delay the inevitable. In the meantime, the problem gets bigger, or the window of opportunity closes.)
- "*The research will show that our latest ad campaign was effective.*" (They're using marketing research to justify past decisions. Rarely should marketing research be done after the fact.)[11]

## 1.6 Is Marketing Research Always Correct?

To be sure, marketing research can help companies avoid making mistakes. Take Tim Hortons, a popular coffee chain in Canada, which has been expanding in the United States and internationally. Hortons recently opened some self-serve kiosks in Ireland, but the service was a flop. Why? Because cars in Ireland don't have cup holders. Would marketing research have helped? Probably. So would a little bit of market intelligence. It would have been easy for an observer to see that trying to drive a car and hold a cup of hot coffee at the same time is difficult.

That said, we don't want to leave you with the idea that marketing research is infallible. As we indicated at the beginning of the chapter, the process isn't foolproof. In fact, marketing research studies have rejected a lot of good ideas. The idea for telephone answering machines was initially rejected following marketing research. So was the hit sitcom *Seinfeld*, a show that in 2002 *TV Guide* named the number-one television program of all time. In the next section of this chapter, we'll discuss the steps related to conducting marketing research. As you will learn, many things can go wrong along the way that can affect the results of research and the conclusions drawn from it.

**KEY TAKEAWAY**

Many marketing problems and opportunities can be solved by gathering information from a company's daily operations and analyzing it. Market intelligence involves gathering information on a regular, ongoing basis to stay in touch with what's happening in the marketplace. Marketing research is what a company has to resort to if it can't answer a question by using market intelligence, internal company data, or analytical software. Marketing research is not infallible, however.

**REVIEW QUESTIONS**

1. Why do companies gather market intelligence and conduct marketing research?
2. What activities are part of market intelligence gathering?
3. How do marketing professionals know if they have crossed a line in terms of gathering marketing intelligence?
4. How does the time frame for conducting marketing intelligence differ from the time frame in which marketing research data is gathered?

# 2. STEPS IN THE MARKETING RESEARCH PROCESS

**LEARNING OBJECTIVE**

1. **Describe the basic steps in the marketing research process and the purpose of each step.**

The basic steps used to conduct marketing research are shown in Figure 10.6. Next, we discuss each step.

**FIGURE 10.6** Steps in the Marketing Research Process

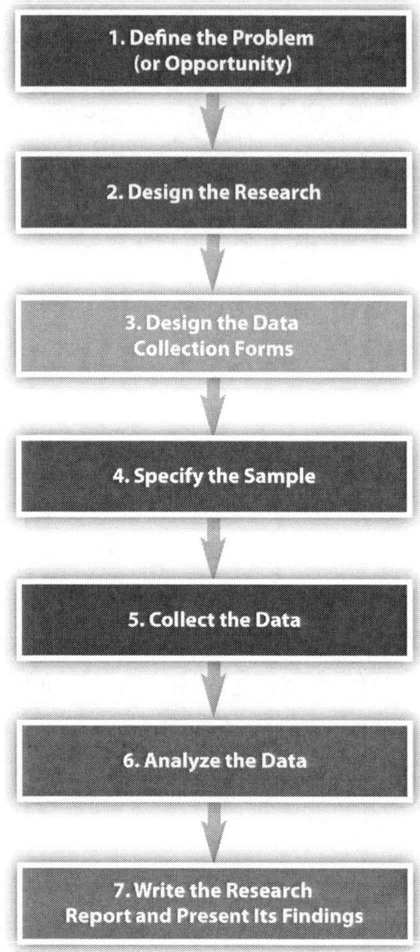


## 2.1 Step 1: Define the Problem (or Opportunity)

There's a saying in marketing research that a problem half defined is a problem half solved. Defining the "problem" of the research sounds simple, doesn't it? Suppose your product is tutoring other students in a subject you're a whiz at. You have been tutoring for a while, and people have begun to realize you're darned good at it. Then, suddenly, your business drops off. Or it explodes, and you can't cope with the number of students you're being asked help. If the business has exploded, should you try to expand your services? Perhaps you should subcontract with some other "whiz" students. You would send them students to be tutored, and they would give you a cut of their pay for each student you referred to them.

Both of these scenarios would be a problem for you, wouldn't they? They are problems insofar as they cause you headaches. But are they really *the* problem? Or are they the symptoms of something bigger? For example, maybe your business has dropped off because your school is experiencing financial trouble and has lowered the number of scholarships given to incoming freshmen. Consequently, there are fewer total students on campus who need your services. Conversely, if you're swamped with people who want you to tutor them, perhaps your school awarded more scholarships than usual, so there are a greater number of students who need your services. Alternately, perhaps you ran an ad in your school's college newspaper, and that led to the influx of students wanting you to tutor them.

Businesses are in the same boat you are as a tutor. They take a look at symptoms and try to drill down to the potential causes. If you approach a marketing research company with either scenario—either too much or too little business—the firm will seek more information from you such as the following:

- In what semester(s) did your tutoring revenues fall (or rise)?
- In what subject areas did your tutoring revenues fall (or rise)?

- In what sales channels did revenues fall (or rise): Were there fewer (or more) referrals from professors or other students? Did the ad you ran result in fewer (or more) referrals this month than in the past months?
- Among what demographic groups did your revenues fall (or rise)—women or men, people with certain majors, or first-year, second-, third-, or fourth-year students?

The key is to look at all potential causes so as to narrow the parameters of the study to the information you actually need to make a good decision about how to fix your business if revenues have dropped or whether or not to expand it if your revenues have exploded.

The next task for the researcher is to put into writing the research objective. The **research objective** is the goal(s) the research is supposed to accomplish. The marketing research objective for your tutoring business might read as follows:

**research objective**
The goal(s) marketing research is supposed to accomplish.

To survey college professors who teach 100- and 200-level math courses to determine why the number of students referred for tutoring dropped in the second semester.

This is admittedly a simple example designed to help you understand the basic concept. If you take a marketing research course, you will learn that research objectives get a lot more complicated than this. The following is an example:

> *"To gather information from a sample representative of the U.S. population among those who are "very likely" to purchase an automobile within the next 6 months, which assesses preferences (measured on a 1–5 scale ranging from "very likely to buy" to "not likely at all to buy") for the model diesel at three different price levels. Such data would serve as input into a forecasting model that would forecast unit sales, by geographic regions of the country, for each combination of the model's different prices and fuel configurations.[12] "*

Now do you understand why defining the problem is complicated and half the battle? Many a marketing research effort is doomed from the start because the problem was improperly defined. Coke's ill-fated decision to change the formula of Coca-Cola in 1985 is a case in point: Pepsi had been creeping up on Coke in terms of market share over the years as well as running a successful promotional campaign called the "Pepsi Challenge," in which consumers were encouraged to do a blind taste test to see if they agreed that Pepsi was better. Coke spent four years researching "the problem." Indeed, people seemed to like the taste of Pepsi better in blind taste tests. Thus, the formula for Coke was changed. But the outcry among the public was so great that the new formula didn't last long—a matter of months—before the old formula was reinstated. Some marketing experts believe Coke incorrectly defined the problem as "How can we beat Pepsi in taste tests?" instead of "How can we gain market share against Pepsi?"[13]

## Video Clip

**New Coke Is It! 1985**

This video documents the Coca-Cola Company's ill-fated launch of New Coke in 1985.

View the video online at: http://www.youtube.com/embed/W6t7deaplgY

**Video Clip**

**1985 Pepsi Commercial—"They Changed My Coke"**
This video shows how Pepsi tried to capitalize on the blunder.

View the video online at: http://www.youtube.com/embed/8_hvOBnsirl

## 2.2 Step 2: Design the Research

The next step in the marketing research process is to do a research design. The **research design** is your "plan of attack." It outlines what data you are going to gather and from whom, how and when you will collect the data, and how you will analyze it once it's been obtained. Let's look at the data you're going to gather first.

**research design**

An outline that specifies the research data to be gathered, from whom, how, and when the data will be analyzed once it has been obtained.

There are two basic types of data you can gather. The first is primary data. **Primary data** is information you collect yourself, using hands-on tools such as interviews or surveys, specifically for the research project you're conducting. **Secondary data** is data that has already been collected by someone else, or data you have already collected for another purpose. Collecting primary data is more time consuming, work intensive, and expensive than collecting secondary data. Consequently, you should always try to collect secondary data first to solve your research problem, if you can. A great deal of research on a wide variety of topics already exists. If this research contains the answer to your question, there is no need for you to replicate it. Why reinvent the wheel?

**primary data**

Data collected using hands-on tools such as interviews or surveys to answer a question for a specific research project.

**secondary data**

Data already collected by your firm or another organization for purposes other than the marketing research project at hand.

### Sources of Secondary Data

Your company's internal records are a source of secondary data. So are any data you collect as part of your marketing intelligence gathering efforts. You can also purchase syndicated research. **Syndicated research** is primary data that marketing research firms collect on a regular basis and sell to other companies. J.D. Power & Associates is a provider of syndicated research. The company conducts independent, unbiased surveys of customer satisfaction, product quality, and buyer behavior for various industries. The company is best known for its research in the automobile sector. One of the best-known sellers of syndicated research is the Nielsen Company, which produces the Nielsen ratings. The Nielsen ratings measure the size of television, radio, and newspaper audiences in various markets. You have probably read or heard about TV shows that get the highest (Nielsen) ratings. Nielsen, along with its main competitor, Information Resources, Inc. (IRI), also sells businesses **scanner-based research**. Scanner-based research is information collected by scanners at checkout stands in stores. Each week Nielsen and IRI collect information on the millions of purchases made at stores. The companies then compile the information and sell it to firms in various industries that subscribe to their services. The Nielsen Company has also recently teamed up with Facebook to collect marketing research information. Via Facebook, users will see surveys in some of the spaces in which they used to see online ads.[14]

**syndicated research**

Primary data marketing research firms collect on a regular basis and sell to other companies.

**scanner-based research**

Information collected by scanners at checkout stands in stores.

By contrast, MarketResearch.com is an example of a marketing research aggregator. A **marketing research aggregator** is a marketing research company that doesn't conduct its own research and sell it. Instead, it buys research reports from other marketing research companies and then sells the reports in their entirety or in pieces to other firms. Check out MarketResearch.com's Web site. As you will see there are a huge number of studies in every category imaginable that you can buy for relatively small amounts of money.

**marketing research aggregator**

A marketing research company that doesn't conduct its own research but instead buys it from other marketing research companies and then sells the reports in their entirety or in pieces to other firms.

## FIGURE 10.7

Market research aggregators buy research reports from other marketing research companies and then resell them in part or in whole to other companies so they don't have to gather primary data.

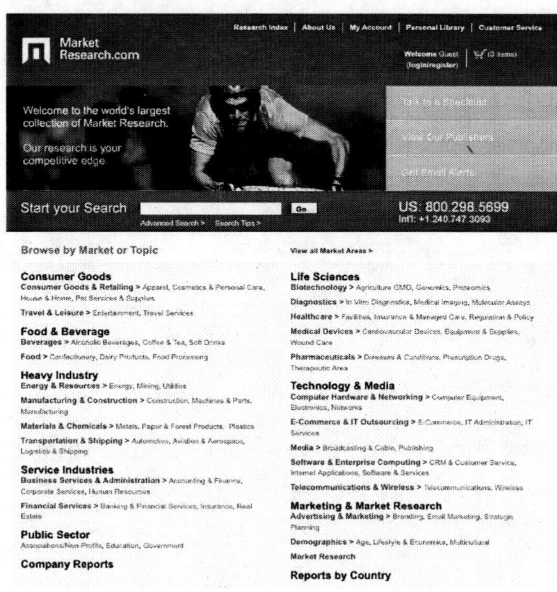


*Source: http://www.marketresearch.com.*

Your local library is a good place to gather free secondary data. It has searchable databases as well as handbooks, dictionaries, and books, some of which you can access online. Government agencies also collect and report information on demographics, economic and employment data, health information, and balance-of-trade statistics, among a lot of other information. The U.S. Census Bureau collects census data every ten years to gather information about who lives where. Basic demographic information about sex, age, race, and types of housing in which people live in each U.S. state, metropolitan area, and rural area is gathered so that population shifts can be tracked for various purposes, including determining the number of legislators each state should have in the U.S. House of Representatives. For the U.S. government, this is primary data. For marketing managers it is an important source of secondary data.

The Survey Research Center at the University of Michigan also conducts periodic surveys and publishes information about trends in the United States. One research study the center continually conducts is called the "Changing Lives of American Families" (http://www.isr.umich.edu/home/news/research-update/2007-01.pdf). This is important research data for marketing managers monitoring consumer trends in the marketplace. The World Bank and the United Nations are two international organizations that collect a great deal of information. Their Web sites contain many free research studies and data related to global markets. Table 10.1 shows some examples of primary versus secondary data sources.

**TABLE 10.1** Examples of Primary Data Sources versus Secondary Data Sources

| Primary Data Sources | Secondary Data Sources |
|---|---|
| Interviews | Census data |
| Surveys | Web sites |
| | Publications |
| | Trade associations |
| | Syndicated research and market aggregators |

### Gauging the Quality of Secondary Data

When you are gathering secondary information, it's always good to be a little skeptical of it. Sometimes studies are commissioned to produce the result a client wants to hear—or wants the public to hear. For example, throughout the twentieth century, numerous studies found that smoking was good for people's health. The problem was the studies were commissioned by the tobacco industry. Web research can also pose certain hazards. There are many biased sites that try to fool people that they are providing good data. Often the data is favorable to the products they are trying to sell. Beware of product reviews as well. Unscrupulous sellers sometimes get online and create bogus ratings for products. See below for questions you can ask to help gauge the credibility of secondary information.

#### Gauging the Credibility of Secondary Data: Questions to Ask

- Who gathered this information?
- For what purpose?
- What does the person or organization that gathered the information have to gain by doing so?
- Was the information gathered and reported in a systematic manner?
- Is the source of the information accepted as an authority by other experts in the field?
- Does the article provide objective evidence to support the position presented?

### Types of Research Design

Now let's look specifically at the types of research designs that are utilized. By understanding different types of research designs, a researcher can solve a client's problems more quickly and efficiently without jumping through more hoops than necessary. Research designs fall into one of the following three categories:

1. Exploratory research design
2. Descriptive research design
3. Causal research design (experiments)

An **exploratory research design** is useful when you are initially investigating a problem but you haven't defined it well enough to do an in-depth study of it. Perhaps via your regular market intelligence, you have spotted what appears to be a new opportunity in the marketplace. You would then do exploratory research to investigate it further and "get your feet wet," as the saying goes. Exploratory research is less structured than other types of research, and secondary data is often utilized.

**exploratory research design**

A less-structured type of research design used to initially investigate a marketing research project that hasn't yet been defined well enough for an in-depth study to be conducted.

The **depth interview**—engaging in detailed, one-on-one, question-and-answer sessions with potential buyers—is an exploratory research technique. However, unlike surveys, the people being interviewed aren't asked a series of standard questions. Instead the interviewer is armed with some general topics and asks questions that are open ended, meaning that they allow the interviewee to elaborate. "How did you feel about the product after you purchased it?" is an example of a question that might be asked. A depth interview also allows a researcher to ask logical follow-up questions such as "Can you tell me what you mean when you say you felt uncomfortable using the service?" or "Can you give me some examples?" to help dig further and shed additional light on the research problem. Depth interviews can be conducted in person or over the phone. The interviewer either takes notes or records the interview.

**depth interview**

An exploratory research technique of engaging in detailed, one-on-one, question-and-answer sessions with potential buyers.

Focus groups and case studies are often utilized for exploratory research as well. A **focus group** is a group of potential buyers who are brought together to discuss a marketing research topic with one another. A moderator is used to focus the discussion, the sessions are recorded, and the main points of consensus are later summarized by the market researcher. Textbook publishers often gather groups of professors at educational conferences to participate in focus groups. However, focus groups can also be conducted on the telephone, in online chat rooms, or both, using meeting software like WebEx. The basic steps of conducting a focus group are outlined below.

**focus group**

A group of potential buyers brought together to discuss a marketing research topic with one another.

#### The Basic Steps of Conducting a Focus Group

1. Establish the objectives of the focus group. What is its purpose?
2. Identify the people who will participate in the focus group. What makes them qualified to participate? How many of them will you need and what they will be paid?

3. Obtain contact information for the participants and send out invitations (usually e-mails are most efficient).
4. Develop a list of questions.
5. Choose a facilitator.
6. Choose a location in which to hold the focus group and the method by which it will be recorded.
7. Conduct the focus group. If the focus group is not conducted electronically, include name tags for the participants, pens and notepads, any materials the participants need to see, and refreshments. Record participants' responses.
8. Summarize the notes from the focus group and write a report for management.

A **case study** looks at how another company solved the problem that's being researched. Sometimes multiple cases, or companies, are used in a study. Case studies nonetheless have a mixed reputation. Some researchers believe it's hard to generalize, or apply, the results of a case study to other companies. Nonetheless, collecting information about companies that encountered the same problems your firm is facing can give you a certain amount of insight about what direction you should take. In fact, one way to begin a research project is to carefully study a successful product or service.

**case study**

A study that looks at how another company, or companies, solved a problem being researched.

Two other types of qualitative data used for exploratory research are ethnographies and projective techniques. In an **ethnography**, researchers interview, observe, and often videotape people while they work, live, shop, and play. The Walt Disney Company has recently begun using ethnographers to uncover the likes and dislikes of boys aged six to fourteen. This is a financially attractive market segment for Disney, but one in which the company has been losing market share. The ethnographers visit the homes of boys, observe the things they have in their rooms to get a sense of their hobbies, and accompany them and their mothers when they shop to see where they go, what the boys are interested in, and what they ultimately buy. (The children get seventy-five dollars out of the deal, incidentally.)[15]

**ethnography**

A type of study whereby marketing researchers interview, observe, and often videotape people while they work, live, shop, and play.

**Projective techniques** are used to reveal information research respondents might not reveal by being asked directly. Asking a person to complete sentences such as the following is one technique:

*People who buy Coach handbags* __________.

(Will he or she reply with "are cool," "are affluent," or "are pretentious," for example?)

*KFC's grilled chicken is* ______.

Or the person might be asked to finish a story that presents a certain scenario. Word associations are also used to discern people's underlying attitudes toward goods and services. Using a word-association technique, a market researcher asks a person to say or write the first word that comes to his or her mind in response to another word. If the initial word is "fast food," what word does the person associate it with or respond with? Is it "McDonald's"? If many people reply that way, and you're conducting research for Burger King, that could indicate Burger King has a problem. However, if the research is being conducted for Wendy's, which recently began running an advertising campaign to the effect that Wendy's offerings are "better than fast food," it could indicate that the campaign is working.

**projective technique**

An exploratory research technique used to reveal information research respondents might not reveal by being asked directly.

Completing cartoons is yet another type of projective technique. It's similar to finishing a sentence or story, only with the pictures. People are asked to look at a cartoon such as the one shown in Figure 10.8. One of the characters in the picture will have made a statement, and the person is asked to fill in the empty cartoon "bubble" with how they think the second character will respond.

**FIGURE 10.8** Example of a Cartoon-Completion Projective Technique

In some cases, your research might end with exploratory research. Perhaps you have discovered your organization lacks the resources needed to produce the product. In other cases, you might decide you need more in-depth, quantitative research such as descriptive research or causal research, which are discussed next. Most marketing research professionals advise using both types of research, if it's feasible. On the one hand, the qualitative-type research used in exploratory research is often considered too "lightweight." Remember earlier in the chapter when we discussed telephone answering machines and the hit TV sitcom *Seinfeld*? Both product ideas were initially rejected by focus groups. On the other hand, relying solely on quantitative information often results in market research that lacks ideas.

**Video Clip**

**The Stone Wheel—What One Focus Group Said**

Watch the video to see a funny spoof on the usefulness—or lack of usefulness—of focus groups.

View the video online at: http://www.youtube.com/embed/OORnMYoWX9c

### Descriptive Research

Anything that can be observed and counted falls into the category of descriptive research design. A study using a **descriptive research design** involves gathering hard numbers, often via surveys, to describe or measure a phenomenon so as to answer the questions of *who*, *what*, *where*, *when*, and *how*. "On a scale of 1–5, how satisfied were you with your service?" is a question that illustrates the information a descriptive research design is supposed to capture.

**descriptive research design**

A study that involves gathering hard numbers, often via surveys, to describe or measure a phenomenon so as to answer the questions of *who, what, where, when,* and *how.*

Physiological measurements also fall into the category of descriptive design. **Physiological measurements** measure people's involuntary physical responses to marketing stimuli, such as an advertisement. Recall in Chapter 3 we explained that researchers have gone so far as to scan the brains of consumers to see what they *really* think about products versus what they say about them. Eye tracking is another cutting-edge type of physiological measurement. It involves recording the movements of a person's eyes when they look at some sort of stimulus, such as a banner ad or a Web page. The Walt Disney Company has a research facility in Austin, Texas, that it uses to take physical measurements of viewers when they see Disney programs and advertisements. The facility measures three types of responses: people's heart rates, skin changes, and eye movements (eye tracking).[16]

**physiological measurements**

Measurements that record people's involuntary physical responses to marketing stimuli, such as an advertisement.

A strictly descriptive research design instrument—a survey, for example—can tell you how satisfied your customers are. It can't, however, tell you why. Nor can an eye-tracking study tell you *why* people's eyes tend to dwell on certain types of banner ads—only that they do. To answer "why" questions an exploratory research design or causal research design is needed.[17]

**FIGURE 10.9**

A woman shows off her headgear for an eye-tracking study. The gear's not exactly a fashion statement but . . .

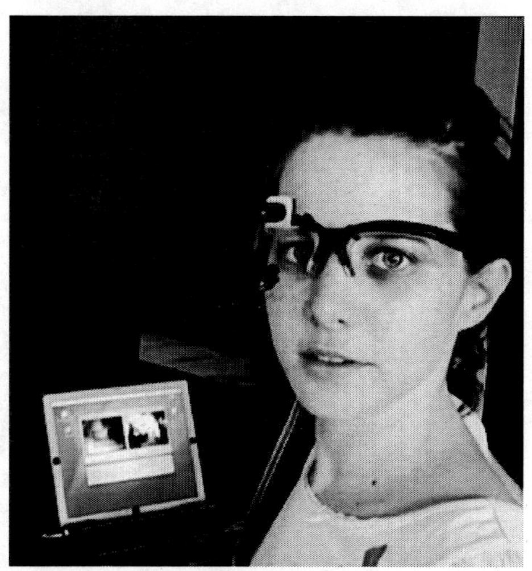

*Source: http://www.jasonbabcock.com/eyetracking_hardware.html.*

### Causal Research

**Causal research design** examines cause-and-effect relationships. Using a causal research design allows researchers to answer "what if" types of questions. In other words, if a firm changes $X$ (say, a product's price, design, placement, or advertising), what will happen to $Y$ (say, sales or customer loyalty)? To conduct causal research, the researcher designs an experiment that "controls," or holds constant, all of a product's marketing elements except one. The one variable is changed, and the effect is then measured. Sometimes the experiments are conducted in a laboratory using a simulated setting designed to replicate the conditions buyers would experience. Or the experiments may be conducted in a virtual computer setting.

You might think setting up an experiment in a virtual world such as the online game Second Life would be a viable way to conduct controlled marketing research. Some companies have tried to use Second Life for this purpose, but the results have been somewhat mixed as to whether or not it is a good medium for marketing research. The German marketing research firm Komjuniti was one of the first "real-world" companies to set up an "island" in Second Life upon which it could conduct marketing research. However, with so many other attractive fantasy islands in which to play, the company found it difficult to get Second Life residents, or players, to voluntarily visit the island and stay long enough so meaningful research could be conducted. (Plus, the "residents," or players, in Second Life have been known to protest corporations invading their world. When the German firm Komjuniti created an island in Second Life to conduct marketing research, the residents showed up waving signs and threatening to boycott the island.)[18]

**causal research design**

A type of research design that examines cause-and-effect relationships to allow researchers to answer "what if" types of questions.

Why is being able to control the setting so important? Let's go back to our American flag example. Suppose prior to 9/11 Walmart had been in the process of conducting an experiment to see where in its stores American flags should be placed so as to increase their sales. Obviously, the terrorist attacks in the United States would have skewed the experiment's data.

An experiment conducted in a natural setting such as a store is referred to as a **field experiment**. Companies sometimes do field experiments either because it is more convenient or because they want to see if buyers will behave the same way in the "real world" as in a laboratory or on a computer. The place the experiment is conducted or the demographic group of people the experiment is administered to is considered the **test market**. Before a large company rolls out a product to the entire marketplace, it will often place the offering in a test market to see how well it will be received. For example, to compete with MillerCoors' sixty-four-calorie beer MGD 64, Anheuser-Busch recently began testing its Select 55 beer in certain cities around the country.[19]

**field experiment**

A marketing research experiment conducted in a natural setting such as a store versus a simulated setting in a laboratory or on a computer.

**test market**

The place an experiment is conducted or the demographic group of people an experiment is administered to.

**FIGURE 10.10** Select 55 beer: Coming soon to a test market near you? (If you're on a diet, you have to hope so!)

Many companies use experiments to test all of their marketing communications. For example, the online discount retailer Overstock.com carefully tests all of its marketing offers and tracks the results of each one. One study the company conducted combined twenty-six different variables related to offers e-mailed to several thousand customers. The study resulted in a decision to send a group of e-mails to different segments. The company then tracked the results of the sales generated to see if they were in line with the earlier experiment it had conducted that led it to make the offer.

## 2.3 Step 3: Design the Data-Collection Forms

If the behavior of buyers is being formally observed, and a number of different researchers are conducting observations, the data obviously need to be recorded on a standardized data-collection form that's either paper or electronic. Otherwise, the data collected will not be comparable. The items on the form could include a shopper's sex; his or her approximate age; whether the person seemed hurried, moderately hurried, or unhurried; and whether or not he or she read the label on products, used coupons, and so forth.

The same is true when it comes to surveying people with questionnaires. Surveying people is one of the most commonly used techniques to collect quantitative data. Surveys are popular because they can be easily administered to large numbers of people fairly quickly. However, to produce the best results, the questionnaire for the survey needs to be carefully designed.

### Questionnaire Design

Most questionnaires follow a similar format: They begin with an introduction describing what the study is for, followed by instructions for completing the questionnaire and, if necessary, returning it to the market researcher. The first few questions that appear on the questionnaire are usually basic, warm-up type of questions the respondent can readily answer, such as the respondent's age, level of education, place of residence, and so forth. The warm-up questions are then followed by a logical progression of more detailed, in-depth questions that get to the heart of the question being researched. Lastly, the questionnaire wraps up with a statement that thanks the respondent for participating in the survey and information and explains when and how they will be paid for participating. To see some examples of questionnaires and how they are laid out, click on the following link: http://cas.uah.edu/wrenb/mkt343/Project/Sample%20Questionnaires.htm.

How the questions themselves are worded is extremely important. It's human nature for respondents to want to provide the "correct" answers to the person administering the survey, so as to seem agreeable. In other words, there is always a hazard that people will try to tell you what you want to hear on a survey. Consequently, care needs to be taken that the survey questions are written in an unbiased, neutral way. In other words, they shouldn't lead a person taking the questionnaire to answer a question one way or another by virtue of the way you have worded it. The following is an example of a leading question.

*Don't you agree that teachers should be paid more?*

The questions also need to be clear and unambiguous. Consider the following question:

*Which brand of toothpaste do you use?*

The question sounds clear enough, but is it really? What if the respondent recently switched brands? What if she uses Crest at home, but while away from home or traveling, she uses Colgate's Wisp portable toothpaste-and-brush product? How will the respondent answer the question? Rewording the question as follows so it's more specific will help make the question clearer:

*Which brand of toothpaste have you used at home in the past six months? If you have used more than one brand, please list each of them.*[20]

Sensitive questions have to be asked carefully. For example, asking a respondent, "Do you consider yourself a light, moderate, or heavy drinker?" can be tricky. Few people want to admit to being heavy drinkers. You can "soften" the question by including a range of answers, as the following example shows:

*How many alcoholic beverages do you consume in a week?*

- __0–5 alcoholic beverages
- __5–10 alcoholic beverages
- __10–15 alcoholic beverages

Many people don't like to answer questions about their income levels. Asking them to specify income ranges rather than divulge their actual incomes can help.

Other research question "don'ts" include using jargon and acronyms that could confuse people. "How often do you IM?" is an example. Also, don't muddy the waters by asking two questions in the same question, something researchers refer to as a **double-barreled question**. "Do you think parents should spend more time with their children and/or their teachers?" is an example of a double-barreled question.

**Open-ended questions**, or questions that ask respondents to elaborate, can be included. However, they are harder to tabulate than **closed-ended questions**, or questions that limit a respondent's answers. Multiple-choice and yes-and-no questions are examples of closed-ended questions.

**double-barreled question**

A survey question that is potentially confusing because it asks two questions in the same question.

**open-ended questions**

Questions that ask respondents to elaborate upon, or explain, their answers.

**closed-ended questions**

Questions that limit a respondent's answers. Multiple-choice and yes-and-no questions are examples of closed-ended questions.

### Testing the Questionnaire

You have probably heard the phrase "garbage in, garbage out." If the questions are bad, the information gathered will be bad, too. One way to make sure you don't end up with garbage is to test the questionnaire before sending it out to find out if there are any problems with it. Is there enough space for people to elaborate on open-ended questions? Is the font readable? To test the questionnaire, marketing research professionals first administer it to a number of respondents face to face. This gives the respondents the chance to ask the researcher about questions or instructions that are unclear or don't make sense to them. The researcher then administers the questionnaire to a small subset of respondents in the actual way the survey is going to be disseminated, whether it's delivered via phone, in person, or by mail.

Getting people to participate and complete questionnaires can be difficult. If the questionnaire is too long or hard to read, many people won't complete it. So, by all means, eliminate any questions that aren't necessary. Of course, including some sort of monetary incentive for completing the survey can increase the number of completed questionnaires a market researcher will receive.

## 2.4 Step 4: Specify the Sample

Once you have created your questionnaire or other marketing study, how do you figure out who should participate in it? Obviously, you can't survey or observe all potential buyers in the marketplace. Instead, you must choose a sample. A **sample** is a subset of potential buyers that are representative of your *entire* target market, or **population** being studied. Sometimes market researchers refer to the population as the *universe* to reflect the fact that it includes the entire target market, whether it consists of a million people, a hundred thousand, a few hundred, or a dozen. "All unmarried people over the age of eighteen who purchased Dirt Devil steam cleaners in the United States during 2009" is an example of a population that has been defined.

**sample**

A small amount of a product given to consumers to try for free.

**population**

The entire target market being studied.

Obviously, the population has to be defined correctly. Otherwise, you will be studying the wrong group of people. Not defining the population correctly can result in flawed research, or sampling error. A **sampling error** is any type of marketing research mistake that results because a sample was utilized. One criticism of Internet surveys is that the people who take these surveys don't really represent the overall population. On average, Internet survey takers tend to be more educated and tech savvy. Consequently, if they solely constitute your population, even if you screen them for certain criteria, the data you collect could end up being skewed.

**sampling error**

Any type of marketing research mistake that results because a sample was utilized.

The next step is to put together the **sampling frame**, which is the list from which the sample is drawn. The sampling frame can be put together using a directory, customer list, or membership roster.[21] Keep in mind that the sampling frame won't *perfectly* match the population. Some people will be included on the list who shouldn't be. Other people who should be included will be inadvertently omitted. It's no different than if you were to conduct a survey of, say, 25 percent of your friends, using friends' names you have in your mobile phone. Most of your friends' names are likely to be programmed into your phone, but not all of them. As a result, a certain degree of sampling error always occurs.

**sampling frame**

The list from which a research sample is drawn. The sampling frame won't perfectly match the population.

There are two main categories of samples in terms of how they are drawn: probability samples and nonprobability samples. A **probability sample** is one in which each would-be participant has a known and equal chance of being selected. The chance is known because the total number of people in the sampling frame is known. For example, if every other person from the sampling frame were chosen, each person would have a 50 percent chance of being selected.

**probability sample**

A research sample in which each would-be participant has a known and equal chance of being selected.

**nonprobability sample**

A research sample that's not drawn in a systematic way.

**convenience sample**

Type of nonprobability sample that's drawn because it's readily available and convenient to do so.

A **nonprobability sample** is any type of sample that's not drawn in a systematic way. So the chances of each would-be participant being selected can't be known. A **convenience sample** is one type of nonprobability sample. It is a sample a researcher draws because it's readily available and convenient to do so. Surveying people on the street as they pass by is an example of a convenience sample. The question is, are these people representative of the target market?

For example, suppose a grocery store needed to quickly conduct some research on shoppers to get ready for an upcoming promotion. Now suppose that the researcher assigned to the project showed up between the hours of 10 a.m. and 12 p.m. on a weekday and surveyed as many shoppers as possible. The problem is that the shoppers wouldn't be representative of the store's entire target market. What about commuters who stop at the store before and after work? Their views wouldn't be represented. Neither would people who work the night shift or shop at odd hours. As a result, there would be a lot of room for sampling error in this study. For this reason, studies that use nonprobability samples aren't considered as accurate as studies that use probability samples. Nonprobability samples are more often used in exploratory research.

Lastly, the size of the sample has an effect on the amount of sampling error. Larger samples generally produce more accurate results. The larger your sample is, the more data you will have, which will give you a more complete picture of what you're studying. However, the more people surveyed or studied, the more costly the research becomes.

Statistics can be used to determine a sample's optimal size. If you take a marketing research or statistics class, you will learn more about how to determine the optimal size.

Of course, if you hire a marketing research company, much of this work will be taken care of for you. Many marketing research companies maintain panels of prescreened people they draw upon for samples. In addition, the marketing research firm will be responsible for collecting the data or contracting with a company that specializes in data collection. Data collection is discussed next.

## 2.5 Step 5: Collect the Data

**mystery shopper**

A person who is paid to shop at a firm's establishment or one of its competitors' to observe the level of service, cleanliness of the facility, and so forth, and report his or her findings to the firm.

As we have explained, primary marketing research data can be gathered in a number of ways. Surveys, taking physical measurements, and observing people are just three of the ways we discussed. If you're observing customers as part of gathering the data, keep in mind that if shoppers are aware of the fact, it can have an effect on their behavior. For example, if a customer shopping for feminine hygiene products in a supermarket aisle realizes she is being watched, she could become embarrassed and leave the aisle. This would adversely affect your data. To get around problems such as these, some companies set up cameras or two-way mirrors to observe customers. Organizations also hire mystery shoppers to work around the problem. A **mystery shopper** is someone who is paid to shop at a firm's establishment or one of its competitors to observe the level of service, cleanliness of the facility, and so forth, and report his or her findings to the firm.

**Video Clip**

**Make Extra Money as a Mystery Shopper**

Watch the YouTube video to get an idea of how mystery shopping works.

View the video online at: http://www.youtube.com/embed/Rsth2qvWFfw

Survey data can be collected in many different ways and combinations of ways. The following are the basic methods used:

- Face-to-face (can be computer aided)

- Telephone (can be computer aided or completely automated)
- Mail and hand delivery
- E-mail and the Web

A face-to-face survey is, of course, administered by a person. The surveys are conducted in public places such as in shopping malls, on the street, or in people's homes if they have agreed to it. In years past, it was common for researchers in the United States to knock on people's doors to gather survey data. However, randomly collected door-to-door interviews are less common today, partly because people are afraid of crime and are reluctant to give information to strangers.[22]

Nonetheless, "beating the streets" is still a legitimate way questionnaire data is collected. When the U.S. Census Bureau collects data on the nation's population, it hand delivers questionnaires to rural households that do not have street-name and house-number addresses. And Census Bureau workers personally survey the homeless to collect information about their numbers. Face-to-face surveys are also commonly used in third world countries to collect information from people who cannot read or lack phones and computers.

A plus of face-to-face surveys is that they allow researchers to ask lengthier, more complex questions because the people being surveyed can see and read the questionnaires. The same is true when a computer is utilized. For example, the researcher might ask the respondent to look at a list of ten retail stores and rank the stores from best to worst. The same question wouldn't work so well over the telephone because the person couldn't see the list. The question would have to be rewritten. Another drawback with telephone surveys is that even though federal and state "do not call" laws generally don't prohibit companies from gathering survey information over the phone, people often screen such calls using answering machines and caller ID.

Probably the biggest drawback of both surveys conducted face-to-face and administered over the phone by a person is that they are labor intensive and therefore costly. Mailing out questionnaires is costly, too, and the response rates can be rather low. Think about why that might be so: if you receive a questionnaire in the mail, it is easy to throw it in the trash; it's harder to tell a market researcher who approaches you on the street that you don't want to be interviewed.

By contrast, gathering survey data collected by a computer, either over the telephone or on the Internet, can be very cost effective and in some cases free. SurveyMonkey and Zoomerang are two Web sites that will allow you to create online questionnaires, e-mail them to up to one hundred people for free, and view the responses in real time as they come in. For larger surveys, you have to pay a subscription price of a few hundred dollars. But that still can be extremely cost effective. The two Web sites also have a host of other features such as online-survey templates you can use to create your questionnaire, a way to set up automatic reminders sent to people who haven't yet completed their surveys, and tools you can use to create graphics to put in your final research report. To see how easy it is to put together a survey in SurveyMonkey, click on the following link: http://help.surveymonkey.com/app/tutorials/detail/a_id/423.

Like a face-to-face survey, an Internet survey can enable you to show buyers different visuals such as ads, pictures, and videos of products and their packaging. Web surveys are also fast, which is a major plus. Whereas face-to-face and mailed surveys often take weeks to collect, you can conduct a Web survey in a matter of days or even hours. And, of course, because the information is electronically gathered it can be automatically tabulated. You can also potentially reach a broader geographic group than you could if you had to personally interview people. The Zoomerang Web site allows you to create surveys in forty different languages.

Another plus for Web and computer surveys (and electronic phone surveys) is that there is less room for human error because the surveys are administered electronically. For instance, there's no risk that the interviewer will ask a question wrong or use a tone of voice that could mislead the respondents. Respondents are also likely to feel more comfortable inputting the information into a computer if a question is sensitive than they would divulging the information to another person face-to-face or over the phone. Given all of these advantages, it's not surprising that the Internet is quickly becoming the top way to collect primary data. However, like mail surveys, surveys sent to people over the Internet are easy to ignore.

Lastly, before the data collection process begins, the surveyors and observers need to be trained to look for the same things, ask questions the same way, and so forth. If they are using rankings or rating scales, they need to be "on the same page," so to speak, as to what constitutes a high ranking or a low ranking. As an analogy, you have probably had some teachers grade your college papers harder than others. The goal of training is to avoid a wide disparity between how different observers and interviewers record the data.

**FIGURE 10.11**

Training people so they know what constitutes different ratings when they are collecting data will improve the quality of the information gathered in a marketing research study.

For example, if an observation form asks the observers to describe whether a shopper's behavior is hurried, moderately hurried, or unhurried, they should be given an idea of what defines each rating. Does it depend on how much time the person spends in the store or in the individual aisles? How fast they walk? In other words, the criteria and ratings need to be spelled out.

### Collecting International Marketing Research Data

Gathering marketing research data in foreign countries poses special challenges. However, that doesn't stop firms from doing so. Marketing research companies are located all across the globe, in fact. Eight of the ten largest marketing research companies in the world are headquartered in the United States. However, five of these eight firms earn more of their revenues abroad than they do in the United States. There's a reason for this: many U.S. markets were saturated, or tapped out, long ago in terms of the amount that they can grow. Coke is an example. As you learned earlier in the book, most of the Coca-Cola Company's revenues are earned in markets abroad. To be sure, the United States is still a huge market when it comes to the revenues marketing research firms generate by conducting research in the country: in terms of their spending, American consumers fuel the world's economic engine. Still, emerging countries with growing middle classes, such as China, India, and Brazil, are hot new markets companies want to tap.

What kind of challenges do firms face when trying to conduct marketing research abroad? As we explained, face-to-face surveys are commonly used in third world countries to collect information from people who cannot read or lack phones and computers. However, face-to-face surveys are also common in Europe, despite the fact that phones and computers are readily available. In-home surveys are also common in parts of Europe. By contrast, in some countries, including many Asian countries, it's considered taboo or rude to try to gather information from strangers either face-to-face or over the phone. In many Muslim countries, women are forbidden to talk to strangers.

And how do you figure out whom to research in foreign countries? That in itself is a problem. In the United States, researchers often ask if they can talk to the heads of households to conduct marketing research. But in countries in which domestic servants or employees are common, the heads of households aren't necessarily the principal shoppers; their domestic employees are.[23]

Translating surveys is also an issue. Have you ever watched the TV comedians Jay Leno and David Letterman make fun of the English translations found on ethnic menus and products? Research tools such as surveys can suffer from the same problem. Hiring someone who is bilingual to translate a survey into another language can be a disaster if the person isn't a native speaker of the language to which the survey is being translated.

**back translation**

A process whereby a native speaker translates a research instrument such as a survey into a foreign language and then back again to the original language to determine if there are gaps in meaning.

One way companies try to deal with translation problems is by using back translation. When **back translation** is used, a native speaker translates the survey into the foreign language and then translates it back again to the original language to determine if there were gaps in meaning—that is, if anything was lost in translation. And it's not just the language that's an issue. If the research involves any visual images, they, too, could be a point of confusion. Certain colors, shapes, and symbols can have negative connotations in other countries. For example, the color white represents purity in many Western cultures, but in China, it is the color of death and mourning.[24] Also, look back at the cartoon-completion exercise in Figure 10.8. What would women in Muslim countries who aren't allowed to converse with male sellers think of it? Chances are, the cartoon wouldn't provide you with the information you're seeking if Muslim women in some countries were asked to complete it.

One way marketing research companies are dealing with the complexities of global research is by merging with or acquiring marketing research companies abroad. The Nielsen Company is the largest marketing research company in the world. The firm operates in more than a hundred countries and employs more than forty thousand people. Many of its expansions have been the result of acquisitions and mergers.

## 2.6 Step 6: Analyze the Data

Step 6 involves analyzing the data to ensure it's as accurate as possible. If the research is collected by hand using a pen and pencil, it's entered into a computer. Or respondents might have already entered the information directly into a computer. For example, when Toyota goes to an event such as a car show, the automaker's marketing personnel ask would-be buyers to complete questionnaires directly on computers. Companies are also beginning to experiment with software that can be used to collect data using mobile phones.

Once all the data is collected, the researchers begin the **data cleaning**, which is the process of removing data that have accidentally been duplicated (entered twice into the computer) or correcting data that have obviously been recorded wrong. A program such as Microsoft Excel or a statistical program such as Predictive Analytics Software (PASW, which was formerly known as SPSS) is then used to tabulate, or calculate, the basic results of the research, such as the total number of participants and how collectively they answered various questions. The programs can also be used to calculate averages, such as the average age of respondents, their average satisfaction, and so forth. The same can done for percentages, and other values you learned about, or will learn about, in a statistics course, such as the standard deviation, mean, and median for each question.

**data cleaning**

The process of removing research data that have accidentally been duplicated (entered twice into the computer) or correcting data that have obviously been recorded wrong.

The information generated by the programs can be used to draw conclusions, such as what *all* customers might like or not like about an offering based on what the sample group liked or did not like. The information can also be used to spot differences among groups of people. For example, the research might show that people in one area of the country like the product better than people in another area. Trends to predict what might happen in the future can also be spotted.

If there are any open-ended questions respondents have elaborated upon—for example, "Explain why you like the current brand you use better than any other brand"—the answers to each are pasted together, one on top of another, so researchers can compare and summarize the information. As we have explained, qualitative information such as this can give you a fuller picture of the results of the research.

Part of analyzing the data is to see if it seems sound. Does the way in which the research was conducted seem sound? Was the sample size large enough? Are the conclusions that become apparent from it reasonable?

The two most commonly used criteria used to test the soundness of a study are (1) validity and (2) reliability. A study is **valid** if it actually tested what it was designed to test. For example, did the experiment you ran in Second Life test what it was designed to test? Did it reflect what could really happen in the real world? If not, the research isn't valid. If you were to repeat the study, and get the same results (or nearly the same results), the research is said to be **reliable**. If you get a drastically different result if you repeat the study, it's not reliable. The data collected, or at least some it, can also be compared to, or reconciled with, similar data from other sources either gathered by your firm or by another organization to see if the information seems on target.

**valid (study)**

A study that actually tests what it was designed to test and not something else.

**reliable (study)**

A study that, when repeated, produces the same or nearly the same result.

## 2.7 Stage 7: Write the Research Report and Present Its Findings

If you end up becoming a marketing professional and conducting a research study after you graduate, hopefully you will do a great job putting the study together. You will have defined the problem correctly, chosen the right sample, collected the data accurately, analyzed it, and your findings will be sound. At that point, you will be required to write the research report and perhaps present it to an audience of decision makers. You will do so via a written report and, in some cases, a slide or PowerPoint presentation based on your written report.

The six basic elements of a research report are as follows.

1. **Title Page.** The title page explains what the report is about, when it was conducted and by whom, and who requested it.
2. **Table of Contents.** The table of contents outlines the major parts of the report, as well as any graphs and charts, and the page numbers on which they can be found.
3. **Executive Summary.** The executive summary summarizes all the details in the report in a very quick way. Many people who receive the report—both executives and nonexecutives—won't have time to read the entire report. Instead, they will rely on the executive summary to quickly get an idea of the study's results and what to do about those results.
4. **Methodology and Limitations.** The methodology section of the report explains the technical details of how the research was designed and conducted. The section explains, for example, how the data was collected and by whom, the size of the sample, how it was chosen, and whom or what it consisted of (e.g., the number of women versus men or children versus adults). It also includes information about the statistical techniques used to analyze the data.

   Every study has errors—sampling errors, interviewer errors, and so forth. The methodology section should explain these details, so decision makers can consider their overall impact. The **margin of error** is the overall tendency of the study to be off kilter—that is, how far it could have gone wrong in either direction. Remember how newscasters present the presidential polls before an election? They always say, "This candidate is ahead 48 to 44 percent, plus or minus 2 percent." That "plus or minus" is the margin of error. The larger the margin of error is, the less likely the results of the study are accurate. The margin of error needs to be included in the methodology section.

**margin of error**

A measure of the possible inaccuracy of the data reported in a survey.

5. **Findings**. The findings section is a longer, fleshed-out version of the executive summary that goes into more detail about the statistics uncovered by the research that bolster the study's findings. If you have related research or secondary data on hand that back up the findings, it can be included to help show the study did what it was designed to do.
6. **Recommendations**. The recommendations section should outline the course of action you think should be taken based on the findings of the research and the purpose of the project. For example, if you conducted a global market research study to identify new locations for stores, make a recommendation for the locations.[25]

As we have said, these are the basic sections of a marketing research report. However, additional sections can be added as needed. For example, you might need to add a section on the competition and each firm's market share. If you're trying to decide on different supply chain options, you will need to include a section on that topic.

As you write the research report, keep your audience in mind. Don't use technical jargon decision makers and other people reading the report won't understand. If technical terms must be used, explain them. Also, proofread the document to ferret out any grammatical errors and typos, and ask a couple of other people to proofread behind you to catch any mistakes you might have missed. If your research report is riddled with errors, its credibility will be undermined, even if the findings and recommendations you make are extremely accurate.

Many research reports are presented via PowerPoint. If you're asked to create a slideshow presentation from the report, don't try to include every detail in the report on the slides. The information will be too long and tedious for people attending the presentation to read through. And if they do go to the trouble of reading all the information, they probably won't be listening to the speaker who is making the presentation.

Instead of including all the information from the study in the slides, boil each section of the report down to key points and add some "talking points" only the presenter will see. After or during the presentation, you can give the attendees the longer, paper version of the report so they can read the details at a convenient time, if they choose to.

## KEY TAKEAWAY

Step 1 in the marketing research process is to define the problem. Businesses take a look at what they believe are symptoms and try to drill down to the potential causes so as to precisely define the problem. The next task for the researcher is to put into writing the research objective, or goal, the research is supposed to accomplish. Step 2 in the process is to design the research. The research design is the "plan of attack." It outlines what data you are going to gather, from whom, how, and when, and how you're going to analyze it once it has been obtained. Step 3 is to design the data-collection forms, which need to be standardized so the information gathered on each is comparable. Surveys are a popular way to gather data because they can be easily administered to large numbers of people fairly quickly. However, to produce the best results, survey questionnaires need to be carefully designed and pretested before they are used. Step 4 is drawing the sample, or a subset of potential buyers who are representative of your *entire* target market. If the sample is not correctly selected, the research will be flawed. Step 5 is to actually collect the data, whether it's collected by a person face-to-face, over the phone, or with the help of computers or the Internet. The data-collection process is often different in foreign countries. Step 6 is to analyze the data collected for any obvious errors, tabulate the data, and then draw conclusions from it based on the results. The last step in the process, Step 7, is writing the research report and presenting the findings to decision makers.

## REVIEW QUESTIONS

1. Explain why it's important to carefully define the problem or opportunity a marketing research study is designed to investigate.
2. Describe the different types of problems that can occur when marketing research professionals develop questions for surveys.
3. How does a probability sample differ from a nonprobability sample?
4. What makes a marketing research study valid? What makes a marketing research study reliable?
5. What sections should be included in a marketing research report? What is each section designed to do?

# 3. DISCUSSION QUESTIONS AND ACTIVITIES

## DISCUSSION QUESTIONS

1. Are small business owners at a disadvantage if they lack the marketing research resources large companies have? Why or why not?
2. Online marketing research seems to be the wave of the future. What drawbacks do you see associated with online research? What are the privacy issues?
3. Why do you think so many marketing research companies are conglomerating—that is, merging with or acquiring one another? Is it solely to conduct global marketing research?

## ACTIVITIES

1. In this activity, you will conduct a survey using either Zoomerang.com or SurveyMonkey.com. Divide into groups of four people. Each group should do the following:
    a. Choose a food-service establishment on or near your campus. Then create a ten-question survey designed to gauge how satisfied customers are with the establishment's food and service.
    b. Decide how you will deliver the questionnaire you've created. Choose a sampling frame, or list of people from which you will draw your sample.
    c. Administer the survey. After you have collected the results, analyze them and write a research report with the sections outlined in the chapter.
    d. Contact the owner or manager of the establishment, and present him or her with the findings. If your research is helpful to the manager, who knows? It might earn you a free meal or at least some money-off coupons.
2. Would you like to own an all-electric car? Do you think there is a viable market for such a product? Team up into small groups of three or four people. As a team, use secondary data to research the viability of selling electric cars profitably. Utilize some of the sources mentioned in the chapter. Try to determine the population of electric-car buyers. Lastly, write a research report based on your findings. Each group should present its findings to the class. Do the findings differ from group to group? If so, why?

# ENDNOTES


1. Seth Stern, "The Museum of Food Failures," *Christian Science Monitor*, July 2, 2002, http://www.csmonitor.com/2002/0702/p18s03-hfks.html (accessed December 14, 2009).
2. Stephen Baker, "The Web Knows What You Want," *BusinessWeek*, July 24, 2009, http://www.businessweek.com/magazine/content/09_30/b4140048486880.htm (accessed December 14, 2009).
3. Christina Zarello, "Hunting for Gold in the Great Outdoors," *Rental Information Systems News*, May 5, 2009, http://www.risnews.com/ME2/dirmod.asp?sid=&nm=&type=MultiPublishing&mod=PublishingTitles&mid=2E3DABA5396D4649BABC55BEADF2F8FD&tier=4&id=7BC8781137EC46D1A759B336BF50D2B6 (accessed December 14, 2009).
4. Christina Zarello, "Hunting for Gold in the Great Outdoors," *Rental Information Systems News*, May 5, 2009, http://www.risnews.com/ME2/dirmod.asp?sid=&nm=&type=MultiPublishing&mod=PublishingTitles&mid=2E3DABA5396D4649BABC55BEADF2F8FD&tier=4&id=7BC8781137EC46D1A759B336BF50D2B6 (accessed December 14, 2009).
5. Jan Gardner, "Competitive Intelligence on a Shoestring," *Inc.*, September 24, 2001, http://www.inc.com/articles/2001/09/23436.html (accessed December 14, 2009).
6. Judith Nemes, "Dumpster Diving: From Garbage to Gold," *Greenbiz.com*, January 16, 2009, http://www.businessgreen.com/business-green/analysis/2234107/dumpster-diving-garbage-gold (accessed December 14, 2009).
7. "P&G Admits to Dumpster Diving," *PRWatch.org*, August 31, 2001, http://www.prwatch.org/node/663 (accessed December 14, 2009).
8. "Microsoft Suit Alleges Ex-Worker Stole Trade Secrets," *CNET*, January 30, 2009, http://news.cnet.com/8301-10805_3-10153616-75.html (accessed December 14, 2009).
9. Jack Anderson, "Bugging Air France First Class," *Ellensburg Daily News*, March 25, 1995, 3, http://news.google.com/newspapers?nid=860&dat=19950320&id=ddYPAAAAIBAJ&sjid=F48DAAAAIBAJ&pg=4554,2982160 (accessed April 13, 2012).
10. "SCIP Code of Ethics for CI Professionals," Society of Competitive Intelligence Professionals, http://www.scip.org/About/content.cfm?ItemNumber=578&navItemNumber=504 (accessed December 14, 2009).
11. Alex J. Caffarini, "Ten Costly Marketing Mistakes and How to Avoid Them," Analysights, LLC, http://analysights.com/Documents/10_Costly_MR_Mistakes.pdf (accessed December 14, 2009).
12. Alvin Burns and Ronald Bush, *Marketing Research*, 6th ed. (Upper Saddle River, NJ: Prentice Hall, 2010), 85.
13. Alvin Burns and Ronald Bush, *Marketing Research*, 6th ed. (Upper Saddle River, NJ: Prentice Hall, 2010), 87–88.
14. Alan Rappeport and David Gelles, "Facebook to Form Alliance with Nielsen," *Financial Times*, September 23, 2009, 16.
15. Brook Barnes, "Disney Expert Uses Science to Draw Boy Viewers," *New York Times*, April 15, 2009, http://www.nytimes.com/2009/04/14/arts/television/14boys.html?pagewanted=1&_r=1 (accessed December 14, 2009).
16. Todd Spangler, "Disney Lab Tracks Feelings," *Multichannel News* 30, no. 30 (August 3, 2009): 26.
17. James Wagner, "Marketing in Second Life Doesn't Work…Here Is Why!" *GigaOM*, April 4, 2007, http://gigaom.com/2007/04/04/3-reasons-why-marketing-in-second-life-doesnt-work (accessed December 14, 2009).
18. James Wagner, "Marketing in Second Life Doesn't Work…Here Is Why!" *GigaOM*, April 4, 2007, http://gigaom.com/2007/04/04/3-reasons-why-marketing-in-second-life-doesnt-work/ (accessed December 14, 2009).
19. Jeremiah McWilliams, "A-B Puts Super-Low-Calorie Beer in Ring with Miller," *St. Louis Post-Dispatch*, August 16, 2009, http://www.stltoday.com/business/next-matchup-light-weights-a-b-puts-super-low-calorie/article_47511bfe-18ca-5979-bdb9-0526c97d4edf.html (accessed April 13, 2012).
20. "Questionnaire Design," *QuickMBA*, http://www.quickmba.com/marketing/research/qdesign (accessed December 14, 2009).
21. Bruce Wrenn, Robert E. Stevens, and David L. Loudon, *Marketing Research: Text and Cases*, 2nd ed. (Binghamton, NY: Haworth Press, 2007), 180.
22. Carl D. McDaniel and Roger H. Gates, *Marketing Research Essentials*, 2nd ed. (Cincinnati: South-Western College Publishing, 1998), 61.
23. Naresh Malhotra, *Marketing Research: An Applied Approach*, 6th ed. (Upper Saddle River, NJ: Prentice Hall), 764.
24. Malika Zouhali-Worrall, "Found in Translation: Avoiding Multilingual Gaffes," *CNNMoney.com*, July 14, 2008, http://money.cnn.com/2008/07/07/smallbusiness/language_translation.fsb/index.htm (accessed December 14, 2009).
25. Sherrie Mersdorf, "How to Organize Your Next Survey Report," *Cvent*, August 24, 2009, http://survey.cvent.com/blog/cvent-survey/0/0/how-to-organize-your-next-survey-report (accessed December 14, 2009).

# CHAPTER 11
# Advertising, Integrated Marketing Communications, and the Changing Media Landscape

Communication helps businesses grow and prosper, creates relationships, strengthens the effectiveness of organizations, and allows people to learn about one another. Technology such as the Internet and cell phones affects the way we communicate and is changing the type of messaging strategy organizations use.

Do you feel lost without your cell phone? Are you more likely to respond to text messages than phone calls? Do you use the print publications (magazines, newspapers, references) at the library or do you find all your references online? Do your grandparents prefer different methods of communication? Think about how you get information and then think about how organizations can communicate with you and other target markets about their products, services, or causes. As we find new sources of information, the media and message strategies used by businesses must also change. However, organizations still want consumers to get a consistent message.

## 1. INTEGRATED MARKETING COMMUNICATIONS (IMC) AND NEW MEDIA

**LEARNING OBJECTIVES**

1. **Understand what integrated marketing communications (IMC) are.**
2. **Understand why organizations may change their promotional strategies to reach different audiences.**

Once they have developed products and services, organizations must communicate the value and benefits of the offerings to both current and potential customers in both business-to-business and business-to-consumer markets. **Integrated marketing communications (IMC)** provide an approach designed to deliver one consistent message to buyers across an organization's promotions that may span all different types of media—TV, radio, magazines, the Internet, mobile phones, and so forth. For example, Campbell's Soup Company typically includes the "Mm, mm good" slogan in the print ads it places in newspapers and magazines, in ads on the Internet, and in commercials on television and radio. A company's ads should communicate a consistent message even if it is trying to reach different audiences. For example, although the messages are very similar, Campbell's uses two variations of commercials designed to target different consumers. Watch the two YouTube videos below. You'll notice that the message Campbell's gets across is consistent. But can you figure out who the two target audiences consist of?

**integrated marketing communications (IMC)**

Approach designed to deliver one consistent message to buyers across an organization's promotions.

### Video Clip

**A Meal That's Always Popular with the Group**

Campbell's soup provides a good meal.

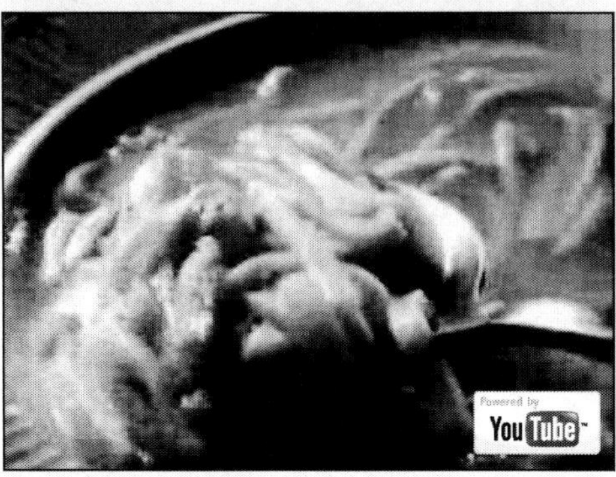


View the video online at: http://www.youtube.com/embed/W5ZM1cqpdT0

### Video Clip

**So Many Possibilities for Enjoying Soup**

Campbell's soup pleases people of all ages.

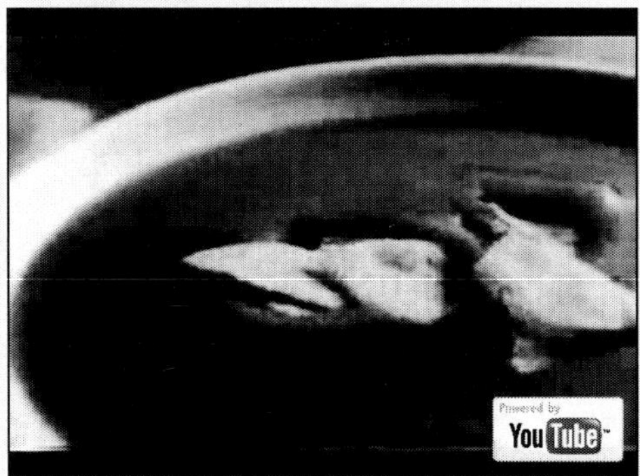


View the video online at: http://www.youtube.com/embed/IN3c4rZJNd4

Changes in communication technology and instant access to information through tools such as the Internet explain one of the reasons why integrated marketing communications have become so important. Delivering consistent information about a brand or an organization helps establish the brand in the minds of consumers and potential customers. Many consumers and business professionals seek information and connect with other people and businesses from their computers and phones. The work and social environments are changing, with more people having virtual offices and texting on their cell phones or communicating through social media such as Facebook. Text messaging, Internet, cell phones, blogs—the way we communicate continues to change the way companies are doing business and reaching their customers. As a result, organizations have realized they need to change their promotional strategies as well to reach specific audiences.

Many college students are part of the millennial generation, and it is consumers from this generation (people like you perhaps) who are driving the change toward new communication technologies. As we discussed in Chapter 5 you might opt to get promotions via **mobile marketing**—say, from stores on your cell phone as you walk by them or via a mobile gaming device that allows you to connect to the Web. Likewise, advertisements on Facebook are becoming more popular as businesses explore social media. For example, when Honda let people on Facebook use the Honda logo to give heart-shaped virtual gifts on Valentine's Day, over one and a half million people participated in the event and viewed the Honda Fit online in the process. Imagine the brand awareness generated for the Honda Fit.

**FIGURE 11.1**

Some consumers feel lost without their cell phones. Phones such as the one pictured provide a source of information for consumers and a new medium for advertisers to deliver information.

© 2010 *Jupiterimages Corporation*

**mobile marketing**

Marketing media that is available in different places such as cell phones or on forms of transportation.

**FIGURE 11.2**

Marketing based on the Internet and wireless technology is popular.

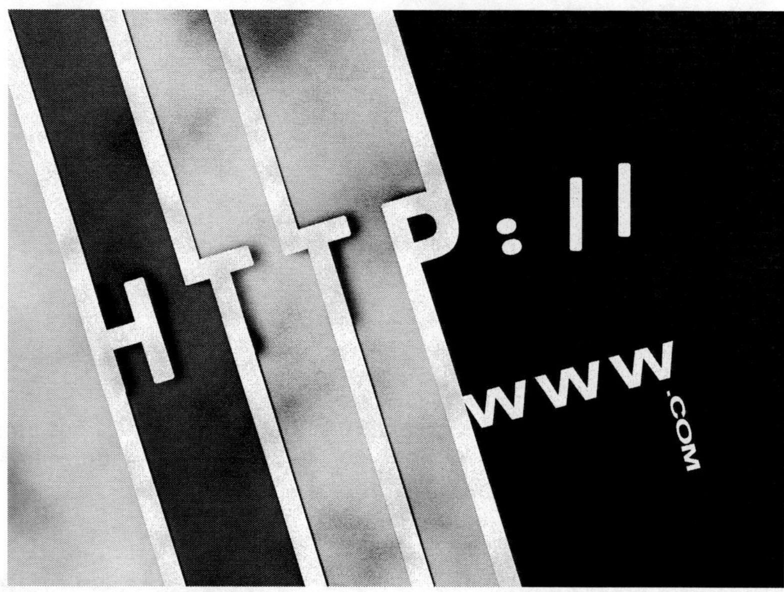


© 2010 *Jupiterimages Corporation*

Traditional media (magazines, newspapers, television) now compete with media such as the Internet, texting, and mobile phones; user-generated content such as blogs and YouTube; and **out-of-home advertising** such as billboards and movable promotions. You might have noticed that the tray tables on airplanes sometimes have ads on them. You have probably also seen ads on the inside of subway cars, in trains and buses, and even in bathroom stalls. These, too, are examples of out-of-home advertising.

**out-of-home advertising**

Billboards and movable promotions that are displayed in a broad range of public spaces including tray tables on airplanes, the inside of subways, trains, buses, and even in bathroom stalls.

**FIGURE 11.3**

The inside walls of many subways provide an opportunity for advertisers to reach commuters with their messages.

As the media landscape changes, the money organizations spend on different types of communication will change as well. Some forecasts indicate that in the next five years companies will increase their expenditures on new media from approximately 16 percent of their total promotional budgets to almost 27 percent of their budgets, or $160 billion by 2012.[1]

## KEY TAKEAWAY

As the media landscape changes, marketers may change the type of promotions they use in order to reach their target markets. With changing technology and social media (e.g., Facebook), less money is being budgeted for traditional media such as magazines and more money is budgeted for "new media." Regardless of the type of media used, marketers use integrated marketing communications (IMC) to deliver one consistent message to buyers.

## REVIEW QUESTIONS

1. Explain the concept of integrated marketing communications.
2. How is the media used by organizations changing? What age group is driving the change?
3. What factors are causing the media landscape to change?

# 2. THE PROMOTION (COMMUNICATION) MIX

## LEARNING OBJECTIVES

1. **Understand the different components of the promotion mix.**
2. **Understand the different types of media and vehicles.**

Although the money organizations spend promoting their offerings may go to different media channels, a company still wants to send its customers and potential consumers a consistent message (IMC). The different types of marketing communications an organization uses compose its **promotion or communication mix**, which consists of advertising, sales promotions, public relations and publicity, personal selling, and direct marketing.

**promotion or communication mix**

Communication tools that may include advertising, sales promotions, public relations and publicity, personal selling, and direct marketing.

**Advertising** involves paying to disseminate a message that identifies a brand (product or service) or an organization being promoted to many people at one time. The typical media that organizations utilize for advertising of course include television, magazines, newspapers, the Internet, direct mail, and radio. As we explained, businesses are also advertising on social media such as Facebook, blogs, Twitter, and mobile devices. Each medium (television or magazines or mobile phones) has different advantages and disadvantages. A few examples of advantages and disadvantages are discussed below.

**advertising**

A message that is paid for and sent to large groups of the population at one time with an identified organization or brand (product or service) being promoted.

For example, mobile phones provide continuous access to people on the go although reception may vary in different markets. Radios, magazines, and newspapers are also portable. People tend to own more than one radio, but there are so many radio stations in each market that it may be difficult to reach all target customers. People typically are doing another activity (e.g., driving or studying) while listening to the radio, and without visuals, radio relies solely on audio. Both television and radio must get a message to consumers quickly. Although many people change channels or leave the room during commercials, television does allow for demonstrations. In an effort to get attention, advertisers have changed the volume for television commercials for years. However, the Federal Trade Commission passed a new regulation effective in 2010 that prohibits advertisers from changing the volume level of commercials on television.

People may save magazines for a long time, but advertisers must plan in advance to have ads in certain issues. With the Internet, both magazines and newspapers are suffering in terms of readership and advertising dollars. Many major newspapers, such as papers in Seattle and Chicago, have gone out of business. Local news and the fact that local retailers get cheaper rates for advertising in local newspapers may encourage both local businesses and consumers to support newspapers in some markets.

One of the biggest factors an organization must determine is which medium or media provides the biggest bang for the buck, given a product's characteristics and target market. For example, a thirty-second ad aired during Super Bowl XLII cost $2.7 million. However, a record number of 97.5 million people watched the game, so the cost per ad was less than three cents per viewer. But do the ads pay off for companies in terms of sales? Many advertising professionals believe many of the ads don't. However, the ads probably do have a brand awareness or public relations type of effect.

**FIGURE 11.4**

The first issue of *Sports Illustrated* was published August 16, 1954. Today, the companies that advertise in *Sports Illustrated* do so not only in the magazine but also on the Web site.

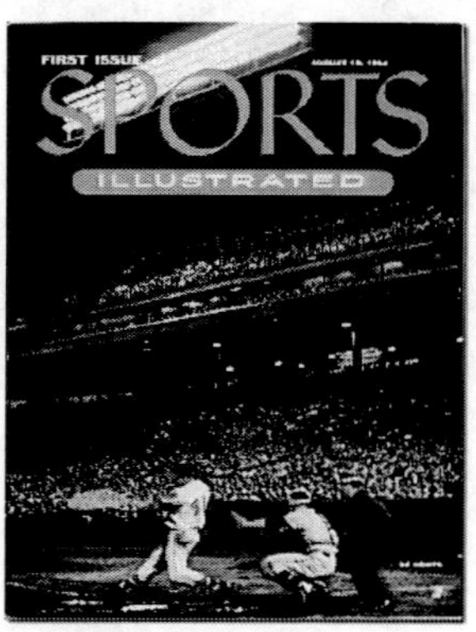


*Source: Wikipedia.*

**vehicle**

The specific means, such as a particular magazine or a specific television show, within a medium to reach a selected target market.

Within each different medium, an organization might select a different vehicle. A **vehicle** is the specific means within a medium to reach a selected target market. For example, if a company wants to develop commercials on television to reach teenagers, it might select *Gossip Girl* on the CW as the best vehicle. If an organization wants to use magazines to reach males interested in sports, it might use *Sports Illustrated*. As technology changed, *Sports Illustrated* launched SI.com so readers could get up-to-date information on the Web. On SI.com, readers can also access links to popular articles and "SIVault" (http://vault.sportsillustrated.cnn.com/vault), where they can search articles and pictures that have run in the magazine since it was launched in 1954.

**personal selling**

An interactive, personal, paid promotional approach between a buyer and a seller.

**Personal selling** is an interactive, paid approach to marketing that involves a buyer and a seller. The interaction between the two parties can occur in person, by telephone, or via another technology. Whatever medium is used, developing a relationship with the buyer is usually something the seller desires.

When you interview for internships or full-time positions and try to convince potential employers to hire you, you are engaging in personal selling. The interview is very similar to a buyer-seller situation. Both the buyer and seller have objectives they hope to achieve. Although business-to-business markets utilize more personal selling, some business-to-consumer markets do as well. If you have ever attended a Pampered Chef or Tupperware party or purchased something from an Amway or Mary Kay representative, you've been exposed to personal selling. Chapter 13 discusses personal selling in more detail and when it should and should not be used.

**public relations (PR)**

The process of creating a positive image for a company, an offering, or a person via publicity.

**Public relations (PR)** helps improve and promote an organization's image and products by putting a positive spin on news stories. Public relations materials include press releases, publicity, product placement, and sponsorships. Companies also use PR to promote products and to supplement their sales efforts. PR is often perceived as more neutral and objective than other forms of promotion because much of the information is tailored to sound as if it has been created by an organization independent of the seller. Many companies have internal PR departments or hire PR firms to find and create public relations opportunities for them. As such, PR is part of a company's promotion budget. In Chapter 12 we'll discuss the specific PR tools companies use as part of their integrated marketing communications.

**sales promotion**

Other forms of promotions (coupons, contests, rebates, mail-in offers) not included as a component of a communication mix.

**Sales promotions** consist of other types of promotions—coupons, contests, games, rebates, mail-in offers, and so forth—that are not included as part of another component of the communication mix. Sales promotions are often developed to get customers and potential customers to take action quickly, make larger purchases, and make repeat purchases. Many stores now place coupons next to products to encourage consumers to select a particular brand and products.

In business-to-business marketing, sales promotions are typically called **trade promotions** because they are targeted to channel members who conduct business or trade with consumers. Trade promotions include trade shows, sponsorships, event marketing, and special incentives given to retailers, such as extra money, in-store displays, and prizes to market particular products and services. Sales promotions are often used to supplement advertising and create incentives for customers to buy products more quickly. Chapter 12 also discusses the different types of sales promotion tools companies have available.

**FIGURE 11.5**

Consumers cut out and use more coupons in a weak economy.

**trade promotions**

Sales promotions aimed at businesses.

**Direct marketing** involves delivering personalized promotional materials directly to individual consumers. It provides an interactive approach for organizations to reach consumers in hopes of getting consumers to take action. Materials may be delivered via mail, catalogs, Internet, e-mail, telephone, or direct-response advertising. Several benefits of direct marketing include the ability to target a specific set of customers, measure the return on investment (ROI), and test different strategies before implementing to all targeted consumers. However, direct marketing is very intrusive and many consumers may ignore attempts to reach them.

**Telemarketing** involves direct marketing by phone. You just sat down for dinner and the phone rings. It's a local charity calling to raise money. The calls always seem to come at dinner or at other inconvenient times. Although expensive, telemarketing can be extremely effective for charitable organizations and different service firms and retailers. However, because some consumers have negative perceptions of telemarketers many organizations do not use it. The **Do Not Call Registry**, which was established in 2008, prevents organizations from calling any numbers registered with the Federal Trade Commission.

Catalogs and **direct mail** provide popular alternatives for many marketers although the volume sent drops significantly in a weak economy. Direct mail can be personalized and ask consumers to make a **call to action**, which is a certain response the organization requests.

**Direct response advertising** includes an offer and a call to action. You're watching television and an interesting product is shown. The announcer says, "Call now and receive a bonus package." They want consumers to call to purchase the product or to get more information. However, the Internet provides the preferred direct-response medium because it is less expensive and easier for the organization. The Internet is also an important medium for direct marketing.

**direct marketing**

Delivering personalized promotional materials directly to individual consumers. Materials may be delivered via mail, catalogs, Internet, e-mail, or telephone, or in person.

**telemarketing**

A form of direct marketing that involves contacting people by phone.

**Do Not Call Registry**

Established by the Federal Trade Commission (FTC) in 2008, the service prevents organizations from calling any phone numbers registered with the FTC.

**direct mail**

A form of direct marketing that is mailed to consumers. It can be personalized and ask consumers to make a certain response. Catalogs are often part of direct mail campaigns.

**call to action**

In direct marketing, requesting consumers to make a specific response such as a purchase or a call for more information.

**direct response advertising**

Direct marketing that includes an offer and a call to action.

## KEY TAKEAWAY

The promotion (communication) mix is composed of advertising, personal selling, public relations, sales promotion, and direct marketing. Once a company decides on a component of the promotion mix, such as advertising, it must still decide which medium (e.g., television, cell phones, magazines) or media (more than one medium) to use. Within each medium, the company must also select a vehicle, which may be a particular television show, radio station, or magazine.

## REVIEW QUESTIONS

1. Define each component of the promotion (communication) mix.
2. What is the difference between a medium and a vehicle?
3. Identify examples of traditional media and new media.

# 3. THE PROMOTION MIX, COMMUNICATION, AND BUYERS' PERCEPTIONS

**LEARNING OBJECTIVES**

1. **Understand that different factors can affect the promotion mix.**
2. **Understand the communication process.**
3. **Understand buyers' perceptual processes.**

## 3.1 The Promotion Mix

A marketing manager from one company might decide to focus on social media, whereas a marketing manager from another company might decide to focus her company's efforts on television commercials. Why do companies select different types of media for what may be perceived as similar messages? As Figure 11.6 shows, a number of factors affect the choice of promotion mix elements.

**FIGURE 11.6** Factors That Influence Selection of Promotion Mix

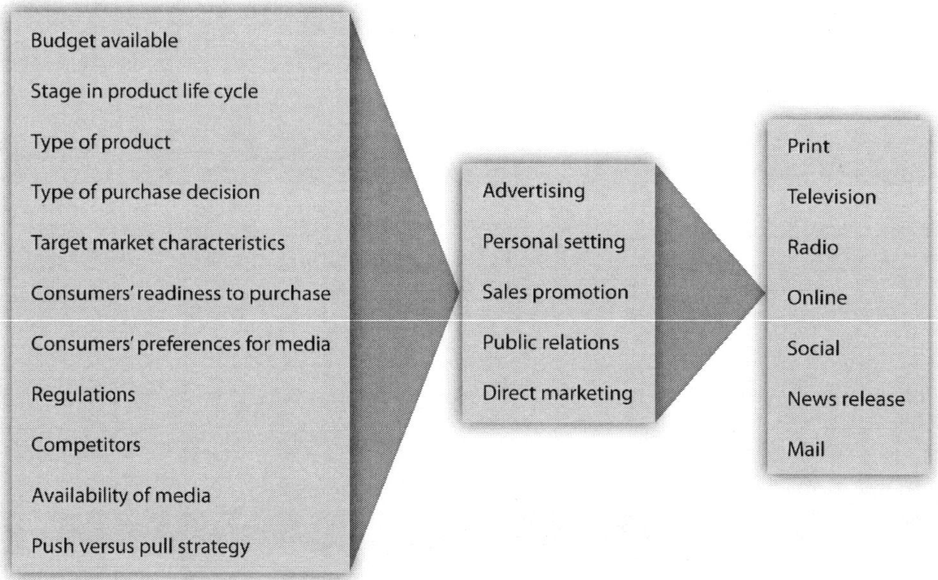


**reach**

The number of people exposed to a message.

**frequency**

How often people are exposed to a message.

*Budget Available.* For many companies, the budget available to market a product determines what elements of the promotion mix are utilized. The budget affects a promotion's **reach** (number of people exposed to the message) and **frequency** (how often people are exposed). For example, many smaller companies may lack the money to create and run commercials on top-rated television shows or during the Super Bowl. As a result, they may not get the exposure they need to be successful. Other firms such as McDonald's may come up with creative ways to reach different target markets. For example, For example, McDonald's targeted college students with a special promotion that it filmed live in a Boston University lecture.

*Stage in the product life cycle.* The stage in the product life cycle also affects the type and amount of promotion used. Products in the introductory stages typically need a lot more promotional dollars to create awareness in the marketplace. Imagine how much more fuel an airplane needs for takeoff than it needs once it is in the air. The same is true of communication. More "fuel" is needed in the beginning to help with the takeoff.

*Type of product and type of purchase decision.* Different products also require different types of promotion. Very technical products and very expensive products often need personal selling so the customer understands how the product operates and its different features. By contrast, advertising is often relied upon to sell convenience goods and products purchased routinely since customers are familiar with the products.

*Target market characteristics and consumers' readiness to purchase.* In order to select the best method to reach their target market(s), organizations must also understand how ready different target markets are to make purchases. For example, some people are early adopters and want to try new things as soon as they are available, and other groups wait until products have been on the market for a while. Some consumers might not have the money to purchase different products, although they will need the product later. For example, are most college freshmen ready to purchase new cars?

*Consumers' preferences for various media.* We've already explained that different types of consumers prefer different types of media. In terms of target markets, as we mentioned, college-aged students prefer online, cell phone, and social media more than older consumers do. Consumers' media preferences have been researched extensively by academics and marketing research companies. Companies also do their own research and conduct surveys of their consumers to find out how they want to be reached.

*Regulations, competitors, and environmental factors.* Regulations can affect the type of promotion used. For example, laws in the United States prohibit tobacco products from being advertised on television. In some Asian countries, controversial products such as alcohol cannot be advertised during Golden (prime) time on television. The hope is that by advertising late at night, young children do not see the advertisements. The strength of the economy can have an impact as well. In a weak economy, some organizations use more sales promotions such as coupons to get consumers into their stores. The risk is that consumers may begin to expect coupons and not want to buy items without a special promotion.

*Availability of media.* Organizations must also plan their promotions based on availability of media. The top-rated television shows and Super Bowl ad slots, for example, often sell out quickly. Magazines tend to have a longer lead time, so companies must plan far in advance for some magazines. By contrast, because of the number of radio stations and the nature of the medium, organizations can often place radio commercials the same day they want them to be aired. Uncontrollable events can affect a company's promotions, too. For example, when a disaster occurs, TV stations often cut advertisements to make way for continuous news coverage. If there is a crisis or disaster and your company is in the middle of a promotion being advertised on TV, you will likely have to scramble to reach consumers via another medium.

*Push versus pull strategy.* Businesses must also decide whether to use a push strategy, a pull strategy, or both push and pull strategies. A **push strategy** involves promoting a product to middlemen, such as wholesalers and retailers, who then promote the product to consumers. Manufacturers may set up displays in retail outlets for new products so the retailer can promote the product to consumers. A **pull strategy** involves promoting a product to final consumers. For example, a manufacturer promotes its new product on television to consumers and places coupons in the newspaper inserts to get the consumers demanding the product. Their pull causes wholesalers and retailers to buy the product to try to meet their demand. Many manufacturers use both a push strategy and a pull strategy. More details on push and pull strategies are discussed in Chapter 12.

**push strategy**

A strategy in which businesses are the target of promotions so products get "pushed" through their marketing channels and sold to consumers.

**pull strategy**

A strategy in which consumers are targeted with sales promotions such as coupons, contests, games, rebates, mail-in offers.

## 3.2 The Communication Process

Do you use TiVo or a digital video recorder (DVR) to record movies or television shows so you can watch them when you want without television commercials? Do you ever use the remote to skip the commercials or to look at different shows? Think about which television shows you choose to watch, which magazines you read, which radio stations you select. Think about what else you are doing when you watch television or when you are studying or when you are listening to the radio.

It's a hot day in July and you're enjoying a day at the beach. Your friends brought a radio to the beach and the volume is turned up so you can hear all the music. If you're listening to the music or talking to a friend at the beach while you're listening to the radio, do you hear or pay attention to the commercials? Do you remember which products were advertised?

The communication process illustrates how messages are sent and received, as shown in Figure 11.7. The source (or sender) **encodes**, or translates, a message so that it's appropriate for the message channel—say, for a print advertisement, TV commercial, or store display—and shows the benefits and value of the offering. The receiver (customer or consumer) then **decodes**, or interprets, the message. For effective communication to occur, the receiver must interpret the message as the sender intended.

**encode**

Senders must translate or convert benefits and value of a product or service into a message for the message channel selected.

**decode**

Receivers interpret messages.

You're ready to go home on a Friday afternoon and you hear someone mention an upcoming event on Saturday. However, you did not listen to all the details and assume the event is the next day, not the following Saturday. Since you already made other plans for the next day, you don't even consider showing up the following Saturday. Has this ever happened to you? You don't show up at an event because you didn't interpret the message correctly? If you do not hear someone correctly, misread information, or misinterpret a message, you might think a product or service provides different benefits or is easier or harder to use than it really is.

**interference**

Any distractions or noise that senders and receivers face during the transmission of a message.

**Interference**, or noise, can distort marketing messages. Interference includes any distractions receivers and senders face during the transmission of a message. For example, when you were growing up did you see commercials for toys such as the pogo ball, which appeared to be so easy to use but when you tried to jump up and down on it, you found out it was extremely difficult? The same thing may happen if you're studying for an exam while you're talking on the phone. The conversation interferes with remembering what you're reading. Factors such as poor reception, poor print quality, problems with a server, or a low battery can also interfere with your getting messages.

**feedback**

Means of telling sellers you saw their information and wanted to try their product.

Purchasing a product provides the sender with **feedback**, which often tells the seller that you saw information and wanted to try the product. If you use any coupons or promotions when you buy a product, the advertiser knows which vehicle you used to get the information. Market research and warranty registration also provide feedback.

**FIGURE 11.7** The Communication Process

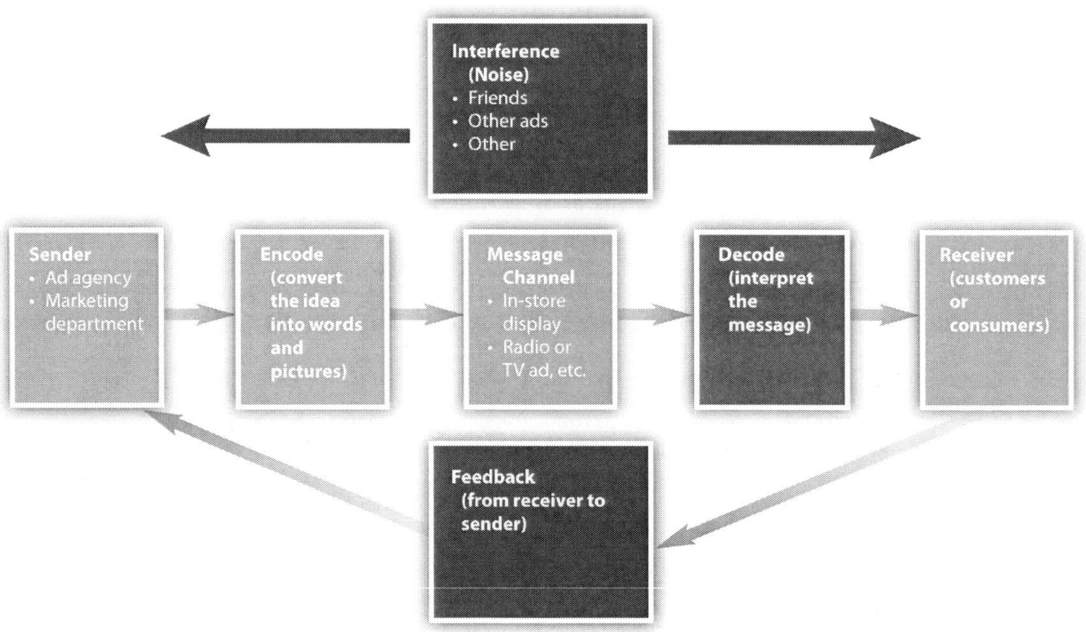


## 3.3 Perceptual Processes

**perceptual processes**

The way in which people select to be exposed to information, pay attention to it, interpret it, and retain it.

Recall that we first discussed perception when we discussed buyer behavior in Chapter 3. The **perceptual process** is how a person decides what to pay attention to and how to interpret and remember different things, among them information included in advertising. When you choose to take an elective class or select a television show, a magazine, or a radio station, you are selecting what information you are exposed to and also deciding what gets your attention.

Think about being at the beach again. You're with a friend, but when you hear someone else say your name, you may pay more attention to the person talking about you than to your friend. The same thing happens when you watch a television show or read a magazine. You might be watching a show when the phone rings and then pay more attention to the person on the phone than to what is on the television. You might be studying for a test and your friends show up and your attention shifts to them. With so many different types of distractions and technology such as recording devices, imagine how difficult it is for an advertiser to get your attention.

If an advertiser does get your attention, do you interpret the information correctly or do you change (distort) it? If a friend tells you a story, then you tell another friend, and that person tells someone else, will the message be the same after it is relayed to multiple people? If you miss class and borrow someone else's notes, do you understand what they mean? Not only must advertisers try to present consistent messages (IMC), they must also try to ensure that you interpret the message as they intended.

Advertisers also want you to remember their brands and organizations. When you study for an exam and memorize key terms, you may not remember them after the test. But hopefully if you hear the terms multiple times, you will remember them. Advertisers use the same strategy to try to get you to retain their messages. Not only do you see the same commercial or message in multiple places, but you may also see it multiple times in each place. However, advertisers must also be careful that consumers don't get so tired of the message that there is a negative effect.

Do you remember information from classes your freshman year? Do you know your friends' phone numbers or e-mail addresses, or do you just find their names on your contact list? Which commercials do you remember? What gets your attention? Sometimes annoying or humorous messages get your attention and you remember the commercial. Advertisers want you to remember their brand. A great promotion is not effective if people don't remember the brand. We tend to remember information that has some relevance to our personal situation or beliefs. For example, if you have no need for a product or service, you might not pay attention to or remember the messages used to market it.

**KEY TAKEAWAY**

Many factors, such as a firm's marketing budget, the type of product, regulations, target customers, and competitors, influence what composes the promotion mix. Depending on what medium is used, marketers use the communication process to encode or translate ideas into messages that can be correctly interpreted (decoded) by buyers. However, marketers must determine how to get consumers' attention and avoid as much interference and noise as possible. Perceptual processes include how a person decides what to pay attention to and how to interpret and remember different things.

**REVIEW QUESTIONS**

1. Explain the communication process and factors that can interfere with interpretation of messages.
2. What is the perceptual process and how does it relate to promotion?
3. What is the difference between encoding and decoding a message?

# 4. MESSAGE STRATEGIES

**LEARNING OBJECTIVES**

1. **Understand what a unique selling proposition is and how it is used.**
2. **Understand different types of promotion objectives.**
3. **Identify different message strategies.**

## 4.1 Utilizing a Product's Unique Selling Proposition (USP)

When organizations want to communicate value, they must determine what message strategies work best for them. Smart organizations determine a product's **unique selling proposition (USP)**, or specific benefit consumers will remember. Domino's "Pizza delivered in 30 minutes or it's free" is a good example of a unique selling proposition. Likewise, Nike's global slogan "Just Do It" helps athletes and other consumers realize their potential, and many consumers may think of all the things that they do when they use Nike products. Watch the video below on Nike to get an idea of the many different activities people from different countries do when using Nike products.

**unique selling proposition (USP)**

A specific product benefit consumers will remember.

## Video Clip

**People around the World Use Nike Products**

Nike products are used for many different sports by all types of athletes.

View the video online at: http://www.youtube.com/embed/Pp5dZZBKTXQ

Nike and Coca-Cola have been extremely successful in adapting their promotions to different international markets. Both companies have very popular global brands. Sometimes the same promotions work in different cultures (countries), but others must be adapted for different international audiences—similar to the way products may be adapted for international markets. Companies must be careful of how words translate, how actions are interpreted, how actors (or models) look, and what different colors in ads may mean.

When deciding on a message strategy, organizations must consider the audience, the objectives of the promotion, the media, and the budget, as well as the USP and the product. Knowing your audience and whom you are trying to reach is critical. The more advertisers know about the consumers (or businesses) exposed to the message, the better. Commercials for golf products shown during golf tournaments focus specifically on golfers. Other commercials, such as several recent ones for the fast-food chain Hardee's, are on the risqué side. They may appeal to some college students but may offend other consumers such as senior citizens. What do you think? Do you think Hardee's is trying to reach a younger demographic? Do the ads make you more inclined to purchase fast food from Hardee's? See the Hardee's commercial in the video below.

## Video Clip

**Commercial for Hardee's Thickburger**

This commercial that may be offensive to some consumers.

View the video online at: http://www.youtube.com/embed/Avq2LAcPdj0

## 4.2 The Organization's Promotion Objectives

Advertisers must also examine their promotion objectives. What are they trying to accomplish with their promotions? Are they trying to build awareness for a new product, are they wanting to get people to take action immediately, or are they interested in having people remember their brand in the future? Building **primary demand**, or demand for a product category, such as orange juice, might be one objective, but a company also wants to build **selective demand**, or demand for its specific brand(s), such as Tropicana orange juice.

**primary demand**

Demand for a product category (e.g., orange juice) versus a product brand (e.g., Tropicana).

**selective demand**

Demand for a specific brand (Tropicana orange juice).

Other common objectives follow the **AIDA model** (attention, interest, desire, and action). AIDA objectives typically are achieved in steps. First, companies focus on attention and awareness of a product or service, which is especially important for new offerings. If a consumer or business is not aware of a product or service, they won't buy it. Once consumers or businesses are aware of products or services, organizations try to get consumers interested and persuade them that their brands are best. Ultimately, companies want consumers to take action or purchase their products or services.

**AIDA model**

A model that includes several different promotion objectives, including attention, interest, desire, and action. One objective may be to get attention. Other objectives of promotion may be to generate interest and desire. The ultimate objective is to get customers to take action or purchase the product or service.

## 4.3 Message Characteristics

Organizations must also determine what type of appeal to use and how to structure their messages. Some of the common advertising appeals are humorous, emotional, frightening (fear), rational (informative), and environmentally conscious. If you were asked to name your favorite commercial, would it be one with a humorous appeal? Many people like commercials that use humor because they are typically entertaining and memorable. Humor sells, but firms must be careful that the brand is remembered. Some commercials are very entertaining, but consumers cannot remember the brand or product.

Each year, some of the most talked-about commercials take place during the Super Bowl. Many people watch the game just to see the commercials. Watch the following YouTube videos to see one of the top ten Super Bowl commercials of all time and how newer commercials relied on a similar approach. Notice how many of them use a humorous appeal. But do you think some are more effective than others? In other words, will viewers actually buy the product(s)?

### Video Clip

**Often Rated the Best Super Bowl Commercial Ever**

This commercial uses a child and fun to appeal to many consumers.

View the video online at: http://www.youtube.com/embed/Lc0izCGKxP8

## Video Clip

**Rated One of the Best Super Bowl Commercials of 2009**

Coke Zero uses the same approach in 2009 as the award-winning commercial in the 1980 Super Bowl.

View the video online at: http://www.youtube.com/embed/v_pYddCq7Hg

## Video Clip

**Pepsi's Version of "Asking for a Shirt"**

Pepsi uses a humorous approach for a commercial although it was not a Super Bowl commercial.

View the video online at: http://www.youtube.com/embed/Jx38M9lIRtA

Companies must also be careful when using fear appeals so consumers don't get too alarmed or frightened. A few years ago, Reebok had to discontinue a TV ad because it upset so many people. The ad showed a bungee jumper diving off a bridge, followed by a shot of just his shoes hanging from the bridge by the bungee cord. That ad provoked people because it implied the jumper had fallen to his death.

**open-ended message**

A promotional message that allows the consumer to draw his or her own conclusions.

**closed-ended message**

A promotional message that draws a logical conclusion.

Firms also decide whether to use strategies such as an open-ended or closed-ended message; whether to use a one-sided or two-sided message; and whether to use slogans, characters, or jingles. An **open-ended message** allows the consumer to draw his or her own conclusion, such as a commercial for perfume or cologne. A **closed-ended message** draws a logical conclusion. Most messages are one sided, stressing only the positive aspects, similar to what you include on your résumé. However, two-sided messages are often utilized as well. Pharmaceutical companies often show both the positive aspects (benefits) of using a drug and the negative aspects of not using it. (Of course, U.S. laws require companies to list the side effects of prescriptions—hence the long "warnings" you hear and read about in conjunction with drug ads.)

## Video Clip

**Example of an Open-Ended Commercial**

Do you interpret cologne and perfume ads the same way you see them portrayed on television?

View the video online at: http://www.youtube.com/embed/bEmrdO8tW3w

The order of presentation also affects how well consumers remember a brand. If you forgot about a twenty-five-page term paper that you had to write before the next day of class, which sections of the paper would be the strongest? Would the beginning, the end, or the middle be the best section? Many students argue that either the beginning or the end is most important, hoping that the instructor does not read the entire paper carefully. The same strategy is true for commercials and advertisements. The beginning and the end of the message should be strong and include the brand name. That way, if consumers hear or read only part of the message, they will hopefully remember the brand name.

Some companies use characters or mascots and/or jingles or slogans. Although media is changing, many of the characters and jingles have stayed the same for decades. When you think of Campbell's soup, do you think "Mm, mm good"? Just as the commercials viewed in the beginning of the chapter focused on "Mm, mm good," Campbell's has used the same slogan since the early 1900s, and the Campbell Soup Kids were created in 1904. Although Campbell's changed its slogan in 1998, the company still uses the "Mm, mm good" slogan in most of its promotions across different media. Apparently, the slogan still resonates with consumers. Other jingles, characters (mascots), or symbols you may be familiar with include the Jolly Green Giant, the Wienermobile, and the Pillsbury Doughboy known as Poppin' Fresh. The following figures illustrate some of these characters and symbols.

**FIGURE 11.8**

The Jolly Green Giant helped kids remember the Green Giant jingle and hopefully reminded them to eat their vegetables.

*Source: Wikimedia Commons.*

**FIGURE 11.9**

The Wienermobile tours the country.

*Source: Wikimedia Commons.*

**FIGURE 11.10**

The Pillsbury Doughboy, Poppin' Fresh, is popular around the world and is shown on this box of pancake mix in Israel.

*Source: Wikipedia.*

Do you remember the Oscar Mayer jingles? Watch the video below and see if you find yourself singing along. The jingle was originally developed in 1963 and is now recorded in different languages. In 2006 Oscar Mayer promoted a singing contest for the jingle, which still remains popular. Kraft's promotions are also consistent across media, using the visuals from commercials as pictures in their print ads in both English and Spanish versions, following the IMC concept.

## Video Clip

**The Original Oscar Mayer Wiener Song**

Often considered one of the best original ads on TV, the Oscar Mayer Wiener song is known by people of all ages.

View the video online at: http://www.youtube.com/embed/aNddW2xmZp8

## Video Clip

**The Oscar Mayer Bologna Song**

The Oscar Mayer Bologna song is also well known among consumers of all ages.

View the video online at: http://www.youtube.com/embed/rmPRHJd3uHI

## KEY TAKEAWAY

Organizations must determine promotion objectives, or what they want to accomplish with their promotions. For example, if a company has a new brand they may want to generate awareness or attention. Later, they may focus on persuading customers to buy their brand. Each brand needs to have a unique selling proposition (USP) for customers to remember and want their product. Depending on their objectives and their USP, marketers must develop a message strategy. Some companies prefer humor or rational appeals while others may use a fear appeal.

### REVIEW QUESTIONS

1. Identify the different promotion objectives companies may use.
2. What are some of the message strategies organizations use?
3. What is the difference between an open-ended and a closed-ended message?

# 5. THE PROMOTION BUDGET

### LEARNING OBJECTIVES

1. **Understand different ways in which promotion budgets can be set.**
2. **Understand how the budget can be allocated among different media.**

An offering's budget is a critical factor when it comes to deciding which message strategies to pursue. Several methods can be used to determine the promotion budget. The simplest method for determining the promotion budget is often merely using a **percentage of last year's sales** or the projected sales for the next year. This method does not take into account any changes in the market or unexpected circumstances. However, many firms use this method because it is simple and straightforward.

**percent-of-sales method**

A budgeting technique based on a set percentage of current or projected sales.

The **affordable method**, or what you think you can afford, is a method used often by small businesses. Unfortunately, things often cost more than anticipated, and you may not have enough money. Many small businesses think they're going to have money for promotion, but they run out and cannot spend as much on promotion as they had hoped. Such a situation may have happened to you when you planned a weekend trip based on what you thought you could afford, and you did not have enough money. As a result, you had to modify your plans and not do everything you planned.

**affordable method**

A budgeting technique whereby companies spend what they think they can afford promoting a product.

Other companies may decide to use **competitive parity**—that is, they try to keep their promotional spending comparable to the competitors' spending level. This method is designed to keep a brand in the minds of consumers. During a recession, some firms feel like they must spend as much—if not more—than their competitors to get customers to buy from them. Other companies are forced to cut back on their spending or pursue more targeted promotions. When Kmart faced bankruptcy, they cut back on expenditures, yet they kept their advertising inserts (free-standing inserts, or FSI) in Sunday newspapers to remain competitive with other businesses that had an FSI.

**competitive parity**

A budgeting method whereby companies make sure their promotion budgets are comparable to their competitors'.

A more rational approach is the **objective and task method**, whereby marketing managers first determine what they want to accomplish (objectives) with their communication. Then they determine what activities—commercials, sales promotions, and so on—are necessary to accomplish the objectives. Finally, they conduct research to figure out how much the activities, or tasks, cost in order to develop a budget.

**objective and task method**

A budget based on a company's promotion objectives and the costs of the activities and tasks necessary to accomplish those objectives.

Part of the budgeting process includes deciding how much money to allocate to different media. Although most media budgets are still spent predominantly on traditional media, shifts in spending are occurring as the media landscape continues to change. Mobile marketing continues to become more popular as a way to reach specific audiences. One estimate shows that over one-third of cell phone users were exposed to mobile advertising in 2009 and that 16 percent of the people exposed to mobile advertising responded to the ads via text messaging. Younger people are typically the most accepting of mobile advertising.[2]

**FIGURE 11.11** Stubb's Bar-B-Q Trailer—Out-of-Home Advertising That Is Mobile Marketing

The Stubb's Bar-B-Q trailer travels around the country promoting the brand name and product.

*Source: Photo courtesy of Stubb's Legendary Kitchen.*

The manufacturers of most major brands plan to use texting and multimedia messages in the future. Mobile marketing allows advertisers to communicate with consumers and businesses on the go. Over half of Chinese, Korean, Indian, and Thai Internet users access social media sites through their phones rather than through computers.[3] While many marketers plan to use electronic devices for their mobile-marketing strategies, other firms may use movable or mobile promotions (see Figure 11.11), which, as discussed earlier, are also considered out-of-home advertising. It is anticipated that the percentage companies spend on mobile media may be as much as 25 percent of their total promotional budgets by 2011.[4]

**KEY TAKEAWAY**

Companies can determine how much to spend on promotion several different ways. The percent of sales method, in which companies use a set percentage of sales for their promotion, is often the easiest method to use. Small companies may focus on what they think they can afford while other organizations may try to keep their promotions relatively equal to their competitors'. The objective and task approach takes objectives into consideration and the costs of the tasks necessary to accomplish objectives in order to determine the promotion budget.

**REVIEW QUESTIONS**

1. Explain four different ways to set a product's promotion budget.
2. What is mobile marketing?

# 6. DISCUSSION QUESTIONS AND ACTIVITIES

**DISCUSSION QUESTIONS**

1. Provide an example of how an organization uses different media to present a consistent message using integrated marketing communications (IMC).
2. In your opinion, what are the advantages and disadvantages of advertising on the radio, in magazines, on television, through direct marketing, and on the Internet?
3. Give an example of an organization's promotional strategy and how it gets consumers to select it, pay attention to it, and retain it as intended.
4. Give an example of the unique selling proposition for one of your favorite brands.
5. Explain why companies might use different budgeting methods to set their promotional budgets.

## ACTIVITIES

1. Identify your three favorite and least favorite commercials and explain why you like or don't like each one. Notice whether there are similarities in your preferences. In other words, are your favorite commercials humorous? Are your least favorite commercials annoying?
2. Create a message strategy for a cover letter to go with your résumé.
3. Outline three message strategies that you feel would get consumers' attention in television commercials and in print ads.

# ENDNOTES


1. "PQ Media: New Media Spend to Hit $160B in 2012," *MarketingVOX*, March 26, 2008, http://www.marketingvox.com/pq-media-new-media-spend-to-hit-160b-in-2012-037592 (accessed December 15, 2009).
2. Jack Loechner. "Advertising Growth Spreads in All Mobile Formats," Research Brief, *MediaPost Blogs*, May 27, 2009, http://www.mediapost.com/publications/article/106675/ (accessed April 13, 2012).
3. "Social Network Site Users Ready to Go Mobile But Telecom Carriers Need to Set the Stage for Mass Adoption, Says IDC," *IDC*, November 17, 2009, http://www.idc.com/AP/pressrelease.jsp?containerId=prSG22084309 (accessed January 20, 2010).
4. "89% of Major Brands Planning to Market via Mobile Phones by 2008," *Mobile Europe*, February 20, 2006, http://www.mmaglobal.com/research/89-major-brands-planning-market-mobile-phones-2008-mobile-marketing-accelerate-more-half-br (accessed April 13, 2012).

# CHAPTER 12
# Public Relations and Sales Promotions

You just finished reading a great newspaper story about a local restaurant even though you know the company has experienced several lawsuits and many customer complaints. The news story makes the restaurant sound like a great corporate citizen and the best place to eat in town. Sometimes a company gets "free" **publicity** such as news stories or reviews about its products and services in the mass media, even though the organization has no control over the content of the stories and might not even know about their publication. How did a restaurant with so many complaints manage to get such a great story written about it? How did it get good coverage when it might not be deserved? Perhaps the restaurant used part of its promotion budget to pay for public relations efforts to generate positive stories and positive publicity.

**publicity**

Publicized information such as news stories about products and services, people, and organizations.

**Public relations (PR)** includes information that an organization wants its public (customers, employees, stakeholders, general public) to know. PR involves creating a positive image for a company, an offering, or a person via publicity. PR has become more important in recent years because there are now so many media outlets people pay attention to, including YouTube, social networking sites, and blogs. It's pretty easy for anyone to say anything about a company in public forum. Indeed, publicity is a double-edged sword; it can result in negative news, such as a poor review of a movie, restaurant, or car, or positive news. Organizations work hard to get favorable news stories, so while publicity sounds free, building relationships with journalists does cost money. Just like advertising (see Chapter 11 for discussion), public relations and sales promotions are critical components of the promotion budget for many firms.

**public relations (PR)**

The process of creating a positive image for a company, an offering, or a person via publicity.

Organizations also use sales promotions to generate positive customer perceptions and sales. **Sales promotions** are promotional activities companies do in addition to advertising, public relations, and personal selling in order to sell a product. Issuing coupons, running contests and games, and offering rebates and mail-in offers are examples of sales promotions. In this chapter, we examine the public relations and sales promotion tools that organizations use and how they contribute to a company's success.

**sales promotion**

Other forms of promotions (coupons, contests, rebates, mail-in offers) not included as a component of a communication mix.

# 1. PUBLIC RELATIONS ACTIVITIES AND TOOLS

**LEARNING OBJECTIVES**

1. Understand the concept of public relations and why organizations allocate part of their promotional budgets to it.
2. Understand what the different types of public relations tools are.
3. Explain how companies use different public relations tools to their advantage.

Good public relations efforts can help a firm create rapport with its customers, promote what it has to offer, and supplement its sales efforts. Many organizations that engage in public relations have in-house PR departments, media relations groups, or investor relations groups. Other organizations sometimes hire external PR firms or advertising agencies to find and create public relations opportunities for them. PR specialists must build relationships with people at different media outlets to help get their stories placed. Universities, hospitals, government organizations, and charitable organizations often hire PR people to help disseminate positive information about their services and to increase interest in what they do.

PR specialists also help political campaign managers generate positive information in the press. PR specialists can handle damage control and put a positive view on situations when something bad happens to an organization or person. In foreign markets, PR agencies may help ensure product concepts are understood correctly. Getting all PR stories placed in desired media is not guaranteed. A lot of time and effort is spent getting to know people who can help publish or announce the information to the public.

Companies use a variety of tools for their public relations purposes, including annual reports, brochures and magazines for both employees and the public, Web sites to show good things they're doing, speeches, blogs, and podcasts. Some of the most commonly used PR tools include press releases, sponsorships, product placements, and social media. Social media is discussed in Chapter 14.

## 1.1 Press Releases

**press release**

A news story written by an organization to promote a product, service, or person.

Part of a company's public relations efforts includes putting a positive spin on news stories. As we explained in Chapter 11, a **press release** is a news story written by an organization to promote a product, organization, or person. Consider how much better a story or a product recommendation is likely to be perceived when the receiver thinks the content is from an objective third party rather than an organization writing about itself. Public relations personnel frequently prepare press releases in hopes that the news media will pick them up and disseminate the information to the public. However, there is no guarantee that the media will use a press release. Some of the PR opportunities that companies may seek to highlight in their press releases include charity events, awards, new products, company reports, and things they are doing to improve the environment or local community.

Read the following two examples of press releases. The first story sounds like it was written by a news organization, but it was created by Apple and their public relations people to highlight the introduction of the new iPhone 3G. The second press release and picture (see Figure 12.1) provide an example of how a company like Stubb's Bar-B-Q teams up with Mobile Loaves & Fishes, a charity that helps feed the hungry, to help feed homeless and poor people and restock food banks around the country. The story enhances the positive image of both organizations.

### An Example of a Press Release to Introduce a New Product

#### Apple Introduces the New iPhone 3G

*Twice as Fast at Half the Price*

SAN FRANCISCO—June 9, 2008—Apple® today introduced the new iPhone™ 3G, combining all the revolutionary features of iPhone with 3G networking that is twice as fast* as the first generation iPhone, built-in GPS for expanded location-based mobile services, and iPhone 2.0 software which includes support for Microsoft Exchange ActiveSync and runs the hundreds of third party applications already built with the recently released iPhone SDK. In the US the new iPhone 3G is priced at a stunning $199 for the 8GB model, and just $299 for the

16GB model.** iPhone 3G will be available in more than 70 countries later this year, beginning with customer availability in 22 countries—Australia, Austria, Belgium, Canada, Denmark, Finland, France, Germany, Hong Kong, Ireland, Italy, Japan, Mexico, Netherlands, New Zealand, Norway, Portugal, Spain, Sweden, Switzerland, UK and the US—on July 11.

*Based on 3G and EDGE testing. Actual speeds vary by site conditions.

**Based on iPhone 3G (8GB) and first generation iPhone (8GB) purchases. Requires new two year AT&T rate plan, sold separately.[1]

## An Example of a Press Release to Show How a Company Helps Feed the Hungry and Restock Food Banks around the Country

### Stubb's Teams Up with Mobile Loaves & Fishes to Launch "Feed the World Tour"

*Tuesday, May 26, 5 p.m. @ Wooldridge Park*

AUSTIN—Stubb's Legendary Kitchen will kick off its 12-city "Feed the World Tour" this Tuesday, May 26 at 5 p.m. in Wooldridge Square Park, 9th and Guadalupe Streets, by serving chopped beef sandwiches with famous Stubb's barbecue sauce to homeless and working poor people from one of Mobile Loaves & Fishes' special catering trucks, which serve people in six cities every day.

Kurt Koegler, president of Stubb's Legendary Kitchen, will join Alan Graham, Mobile Loaves' founder/president, and volunteers from the company and MLF volunteers to serve the sandwiches and distribute Stubb's T-shirts. The Austin-based company chose Mobile Loaves as its partner to kick off the "Feed the World Tour," which is named for the stated mission of Texas Bar-B-Q legend, C.B. "Stubb" Stubblefield, who said: "I was born hungry I want to feed the world."

After leaving Austin, the tour will swing through the Southeast, up the East Coast and into Washington, D.C. where the Stubb's team will compete at the annual BBQ Battle on Pennsylvania Avenue. In each city, Stubb's Legendary Kitchen and company president Koegler will barbecue for the homeless and help restock depleted food banks.

"Stubb was a cook but more than that, a lover of people. The values that guided his life still guide the company that bears his name. Stubb's life truly is in every bottle of sauce and marinade we make. All of us at Stubb's are thrilled to be working with Mobile Loaves and bringing all of Stubb's Love and Happiness to those who all too often need it most" said Koegler.

*"The economy has placed greater demand on organizations like Mobile Loaves and local food banks, so we couldn't think of a better time to show our support," Koegler said. "Stubb's greatest joy was feeding the people who came from all around for a taste of his famous barbecue, and it is an honor for us to fulfill his mission with our Feed the World Tour."*

"We're honored to be selected as Stubb's charity partner for the kick-off of this awesome tour," Graham said. "As someone who once was poor and hungry, C.B. 'Stubb' Stubblefield is smiling in heaven to know that his creation is helping feed brothers and sisters on the street here in Austin and around the country. We look forward to connecting Stubb's with people on the streets here and in the other cities we serve."[2]

**A Picture of Stubb's Legendary Kitchen's "Feed the World Tour"**

*Source: Photo courtesy of Stubb's Legendary Kitchen.*

**damage control**

Crisis management PR effort aimed to minimize any negative effects a company gets from bad publicity.

Press releases and other PR activities can also be used for damage control purposes. **Damage control** is the process of countering the extreme negative effects a company gets when it receives bad publicity. Domino's Pizza was forced to engage in damage control after two of its employees created a video doing disgusting things to pizzas and then posting it to YouTube. If the publicity is particularly bad, as it was for Domino's, a company might hold a press conference or prepare a speech for the top executive to give. For example, the president of Domino's spoke on video to try to control the damage to Domino's business. The company then posted the video on YouTube (see the video below).

**Video Clip**

**An Example of Damage Control**

Patrick Doyle, the president of Domino's, responds on YouTube to a video created by two Domino's employees, who were subsequently fired by the pizza chain.

View the video online at: http://www.youtube.com/embed/dem6eA7-A2I

Similarly, companies that move into foreign markets are sometimes perceived negatively by locals because they have little information about the firms. In India, the reputation of companies is very important to workers and their families. As a result, U.S. employers recruiting in the tech industry in India often have to work hard to make their brands and products known so people will want to work for them. The firms do so via various PR efforts.

Just as press releases can be used to promote the good things an organization or person does, press conferences can also be held when a company is simply seeking good PR. An organization might hold a press conference to announce that it has hired new, highly sought-after executives, that it is breaking ground on a new building, or to talk about its community service projects.

## 1.2 Sponsorships

Many of you have heard of the Staples Center (Figure 12.2), where the Los Angeles Lakers play basketball. But imagine how many *more* people heard about the Staples Center following the announcement that Michael Jackson's public memorial would take place there. All the news stories talking about tickets and information about the memorial provided "free" publicity for the center and for the office supplies store, Staples, for which the center is named. Staples paid $375 million for naming rights of the center, which was built in 1998.[3] Indeed, the chain has gotten a huge return on its sponsorship of the center.

A **sponsorship** involves paying a fee to have your name associated with different things, such as the following:

- A particular venue (Wrigley Field; the Staples Center)
- A superstar's apparel (Tiger Woods wearing Nike hats and shirts)
- An event (the AT&T National Golf Tournament; the Chick-fil-A Peach Bowl)
- A cause (M&M's support of the Special Olympics)
- An educational workshop or information session
- A NASCAR vehicle (by Pfizer, the maker of Viagra; see Figure 12.3)

Even though sponsorships are expensive, they are growing in popularity as corporations seek ways to strengthen their corporate image, increase their brand awareness, differentiate their products, and reach their target markets. Worldwide, corporations spent over $43 billion on sponsorships in 2008;[4] however, the recession has taken a toll and the new stadium for the Dallas Cowboys still doesn't have a sponsor with naming rights. Over two-thirds of the sponsorships in North America are for sports, followed by entertainment (e.g., music and performing arts) and causes (e.g., the Susan G. Komen Race for the Cure and "alternative spring breaks" for college students). Other organizations and structures, such as buildings and bridges, may seek sponsorships as a means of generating revenue. Imagine how many people drive across the Brooklyn Bridge in New York or the Golden Gate Bridge in San Francisco and how much awareness an organization would get if they were allowed to pay to have their name on either of the bridges.

**FIGURE 12.2**

The Staples Center in Los Angeles is an example of a venue sponsorship. The office supplies store Staples paid for the naming rights to the stadium.

*Source: Wikipedia.*

**sponsorship**

Paying a fee to have your name associated with different things such a particular venue, person's apparel, or event, or even a NASCAR vehicle.

**Cause-related marketing** is one of the fastest-growing types of sponsorships. It occurs when a company supports a nonprofit organization in some way. For example, M&M's sponsors the Special Olympics and American Airlines raises money for breast cancer research with an annual celebrity golf and tennis tournament. The airline also donates frequent flier miles to the cause. Yoplait Yogurt donates money for breast cancer research for every pink lid that is submitted. Cause-related marketing can have a positive PR impact by strengthening the affinity people have for a company that does it.

**Video Clip**

**An Example of Sponsoring a Cause**

M&M's sponsors the Special Olympics.

View the video online at: http://www.youtube.com/embed/P6SNLE7JPf0

**FIGURE 12.3**

Pfizer, the maker of Viagra, is one of the many companies that sponsor NASCAR racing teams.

*Source: Flickr.*

**cause-related marketing**

When a company supports a nonprofit organization in some way in order to generate positive public relations.

## 1.3 Product Placements

Getting a company's product included as part of a television show, movie, video game, special event, or book is called a **product placement**. When you watch reruns of *Seinfeld*, you often see different Coca-Cola products being consumed. Likewise, you might see a Nissan Maxima on *Desperate Housewives*. Over four hundred product placements typically appear in each episode of *The Biggest Loser*. Apple placed products in twenty-four movies that reached number one between August 1, 2008, and August 1, 2009, while Ford products appeared twenty times and Budweiser products appeared twelve times.[5]

**product placement**

Getting a company's product included as part of a television show, movie, video game, special event.

## Video Clip

**Example of Product Placement**

Although the video sounds like a paid commercial, it is actually part of an episode of *30 Rock*.

View the video online at: http://www.youtube.com/embed/d36wUmJGzvA

Typically, a company pays a fee to have one of its products placed. But sometimes the company pays nothing if the product is needed for a show in some way or as part of the plot. FedEx did not pay for product placement in the movie *Castaway*.[6] Product placement can improve a brand's awareness and exposure and often increase its sales. Given the number of exposures an organization receives with product placement, the cost of a product placement can be less expensive than commercials might cost.

Although most product placements appear in television shows and movies, corporations are pursuing other options. For example, they are now placing products in online videos, computer games, and books. The number of product placements is expected to increase as consumers continue to skip commercials and advertisements using digital video recorders (DVRs).

### KEY TAKEAWAY

Public relations (PR) are the activities organizations engage in to create a positive image for a company, product, service, or a person. Press releases, sponsorships, and product placements are three commonly used PR tools. Press releases are designed to generate publicity, but there is no guarantee the media will use them in the stories they write. Sponsorships are designed to increase brand awareness, improve corporate image, and reach target markets. Product placements are designed to generate exposure, brand awareness, and interest.

### REVIEW QUESTIONS

1. Why are public relations efforts funded by firms?
2. Who does the public relations for a firm?
3. Identify three public relation tools.

# 2. SALES PROMOTIONS

## LEARNING OBJECTIVES

1. **Learn about different types of sales promotions companies use to get customers to buy their products.**
2. **Understand the different types of sales promotions companies use with their business customers.**
3. **Understand why sales promotions have become such an integral part of an organization's promotion mix.**
4. **Differentiate between a push and pull strategy.**

Sales promotions are activities that supplement a company's advertising, public relations, and personal selling efforts. Sales promotions are often temporary, but when the economy is weak sales promotions such as coupons become even more popular for consumers and are used more frequently by organizations. The goal of sales promotions is to persuade customers to take action quickly and make larger purchases. As discussed in Chapter 11, sales promotions in business-to-business (B2B) settings are typically called **trade promotions**; they are referred to as such because businesses "trade" or do business with other businesses.

**trade promotions**

Sales promotions aimed at businesses.

Also as discussed in Chapter 11, companies use a **pull strategy** when they target consumers with promotions. In other words, a company promotes it products and services to the final consumer to *pull* a consumer to the stores or get the consumer asking for the product. If a company sends coupons to the consumer, hopefully the consumer will take the coupon (sales promotion) to the store and buy the product. A **push strategy** is used when businesses are the target of sales promotions so that products may be *pushed* through the channel to final consumers. For example, a manufacturer may provide incentives such as price discounts to the retailer who then promotes or pushes the product to the final consumer. Figure 12.4 shows how push strategy differs from a pull strategy. Many organizations use both a pull and push strategy, promoting their products and services to both final consumers and their trade partners (retailers, wholesalers).

**pull strategy**

A strategy in which consumers are targeted with sales promotions such as coupons, contests, games, rebates, mail-in offers.

**push strategy**

A strategy in which businesses are the target of promotions so products get "pushed" through their marketing channels and sold to consumers.

**FIGURE 12.4** A Push versus a Pull Strategy

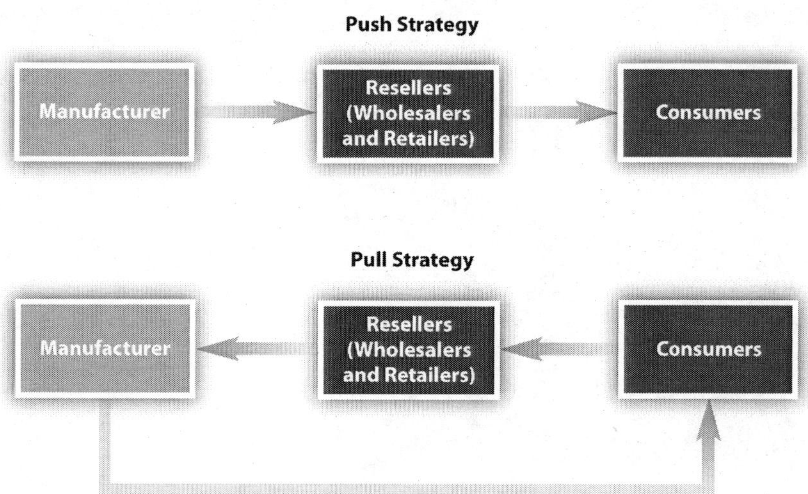


## 2.1 Types of Consumer Sales Promotions

Do you like free samples? Most people do. A **sample** is a sales promotion in which a small amount of a product that is for sale is given to consumers to try. Samples increase awareness, so the strategy encourages trial and builds awareness. You have probably purchased a product that included a small free sample with it—for example, a small amount of conditioner packaged with your shampoo. Have you ever gone to a store that provided free samples of different food items? The idea for giving away samples is to get people to buy a product. Although sampling is an expensive strategy, it is usually very effective for food products. People try the product, the person providing the sample tells consumers about the product, and mentions any special prices for the product.

**sample**

A small amount of a product given to consumers to try for free.

**coupons**

Provide an immediate price reduction off an item and the amount of the coupon is reimbursed to the retailer by the manufacturer.

In many retail grocery stores, coupons are also given to consumers with the samples. **Coupons** provide an immediate price reduction off an item. The amount of the coupon is later reimbursed to the retailer by the manufacturer. The retailer also gets a handling fee for accepting coupons. When the economy is weak, more consumers cut out coupons and look for special bargains such as double coupons and buy-one-get-one-free (BOGO) coupons. While many consumers cut coupons from the inserts in Sunday newspapers, other consumers find coupons for products and stores online. Stores may also provide coupons for customers with a loyalty card.

Consumers can also download coupons on many mobile phones. Mobile marketing and the Internet provide consumers in international markets access to coupons and other promotions. In India, the majority of coupons used are digital, while paper coupons have the largest share in the United States. Over 80 percent of diapers are purchased with coupons; imagine how much easier and less wasteful digital coupons scanned from a mobile phone are for both organizations and consumers.

**point-of-purchase displays**

In-store displays designed to encourage consumers to buy products immediately.

**Point-of-purchase displays**, including coupon machines placed in stores, encourage consumers to buy a product immediately. When a consumer sees a special display or can get a coupon instantly, manufacturers hope the sales promotion increases sales. Other sales promotions are conducted online. Online sales promotions include incentives such as free items, free shipping, coupons, and sweepstakes. For example, many online merchants such as Shoe Station and Zappos offer free shipping and free return shipping to encourage consumers to shop online. Some firms have found that the response they get to their online sales promotions is better than response they get to traditional sales promotions.

**premiums**

Something consumers get for free or a small handling charge with proof of purchase.

Another very popular sales promotion for consumers is a premium. A **premium** is something you get either for free or for a small shipping and handling charge with your proof of purchase (sales receipt or part of package). Remember wanting your favorite cereal because there was a toy in the box? The toy is an example of a premium. Sometimes you might have to mail in a certain number of proofs of purchase to get a premium. The purpose of a premium is to motivate you to a buy product multiple times. What many people don't realize is that when they pay the shipping and handling charges, they may also be paying for the premium.

**contests**

Sales promotions that people enter or participate in order to win a prize.

Contests or sweepstakes also attract a lot of people. **Contests** are sales promotions people enter or participate in to have a chance to win a prize. The Publisher's Clearing House Sweepstakes and the Monopoly Game at McDonald's are both examples. The organization that conducts the sweepstakes or contest hopes you will not only enter its contest but buy some magazines (or more food) when you do.

**Video Clip**

**Want to Subscribe?**

The Fantanas are back! Watch the video for a contest being conducted by Fanta soft drinks. As with other sales promotion tools, the idea is to get you to buy a product and more specifically to make repeat purchases.

View the video online at: http://www.youtube.com/embed/TW4TSbYrn_4

**loyalty programs**

Marketing efforts that reward the frequent purchase and consumption of an offering.

**Loyalty programs** are sales promotions designed to get repeat business. Loyalty programs include things such as frequent flier programs, hotel programs, and shopping cards for grocery stores, drugstores, and restaurants. Sometimes point systems are used in conjunction with loyalty programs. After you accumulate so many miles or points, an organization might provide you with a special incentive such as a free flight, free hotel room, or free sandwich. Many loyalty programs, especially hotel and airline programs, have partners to give consumers more ways to accumulate and use miles and points.

**Rebates** are popular with both consumers and the manufacturers that provide them. When you get a rebate, you are refunded part (or all) of the purchase price of a product back after completing a form and sending it to the manufacturer with your proof of purchase. The trick is completing the paperwork on time. Many consumers forget or wait too long to do so. Consequently, they do not get any money back. This is why rebates are also popular with manufacturers. Rebates sound great to consumers until they forget to send it back.

**rebates**

A promotion whereby part of the purchase price of an offering is refunded to a customer after the customer completes a form and sends in the proof of purchase (sales receipt).

## 2.2 Types of Trade Promotions

One of the most common types of sales promotions in B2B markets are trade shows. A **trade show** is an event in which firms in a particular industry display and demonstrate their offerings to other organizations they hope will buy them. There are typically many different trade shows in which one organization can participate. Using displays, brochures, and other materials, representatives at trade shows can identify potential customers (prospects), inform customers about new and existing products, and show them products and materials. Representatives can also get feedback from prospects about their company's products and materials, and perhaps about competitors.

**trade show**

An event in which firms in a particular industry display and demonstrate their offerings to other organizations they hope will buy them.

Companies also gather competitive information at trade shows because they can see the products other firms are exhibiting and how they are selling them. While approximately 75 percent of representatives attending trade shows actually buy the product(s) they see, 93 percent of attendees are influenced by what they see at the trade shows. However, only 20 percent of organizations follow up on leads obtained at trade shows and only 17 percent of buyers are called upon after they express interest in a particular company's products.[7] Figure 12.5 is an example of a booth display at a trade show showcasing the Korean electronics firm, Samsung.

**FIGURE 12.5** A Samsung Display at the Consumer Electronics (CES) Trade Show in Las Vegas, Nevada, in 2009

*Source: Wikipedia.*

**Conventions**, or meetings, with groups of professionals also provide a way for sellers to show potential customers different products. For example, a medical convention might be a good opportunity to display a new type of medical device. Sales representatives and managers often attend conventions to market their products.

**conventions**

Meetings of groups of professionals that provide a way for sellers to showing potential customers different products.

**FIGURE 12.6**

Intuitive Surgical is the maker of the da Vinci robot, a new type of technology used to make surgeries easy to perform and less invasive. Intuitive Surgical often demonstrates the robot at surgical conventions.

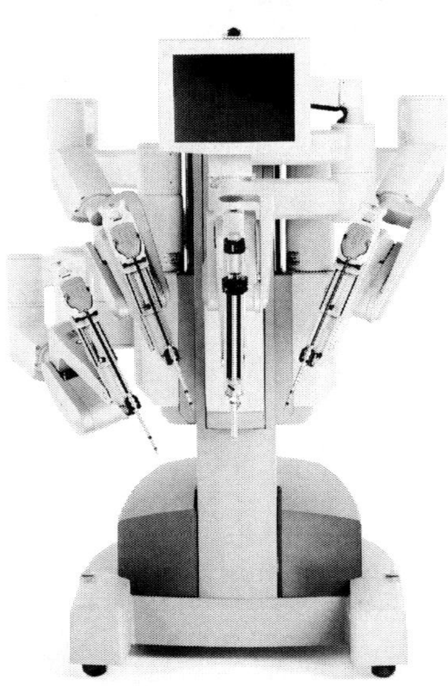



**sales contests**

Contests designed to motivate salespeople to increase their sales of particular products.

**trade allowances**

Discounts an organization gives its channel partners for performing different functions.

**advertising allowance**

An allowance (money) a manufacturer provide retailers to advertise its products in local newspapers.

**training**

Assistance an organization offers its channel partner's salespeople. The goal is to help them understand how the organization's products work and how consumers can be enticed to buy them.

**product demonstrations**

A demonstration designed to show a channel partner's customers how products work and answer any questions they might have.

**Sales contests**, which are often held by manufacturers or vendors, provide incentives for salespeople to increase their sales. Often, the contests focus on selling higher-profit or slow-moving products. The sales representative with the most sales of the product wins a prize such as a free vacation, company recognition, or cash.

**Trade allowances** give channel partners—for example, a manufacturer's wholesalers, distributors, retailers, and so forth—different incentives to push a product. One type of trade allowance is an **advertising allowance** (money) to advertise a seller's products in local newspapers. An advertising allowance benefits both the manufacturer and the retailer. Typically, the retailer can get a lower rate than manufacturers on advertising in local outlets, saving the manufacturer money. The retailer benefits by getting an allowance from the manufacturer.

Another sales promotion tool manufacturers offer businesses is **training** to help their salespeople understand how the manufacturers' products work and how consumers can be enticed to buy them. Many manufacturers also provide in-store **product demonstrations** to show a channel partner's customers how products work and answer any questions they might have. Demonstrations of new video game systems and computers are extremely popular and successful in generating sales.

**Free merchandise**, such as a tool, television, or other product produced by the manufacturer, can also be used to get retailers to sell products to consumers. In other words, a manufacturer of televisions might offer the manager of a retail electronics store a television to push its products. If a certain number of televisions are sold, the manager gets the television.

**free merchandise**

A product or service a seller offers retailers in order to get them to push it toward consumers.

Have you ever been to an electronics store or a furniture store and felt like the salesperson was pushing one particular television or one particular mattress? Perhaps the salesperson was getting **push money**, or a cash incentive from the manufacturer to *push* a particular item. The push to the sell item might be because there is a large amount of inventory of it, it is being replaced by a new model, or the product is not selling well.

**push money**

A cash incentive a manufacturer provides its channel partners to sell particular items.

Figure 12.7 recaps the different types of sales promotions designed for both consumers and businesses. Although different types of sales promotions work best for different organizations, rebates are very profitable for companies because, as you have learned, many consumers forget to send in their rebate forms. In a weak economy, consumers tend to use more coupons, but they also buy more store brands. Coupons available online or at the point of purchase are being used more often by consumers. Trade shows can be very successful, although the companies that participate in them need to follow-up on the leads generated at the shows.

**FIGURE 12.7** Examples of Sales Promotions

| Consumer Sales Promotions | Business-to-Business Sales Promotions |
|---|---|
| Coupons | Trade shows and conventions |
| Sweepstakes or contests | Sales contests |
| Premiums | Trade and advertising allowances |
| Rebates | Product demonstrations |
| Samples | Training |
| Loyalty programs | Free merchandise |
| Point-of-purchase displays | Push money |

## KEY TAKEAWAY

Companies use sales promotions to get customers to take action (make purchases) quickly. Sales promotions increase the awareness of products, help introduce new products, and often create interest in the organizations that run the promotions. Coupons, contests, samples, and premiums are among the types of sales promotions aimed at consumers. Trade promotions, or promotions aimed at businesses, include trade shows, sales contests, trade allowances, and push money.

## REVIEW QUESTIONS

1. What are the objectives of sales promotions?
2. What is a trade promotion?
3. Identify and provide an example of three sales promotion tools targeted at consumers.
4. Identify and provide an example of three sales promotion tools targeted at businesses.
5. Explain the difference between a push strategy and pull strategy.

# 3. DISCUSSION QUESTIONS AND ACTIVITIES

## DISCUSSION QUESTIONS

1. Explain three different types of public relations tools that a company can use to generate interest in its products.
2. As the manufacturer of small appliances, explain how you might plan to use both a push strategy and pull strategy.
3. What type of sales promotions do you feel are most effective for college students?

## ACTIVITIES

1. Create a sales promotion you think will attract a lot of students to your favorite fast-food restaurant.
2. Write a press release about special activities your college or university is doing to help the environment or community.

# ENDNOTES

1. Apple, Inc., "Apple Introduces the New iPhone 3G," http://www.apple.com/pr/library/2008/06/09iphone.html (accessed December 9, 2009).
2. Mobile Loaves & Fishes Blog, "Stubb's Teams Up With MLF to Launch 'Feed The World' Tour!" May 22, 2009, http://mobileloavesandfishes.typepad.com/weblog/2009/05/stubbs-teams-up-with-mlf-to-launch-feed-the-world-tour-homeless.html (accessed December 9, 2009).
3. http://en.wikipedia.org/wiki/Staples_Center (accessed December 9, 2009).
4. "Events and Sponsorship 2008 Marketing Fact Book," *Marketing News*, July 15, 2008, 26.
5. http://brandchannel.com/features_effect.asp?pf_id=489 (accessed December 9, 2009).
6. http://en.wikipedia.org/wiki/Cast_Away (accessed December 9, 2009).
7. John F. Tanner, Jr., and Dennis Pitta, "Identifying and Creating Customer Value" (special session presentation, Summer Educators' Conference, Chicago, 2009).

# CHAPTER 13
# Professional Selling

The clock in Ted Schulte's home office was striking 11:00 p.m. His children had gone to bed hours ago. Yet Schulte, an account representative who sells pacemakers for Guidant, was on the phone talking to one of his clients, a cardiologist. The cardiologist was performing surgery at 7:00 a.m. the next day. His patient had a number of health problems that caused the doctor to question which pacemaker would best suit her needs. The cardiologist's questions had to be answered immediately so the right materials and tools would be available for the procedure. The best expert on the matter was not another physician in this case—it was Schulte.

When you visit your physician, you want to think that her training and education have completely prepared her for dealing with whatever condition sent you there. The reality is, however, that salespeople play a major role in her continuing education. Similarly, the house or apartment you live in may have been designed by an architect, but that architect's choices in materials and design elements were influenced by salespeople, each of whom are experts in a particular product category. Not only was the food you eat sold to the grocery store by a salesperson, but the ingredients were also sold to the food companies by salespeople.

**Audio Clip**

**Interview with Ted Schulte**
Listen as Ted Schulte describes his start as a salesperson.

Salespeople play an important role in our economy. They are vital to customers and companies alike. In this chapter, we explore the role professional selling plays in terms of a company's marketing strategy. We also look at the factors that enhance a firm's success when it markets and sells its products through salespeople.

## 1. THE ROLE PROFESSIONAL SALESPEOPLE PLAY

**LEARNING OBJECTIVES**

1. **Recognize the role professional selling plays in society and in firms' marketing strategies.**
2. **Identify the different types of sales positions.**

You've created a great product, you've priced it right, and you've set a wonderful marketing communication strategy in motion. Now you can just sit back and watch the sales roll in, right? Probably not. Unless your company is able to sell the product entirely over the Internet, you probably have a lot more work to do. For example, if you want consumers to be able to buy the product in a retail store, someone will first have to convince the retailer to carry the product.

"Nothing happens until someone sells something," is an old saying in business. But in reality, a lot must happen before a sale can be made. Companies count on their sales and marketing teams not only to sell products but to the lay the groundwork that makes it happens. However, salespeople are expensive. Often they are the most expensive element in a company's marketing strategy. As a result, they have to generate business in order to justify a firm's investment in them.

## 1.1 What Salespeople Do

Salespeople act on behalf of their companies by doing the following:

- Creating value for their firms' customers
- Managing relationships
- Relaying customer and market information back to their organizations

In addition to acting on behalf of their firms, sales representatives also act on behalf of their customers. Whenever a salesperson goes back to her company with a customer's request, be it for quicker delivery, a change in a product feature, or a negotiated price, she is voicing the customer's needs. Her goal is to help the buyer purchase what serves his or her needs the best. Like Ted Schulte, the salesperson is the expert.

From society's perspective, selling is wonderful when professional salespeople act on behalf of both buyers and sellers. The salesperson has a fiduciary responsibility (in this case meaning something needs to be sold) to the company and an ethical responsibility to the buyer. At times, however, the two responsibilities conflict with one another. For example, what should a salesperson do if her product meets only most of a buyer's needs, while a competitor's product is a perfect fit?

Salespeople also face conflicts within their companies. When a salesperson tells a customer a product will be delivered in three days, she has made a promise that will either be kept or broken by her company's shipping department. When the salesperson accepts a contract with certain terms, she has made a promise to the customer that will either be kept or broken by her company's credit department. What if the credit department and shipping department can't agree on the shipping terms the customer should receive? Which group should the salesperson side with? What if managers want the salesperson to sell a product that's unreliable and will swamp the company's customer service representatives with buyers' complaints? Should she nonetheless work hard to sell the offering?

**role conflict**

A situation in which someone faces competing expectations from two or more people or groups; for example, a salesperson who has a customer who wants one thing and a boss who wants another.

Situations such as these create role conflict. **Role conflict** occurs when the expectations people set for you differ from one another. Now couple the situation we just mentioned with the fact that the salesperson has a personal interest in whether the sale is made or not. Perhaps her income or job depends on it. Can you understand how role conflict might result in a person using questionable tactics to sell a product?

So are salespeople dishonest? You might be surprised to learn that one study found that salespeople are less likely to exaggerate in order to get what they want than politicians, preachers, and professors. Another study looked at how business students responded to ethical dilemmas versus how professional salespeople responded. What did the study find? That salespeople were more likely to respond ethically than students were.

In general, salespeople handle these conflicting expectations well. Society benefits because salespeople help buyers make more informed decisions and help their companies succeed, which, in turn, creates jobs for people and products they can use. Most salespeople also truly believe in the effectiveness of their company's offerings. Schulte, for example, is convinced that the pacemakers he sells are the best there are. When this belief is coupled with a genuine concern for the welfare of the customer—a concern that most salespeople share—society can't lose.

## 1.2 Creating Value

Consider the following situations:

- At the beginning of the chapter, we described a real-life situation—a cardiac surgeon with a high-risk patient is wondering what to do. The physician calls Ted Schulte at Guidant to get his input on how to handle the situation. Schulte recommends the appropriate pacemaker and offers to drive one hundred miles early in the morning in order to be able to answer any questions that might arise during the surgery.
- A food wholesaler is working overtime to prepare invoices. Unfortunately, one out of five has a mistake. The result is that customers don't get their invoices in a timely fashion, so they don't pay quickly and don't pay the correct amounts. Consequently, the company has to borrow money fulfill its payroll obligations. John Plott, a salesperson from Sri-IIST, a document-management company, recommends the wholesaler purchase an electronic invoicing system. The wholesaler does. Subsequently, it takes the wholesaler just days to get invoices ready, instead of weeks. And instead of the invoices being only 80 percent accurate, they are close to being 100 percent accurate. The wholesaler no longer has trouble meeting its payroll because customers are paying more quickly.
- Sanderson Farms, a chicken processor, wants to build a new plant near Waco, Texas. The chambers of commerce for several towns in the area vie for the project. The chamber

representative from Waco, though, locates an enterprise zone that reduces the company's taxes for a period of time, and then works with a local banker to get the company better financing. In addition, the rep gets a local technical college involved so Sanderson will have enough trained employees. These factors create a unique package that sells the company on setting up shop in Waco.

All these are true stories of how salespeople create value by understanding the needs of their customers and then create solutions to meet those needs. Salespeople can adapt the offering, such as in the Sanderson Farms example, or they can adapt how they present the offering so that it is easier for the client to understand and make the right decision.

Adapting a message or product on the fly isn't something that can be easily accomplished with other types of marketing communication. Granted, some Web sites are designed to adapt the information and products they display based on what a customer appears to be interested in while he or she is looking at the sites. But unless the site has a "chat with a representative" feature, there is no real dialog occurring. The ability to engage in dialog helps salespeople better understand their customers and their needs and then create valuable solutions for them.

Note also that creating value means making sales. Salespeople sell—that's the bulk of the value they deliver to their employers. There are other ways in which they deliver value, but it is how much they sell that determines most of the value they deliver to their companies.

Salespeople aren't appropriate channels for companies in all situations, however. Some purchases don't require the salesperson's expertise. Or the need to sell at a very low cost may make retail stores or online selling more attractive. But in situations requiring adaptation, customer education, and other value-adding activities, salespeople can be the best channel to reach customers.

## 1.3 Managing Relationships

Because their time is limited, sales representatives have to decide which accounts they have the best shot at winning and which are the most lucrative. Once a salesperson has decided to pursue an account, a strategy is devised and implemented, and if a sale happens, the salesperson is also responsible for ensuring that the offering is implemented properly and to the customer's satisfaction.

We've already emphasized the notion of "customers for life" in this book. Salespeople recognize that business is not about making friends, but about making and retaining customers. Although buyers tend to purchase products from salespeople they like, being liked is not enough. Salespeople have to ensure that they close the deal with the customer. They also have to recognize that the goal is not to just close one deal, but as many deals as possible in the future.

## 1.4 Gathering Information

Salespeople are **boundary spanners**, in that they operate outside the firm and in the field. As such, they are the first to learn about what competitors are doing. An important function for them, then, is to report back to headquarters about their competitors' new offerings and strategies.

**boundary spanners**

People who work both inside and outside their organizations. Salespeople are boundary spanners.

Similarly, salespeople interact directly with customers and, in so doing, gather a great deal of useful information about their needs. The salespeople then pass the information along to their firms, which use it to create new offerings, adjust their current offerings, and reformulate their marketing tactics. The trick is getting the information to the right decision makers in firms. Many companies use customer relationship management (CRM) software like Aplicor or Salesforce.com to provide a mechanism for salespeople to enter customer data and others to retrieve it. A company's marketing department, for example, can then use that data to pinpoint segments of customers to communicate directly with. In addition to using the data to improve and create and marketing strategies, the information can also help marketing decision makers understand who makes buying decisions, resulting in such decisions as targeting trade shows where potential buyers are likely to be. In other words, marketing managers don't have to ask salespeople directly what customers want; they can pull that information from a customer database. (For an online demonstration of Aplicor, visit http://www.aplicor.com/product_tour.php.)

## FIGURE 13.1

Aplicor is a computer software program that enables salespeople to capture and track information on their accounts. This information can then be used by marketing mangers to design better marketing strategies and offerings. The system also helps salespeople manage their accounts better, because they have access to more customer information.

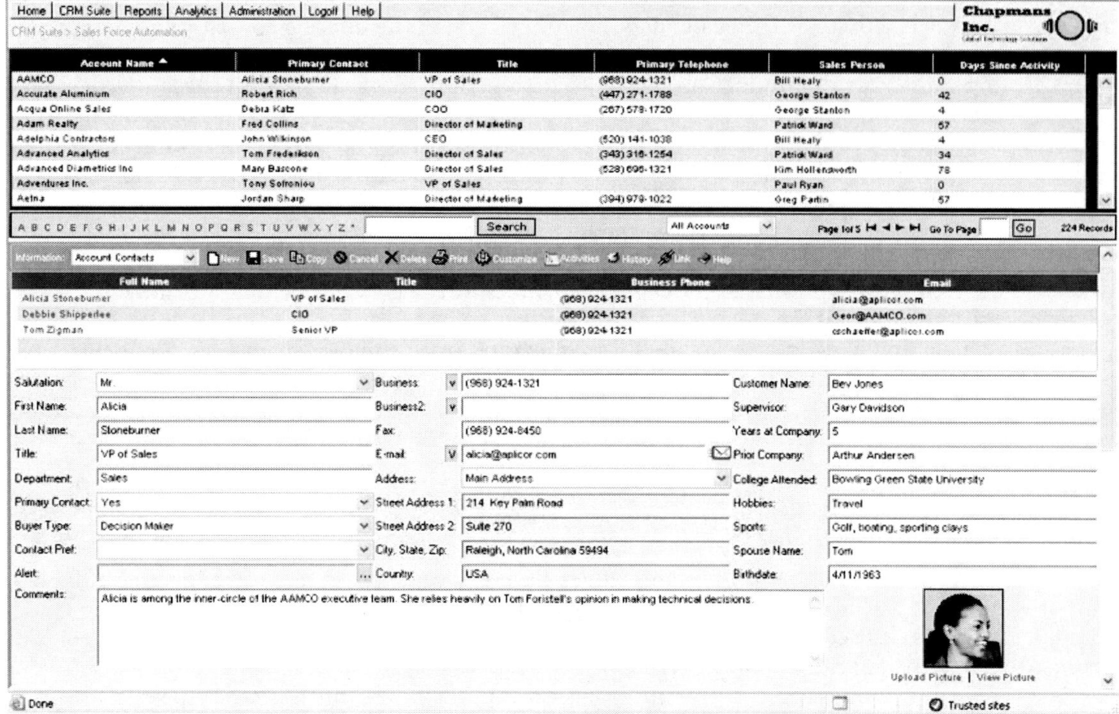


*Source: Aplicor, used with permission.*

## 1.5 Types of Sales Positions

There are different ways to categorize salespeople. They can be categorized by the customers they work with, such as whether they are consumers, other businesses, or government institutions. Another way to categorize salespeople is by the size of their customers. For the purposes of this book, we will categorize salespeople by their activities. Using activities as a basis, there are four basic types of salespeople: missionary salespeople, trade salespeople, prospectors, and account managers. Most professional sales positions involve selling to other businesses, but many also sell to consumers like you. Next, we discuss each of the types of salespeople.

### Missionary Salespeople

**missionary salesperson**

A salesperson who calls on people who make decisions about products but don't actually buy them.

A **missionary salesperson** calls on people who make decisions about products but don't actually buy them, and while they call on individuals, the relationship is business-to-business. For example, a pharmaceutical representative might call on a physician to provide the doctor with clinical information about a medication's effectiveness. The salesperson hopes the doctor will prescribe the drug. Patients, not doctors, actually purchase the medication. Similarly, salespeople call on your professors urging them to use certain textbooks. But you, the student, choose whether or not to actually buy the books.

There are salespeople who also work with "market influencers." Mary Gros works at Teradata, a company that develops data warehousing solutions. Gros calls on college faculty who have the power to influence decision makers when it comes to the data warehouses they use, either by consulting for the them, writing research papers about data warehousing products, or offering opinions to students on the software. In an effort to influence what they write about Teradata's offerings, Gros also visits with analysts who write reviews of products.

### Trade Salespeople

A **trade salesperson** is someone who calls on retailers and helps them display, advertise, and sell products to consumers. Eddy Patterson is a trade salesperson. Patterson calls on major supermarket chains like HEB for Stubb's Bar-B-Q, a company that makes barbecue sauces, rubs, marinades, and other barbecuing products. Patterson makes suggestions about how Stubb's products should be priced and where they should be placed in store so they will sell faster. Patterson also works with his clients' advertising departments in order to create effective ads and fliers featuring Stubb's products.

**trade salesperson**

Someone who calls on retailers and provides them assistance with merchandising and selling products to consumers.

**FIGURE 13.2**

Trade salespeople like Eddy Patterson for Stubb's help retailers promote and sell products to consumers.

*Source: Photo courtesy of Stubb's Legendary Kitchen.*

### Prospectors

A **prospector** is a salesperson whose primary function is to find prospects, or potential customers. The potential customers have a need, but for any number of reasons, they are not actively looking for products to meet those needs—perhaps because they lack information about where to look for them or simply haven't had the time to do so. Prospectors often knock on a lot of doors and make a lot of phone calls, which is called *cold calling* because they do not know the potential accounts and are therefore talking to them "cold." Their primary job is to sell, but the activity that drives their success is prospecting. Many salespeople who sell to consumers would be considered prospectors, including salespeople such as insurance or financial services salespeople, or cosmetic salespeople such as those working for Avon or Mary Kay.

**prospector**

A salesperson whose primary responsibility is prospecting, or finding potential customers. The salesperson might be responsible for closing the sales or simply turning the prospects over to someone else to close.

In some B2B situations, the prospector finds a prospect and then turns it over to another salesperson to close the deal. Or the prospector may take the prospect all the way through the sales process and close the sale. The primary responsibility is to make sales, but the activity that drives the salesperson's success is prospecting.

### Account Managers

**Account managers** are responsible for ongoing business with a customer who uses a product. A new customer may be found by a prospector and then turned over to an account manager, or new accounts may be so rare that the account manager is directly responsible for identifying and closing them. For example, if you sold beds to hospitals, new hospital organizations are rare. A new hospital may be built, but chances are good that it is replacing an existing hospital or is part of an existing hospital chain, so the account would already have coverage.

**account manager**

A salesperson responsible for ongoing business with a customer who uses a product. Satisfying long-term customers and persuading them to reorder products are important activities for account managers.

Taylor Bergstrom, a Baylor University graduate, began his career as a sales representative prospecting for the Texas Rangers baseball team. Bergstrom spent a lot of time calling people who had purchased single game tickets in an effort to sell them fifteen-game packages or other special-ticket packages. Today, Bergstrom is an account manager for the club. He works with season ticket holders to ensure that they have a great experience over the course of a season, regardless of whether the Rangers win or lose. His sales goals include upgrading season ticket holders to more expensive seats, identifying referral opportunities for new season-ticket sales, and selling special-event packages, such as party packages to box-seat holders. While most account managers sell to businesses, some, like Bergstrom, sell to individual consumers.

Account managers also have to identify lead users (people or organizations likely to use new, cutting-edge products) and build relationships with them. (Recall that we discussed lead users in Chapter 6.) Lead users are in a good position to help improve a company's offerings or develop new ones. Account managers work closely with these lead users and build relationships across both their companies so that the two organizations can innovate together.

**FIGURE 13.3**

Taylor Bergstrom, who began his career as a sales representative for the Texas Rangers baseball team, is now an account manager for the club. Some of the deals he closes are worth hundreds of thousands of dollars.

*Source: Taylor Bergstrom, used with permission.*

### KEY TAKEAWAY

Salespeople act as representatives for other people, including employees who work in other parts of their companies. Salespeople create value for their customers, manage relationships, and gather information for their firms. There are four types of salespeople: missionary salespeople, trade salespeople, prospectors, and account managers.

### REVIEW QUESTIONS

1. Salespeople play three primary roles. What are they?
2. Salespeople create value in what two ways?
3. How does each type of salesperson create value?

# 2. CUSTOMER RELATIONSHIPS AND SELLING STRATEGIES

### LEARNING OBJECTIVES

1. **Understand the types of selling relationships that firms seek.**
2. **Be able to select the selling strategy needed to achieve the desired customer relationship.**

## 2.1 Customer Relationships

Some buyers and sellers are more interested than others in building strong relationships with each other. Generally speaking, however, all marketers are interested in developing stronger relationships with large customers. Why? Because serving one large customer can often be more profitable than serving several smaller customers, even when the large customer receives quantity discounts. Serving many small customers—calling on them, processing all their orders, and dealing with any complaints—is time consuming and costs money. To illustrate, consider the delivery process. Delivering a large load to one customer can be accomplished in just one trip. By contrast, delivering smaller loads to numerous customers will require many more trips. Marketers, therefore, want bigger, more profitable customers. Big box retailers such as Home Depot and Best Buy are examples of large customers that companies want to sell to because they expect to make more profit from the bigger sales they can make.

Marketers also want stronger relationships with customers who are innovative, such as lead users. Similarly, marketers seek out customers with status or who are recognized by others for having expertise. For example, Holt Caterpillar is a Caterpillar construction equipment dealer in Texas and is recognized among Caterpillar dealers for its innovativeness. Customers such as Holt influence others (recall that we discussed these opinion leaders in Chapter 3). When Holt buys or tries something new and it works, other Cat dealers are quick to follow. Some companies are reaching out to opinion leaders in an attempt to create stronger relationships. For example, JCPenney uses e-mail and Web sites to form relationships with opinion leaders who will promote its products. We'll discuss how the company does so in the next chapter.

**FIGURE 13.4**

Firms can often achieve economies of scale, such as lower delivery costs by sending full trucks, when they sell to bigger customers.

*Source: Wikimedia Commons.*

**Audio Clip**

**Interview with Ted Schulte**

Listen as Ted Schulte discusses the benefits of relationship selling.

Salespeople are also tasked with maintaining relationships with market influencers who are not their customers. As mentioned earlier, Mary Gros at Teradata works with professors and with consultants so that they know all about Teradata's data warehousing solutions. Professors who teach data warehousing influence future decision makers, whereas consultants and market analysts influence today's decision makers. Thus, Gros needs to maintain relationships with both groups.

## 2.2 Types of Sales Relationships

Think about the relationships you have with your friends and family. Most relationships operate along a continuum of intimacy or trust. The more you trust a certain friend or family member, the more you share intimate information with the person, and the stronger your relationship is. The relationships between salespeople and customers are similar to those you have, which range from acquaintance to best friend (see Figure 13.5).

**FIGURE 13.5** The Relationship Continuum

As this figure depicts, business relationships range from transactional, or one-time purchases, to strategic partnerships that are often likened to a marriage. Somewhere in between are functional and affiliative relationships that may look like friendships.

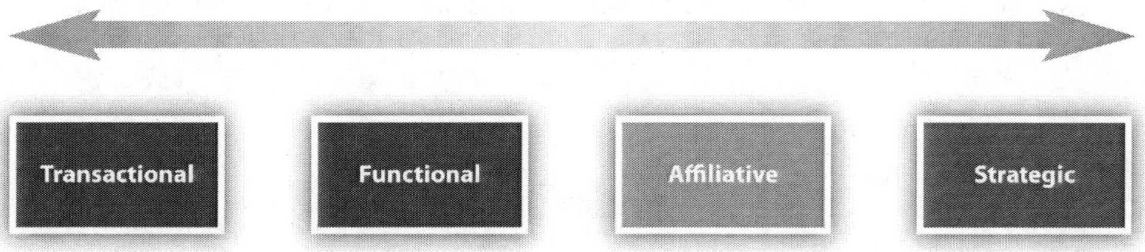


At one end of the spectrum are *transactional relationships*; each sale is a separate exchange, and the two parties to it have little or no interest in maintaining an ongoing relationship. For example, when you fill up your car with gas, you might not care if it's gas from Exxon, Shell, or another company. You just want the best price. If one of these companies went out of business, you would simply do business with another.

*Functional relationships* are limited, ongoing relationships that develop when a buyer continues to purchase a product from a seller out of habit, as long as her needs are met. If there's a gas station near your house that has good prices, you might frequently fill up there, so you don't have to shop around. If this gas station goes out of business, you will be more likely to feel inconvenienced. MRO (maintenance, repair, and operations) items, such as such as nuts and bolts used to repair manufacturing equipment are often sold on the basis of functional relationships. There are small price, quality, and services differences associated with the products. By sticking with the product that works, the buyer reduces his costs.

*Affiliative selling relationships* are more likely to occur when the buyer needs a significant amount of expertise needed from the seller and trust is an issue. Ted Schulte describes one segment of his market as affiliative; the people in this segment trust Schulte's judgment because they rely on him to help them make good decisions on behalf of patients. They know that Schulte wouldn't do anything to jeopardize that relationship.

A *strategic partnership* is one in which both the buyer and seller to commit time and money to expand "the pie" for both parties. This level of commitment is often likened to a marriage. For example, GE manufactures the engines that Boeing uses in the commercial planes it makes. Both companies work together to advance the state of engine technology because it gives them both an edge. Every time Boeing sells an airplane, GE sells one or more engines. A more fuel-efficient or faster engine can mean more sales for Boeing as well as GE. As a result, the engineers and other personnel from both companies work very closely in an ongoing relationship.

**FIGURE 13.6**

GE's GEnx aircraft engines were developed to meet air travel and cargo companies' needs for better fuel efficiency and faster flights. GE works together with Boeing to integrate the new engines into 747s.

*Source: Wikimedia Commons.*

Going back to the value equation, in a transactional relationship, the buyer calculates the value gained after every transaction. As the relationship strengthens, value calculations become less transaction oriented and are made less frequently. There will be times when either the buyer or the seller engages in actions that are not related directly to the sale but that make the relationship stronger. For example, a GE engineer may spend time with Boeing engineers simply educating them on a new technology. No specific sale may be influenced, but the relationship is made stronger by delivering more value.

Note that these types of relationships are not a process—not every relationship starts at the transactional level and moves through functional and affiliative to strategic. Nor is it the goal to make every relationship a strategic partnership. From the seller's perspective, the motivation to relate is a function of an account's size, innovation, status, and total lifetime value.

## 2.3 Selling Strategies

A salesperson's selling strategies will differ, depending on the type of relationship the buyer and seller either have or want to move toward. There are essentially four selling strategies: script-based selling, needs-satisfaction selling, consultative selling, and strategic partnering.

### Script-Based Selling

**script-based selling**

A form of selling in which the salesperson memorizes a sales pitch and delivers it verbatim to each prospective customer.

Salespeople memorize and deliver sales pitches verbatim when they utilize a **script-based selling** strategy. Script-based selling is also called *canned selling*. The term "canned" comes from the fact that the sales pitch is standardized, or "straight out of a can." Back in the late 1880s, companies began to use professional salespeople to distribute their products. Companies like National Cash Register (NCR) realized that some salespeople were far more effective than others, so they brought those salespeople into the head office and had them give their sales pitches. A stenographer wrote each pitch down, and then NCR's sales executives combined the pitches into one effective script. In 1894, the company started one of the world's first sales schools, which taught people to sell using the types of scripts developed by NCR.

Script-based selling works well when the needs of customers don't vary much. Even if they do, a script can provide a salesperson with a polished and professional description of how an offering meets each of their needs. The salesperson will ask the customer a few questions to uncover his or her need, and then provides the details that meet it as spelled out in the script. Scripts also ensure that the salesperson includes all the important details about a product.

### Needs-Satisfaction Selling

The process of asking questions to identify a buyer's problems and needs and then tailoring a sales pitch to satisfy those needs is called **needs-satisfaction selling**. This form of selling works best if the needs of customers vary, but the products being offered are fairly standard. For example, you might wander onto a car lot with a set of needs for a new vehicle. Someone else might purchase the same vehicle but for an entirely different set of reasons. Perhaps this person is more interested in the miles per gallon, or how big a trailer the vehicle can tow, whereas you are more interested in the vehicle's style and the amount of legroom and headroom it has. The effective salesperson would ask you a few questions, determine what your needs are, and then offer you the right vehicle, while emphasizing those points that meet your needs best. The vehicle's miles per gallon and towing capacity wouldn't be mentioned in the conversation.

**FIGURE 13.7**

National Cash Register, now NCR, was one of the first companies to professionalize selling with a sales school in 1894. Today, the company is a major seller of not only cash registers but also many other products, such as the scanner shown here, which you may see in a grocery or clothing store.

*Source: NCR, used with permission.*

### Consultative Selling

To many students, needs-satisfaction selling and consultative selling seem the same. The key difference between the two is the degree to which a customized solution can be created. With **consultative selling**, the seller uses special expertise to solve a complex problem in order to create a somewhat customized solution. For example, TAC is a company that creates customized solutions to make office and industrial buildings more energy efficient. TAC salespeople work with their customers over the course of a year or longer, as well as with engineers and other technical experts, to produce a solution.

### Strategic-Partner Selling

When the quality of the relationship between the buyer and seller moves toward a strategic partnership, the selling strategy gets more involved than even consultative selling. In **strategic-partner selling**, both parties invest resources and share their expertise with each other to create solutions that jointly grow one another's businesses. Schulte, for example, positions himself as a strategic partner to the cardiologists he works with. He tries to become a trusted partner in the patient care process.

**needs-satisfaction selling**

The process of asking questions to identify a potential buyer's needs and then tailoring the sales pitch to satisfy those needs.

**consultative selling**

A selling strategy in which a salesperson uses special expertise to create a somewhat customized solution to a buyer's problem.

**strategic-partner selling**

A situation in which a buyer and seller jointly invest resources and share their expertise to create solutions designed to grow one another's businesses.

## 2.4 Choosing the Right Sales Strategy for the Relationship Type and Selling Stage

The sales-strategy types and relationship types we discussed don't always perfectly match up as we have described them. Different strategies might be more appropriate at different times. For example, although script-based selling is generally used in transactional sales relationships, it can be used in other types of sales relationships as well, such as affiliative-selling relationships. An affiliative-sales position may still, for example, need to demonstrate new products, a task for which a script is useful. Likewise, the same questioning techniques used in needs-satisfaction selling might be used in relationships characterized by consultative selling and strategic-partner selling.

So when is each method more appropriate? Again, it depends on how the buyer wants to buy and what information the buyer needs to make a good decision.

The typical sales process involves several stages, beginning with the approach and ending with customer service. In between are other stages, such as the needs-identification stage, presentation stage, and closing stage (see Figure 13.8).

In the approach, the salesperson attempts to capture enough of the prospective customer's attention and interest in order to continue the sales call. If it is a first-time call, introductions are needed. A benefit that could apply to just about any customer may also be offered to show that the time will be worthwhile.

**FIGURE 13.8** The Typical Sales Process

A typical sales process starts with the approach and move through several stages to the close. Good salespeople continue with making sure the customer gets the product, uses it right, and is happy with it.

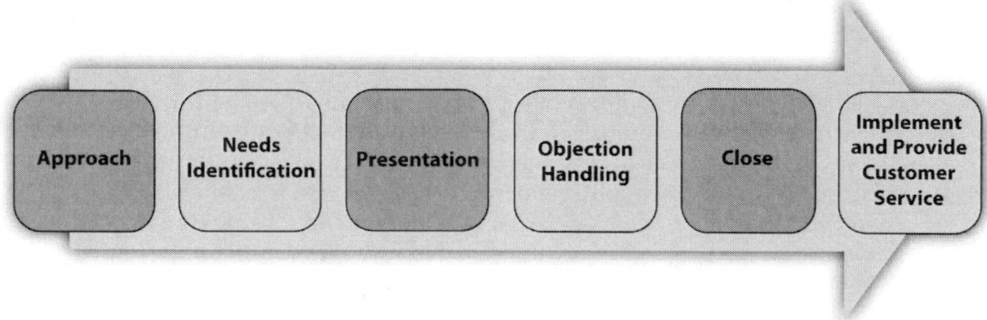


With the buyer's permission, the salesperson then moves into a needs identification section. In complex situations, many questions are asked, perhaps over several sales calls. In simpler situations, needs may not vary across customers so a canned presentation is more likely. Then, instead of identifying needs, needs are simply listed as solutions are described.

A presentation is then made that shows how the offering satisfies the needs identified earlier. One approach to presenting solutions uses statements called *FEBAs*. FEBA stands for feature, evidence, benefit, and agreement. The salesperson says something like, "This camera has an automatic zoom [Feature]. If you look at the viewfinder as I move the camera, you can see how the camera zooms in and out on the objects it sees [Evidence]. This zoom will help you capture those key moments in Junior's basketball games that you were telling me you wanted to photograph [Benefit]. Won't that add a lot to your scrapbooks [Agreement]?"

Note that the benefit was tied to something the customer said was important. A benefit only exists when something is satisfying a need. The automatic zoom would provide no benefit if the customer didn't want to take pictures of objects both near and far.

**objection**

A statement by a buyer of concern about an offer or salesperson.

**Objections** are concerns or reasons not to continue that are raised by the buyer, and can occur at any time. A prospect may object in the approach, saying there isn't enough time available for a sales call or nothing is needed right now. Or, during the presentation, a buyer may not like a particular feature. For example, the buyer might find that the automatic zoom leads the camera to focus on the wrong object. Salespeople should probe to find out if the objection represents a misunderstanding or a hidden need. Further explanation may resolve the buyer's concern or there may need to be a trade-off; yes, a better zoom is available but it may be out of the buyer's price range, for example.

When all the objections are resolved to the buyer's satisfaction, the salesperson should ask for the sale. Asking for the sale is called the *close*. In complex selling situations that require many sales calls, the close may be a request for the next meeting or some other action. When the close involves an actual sale, the next step is to deliver the goods and make sure the customer is happy.

The sales process used to sell products is generally the same regardless of the selling strategy used. However, the stage being emphasized will affect the strategy selected in the first place. For example, if the problem is a new one that requires a customized solution, the salesperson and buyer are likely to spend more time in the needs identification stage. Consequently, a needs-satisfaction strategy or consultation strategy is likely to be used. Conversely, if it's already clear what the client's needs are, the presentation stage is likely to be more important. In this case, the salesperson might use a script-based selling strategy, which focuses on presenting a product's benefits rather than questioning the customer.

**KEY TAKEAWAY**

Some buyers and sellers are more interested in building strong relationships with one another than others. The four types of relationships between buyers and sellers are transactional, functional, affiliative, and strategic. The four basic sales strategies salespeople use are script-based selling, needs-satisfaction selling, consultative selling, and strategic-partner selling. Different strategies can be used with in different types of relationships. For example, the same questioning techniques used in needs-satisfaction selling might be used in relationships characterized by consultative selling and strategic-partner selling. The sales process used to sell products is generally the same regardless of the selling strategy used. However, the strategy chosen will depend on the stage the seller is focusing on. For example, if the problem is a new one that requires a customized solution, the salesperson and buyer are likely to spend more time in the needs identification stage. Consequently, a needs-satisfaction strategy or consultation strategy is likely to be used.

**REVIEW QUESTIONS**

1. Do customer relationships begin as transactional and move toward strategic partnerships?
2. How does each sales strategy vary?
3. Which step of the sales process is most important and why? How would the steps of the sales process vary for each type of sales position?

# 3. SALES METRICS (MEASURES)

**LEARNING OBJECTIVES**

1. **Describe the sales cycle.**
2. **Understand the selling metrics that salespeople use.**
3. **Understand the selling metrics that sales managers and executives use.**

## 3.1 The Sales Cycle

A key component in the effectiveness of salespeople is the sales cycle. The **sales cycle**—how long it takes to close a sale—can be measured in steps, in days, or in months. As Figure 13.9 shows, the sales cycle is depicted as a **funnel** because not all the people and firms a salesperson talks to will become buyers. In fact, most of them won't.

**sales cycle**

The amount of time or number of steps it takes to make a sale; also called the sales pipeline or funnel.

**funnel**

The amount of time or number of steps it takes to make a sale; also called the sales cycle or pipeline.

**FIGURE 13.9** The Sales Cycle

The sales cycle starts with leads, some of whom become suspects. Some suspects become prospects, and some prospects become customers.

The cycle starts with a **lead**, which is nothing more than contact information of someone who might be interested in the salesperson's product. To follow up on the lead, the salesperson might phone or drop by to see the person identified in the lead. This beginning of the sales process is called the **approach**. During the approach, the salesperson introduces himself or herself and his or her company to the buyer. If the buyer shows interest, the salesperson then moves to the next step in the sales process.

A **suspect** is a person or organization that has an interest in an offering, but it is too early to tell what or if they are going to buy. They've agreed to meet with the salesperson and will possibly listen to the sales script or participate in a needs-identification process. During the needs-identification stage, the salesperson is trying to qualify the account as a prospect. **Qualifying** a prospect is a process of asking questions to determine whether the buyer is likely to become a customer. A **prospect** is someone with the budget, authority, need, and time (**BANT**) to make a purchase. In other words, the person has the money to make the purchase and the authority to do so; the person also needs the type of product the salesperson is selling and is going to buy such a product soon.

Once the purchase has been made, the sales cycle is complete. If the relationship between the company and the buyer is one that will be ongoing, the buyer is considered one of the salesperson's "accounts." Note that the buyer made a decision each step of the way in the cycle, thereby moving further down the funnel. She decided to consider what the salesperson was selling and became a suspect. She then decided to buy something and became a prospect. Lastly, she decided to buy the salesperson's product and became a customer.

## 3.2 Metrics Used by Salespeople

As you know, the key metric, or measure, salespeople are evaluated on are the revenues they generate. Sometimes the average revenue generated per customer and the average revenue generated per sales call are measured to determine if a salesperson is pursuing customers that are the most lucrative. How many prospects and suspects a salesperson has in the **pipeline** are two other measures. The more potential buyers there are in the pipeline, the more revenue a salesperson is likely to generate.

Conversion ratios are an extremely important metric. **Conversion ratios** measure how good a salesperson is at moving customers from one stage in the selling cycle to the next. For example, how many leads did the salesperson convert to suspects? A 10:1 ratio means it took ten leads for the salesperson to get one suspect who agreed to move to the next step. A salesperson with a 5:1 ratio only needs to pursue five leads to get a suspect. So, if the representative can make only ten sales calls in a day, then the salesperson with the 5:1 ratio will have produced two suspects versus just one suspect for the other salesperson. As a result, the second rep will have more suspects in the pipeline at the end of the day. Similarly, how many suspects did the salesperson convert to prospects and finally to customers? If all the other conversion ratios (suspect-to-prospect ratio and prospect-to-customer ratio) are the same for the two salespeople, then the rep with the 5:1 ratio will close twice as many sales as the one with a 10:1 ratio.

Salespeople can track their conversion ratios to identify which stages of the sales cycle they need to work on. For example, the sales representative with 10:1 ratio can study what the rep with the 5:1 ratio is doing in order to try to improve his efficiency and sales levels. His conversion ratios also tell him how many sales calls he has to make each day or week to generate a sale and how many calls must be made on leads, suspects, and prospects to convert them.

How many sales calls of each type a representative has to make in a certain period of time are **activity goals**. As Figure 13.10 illustrates, activities and conversions drive sales. More calls translate into more conversions, and more conversions translate into more sales. You can think of it as sort of a domino effect.

**lead**

The contact information for someone who might be interested a salesperson's product.

**approach**

The first step in the sales process. The salesperson introduces himself or herself and the company to the buyer and determines if the buyer has any interest in purchasing the firm's products.

**suspect**

A person or organization that has an interest in an offering but hasn't indicated if they are going to purchase.

**qualifying**

A process of asking questions to determine whether a buyer is likely to become a customer.

**prospect**

Someone who has the budget, authority, need for, and time to purchase a product.

**BANT**

An acronym for the characteristics of a qualified prospect. A BANT has the budget, authority, need for, and time to purchase a product.

**pipeline**

The amount of time or number of steps it takes to make a sale; also called the sales cycle or funnel.

**conversion ratios**

The rate at which a salesperson moves, or converts, potential customers from one stage of the sales cycle to the next.

**activity goals**

The number and type of sales calls a representative is expected to make in a certain period of time.

A **win-loss analysis** is an "after the battle" review of how well a salesperson performed given the opportunities she faced. Each sales opportunity after the customer has bought something (or decided to buy nothing) is examined to determine what went wrong and what went right. (Keep in mind that to some extent, all salespeople think back through their sales call to determine what they could have said or done differently and what they should say or do again in the future.) When several professionals are involved in the selling process, a win-loss analysis can be particularly effective because it helps the sales team work together more effectively in the future. Like a team watching a film after a football game, each member of the sales team can review the process for the purpose of improvement. When the results are fed to managers, the analysis can help a company develop better products. A marketing manager who listens carefully to what salespeople say during a win-loss analysis can develop better advertising and marketing campaigns. Communicating the same message to the entire market can help shorten the sales cycle for all a company's sales representatives.

**win-loss analysis**

The process of reviewing each sales cycle after it is completed to identify key factors that accounted for the win or the loss of a sale.

**FIGURE 13.10** How Activities and Conversions Drive Sales

Activities, or sales calls of various types, drive conversions, which then drive sales.

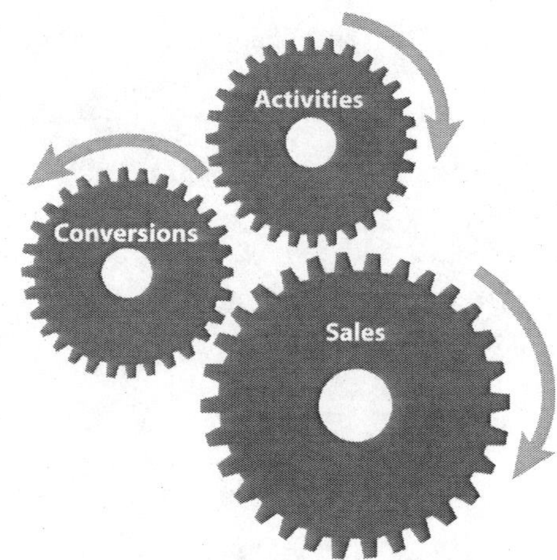


Another important metric used by many salespeople is how much money they will make. Most salespeople are paid some form of incentive pay, such as a bonus or commission, which is determined by how much they sell. A **bonus** is paid at the end of a period of time based on the total amount sold, while a **commission** is typically thought of as a payment for each sale. A bonus plan can be based on how well the company, the individual salesperson, or the salesperson's team does. Some salespeople are paid only on the basis of commission, but most are paid a salary plus a commission or a bonus.

Commissions are more common when sales cycles are short and selling strategies tend to be more transactional than relationship oriented. Perhaps one exception is financial services. Many financial services salespeople are paid a commission but expected to also build a long-lasting relationship with clients. Some salespeople are paid only salary. As might be expected, these salespeople sell very expensive products that have a very long sales cycle. If they were only paid on commission, they would starve before the sale was made. They may get a bonus to provide some incentive, or if they receive a commission, it may be a small part of their overall compensation.

**bonus incentive**

Pay based on overall sales performance; it may be based on how well an individual salesperson does, how the team does, or how the company performs.

**commission incentive**

Pay based on a single sale.

## 3.3 Metrics Used by Sales Managers

The sales manager is interested in all the same metrics as the salesperson, plus others. The metrics we discussed earlier can be used by the sales manager to evaluate salespeople, promote them, or pinpoint areas in which they need more training. Sales managers also use sales cycle metrics to make broader decisions. Perhaps everyone needs training in a particular stage of the sales process, or perhaps the leads generated by marketing are not effective, and new marketing ideas are warranted. Sales cycle metrics at the aggregate level can be very useful for making effective managerial decisions.

Sales managers also look at other measures such as *market share*, or how much of the market is buying from the firm versus its competitors; sales by product or by customer type; and sales per salesperson. Sales by product or by product line, especially viewed over time, can provide the sales executive with insight into whether a product should be divested or needs more investment. If the sales for the product line are declining but the product's market share is holding firm, then the entire market is shrinking. A shrinking market can mean the firm needs to look for new markets or develop new offerings.

**sales quota**

The minimum level of sales performance for an individual salesperson.

Time is yet another element that sales managers look at. If the firm's sales are declining, is the company in a seasonal slump it will come out of, or does the firm have a serious, ongoing problem? Sales executives are also constantly concerned about what the firm's sales are doing relative to what was forecasted for them. Forecasts turn in to **sales quotas**, or minimum levels of sales performance for each salesperson. In addition, forecasts turn into orders for raw materials and component parts, inventory levels, and other expenditures of money. If the forecast is way off, then money is lost, either because the company ran out of products or because too much was spent to build up inventories that didn't sell.

In Figure 13.11, you can see a sample of data a sales manager may review. As you can see, most of the sales teams are performing near quota. But what about the Midwest? Selling 7 percent more is a good thing, but an astute manager would want to know why sales were short by over $200,000. Inventory can be balanced against the Southeast's shortfall, but that adds cost to ship from the plant to Atlanta, then to Chicago. Accurate forecasts would have put that product in the Midwest's Chicago warehouse to start with.

**FIGURE 13.11** An Example of the Sales Data Sales Managers Utilize

Tables such as this provide information that managers use to evaluate sales performance against expected sales, or quota.

**Analysis by U.S. Region**

| Region | Quota | Actual | Difference | Performance |
|---|---|---|---|---|
| Northeast | $ 4,167,000 | $ 4,147,400 | -$ 19,600 | 99.5% |
| Southeast | $ 3,588,250 | $ 3,425,100 | -$ 163,150 | 95% |
| Midwest | $ 3,472,500 | $ 3,698,875 | $ 226,375 | 107% |
| Northwest | $ 5,093,000 | $ 5,209,880 | $ 116,880 | 102% |
| Southwest | $ 5,112,750 | $ 5,120,250 | $ 7,500 | 100% |
| Western | $ 4,861,500 | $ 4,948,920 | $ 87,420 | 102% |
| Total | $26,295,000 | $26,550,425 | $ 255,425 | 101% |

**Analysis by Salesperson (Southwest Region)**

| Salesperson | Quota | Actual | Difference | Performance |
|---|---|---|---|---|
| Becky (Atlanta—South) | $ 868,000 | $ 851,000 | -$ 17,000 | 98% |
| Juan (South Florida) | $ 804,000 | $ 810,000 | +$ 6,000 | 101% |
| Jerry (Carolinas) | $ 592,000 | $ 416,000 | -$176,000 | 70% |
| Mack (Alabama/Miss.) | $ 370,000 | $ 372,000 | +$ 2,000 | 103% |
| Earl (Atlanta—North) | $ 609,000 | $ 631,000 | +$ 22,000 | 104% |
| Dave (Tennessee) | $ 345,000 | $ 345,000 | 0 | 100% |
| Total | $3,588,000 | $3,425,000 | -$163,000 | 95% |

Similarly, a manager would be concerned about Jerry's lack of sales. That one salesperson accounts for the entire region's shortfall against quota. Was the shortfall due to Jerry's inability to sell, or did something happen in the territory? For example, if a hurricane came ashore in the Carolinas or if Jerry had a health problem arise, the manager's concern would be different than if Jerry lost a major account or had a history of failing to reach quota.

Sales executives don't just focus on sales, though. They also focus on costs. Why? Because many sales executives are held accountable not only for their firms' sales levels but also for profit levels. Money has to be spent to sell products, of course: If the firm spends too little, the sales force will be unable to perform effectively. If the budget to attend trade shows is cut, for example, the quantity and quality of leads salespeople get could fall—and so could their sales. But if the firm spends too much on trade shows, the cost per lead generated increases with no real improvement in the sales force's productivity. Perhaps the "additional" leads are duplicates or take too much time to follow up on.

Customer satisfaction is another important metric. Salespeople and their bosses want satisfied customers. Dissatisfied customers not only stop buying a company's products, they often tell their friends and family members about their bad purchasing experiences. Sometimes they go so far as to write blogs or bad product reviews on Web sites such as Epinions.com. Some research studies have shown that average customer satisfaction scores are less important than the number of complaints a company gets. Perhaps it's because of the negative word-of-mouth that unhappy customers generate.

In addition to tracking complaints, companies measure customer satisfaction levels through surveys. An average score of 3 on a scale of 1 to 5 could mean two things. The score could mean that everyone is, on average, happy and therefore gave the company a rating of 3.0. Or the score could mean that half of the customers are wildly enthusiastic and gave the company a 5 while the other half was bitterly disappointed and rated the company a 1. If the latter is the case, then half of the company's customers are telling their friends about their negative experience and discouraging many others from buying. Sometimes companies hire firms like TeleSight, an organization capable of tracking satisfaction scores for an entire industry. Using a service like this, the sales executive can not only track the company's customer satisfaction scores but also see how they compare with the scores of the industry overall.

## KEY TAKEAWAY

The sales cycle is a basic unit of measurement indicating how long it takes to close a sale. Salespeople examine their performance at each stage of the sales cycle in order to identify specific areas for improvement. A salesperson who shortens the cycle is able to generate more revenue with the same amount of effort. Salespeople also track their conversion ratios to identify which stages of the sales cycle they need to work on.

Sales executives track the same metrics as individual salespeople but at the aggregate level. If many salespeople are struggling with one stage of the sales cycle, for example, then additional training or marketing may be needed, or a new strategy is necessary. Sales executives also look at their firm's sales relative to their forecasts in order to spot possible trends. A firm's sales trends affect many of the other decisions the company's executives have to make, including manufacturing and output decisions. Sales managers also have to manage their company's selling costs. Sales managers are often responsible for a firm's sales and its profit levels.

## REVIEW QUESTIONS

1. How might the sales cycle vary across the types of sales positions? How do salespeople use the sales cycle to manage their performance?
2. What is the relationship between conversion ratios and activity goals? How do salespeople use this information? How do sales executives use the information?
3. What metrics do sales executives use that salespeople are less concerned with?

# 4. ETHICS IN SALES AND SALES MANAGEMENT

**LEARNING OBJECTIVES**

1. **Compare and contrast common ethical challenges facing salespeople and sales managers.**
2. **Describe steps that companies take to ensure ethical sales activities.**

When faced with an opportunity to exaggerate in job interviews, who would exaggerate more: professors, politicians, preachers, or salespeople? Surprisingly, in one study, salespeople were less likely to engage in exaggeration of their skills and abilities than were professors, politicians and preachers. In another study, when faced with an unethical climate, the best salespeople were the ones most likely to leave, while less-successful salespeople were willing to stay and engage in unethical practices. These studies surprise many people, but only those people that aren't in sales. Most salespeople are scrupulously ethical and, like Ted Schulte mentioned at the start of the chapter, they are in sales because they really enjoy working to help people solve problems.

## 4.1 Common Ethical Issues for Salespeople

What are the most common ethical issues facing salespeople? Many of the most common situations you could face as a salesperson involve issues such as the following:

- A customer asking for information about one of their competitors, who happens to be one of your customers
- Deciding how much to spend on holiday season gifts for your customers
- A buyer asking for something special, which you could easily provide, but aren't supposed to give away
- Deciding to play golf on a nice day, since no one knows if you are actually at work or not

Let's examine each of the issues. In the first issue, a customer owns the information about their business. The salesperson may hold that information, such as how many cases of the product they purchase or who their customers are, but that salesperson does not have the right to share that information with the customer's competitor. In many instances, a buyer may ask the seller to sign a nondisclosure agreement because, in order to serve the buyer, the seller will gain access to important private information about that buyer. But even if there is no nondisclosure agreement, courts are likely to agree with the buyer that the seller has an obligation to protect the buyer's information.

In the second issue, the concern is whether the gift is so extravagant that it is considered a bribe. In some companies, such as IBM and Walmart, buyers are not allowed to accept so much as a free cup of coffee from a seller. These companies do not allow their buyers to receive promotional items such as a pen or coffee cup with the seller's logo on it because they want every vendor to have free access to sales opportunities and earn the business on their merits, not their freebies. Many buyers would question the motives of a salesperson giving too large a gift. Most salespeople agree that lavish entertainment and gifts are becoming less important in business because decision makers know these add to the costs of doing business and they'd rather get a better price than be entertained.

The third issue is tough for salespeople because there are two factors involved: a possible violation of company policy and providing an unfair advantage to one customer. Customers may not know that their special request could get the salesperson in trouble and the request may be reasonable, just against company policy. In that instance, the salesperson should not follow through on the request, though it might make sense to see if the policy can be changed. The second factor, though, is a bit more difficult because the request can be unfair to other customers, and may cause legal problems. As long as the special request can be provided to anyone who asks for it, no law is broken. What if the special request is for a discount? Pricing discrimination laws could come into play if such a discount is not made available to all who ask. What if the request isn't illegal, but other customers find out and get upset that they weren't offered the same benefit? Then the salesperson may get a reputation for being untrustworthy.

In the final issue, the question is whether the salesperson is cheating the company out of time and effort. Some argue that a salesperson who is paid straight commission (paid by the sale) is not stealing anything from the company, but others argue that even in that instance, the company is being deprived of possible sales that would be gained if the salesperson was working.

**FIGURE 13.12**

Lavish gifts like this watch may be nice, but many buyers will consider it too lavish and wonder about the salesperson's motives.

These are not the only issues that salespeople face. In the United States, two basic principles of business are that everyone should have an equal opportunity to earn business, and the customer remains free to make a choice. Manipulation, a form of unethical sales behavior, unfairly reduces or eliminates a buyer's ability or opportunity to make a choice. Persuasion, on the other hand, may influence a buyer's decision, but the decision remains the buyer's. Manipulation can include misrepresentation, or claiming a product does something it doesn't, but it can also include withholding important information, using hard-sell tactics, and other unfair sales tactics.

However, as mentioned earlier, salespeople tend to be ethical people. The use of manipulative sales tactics is actually pretty rare.

## 4.2 Company Safeguards

Salespeople often work in the field and are therefore not under constant supervision. Even inside salespeople may be able to get away with less than ethical behavior as no supervisor can watch or hear everything. So how do companies manage ethical practices?

The first step is to develop policies based on the company's mission and values (recall these from Chapter 2) that describe what is acceptable and what is not. Good ethical policies not only list or describe appropriate and inappropriate behaviors; they also describe the underlying principles. Not all ethical dilemmas can be listed in a policy, so by detailing the principles and values that make up the reasoning behind the policies, salespeople and sales managers will be more prepared to respond appropriately.

Codes of ethics, or ethics policies, can be pretty detailed. Shell's ethics policy, for example, is a book over twenty pages long! Not only do these cover how salespeople (and other company representatives) should interact with customers, they also detail how employees should treat each other and how the company's vendors should be treated. (To see an example of a brief code of ethics for salespeople, visit Sales and Marketing Executives International's Web site, http://www.smei.org/displaycommon.cfm?an=1&subarticlenbr=16.)

**FIGURE 13.13**

Even though it is a beautiful day for golf, a salesperson who takes time away from the job is stealing time from the company, and losing sales opportunities as well. Taking a customer to play may be a different story; such a game may be a time to strengthen a relationship, as long as the customer does not feel manipulated or obligated.

A good second step is to train all salespeople and sales managers on the policy. One reason for such training is to secure greater support and application of the policy, but another reason is that, should a salesperson engage in an unethical or illegal activity, the company is protected. The Federal Sentencing Guidelines (FSG) were first developed in 1987 and then updated in 2007, and specify what happens to companies when employees commit breaches of ethics. Companies that have solid policies and train all employees on those policies can, rightfully under the FSG, claim that any unethical employee was acting against company policies and on his or her own, should anyone file charges against the company. Solid policies and employee training can then be used as a defense against such charges, and the company would not be held liable.

Yet training alone is insufficient. The company must also enforce the policy and have procedures in place that make enforcement possible. For example, a company should have a mechanism for reporting unethical activity in a way that protects the person making the report. Many companies have anonymous message boxes that enable an employee to report unethical activity. One similar and common practice is to have an ethics office, charged with investigating any complaints. The FSG requires that companies also have internal auditing procedures to ensure that misconduct can be detected.

Note that these codes of ethics, the FSG, and the policies and procedures affect all employees. These were not created just because of salespeople. Marketers have faced ethics challenges in how claims are made in advertising, while supply chain managers have encountered dilemmas in dealing ethically with vendors. Managers, in any area of the firm, encounter challenges regarding equal opportunity and creating an appropriately professional work environment.

## 4.3 Challenges Facing Sales Managers

Sales managers face the same challenges in managing salespeople that all managers face. These include ensuring that hiring, compensation, and other management practices are not discriminatory; that sexual harassment finds no home in the workplace; and that employees are treated with dignity and respect.

Other challenges may arise, though. For example, salespeople have to be in front of customers when customers are available. Earlier, we discussed how the number of calls made can impact a salesperson's success. So should a sales manager schedule all training sessions on weekends, when buyers are at home and not available for sales calls? Does the answer to that question change if the salesperson is paid a salary or a commission?

Recently, one sales manager reported a customer who said he did not want Muslims calling on him. Another sales manager said when she and her salesperson (another woman) sat down with a buyer (a male), the buyer had pornography on his computer monitor. Do those sales managers assign new salespeople to the accounts? Or do they "fire" the customer? If the customer was to be fired, the salesperson would lose commission. Yet in both instances, the managers said they fired the customer, an action that both salespeople were happy with, and they were reassured that the loss of the sale wouldn't be held against them. The loss of the commission was worth it.

In sales, several laws apply that also apply in other areas of marketing but are more prominent in sales. For example, the Uniform Commercial Code (UCC) determines when a sale is a sale. Typically, a sale is a sale when the product is delivered and accepted by the buyer. In most instances, the customer can cancel the order with no penalty unless accepted. Sales managers have to be aware of such laws in order to avoid creating policies that can be illegal.

Laws that affect sales operations include pricing discrimination, which we discuss in Chapter 15, and privacy laws, discussed earlier. In addition, laws regarding hiring practices, workplace safety, and others can affect sales managers. If global sales situations arise, the Federal Corrupt Practices Act—which prohibits bribery and other practices that might be culturally acceptable elsewhere but that are illegal in the United States—comes into play.

For these reasons, sales managers should develop close working relationships with the human resources department. These professionals, along with the legal department, are charged with staying abreast of legal changes that influence management practice.

### KEY TAKEAWAY

Salespeople are, for the most part, caring, ethical professionals. They do face unique ethical challenges because of their job, including how to handle unethical requests from customers and making sure that they know and follow all company policies for interacting with customers. American salespeople have the added constraint that what's illegal in the United States is illegal for them in other countries because of the Foreign Corrupt Practices Act, even if the behavior in question is acceptable to those countries' laws and practices.

Sales managers have all the usual management concerns, such as fair hiring practices. According to the Federal Sentencing Guidelines, managers also have to develop policies and practices that codify ethical behaviors, train salespeople on the ethics policies, and ensure that the policies are followed. In addition, sales managers have to be aware of laws such as the Universal Commercial Code and others that govern sales transactions.

### REVIEW QUESTIONS

1. Do salespeople deserve the image or negative stereotype? Why or why not?
2. Do ethics get in the way of success in sales? Why or why not?
3. What safeguards do companies enact to ensure ethical behavior among salespeople and sales managers?

# 5. INTEGRATING SALES AND MARKETING

**LEARNING OBJECTIVES**

1. Identify the ways in which the marketing function supports the sales function.
2. Describe how the sales group of a company can support its marketing efforts.

Traditionally, sales and marketing are like oil and water—the departments don't mix well. Salespeople are typically among the highest paid employees in an organization. At the national printing company Moore-Wallace, for example, salespeople are five of the seven top-paid employees, with the CEO coming in at number three and the CFO at number five. As a result, jealousy can occur.

University of Georgia professor Tom Leigh was consulting with an organization when he asked salespeople to describe marketing. One salesperson said the marketing department was a black hole that sucked in money and gave nothing back. In the same company, a marketing manager described salespeople as selfish glad-handers who often skated on the wrong side of ethics. Unfortunately, these perceptions exist at too many organizations.

## 5.1 What Marketing Does for Sales

A firm's sales and marketing groups can work well together. We'll focus first on how marketing managers help salespeople.

### Marketing Shortens the Sales Cycle

A company's marketing activities include creating advertising and promotional campaigns, participating in trade shows, and preparing collateral. **Collateral** is printed or digital material salespeople use to support their message. It can consist of brochures, position papers, case studies, clinical studies, market studies, and other documents.

**collateral**

Printed or digital material, such as brochures, position papers, case studies, clinical studies, market studies, or other documents created by marketing professionals.

Salespeople use collateral to support their claims. Although a pharmaceutical rep selling a drug might claim it works faster than competing medications, a clinical study would carry more weight. If such a study existed, the drug maker's marketing department would prepare a brochure to give to doctors that highlight those findings.

**FIGURE 13.14**

This "sell sheet" for a color photocopier is an example of collateral used by the salespeople who work for Konical-Minolta Business Services (KMBS). Collateral is printed or digital material salespeople use to support their messages.

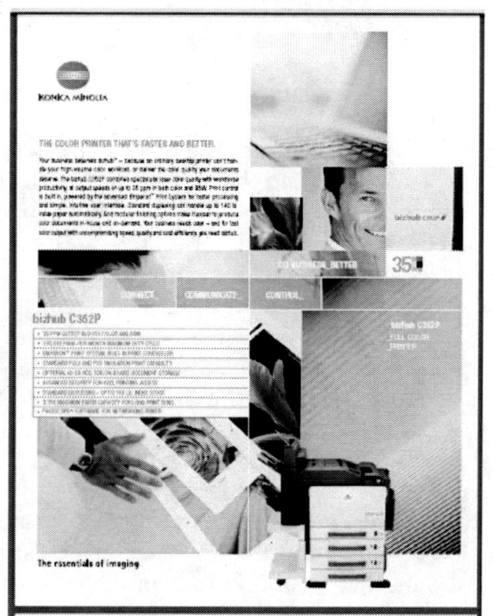


*Source: Konical-Minolta Business Systems, used with permission.*

Traditionally, firms have used their marketing groups to create awareness for their offerings and brand names through advertising. Brand awareness opens doors for salespeople. Few businesspeople sit in their offices hoping a salesperson will drop by. They are too busy to entertain every salesperson who walks in! But when a salesperson does come by from a well-known company, the businessperson is far more likely to be courteous and listen, however briefly, to see if there is some value in continuing the conversation.

**lead management**

The process of identifying and qualifying leads in order to capture new business.

**closed-loop lead management systems**

Information systems that track sales leads from the point at which the marketer identifies them to the point at which they are closed.

Marketing professionals also support salespeople by providing them with lead management. **Lead management** is the process of identifying and qualifying leads in order to grow new business. **Closed-loop lead management systems** are information systems that are able to track leads all the way from the point at which the marketer identifies them to when they are closed. Figure 13.15 illustrates the process and shows how marketing groups use the information to evaluate which of their activities are earning their companies the biggest bang for their buck.

**FIGURE 13.15** How a Closed-Loop Management System Works

A closed-loop lead management system can result in better investment decisions for marketing managers because they can learn what marketing actions shorten sales cycles and create more sales.

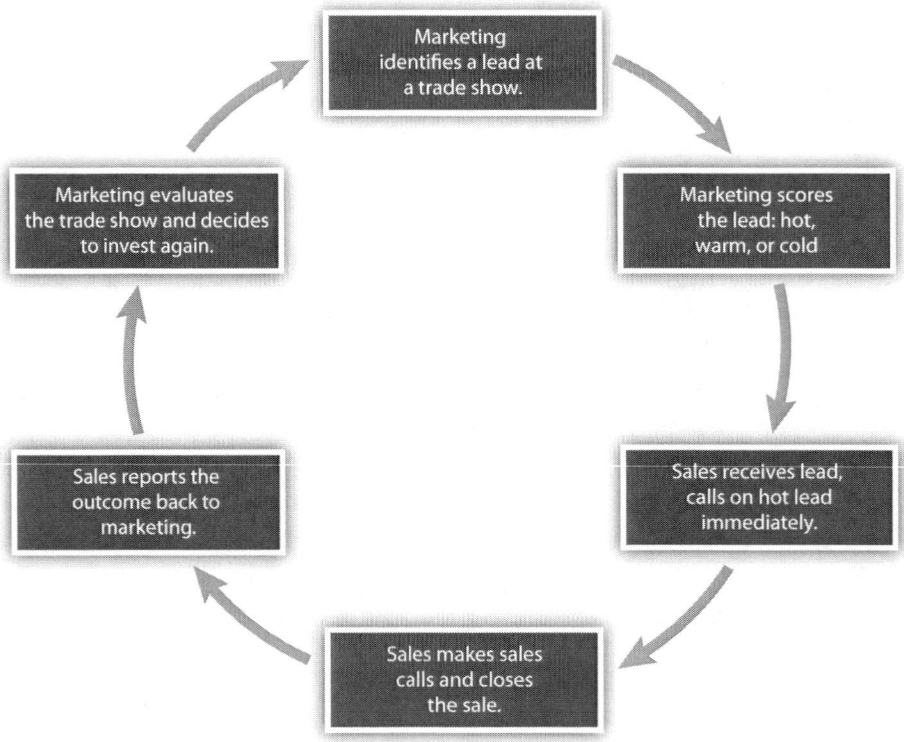


Unfortunately, many companies lack such a system. So in many cases, marketing personnel identify leads, turn them over to sales representatives, and that's the last they hear of them. Was the lead a good one, and did it ultimately lead to a purchase? Was the trade show that produced the lead worth the money spent attending it? These companies don't know. Closing the loop (meaning closing the feedback loop to marketing) gives marketing personnel insight into what works and what doesn't.

Ram Ramamurthy is a marketing professional for Sri-IIST, a company that has a closed-loop lead management system. Ramamurthy met Frank Zapata, a potential customer, at an industry trade show held annually in Las Vegas and gave Zapata a demonstration of his company's new offering, a software service called DG Vault. So when Curtis Hamm, the Sri-IIST salesperson who handles Zapata's account, followed up on the lead, he knew that Zapata had already seen the product. Instead of two or three sales calls to build interest in DG Vault, Hamm only needed to ask Zapata to gather all the appropriate personnel together to review the service, and then present its financial benefits to Zapata's CFO. Because of the meeting at the trade show, at least two stages in the sales cycle were eliminated. After Hamm closed the sale, he also closed the loop, providing feedback to Ramamurthy about any lingering questions Zapata may have had. Using that feedback, Ramamurthy can strengthen the next trade show presentation.

### Marketing Improves Conversion Ratios by Scoring Leads

Marketing groups also help their firms' salespeople improve their conversion ratios by scoring the leads they send them. **Lead scoring** is a process by which marketing personnel rate the leads to indicate whether a lead is hot (ready to buy now), warm (going to buy soon), or cold (interested but with no immediate plans to buy). As you can imagine, someone who has had a conversation at a trade show with a company representative, seen a demonstration, and answered questions about her budget, authority, need, and time, is close to being a prospect already. The more hot leads you put into the sales cycle, the more conversions to prospects and customers you can expect.

**lead scoring**

The process of rating leads based on the readiness of potential buyers to purchase products.

Lead scoring is not just a function of asking questions, however. A potential customer who visits your company's Web site, downloads a case study about how a product solved certain problems for a customer, and then clicks a link on a follow-up e-mail to watch an online demo of the offering has shown a significant amount of interest in the product. True, the lead has not answered questions concerning BANT. The buyer's behavior, though, indicates a strong interest—a much stronger interest than someone who clicked a link in an e-mail and only watched a portion of the demo.

When should marketing pass a lead on to sales? If the lead was generated at a trade show, then the salesperson should get the lead immediately. The people and organizations designated in Leads generated through other means, however, might be targeted to receive additional marketing messages before being passed along to a salesperson. Closed-loop lead management systems provide marketing managers with the information they need to know when to pass the lead along and when more marketing conversations are effective.

Improving conversions is not just a matter of finding more hot leads, however. Marketing personnel can improve salespeople's conversions by providing materials that help buyers make good decisions. Advertising, a company's Web site, activities at trade shows, and collateral can all help, and in the process, improve a sales force's conversion ratios. To be sure, some educated buyers, once they have more information about a product, will realize they don't need or want it and will go no further. But this is better than their buying the product and becoming angry when it fails to meet their expectations.

## 5.2 What Sales Does for Marketing

Without the help of their firms' salespeople, marketers would be at a serious disadvantage. Salespeople talk to customers every day. They are the "eyes and ears" of their companies. More than anyone else in an organization, they know what customers want.

### Salespeople Communicate Market Feedback

Salespeople are responsible for voicing their customers' ideas and concerns to other members of the organization. After all, if marketing managers are going to create collateral to educate them, they need to know what they need and want in the way of information. That knowledge comes from salespeople. How the information is conveyed, though, varies from situation to situation and company to company.

**Audio Clip**

**Interview with Ted Schulte**

Ted Schulte describes the relationship between sales and marketing at Boston Scientific.

Accenture, the management consulting firm, engages in projects with clients that cost hundreds of thousands of dollars, if not millions. After each sale is concluded, the account management team reviews the process in excruciating detail, win or lose. Questions such as "Did we have the right information to give to the client at the right time?" or "Were our offerings aligned with their needs?" are answered. After the review, executives then decide whether the company needs to produce additional marketing material to support the offering, create new offerings, or follow up on any other ideas generated by the review.

By contrast, KMBS salespeople sell copiers and printers that range from $5,000 to $150,000. A KMBS sale generally isn't as large as an Accenture sale, but KMBS has many more sales going on at any given time than Accenture does. The sheer volume of sales at KBMS makes it harder for salespeople to get the information related to those sales to the company's decision makers. For that reason, KMBS uses CRM software to track all its prospects and their key buying criteria. If the sale is lost, the reasons for it can be entered into the software, as well as information about the competing product the buyer purchased. Marketing personnel then use this information to improve KBMS's sales efforts.

**FIGURE 13.16**

This elegant sushi bar is actually part of a trade show booth used by Durcon, a company that manufactures impermeable countertop. The elegance of the countertop, with its black and white design, reflects a key sales message the marketing manager responsible for the exhibit gathered from Durcon's salespeople. Specifically, the salespeople wanted buyers to see how Durcon's product could be customized for any elegant décor requirement.

*Source: Durcon, Inc., used with permission.*

Astute marketing professionals, however, do not rely totally on CRM software to understand what makes markets tick. As we have explained, they also spend time with real customers and with salespeople. Andrea Wharton, a marketing executive with Alcatel, is responsible for her company's presence at trade shows. Wharton spends a great deal of time talking to salespeople in order to find out what messages are effective, and she uses that information to create Alcatel's exhibit booths for trade shows. She then works in the booth at the shows so she can talk directly with customers and get their reactions firsthand.

Changing the offering can be the outcome of what occurs when salespeople convey information provided by their customers. Perhaps customers are asking for additional product features, faster delivery, or better packing to reduce the number of damaged products shipped. The fast-food chain Wendy's provides us with an example. When Wendy's began testing the idea of offering salads in its restaurants, it had a problem. Previously, the restaurant had only packaged food in paper products such as cardboard. Plastic was never used. The company had made a commitment to environmental sustainability and not using plastic was a point of pride for the organization.

For help, Wendy's turned to the food-packaging company Pak-Sher. Wendy's Pak-Sher sales representative could have pulled a number of different products from Pak-Sher's shelves that would have worked *marginally* well for Wendy's salads, but he knew more than that was needed. He assembled a team of packaging engineers, and they visited Wendy's test kitchens. Together with the Wendy's product developers, the Pak-Sher engineers created the plastic packaging Wendy's "Garden Sensations" salads are sold in. While the plastic packaging required Wendy's to reevaluate its position on the use of plastics, Pak-Sher engineers also incorporated recycled material to support Wendy's sustainability goals. Pak-Sher changed its offering to meet the sustainability desires of its customer.

In this instance, the salesperson did not carry the voice of the customer back to the company so much as carry the company directly to the customer. Managing the collaboration in new product design is often the function of salespeople when products are customized. For example, Tim Pavlovich is a salesperson for Dell, but what he sells are called "appliances." These appliances are Dell computers that are installed inside of the customer's product. When you go to the kiosk at the airport and swipe a credit card in order to print your own boarding pass, chances are good that inside that kiosk is a Dell computer. Pavlovich works with Dell's engineers to make sure that the customer gets the right component or appliance; in turn, the engineers obtain valuable customer insights that translate into new Dell products.

**FIGURE 13.17**

Kiosks, like this one made for American Airlines, contain computers made by other companies such as Dell. Salespeople from Dell worked with the kiosk manufacturer to design in the best computer solution for the job. The kiosk manufacturer's salespeople then worked with American Airlines to provide the hardware and software solutions.

*Source: American Airlines, used with permission.*

### Salespeople Monitor the Competition

Salespeople also track the actions of their competitors, what customers buy, and enter the information into their firms' CRM systems. When marketing managers examine the marketing and sales efforts of their competitors, they are looking for their weak spots and strengths. The weak spots can be capitalized on, whereas the strengths need to be minimized.

More specifically, marketing managers need to know which companies are the strongest competitors based on the percentage of deals they win. Knowing this information can help a firm analyze its own competitive strengths and weaknesses and develop better marketing messages, sales strategies, offerings, or a combination of the three. Marketing managers also want to know which competitors the sales force most frequently finds itself competing against. If prospects consider the same competitor's product time and time again relative to your product, then the competitor's marketing and sales efforts are very similar to yours. In this case, you might need to develop some countertactics your salespeople can use to eliminate the product from the prospect's consideration set. Those tactics could include focusing on certain features only your product has or helping your buyers feel secure in the purchase by pointing out how long you've been in business.

**KEY TAKEAWAY**

Marketing personnel support a firm's sales force by shortening the sales cycle and improving conversions. The sales cycle is shortened whenever a marketing activity or marketing communication either eliminates a prospect's need to take a step in the sales cycle or speeds up the stages in the cycle. Marketing managers also create printed and digital materials called collateral designed to help persuade buyers.

Lead management and lead scoring are two other ways in which marketing professionals help their firm's salespeople. If a closed-loop lead management is used, marketing managers can determine what tactics and messages works best and make sound marketing investments.

In turn, salespeople support marketing personnel by communicating their customers' needs and ideas back to them. Salespeople are also the first to spot the actions of competing firms, including which companies and products are the strongest competitors. The marketing department then uses the information to create better marketing messages, sales strategies, offerings, or a combination of the three.

**REVIEW QUESTIONS**

1. What marketing activities support salespeople, and how does that support help them? Be specific.
2. What do salespeople do to support marketing managers? Be specific.
3. What is a closed-loop lead management and what are its benefits to salespeople?

# 6. OUTSOURCING THE SALES FUNCTION

**LEARNING OBJECTIVES**

1. **Identify the primary types of outsourcing salespeople.**
2. **Characterize the strengths and weaknesses of outsourcing sales groups.**

Some companies outsource certain sales functions. In this section, we'll introduce several types of outsourced salespeople, as well as the reasons for and challenges associated with outsourcing various sales activities.

## 6.1 Types of Outsourced Salespeople

A company can outsource part or all of the sales cycle. When a company hires a call center to make phone calls and set up appointments, it is outsourcing only the lead-to-suspect conversion portion of the sales cycle. In other words, every appointment the center sets up would be with a suspect. The suspect-to-prospect and prospect-to-customer conversions could then be the responsibility of either the outsourcer or another type of sales organization it hires for that purpose.

**Independent agents** are salespeople who are not employees of the company. They set their own hours, determine their own activities, and for the most part, manage themselves. Typically, they are paid on a straight commission basis—that is, based only on the revenues they generate for the company. Sometimes, however, they receive base pay, too. Independent agents often sell competing products from competing companies and are common in insurance markets. In other industries, agents are less likely to sell for competing companies. From the buyer's point of view, an independent agent representing multiple products lines should mean the buyer is in a better position to find the best offering with the least amount of hassle.

**independent agents**

Independent salespeople a company hires to sell its products. Independent agents set their own hours, determine their own activities, and for the most part, manage themselves.

**manufacturer's representative**

A type of independent agent who represents manufacturers. Typically, the person represents noncompeting manufacturers that sell complementary products.

A **manufacturer's representative** is an agent that sells a manufacturer's product. Typically, they don't sell competing products; rather, they sell complementary products—products that the same buyer wants to purchase. So for example, an agent that sells bathroom faucets for one manufacturer might sell bathroom towel rods and mirrors for another manufacturer. When a company hires a manufacturer's rep, it does so because the rep is already selling to the desired market. Buyers are more willing to see the rep because of the broad array of products he or she offers.

We discussed distributors in Chapter 8. Distributors often have salespeople who complete the entire sales cycle. Recall that distributors receive and manage inventory. However, they may or may not take title to the inventory before reselling it. Industrial distributors often employ both field salespeople, who call on customers where they are located, and employ inside salespeople, who may sell products by phone or by e-mail at the distributors' locations as well as handle customers who come to those locations. Distributors are like manufacturer's representatives in that they can sell offerings from multiple manufacturers. Some distributors are exclusive, meaning they sell the products of only one manufacturer.

## 6.2 Advantages and Disadvantages of Outsourcing

Outsourcing some of its sales efforts can provide a producer with several advantages. We've already mentioned a few, such as gaining access to more buyers because the organizations and people to which the company has outsourced the work sells a broader array of products. Having a broad array to choose from is more desirable from a buyer's perspective. Moreover, outsourced salespeople have existing relationships with the buyers that can be leveraged. Thus, entering new markets, such as new product markets or new countries, via distributors, independent agents, or manufacturer's representatives can increase the speed at which the company's offerings penetrate a market. These people and organizations also possess key market information and understand competitors and their strategies—information marketers can leverage.

In terms of a company's costs, outsourcing can be less expensive. The company that outsources the work doesn't bear the responsibility and expense of training the salespeople, except to inform them about the company's products. In addition, because the salespeople often work on a straight commission basis, the company only pays them when they sell its products.

The disadvantages of outsourcing can be boiled down to one word: control. Distributors, manufacturer's representatives, and agents are independent. They can decide what to sell and when to sell it. Unlike an employee who can be required to offer your product, they can choose to offer a customer a competing product or simply a different product than the one you sell. Nor can you force them to make sales calls. If it is a beautiful day and the golf course beckons, you may find your rep somewhere on the links.

**spiffs**

A word that originally meant "special promotion incentive funds" and now is used for any short-term bonus payments companies use to encourage salespeople to sell certain products.

To deal with control issues, companies often create incentive programs to motivate independent agents and manufacturer's representatives. Attractive commissions are more likely to get your product mentioned on every call. So are spiffs. **Spiffs** (a term that began as an acronym for *special promotion incentive funds*) are short-term bonus payments companies use to encourage salespeople to sell certain products. Also keep in mind that salespeople want to pitch products that are easy to sell and have short sales cycles. Why? Because they get rewarded for making sales. To the extent you can shorten a product's sales cycle and increase their conversions, you will gain their attention, time, and effort.

In addition to creating incentives for independent salespeople, a company will usually employ a sales manager to work with independent them. The sales manager's job is about selling as much as it is about managing, though. The manager has to constantly sell the agents on selling the company's offerings, and provide them with product information and tips that help them do so.

Finally, just as they listen to their own sales forces, good marketing professionals pay attention to what the independent salespeople and organizations they work with are saying. Not only can marketing managers create better strategies by doing so, they will create strategies that get used. In other words, the salespeople will be more likely to support those strategies with their own efforts because they believe in them.

**KEY TAKEAWAY**

Outsourcing the sales function can be done through distributors, independent agents, and manufacturers' representatives, as well as other types of sales organizations. The entire sales cycle can be outsourced or only parts of it. Outsourcing can cost less and requires less investment than a company-employed sales force. Moreover, independent agents, distributors, and manufacturers' representatives often have established relationships that make it easier for a company to enter and penetrate new markets.

Outsourcing the sales function(s) means that a company will lose some control over its sales activities. To counteract that loss of control, companies try to devise attractive compensation schemes, as well as effective marketing strategies for the independent sales organizations and people with whom they work. Companies also hire sales managers to manage the relationships with the outsourced sales staff.

**REVIEW QUESTIONS**

1. Which parts of the sales cycle can be outsourced and to whom?
2. When does outsourcing make the most sense? The least sense? Why?
3. What can marketers do to make outsourced sales functions more likely to succeed?

# 7. DISCUSSION QUESTIONS AND ACTIVITIES

**DISCUSSION QUESTIONS**

1. As a customer, would it be important for you to know how your salesperson was paid? Why or why not?
2. Should salespeople be responsible for handling all their customers' complaints or should customers be told to call the departments responsible for the complaints? Explain your answer.
3. What impact would a service-dominant logic approach have on how you craft sales strategy?
4. Assume you sell plumbing supplies via a distributor that sells to retailers.
    a. What can you do to shorten the distributor's sales cycle? To improve its conversions?
    b. Assume you are the distributor and you have five salespeople working for you. Two call on plumbing companies and large construction companies at job sites, whereas the other three work as salespeople in your warehouse. What can you do to shorten the sales cycle of each group? How might your efforts affect the performance each group differently?
5. Assume you invented a new plastic-shaping technology that allows plastic products to be manufactured much more cheaply. When you talk to manufacturers, though, they are skeptical because the new method is so radically different from any technology they have ever used before.
    a. What do you think the sales cycle for the technology would look like? What would the most important step of the sales cycle be? Why?
    b. What type of sales force would you utilize and why?
    c. What marketing activities could help you shorten the sales cycle and how?
6. In many organizations, marketing and sales do not get along very well. Describe what you would expect to be the results in an organization such as this.
7. Based on this chapter, what are three questions you would want to ask in a job interview if you were interviewing for an entry-level marketing position?
8. Salespeople are often viewed with disdain by the general public. What has this chapter taught that could change those perceptions?

## ACTIVITIES

1. Contact a salesperson and ask if you can spend a half-day observing sales calls. Whether you are able to observe or not, ask these questions: What are the segments within that salesperson's territory? How do they make decisions and what are the key sales activities?
2. Contact a professional who works with salespeople. This exercise can be done with physicians who have reps call on them, professors who have sales reps call on them, as well as professional purchasing agents. What do they think of salespeople and the value that these professionals get from their salespeople? What separates the good salespeople from the ones that are not so good?

# CHAPTER 14
# Customer Satisfaction, Loyalty, and Empowerment

**customer empowerment**
Providing tools that enable customers to take control or influence marketing.

The marketing concept, described in Chapter 1, reminds us that the customer should be at the center of a firm's activities and that the company that thrives is the one that serves customers' needs better than the competition. Yet often it is the customer who is most adept at serving the customer's needs. Consumers being able to take control of the marketing activities aimed at them is what **customer empowerment** is about. Today, technology is making it more possible for the customer to do exactly that. In a recent survey, the chief marketing officers of 250 top companies were asked about the key factors that influence the performance of their companies. The officers' response? A company's ability to interact and respond to its customers as well as empower them.[1]

Research shows that customer empowerment is a function of three things: creating feedback channels that are easy and widely available, asking for and encouraging feedback about products, and enabling customers to participate in the design of products. In Chapter 5, we discussed how customers can participate in the design of products, or offerings. In this chapter, we focus on those ubiquitous feedback channels, as well as strategies to solicit and encourage feedback.

Take JCPenney, for example. You might think that a company as large as JCPenney would be unable to give customers the ability to create their own types of shopping experiences—that standardizing the products and services they receive would be necessary. But JCPenney is an excellent example of how a firm can use the Internet and other technology to engage its customers and provide them with more control over the products and marketing communications they receive.

**Audio Clip**

**Interview with Laura Carros**
Listen to an interview with Laura Carros, a JCPenney executive responsible for many of the company's customer initiatives.

## 1. CUSTOMER COMMUNITIES

### LEARNING OBJECTIVES

1. **Understand strategies involving online and personal forms of influencer marketing.**
2. **Relate influencer marketing to other forms of social communities and marketing strategies.**

If you are about to buy a new high-definition television, where do you go to learn about which one is best? Like many buyers, you probably turn to the Internet and visit sites such as Epinions.com or ConsumerSearch.com. Do you want to learn about the products of a specific retailer? More than 4,700 JCPenney products have been reviewed on Epinions.

**word of mouth**

The passing of information and opinions verbally.

**buzz**

Word of mouth that includes blogs, articles, and other forms of promotion.

The point is that consumers talk. They talk to each other, and they post their thoughts and opinions online. **Word of mouth**, or the passing of information and opinions verbally, has a powerful influence on purchasing decisions. You rely on word of mouth when you register for classes. For example, you ask other students about which professors are best and how hard their classes are. If you have no one to ask, you can look at online sites such as ratemyprofessors.com.

**Buzz** refers to the amount of word of mouth going on in a market. However, in addition to traditional word of mouth, buzz includes blogs, articles, and other information about an offering.

Companies try to create buzz about their products by sending press releases, holding events, offering free samples, writing blogs, or releasing podcasts. Some marketing managers actually spend time "trolling" the Web looking for postings about their products. If a negative posting appears to be a legitimate complaint, then the marketing manager can take action to fix the customer's problem, and future complaints of the same nature can be avoided.

## 1.1 Influencer Panels

**influencer marketing**

Targeting individuals known to influence others so they will use their influence in the marketer's favor.

A marketing strategy being used increasingly often is **influencer marketing**, or targeting people known to influence others so that they will use their influence in the marketer's favor. These influencers are the lead users we discussed in the chapter on designing offerings. If you spend some time on Procter & Gamble's (P&G) Crest toothpaste Web site, you might be given a chance to complete a survey. (Someone who is very interested in dental care is more likely to take the survey.) The survey asks if you talk about dental care products, if you research such products, and if you influence others. These questions and questions like them are used to identify influencers. P&G then provides influencers with product samples and opportunities to participate in market research. The idea is that new offerings should be cocreated with influencers because they are more likely to be both lead users, early adopters of new offerings, and influence other people's decisions to buy them.

**community**

A form of a social group that centers its attention around a particular brand or product category.

**social network**

A community or social group that centers its attention on a particular brand or product category.

That was the idea behind JCPenney's Ambrielle lingerie community. Carros and other JCPenney employees on the Ambrielle marketing team devised a strategy of identifying women who would be willing to join a special community. A **community**, in the marketing sense, is a social group that centers its attention on a particular brand or product category. Another term for a community is a **social network**. The social network for Ambrielle lingerie is illustrated in Figure 14.1.

**FIGURE 14.1** A Social Network

Each circle represents a person in the social network, and the arrows represent the ties between them. You can see that some are JCPenney customers as represented by the arrows between the company (the star) and the individuals. Others are not, but are in contact with JCPenney customers.

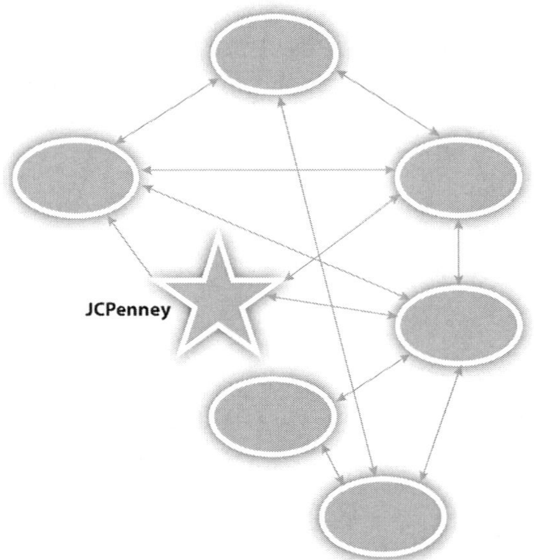

**Audio Clip**

**Interview with Laura Carros**

Listen to hear more about how Laura Carros created the Ambrielle community.

Some communities are organized by companies. For example, the Harley Owners Group (HOG), a club for Harley motorcycle owners, was organized by Harley-Davidson. But many communities spring up naturally, without any help from a marketer. A local arts community is an example. In the case of Ambrielle, JCPenney created and manages the group; in the case of the HOG, Harley-Davidson manages the group in conjunction with its members.

Another difference between the Ambrielle community and HOG is that the Ambrielle community is only composed of influencers. By contrast, anyone who owns a Harley can be a member of HOG. Ambrielle influencers provide feedback about products to JCPenney and take an active role in designing the company's offerings. In other words, the influencers participate regularly in marketing research activities. Another term for this type of community is an **influencer panel**.

**influencer panel**

A special type of community that participates regularly in marketing research activities.

## Organizing and Managing Influencer Panels

Table 14.1 lists the different characteristics used to qualify members of an influencer panel. Note that there are multiple types of influencers represented in the Ambrielle community. Because JCPenney has also gathered lifestyle, demographic, and psychographic information about them, the firm has a fairly complete picture of each member. This information is invaluable because JCPenney can use the knowledge to segment the group more precisely. Thus, when the company test markets communications or offerings with the group, it can gain a better understanding of how well those efforts will work with different types of consumers.

**TABLE 14.1** Characteristics Used to Qualify the Members of Influencer Panels

| Characteristic | Definition |
|---|---|
| Active Influencer | Willing to tell others, but more important, others listen and act on the influencer's opinion. |
| Interested | Has a greater intrinsic interest in the product category than the average user. |
| Heavy User | Actually uses or consumes the offering regularly, preferably more than the average user. |
| Loyal | Sticks to one brand when it works. Note, however, that this category could include someone who isn't loyal because the right offering meeting his or her needs hasn't yet been created. |
| Lead User | Willing to try new products and offer feedback. In some instances, it's possible to modify an offering to suit an individual consumer; when it is, you want lead users to suggest the modifications so you can see how and why they do so. |

An influencer panel does not necessarily become a community. If the communication that occurs is only between the marketer and the individual members of the panel, no community forms. The members must communicate with one another for a community to exist.

As a marketing professional, how do you find influencers? The answer is that they have to be actively recruited. As you learned earlier in the chapter, P&G surveys people looking at its Web sites. If you answer the survey questions in a way that shows you meet the criteria listed in Table 14.1, you might be asked to join a P&G panel. Another method is to ask a customer whose complaint you have just resolved to take a survey. After all, someone who has taken the time to complain might also be motivated to participate on a panel. Still another recruiting method is to send random surveys to households to identify people who would be good panel participants.

Once you create an influencer panel, you have to activate it. After all, influencers do not want to be singled out only to be ignored. However, marketing professionals should be able to answer the following three questions before they activate a panel:

1. **What do we want from the influencer panel?** Usually, companies want feedback on new offerings and new marketing communications, as well as active word-of-mouth promotions. Panelists need to know when you are merely testing a new offering versus introducing it to the marketplace. You don't want word of mouth about a new product that isn't yet ready to be sold.
2. **How much are the panel members willing to do?** Companies want to keep their panelists actively engaged, which requires asking how often they want to participate on the panel, as well as giving them the right to "opt out" of a particular activity if they must. In some instances, you may put out a general call for help, such as posting a notice on an online bulletin board that you need volunteers to test a product. Or, you might just simply send influencers product samples, ask

them to try them, and respond to a questionnaire. In addition, the processes by which they engage have to be easy for them to complete. For example, asking a lot of information up front makes the sign-up process more difficult. If all you need is an e-mail address, just ask for the e-mail address. Any additional information can be gathered later.

3. **What's in it for the panel members?** What do they get out of participating? They of course get to try free, new products that might improve their lives—or will one day improve their lives if a company heeds their advice. For many influencers, the product category is one that was already important to them. The chance to try a product before anyone else does and provide feedback to a manufacturer who has singled them out for their opinion might be all these people want.

## 1.2 Social Networking Sites and Other Social Media

**social networking site**

A communication medium for communities, or social networks.

As we have indicated, communities spring up naturally. Online, **social networking sites** like Facebook and MySpace are used to create communities. Everyone you are friends with on sites such as these are people that you already knew. The sites are simply the communication medium. What is interesting is that Facebook and other social networking sites can't tell the difference between close friends and acquaintances. From a marketing perspective, since each tie or relationship is treated the same, social networking sites provide interesting ways to reach people. One, perhaps not so interesting way, is as a broadcast medium for advertising. A company targets consumers by placing ads on a person's site based on what Facebook or MySpace knows about the person—just as ads are placed on a radio or television station and matched to certain audiences.

The more interesting way is by consumers sending other consumers links and other information. For example, when a marketer creates a Facebook or MySpace page for an offering such as a movie, a community can form around the movie. Then if you join the group that loves the movie, Facebook notifies all of your friends that you are promoting the movie. A community such as this might not be as enduring as the Ambrielle or HOG groups, but it serves its purpose—at least until the movie is old news and newer movies come out and get attention. When you become a "fan" of something like a movie, you are part of the buzz.

Marketers are looking at many ways to use Facebook and other social networking sites to create buzz. Facebook has a "gift-giving" application that allows people to give "gifts" to each other. The gifts are really just icons (pictures) within Facebook. Enter GiveReal, an online service that allows people to give one another real gifts online. GiveReal developed a promotion with Bombay Sapphire, a leading premium gin, and Facebook. The promotion allows Facebook users to give their friends electronic coupons (downloadable to a credit card) for mixed drinks that use Bombay Sapphire. These coupons can then be redeemed at restaurants and bars that accept credit cards.[2]

**viral marketing**

The spread of the company's message (like a virus) through a community.

One result of social networking is **viral marketing**, or the spread of the company's message (like a computer virus) through the community. Some companies have enhanced the viral marketing of their offerings with interactive Web sites that might feature, say, a game built around an offering. Consumers then e-mail their friends with links to the game or Web site. Examples include the viral campaign by Nine Inch Nails for its concept album, *Year Zero*. An online alternate reality game was created involving characters and situations drawn from the music on the album. The album and game were so popular that HBO has even considered creating a series around the dark, futuristic tale told on the album.

Blogs are one form of online communication that helps spread viral marketing messages. Some blogs are written by corporate marketing officers who "spin" the information. But blogs can be written by anyone. Blogs can serve as a "voice" for a community. For example, the chief executive of the National Thoroughbred Horseracing Association (the NASCAR of horseracing) writes a blog for the organization that is posted on its Web site. However, anyone can leave a comment on the blog. Blogs have become much more like dialog in a town hall meeting than a one-way marketing message.

Twitter is another application that facilitates viral marketing by enabling people to "follow" someone. When an organization or a person posts something on Twitter, the post—called a "tweet"—is sent as a text message to all followers of that organization or person. Ashton Kutcher made headlines by being the first person to collect a million followers. However, the first company to generate a million dollars in revenue through Twitter is probably Dell. Dell uses Twitter to communicate special deals via its tweets—offers that are extremely limited. Followers can then contact the company to place their orders for the products. Dell estimated that in 2009, it would earn more than $3 million through Twitter.[3]

Communities are not just a consumer phenomenon, nor are they a function of technology. In the B2B world, communities can be formalized into users' groups. For example, the customers of Teradata, a data warehousing company, have formed a users group. Annually, the group holds a conference in which members talk about how they use Teradata's products. So others users might learn from her company's experience, Laura Carros spoke at one of the conferences about how using CRM technology and Teradata's data warehousing function helped JCPenney create the Ambrielle community.

**Social media** is a catchall phrase for the online channels of communication that build communities. Social media includes social networking sites, blogs, podcasts, wikis, vlogs (video blogs), and other Internet-based applications that enable consumers to contribute content. Social media spending for marketing purposes doubled in 2008 and continued to rise in 2009 despite the poor economy. In fact, Forester, a respected research company, predicts spending to top over $50 billion in 2009![4]

**FIGURE 14.2**

Ashton Kutcher was the first person to have over a million followers on Twitter.

*Source: Wikimedia Commons.*

**social media**

A catchall phrase for online channels of communication that build communities including social networking sites, blogs, podcasts, wikis, vlogs (video blogs), and other Internet-based applications that enable consumers to contribute content.

**KEY TAKEAWAY**

Customer communities form around social networks, which marketers can use to both promote offerings and gather market information. Companies create influencer panels that provide insight into effective offerings and provide word of mouth.

**REVIEW QUESTIONS**

1. Is an influencer panel the same as a community?
2. If a company doesn't create an influencer panel, are there still influencers? If so, who are they influencing and how?
3. What Internet tools, other than influencer panels, create word of mouth?

# 2. LOYALTY MANAGEMENT

**LEARNING OBJECTIVES**

1. **Understand the value of customer loyalty.**
2. **Distinguish attitudinal loyalty from behavioral loyalty.**
3. **Describe the components of a successful loyalty program.**

It's 8:00 p.m. and you're starving. You open the refrigerator and find a leftover chicken breast, half an onion, and some ketchup. But what can you do with these ingredients? You could search online for recipes that contain them, or you could post a question about what to do with them at a Web site like Kraft.com.

Companies like Kraft build Web sites such as Kraft.com in order to create the types of communities we discussed earlier. If you posted your question at Kraft.com, you might have an experience like one woman did—in 24 hours, 853 people viewed the question, and she had 22 answers to choose from. Another question had 3,341 viewers over 10 days. Why has Kraft's Web marketing team worked so hard to create an environment in which people can do this?

One important reason is loyalty. Kraft wants loyal customers—customers who buy Kraft products instead of other brands at every opportunity, who recommend its products to their friends, and are willing to pay a little more to get Kraft quality. Early research on loyalty showed that loyal customers were less expensive to market to, more willing to pay a premium for a particular brand, more willing to try new products under the brand name, more likely to recommend the brand to their friends, and more willing to overlook a problem related to the brand.[5] That said, more recent research shows that the benefits that come from loyal customers are not automatic and that it takes careful management for those benefits to be sustained.[6]

**behavioral loyalty**

The degree to which a customer habitually buys a product and does not respond to competitors' offerings.

**attitudinal loyalty**

The degree to which a customer prefers or likes a brand.

Loyalty has two dimensions. One dimension of loyalty is **behavioral loyalty**, meaning that the customer buys the product regularly and does not respond to competitors' offerings. The second dimension is **attitudinal loyalty**, which is the degree to which the customer prefers or likes the brand.

## 2.1 Behavioral Loyalty

Most marketers would be happy with behavioral loyalty because it does, after all, result in sales. Yet behavioral loyalty doesn't mean that the customer is immune to your competitors' offerings. Nor does it mean the customer is willing to pay more for your brand. For example, a business person might regularly book trips on American Airlines because it flies to the one or two destinations the traveler has to visit regularly. But a lower price on another airline or one scheduled at a more convenient time might persuade the flier to switch to another carrier.

Habitual purchases are a form of behavioral loyalty. Comparison shopping takes time and effort, so buyers are often willing to forego looking for substitute products. Habitual purchases are commonly made for low-involvement offerings. You might regularly purchase a Coke at a drive-thru restaurant near your house rather than take the time, energy, and gasoline to look for a Coke that's cheaper.

Marketers engage in many activities to both encourage and discourage behavioral loyalty. Loyalty programs, such as an airline offering travelers frequent-flier miles, can encourage behavioral loyalty. But coupons and other special price promotions can break behavioral loyalty patterns. We'll discuss loyalty programs in more detail later in this chapter.

## 2.2 Attitudinal Loyalty

As we explained, attitudinal loyalty refers to how much someone likes a brand and is willing to act on that preference. Keep in mind, however, that a person's *willingness* to act on a preference doesn't necessarily mean she will purchase your product: If you sell Ferraris, and she is unemployed, she might be unable to afford one.

**cause-related marketing**

When a company supports a nonprofit organization in some way in order to generate positive public relations.

Cause-related marketing, which we discussed in Chapter 12, can foster attitudinal loyalty among a company's community of customer. Companies that engage in **cause-related marketing** choose causes that are important to the customer communities in which they operate. American Airlines sponsors the Susan G. Komen Foundation, an organization that is working to cure breast cancer. KitchenAid sponsors Cook for the Cure, which also benefits the foundation. Both companies support breast cancer awareness because the cause is important to their female customers.

Note, however, that cause-related marketing should be sincere. You can probably quickly tell when a person or organization is insincere. So can your customers. Sincerity also breeds trust. For example, when Eunice Azzani volunteered for the San Francisco AIDS Foundation, she did so because the cause was important to her and Korn/Ferry International, the executive search firm for which she is a managing director. While working for the cause, Azzani met executives with Mervyn's, Wells Fargo, and other major corporations who later engaged her company to conduct executive searches. They knew they could trust her to do high-quality work and that she was sincere about her place in the community.[7]

Of course, there are many other methods of building attitudinal loyalty. As we mentioned, advertising can create feelings for a brand, as can sponsoring a sports team or cultural event. In the next section, we discuss loyalty programs, one way that companies try to manage both affective and behavioral dimensions of loyalty.

**FIGURE 14.3**

American Airlines is a Lifetime Promise Partner, a program designed to support breast cancer awareness and the Susan G. Komen Foundation. The company has painted Komen's signature pink ribbon on planes as a way to support the foundation. Companies support charities that are important to the communities in which they operate.

*Source: American Airlines, used with permission.*

**Audio Clip**

**Interview with Laura Carros**

Listen to Laura Carros describe some of the marketing efforts she uses to engage loyal customers.

## 2.3 Loyalty Programs

**Loyalty programs** are marketing efforts that reward a person or organization for frequent purchases and the consumption of offerings. For example, Lone Star Park's Star Player Rewards program awards members points for each dollar they spend at the track. The more points they earn, the better the prize is for which they can redeem their points.

**loyalty programs**

Marketing efforts that reward the frequent purchase and consumption of an offering.

**FIGURE 14.4**

Lone Star Park is a horseracing track in Grand Prairie, Texas. The park rewards frequent attendees through its Star Player Rewards program, which tracks members' purchases and bets. Members can also compete in special contests and participate in special events, such as being able to meet famous jockeys.

*Source: Lone Star Park, used with permission.*

The data a firm collects from a loyalty program can be very useful in terms of designing and improving the company's offerings. When members initially sign up for a loyalty program, they provide a great deal of demographic information to the organization. Their behavior can then be tracked as well. For example, Lone Star Park can determine who sits in what section of the track by what tickets members purchase, as well as where they purchase their refreshments or place their bets. The track can also determine members' preferences for food and drink products or services such as betting clerks and betting machines. When the track has nonracing events, such as a concert, the events can be promoted to

Star Players. Depending on how the members respond, additional offers can be made, or not made, to them.

Lone Star Park might also team up to create an offering with American Airlines. For example, the track and the airline could compare customer lists and determine which Star Players members are also members of American's AAdvantage frequent-flier program. These individuals could then be offered discounts on trips to Louisville, Kentucky, where the Kentucky Derby is held. Such an offer is called **cross-promotion marketing**. A cross-promotion can be used to introduce new marketing members to a community; in this case, Lone Star Park is introducing American to the horseracing community. The cross-promotion creates credibility for the new member, just as you are more likely to accept a recommendation from a friend.

**FIGURE 14.5**

The horse that came in second in this Lone Star Park race is owned by one of the authors of this textbook. Note the advertisers in the background of the photo. The advertisers want to reach the same community as Lone Star Park, and they want their products to become the products of choice for that community. As you can tell, advertising at the track isn't just about reaching eyeballs—it's about being viewed as a member of the community, which could result in greater brand loyalty among the community's customers.

**cross-promotion marketing**

A method in which two or more groups act together to reach potential customers.

## The Positive Effects of Loyalty Programs

When loyalty programs work, they result in one or more of the four effects of loyalty: the blocker effect, the spreader effect, the accelerator effect, and the longevity effect. We'll start by describing the longevity effect.

**FIGURE 14.6** The Positive Effects of Loyalty Programs

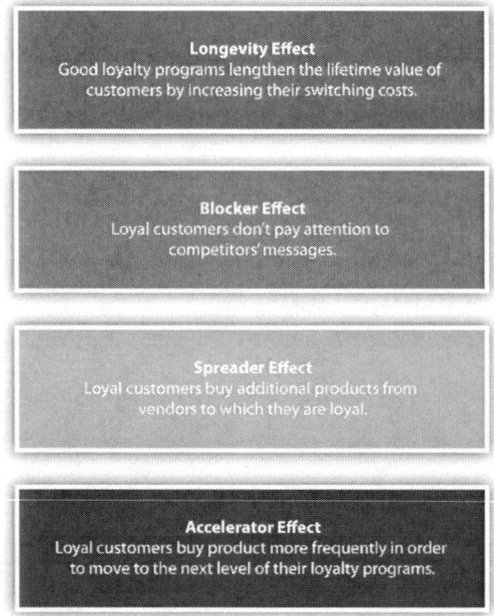


### The Longevity Effect

The **longevity effect** is lengthening the lifetime value of a customer. We discussed customer lifetime value (CLV) in earlier chapters. One result of a good loyalty program is that your buyers remain your customers for longer. Because a loyalty company has better information about its customers, it can create offerings that are more valuable to them and keep them coming back. Consider a loyalty program aimed at customers as they progress through their life stages. A grocery store might send diaper coupons to the mother of a new baby and then, five years later, send the mother coupons for items she can put in her child's school lunches.

**longevity effect**

The process of lengthening the a customer's lifetime value over time.

Loyalty programs also affect the longevity of customers by increasing their switching costs. **Switching costs** are the costs associated with moving to a new supplier. For example, if you are a member of a frequent-flier program, you might put up with some inconveniences rather than switching to another airline. So, if you are a member of American's AAdvantage program, you might continue to fly American even though it cancelled one of your flights, made you sit on a plane on the ground for two hours, and caused you to miss an important meeting. Rather than starting over with Continental's Elite Pass program, you might be inclined to continue to book your flights on American so you can take a free trip to Europe sooner.

**switching costs**

The costs associated with moving to a new supplier of an offering.

### The Blocker Effect

The blocker effect is related to switching costs. The **blocker effect** works this way: The personal value equation of a loyalty program member is enhanced because he or she doesn't need to spend any time and effort shopping around. And because there is no shopping around, there is no need for the member to be perceptive to competitors' marketing communications. In other words, the member of the program "blocks" them out. Furthermore, the member is less **deal-prone**, or willing to succumb to a special offer or lower price from a competitor.

**blocker effect**

A loyalty program that results in members blocking out marketing communications from competitors.

**deal-prone**

Willing to succumb to a special offer or lower price.

The blocker effect can be a function of switching costs—the costs of shopping around as well as the hassles of having to start a new program over. However, the effect can also be a function of *relevance*. Because the loyalty marketer has both information on whom the buyer is and data on what the buyer has already responded to, more relevant communications can be created and aimed at the buyer. In addition, because belonging to the program has value, any communication related to the program are already more relevant to the buyer.

### The Spreader Effect

The **spreader effect** refers to the fact that members of a loyalty program are more likely to try related products offered by the marketer. For example, an American Airlines AAdvantage member who also joins the company's Admiral's Club airport lounge creates additional revenue for the airline, as a does the member's purchase of a family vacation through American's Vacation services.

**spreader effect**

A loyalty program that results in buyers being more likely to try related products offered by a marketer.

The spreader effect becomes even more pronounced when a cross-promotion is added to the mix. Earlier we mentioned Lone Star Park might team with American to offer a trip package to the Kentucky Derby. Another example is Citibank offering you AAdvantage miles if you get a Citibank Visa card through American's AAdvantage program. Cross-promotions such as these encourage loyalty program members to try even more products from more producers.

### The Accelerator Effect

When rats running in a maze get closer to the cheese, they speed up. Like rats in a maze, consumers speed up, or accelerate, purchases when they are about to reach a higher award level in a loyalty program, called the **accelerator effect** of a loyalty program. In American's AAdvantage program, for example, a member gets "Platinum" status after flying sixty flights or fifty thousand miles. Platinum members get special awards, like more frequent upgrades to first class, boarding ahead of everyone else, not having to pay for luggage and other fees, and double mileage toward free flights. Someone who has fifty flights and just needs ten more to become Platinum will start to fly American more frequently until the Platinum level is reached. Then, American hopes that the other effects (blocker, spreader, etc.) will occur.

**accelerator effect**

The effect of a loyalty program that, as a consumer approaches the next level of benefits, the rate of consumer's purchases increases.

Companies can capitalize on the accelerator effect by making it easy for members to track their progress and notifying them when they are close to reaching subsequent levels. American helps its Advantage fliers track their progress by sending them monthly updates on their levels. Couple such a notification with a special offer, and a company is likely to see even greater acceleration. The accelerator effect can also be used with promotions that create short-term, loyal behavior. Pepsi created a promotion with Amazon in which purchasers could accumulate points toward free music downloads. The promotion, launched with a Justin Timberlake Super Bowl ad, was a knock-off of Coca-Cola's MyCokeRewards.com. Although they weren't formal loyalty programs, both promotions led to an accelerator effect as customers got close to the award levels they needed to redeem prizes.

## Criteria for Successful Loyalty Programs

Just having a loyalty program is no guarantee of success, though. Eight studies of more than a dozen grocery-store loyalty programs in the United States and Europe showed that five programs had no impact on the loyalty of customers, two increased sales but not profits, two had mixed results, and five had positive results.[8] There are, however, several characteristics of loyalty programs that can make them effective, each of which is discussed next.

### Good Performance by a Company

The first characteristic of an effective loyalty program is performance. No loyalty program can overcome a company's poor performance. Even the most loyal buyer can put up with subpar performance for only so long.

### Responsiveness by a Company

*Responsiveness* is how well a company can take customer information (such as complaints) and alter what they do to satisfy the customer. Loyal customers are more willing to complete surveys and participate in market research, but they expect companies to use the information wisely. For example, when customers complain, they expect their problems to be fixed and the company to use the information so that the same problems don't reoccur. Likewise, the members of influencer panels expect to be listened to. If you ignore their input, you are likely to alienate them, causing them to switch other brands.

A company's responsiveness—or lack thereof—also becomes evident to buyers when they spot a better offer. Precisely at that moment, they realize that the company that created the better offer was more responsive and worked harder to meet their needs.

### Shared Identity among Participants

Loyal customers are like sports fans—they wear their "team's" colors. That's why loyalty programs have names that sound prestigious, like Continental's "Elite Pass" program or American's "Executive Platinum" program. Loyal customers also want to be recognized for their loyalty. Hampton Inn, which is part of the Hilton family of hotels, is one company that could do a better of job of recognizing its customers—literally. One of the authors stays regularly at the same Hampton Inn, only to be greeted every time on arrival with the question, "Is this your first stay with us?" The author is not only a regular guest at that hotel but a member of Hilton Honors, the hotel's loyalty program. But apparently the Hampton Inn's reservation system doesn't provide that information to its front desk clerks. If you fail to recognize customers who are loyal, you are essentially telling them that their business isn't that important to you.

**FIGURE 14.7**

When customers stay regularly at the same hotel, welcoming them back is an example of recognizing their loyalty. Good loyalty programs allow service personnel to identify loyal customers so they can be given special treatment.

*© 2010 Jupiterimages Corporation*

### Clear Benefits

What are the benefits of being loyal? A loyalty program should make those benefits clear. For example, Continental Airlines has a special boarding lane for its Elite Pass members. Travelers who are not Elite Pass members can easily see the special treatment members receive. If the elements of scarcity and status can be created by a loyalty program, the benefits of belonging to it will be obvious to customers.

### Community Development

Finally, marketers who can put loyal customers together with other loyal customers are likely to build a community around the common experience of consumption. At Lone Star Park or American Airlines, common consumption is obvious—people are actually together. Building a community in which people don't actually consume goods and services together can be a bit more difficult, but recall that Kraft has done so with its online presence. Members of Kraft.com still share their experiences, their recipes, their questions, and their answers, thereby creating a sense of "we're in this together." Some of the postings might be related directly to Kraft products, whereas others might only be indirectly related. Nonetheless, they all provide Kraft with insight into what its customers are thinking. Meanwhile, its customers become more loyal as they participate on the Web site.

Keep in mind that a loyalty program isn't necessary to create loyalty. Lexus doesn't have a formal loyalty program. Yet studies show that Lexus owners are the most loyal luxury car buyers. Over half of all Lexus owners buy another Lexus. (The brand's slogan is "Once a Lexus buyer, always a Lexus buyer.") By contrast, Mercedes-Benz has a loyalty program, but only 40 percent of its buyers purchase another Mercedes.[9]

A company can also offer its customers loyalty benefits that are not a part of a formal loyalty program. For example, Mercedes-Benz gives loyal buyers an opportunity to suggest new features via a contest, for which there is no prize other than the recognition the winner gets because his idea was selected. And like many other car manufacturers, Mercedes offers owners special trade-in deals. The challenge with loyalty promotions that lie outside loyalty programs is collecting the information marketers need to target customers.

## KEY TAKEAWAY

Customer loyalty is both behavioral and attitudinal. Habitual purchases are a form of behavioral loyalty. Cause-related marketing can foster attitudinal loyalty among a company's community of customers, as can loyalty programs. Loyalty programs can have four positive effects: They can increase the longevity, or lifetime value, of customers; block competitors' marketing efforts; encourage customers to buy related offerings; and accelerate their purchases. Loyalty programs don't automatically create loyalty among customers, though. Loyalty is created when a company performs well, responds to its customers, identifies its loyal customers, makes the benefits of its loyalty program transparent (obvious), and when the firm builds a community among its customers.

**REVIEW QUESTIONS**

1. What are the benefits of having loyal customers? Why or how do those benefits occur?
2. What is the difference between loyalty and loyalty programs?
3. How can you create loyalty without having a loyalty program?

# 3. CUSTOMER SATISFACTION

**LEARNING OBJECTIVES**

1. **Understand satisfaction and satisfaction strategies.**
2. **Design a customer satisfaction measurement system.**
3. **Describe complaint management strategies.**

## 3.1 Customer Satisfaction Defined

What comes to mind when you hear someone say, "A satisfied customer"? Perhaps it is an image of someone smiling with the pride of knowing he got a good deal. Or perhaps it is the childlike look of happiness someone exhibits after purchasing a new pair of shoes that are just the right color. Whatever your picture of a satisfied customer is, **customer satisfaction** is typically defined as the feeling that a person experiences when an offering meets his or her expectations. When an offering meets the customer's expectations, the customer is satisfied.

**customer satisfaction**

The feeling that results when an offering meets a consumer's expectations.

Improving customer satisfaction is a goal sought by many businesses. In fact, some companies evaluate their salespeople based on how well they satisfy their customers; in other words, not only must the salespeople hit their sales targets, they have to do so in ways that satisfy customers. Teradata is one company that pays its salespeople bonuses if they meet their customer satisfaction goals.

Customer satisfaction scores have been relatively stable for the past few years as illustrated in Table 14.2. You might think that if increasing the satisfaction of customers were, indeed, the goal of businesses, the scores should show a steady increase. Why don't they? Maybe it's because just satisfying your customers is a *minimal* level of performance. Clearly customer satisfaction is important. However, it isn't a good predictor of a customer's future purchases or brand loyalty. For example, one study of customer satisfaction examined car buyers. Although the buyers rated their satisfaction levels with their purchases 90 percent or higher, only 40 percent of them purchased the same brand of car the next time around.[10]

**TABLE 14.2** Industry-Average Customer Satisfaction Scores, 2000–2008

| | 2000 | 2001 | 2002 | 2003 | 2004 | 2005 | 2006 | 2007 | 2008 |
|---|---|---|---|---|---|---|---|---|---|
| Appliances | 85 | 82 | 82 | 81 | 82 | 80 | 81 | 82 | 80 |
| Computers | 72 | 74 | 71 | 71 | 72 | 74 | 77 | 75 | 74 |
| Electronics | 83 | 81 | 81 | 84 | 82 | 81 | 80 | 83 | 83 |
| Cars | 80 | 80 | 80 | 80 | 79 | 80 | 81 | 82 | 82 |

Keep in mind, though, that satisfaction scores are a function of what the customer expected as well as what the company delivered. So the flat scores in Table 14.2 reflect rising customer expectations as well as improved products. In other words, the better products get, the more it takes to satisfy consumers.

There is also a downside to continuously spending more to satisfy your customers. Recent research shows that firms that do so can experience higher sales revenues. However, after the additional spending costs are factored in, the net profits that result are sometimes marginal or even negative. Nonetheless, satisfaction is not unimportant. A company's performance on key factors is critical both in terms of the loyalty and satisfaction it generates among its customers.[11]

## 3.2 Customer Satisfaction Strategies

So what or how much should you do to improve the satisfaction of your customer? If customer satisfaction can be defined as the feeling a person experiences when an offering meets his or her expectations, then there are two critical ways to improve customer satisfaction. The first is to establish appropriate expectations in the minds of customers. The second is to deliver on those expectations.

We know that dissatisfied customers are likely to tell many more friends about their negative experiences than satisfied customers are about good experiences. Why? Because there's more drama in unmet expectations. A story about met expectations—telling a friend about a night out that was average, for example—is boring. Jan Carlson, a former Scandinavian Airlines executive, was famous for promoting the concept of "delighted" customers. Carlson's idea was that delighting customers by overexceeding their expectations should result in both repeat business and positive word of mouth for a firm. The fact that stories about plain old satisfaction are boring is also why influencer communities, such as JCPenney's Ambrielle community, are so important. Influencers have new offerings to talk about, which are interesting topics, and other buyers want to know their opinions.

Establishing appropriate expectations in the minds customers is a function of the prepurchase communications the seller has with them. If you set the expectations too low, people won't buy your offering. But if you set the expectations too high, you run the risk that your buyers will be dissatisfied. A common saying in business is "underpromise and overdeliver." In other words, set consumers' expectations a bit low, and then exceed those expectations in order to create delighted customers who are enthusiastic about your product. A seller hopes that enthusiastic customers will tell their friends about the seller's offering, spreading lots of positive word of mouth about it.

**FIGURE 14.8**

Ritz-Carlton's employees are empowered and even given a budget to provide services that delight customers—not just meet their expectations.

*© 2010 Jupiterimages Corporation*

One customer satisfaction strategy that grew out of Carlson's idea of delighting customers is to empower customer-facing personnel. Customer-facing personnel are employees that meet and interact with customers. In a hotel, this might include desk clerks, housekeepers, bellman, and other staff. Empowering these employees to drop what they're doing in order to do something special for a customer, for example, can certainly delight customers. In some organizations, employees are even given a budget for such activities.

Ritz-Carlton employees each have an annual budget that can be spent on customer service activities, such as paying for dry cleaning if a customer spilled red wine on a dress in the hotel's restaurant. Sewell Cadillac is famous for how its employees serve its customers. An employee will even pick up a customer up on a Sunday if a Sewell-purchased car breaks down. Other dealers might delegate such a service to another company, but at Sewell, the same salesperson who sold the car might be the person who handles such a task. To Sewell, customer service is too important to trust to another company—a company that perhaps won't feel the same sense of urgency to keep car buyers as satisfied as Sewell does.

Empowerment is more than simply a budget and a job description—frontline employees also need customer skills. Companies like Ritz-Carlton and Sewell spend a great deal of time and effort to ensure that employees with customer contact responsibilities are trained and prepared to handle small and large challenges with equal aplomb.

Another customer satisfaction strategy involves offering customers warranties and guarantees. Warranties serve as an agreement that the product will perform as promised or some form of restitution will be made to the customer. Customers who are risk-averse find warranties reassuring.

**postpurchase dissonance**

A situation in which consumers rethink their decisions after purchasing products and wonder if they made the best decision.

One form of dissatisfaction is **postpurchase dissonance**, which we described in Chapter 3. Recall that it is also called *buyer's remorse.* Postpurchase dissonance is more likely to occur when an expensive product is purchased, the buyer purchases it infrequently and has little experience with it, and there is a perception that it is a high-risk purchase. Many marketers address postpurchase dissonance by providing their customers with reassuring communications. For example, a boat dealer might send a buyer a letter that expresses the dealer's commitment to service the boat and that also reminds the buyer of all the terrific reasons he or she purchased it. Alternatively, the dealer could have the salesperson who sold the boat telephone the buyer to answer any questions he or she might have after owning and operating the boat for a couple of weeks.

## 3.3 Measuring Customer Satisfaction

To measure customer satisfaction, you need to able to understanding what creates it. Just asking customers, "Are you satisfied?" won't tell you much. Yet many companies often measure the satisfaction of their customers on the basis of only a few questions: "How satisfied were you today?" "Would you recommend us to your friends?" and "Do you intend to visit us again?"

Effective customer satisfaction measures have several components. The two general components are the customer's expectations and whether the organization performed well enough to meet them. A third component is the degree of satisfaction, or to put it in terms we've used to describe exceptional performance, is the customer delighted?

To figure out if a customer's expectations were met and they are delighted, more detail is usually required. Companies might break the offering into major components and ask how satisfied customers were with each. For example, a restaurant might ask the following:

- Were you greeted promptly by a host? By your server at your table?
- Was your order taken promptly?
- How long did you wait for your food?
- Was the food served at the appropriate temperature?

These questions assume that each aspect of the service is equally important to the customer. However, some surveys ask customers to rate how important they are. Other surveys simply "weight," or score, questions so that aspects that are known to be more important to customers have a greater impact on the overall satisfaction score. For example, a restaurant might find that prompt service, good taste, and large portions are the only three factors that usually determine customers' overall satisfaction. In that case, the survey can be shortened considerably. At the same time, however, space should be left on the survey so customers can add any additional information that could yield important insight. This information can be used to find out if there are customer service problems that a firm wasn't aware of or if the preferences of consumers in general are changing.

You will still find customer satisfaction survey cards that just ask, "How satisfied were you today?" "Would you recommend us to your friends?" and "Do you intend to visit us again?" The information obtained from these surveys can still be useful if it's paired with a more comprehensive measurement program. For instance, a sample of customers could be given the opportunity to provide more detailed information via another survey and the two surveys could be compared. Such a comparison can help the company pinpoint aspects that need improvement. In addition, the company has given every customer an opportunity to provide input, which is an important part of any empowerment strategy.

**FIGURE 14.9**

Buy a new boat, and the dealer is likely to engage in reassurance communications designed to reduce any postpurchase dissonance and enhance your satisfaction with the offering. The communications might include phone calls from the salesperson who sold you the boat or letters from the dealer's service department.

## 3.4 Complaint Management Strategies

When buyers want to complain about products or companies, they have many ways to do so. They can complain to the companies they're upset with, tell their friends, or broadcast their concerns on the Internet. People who use every Internet site possible to bash a company are called *verbal terrorists*. The term was coined by Paul Greenberg, a marketing analyst who authored the wildly popular book *CRM at the Speed of Light*.

Should companies worry about verbal terrorists? Perhaps so. A recent study indicates that customer satisfaction scores could be less important to a firm's success or failure than the number of complaints its gets.[12] To measure the tradeoff between the two, customer satisfaction guru Fred Reicheld devised something called the *net promoter score*. The net promoter score is the number of recommenders an offering has minus the number of complainers.[13] The more positive the score, the better the company's performance. According to another recent study, a company with fewer complaints is also more likely to have better financial performance.

Studies also show that if a company can resolve a customer's complaint well, then the customer's attitude toward the company is improved, possibly even beyond the level of his or her original satisfaction. Some experts have argued, perhaps jokingly, that if this is the case, a good strategy might be to make customers mad and then do a good job of resolving their problems. Practically speaking, though, the best practice is to perform at or beyond customer expectations so fewer complaints will be received in the first place.

Customers will complain, though, no matter how hard firms try to meet or exceed their expectations. Sometimes, the complaint is in the form of a suggestion and simply reflects an opportunity to improve the experience. In other instances, the complaint represents a service or product failure.

When a complaint is made, the process for responding to it is as important as the outcome. And consumers judge companies as much for whether their response processes seem fair as whether they got what they wanted. For that reason, some companies create customer service departments with specially trained personnel who can react to complaints. Other companies invest heavily in preparing all customer-facing personnel to respond to complaints. Still other companies outsource their customer service. When the service is technical, marketers sometimes outsource the resolution of complaints to companies that specialize in providing technical service. Computer help lines are an example. Technical-support companies often service the computer help lines of multiple manufacturers. A company that outsources its service nonetheless has to make sure that customer complaints are handled as diligently as possible. Otherwise, customers will be left with a poor impression.

## Handling the Complaint Process

A good customer complaint handling process involves the steps listed below. Note that one step is to acknowledge the customer's feelings. A customer who is angry or upset due to a failure does not want to be patronized or have his or her problems taken lightly. The situation is important to the customer and should be important to the person listening and responding to the complaint.

- Listen carefully to the complaint
- Acknowledge the customer's feelings
- Determine the root cause of the problem
- Offer a solution
- Gain agreement on the solution and communicate the process of resolution
- Follow up, if appropriate
- Record the complaint and resolution

Note that the complaint-resolution process involves communicating that process and gaining agreement on a solution, even if the customer sometimes might not like the outcome. He or she still needs to know what to expect.

Finally, the complaint process includes recording the complaint. We stated earlier that a firm's best strategy is to perform at or beyond the customer's expectations so as to minimize the number of complaints it receives in the first place. Analyzing your company's complaints can help you identify weak points in a service process or design flaws in a product, as well as potential miscommunications that are raising customer' expectations unreasonably. To conduct this analysis, however, you need a complete record of the complaints made.

A complaint record should reflect the main reason an offering failed. Typically, the failure can be attributed to one (or more) of the following four gaps:[14]

1. The **communication gap**. Overstating the offering's performance level, thereby creating unrealistic expectations on the part of customers.
2. The **knowledge gap**. Not understanding the customer's expectations or needs, which then leads a company to create a product that disappoints the customer.
3. The **standards gap**. Setting performance standards that are too low despite what is known about the customers' requirements.
4. The **delivery gap**. Failing to meet the performance standards established for an offering.

**communication gap**

A gap that occurs when a marketer overstates the performance level of a product, thereby creating unrealistic expectations on the part of consumers.

**knowledge gap**

A firm's failure to understand a customer's expectations or needs, which then leads it to create an offering that disappoints the customer.

**standards gap**

A gap that results when a marketer sets performance standards for a product that are too low, in spite of what is known about the customer's requirements.

**delivery gap**

A gap that results when a product fails to meet its performance standards.

You can attribute the complaints your company receives to one of the four gaps and then use the information to figure out what must be done to fix the problem, assuming you have one. If the problem is overstating the performance, then perhaps your firm's marketing promotions materials should be reviewed. If it appears that the offering is simply not meeting the needs of your customers, then more work should be done to identify exactly what they are. If your firm is aware of the needs of its customers but there is a gap between their requirements and the standards set for your firm's performance, then standards should be reviewed. Finally, your company's processes should be examined to ensure that standards are being met.

When the Smokey Bones chain of barbecue restaurants (owned by Darden Restaurants) noticed falling profits, managers cut costs by eliminating some items from the menu. Unfortunately, these were the items that made the chain unique; once they were gone, there was nothing distinctive about the chain's offerings. When customers complained, servers replied, "Yes, a lot of people have complained that those products are no longer available." But apparently, there was no process or way to get those complaints to register with the company's management. As a result, the company didn't realize why it was losing customers, and its profits continued to spiral downward. Many locations were closed and the company filed for bankruptcy.

Keep in mind that the complaint handling process itself is subject to complaints. As we mentioned, customers want a process that's fair, even if the outcome isn't what they hoped for. Consequently, monitoring your firm's customer satisfaction levels also means you must monitor how satisfied customers are with how their complaints were handled.

**KEY TAKEAWAY**

Measuring customer satisfaction is an important element of customer empowerment. But satisfaction alone is a minimal level of acceptable performance. It means that the customer's expectations were met. Getting positive word of mouth requires exceeding those expectations. To minimize the number of complaints a company needs an effective process of both handling complaints and understanding their causes so any problems can be corrected. Because the complaint process itself is subject to complaints, monitoring your firm's customer satisfaction levels also means you must monitor how satisfied customers are with your company's complaint handling system.

**REVIEW QUESTIONS**

1. Should a company be happy or concerned if most customers are satisfied?
2. Why have customer satisfaction scores remained relatively steady over the past few years?
3. What are the desired outcomes, from a marketer's perspective, of a complaint management process?
4. How would marketing management use customer satisfaction survey results?

# 4. ETHICS, LAWS, AND CUSTOMER EMPOWERMENT

**LEARNING OBJECTIVES**

1. **Apply general ethical principles and concepts to online marketing.**
2. **Explain the laws that regulate online and other types of marketing.**

You are about to graduate and move to another city to start a new job. Your employer is paying for your moving expenses, so you go online to see what people have to say about the different moving companies. One company has particularly good reviews so you hire it. Yet what actually happens is vastly different—and a complete disaster. Little surprise, then, when you later discover that the company actually paid people to post those positive reviews!

Unfortunately, such an experience has happened so often that the Federal Trade Commission (FTC) is now considering rewriting rules regarding endorsements and whether companies need to announce their sponsorships of messages.

Once upon a time, before the days of the Internet, any form of selling under another guise or a phony front was called **sugging** (a word created from the first letters of *selling under the guise*, or SUG). The term was primarily applied to a practice in which a salesperson would pretend to be doing marketing research by interviewing a consumer, and then turn the consumer's answers into reasons to buy. More recently, some companies have hired young, good-looking, outgoing men and women to hang out in bars and surreptitiously promote a particular brand of alcohol or cigarettes. Sugging seems to be a good term to apply to fake reviews, as well.

**sugging**

Any form of selling under another guise or under a phony front.

**FIGURE 14.10**

This customer comment, posted on http://www.StubbsBBQ.com, is really from a customer. If it weren't, Stubb's would be lying, yet we expect companies to post true statements if they are positive. More difficult to trust are anonymous reviews; we assume they come from real customers, but that is not always true. And when they aren't from real customers, the company is guilty of sugging.

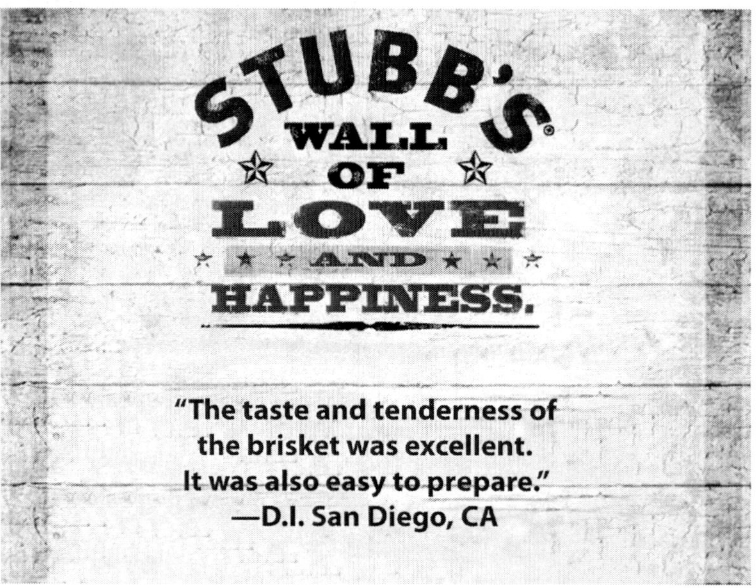


Truly, in no other marketplace should the term *caveat emptor* apply as strongly as it does on the Internet. Caveat emptor means, "let the buyer beware," or "it's your own fault if you buy it and it doesn't work!" Product reviews can be posted by anyone—even by a company or its competitors. So how do you know which ones to trust? Oftentimes you don't. Yet many of us do trust them. One study found that over 60 percent of buyers look for online reviews for their most important purchases, including over 45 percent of senior citizens.[15]

**FIGURE 14.11**

Most of us know that you can't believe everything a salesperson says about a product in a setting like this. But what about online? Whom can you believe? It's caveat emptor, or let the buyer beware, there, too!

*Source: Wikimedia Commons.*

While sugging isn't illegal, it isn't fair. Not only is the content potentially misrepresented, but the source certainly is. As you already know, a marketer cannot make promises about an offering's capabilities unless those capabilities are true. Sugging is similar—it involves misrepresenting or lying about the source of the information in an effort to gain an unfair advantage.

The consequences of being caught while sugging can be high. Even if the information posted was actually an accurate depiction of the offering's capabilities and benefits, consumers will be less likely to believe it—or any of the other the company's marketing communications, for that matter. The loss of trust makes building any kind of lasting relationship with a buyer extremely difficult to do.

## 4.1 Legal Requirements

So far, there are no regulations regarding sugging, although that may change if the FTC decides a crackdown is needed. There are, however, regulations affecting how one uses e-mail to sell.

Specifically, the **CAN-SPAM Act** prohibits the use of e-mail, faxes, and other technology to randomly push a message to a potential consumer. **Spam** is a term for unwanted commercial e-mail similar to junk mail. Using e-mail and other forms of technology to sell is legal if the seller and the buyer have a preexisting relationship or if the buyer has given his or her permission.

*Permission marketing* is a term that was created to suggest that marketers should always ask for permission to sell or to offer buyers marketing messages. The idea was that when permission is granted, the buyer is willing to listen. Now, however, anything "free" online requires that you sign up and give "permission," not just to get the freebie but also all kinds of future spam and annoying messages. You might also inadvertently give a seller permission or allow it sell your name and contact information. When you sign up for contests or agree to the seller's privacy statement when you order something online, you may have given them permission to resell your contact information to one of their "partners."

**CAN-SPAM Act**

A law that prohibits the use of e-mail, fax, and other technology to randomly send messages to potential consumers.

**SPAM**

Any unwanted commercial e-mail similar to junk mail.

Because of trust issues and the overuse of permission marketing, many consumers create **dump accounts**, or e-mail addresses they use whenever they need to register for something online. The dump account is used only for this purpose, so that all spam goes to that account and not the person's personal account. Many consumers find it easier to use dump accounts rather than read every privacy policy and try to remember which vendors won't sell the e-mail addresses to their "partners" for marketing purposes. Therefore, when you are a marketing manager, don't expect all the e-mail addresses you collect from a free offer to be valid.

**dump account**

An e-mail account that is used for registering when buying products online in order to ignore spam and other junk e-mail later.

**FIGURE 14.12**

Attendees to the LinuxWorld trade show agree when they buy their tickets to allow the exhibitors to send them e-mail, postal mail, and marketing messages through a variety of channels. Some companies use preshow e-mails to get attendees to visit their booths. Postshow e-mails might be part of a follow-up campaign.

*Source: Wikimedia Commons.*

In the B2B world, when attendees sign up for a trade show, they often give the show's exhibitors permission to send them e-mails and other information. Most sellers won't send marketing communication to fax machines because they are often shared by a number of people, and there is no guarantee that the intended person will receive the fax. Using e-mail, however, is acceptable because the buyer gave permission.

## Privacy Laws

U.S. **privacy laws** apply to both Internet marketing and other forms of commerce. The laws limit the amount and type of information a company can collect about a consumer and also specify how that information can be used or shared. In the EU, the types of data a company can collect are fewer, and the sharing of information is far more restricted. For example, a company cannot share information about customers in one division with another division. (Sending out unsolicited e-mails to potential buyers is also restricted in Europe.)

**privacy laws**

Laws that limit the amount and type of information a company can collect about a consumer and also specify how that information can be used or shared.

**Gramm-Leach-Bliley Act**

A legal act that requires certain institutions to provide written notice of their privacy policies.

**privacy policies**

Statements about how a company will use and protect a consumer's private data.

The **Gramm-Leach-Bliley Act** of 1999 requires financial institutions to provide written notice of their privacy policies. **Privacy policies** are statements regarding how a company will use and protect a consumer's private data. The law was broadened in 2003 to apply to a wider array of companies and consumer information.

The FTC requires a company to follow its policy or face severe penalties, even if the company is not required by the Gramm-Leach-Bliley Act to have a privacy policy. So, if you own a bookstore and you have a privacy policy, even though the law doesn't require you to have one, you have to follow the FTC's rules. And if you decide to change your privacy policy (for example, you decide to sell your customer list to Amazon), you have to notify your customers of the new policy.

For an example of a privacy policy, take a look at Amazon's. You can find it at http://www.amazon.com/gp/help/customer/display.html?ie=UTF8&nodeId=468496 or just go to http://www.amazon.com and click on the "Privacy Notice" link at the bottom of their page.

What kind of data do companies want on you? (Think back to Chapter 3 and Chapter 5.) They want to know where you live so they can apply PRIZM or VALS data to know you better and create marketing messages more likely to persuade you to buy something. They want to know how much you make to see if you can afford a higher-priced product. They want to know about the other things you buy, because that will likely affect what you buy in the future. If you own a boat, for example, you're more likely to buy fishing gear in the future. If you buy fishing gear, you're more likely to buy clothes from Columbia. And so on. The more they know, the more they can create offers tailored to fit your lifestyle and to entice you to buy.

**FIGURE 14.13**

Your university may know a lot about you, including your health history, your financial situation, and even the car you drive—not just the make and model, but the specific car. The Gramm-Leach-Bliley Act requires your school to protect that data so your privacy is protected.

*Source: Wikimedia Commons.*

Some organizations also have data, such as your social security number, that criminals could use to steal your identity. For example, think about how much information your university has on you. They not only have your social security number, but they may also have your financial information (through financial aid), your health information (through the campus health center), and your vehicle information (through parking fees). Protecting that information so you aren't harmed is a huge responsibility for the university.

Privacy policies and privacy laws apply to both business customers and individual consumers. As we explained in Chapter 8, many business buyers require vendors to sign nondisclosure agreements (NDAs) that specify what information is proprietary, or owned by the customer, and how, if at all, the seller can use that information. NDAs are not an online tool specifically but are often used in the normal course of business.

What about the offering itself? When you buy something online, you don't get to see it first, so how do you know it is what the seller says it is, and what can you do if it isn't? The **Uniform Commercial Code (UCC)** (first mentioned in Chapter 13) is a group of laws that govern commercial practices in the United States. The UCC defines many aspects of sales, such as when a sale actually takes place and what warranties buyers can expect.

**Uniform Commercial Code (UCC)**

A group of laws that govern commercial practices in the United States.

## Warranties and Promises

A **warranty** is a promise by the seller that an offering will perform as the seller said it would. The UCC makes a distinction between two types of warranties. The first is an **expressed warranty**, which is an oral or written statement by the seller regarding how the product should perform and the remedies available to the consumer in the event the offering fails.

An **implied warranty** is an obligation for the seller to provide an offering of at least average quality, beyond any written statements. For example, when you buy a new car, there is an implied warranty that it will run as promised after you drive it off the lot. You also have the right to expect average quality for any characteristic of a product that you buy online, except for those characteristics specifically described in the online material. If you were able to inspect the product before you bought it, such as looking at it in a store, the implied warranty only applies to those aspects you couldn't inspect or observe in the store.

Where the law gets tricky is when it comes to other forms of writing. Marketing messages, whether written in a brochure or advertisement or stated by a salesperson, are considered implied warranties. Any written statement about what the offering does has to be true, or it violates the UCC's definition of an implied warranty (and is therefore punishable by law).

Keep in mind that a salesperson can create an implied warranty in an e-mail or during an online chat session if he or she makes a promise. Even if the salesperson says something that contradicts a company's written material elsewhere, the consumer has the right to believe what the salesperson says. As such, the salesperson promise is legally binding.

**warranty**

A promise or assurance by a seller that an offering will perform as the seller represented it would.

**expressed warranty**

An oral or written statement by the seller regarding how a product should perform and the remedies available to the consumer in the event of its failure.

**implied warranty**

An obligation for a seller to provide an offering of at least average quality, beyond any written statements.

## Protecting Your Company

As marketer, you have an obligation to protect your company from consumers who might not have honest intentions. For example, have you noticed how you sometimes have to reproduce a strange-looking set of letters or words before you are allowed to make a purchase when buying something online? That simple step prevents automatic ordering by bots. A **bot**, which is short for *robot*, is a kind of program that performs automatic functions online. One of those functions could be to purchase products, such as tickets to a highly desirable sporting event, that the buyer can then resell at a higher price. Or a bot could be used to obtain many units of a freebie that someone can then resell. Bots can be used for many illicit purposes; a good marketer anticipates their uses and creates barriers to prevent being taken advantage of.

**bot**

Short for robot; a kind of program that perform automatic functions online.

A legal tool to help protect your company is the Digital Millennium Copyright Act. This act is designed to prevent copyrighted material from being pirated online. While prominent cases involve downloading music, your marketing information is also included. When you find a good way to market your offerings online, a competitor can't just steal your communications and insert their name. You are protected by this act.

What is very difficult to protect against is **phishing**, or soliciting personal information in order to steal an identity and use it to generate cash fraudulently. However, you may find it reassuring to your customers to remind them of your privacy policies and your customer contact practices. For example, a bank may remind its customers that it will never ask for a social security number by e-mail. Making sure your customer contact policies protect your customers can also help protect them against phishing from someone pretending to be you or your company.

**phishing**

Soliciting personal information in order to steal an identity and use it to generate cash fraudulently.

### KEY TAKEAWAY

Sugging is selling under any phony type of front. It includes posting fake reviews about products online. Sugging damages a seller's trust among buyers and should never be done. U.S. laws govern how products can be marketed, both those that are sold electronically and through more traditional channels. Companies must have permission before they can send you spam, and they have to tell you how they will gather and use your personal information. Warranties—expressed and implied—are binding no matter how companies deliver them. Good marketers anticipate less-than-honest activities by individuals and take steps to prevent them. Bots are online robots that some people use to take advantage of marketers.

### REVIEW QUESTIONS

1. What damage is done by sugging? If the customer buys your product, was the sugging OK? How does sugging differ online versus in person?
2. What does the CAN-SPAM Act do?
3. When do you mind a company having a lot of information on you and when is it OK? Are there advantages to you as a consumer when a company knows a lot about you? Are there disadvantages? What safeguards are there for consumers?
4. How can a bot hurt a marketer?

# 5. DISCUSSION QUESTIONS AND ACTIVITIES

### DISCUSSION QUESTIONS

1. Do you have a dump account? What are some other ways that consumers resist marketing attempts? What can, or should, marketers do to get their messages through, or around, such attempts to block or avoid messages?
2. Are you especially loyal to any one brand? If so, what is it and why are you so loyal? When successfully building loyalty and community, trust seems to be the biggest factor. How can a company build trust? Should consumers trust companies? Why or why not? Do you think some consumers are just more prone to be loyal to companies and other consumers are not? Why or why not?
3. How does a company demonstrate responsiveness? How would you design a feedback system so that your company could be responsive? How would it vary if your company sold to other companies versus selling to consumers?
4. A *USA Today* article described how schools sell directories to companies that then market to the students.[16] The schools included public school districts as well as colleges and universities. Have you noticed any marketing to you that probably came as a result of your school selling its directory? If so, what was being sold? Should schools continue to sell directory information (name, address, and phone numbers) or should that information remain private?

### ACTIVITIES

1. Go online to the M&Ms Web site (http://www.mms.com/us/index.jsp) and evaluate it. You will have to go through more than just the main landing page—click on the current contests and other pages to get all the data you need. What does the company do to build loyalty? To build community? Are there opportunities for feedback? Does the company partner with other organizations to leverage the loyalty those other companies enjoy with their customers? If so, what is M&Ms doing? Overall, what do you think is most effective about the site? What is the least effective?
2. Many schools are trying to build loyalty programs that strengthen alumni ties. Assess and critique any loyalty program your school has (take a look at athletics first, as that's usually where they start). Then redesign it. Be explicit in describing how your program will create the four effects of a loyalty program.

# ENDNOTES


1. Girish Ramani and V. Kumar, "Interaction Orientation and Firm Performance," *Journal of Marketing* 72, no. 1 (2008): 27–41.
2. Anonymous, "Give Real; Leading Online Gifting Service GiveReal.com Partners with Bombay Sapphire to Serve Up the Perfect Summer Cocktail through the Web," *Marketing Weekly News*, July 4, 2009, 225.
3. John C. Abell, "Dude—Dell's Making Money off Twitter!" *Wired*, June 12, 2009, http://www.wired.com/epicenter/2009/06/dude-%E2%80%94-dells-making-money-off-twitter (accessed August 24, 2009).
4. Andy Beal, "Forrester Predicts Huge Growth for Social Media Marketing," April 24, 2009, http://www.marketingpilgrim.com/2009/04/forrester-social-media-growth.html (accessed August 26, 2009).
5. Fred Reicheld and Thomas Teal, *The Loyalty Effect: The Hidden Force Behind Growth, Profits and Lasting Value* (Boston: Harvard Business Press, 2001).
6. Werner J. Reinartz and V. Kumar, "The Impact of Customer Relationship Characteristics on Profitable Lifetime Duration," *Journal of Marketing* 67, no. 1 (2003): 77–96.
7. Steven Van Yoder, "Cause-Related Marketing," http://www.streetdirectory.com/travel_guide/5529/marketing/cause_related_marketing.html (accessed October 10, 2008).
8. John F. Tanner, Jr., and Deepa Morris, "Customer Empowerment" (white paper published by BPT Partners, LLC, March 2009).
9. Nelson Ireson, "Lexus First in Owner Loyalty Survey, Saab Last," September 3, 2008, http://www.motorauthority.com/jd-power-lexus-first-in-luxury-owner-loyalty-saab-last.html (accessed July 13, 2009).
10. Raphaelle Lambert-Pandraud, Gilles Laurent, and Eric Lapersonne, "Repeat Purchasing of New Automobiles by Older Consumers: Empirical Evidence and Interpretations," *Journal of Marketing* 69, no. 2 (2005): 97–106.
11. Gustavo Souki and Cid G. Filho, "Perceived Quality, Satisfaction and Customer Loyalty: An Empirical Study in the Mobile Phones Sector in Brazil," *International Journal of Internet and Enterprise Management* 5, no. 4 (2008): 298–314.
12. X. Lou and C. Homburg, "Satisfaction, Complaint, and the Stock Value Gap," *Journal of Marketing* 72, no. 3 (2008): 29–43.
13. Fred Reicheld, *The Ultimate Question: Driving Good Profits and True Growth* (Boston: Harvard Business Press, 2006).
14. Michael Levy and Barton Weitz, *Retailing Management*, 7th ed. (Burr Ridge, IL: McGraw-Hill, 2009.)
15. Jack Neff, "Spate of Recalls Boost Potency of User Reviews," *Advertising Age* 78, no. 43 (2007): 3–4.
16. Jeff Martin, "Privacy Concerns Arise over Student Data," *USA Today*, August 24, 2009, http://www.usatoday.com/news/education (accessed August 25, 2009).

CHAPTER 15

# Price, the Only Revenue Generator

Many people will stand in line for something free, even if it takes hours. When Chick-fil-A opens new locations, they offer the first one hundred customers a free meal every week for a year. Customers camp out to get the free meals. When KFC introduced its grilled chicken, they put coupons good for a free piece of chicken in many Sunday newspaper magazines. So how do sellers make any money if they always offer goods and services on sale or for a special deal? Many sellers give customers something for free hoping they'll buy other products, but a careful balance is needed to make sure a profit is made. Are free products a good pricing strategy?

In previous chapters, we looked at the offering (products and services), communication (promotion), and place (the other marketing mix variables), all of which cost firms money. Price is the only marketing mix variable or part of the offering that generates revenue. Buyers relate the price to value. They must feel they are getting value for the price paid. Pricing decisions are extremely important. So how do organizations decide how to price their goods and services?

**FIGURE 15.1**

Some of shoppers' favorite four-letter words include FREE, SALE, and BOGO (Buy One Get One Free).

© 2010 Jupiterimages Corporation

## 1. THE PRICING FRAMEWORK AND A FIRM'S PRICING OBJECTIVES

**LEARNING OBJECTIVES**

1. **Understand the factors in the pricing framework.**
2. **Explain the different pricing objectives organizations have to choose from.**

Prices can be easily changed and easily matched by your competitors. Consequently, your product's price alone might not provide your company with a sustainable competitive advantage. Nonetheless, prices can attract consumers to different retailers and businesses to different suppliers.

Organizations must remember that the prices they charge should be consistent with their offerings, promotions, and distribution strategies. In other words, it wouldn't make sense for an organization to promote a high-end, prestige product, make it available in only a limited number of stores, and then sell it for an extremely low price. The price, product, promotion (communication), and placement (distribution) of a good or service should convey a consistent image. If you've ever watched the television show *The Price Is Right*, you may wonder how people guess the exact price of the products. Watch the video clip below to see some of the price guessing on *The Price Is Right*.

**Video Clip**

**Perfect Bid on** *The Price Is Right*
Contestant guesses exact price of prizes.

View the video online at: http://www.youtube.com/embed/JMFFGFmn20k

**Video Clip**

**Trying to Figure Out When** *The Price Is Right*
How do consumers get so close when guessing the prices of products?

View the video online at: http://www.youtube.com/embed/pR1Mmxr2Cb4

## 1.1 The Pricing Framework

**pricing objectives**

What an organization wants to accomplish with its pricing.

Before pricing a product, an organization must determine its **pricing objectives**. In other words, what does the company want to accomplish with its pricing? Companies must also estimate demand for the product or service, determine the costs, and analyze all factors (e.g., competition, regulations, and economy) affecting price decisions. Then, to convey a consistent image, the organization should choose the most appropriate pricing strategy and determine policies and conditions regarding price adjustments. The basic steps in the pricing framework are shown in Figure 15.2.

**FIGURE 15.2** The Pricing Framework

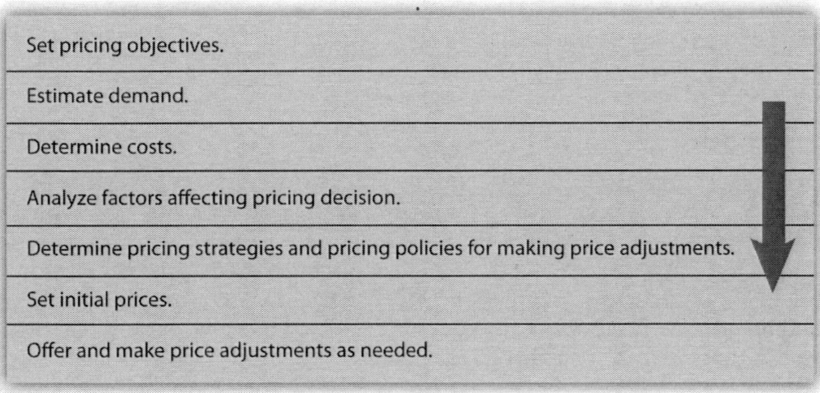


## 1.2 The Firm's Pricing Objectives

Different firms want to accomplish different things with their pricing strategies. For example, one firm may want to capture market share, another may be solely focused on maximizing its profits, and another may want to be perceived as having products with prestige. Some examples of different pricing objectives companies may set include profit-oriented objectives, sales-oriented objectives, and status quo objectives.

### Earning a Targeted Return on Investment (ROI)

ROI, or return on investment, is the amount of profit an organization hopes to make given the amount of assets, or money, it has tied up in a product. ROI is a common pricing objective for many firms. Companies typically set a certain percentage, such as 10 percent, for ROI in a product's first year following its launch. So, for example, if a company has $100,000 invested in a product and is expecting a 10 percent ROI, it would want the product's profit to be $10,000.

### Maximizing Profits

Many companies set their prices to increase their revenues as much as possible relative to their costs. However, large revenues do not necessarily translate into higher profits. To maximize its profits, a company must also focus on cutting costs or implementing programs to encourage customer loyalty.

In weak economic markets, many companies manage to cut costs and increase their profits, even though their sales are lower. How do they do this? The Gap cut costs by doing a better job of controlling its inventory. The retailer also reduced its real estate holdings to increase its profits when its sales were down during the latest economic recession. Other firms such as Dell, Inc., cut jobs to increase their profits. Meanwhile, Walmart tried to lower its prices so as to undercut its competitors' prices to attract more customers. After it discovered that wealthier consumers who didn't usually shop at Walmart before the recession were frequenting its stores, Walmart decided to upgrade some of its offerings, improve the checkout process, and improve the appearance of some of its stores to keep these high-end customers happy and enlarge its customer base. Other firms increased their prices or cut back on their marketing and advertising expenses. A firm has to remember, however, that prices signal value. If consumers do not perceive that a product has a high degree of value, they probably will not pay a high price for it. Furthermore, cutting costs cannot be a long-term strategy if a company wants to maintain its image and position in the marketplace.

### Maximizing Sales

Maximizing sales involves pricing products to generate as much revenue as possible, regardless of what it does to a firm's profits. When companies are struggling financially, they sometimes try to generate cash quickly to pay their debts. They do so by selling off inventory or cutting prices temporarily. Such cash may be necessary to pay short-term bills, such as payroll. Maximizing sales is typically a short-term objective since profitability is not considered.

### Maximizing Market Share

Some organizations try to set their prices in a way that allows them to capture a larger share of the sales in their industries. Capturing more market share doesn't necessarily mean a firm will earn higher profits, though. Nonetheless, many companies believe capturing a maximum amount of market share is downright necessary for their survival. In other words, they believe if they remain a small competitor they will fail. Firms in the cellular phone industry are an example. The race to be the biggest cell phone provider has hurt companies like Motorola. Motorola holds only 10 percent of the cell phone market, and its profits on their product lines are negative.

### Maintaining the Status Quo

**status quo**

An objective a firm sets to maintain its current prices and/or its competitors' prices.

Sometimes a firm's objective may be to maintain the **status quo** or simply meet, or equal, its competitors' prices or keep its current prices. Airline companies are a good example. Have you ever noticed that when one airline raises or lowers its prices, the others all do the same? If consumers don't accept an airline's increased prices (and extra fees) such as the charge for checking in with a representative at the airport rather than checking in online, other airlines may decide not to implement the extra charge and the airline charging the fee may drop it. Companies, of course, monitor their competitors' prices closely when they adopt a status quo pricing objective.

**KEY TAKEAWAY**

Price is the only marketing variable that generates money for a company. All the other variables (product, communication, distribution) cost organizations money. A product's price is the easiest marketing variable to change and also the easiest to copy. Before pricing a product, an organization must determine its pricing objective(s). A company can choose from pricing objectives such as maximizing profits, maximizing sales, capturing market share, achieving a target return on investment (ROI) from a product, and maintaining the status quo in terms of the price of a product relative to competing products.

**REVIEW QUESTIONS**

1. What are the steps in the pricing framework?
2. In addition to profit-oriented objectives, what other types of pricing objectives do firms utilize?

# 2. FACTORS THAT AFFECT PRICING DECISIONS

**LEARNING OBJECTIVES**

1. **Understand the factors that affect a firm's pricing decisions.**
2. **Understand why companies must conduct research before setting prices in international markets.**
3. **Learn how to calculate the breakeven point.**

Having a pricing objective isn't enough. A firm also has to look at a myriad of other factors before setting its prices. Those factors include the offering's costs, the demand, the customers whose needs it is designed to meet, the external environment—such as the competition, the economy, and government regulations—and other aspects of the marketing mix, such as the nature of the offering, the current stage of its product life cycle, and its promotion and distribution. If a company plans to sell its products or services in international markets, research on the factors for each market must be analyzed before setting prices. Organizations must understand buyers, competitors, the economic conditions, and political regulations in other markets before they can compete successfully. Next we look at each of the factors and what they entail.

## 2.1 Customers

How will buyers respond? Three important factors are whether the buyers perceive the product offers value, how many buyers there are, and how sensitive they are to changes in price. In addition to gathering data on the size of markets, companies must try to determine how price sensitive customers are. Will customers buy the product, given its price? Or will they believe the value is not equal to the cost and choose an alternative or decide they can do without the product or service? Equally important is how much buyers are willing to pay for the offering. Figuring out how consumers will respond to prices involves judgment as well as research.

**Price elasticity**, or people's sensitivity to price changes, affects the demand for products. Think about a pair of sweatpants with an elastic waist. You can stretch an elastic waistband like the one in sweatpants, but it's much more difficult to stretch the waistband of a pair of dress slacks. Elasticity refers to the amount of stretch or change. For example, the waistband of sweatpants may stretch if you pull on it. Similarly, the demand for a product may change if the price changes. Imagine the price of a twelve-pack of sodas changing to $1.50 a pack. People are likely to buy a lot more soda at $1.50 per twelve-pack than they are at $4.50 per twelve-pack. Conversely, the waistband on a pair of dress slacks remains the same (doesn't change) whether you pull on it or not. Likewise, demand for some products won't change even if the price changes. The formula for calculating the price elasticity of demand is as follows.

**price elasticity**

The amount of sensitivity to price changes, which affects the demand for a product.

Price elasticity = percentage change in quantity demanded ÷ percentage change in price

When consumers are very sensitive to the price change of a product—that is, they buy more of it at low prices and less of it at high prices—the demand for it is **price elastic**. Durable goods such as TVs, stereos, and freezers are more price elastic than necessities. People are more likely to buy them when their prices drop and less likely to buy them when their prices rise. By contrast, when the demand for a product stays relatively the same and buyers are not sensitive to changes in its price, the demand is **price inelastic**. Demand for essential products such as many basic food and first-aid products is not as affected by price changes as demand for many nonessential goods.

**price elastic**

Consumers are very sensitive to price changes and buy more at low prices and less at high prices.

**price inelastic**

Buyers are not sensitive to price changes and demand is relatively unchanged.

The number of competing products and substitutes available affects the elasticity of demand. Whether a person considers a product a necessity or a luxury and the percentage of a person's budget allocated to different products and services also affect price elasticity. Some products, such as cigarettes, tend to be relatively price inelastic since most smokers keep purchasing them regardless of price increases and the fact that other people see cigarettes as unnecessary. Service providers, such as utility companies in markets in which they have a monopoly (only one provider), face more inelastic demand since no substitutes are available.

## 2.2 Competitors

How competitors price and sell their products will have a tremendous effect on a firm's pricing decisions. If you wanted to buy a certain pair of shoes, but the price was 30 percent less at one store than another, what would you do? Because companies want to establish and maintain loyal customers, they will often match their competitors' prices. Some retailers, such as Home Depot, will give you an extra discount if you find the same product for less somewhere else. Similarly, if one company offers you free shipping, you might discover other companies will, too. With so many products sold online, consumers can compare the prices of many merchants before making a purchase decision.

The availability of substitute products affects a company's pricing decisions as well. If you can find a similar pair of shoes selling for 50 percent less at a third store, would you buy them? There's a good chance you might. Recall from the five forces model discussed in Chapter 2 that merchants must look at substitutes and potential entrants as well as direct competitors.

## 2.3 The Economy and Government Laws and Regulations

The economy also has a tremendous effect on pricing decisions. In Chapter 2 we noted that factors in the economic environment include interest rates and unemployment levels. When the economy is weak and many people are unemployed, companies often lower their prices. In international markets, currency exchange rates also affect pricing decisions.

Pricing decisions are affected by federal and state regulations. Regulations are designed to protect consumers, promote competition, and encourage ethical and fair behavior by businesses. For example, the **Robinson-Patman Act** limits a seller's ability to charge different customers different prices for the same products. The intent of the act is to protect small businesses from larger businesses that try to extract special discounts and deals for themselves in order to eliminate their competitors. However, cost differences, market conditions, and competitive pricing by other suppliers can justify price differences in some situations. In other words, the practice isn't illegal under all circumstances. You have probably noticed that restaurants offer senior citizens and children discounted menus. The movies also charge different people different prices based on their ages and charge different amounts based on the time of day, with matinees usually less expensive than evening shows. These price differences are legal. We will discuss more about price differences later in the chapter.

**Robinson-Patman Act**

A U.S. act that limits price discrimination (charging different customers different prices for the same product and quantities of it purchased).

**price fixing**

When firms get together and agree to charge the same prices.

**Price fixing**, which occurs when firms get together and agree to charge the same prices, is illegal. Usually, price fixing involves setting high prices so consumers must pay a high price regardless of where they purchase a good or service. Video systems, LCD (liquid crystal display) manufacturers, auction houses, and airlines are examples of offerings in which price fixing existed. When a company is charged with price fixing, it is usually ordered to take some type of action to reach a settlement with buyers.

Price fixing isn't uncommon. Nintendo and its distributors in the European Union were charged with price fixing and increasing the prices of hardware and software. Sharp, LG, and Chungwa collaborated and fixed the prices of the LCDs used in computers, cell phones, and other electronics. Virgin Atlantic Airways and British Airways were also involved in price fixing for their flights. Sotheby's and Christie's, two large auction houses, used price fixing to set their commissions.

One of the most famous price-fixing schemes involved Robert Crandall, the CEO of American Airlines in the early 1990s. Crandall called Howard Putnam, the CEO of Braniff Airlines, since the two airlines were fierce competitors in the Dallas market. Unfortunately for Crandall, Putnam taped the conversation and turned it over to the U.S. Department of Justice. Their conversation went like this:

> *Crandall: "I think it's dumb—to pound—each other and neither one of us making a [expletive] dime."*
>
> *Putnam: "Well…"*
>
> *Crandall: "I have a suggestion for you. Raise your—fares twenty percent. I'll raise mine the next morning."*
>
> *Putnam: "Robert, we—*
>
> *Crandall: "You'll make more money and I will too.*
>
> *Putnam: "We can't talk about pricing."*
>
> *Crandall: "Oh, [expletive] Howard. We can talk about any [expletive] thing we want to talk about."[1] "*

**unfair trade laws**

State laws requiring sellers to keep a minimum price level for similar products.

**predatory pricing**

When companies act in a predatory manner by setting low prices to drive competitors out of business.

**bait and switch**

A pricing tactic a seller uses to lure in, or "bait," customers with a low-priced product. The seller then attempts to persuade the buyer to purchase higher-priced products, perhaps by telling him or her that the low-priced product is no longer available.

By requiring sellers to keep a minimum price level for similar products, **unfair trade laws** protect smaller businesses. Unfair trade laws are state laws preventing large businesses from selling products below cost (as loss leaders) to attract customers to the store. When companies act in a predatory manner by setting low prices to drive competitors out of business, it is a **predatory pricing** strategy.

Similarly, bait-and-switch pricing is illegal in many states. **Bait and switch**, or bait advertising, occurs when a business tries to "bait," or lure in, customers with an incredibly low-priced product. Once customers take the bait, sales personnel attempt to sell them more expensive products. Sometimes the customers are told the cheaper product is no longer available.

You perhaps have seen bait-and-switch pricing tactics used to sell different electronic products or small household appliances. While bait-and-switch pricing is illegal in many states, stores can add disclaimers to their ads stating that there are no rain checks or that limited quantities are available to justify trying to get you to buy a different product. However, the advertiser must offer at least a limited quantity of the advertised product, even if it sells out quickly.

## 2.4 Product Costs

The costs of the product—its inputs—including the amount spent on product development, testing, and packaging required have to be taken into account when a pricing decision is made. So do the costs related to promotion and distribution. For example, when a new offering is launched, its promotion costs can be very high because people need to be made aware that it exists. Thus, the offering's stage in the product life cycle can affect its price. Keep in mind that a product may be in a different stage of its life cycle in other markets. For example, while sales of the iPhone remain fairly constant in the United States, the Koreans felt the phone was not as good as their current phones and was somewhat obsolete. Similarly, if a company has to open brick-and-mortar storefronts to distribute and sell the offering, this too will have to be built into the price the firm must charge for it.

**breakeven point (BEP)**

The amount (in units or dollars) where total revenue equals total costs.

The point at which total costs equal total revenue is known as the **breakeven point (BEP)**. For a company to be profitable, a company's revenue must be greater than its total costs. If total costs exceed total revenue, the company suffers a loss.

**Total costs** include both fixed costs and variable costs. **Fixed costs**, or overhead expenses, are costs that a company must pay regardless of its level of production or level of sales. A company's fixed costs include items such as rent, leasing fees for equipment, contracted advertising costs, and insurance. As a student, you may also incur fixed costs such as the rent you pay for an apartment. You must pay your rent whether you stay there for the weekend or not. **Variable costs** are costs that change with a company's level of production and sales. Raw materials, labor, and commissions on units sold are examples of variable costs. You, too, have variable costs, such as the cost of gasoline for your car or your utility bills, which vary depending on how much you use.

Consider a small company that manufactures specialty DVDs and sells them through different retail stores. The manufacturer's selling price (MSP) is $15, which is what the retailers pay for the DVDs. The retailers then sell the DVDs to consumers for an additional charge. The manufacturer has the following charges:

| | |
|---|---|
| Copyright and distribution charges for the titles | $150,000 |
| Package and label designs for the DVDs | $10,000 |
| Advertising and promotion costs | $40,000 |
| Reproduction of DVDs | $5 per unit |
| Labels and packaging | $1 per unit |
| Royalties | $1 per unit |

In order to determine the breakeven point, you must first calculate the fixed and variable costs. To make sure all costs are included, you may want to highlight the fixed costs in one color (e.g., green) and the variable costs in another color (e.g., blue). Then, using the formulas below, calculate how many units the manufacturer must sell to break even.

The formula for BEP is as follows:

$$\text{BEP} = \text{total fixed costs (FC)} \div \text{contribution per unit (CU)}$$

$$\text{contribution per unit} = \text{MSP} - \text{variable costs (VC)}$$

$$\text{BEP} = \$200{,}000 \div (\$15 - \$7) = \$200{,}000 \div \$8 = 25{,}000 \text{ units to break even}$$

To determine the breakeven point in dollars, you simply multiply the number of units to break even by the MSP. In this case, the BEP in dollars would be 25,000 units times $15, or $375,000.

**total cost**

Fixed costs plus variable costs.

**fixed costs**

Overhead or costs that remain the same regardless of the level of production or the level of sales.

**variable costs**

Costs that change with the level of production or service delivery.

## KEY TAKEAWAY

In addition to setting a pricing objective, a firm has to look at a number of factors before setting its prices. These factors include the offering's costs, the customers whose needs it is designed to meet, the external environment—such as the competition, the economy, and government regulations—and other aspects of the marketing mix, such as the nature of the offering, the stage of its product life cycle, and its promotion and distribution. In international markets, firms must look at environmental factors and customers' buying behavior in each market. For a company to be profitable, revenues must exceed total costs.

## REVIEW QUESTIONS

1. What factors do organizations consider when making price decisions?
2. How do a company's competitors affect the pricing decisions the firm will make?
3. What is the difference between fixed costs and variable costs?

# 3. PRICING STRATEGIES

## LEARNING OBJECTIVES

1. **Understand introductory pricing strategies.**
2. **Understand the different pricing approaches that businesses use.**

Once a firm has established its pricing objectives and analyzed the factors that affect how it should price a product, the company must determine the pricing strategy (or strategies) that will help it achieve those objectives. As we have indicated, firms use different pricing strategies for their offerings. And oftentimes, the strategy depends on the stage of life cycle the offerings are in currently. Products may be in different stages of their life cycle in various international markets. Next, we'll examine three strategies businesses often consider when a product is first introduced and then look at several different pricing approaches that companies utilize during the product life cycle.

## 3.1 Introductory Pricing Strategies

**skimming price strategy**

A strategy whereby a company sets a high initial price for a product. The idea is to target buyers who are willing to pay a high price (top of the market) and buy products early.

Think of products that have been introduced in the last decade and how products were priced when they first entered the market. Remember when the iPhone was first introduced, its price was almost $700. Since then, the price has dropped considerably even for new models. The same is true for DVD players, LCD televisions, digital cameras, and many high-tech products. As mentioned in Chapter 7, a **skimming price strategy** is when a company sets a high initial price for a product. The idea is to go after consumers who are willing to pay a high price (top of the market) and buy products early. This way, a company recoups its investment in the product faster.

The easy way to remember a skimming approach is to think of the turkey gravy at Thanksgiving. When the gravy is chilled, the fat rises to the top and is often "skimmed" off before serving. Price skimming is a pricing approach designed to skim that top part of the gravy, or the top of the market. Over time, the price of the product goes down as competitors enter the market and more consumers are willing to purchase the offering.

**penetration pricing strategy**

A strategy in which an organization offers a low initial price on a product so that it captures as much market share as possible.

In contrast to a skimming approach, a **penetration pricing strategy** is one in which a low initial price is set. Often, many competitive products are already in the market. The goal is to get as much of the market as possible to try the product. Penetration pricing is used on many new food products, health and beauty supplies, and paper products sold in grocery stores and mass merchandise stores such as Walmart, Target, and Kmart.

**everyday low pricing**

The practice of charging a low initial price for an offering and maintaining that price throughout the offering's product life cycle.

Another approach companies use when they introduce a new product is **everyday low prices**. That is, the price initially set is the price the seller expects to charge throughout the product's life cycle. Companies like Walmart and Lowe's use everyday low pricing. Lowe's emphasizes their everyday low pricing strategy with the letters in their name plus the letter "t" (Lowest).

**FIGURE 15.3**

New flavors of snacks, candy, cereal, and shampoo sold in grocery stores and by mass merchandisers similar to the one in this picture are priced using a penetration pricing strategy to get consumers to try the products.

*© 2010 Jupiterimages Corporation*

## 3.2 Pricing Approaches

Companies can choose many ways to set their prices. We'll examine some common methods you often see. Many stores use **cost-plus pricing**, in which they take the cost of the product and then add a profit to determine a price. Cost-plus pricing is very common. The strategy helps ensure that a company's products' costs are covered and the firm earns a certain amount of profit. When companies add a **markup**, or an amount added to the cost of a product, they are using a form of cost-plus pricing. When products go on sale, companies mark down the prices, but they usually still make a profit. Potential **markdowns** or price reductions should be considered when deciding on a starting price.

Many pricing approaches have a psychological appeal. **Odd-even pricing** occurs when a company prices a product a few cents or a few dollars below the next dollar amount. For example, instead of being priced $10.00, a product will be priced at $9.99. Likewise, a $20,000 automobile might be priced at $19,998, although the product will cost more once taxes and other fees are added. See Figure 15.4 for an example of odd-even pricing.

**cost-plus pricing**

A pricing strategy where a certain amount of profit is added to the total cost of a product in order to determine its price.

**markup**

A certain amount of money added to the cost of a product to set the final price.

**markdown**

The amount (in dollars or percent) taken off the price.

**odd-even pricing**

A strategy in which a company prices products a few cents below the next dollar amount or a few dollars (for high-cost products such as automobiles) below the next hundred- or thousand-dollar value.

**FIGURE 15.4**

The charcoal shown in the photo is priced at $5.99 a bag, which is an example of odd-even pricing, or pricing a product slightly below the next dollar amount.

*Source: Photo courtesy of Stubb's Legendary Kitchen.*

**prestige pricing**

The practice of pricing a product higher to signal that it is of high quality.

**price lining (price levels)**

Pricing a group of similar products (e.g., neckties) at a few different price levels (e.g., $25, $50, and $75).

**demand backward pricing**

Pricing a product based on what customers are willing to pay for it and then creating the offering based on that price.

**leader pricing**

A strategy of offering low prices on one or more items as "lead" items in advertisements to attract customers.

**loss leaders**

Products priced below cost; this is illegal in some states.

**sealed bid pricing**

The process of offering to buy or sell products at prices designated in sealed bids.

**Prestige pricing** occurs when a higher price is utilized to give an offering a high-quality image. Some stores have a quality image, and people perceive that perhaps the products from those stores are of higher quality. Many times, two different stores carry the same product, but one store prices it higher because of the store's perceived higher image. Neckties are often priced using a strategy known as **price lining**, or *price levels*. In other words, there may be only a few price levels ($25, $50, and $75) for the ties, but a large assortment of them at each level. Movies and music often use price lining. You may see a lot of movies and CDs for $15.99, $9.99, and perhaps $4.99, but you won't see a lot of different price levels.

Remember when you were in elementary school and many students bought teachers little gifts before the holidays or on the last day of school. Typically, parents set an amount such as $5 or $10 for a teacher's gift. Knowing that people have certain maximum levels that they are willing to pay for gifts, some companies use **demand backward pricing**. They start with the price demanded by consumers (what they want to pay) and create offerings at that price. If you shop before the holidays, you might see a table of different products being sold for $5 (mugs, picture frames, ornaments) and another table of products being sold for $10 (mugs with chocolate, decorative trays, and so forth). Similarly, people have certain prices they are willing to pay for wedding gifts—say, $25, $50, $75, or $100—so stores set up displays of gifts sold at these different price levels. IKEA also sets a price for a product—which is what the company believes consumers want to pay for it—and then, working backward from the price, designs the product.

**Leader pricing** involves pricing one or more items low to get people into a store. The products with low prices are often on the front page of store ads and "lead" the promotion. For example, prior to Thanksgiving, grocery stores advertise turkeys and cranberry sauce at very low prices. The goal is to get shoppers to buy many more items in addition to the low-priced items. Leader or low prices are legal; however, as you learned earlier, **loss leaders**, or items priced below cost in an effort to get people into stores, are illegal in many states.

**Sealed bid pricing** is the process of offering to buy or sell products at prices designated in sealed bids. Companies must submit their bids by a certain time. The bids are later reviewed all at once, and the most desirable one is chosen. Sealed bids can occur on either the supplier or the buyer side. Via sealed bids, oil companies bid on tracts of land for potential drilling purposes, and the highest bidder is awarded the right to drill on the land. Similarly, consumers sometimes bid on lots to build houses. The highest bidder gets the lot. On the supplier side, contractors often bid on different jobs and the lowest bidder is awarded the job. The government often makes purchases based on sealed bids. Projects funded by stimulus money were awarded based on sealed bids.

**FIGURE 15.5**

When people think of auctions, they may think of the words, "Going, going, gone." Online auctions use a similar bidding process.

Bids are also being used online. **Online auction** sites such as eBay give customers the chance to bid and negotiate prices with sellers until an acceptable price is agreed upon. When a buyer lists what he or she wants to buy, sellers may submit bids. This process is known as a **forward auction**. If the buyer not only lists what he or she wants to buy but also states how much he or she is willing to pay, a **reverse auction** occurs. The reverse auction is finished when at least one firm is willing to accept the buyer's price.

**Going-rate pricing** occurs when buyers pay the same price regardless of where they buy the product or from whom. Going-rate pricing is often used on commodity products such as wheat, gold, or silver. People perceive the individual products in markets such as these to be largely the same. Consequently, there's a "going" price for the product that all sellers receive.

**Price bundling** occurs when different offerings are sold together at a price that's typically lower than the total price a customer would pay by buying each offering separately. Combo meals and value meals sold at restaurants are an example. Companies such as McDonald's have promoted value meals for a long time in many different markets. See the video clips below for early promotions of value meals in the United States, Greece, and Japan. Other products such as shampoo and conditioner are sometimes bundled together. Automobile companies bundle product options. For example, power locks and windows are often sold together, regardless of whether customers want only one or the other. The idea behind bundling is to increase an organization's revenues.

**online auction**

Bidding and negotiating prices online with buyers and sellers on sites such as eBay.com until an acceptable price is agreed upon.

**forward auction**

The process that occurs when a buyer lists what he or she wants to buy and sellers may submit bids.

**reverse auction**

When the buyer lists what he or she wants to buy and also states how much he or she is willing to pay. The reverse auction is finished when at least one firm is willing to accept the buyer's price.

**going-rate pricing**

Pricing whereby purchasers pay the same price for a product regardless of where they buy it or from whom.

**price bundling**

A strategy of selling different products or services together, typically at a lower price than if each product or service is sold separately.

## Video Clip

**McDonald's Introduced Value Meals in 1985**
Look at the cost and the amount of food in the original value meal.

View the video online at: http://www.youtube.com/embed/VoP0tAvHcGY

## Video Clip

**McDonald's Uses Humor in Greece to Sell Big Macs**

View the video online at: http://www.youtube.com/embed/3GBzl6hSB68

## Video Clip

**McDonald's in Japan**
McDonald's is popular around the world.

View the video online at: http://www.youtube.com/embed/11quU3nqkVE

**Captive pricing** is a strategy firms use when consumers must buy a given product because they are at a certain event or location or they need a particular product because no substitutes will work. Concessions at a sporting event or a movie provide examples of how captive pricing is used. Maybe you didn't pay much to attend the game, but the snacks and drinks were extremely expensive. Similarly, if you buy a razor and must purchase specific razor blades for it, you have experienced captive pricing. The blades are often more expensive than the razor because customers do not have the option of choosing blades from another manufacturer.

**captive pricing**

A strategy firms use to price products when they know customers must buy specific replacement parts, such as razor blades, because there are no alternatives.

Pricing products consumers use together (such as blades and razors) with different profit margins is also part of **product mix pricing**. Recall from Chapter 6 that a product mix includes all the products a company offers. If you want to buy an automobile, the base price might seem reasonable, but the options such as floor mats might earn the seller a much higher profit margin. While consumers can buy floor mats at stores like Walmart for $30, many people pay almost $200 to get the floor mats that go with the car from the dealer.

**product mix pricing**

Deciding how to price a firm's products and services that go together, such as power options (locks, windows) on a car.

Most students and young people have cell phones. Are you aware of how many minutes you spend talking or texting and what it costs if you go over the limits of your phone plan? Maybe not if your plan involves two-part pricing. **Two-part pricing** means there are two different charges customers pay. In the case of a cell phone, a customer might pay a charge for one service such as a thousand minutes, and then pay a separate charge for each minute over one thousand. Get out your cell phone and look at how many minutes you have used. Many people are shocked at how many minutes they have used or the number of messages they have sent in the last month.

**two-part pricing**

A pricing strategy in which providers have two different charges for a product, such as the base monthly rate for cell phone coverage and additional charges for extra minutes or texting.

Have you ever seen an ad for a special item only to find out it is much more expensive than what you recalled seeing in the ad? A company might advertise a price such as $25*, but when you read the fine print, the price is really five payments of $25 for a total cost of $125. **Payment pricing**, or allowing customers to pay for products in installments, is a strategy that helps customers break up their payments into smaller amounts, which can make them more inclined to buy higher-priced products.

**payment pricing**

A pricing strategy in which customers are allowed to break down product payments into smaller amounts they pay incrementally.

**Promotional pricing** is a short-term tactic designed to get people into a store or to purchase more of a product. Examples of promotional pricing include back-to-school sales, rebates, extended warranties, and going-out-of-business sales. Rebates are a great strategy for companies because consumers think they're getting a great deal. But as you learned in Chapter 12, many consumers forget to request the rebate. Extended warranties have become popular for all types of products, including automobiles, appliances, electronics, and even athletic shoes. If you buy a vacuum for $35, and it has a one-year warranty from the manufacturer, does it really make sense to spend an additional $15 to get another year's warranty? However, when it comes to automobiles, repairs can be expensive, so an extended warranty often pays for itself following one repair. Buyers must look at the costs and benefits and determine if the extended warranty provides value.

**promotional pricing**

A short-term tactic to get people to purchase a product or more of it.

We discussed **price discrimination**, or charging different customers different prices for the same product, earlier in the chapter. In some situations, price discrimination is legal. As we explained, you have probably noticed that certain customer groups (students, children, and senior citizens, for example) are sometimes offered discounts at restaurants and events. However, the discounts must be offered to all senior citizens or all children within a certain age range, not just a few. Price discrimination is used to get more people to use a product or service. Similarly, a company might lower its prices in order to get more customers to buy an offering when business is slow. Matinees are often cheaper than movies at night; bowling might be less expensive during nonleague times, and so forth.

**price discrimination**

The process of charging different customers different prices for the same product and quantities of it purchased.

## 3.3 Price Adjustments

Organizations must also decide what their policies are when it comes to making **price adjustments**, or changing the listed prices of their products. Some common price adjustments include **quantity discounts**, which involves giving customers discounts for larger purchases. Discounts for paying cash for large purchases and seasonal discounts to get rid of inventory and holiday items are other examples of price adjustments.

**price adjustment**

A change to the listed price of a product.

**quantity discounts**

Discounts buyers get for making large purchases.

**FOB (free on board) origin**

A pricing arrangement that designates that a product's title changes at its origin (the place it's purchased), and the buyer pays the shipping charges.

**FOB (free on board) destination**

A pricing arrangement that designates that a product's title changes at its destination (the place to which it's transported), and the seller pays the shipping charges.

**uniform-delivered pricing**

A pricing strategy in which buyers pays the same shipping charges regardless of their locations.

**trade allowances**

Discounts an organization gives its channel partners for performing different functions.

**reciprocal agreements**

Agreements whereby merchants agree to promote one another's offerings to customers.

A company's price adjustment policies also need to outline the firm's shipping charges. Many online merchants offer free shipping on certain products, orders over a certain amount, or purchases made in a given time frame. *FOB (free on board) origin* and *FOB delivered* are two common pricing adjustments businesses use to show when the title to a product changes along with who pays the shipping charges. **FOB (free on board) origin** means the title changes at the origin—that is, when the product is purchased—and the buyer pays the shipping charges. **FOB (free on board) destination** means the title changes at the destination—that is, after the product is transported—and the seller pays the shipping charges.

**Uniform-delivered pricing**, also called postage-stamp pricing, means buyers pay the same shipping charges regardless of where they are located. If you mail a letter across town, the postage is the same as when you mail a letter to a different state.

Recall that we discussed **trade allowances** in Chapter 12. For example, a manufacturer might give a retail store an advertising allowance to advertise the manufacturer's products in local newspapers. Similarly, a manufacturer might offer a store a discount to restock the manufacturer's products on store shelves rather than having its own representatives restock the items.

**Reciprocal agreements** are agreements in which merchants agree to promote each other to customers. Customers who patronize a particular retailer might get a discount card to use at a certain restaurant, and customers who go to a restaurant might get a discount card to use at a specific retailer. For example, when customers make a purchase at Diesel, Inc., they get a discount coupon good to use at a certain resort. When customers are at the resort, they get a discount coupon to use at Diesel. Old Navy and Great Clips implemented similar reciprocal agreements.

## FIGURE 15.6

When customers made a purchase at the clothing chain Diesel, they were given a bounce back card to be used during certain dates as shown in this photo. The bounce back card gets customers back in the store for additional purchases.

*Source: Photo courtesy of Diesel, Inc.*

**bounce back**

A discount card or coupon purchasers can use on their next shopping visits during set dates.

A promotion that's popular during weak economic times is called a bounce back. A **bounce back** is a promotion in which a seller gives customers discount cards or coupons (see Figure 15.6) after purchasing. Consumers can then use the cards and coupons on their next shopping visits. The idea is to get the customers to return to the store or online outlets later and purchase additional items. Some stores set minimum amounts that consumers have to spend to use the bounce back card.

### KEY TAKEAWAY

Both external and internal factors affect pricing decisions. Companies use many different pricing strategies and price adjustments. However, the price must generate enough revenues to cover costs in order for the product to be profitable. Cost-plus pricing, odd-even pricing, prestige pricing, price bundling, sealed bid pricing, going-rate pricing, and captive pricing are just a few of the strategies used. Organizations must also decide what their policies are when it comes to making price adjustments, or changing the listed prices of their products. Some companies use price adjustments as a short-term tactic to increase sales.

### REVIEW QUESTIONS

1. Explain the difference between a penetration and a skimming pricing strategy.
2. Describe how both buyers and sellers use sealed bid pricing.
3. Identify an example of each of the following: odd-even pricing, prestige pricing, price bundling, and captive pricing.
4. What is the difference between FOB origin and FOB destination when paying for shipping charges?
5. Explain how trade allowances work.

# 4. DISCUSSION QUESTIONS AND ACTIVITIES

### DISCUSSION QUESTIONS

1. What is the difference between leader pricing and a loss leader?
2. Which pricing approaches do you feel work best long term?
3. When is price discrimination legal?
4. Which pricing strategies have you noticed when you shop?
5. What new products have you purchased in the last two years that were priced using either a penetration or a skimming approach?

### ACTIVITIES

1. In order to understand revenues and costs, get a two-liter bottle of soda, ten to twenty cups, and a bucket of ice. Fill each cup with ice and then fill it with soda. Assume each cup of soda sells for at least $1 and you paid $1 for the soda and $1 for the cups. How much profit can you make?
2. Go to a fast-food restaurant for lunch. Figure out how much the price of a bundled meal is versus buying the items separately. Then decide if you think many consumers add a soda or fries because they feel like they're getting a deal.

# ENDNOTES

1. David S. Jackson, John S. Demott, and Allen Pusey, "Dirty Tricks in Dallas," *Time*, March 7, 1983, http://www.time.com/time/magazine/article/0,9171,953755,00.html (accessed December 15, 2009).

CHAPTER 16

# The Marketing Plan

The average tenure of a chief marketing officer (CMO) can be measured in months—about twenty-six months or less, in fact.[1] Why? Because marketing is one of those areas in a company in which performance is obvious. If sales go up, the CMO can be lured away by a larger company or promoted.

Indeed, successful marketing experience can be a ticket to the top. The experience of Paul Polman, a former marketing director at Procter & Gamble (P&G), illustrates as much. Polman parlayed his success at P&G into a division president's position at Nestlé. Two years later, he became the CEO (chief executive officer) of Unilever.[2]

However, if sales go down, CMOs can find themselves fired. Oftentimes nonmarketing executives have unrealistic expectations of their marketing departments and what they can accomplish.[3] "Sometimes CEOs don't know what they really want, and in some cases CMOs don't really understand what the CEOs want," says Keith Pigues, a former CMO for Cemex, the world's largest cement company. "As a result, it's not surprising that there is a misalignment of expectations, and that has certainly led to the short duration of the tenure of CMOs."

Moreover, many CMOs are under pressure to set rosy sales forecasts in order to satisfy not only their executive teams but also investors and Wall Street analysts. "The core underpinning challenge is being able to demonstrate you're adding value to the bottom line," explains Jim Murphy, former CMO of the consulting firm Accenture. The problem is that when CMOs overpromise and underdeliver, they set themselves up for a fall.

Much as firms must set their customers' expectations, CMOs must set their organization's marketing expectations. Marketing plans help them do that. A well-designed marketing plan should communicate realistic expectations to a firm's CEO and other stakeholders. Another function of the **marketing plan** is to communicate to everyone in the organization who has what marketing-related responsibilities and how they should execute those responsibilities.

**marketing plan**

A document that is designed to communicate the marketing strategy for an offering. The purpose of the plan is to influence executives, suppliers, distributors, and other important stakeholders of the firm so they will invest money, time, and effort to ensure the plan is a success.

**Audio Clip**

**Katie Scallan-Sarantakes**

Katie Scallan-Sarantakes develops and executes marketing plans for the Gulf States region of Toyota. Her path to this position is not unusual. Listen as she describes what she did to prepare herself for a position running a regional marketing office of a major global automaker.

## 1. MARKETING PLANNING ROLES

### LEARNING OBJECTIVE

1. **Identify the people responsible for creating marketing plans in organizations.**

Who, within an organization, is responsible for creating its marketing plans? From our discussion above, you might think the responsibility lies with the organization's chief marketing officer (CMO). The reality is that a team of marketing specialists is likely to be involved. Sometimes multiple teams are involved. Many companies create marketing plans at the divisional level. For example, Rockwell International has so many different business areas that each does its own strategic planning. The division responsible for military avionics, for instance, creates its own marketing plans and strategies separately from the division that serves the telecommunications industry. Each division has its own CMO.

### FIGURE 16.1

Rockwell International's many divisions serve a diverse set of industries, from military avionics and communications to consumer and business telecommunications. That's why Rockwell develops marketing plans at the division level (business-unit level).

Some of the team members specialize in certain areas. For example, the copier company Xerox has a team that specializes in competitive analysis. The team includes an engineer who can take competitors' products apart to see how they were manufactured, as well as a systems analyst who tests them for their performance. Also on the team is a marketing analyst who examines the competition's financial and marketing performance.

Some marketing-analyst positions are entry-level positions. You might be able to land one of these jobs straight out of college. Other positions are more senior and require experience, usually in sales or another area of marketing. Marketing analysts, who are constantly updating marketing information, are likely to be permanent members of the CMO's staff.

In some consumer-goods companies with many brands (such as P&G and SC Johnson), product—or brand—managers serve on their firm's marketing planning teams on an as-needed basis. These individuals are not permanent members of the team but participate only to the extent that their brands are involved. Many other members of the firm will also participate on marketing planning teams as needed. For example, a marketing researcher is likely to be part of such a team when it needs data for the planning process.

### KEY TAKEAWAY

The CMO of a business unit is likely to be responsible for the creation of its marketing plan. However, the CMO is generally assisted by marketing professionals and other staff members, who often work on marketing planning teams as needed. Marketing analysts, however, are permanent members of the CMO's staff.

### REVIEW QUESTIONS

1. Who is involved in the creation of a marketing plan?
2. In addition to marketing analysts, what other members of an organization help create marketing plans?

# 2. FUNCTIONS OF THE MARKETING PLAN

**LEARNING OBJECTIVES**

1. **Understand the functions of a marketing plan.**
2. **Write a marketing plan.**

In Chapter 1, we introduced the marketing plan and its components. Recall that a marketing plan should do the following:

a. Identify customers' needs.

b. Evaluate whether the organization can meet those needs in some way that allows for profitable exchanges with customers to occur.

c. Develop a mission statement, strategy, and organization centered on those needs.

 1. Create offerings that are the result of meticulous market research.
 2. Form operations and supply chains that advance the successful delivery of those offerings.

d. Pursue advertising, promotional, and public relations campaigns that lead to continued successful exchanges between the company and its customers.

e. Engage in meaningful communications with customers on a regular basis.

## 2.1 The Marketing Plan's Outline

The actual marketing plan you create will be written primarily for executives, who will use the forecasts in your plan to make budgeting decisions. These people will make budgeting decisions not only for your marketing activities but also for the firm's manufacturing, ordering, and production departments, and other functions based on your plan.

In addition to executives, many other people will use the plan. Your firm's sales force will use the marketing plan to determine its sales strategies and how many salespeople are needed. The entire marketing staff will rely on the plan to determine the direction and nature of their activities. The advertising agency you hire to create your promotional campaigns will use the plan to guide its creative team. Figure 16.2 shows a complete outline of a marketing plan (you may also want to go to http://www.morebusiness.com/templates_worksheets/bplans/printpre.brc for an example). Next, we will discuss the elements in detail so you will know how to prepare a marketing plan.

**FIGURE 16.2** Marketing Plan Outline

**The Marketing Plan: An Outline**

I. Executive Summary
II. The Business Challenge
   a. A brief description of the offering and the goals of the plan. This section serves as an introduction.
III. The Market
   a. Customers: Who are they, and what do they need?
   b. Company analysis: Your firm's strengths and weaknesses relative to this market and the offering.
   c. Collaborators: Your collaborators could include suppliers and/or distributors or retailers.
   d. Competitors: Who are they, and what are they doing?
   e. Business climate: The business climate includes the opportunities and threats created by environmental forces, such as government regulations and legislation, the economy, and social, cultural, and technological forces.
IV. The Strategy
   a. The strategy: Why did you choose the strategy you did? Consider including a brief discussion of alternatives that were considered and discarded.
   b. The offering: Provide details on the features and benefits of the offering, as well as its pricing options.
   c. The communication plan: How will the offering be launched? What will the ongoing communication strategies be? This section is likely to be fairly broad and will require collaboration with communication partners such as your firm's advertising agency.
   d. Distribution: How will the offering be sold? Who will sell it? Who will ship it? Who will service it?
V. Budget
   a. Investment: Provide details about the budget needed to launch and maintain the offering.
   b. Return: List both the short-term and long-term financial goals of the offering, including its projected sales, costs, and net income.
   c. Other resources required.
VI. Conclusion

## 2.2 The Executive Summary

A marketing plan starts with an executive summary. An executive summary should provide all the information your company's executives need to make a decision without reading the rest of the plan. The summary should include a brief description of the market, the product to be offered, the strategy behind the plan, and the budget. Any other important information, such as how your competitors and channel partners will respond to the actions your firm takes, should also be summarized. Because most executives will be reading the plan to make budgeting decisions, the budgeting information you include in the summary is very important. If the executives want more detail, they can refer to the "budget" section, which appears later in the plan. The executive summary should be less than one page long; ideally, it should be about a half page long. Most marketing plan writers find it easier to write a plan's summary last, even though it appears first in the plan. A summary is hard to write when you don't know the whole plan, so waiting until the plan is complete makes writing the executive summary easier.

## 2.3 The Business Challenge

In the "business challenge" section of the plan, the planner describes the offering and provides a brief rationale for why the company should invest in it. In other words, why is the offering needed? How does it fit in with what the company is already doing and further its overall business goals? In addition, the company's mission statement should be referenced. How does the offering and marketing plan further the company's mission?

Remember that a marketing plan is intended to be a persuasive document. You are trying not only to influence executives to invest in your idea but also to convince other people in your organization to buy into the plan. You are also trying to tell a compelling story that will make people outside your organization—for example, the director of the advertising agency you work with, or a potential supplier or channel partner—invest money, time, and effort into making your plan a success. Therefore, as you write the plan you should constantly be answering the question, "Why should I invest in this plan?" Put your answers in the business challenge section of the plan.

**FIGURE 16.3**

Your marketing plan has to convince busy executives and other stakeholders that your idea is worth investing in.

## 2.4 The Market

The market section of the plan should describe your customers and competitors, any other organizations with which you will collaborate, and the state of the market. We suggest that you always start the section by describing the customers who will purchase the offering. Why? Because customers are central to all marketing plans. After that, discuss your competitors, the climate, and your company in the order you believe readers will find most persuasive. In other words, discuss the factor you believe is most convincing first, followed by the second-most convincing factor, and so on.

### Customers

Who does your market consist of? What makes these people decide to buy the products they do, and how do they fulfill their personal value equations? What is their buying process like? Which of their needs does your offering meet?

Break the market into customer segments and describe each segment completely, answering those questions for each segment. When you write your plan, begin with the most important segment first and work your way to the least important segment. Include in your discussion the market share and sales goals for each segment.

For example, Progresso Soups' primary market segments might include the following:

- Families in colder regions
- People who need a good lunch but have to eat at their desks
- Busy young singles
- Older, perhaps retired, empty-nesters

These segments would be based on research that Progresso has completed showing that these are the groups that eat the most soup.

Your discussion of each segment should also include how to reach the customers within it, what they expect or need in terms of support (both presales and postsales support), and other information that helps readers understand how each segment is different from the others. After reading the section, a person should have a good grasp of how the segments differ yet understand how the needs of each are satisfied by the total offering.

**FIGURE 16.4**

Progresso Soups may divide their market into several groups. This family photo might actually represent three different markets: a person who eats lunch at his or her desk at work and needs something quick and filling; a retired but active couple that wants something hot and nourishing; and a busy young family looking for easy meals to prepare.

**Audio Clip**

**Katie Scallan-Sarantakes**

A marketing plan has to account for many factors: customers, competitors, and more. Listen as Katie Scallan-Sarantakes describes how she had to consider these factors when creating marketing plans for Toyota.

### Company Analysis

Include the results of your analysis of your company's strengths and weaknesses in this section. How is the company perceived by the customers you described earlier? Why is the company uniquely capable of capitalizing on the opportunity outlined in the plan? How sustainable is the competitive advantage you are seeking to achieve?

You will also need to identify any functional areas in which your company might need to invest for the plan to succeed. For example, money might be needed for new production or distribution facilities and to hire new marketing or sales employees and train existing ones.

**SWOT analysis**

An acronym for strengths, weaknesses, opportunities, and threats, the SWOT analysis is a tool that frames the situational analysis.

One tool that is useful for framing these questions is the **SWOT analysis**. SWOT stands for strengths, weaknesses, opportunities, and threats. Strengths and weaknesses are internal, meaning they are conditions of the company. Either these conditions are positive (strengths) or negative (weaknesses). Opportunities and threats are external to the company, and could be due to potential or actual actions taken by competitors, suppliers, or customers. Opportunities and threats could also be a function of government action or changes in technology and other factors.

When working with executives, some consultants have noted the difficulty executives have in separating opportunities from strengths, weaknesses from threats. Statements such as "We have an opportunity to leverage our strong product features" indicate such confusion. An opportunity lies in the market, not in a strength. Opportunities and threats are external; strengths and weaknesses are internal. Assuming demand (an external characteristic) for a strength (an internal characteristic) is a common marketing mistake. Sound marketing research is therefore needed to assess opportunity.

Other factors that make for better SWOT analysis are these:

- **Honest.** A good SWOT analysis is honest. A better way to describe those "strong" product features mentioned earlier would be to say "strong reputation among product designers," unless consumer acceptance has already been documented.
- **Broad.** The analysis has to be broad enough to capture trends. A small retail chain would have to look beyond its regional operating area in order to understand larger trends that may impact the stores.
- **Long term.** Consider multiple time frames. A SWOT analysis that only looks at the immediate future (or the immediate past) is likely to miss important trends. Engineers at Mars (makers of Skittles, M&Ms, and Snickers) visit trade shows in many fields, not just candy, so that they can identify trends in manufacturing that may take a decade to reach the candy industry. In this way, they can shorten the cycle and take advantage of such trends early when needed.
- **Multiple perspectives.** SWOT analyses are essentially based on someone's perception. Therefore, a good SWOT should consider the perspective of all areas of the firm. Involve people from shipping, sales, production, and perhaps even from suppliers and channel members.

The SWOT analysis for a company, or for any organization, is both internal and external in focus. Some of the external areas for focus are collaborators (suppliers, distributors, and others), competitors, and the business climate.

### Collaborators

Along with company strengths and weaknesses, identify any actual or potential partners needed to pull the plan off. Note that collaborators are more than just a list of suppliers and distributors. Collaborators are those organizations, either upstream or downstream in the value chain, you need to partner with to cocreate value.

For example, AT&T collaborated with Apple to develop the iPhone. AT&T is downstream in the value chain, providing the needed cell service and additional features that made the iPhone so revolutionary. At the same time, however, AT&T was a part of the development of the iPhone and the attendant marketing strategy; the partnership began well before the iPhone was launched.

### Competitors

Your marketing plan, if it is any good at all, is likely to spark retaliation from one or more competitors. For example, Teradata and Unica operate in the same market. Both sell data-warehousing products to companies. Teradata primarily focuses on the information technology departments that support the data warehouse, whereas Unica focuses on the marketing departments that actually use the data warehouse. Nonetheless, Teradata is well aware of Unica's marketing strategy and is taking steps to combat it by broadening its own market to include data-warehousing users in marketing departments. One step was to teach their salespeople what marketing managers do and how they would use a data warehouse as part of their job so that when these salespeople are talking to marketing managers, they can know what they're talking about.

Teradata marketing planners also have to be aware of potential competitors. What if IBM or HP decided to enter the market? Who is most likely to enter the market, what would their offering look like, and how can we make it harder for them to want to enter the market? If your company captures their market before they can enter, then they may choose to go elsewhere.

Identify your competitors and be honest about both their strengths and weaknesses in your marketing. Remember that other people, and perhaps other organizations, will be using your plan to create their own plans. If they are to be successful, they have to know what competition they face. Include, too, in this section of the plan how quickly you expect your competitors to retaliate and what the nature of that retaliation will be. Will they lower their prices, create similar offerings, add services to drive up the value of their products, spend more on advertising, or a combination of these tactics?

A complete competitive analysis not only anticipates how the competition will react; it also includes an analysis of the competition's financial resources. Do your competitors have money to invest in a competitive offering? Are they growing by acquiring other companies? Are they growing by adding new locations or new sales staff? Or are they growing simply because they are effective? Maybe they are not growing at all. To answer these questions, you will need to carefully review your competitors' financial statements and all information publicly available about them. This can include an executive quoted in an article about a company's growth for a particular product or an analyst's projection for future sales within a specific market.

### Business Climate

You may have already addressed some of the factors in the business environment that are creating the opportunity for your offering. For example, when you discussed customers, you perhaps noted a new technology they are beginning to use.

A complete coverage of the climate would include the following (the PEST analysis):

- Political climate
- Economic climate
- Social and cultural environment
- Technological environment

A scan of the political climate should include any new government regulations as well as legislation. For example, will changes in the tax laws make for more or less disposable income among our customers? Will the tightening of government regulations affect how salespeople can call on doctors, for example, hindering your marketing opportunity? Will federal policies that affect exchange rates or tariffs make global competitors stronger or weaker? For example, the government introduced the Cash for Clunkers program to encourage people to buy new cars. Within only a few weeks, 250,000 new cars were sold through the program and it ran out of money. Auto dealers were caught unprepared and many actually ran out of popular vehicles.

The economic climate is also important to consider. While 2008 saw tremendous swings in gas prices, other factors such as the subprime lending crisis and decline of the housing market affected everything from the price of corn to the sales of movie tickets. Such volatility is unusual, but it is important nonetheless to know what the economy is doing.

The social and cultural environment is also important to watch. Marketers, for example, may note the rise in the Hispanic population as a market segment, but it is also important to recognize the influence of the Hispanic culture. Understanding the Hispanic culture is important in reaching this market segment with the right marketing mix. In creating marketing campaigns for something such as a financial product, it's very important to understand the history that Hispanics have had with financial institutions in their home countries. Understanding that culturally Hispanics might not trust financial institutions and developing campaigns that generate positive word of mouth, such as refer-a-friend and influencer tactics, can be explosive once the wall has been torn down.

Finally, the technological environment should be considered. Technology is the application of science to solve problems. It encompasses more than just information (computer) technology. For example, when Ted Schulte (profiled in Chapter 13) discusses a pacemaker with a cardiac surgeon, Ted is describing the latest technology available. The new technology could be related to the battery used to power the pacemaker, the materials used in the leads (the wires that connect the pacemaker to the body), or even the material that encases the pacemaker. Understanding the technological environment can provide you with a greater understanding of a product's life cycle and the direction the market is taking when it comes to newer technologies.

**FIGURE 16.5**

The housing crisis was caused by a failure in the subprime lending market, an economic condition that affected many other businesses.

**FIGURE 16.6**

Technology encompasses more than just information technology. Produced by Guidant Technologies, this pacemaker utilizes information technology to record heart-function data a doctor can read later. But the product might also utilize other new technologies, such as a new battery, materials used to connect the pacemaker to the heart, and the casing for the pacemaker, all of which affect its performance.

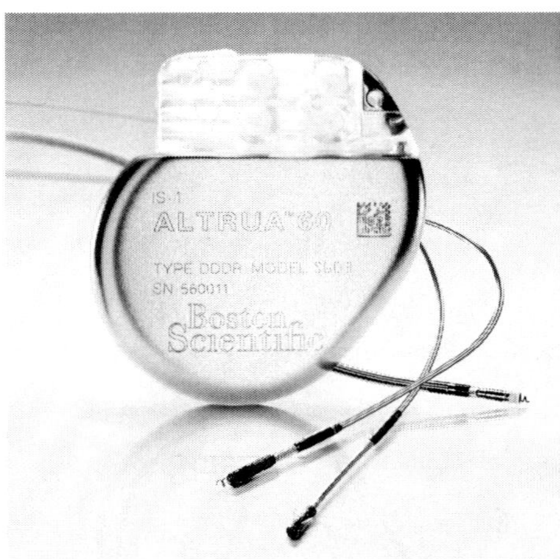


*Source: Guidant Technologies, used with permission.*

Many of the environmental factors we mentioned impact other factors. For example, technological changes are altering the social and cultural environment. Instead of writing letters to one another, families and friends use e-mail and social networking sites to communicate and maintain relationships. Online communication has affected any number of businesses, including the greeting card business and the U.S. Postal Service, which recently announced it was closing many facilities.

Likewise, the economic environment influences the political environment and vice versa. The huge bailout of the banks by the government is an example of how the economic environment affects the political environment. The laws passed as a result of the bank bailout, which include more-restrictive lending practices, are affecting banks, businesses, and consumers. Any looming changes in the business climate such as this need to be included in your marketing plan.

## 2.5 The Strategy

The next section of the plan details the strategy your organization will use to develop, market, and sell the offering. This section is your opportunity to create a compelling argument as to what you intend to do and why others should invest in the strategy. Your reader will be asking, "Why should we adopt this strategy?" To answer that question, you may need to include a brief discussion of the strategic alternatives that were considered and discarded. When readers complete the section, they should conclude that the strategy you proposed is the best one available.

### The Offering

Provide detail on the features and benefits of the offering, including pricing options, in this section. For example, in some instances, your organization might plan for several variations of the offering, each with different pricing options. The different options should be discussed in detail, along with the market segments expected to respond to each option. Some marketing professionals like to specify the sales goals for each option in this section, along with the associated costs and gross profit margins for each. Other planners prefer to wait until the budget section of the plan to provide that information.

The plan for the offering should also include the plan for introducing offerings that will follow the initial launch. For example, when should Progresso introduce new soup flavors? Should there be seasonal flavors? Should there be smaller sizes and larger sizes, and should they be introduced all at the same time or in stages?

Part of an offering is the service support consumers need to extract the offering's full value. The support might include presales support as well as postsales support. For example, Teradata has a team of finance specialists who can help customers document the return on investment they would get from purchasing and implementing a Teradata data warehouse. This presales support helps potential buyers make a stronger business case for buying Teradata's products with executives who control their companies' budgets.

Postsales support can include technical support. In B2B (business-to-business) environments, sellers frequently offer to train their customers' employees to use products as part of their postsales support. Before you launch an offering, you need to be sure your firm's support services are in place. That means training service personnel, creating the appropriate communication channels for customers to air their technical concerns, and other processes.

### The Communication Plan

How will the offering be launched? Will it be like Dow Corning's launch of a new silicon acrylate copolymer, a product used to add color to cosmetics? That product was announced at the In-Cosmetics trade show in Barcelona. Or will you invite customers, media, and analysts from around the globe to your company's offices for the launch, as SAS did with its SAS 9 software product?

In addition to the announcement of the new product, the communication plan has to specify how ongoing customer communications will be conducted. The mechanisms used to gather customer feedback as well as how the offering will be promoted to customers need to be spelled out. For example, will you create an online community like Laura Carros did with the JCPenney Ambrielle line?

The discussion of the communication plan can be fairly broad. You can put additional details in a separate planning document that outlines the product's advertising strategies, event strategies (such as trade shows and special events like customer golf tournaments that will be used to promote the product), and sales strategies.

**FIGURE 16.7**

Prior to launching a new offering, the presales and postsales support personnel for it have to be trained and the appropriate work processes created so that the right level of support is provided. These call-center technicians had to first learn the offering's technical processes before it could be launched.

### Distribution

This section should answer questions about where and how the offering will be sold. Who will sell it? Who will ship it? Who will service and support it? In addition, the distribution section should specify the inventories that need to be maintained in order to meet customer expectations for fast delivery and where those inventories should be kept.

## 2.6 Budget

The budget section is more than just a discussion of the money needed to launch the new offering. A complete budget section will cover all the resources, such as new personnel, new equipment, new locations, and so forth, for the launch to be a success. Of course, these resources have costs associated with them. In some instances, the budget might require that existing resources be redeployed and a case made for doing so.

The first portion of the budget will likely cover the investment required for the launch. The plan might point out that additional funds need to be allocated to the offering to make it ready for the market. For example, perhaps additional beta testing or product development over and above what the firm normally commits to new products is needed. Certainly, marketing funds will be needed to launch the offering and pay for any special events, advertising, promotional materials, and so forth. Funds might also be needed to cover the costs of training salespeople and service personnel and potentially hiring new staff members. For example, Teradata introduced a new offering that was aimed at an entirely new market. The new market was so different that it required a new sales force. Details for the sales force, such as how many salespeople, sales managers, and support personnel will be needed, would go in this section.

The budget section should include the costs associated with maintaining the amount of inventory of the product to meet customers' needs. The costs to provide customers with support services should also be estimated and budgeted. Some products will be returned, some services will be rejected by the consumer, and other problems will occur. The budget should include projections and allowances for these occurrences.

The budget section is also the place to forecast the product's sales and profits. Even though the plan likely mentioned the sales goals set for each market segment, the budget section is where the details go. For example, the cost for advertising, trade shows, special events, and salespeople should be spelled out. The projections should also include timelines. The sales costs for one month might be estimated, as well as two months, six months, and so forth, as Figure 16.8 shows.

Note that Figure 16.8 shows that the product's costs are high early on and then decrease before leveling out. That cost line assumes there is a heavy upfront investment to launch the offering, which is usually true for new products. The sales of the offering should grow as it gathers momentum in the market. However, the market potential stays the same, assuming that the potential number of customers stays the same. That might not always be the case, though. If we were targeting mothers of babies, for example, the market potential might vary based on the projected seasonality in birth rates because more babies tend to be born in some months than others.

**FIGURE 16.8** A Marketing Plan Timeline Illustrating Market Potential, Sales, and Costs

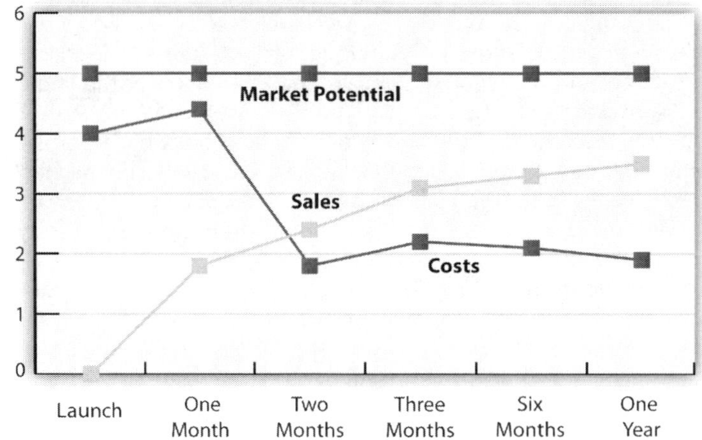


## 2.7 Conclusion

In the conclusion, repeat the highlights. Summarize the target market, the offer, and the communication plan. Your conclusion should remind the reader of all the reasons why your plan is the best choice.

Of course, the written plan is itself a marketing tool. You want it to convince someone to invest in your ideas, so you want to write it down on paper in a compelling way. Figure 16.9 offers some tips for effectively doing so. Also, keep in mind that a marketing plan is created at a single point in time. The market, though, is dynamic. A good marketing plan includes how the organization should respond to various scenarios if the market changes. In addition, the plan should include "triggers" detailing what should happen under the scenarios. For example, it might specify that when a certain percentage of market share is reached, then the price of the product will be reduced (or increased). Or the plan might specify the minimum amount of the product that must be sold by a certain point in time—say, six months after the product is launched—and what should happen if the mark isn't reached. Also, it should once again be noted that the marketing plan is a communication device. For that reason, the outline of a marketing plan may look somewhat different from the order in which the tasks in the outline are actually completed.

**FIGURE 16.9** Tips for Writing an Effective Marketing Plan

- Be brief—executives are busy.
- Anticipate and answer questions your organization's executives might have.
- Use active (not passive) voice when you write your plan.
- Use visuals and bullet points. Some people are visual learners and others are verbal. Meet the needs of both types of people.
- Read, proofread, and have someone else proofread the plan.

**KEY TAKEAWAY**

A marketing plan's executive summary should include a brief summary of the market, the product to be offered, the strategy behind the plan, and the budget, as well as any other important information. In this section of the plan, the planner describes the offering and a brief rationale for why the company should invest in it. The market section of the plan should describe a firm's customers, competitors, any other organizations with which it will collaborate, and the climate of the market. The strategy section details the tactics the organization will use to develop, market, and sell the offering. When readers complete the strategy section, they should conclude that the proposed strategy is the best one available.

The budget section of the marketing plan covers all the resources, such as new personnel, new equipment, new locations, and so forth, needed to successfully launch the product, as well as details about the product's costs and sales forecasts.

**REVIEW QUESTIONS**

1. What is a marketing plan and how is it used?
2. Which section of the marketing plan is most important? Why? The least important?
3. What is the purpose of scenario planning?

# 3. FORECASTING

**LEARNING OBJECTIVES**

1. **List steps in the forecasting process.**
2. **Identify types of forecasting methods and their advantages and disadvantages.**
3. **Discuss the methods used to improve the accuracy of forecasts.**

Creating marketing strategy is not a single event, nor is the implementation of marketing strategy something only the marketing department has to worry about. When the strategy is implemented, the rest of the company must be poised to deal with the consequences. As we have explained, an important component is the sales forecast, which is the estimate of how much the company will actually sell. The rest of the company must then be geared up (or down) to meet that demand. In this section, we explore forecasting in more detail, as there are many choices a marketing executive can make in developing a forecast.

Accuracy is important when it comes to forecasts. If executives overestimate the demand for a product, the company could end up spending money on manufacturing, distribution, and servicing activities it won't need. The software developer Data Impact recently overestimated the demand for one of its new products. Because the sales of the product didn't meet projections, Data Impact lacked the cash available to pay its vendors, utility providers, and others. Employees had to be terminated in many areas of the firm to trim costs.

Underestimating demand can be just as devastating. When a company introduces a new product, it launches marketing and sales campaigns to create demand for it. But if the company isn't ready to deliver the amount of the product the market demands, then other competitors can steal sales the firm might otherwise have captured. Sony's inability to deliver the e-Reader in sufficient numbers made Amazon's Kindle more readily accepted in the market; other features then gave the Kindle an advantage that Sony is finding difficult to overcome.

The marketing leader of a firm has to do more than just forecast the company's sales. The process can be complex, because how much the company can sell will depend on many factors such as how much the product will cost, how competitors will react, and so forth—in fact, much of what you have already read about in preparing a marketing strategy. Each of these factors has to be taken into account in order to determine how much the company is likely to sell. As factors change, the forecast has to change as well. Thus, a sales forecast is actually a composite of a number of estimates and has to be dynamic as those other estimates change.

**market potential**

Total industry-wide sales expected in a particular product category for the time period of interest.

**sales potential**

The maximum total revenue a company hopes to generate from a product or the number of units of it the company can hope to sell.

A common first step is to determine **market potential**, or total industry-wide sales expected in a particular product category for the time period of interest. (The time period of interest might be the coming year, quarter, month, or some other time period.) Some marketing research companies, such as Nielsen, Gartner, and others, estimate the market potential for various products and then sell that research to companies that produce those products.

Once the marketing executive has an idea of the market potential, the company's sales potential can be estimated. A firm's **sales potential** is the maximum total revenue it hopes to generate from a product or the number of units of it the company can hope to sell. The sales potential for the product is typically represented as a percentage of its market potential and equivalent to the company's estimated maximum market share for the time period. As you can see in Figure 16.8, companies sell less than potential because not everyone will make a decision to buy their product: some will put off a decision; others will buy a competitor's product; still others might make do with a substitute product. In your budget, you'll want to forecast the revenues earned from the product against the market potential, as well as against the product's costs.

## 3.1 Forecasting Methods

Forecasts, at their basic level, are simply someone's guess as to what will happen. Each estimate, though, is the product of a process. Several such processes are available to marketing executives, and the final forecast is likely to be a blend of results from more than one process. These processes are judgment techniques and surveys, time series techniques, spending correlates and other models, and market tests.

### Judgment and Survey Techniques

**judgment techniques**

Forecasting methods that rely on someone's estimate(s).

At some level, every forecast is ultimately someone's judgment. Some techniques, though, rely more on people's opinions or estimates and are called **judgment techniques**. Judgment techniques can include customer (or channel member or supplier) surveys, executive or expert opinions, surveys of customers' (or channel members') intentions or estimates, and estimates by salespeople.

#### Customer and Channel Surveys

In some markets, particularly in business-to-business markets, research companies ask customers how much they plan to spend in the coming year on certain products. Have you ever filled out a survey asking if you intend to buy a car or refrigerator in the coming year? Chances are your answers were part of someone's forecast. Similarly, surveys are done for products sold through distributors. Companies then buy the surveys from the research companies or do their own surveys to use as a starting point for their forecasting. Surveys are better at estimating market potential than sales potential, however, because potential buyers are far more likely to know they will buy something—they just don't know which brand or model. Surveys can also be relatively costly, particularly when they are commissioned for only one company.

#### Sales Force Composite

**sales force composite**

An estimate of future sales based on the sum of estimates from all of the company's salespeople.

A **sales force composite** is a forecast based on estimates of sales in a given time period gathered from all of a firm's salespeople. Salespeople have a pretty good idea about how much can be sold in the coming period of time (especially if they have bonuses riding on those sales). They've been calling on their customers and know when buying decisions will be made.

Estimating the sales for new products or new promotions and pricing strategies will be harder for salespeople to estimate until they have had some experience selling those products after they have been introduced, promoted, or repriced. Further, management may not want salespeople to know about new products or promotions until these are announced to the general public, so this method is not useful in situations involving new products or promotions. Another limitation reflects salespeople's natural optimism. Salespeople tend to be optimistic about what they think they can sell and may overestimate future sales. Conversely, if the company uses these estimates to set quotas, salespeople are likely to reduce their estimates to make it easier to achieve quota.

Salespeople are more accurate in their near-term sales estimates, as their customers are not likely to share plans too far into the future. Consequently, most companies use sales force composites for shorter-range forecasts in order to more accurately predict their production and inventory requirements. Konica-Minolta, an office equipment manufacturer, has recently placed a heavy emphasis on improving the accuracy of its sales force composites because the cost of being wrong is too great. Underestimated forecasts result in some customers having to wait too long for deliveries for products, and they may turn to competitors who can deliver faster. By contrast, overestimated forecasts result in higher inventory costs.

### Executive Opinion

**Executive opinion** is exactly what the name implies: the best-guess estimates of a company's executives. Each executive submits an estimate of the company's sales, which are then averaged to form the overall sales forecast. The advantages of executive opinions are that they are low cost and fast and have the effect of making executives committed to achieving them. An executive-opinion-based forecast can be a good starting point. However, there are disadvantages to the method, so it should not be used alone. These disadvantages are similar to those of the sales force composites. If the executives' forecast becomes a quota upon which their bonuses are estimated, they will have an incentive to underestimate the forecast so they can meet their targets. Organizational factors also come into play. A junior executive, for example, is not likely to forecast low sales for a product that his or her CEO is pushing, even if low sales are likely to occur.

**executive opinion**

A forecasting method in which an executive or group of executives provides a best estimate of what will be sold or what will happen.

### Expert Opinion

**Expert opinion** is similar to executive opinion except that the expert is usually someone outside the company. Like executive opinion, expert opinion is a tool best used in conjunction with more quantitative methods. As a sole method of forecasting, however, expert opinions are often very inaccurate. Just consider how preseason college football rankings compare with the final standings. The football experts' predictions are usually not very accurate.

**expert opinion**

A forecasting method in which the forecast is based on an objective third-party expert's best estimate of what will happen in the market and how that will influence sales.

## Time Series Techniques

Time series techniques examine sales patterns in the past in order to predict sales in the future. For example, with a **trend analysis**, the marketing executive identifies the rate at which a company's sales have grown in the past and uses that rate to estimate future sales. For example, if sales have grown 3 percent per year over the past five years, trend analysis would assume a similar 3 percent growth rate next year.

A simple form of analysis such as this can be useful if a market is stable. The problem is that many markets are not stable. A rapid change in any one of a market's dynamics is likely to result in wide swings in growth rates. Just think about auto sales before, during, and after the government's Cash for Clunkers program. What sold the previous month could not account for the effects of the program. Consequently, if an executive were to have estimated auto sales based on the rate of change for the previous period, the estimate would have been way off.

**trend analysis**

A group of forecasting methods that base the future period of sales (or another variable) on the rate of change for previous periods of time.

**FIGURE 16.10**

The federal government's Cash for Clunkers program resulted in a significant short-term increase in new car sales and filled junkyards with thousands of clunkers!

*Source: Wikimedia Commons.*

The Cash for Clunkers program was an unusual situation; many products may have wide variations in demand for other reasons. Trend analysis can still be useful in these situations but adjustments have to be made to account for the swings in rates of change. Two common adjustments are the **moving average**, whereby the rate of change for the past few periods is averaged, and **exponential smoothing**, a type of moving average that puts more emphasis on the most recent period.

**moving average**

A trend analysis type of forecasting method that estimates sales (or other variable) based on an average rate of change over a group of previous periods of time; the rate changes (moves) as the oldest period is dropped off and the most recent period added in.

**exponential smoothing**

A method of trend analysis forecasting that weights more recent periods of time more heavily than more distant periods of time.

## Correlates and Other Models

A number of more sophisticated models can be useful in forecasting sales. One fairly common method is a **correlational analysis**, which is a form of trend analysis that estimates sales based on the trends of other variables. For example, furniture-company executives know that new housing starts (the number of new houses that are begun to be built in a period) predict furniture sales in the near future because new houses tend to get filled up with new furniture. Such a correlate is considered a **leading indicator**, because it leads, or precedes, sales. The Conference Board publishes an Index of Leading Indicators, which is a single number that represents a composite of commonly used leading indicators. Some of these leading indicators are housing starts, wholesale orders, orders for durable goods (items like refrigerators, air conditioning systems, and other long-lasting consumer products), and even consumer sentiment, or how consumers think the economy is doing.

**correlational analysis**

A form of trend analysis that estimates sales based on the trends of other variables.

**leading indicator**

A correlate that occurs before the variable being forecasted (e.g., permits to build new houses is a leading indicator of building material sales because permits are issued before the materials are purchased).

### Response Models

Some companies create sophisticated statistical models called **response models**, which are based on how customers have responded in the past to marketing strategies. JCPenney, for example, takes previous sales data and combines it with customer data gathered from the retailer's Web site. The models help JCPenney see how many customers are price sensitive and only buy products when they are on sale and how many customers are likely to respond to certain offers. The retailer can then estimate the sales for products by market segment based on the offers and promotions directed at those segments.

**response models**

Sophisticated statistical models used in forecasting that are based on how customers have responded in the past to marketing strategies.

## Market Tests

A **market test** is an experiment in which the company launches a new offering in a limited market in order to gain real-world knowledge of how the market will react to the product. Since there isn't any historical data on how the product has done, response models and time-series techniques are not effective. A market test provides some measure of sales in response to the marketing plan, so in that regard, it is like a response model, just based on limited data. The demand for the product can then be extrapolated to the full market. However, remember that market tests are visible to your competitors, and they can undertake actions, such as drastic price cuts, to skew your results.

**market test**

The test launch of a product's complete marketing plan to ensure that it reaches buyers, gets positive reactions, and generates sales of the product.

**FIGURE 16.11**

HEB uses Waco, Texas, as a test market, combining data from its loyalty program with sales data to see who buys what and at what price.

*Source: Wikimedia Commons.*

The grocery chain HEB uses Waco, Texas, as a test site. HEB has a loyalty program that enables it to collect lots of data on its customers. When HEB wants to test market a new product, the firm does it in Waco, where individual customer data can be combined with sales data. Testing in Waco tells HEB who is likely to buy the product and at what price, information that makes extrapolating to their larger market more accurate.

## 3.2 Building Better Forecasts

At best, a forecast is a scientific estimate, but really, a forecast is still just a sophisticated guess. Still, there are steps that can enhance the likelihood of success. The first step is to commit to accuracy. At Konica-Minolta, regional vice presidents are rewarded for being accurate and punished for being wrong about their forecasts, no matter what the direction of them is. As we mentioned earlier, underestimating is considered by Konica-Minolta leadership to be just as bad as overestimating sales.

We've also mentioned how salespeople and managers will lower estimates if the estimates are used to set quotas. Using forecasts properly is another factor that can improve forecasting accuracy. But there are other ways to make forecasts more accurate. These begin with picking the right methods for your business.

### Pick the Right Method(s) for Your Business and Your Decision

Some products have very short selling cycles; others take a long time to produce and sell. What is appropriate for a fast-moving consumer good like toothpaste is not appropriate for a durable good like a refrigerator. A response model might work for Crest toothpaste in the short term, but longer-term forecasts might require a sophisticated time-series technique. By contrast, Whirlpool might find, for example, that channel surveys are better predictors of refrigerator sales over the long term.

### Use Multiple Methods

Since forecasts are estimates, the more estimates generated from various methods, the better. For example, combining expert opinions with a trend analysis could help you understand not only what is happening but also why. Every forecast results in decisions, such as the decision to hire more people, add manufacturing capacity, order supplies, and so forth. In addition, practice makes perfect, as they say. The more forecasts you have to make and resulting decisions you have to live with, the better you will get at forecasting.

### Use Many Variables

Forecasting for smaller business units first can result in greater accuracy. For example, JCPenney may estimate sales by region first, and then roll that information up into a national sales forecast. By forecasting locally, more variables can be considered, and with more variables comes more information, which should help the accuracy of the company's overall sales forecast. Similarly, JCPenney may estimate sales by market segment, such as women over age fifty. Again, forecasting in a smaller segment or business unit can then enable the company to compare such forecasts to forecasts by product line and gain greater accuracy overall.

### Use Scenario-Based Forecasts

One forecast is not enough. Consider what will happen if conditions change. For example, how might your forecast change if your competitors react strongly to your strategy? How might it change if they don't react at all? Or if the government changes a policy that makes your product tax free? All of these factors will influence sales, so the smart executive considers multiple scenarios. While the executive may not expect the government to make something tax free, scenarios can be created that consider favorable government regulation, stable regulation, and negative regulation, just as one can consider light competitive reaction, moderate reaction, or strong reaction.

### Track Actual Results and Adjust

As time goes on, forecasts that have been made should be adjusted to reflect reality. For example, Katie Scallan-Sarantakes may have to do an annual forecast for Scion sales, but as each month goes by, she has hard sales data with which to adjust future forecasts. Further, she knows how strongly competition has reacted and can adjust her estimates accordingly. So, even though she may have an annual forecast, the forecast changes regularly based on how well the company is doing.

**KEY TAKEAWAY**

A forecast is an educated guess, or estimate, of sales in the future. Accuracy is important because so many other decisions a firm must make depend on the forecasts. When a company forecasts sales, it has to consider market potential and sales potential. Many methods of forecasting exist, including expert opinion, channel and customer surveys, sales force composites, time series data, and test markets.

Better forecasts can be obtained by using multiple methods, forecasting for various scenarios, and tracking actual data (including sales) and adjusting future forecasts accordingly.

**REVIEW QUESTIONS**

1. Which forecasting method would be most accurate for forecasting sales of hair-care products in the next year? How would your answer change if you were forecasting for the next month? For home appliances?
2. What is the role of expert opinion in all forecasts?
3. How can forecasting accuracy be improved?

# 4. ONGOING MARKETING PLANNING AND EVALUATION

**LEARNING OBJECTIVES**

1. **Apply marketing planning processes to ongoing business settings.**
2. **Identify the role of the marketing audit.**

Our discussion so far might lead you to believe that a marketing plan is created only when a new offering is being launched. In reality, marketing plans are created frequently—sometimes on an annual basis, or when a new CMO is hired, when market dynamics change drastically and quickly, or just whenever a company's CEO wants one. Moreover, as we indicated, a marketing plan should be something of a "living" document; it should contain triggers that result in a company reevaluating its strategies should different scenarios occur.

Some of those scenarios can occur immediately. For example, when a product is launched, the market reacts. Journalists begin to cover the phenomenon, competitors respond, and regulators may take note. What then should happen if the sales goals for the product are substantially exceeded? Should its price be raised or lowered? Should follow-on offerings be launched sooner? What if a competitor launches a similar offering a week later? Or worse yet, what if the competition launches a much better offering? The key to a successful ongoing marketing strategy is twofold: understanding causality and good execution of the marketing plan. Next we discuss each of these aspects.

**Audio Clip**

**Katie Scallan-Sarantakes**

Katie Scallan-Sarantakes knows firsthand the difficulty of tracking the success of marketing activity. She describes some of those challenges here.

## 4.1 Causality

**causality**

The relationship between two variables whereby one variable is a direct consequence of the other.

**Causality** is the relationship between two variables whereby one variable is a direct consequence of the other. For a scientist in a lab, identifying causality is fairly easy because the causal variable can be controlled and the consequences observed. For marketers, such control is a dream, not a reality. Identifying causality, then, can be a real challenge.

Why is causality so important? Assume you've observed a drop in sales that you think is caused by a competitor's lower price. If you reduce your price to combat the competitor's when, in reality, the poor sales are due simply to seasonal factors, lower prices might give consumers the impression that your product is cheap or low quality. This could send your sales even further downward. Drawing the wrong conclusions about causality can lead to disastrous results.

Control is an important related concept. **Control**, in this context, means not the degree to which you can manipulate an outcome but rather the degree to which you can separate the effects of a variable on a consequence. For example, you have complete control over what the customer pays for the offering. You are able to manipulate that outcome. However, you have no control over seasonal effects. Nonetheless, you can identify what those effects are and account for their influence.

**control**

(a) The degree to which you can manipulate an outcome; (b) the degree to which you can separate the effects of a variable on a consequence.

The first type of control is **managerial control**, whereby you have control over how variables in a marketing plan are implemented. You decide, for example, how many stores will carry your product. You can vary that number and have an effect on sales. The second type of control is **statistical control**, whereby you can remove the influence of the variable on the outcome mathematically. For example, you have no control over seasonality. If you are selling a product for babies and more babies are born in August than any other month, then your sales will go up in September. Statistical control allows you to smooth out the seasonal variance on sales so you can then determine how much of the change in sales is due to other factors, especially those you have control over. Statistical control is something you learned in a regression class. However, the numbers in a statistical analysis can be as easily approximated. You don't necessarily need to utilize complicated equations. Consider the following scenario:

**managerial control**

The ability to manipulate variables, such as how a marketing plan is implemented.

**statistical control**

Mathematically removing the influence of a variable on an outcome so as to isolate the cause of a problem.

1. Over the past five years, you have observed an average decline of 20 percent in sales for the months of June, July, and August, which also happen to be months in which many salespeople and buyers vacation.
2. This year, the decline was 28 percent.
3. You can therefore safely assume that about 20 percent of the decline this year was due to people taking vacations, as they have in years past; you can further assume that the amount of the decline due to factors other than vacations was about 8 percent.

Doing a simple analysis such as this at least gives you some idea that something new is going on that is lowering your sales. You can then explore the problem more completely.

So how do you figure out exactly what *is* the cause of such a decline? In some instances, marketing executives speculate about the potential causes of problems and then research them. For example, if the product's price is perceived to be the problem, conversing with a number of former customers who switched to competing products could either verify this hunch or dispel it. In a B2B environment, salespeople who are aware of a competitor's new lower prices might be the first to identify the problem, rather than marketing executives. Nonetheless, the firm's marketing executives can then try to verify that lower prices led to the sales decline. In consumer-goods markets, there are often many segments of consumers. Rather than asking a few of them what they think, formal market research tools such as surveys and focus groups are used.

## 4.2 The Marketing Audit

Another investigative tool that can be used to research a drop in a company's sales performance is a marketing audit. A **marketing audit** is an examination or snapshot of the state of a company's marketing strategies as they are actually implemented. Here, managerial control becomes important. Was the strategy implemented as intended? Is the strategy working?

**marketing audit**

A snapshot of the state of the company's marketing strategies as they are actually implemented; an examination of the implementation of a marketing plan to determine if it was implemented properly and if it was successful.

For example, when Xerox launched a new workstation, the company ran a promotion giving a customer who bought a workstation a discount on a copier. Despite the promotion, the overall sales of the workstation failed to meet Xerox's expectations. There were, however, geographical areas in which the sales of the product were quite good. What was up?

Upon closer examination, Xerox's managers learned that the firm's salespeople in these areas had actually developed a much more effective selling strategy: they sold the copiers first and then offered the workstation for free by applying the amount of the discount to the workstation, not the copier. Xerox's marketing quickly revamped the promotion and communicated it effectively to the rest of the sales staff.

**FIGURE 16.12**

A marketing audit is an examination of all of the company's marketing activities. Here, an auditor is looking at actual product displays in a retail store to make sure the product is being displayed and priced properly.

**fidelity**

The degree to which a plan is implemented as intended.

**Fidelity** is the degree to which the plan is being implemented as it is supposed to be. In the example of the Xerox workstation, there was substantial fidelity—the plan was being implemented right—but the plan was poor. Usually, though, the problem is that the plan is not executed properly.

More serious issues require more in-depth study. When Mark Hurd took over as Hewlett-Packard's CEO in 2005, he ordered an immediate audit of HP's sales and marketing activities. Metrics such as the win/loss ratios of business deals, the length of time it took to get a proposal approved and presented to a customer, and other factors exposed numerous problems Hurd needed to fix. The audit identified the causes, many of which Hurd and his team were able to deal with quickly. As a result, HP increased market share and captured the lead in the PC market in the first year following Hurd's appointment.

According to the marketing consulting company Copernicus, a marketing audit should assess many factors, but especially those listed below. Does any of the information surprise you?

### Top Ten Factors a Marketing Audit Should Assess

1. Key factors that impacted the business for good or for bad during the past year.
2. Customer satisfaction scores and the number and type of customer complaints.
3. The satisfaction levels of distributors, retailers, and other value chain members.
4. The marketing knowledge, attitudes, and satisfaction of all executives involved in the marketing function.
5. The extent to which the marketing program was marketed internally and "bought into" by top managers and nonmarketing executives.
6. The offering: Did it meet the customer's needs as expected, and was the offering's competitive advantage defensible?
7. The performance of the organization's advertising, promotion, sales, marketing, and research programs with an emphasis on their return on the money invested in them.
8. Whether the marketing plan achieved its stated financial and nonfinancial goals.
9. Whether the individual elements of the marketing plan achieved their stated financial and nonfinancial goals.
10. The current value of the brand and customer equity for each brand in the product portfolio.[4]

You were probably surprised by a few items on the list. For example, did your marketing plan include a plan to market the marketing program to important internal parties, such as the company's managers and employees? We discussed earlier that the marketing plan should persuade others to invest in the plan's success. Part of that persuasion process could actually include a plan to communicate the plan! A marketing audit should assess the extent to which the plan was successful in achieving the goal of getting important people and departments within an organization to buy into the plan.

Do you think the "top ten" list above is prioritized correctly? Some people would argue that the first four or five factors that need to be examined are the most important. Other people would argue that only the financial factors (factors 7–10) matter. Which group is right?

The answer really depends on what's important at the time to a company. Because HP hired Hurd to improve the company's poor financial performance, financial issues were likely his top priority. He knew, however, that the causes of the poor financial performance probably lay elsewhere, so he had his team look deeper. Financial problems are usually the first to prompt a marketing audit.

Many firms don't wait for problems before conducting an audit. Either they hire consultants like Copernicus Marketing Consulting to conduct the audit, or they do the audits themselves. If a firm's budget doesn't allow for a complete audit annually, the company will often focus on one particular area at a time, such as levels of satisfaction among its customers and channel partners. The following year it might audit the company's communications strategy. Rotating the focus ensures that every aspect is audited regularly, if not annually.

**Audio Clip**

**Katie Scallan-Sarantakes**

Marketing is a fun job, but it is more than that. Marketing professionals have to deliver business results with all of the work they do. As Katie Scallan-Sarantakes describes, you have to prove your ability to deliver value.

**KEY TAKEAWAY**

The key to a successful ongoing marketing strategy is twofold: understanding causality and good marketing plan execution. Drawing the wrong conclusions about causality, or what actually causes a change in a company's sales performance, can lead to disastrous results. That's why companies investigate the causes by gathering market feedback and conducting market research. Another tool that can be used to research a change in a company's sales performance is a marketing audit. A marketing audit is an examination or a snapshot of the state of a company's marketing strategies as they are actually implemented. Complete and partial audits can be done internally or by a consulting firm in order to find areas for improvement.

**REVIEW QUESTIONS**

1. What is the difference between managerial control and statistical control? How is statistical control used?
2. What should a marketing audit accomplish?

# 5. DISCUSSION QUESTIONS AND ACTIVITIES

**DISCUSSION QUESTIONS**

1. In addition to CMOs, why do you believe so many other employees participate in marketing planning?
2. What is the most important part of a marketing plan? Why? What is the least important? Why?
3. Why doesn't the execution of a marketing plan necessarily follow the same order as the plan itself?
4. What is the most important part of a marketing audit? Why? What is the least important part? Why?

**ACTIVITIES**

1. Pick a product with which you are very familiar and create a simple marketing plan for it. Focus on one market segment.
2. Conduct an audit of a company's marketing plan as if you were a consultant. Selecting a relatively new consumer product may be easier because it is likely to have more press available that you can use for data.

# ENDNOTES

1. Hallie Mummert, "Sitting Chickens," *Target Marketing* 31, no. 4 (April 2008): 11.
2. David Benady, "Working with the Enemy," *Marketing Week*, September 11, 2008, 18.
3. Quotes in this paragraph are from Kate Maddox, "Bottom-Line Pressure Forcing CMO Turnover," *B2B* 92, no. 17 (December 10, 2007): 3–4.
4. "Marketing Audit: 10 Critical Components," Copernicus Marketing Consulting, http://www.copernicusmarketing.com/our-thinking/blog/2011/07/20/10-critical-components-of-a-marketing-audit/ (accessed April 13, 2012).

# Index